missiological approach that boldly challenges both scholars and practitioners to rethink Pentecostal engagement with ecological crises. This work is indispensable for academics, theologians and missiologists exploring the vibrant intersections of theology, ecology and global Pentecostalism. It makes a profound and lasting contribution to ongoing conversations about faith, justice and responsible stewardship of creation – an essential read for anyone committed to a transformative theology of life and care for our planet.

Chammah J. Kaunda, PhD
Academic Dean, Oxford Centre for Mission Studies, UK
Extraordinary Professor, Christian Spirituality, Church History and Missiology,
University of the Western Cape, South Africa

As this volume amply illustrates, Pentecostal scholars from around the world are now making crucial contributions to Christian ecotheology that express a distinctive vision and lure. Long accused by outsiders of promoting either evangelical escapism or a prosperity gospel, here are authentic Pentecostal voices affirming the need to hold together soil *and* Spirit, earth *and* heaven, God's immanence *and* God's transcendence in God's mission to heal a broken world. Indeed, that is a striking feature of the Pentecostal intuition, namely the uncanny ability to simultaneously do justice to both Spirit baptism on the one hand *and* the appropriate use of technology in worship on the other. Ecumenical ecotheology cannot flourish without such life-giving Pentecostal contributions and the spirit of collaboration that is evident in this volume.

Ernst Conradie, PhD
Professor of Religion and Theology,
University of the Western Cape, South Africa

This diverse edited collection, encompassing an impressive array of authors from numerous global regions, is a crucial contribution to ecotheological literature. It challenges the false assumption that Pentecostalism does not take environmental, ecological and social issues seriously. The division of the collection into biblical, theological, global and ecumenical dimensions within Pentecostalism in their relationships with environmental practices offers an important current map of the field. Weaving in and through this book are concerns for missiology, the ecumenical diversity of witness of varieties of Pentecostalism in earth care, as well as important theological arguments on how the Holy Spirit is active in creation, while also incorporating indigenous and other local cultural studies. This is a scholarly book that deserves to be widely read and discussed.

Celia Deane-Drummond, PhD
Director, *Laudato Si'* Research Institute
Senior Research Fellow,
University of Oxford, UK

This landmark volume is a timely and courageous contribution to both Pentecostal theology and the global conversation on environmental stewardship and care for creation. With scholarly depth, global diversity and profound pastoral concern, *Wonders Above and Signs Below* brings together voices from across the globe to explore the Spirit's call to love, protect and restore the earth. It refuses to separate mission from environmental responsibility, showing how Pentecostal-charismatic communities can respond prophetically to one of the greatest crises of our time. This book is essential reading for pastors, theologians and all who believe the Spirit's renewal embraces the whole creation.

Graham Joseph Hill, PhD, OAM
Associate Professor,
Charles Sturt University, Australia

In his sermon, "A Knock at Midnight," based upon Jesus's parable of the persistent neighbour who comes calling for bread, Martin Luther King Jr. warned that the church could not afford to be in a state of slumber and ignore the moral, social and psychological crises that were compelling people, in the darkness of night, to seek the bread that sustains life. In our present midnight of ecological crisis, creation comes calling. It persistently knocks on the doors of our homes, churches and institutions, asking for help in sustaining the fragile ecology of life. This volume of essay offers a glimpse of how Pentecostal scholars from around the world are opening their doors to creation's midnight call. Within the pages of this book, you will discover a mature and global conversation, one crafted with careful biblical and theological analyses. In my estimation, this timely intervention represents the best of a maturing Pentecostal movement. I rejoice to see this day.

Cheryl Bridges Johns, PhD
Director, Pentecostal House of Study,
Distinguished Visiting Professor,
United Theological Seminary, Ohio, USA

Wonders Above and Signs Below constitutes a significant and timely intervention within the fields of Pentecostal missiology and environmental studies. Despite its relatively brief history, the Pentecostal movement has profoundly shaped global Christianity and this volume extends that influence by critically engaging with the urgent issue of environmental degradation. Through a richly textured, nuanced and intentional dialogue between Pentecostal theologians and others across the ecumenical spectrum, the book offers interdisciplinary insights marked by rigorous scholarship and a truly global perspective. Rooted in a dynamic Christo-pneumatocentric framework, it pioneers a visionary

Wonders Above, Signs Below

GLOBAL LIBRARY

Wonders Above, Signs Below

Pentecostal Missiology and Environmental Degradation

Edited by
Eugene Baron & Amos Yong

GLOBAL LIBRARY

© 2025 Eugene Baron and Amos Yong

Published 2025 by Langham Global Library
An imprint of Langham Publishing
www.langhampublishing.org

Langham Publishing and its imprints are a ministry of Langham Partnership

Langham Partnership
PO Box 296, Carlisle, Cumbria, CA3 9WZ, UK
www.langham.org

ISBNs:
978-1-78641-152-5 Print
978-1-78641-259-1 ePub
978-1-78641-260-7 PDF
DOI: https://doi.org/10.69811/9781786411525

Eugene Baron and Amos Yong hereby assert their moral right to be identified as the Author of the General Editor's part in the Work in accordance with sections 77 and 78 of the Copyright, Designs and Patents Act 1988.

All rights reserved. No part of this publication may be reproduced, stored in a retrieval system or transmitted, in any form or by any means, electronic, mechanical, photocopying, recording or otherwise, without the prior written permission of the publisher or the Copyright Licensing Agency.

Requests to reuse content from Langham Publishing are processed through PLSclear. Please visit www.plsclear.com to complete your request.

Scripture quotations are from the New Revised Standard Version Bible, copyright © 1989 National Council of the Churches of Christ in the United States of America. Used by permission. All rights reserved.

British Library Cataloguing-in-Publication Data
A catalogue record for this book is available from the British Library

ISBN: 978-1-78641-152-5

Cover & Book Design: projectluz.com

Langham Partnership actively supports theological dialogue and an author's right to publish but does not necessarily endorse the views and opinions set forth here or in works referenced within this publication, nor can we guarantee technical and grammatical correctness. Langham Partnership does not accept any responsibility or liability to persons or property as a consequence of the reading, use or interpretation of its published content.

Contents

Contributors xi

Preface xiii

Introduction: Framing the Pentecostal Missiological Concerns
about Environmental Degradation 1
Eugene Baron & Amos Yong

Part I: Scriptural Perspectives

1   The Apocalyptic Destruction of the Earth in Isaiah 24 and its
    Place in a Pentecostal Ecotheology 21
    Anita Davis & Jacqueline N. Grey

2   The Sending and Groaning Spirit: An Eco-Pneumatological
    Reading of Mark's Temptation Narrative and Romans 8:18–27 41
    Jeffrey Lamp

3   Apocalyptic Ecotheology: A Pentecostal Contribution 59
    Jon K. Newton

4   Many Tongues, Many Biocultural Niches: A Pentecostal
    Missiological Response to Language Endangerment and
    Environmental Degradation 81
    Amos Yong

Part II: Theological Perspectives

5   Greening Hollenweger: Retrieving Ecological Dimensions from
    the Dean of Pentecostal Studies 109
    A. J. Swoboda

6   *Missio Dei, Imago Dei* and the *Spiritus Dei*: Oneness Pentecostals
    and Creation Care 129
    Joey Peyton

7   Materiality, Interdependence and Participation: Viewing the
    Renewal of Creation Through the Lens of Pentecostal Experience . . . 143
    Michael J. Frost

8   Beyond Eco-Mission: Toward a Zoological Imperative in
    Theological Discourse 163
    Daniela Rizzo

Part III: Global Perspectives

9   Pentecostals, Poverty and the Environmental Crisis: Recuperating
    an Ecotheology among Pentecostals in Central and Eastern Europe 183
    Melody J. Wachsmuth & Adrian Ana

10 Towards an African Pentecostal Ecotheology of the Forest 209
    Ocen Walter Onen & Tanya Riches

11 "Praying with Holy Ghost Fire in Ghana's Natural Environment":
    A Potential African Pentecostal Contribution to Eco-Missiology... 233
    Kwame Oppong-Konadu & Sarah Korang Sansa

12 Eco-Ecclesiology: Repositioning Classical Ghanaian Pentecostal
    Ecclesiology toward Creation Care 253
    Emmanuel Awudi

13 Not of This World? (Neo)Pentecostal Responses to Climate
    Change and Ecological Crises............................... 271
    Stian Sørlie Eriksen

Part IV: Ecumenical Perspectives

14 Pentecostal Climate Justice: Ecological Activism Meets Restitution. 307
    Harold D. Hunter

15 Incarnation as a Metaphysical Key for Missional Pentecostal
    Ecotheology: A Marian Pentecostal Observation 327
    Sanna Urvas

16 Cosmotheandric Eucharist, Contemplacostal Spirituality and the
    Call to Relational Solidarity 343
    Aizaiah G. Yong

17 Ecological Imagination after Pentecost 359
    Andy Lord

18 Knowing God's Mission as Creation Care: A Missional Pentecostal
    Ecclesiological Conversation 379
    Eugene Baron

Appendix: Possible Next Steps for Spirit-Filled Witness vis-a-vis the
    Environment 403

Contributors

Adrian Ana (Master of Environmental Science, Babes-Bolyai University) is an ordained minister serving in the Pentecostal church, Somesu-Rece, Romania.

Emmanuel Awudi (PhD, Akrofi-Christaller Institute) is a lecturer at Pentecost School of Theology and Mission, Pentecost University, Accra, Ghana.

Eugene Baron (PhD, University of the Western Cape) is editor-in-chief of *HTS Theological Studies*, and professor of Christian studies at the University of Johannesburg, South Africa.

Anita Davis (MA, Alphacrucis College) is a PhD candidate at University of Divinity, Melbourne, Australia.

Stian Sørlie Eriksen (PhD, VID Specialized University) is associate professor of theology and religion at VID Specialized University, Stavanger, Norway, and associate professor of theology and religion at the Norwegian School of Leadership and Theology, Oslo.

Michael J. Frost (PhD, University of Otago) is lecturer in theology at Alphacrucis College, Auckland, New Zealand.

Jacqueline N. Grey (PhD Charles Sturt University) is professor of biblical studies at Alphacrucis University College, Parramatta, Australia.

Harold D. Hunter (PhD, Fuller Seminary) is the International Pentecostal Holiness Church ecumenical officer, an adjunct professor at Oral Roberts University Graduate School of Theology, Oklahoma, USA, and chair of the Pentecostal World Fellowship Creation Care Task Force.

Jeffrey Lamp (PhD, Trinity Evangelical Divinity School) is senior professor of New Testament and instructor of environmental science at Oral Roberts University, Oklahoma, USA.

Andy Lord (PhD, University of Birmingham) is an Anglican minister in Oxford Diocese, UK, and associate lecturer at London School of Theology, UK.

Jon K. Newton (PhD, Deakin University) is associate professor of biblical studies and Pentecostalism at Alphacrucis University College, Melbourne, Australia.

Ocen Walter Onen (MTD, Eastern College Australia) is a PhD candidate at Stellenbosch University, South Africa.

Kwame Oppong-Konadu (MTh, Protestant Theological University) is an affiliated researcher and PhD candidate at the Evangelische Theologische Faculteit, Leuven, Belgium.

Joey Peyton (PhD, Assembly of God Theological Seminary) is a church consultant, pastoral counsellor, mentor, and independent scholar.

Tanya Riches (PhD, Fuller Seminary) is director of Master of Transformational Development at Eastern College Australia, Melbourne.

Daniela Rizzo (PhD, Alphacrucis University College) is lecturer of systematic theology at Alphacrucis University College, Melbourne, Australia.

Sarah Korang Sansa (MTh, Protestant Theological University) is a PhD candidate at the Protestant Theological University, Utrecht, Netherlands.

A. J. Swoboda (PhD, University of Birmingham) is associate professor of Bible and theology at Bushnell University, Oregon, USA, and lead mentor for the Doctor of Ministry program on Christian formation and soul care at Friends University, Kansas, USA.

Sanna Urvas (DTh, University of Helsinki) is professor of systematic theology at the Theological School of Finland, Tampere.

Melody J. Wachsmuth (PhD, Oxford Centre for Mission Studies) is a lecturer at the Evangelical Theological Seminary, Osijek, Croatia, and a board member and lecturer at the travelling Roma Bible School that serves the Balkans region of Eastern Europe.

Aizaiah G. Yong (PhD, Claremont School of Theology) is executive director of the Collegeville Institute of Ecumenical and Cultural Research at Saint John's Abbey and University, Minnesota, USA, and affiliate associate professor of spirituality at the Claremont School of Theology, California, USA.

Amos Yong (PhD, Boston University) is professor of theology and mission at Fuller Seminary, California, USA.

Preface

We are writing this preface during the season of Pentecost, a time that brings together people from across the Christian world to remind them of the pouring out of the Spirit, and hearing the Spirit each in his or her own "language." This book brings together a broad range of Pentecostal scholars into dialogue with one another and with you, each reader, about what we *know* and *feel* about the earth and how it, and we, can flourish. As missiological endeavours across the ecumenical spectrum have in the last generation recognized the ecological crisis and attempted to address it, so in this project Pentecostal theologians and their comrades join the conversation.

This book is also the product of an ecumenical effort. A South African reformed ordained pastor and scholar (Eugene) initiated conversations with a Chinese American Pentecostal minister and scholar (Amos), resulting in a journey together showcasing how theologizing and missiologizing need not be polarizing, but express a prophetic dialogue, generate solidarity across Christian traditions, and hone decolonial commitments, all for the purposes of working towards the flourishing of all life! So many people and institutions need to be appreciated for their invaluable support and contributions on this journey to see the book coming to fruition. We therefore wish to thank all those that made this project possible, as it spanned over almost three years, the careful and exceptional crafting of the chapters by the authors across quite a few continents to make possible such a unique contribution.

The National Research Foundation in South Africa and the University of the Free State that assisted Eugene in the completion of this project providing him the necessary sabbatical at strategic moments to work on it.

Amos thanks Fuller Theological Seminary for sabbatical support that facilitated some of the work on this book. As always, Alma's partnership and accompaniment makes possible and enjoyable the fulfilling of Amos's scholarly vocation, of which this book is another expression.

We are grateful to Langham Publishingfor their willingness to make this work available as a free to access PDF (because of which searching the work is more easily facilitated and thus we have not included any index to the book). Mark Arnold and his team have been wonderful to work with. The Langham copy-editor was particularly helpful in helping us avoid the kinds of confusions so prevalent when navigating interdisciplinary – in this case, Pentecostal studies, theology, missiology and environmental studies – terrain.

Introduction

Framing the Pentecostal Missiological Concerns about Environmental Degradation

Eugene Baron & Amos Yong

Environmental Degradation

There is an emerging global consensus that environmental problems such as climate change, the alarming rate of biodiversity loss (increasing extinction rates), continued deforestation (especially but not only in the Amazon and Southeast Asia),[1] the increase in the various forms of pollution (air, water, soil), the escalation of ocean levels and acidification endangering marine species, and devastating habitat destruction (through the processes of urbanization, agricultural development, and the waste disposal, recycling, and management crises) all need to be addressed as a matter of urgency.

On 5 June 2024, World Environment Day, the Secretary-General of the United Nations (UN), António Guterres, delivered his keynote address on climate action at the American Museum of Natural History in New York. He warned that the Earth has reached so many tipping points that urgent intervention is needed to slow down such phenomena.[2] In terms of the recent statistics on climate change in Europe, May 2024 was recorded as the earth's

---

1. The World Bank states that forests saw annual losses of 5.2 million hectares between 2000 and 2010, despite declines in deforestation rates and increased forest plantations. World Bank, "Toward a Clean, Green, Resilient World for All," strategy summary, undated. For more details, see their website at https://www.worldbank.org/en/topic/environment/publication/environment-strategy-toward-clean-green-resilient-world.

2. Anonymous, "There is an Exit Off 'The Highway to Climate Hell', Guterres Insists," *Climate and Environment*, online article, 5 June 2024.

hottest month on record, and with each new year, the continent's temperature is increasing.³ Therefore he laments, in metaphoric terms, the "telling" by the Earth that something is wrong, but human beings are not "listening." He contends that humans in this crisis are both the danger (causing the crisis) but also the solution (able to resolve it amicably). Guterres argues that recently we have felt the impact globally of the heat waves in Asia that catalyzed droughts and storms in parts of North America, and floods in East Africa and Brazil; these are all related to the climate crisis. Business is already affected, and food insecurity is on the rise. While the rich benefit and maximize profits generated by late market capitalism, the poor and the vulnerable (who are the largest percentage of the world's population) will be the most negatively affected.

The Intergovernmental Science-Policy Platform on Biodiversity and Ecosystem Services raises a deep concern that at least one million of the estimated eight million species of plants and animals are threatened with extinction should the challenge not be prioritized.⁴ It estimates that at least 24,000 of the estimated 28,000 species in the world are at risk of extinction (see Chatham House and United Nations Environmental Programme [UNEP]), including 90 percent of the world's marine fish stocks which are entirely depleted as well as overexploited.⁵ The arguable cause of this is the global food system as increased agricultural development has been identified more specifically as the key driver and threat.⁶ All of these developments lead to deforestation and, according to Antonio Gutierrez, will result in the extinction of 80 percent of medicine that comes from plants and animals. The World Bank, in similar vein, reports that

> Over the past 40 years, there have been significant declines in healthy ecosystems – e.g., forests, mangroves, sea grass beds, coral reefs and their flora and fauna populations, with species

---

3. National Oceanic and Atmospheric Administration. U.S. Department of Commerce. May 2024 was Earth's warmest May on record. The globe saw its 12th-consecutive month of record warmth. News & Features 13 June 2024, https://www.noaa.gov/news/may-2024-was-earths-warmest-may-on-record.

4. Further information and statistics can be found on the website of the United Nations Environmental Programme at https://www.unep.org/facts-about-nature-crisis.

5. See further information at https://unctad.org/news/90-fish-stocks-are-used-fisheries-subsidies-must-stop.

6. Tim Benton, Carling Bieg, Helen Harwatt, Roshan Pudasaini, and Laura Wellesley, "Food System Impacts on Biodiversity," research paper (London: Chatham House, updated 21 March 2021), https://www.chathamhouse.org/2021/02/food-system-impacts-biodiversity-loss.

loss affecting everything from fungi to insects, plants, frogs, tigers, and gorillas.[7]

This situation is further aggravated by the alarming statistics on the global scale of increased pollution. In fact, it is reported that at least 66 percent of the ocean area is polluted through occurrent human activities, most especially through the fisheries industry (see IPBES).[8] The impact of rising CO_2 emissions on the oceans is alarming. According to the U.S. National Oceanic and Atmospheric Administration, nearly 30 percent of these emissions have already been absorbed by the oceans. This has ominous consequences for marine life across the world.

The development of urbanization has indeed brought a steep and profitable increase in the global economy, benefiting mostly the developed world and the new emerging economies, but it has also had an alarming environmental impact. The UNEP reports that at least 70 percent of Earth's land surface has been significantly altered by human actions (IPBES), which in some cases is related to increased deforestation. It reports that as much as 70 percent of the world's greenhouse gas emissions come from cities as their urban ecological footprint increases.[9] The problem is not the development of cities, but the lack of careful consideration on the impact on the environment during the design and building phases of urban planning.

The ecological crisis has had simultaneously an adverse impact on the environment as well as the livelihood of human beings. For instance, the UN reports that at least 25 percent of global greenhouse gas emissions are generated by land clearing, crop production and fertilization.[10] A result of these human actions is that approximately 100,000,000–300,000,000 people are at increased risk of floods and hurricanes because of the loss of coastal habitat. In addition, the report warns that maintaining the recent declines of nature and biodiversity at the current rate will undermine progress towards thirty-five out of forty-four of the targets of Sustainable Development Goals (SDCs)

---

7. World Bank, "Toward a Clean, Green, Resilient World for All," https://www.worldbank.org/en/topic/environment/publication/environment-strategy-toward-clean-green-resilient-world.

8. These statistics are reported by the Intergovernmental Science-Policy Platform on Biodiversity and Ecosystem Services (IPBES). See the report documented by the European Commission Regenerating our Ocean and Waters by 2030. Interim report of the Mission Board Healthy Oceans, Seas, Coastal and Inland Waters, which is available at https://eo4society.esa.int/wp-content/uploads/2020/09/Ocean.en_.pdf.

9. United Nations Environmental Programme, "Facts about the Nature Crisis," News Release, 30 May 2024. https://www.unep.org/facts-about-nature-crisis.

10. United Nations Environmental Programme, "Facts about the Nature Crisis."

that are related to poverty, hunger, health, climate, oceans, and land. Moreover, a recent study conducted by the University of Singapore (1980–2020) found an association between air pollution (from cars, factories, and fires) and 135,000,000 premature deaths globally during that time period.[11] In respect of the above-mentioned global statistics, it becomes important to stress the collective participation of both academia and society, which this book reflects, not only via policymaking, awareness campaigns, etc. but in action through theological reflection towards missiological and other practices that are friendlier towards the environment.

Gutierrez calls for political will, especially from developed countries, to assist the developing countries to deal effectively with reducing carbon emission et cetera. The United Nations has summarized some action steps to slow down environmental degradation:[12]

- "A clearly defined and ambitious Post-2020 Global Biodiversity Framework that is matched by finances and accountability mechanisms to achieve the framework's targets.
- Investments in nature-based solutions to at least triple by 2030 if the world is to meet its climate change, biodiversity, and land degradation targets.
- Prevention of the large-scale collapse of nature through effective conservation of more of the land, inland waters, and oceans, as well as the world delivering on its current commitment to restore at least one billion hectares of degraded land in the next decade.
- The transformation of the food systems to become more sustainable and resilient, reverse environmental degradation, restore ecosystems, and ensure food and nutritional security.
- Reform of tax structures and subsidies to incentivize sustainable production and ensure that environmental degradation no longer profits large corporations.

---

11. Nanyang Technological University, "NTU Singapore-Led Study Estimates That Between 1980 and 2020 135 Million Premature Deaths Could Be Linked to Fine Particulate Matter Pollution," news release, Singapore, 10 June 2024. Available at ntu-singapore-led-study-estimates-that-between-1980-and-2020-135-million-premature-deaths-could-be-linked-to-fine-particulate-matter-pollution.pdf. A peer-reviewed journal article on this study is available at https://www3.ntu.edu.sg/CorpComms2/research%20papers/PM2.5.pdf.

12. United Nations Environmental Programme, "Facts about the Nature Crisis," news release, 30 May 2024; https://www.unep.org/facts-about-nature-crisis.

- Corporations to put sustainability at the heart of decision-making and focus on new sustainable business models to meet society's needs in ways less impactful on the environment.
- All financial players to align their business strategies with global and national sustainability goals including the SDGs, the Paris Agreement and the upcoming Biodiversity Framework.

Theological and Missiological Responses

In light of all of these strategies, what can theologians do to solve such an urgent crisis? The environment, how to responsibly care for it, and ensure that it continues to sustain life is a theme addressed in many disciplines, including the humanities, social sciences, and theology. Numerous publications address the intersections between mission and the environment. However, the different authors in this book were invited to engage these matters via a more specific focus – addressing the concerns of ecological degradation through a critical assessment of the intersections between mission, Pentecostal Christianities, and environmental degradation.

In 2013, the World Council of Churches (WCC) (particularly the Commission on World Mission and Evangelism) engaged in considerable discussion on mission and the flourishing of life. In this regard, the mission statement *Together Towards Life* is an important statement to consider. In the mission statement of the WCC, the Pentecostal and charismatic churches are recognized participants in the life-giving mission of God, perhaps once a marginalized perspective but now an important voice from and to the ecumenical church.[13] In fact, the WCC describes these churches as playing a vital role as God's agents in mission. In their words, God is able to use currently those that were previously ridiculed as "foolish," "poor," and "powerless," to become instrumental in his mission on Earth (1 Cor 1:18–19); this includes Pentecostal Christianities. On the other hand, the mission of life for the whole of creation is one created and transformed by life in the Spirit.[14] These words would indeed find a home within Pentecostal churches. In this regard, the WCC in its statement integrates the three components (mission, environment, and Pentecostalism) and their relationship with one another. However, besides the statement, this intersection needs to be explored, especially the focus on

---

13. Jooseop Keum, ed. *Together Towards Life: Mission and Evangelism in Changing Landscape* (Geneva: World Council of Churches, 2013), 5.
14. Keum, *Together Towards Life*, 4.

the Pentecostal churches. Therefore, what the mission statement of the WCC does not tell us but prompts us towards is indeed a deeper reflection on how this is, or can be done, by these Pentecostal-charismatic communities that emphasize the Spirit of life. However, not long after emphasizing the role of Pentecostal and charismatic communities in the "life-giving" of the Spirit, the mission statement also expresses its concern for "spiritualities" which are respectful to the earth to be developed.[15] This has no direct reference to the Pentecostal churches as such, but a message to all Christian communities, including the Pentecostal and charismatic communities, in which the focus is on spiritualities that might be detrimental or enhance an environmentally friendly attitude. More recently, an edited volume, released to coincide with the start of the 11th WCC Assembly (31 August–8 September 2022), contains a chapter that explores the current issues affecting mission. In it, Allen Yeh uses the cultural mandate derived from Genesis 1:27–29 to argue in favour of creation care, averring that "yes, we may use everything on earth for food, clothing, shelter, etc., but it must be done with care, responsibility, stewardship, and sustainability."[16] This assertion calls on Christians to engage in responsible stewardship of the natural environment and avert ecological degradation.

Since Karl Barth's Brandenburg lecture (1932), as well as the World Mission Conference in Willingen (Germany) in 1952, the emphasis on the *missio Dei* – God sending the Son, the Son sending the Spirit, and the Spirit sending the church – has become crucial in moving from the old paradigm of mission to the new one. This is also intended for "mission churches," that is, those being long recipients of mission which until more recently did not regard themselves as agents of God's mission on earth.[17] This became the rationale for David Bosch's emphasis on the agency and missionary nature of the church.[18] We also take note of similar developments by the "missional church" movement within the North American context which challenges how the churches should understand their "nature" in the world. They should be God's witnesses![19] The missional church movement was coined and adopted primarily by those

---

15. Keum, *Together Towards Life*, 10.

16. Allen Yeh, "Mission and the Age of World Christianity," in *Together in the Mission of God*, ed. Risto Juko (Geneva: World Council of Churches, 2022), 187.

17. Eugene Baron, "The Call for African Missional Consciousness through Renewed Mission Praxis in URCSA," *Studia Historiae Ecclesiasticae* 45, no. 3 (2019): 1–19.

18. David Bosch, *Transforming Mission* (Maryknoll: Orbis, 1991).

19. Darrell L. Guder, *Called to Witness: Doing Missional Theology* (Grand Rapids: Eerdmans, 2015).

belonging to the Reformed tradition, hence more critical thought must go into rethinking the ecclesial nature of Pentecostal churches, in particular.

A Growing Pentecostal Witness

Though most of the early literature on Pentecostalism was focused on or produced by (and for) the North American context, not least given the provenance of the Azusa Street Revival in Los Angeles in the early twentieth century, Pentecostal scholars have in the last generation shown that the global movement cannot be reduced in terms of its origins to one historical location, and, more importantly, its contemporary expressions extend around the world and are manifest in many forms. On the one hand, when the National Association of Evangelicals was formed in 1942 in the United States, some pentecostal churches were quick to affiliate and be associated within that circle and now many are part of the Lausanne network. On the other hand, as early as the 1952 International Missionary Council's Willingen Conference in Germany, there were already some Pentecostals attending and participating in what gave shape to a new ecumenical paradigm in mission (*missio Dei*), even as Pentecostal churches began joining the World Council of Churches starting in the 1960s. And as pentecostal scholarship has emerged in the last generation, there have been extensive debates about whether to include within this category persons, congregations, communities, or groups that have experienced charismatic renewal, or indigenous churches around the world that practice the spiritual or charismatic gifts but may not call themselves either *pentecostal* or *charismatic*. This shows that within the Pentecostal movement itself there are different streams and manifestations stretching across the full spectrum of so-called *fundamentalists* on the right, *evangelicals* closer to the center, and *liberals* or *progressives* on the left.[20]

As Robeck and Yong and their contributors to the *Cambridge Companion to Pentecostalism* have quite eloquently made, Pentecostalism differs in terms of its contextual expressions, therefore one might best talk about Pentecostalisms.[21] It should not be surprising then, that these varieties of Pentecostalisms have generated a broad scope of theological instincts and articulations,

---

20. Historical and other perspectives can be found in Amos Yong et al., ed., *Global Renewal Christianity: Spirit-Empowered Movements Past, Present, and Future*, 4 vols. (Lake Mary: Charisma House, 2016–2017).

21. Cecil M. Robeck and Amos Yong, eds., *The Cambridge Companion to Pentecostalism* (New York: Cambridge University Press, 2014).

correlative with the already-noted full spectrum of evangelical-ecumenical sensibilities. Therefore Pentecostal hermeneutics can range from the literalist readings of the Bible to more reader-response or contextual approaches; Pentecostal epistemologies can be more rationalist(ic) to more experientialist; Pentecostal historical roots may be fed by more Reformed perspectives in some instances and with Wesleyan inclinations in others; Pentecostal cosmologies could presume Western-orientations in those contexts but also be interwoven with indigenous worldviews in global South or majority world contexts. And last but not least, although surely also important to register in any summary of Pentecostal theological commitments, there is the divide – in some cases, chasm – between Oneness (so-called, pejoratively, Jesus-only) and trinitarian presuppositions. However in all of this an emphasis, the working of the Holy Spirit seems the key factor.[22]

Within the emerging Pentecostal theological community, a growing number of scholars are beginning to turn their attention to environmental issues. Leading the way is North American A. J. Swoboda, the only one with his own monograph, another co-authored volume, and an edited volume that includes a range of contributions from within and outside the Pentecostal scholarly and ecclesial community.[23] Jeffrey Lamp, a New Testament scholar who has long taught at Oral Roberts University (ORU), one of the leading schools serving the North American Pentecostal-charismatic community,[24] has also conducted an ecological reading of one of the Christian Testament's books, although specifically focused neither on a "Pentecostal interpretation" nor a "missiological appropriation." Beyond these works, essays and articles on Pentecostal ecotheologies and environmental theologies have emerged across

---

22. For more on how these global pentecostal churches have been theologically generative, see, e.g., Amos Yong, *The Spirit Poured Out on All Flesh: Pentecostalism and the Possibility of Global Theology* (Grand Rapids: Baker Academic, 2005); *In the Days of Caesar: Pentecostalism and Political Theology* (Grand Rapids: Eerdmans, 2010); and *Renewing Christian Theology: Systematics for a Global Christianity*, images and commentary by Jonathan A. Anderson (Waco: Baylor University Press, 2014).

23. See A. J. Swoboda, *Tongues and Trees: Towards a Pentecostal Ecological Theology* (Blandford Forum: Deo, 2013); A. J. Swoboda, ed. *Blood Cries Out: Pentecostals, Ecology & the Groans of Creation* (Eugene: Wipf & Stock, 2014); A. J. Swoboda, Daniel L. Brunner, and Jennifer L. Butler, *Introducing Evangelical Ecotheology: Foundations in Scripture, Theology, History, and Praxis* (Grand Rapids: Baker Academic, 2014).

24. Jeffrey S. Lamp, *The Greening of Hebrews: An Ecological Reading of the Letter to the Hebrews* (Eugene: Wipf & Stock, 2012).

a wide range of peer-reviewed and edited collections, including but not limited to those working at the interface of Pentecostal theology and the sciences.[25]

There is extensive literature in the field of Pentecostal missiology. Yet, Pentecostal missiologists, with few exceptions,[26] have not included creation care, environmental concerns, or ecological issues within their purview. Therefore, as there is a growing missiological literature on the environment, it is time for the global Pentecostal-charismatic missiological community to take up this important issue. Building on emerging eco-theological and social action scholarship among Pentecostal theologians and missiologists, this book brings together twenty-two scholars to consider a range of Pentecostal missiological responses to environmental issues. Our authors derive mostly from across the wide range of Pentecostal churches, with some identifying variously with charismatic streams from across other ecclesial traditions, and even others coming from non-Pentecostal churches but with research background on Pentecostal-charismatic Christianity or interests in ecumenical dialogue with Pentecostal communities. They deploy theological and hermeneutical methods representing this wide spectrum of ecclesial locations, in many cases approaching their work with more recognizably Pentecostal voices and perspectives although in a few instances drawing from a vast repertoire of disciplinary, methodological, and ecclesial resources, albeit always appealing to the work of the Spirit that is one hallmark of Pentecostal-charismatic spirituality. Rather than promoting any one Pentecostal perspective – impossible, as the preceding overview of the dynamic global movement indicates – our goal is to create a spacious site for broader Pentecostal and ecumenical conversation at this relatively unexplored intersection where Pentecostal Christianities meet environmental issues.

Contributors will discuss the role of churches affiliated with the global Pentecostal-charismatic movement in promoting creation care and concerns for the environment. The questions to be taken up include but are not limited to the following: Until now, what have been the views, perceptions, attitudes, and actions regarding the environment and climate change across Pentecostal-charismatic church communities? How might the developing Pentecostal-charismatic tradition theologize or could strategize to address environmental concerns? How can Pentecostal-charismatic theologians and missiologists aid

---

25. See, for example, Amos Yong, ed., *The Spirit Renews the Face of the Earth: Pentecostal Forays in Science and Theology of Creation* (Eugene: Pickwick, 2009).

26. Amos Yong, "The Missio Spiritus: Towards a Pneumatological Missiology of Creation," in *Creation Care in Christian Missio*, Regnum Edinburgh Centenary Series 29, ed. Kapya J. Kaoma (Oxford: Regnum, 2013), 121–33.

church and mission leaders and lay people of the ecclesial community reconsider Christian witness and mission in relationship to the environment? When discussing the Holy Spirit's enabling and empowering Christian mission and witness, how might Pentecostal-charismatic believers be inspired to respond to issues of the environment in the present time?

A Brief Overview of the Chapters

The book is divided into four parts, with the first on "Scriptural Perspectives" that focus on both Old and New Testament passages to encourage and explore the way in which care for the environment among Pentecostals could be missiologically embraced. The first chapter, "The Apocalyptic Destruction of the Earth in Isaiah 24 and Its Place in a Pentecostal Ecotheology," by Jacqueline Grey and Anita Davis (both from Australia), engages a close reading of a prophetic and apocalyptic text that speaks of the degradation of the earth by the hand of Yahweh. They consider how Isaiah 24 contributes to the key concepts of the emerging Pentecostal theology of ecology, showing the connections between Isaiah 24 and Romans 8 of the groaning of creation, as well as unfolding missiological implications.

"The Sending and Groaning Spirit: A Pneumatological Reading of Mark's Temptation Narrative and Romans 8:18–27," by Jeffrey Lamp (USA) argues that the same Spirit that drove Jesus into the wilderness to reclaim the Adamic vocation (from the Markan passage) drives, accompanies, and empowers believers in the present in mission to extend God's benevolent rule for creation in anticipation of their joint eschatological destiny of liberation from corruption. The groaning Spirit facilitates an empathetic identification of the groaning children of God with the groaning creation as the life-giving Spirit leads both to their liberation, evidenced in the care for creation exercised by the children of God.

Jon Newton (Australia) in his chapter, "Apocalyptic Ecotheology: A Pentecostal Contribution," discusses themes and passages in the Christian Bible on the book of Revelation that have been drawn on or are relevant to the challenge of environmental degradation, and explore their implications for Pentecostal praxis. He focuses on God as Creator and Provider; the book of Revelation's language regarding creation worshiping God and the Lamb and its imagery of environmental disaster, critique of an all-consuming empire, and promise of a new/renewed heaven and earth; and also some aspects of Revelation that may be in tension with ecotheology such as its ethical and spiritual dualism and its suspicion of authoritarian or "big" government endeavors or initiatives.

Finally in this section of the book, "Many Tongues, Many Biocultural Niches: A Pentecostal Missiological Response to Language Endangerment and Environmental Degradation" by Amos Yong (USA) reconsiders the Pentecost narrative in Acts 2 in the contemporary context of climate change, particularly in light of the growing literature on biolinguistic diversity that documents the interrelationship between endangered languages (and their ethnic-cultural communities) and ecological degradation. In response, a missiological program for cultural-linguistic revitalization is sketched consistent with the eschatological arc of the Spirit's creative and redemptive work populating those from many nations, tribes, and languages to the ends of the Earth and also before the great throne amid the new creation.

Part two of the book, "Theological Perspectives," draws forth various strands of Pentecostal scholarship in the service of Pentecostal mission that attends to our current global context of environmental degradation. A. J. Swoboda's (USA) "Exploring the Ecological Thought of a Pentecostal Forebear" begins by engaging the ecological thinking of Walter Hollenweger (1927–2016), the dean of Pentecostal scholarship. He provides a thorough examination of Hollenweger's writing to unearth some of the key contributions to his life's work for further construction and implementation of ecological theology and especially mission practice among Pentecostal and charismatic movements in the twenty-first century.

This is followed by Joey Peyton's (USA) chapter, "*Missio Dei, Imago Dei*, and the *Spiritus Dei*: Oneness Pentecostalism and Creation Care," which focuses on how many "oneness" Pentecostals understand and embrace the outpouring of the *Spiritus Dei* with little regards to the larger *missio Dei*, or even in relationship to their own existence in God's present world as the *imago Dei*. He provides an assessment of the involvement and engagement of Oneness Pentecostals in issues of creation care, and urges, in conclusion, that discipleship focus on "being" God's image and living out God's mission for and to the whole of creation.

Michael J. Frost (Australia/New Zealand) in "Materiality, Interdependence and Participation: Viewing the Renewal of Creation through the Lens of Pentecostal Experience" acknowledges how Pentecostal renewal has been understood and experienced in both individualistic and spiritualized terms. These do not position Pentecostalism well to respond to widespread systemic material problems like the climate crisis but, rather, further exacerbate human actions that amplify the problem. Thus, he explores this emerging Pentecostal theological discourse in two directions: that Pentecostal experience and renewal are better understood as embodied and participatory, and that such renewal has cosmic missiological implications.

Lastly for the theological section, the chapter of Daniela Rizzo (Australia), "Beyond Eco-Mission: Toward a Zoological Imperative in Theological Discourse," embarks on a nuanced intersection of theology, spirituality, and conservation by examining the concept of conservation as eco-mission within the context of Pentecostalism. She explores the theological implications of the Pentecostal belief in the universal outpouring of the Holy Spirit, as articulated in the Lukan phrase, "The Spirit poured out on all flesh," and conclusively argues that the endangerment and extinction of animal species (as part of the all flesh baptism of the Spirit) can be viewed as a form of sin, thus highlighting another dimension of the church's missiological role to humanity's responsibility as stewards of creation.

In the third part of the book, "Global Perspectives," attention is drawn to a few case studies around the world illuminating current and emerging Pentecostal environmental mission praxis. In "Pentecostals, Poverty and the Environmental Crisis: Recuperating an Ecotheology among Pentecostals in Central and Eastern Europe," Melody Wachsmuth (Croatia/USA) and Adrian Ana (Romania) probe the diverse reasons for lack of ecological and environmental engagement from Pentecostal communities – ranging from effects of communism, poverty and survival to the abundant flow of premillennial Western missionaries – and discuss possible ways to bridge the gap between current Pentecostal theology in discrete contexts and lived experience, especially their mission commitments. The chapter paper focuses primarily on Romania, Croatia, and Roma Pentecostals.

Tanya Riches (Australia) and Ocen Walter Onen (Uganda), in "Towards an African Pentecostal Ecotheology of the Forest," focus on Habuleleke Full Gospel Congregation and their forest regeneration project in Eastern Uganda as a case study to propose a transformational development approach that would enable a flourishing relationship between a church, their community, and their forest. They extend Nimi Wariboko's concept of friendship to include the forest, now understandable as "an actor" capable of mutual interdependence and with its life force animated by the Spirit. This chapter thus sketches an (East) African Pentecostal transformational development approach enabling flourishing within an interdependent relationship between development workers, church, community, and forest.

Kwame Oppong-Konadu (Ghana/Belgium) and Sarah Korang Sansa's (Ghana/Netherlands) "'Praying with Holy Ghost Fire in Ghana's Natural Environment': A Potential African Pentecostal Contribution to Eco-Missiology," discusses how Pentecostal glossolalia and prayer practices in the Ghanaian environment could spark the missiological imagination in ways that motivate conservation of forest resources and contribute towards environmental sustainability. Adopting a life history and semi-autoethnographic method to present their experiences, our authors call for a deeper analysis of Ghanaian Pentecostal prayer engagements in the environment and advocate for an Afro-eco-Pentecostal missiology – a broader dialogue between the African indigenous worldview and Pentecostal spirituality – to move eco-missiological discourses forward in Ghana and sub-Saharan Africa.

In the chapter, "Eco-Ecclesiology: Repositioning Classical Ghanaian Pentecostal Ecclesiology towards Creation Care," Emmanuel Awudi (Ghana) documents the growing realization within the Pentecostal churches of Ghana that the great commission works in tandem with the first commission to humanity: keeping and guarding the earth. His chapter emerged from his doctoral work in which he explored four classical Pentecostal denominations in Ghana, four Indigenous African Churches, and four African Pentecostal scholars. He enumerates strategies to maximize the impact of classical Pentecostal ecclesiology on eco-care and eco-mission as the tradition's contribution to minimizing climate change and its impact, not only in Ghana but for the greater Pentecostal tradition.

Stian Sørlie Eriksen's (Norway) "Not of This World? (Neo)Pentecostal Responses to Climate Change and Ecological Crises" concludes this section by addressing climate change and ecological initiatives and perspectives in and among a selection of globally oriented Pentecostal-charismatic churches, a selection of neo-Pentecostal churches/movements, and a few neo-Pentecostal anchored universities that have emerged during the last decades. Critically considering their societal and theological contexts, he argues that neo-Pentecostal theology and spirituality can help shed light on ecological and environmental initiatives within their contexts, especially in dialogue with contextual spiritualities (e.g. African), realized eschatological themes, and contextual ecological and climate realities.

The final section of the book, "Ecumenical Perspectives" is a section in which voices from the wider church's catholic past and present are brought into dialogue with Pentecostal ones to explore the issues. It starts off with the chapter, "Pentecostal Climate Justice: Ecological Activism Meets Restitution," by Harold D. Hunter (USA), who takes us on a pilgrimage that witnesses the emerging ecological engagement of Pentecostal churches and organizations around the world. He reviews some materials published in English, most of which come from North America, and listens to indigenous people as well, arguing that a bigger story on the ecological engagement of this community emerges when looking at the global South.

Sanna Urvas (Finland) in her chapter, "Incarnation as a Metaphysical Key for Pentecostal Ecotheology: A Marian Pentecostal Observation," explores a Pentecostal dialogue with the Eastern Christian tradition by utilizing two aspects that are essential in Pentecostal ethos and orientation: incarnation and Mary, as a biblical example of deep experiential connection with Christ. Therefore, the material or fleshly incarnation of Christ is presented as a metaphysical key to ecotheology. The chapter is constructed with a Pentecostal orientation and in dialogue with other Pentecostal voices, but mainly with one theological voice from the past, Ephrem the Syrian.

Aizaiah G. Yong (USA)'s chapter, "Cosmotheandric Eucharist, Contemplacostal Spirituality and the Call to Relational Solidarity," builds upon the cosmotheandric eucharist practice found in the lineage of Raimon Panikkar and seeks to bridge its insights with a "contemplacostal vision" and its call to inter-relational praxis. To Panikkar's cosmotheandric spirituality (which bridges the sacred and the material realms in all-inclusive ways) he introduces a "contemplacostal" lens that cultivates relational solidarity with all beings (and especially those forgotten/oppressed by the dominant culture) and strengthens creative capacities of discernment, courage, and compassion for attentiveness to the present eco-apocalyptic moment.

Next, Andy Lord's (UK) "Ecological Mission Imagination after Pentecost" explores how writers on the environment from beyond the church utilize narratives in many creative ways to develop imaginations that take the ecological crisis seriously. Through a dialogue with Robert Macfarlane's engagement with personal, historical, geographic, geological, political, and religious narratives to suggest how our interactions with the land around us shape our thinking and living, Lord teases out how narrative might contribute to the development of an ecological imagination directed towards mission after Pentecost. He argues that Pentecostal approaches to ecological mission need to engage with and nurture contemporary narratives that feed imaginative action.

The last chapter of this section, South African Eugene Baron's "Knowing God's Mission as Creation Care: A Missional Pentecostal Ecclesiological Conversation," urges that multiple episteme should be explored to communicate and assist congregants to understand their mission as creation care during worship services. He provides some critique on how a Pentecostal epistemology is still quite under-utilized and prioritized in discourses of missional worship. This serves as the primary dialogue partner here with Pentecostal theological and missiological voices and might make them conscious of their responsibility towards the *missio Dei* and creation care.

We are hopeful that especially Pentecostal mission leaders, missionaries, missiologists, and all in Pentecostal-charismatic churches committed to the church's missional witness will find these essays informative and helpful for their efforts. We welcome also Pentecostal scholars, theologians, and ecclesial leaders to engage with these ideas and be in dialogue with ecclesial communities, mission movements, and organizations about how to live more faithfully in the mission of God in a time of climate change. Last but not least, we consider this volume a contribution to the broader conversation on eco-mission from across the wide spectrum of Pentecostal-charismatic experience and perspective knowing that its pages will reflect how much we have learned from the prior and ongoing efforts of our brothers and sisters around the world who are also seeking to bear faithful witness in an era of environmental degradation. We also believe with both humility and confidence, that the Pentecostal tongues borne out across this book will further stimulate thinking and resource missiological praxis for the global church.

Bibliography

Anonymous, "There is an Exit Off 'the Highway to Climate Hell', Guterres Insists." UN News. *Climate and Environment*. Online Article. 5 June 2024. https://news.un.org/en/story/2024/06/1150661.

Baron, Eugene. "The Call for African Missional Consciousness through Renewed Mission Praxis in URCSA." *Studia Historiae Ecclesiasticae* 45, no. 3 (2019): 1–19.

Benton, Tim, Carling Bieg, Helen Harwatt, Roshan Pudasaini, and Laura Wellesley. "Food System Impacts on Biodiversity." Chatham House, research paper, updated 21 March 2021. https://www.chathamhouse.org/2021/02/food-system-impacts-biodiversity-loss.

Bosch, David J. *Transforming Mission*. Maryknoll: Orbis, 1991.

Guder, Darrell L. *Called to Witness: Doing Missional Theology*. Grand Rapids: Eerdmans, 2015.

Intergovernmental Science-Policy Platform on Biodiversity and Ecosystem Services (IPBES). "About." 16 June 2024. https://www.ipbes.net/about.

Keum, Jooseop, ed. *Together Towards Life: Mission and Evangelism in Changing Landscapes*. Geneva: World Council of Churches, 2013.

Lamp, Jeffrey S. *The Greening of Hebrews: An Ecological Reading of the Letter to the Hebrews*. Eugene: Wipf & Stock, 2012.

National Oceanic and Atmospheric Administration. U.S. Department of Commerce. "May 2024 was Earth's warmest May on record." *News & Features.* 13 June 2024. https://www.noaa.gov/news/may-2024-was-earths-warmest-may-on-record.

Robeck, Cecil M., and Amos Yong, eds. *The Cambridge Companion to Pentecostalism.* New York: Cambridge University Press, 2014.

Swoboda, A. J. *Tongues and Trees: Towards a Pentecostal Ecological Theology.* Blandford Forum: Deo, 2013.

Swoboda, A. J., ed. *Blood Cries Out: Pentecostals, Ecology & the Groans of Creation.* Eugene: Wipf & Stock, 2014.

Swoboda, A. J., Daniel L. Brunner, and Jennifer L. Butler. *Introducing Evangelical Ecotheology: Foundations in Scripture, Theology, History, and Praxis.* Grand Rapids: Baker Academic, 2014.

University of Singapore. "NTU Singapore-Led Study Estimates that between 1980 and 2020, 135 Million Premature Deaths Could Be Linked to Fine Particulate Matter Pollution." News Release. 25 May 2024. ntu-singapore-led-study-estimates-that-between-1980-and-2020-135-million-premature-deaths-could-be-linked-to-fine-particulate-matter-pollution.pdf.

United Nations Environmental Programme. "Facts about Nature." 29 May 2024 https://www.unep.org/facts-about-nature crisis#:~:text=Around%203.2%20billion%20people%2C%20or%2040%20percent%20of,generated%20by%20land%20clearing%2C%20crop%20production%20and%20fertilization.

United Nations Environmental Programme, "Facts about the Nature Crisis." News Release. 30 May 2024. https://www.unep.org/facts-about-nature-crisis.

https://unctad.org/system/files/official-document/tc2015d1rev2_S01_P08.pdf.

World Bank. "Toward a Clean, Green, Resilient World for All," Strategy Summary, undated. https://www.worldbank.org/en/topic/environment/publication/environment-strategy-toward-clean-green-resilient-world.

World Council of Churches. "Member Churches." https://www.oikoumene.org/member-churches.

World Meteorological Organization. "Climate Change." 16 June 2014. https://wmo.int/topics/climate.

Yeh, Allen. 2022. "Mission and the Age of World Christianity." In *Together in the Mission of God*, edited by Risto Juko, 181–97. Geneva: World Council of Churches, 2022.

Yong, Amos. *In the Days of Caesar: Pentecostalism and Political Theology.* Grand Rapids: Eerdmans, 2010.

——— "The Missio Spiritus: Towards a Pneumatological Missiology of Creation." In *Creation Care in Christian Mission.* Regnum Edinburgh Centenary Series *29,* edited by Kapya J. Kaoma, 121–33. Oxford: Regnum, 2013.

——— *Renewing Christian Theology: Systematics for a Global Christianity.* Images and commentary by Jonathan A. Anderson. Waco: Baylor University Press, 2014.

——— *The Spirit Poured Out on All Flesh: Pentecostalism and the Possibility of Global Theology.* Grand Rapids: Baker Academic, 2005.

Yong, Amos, ed. *The Spirit Renews the Face of the Earth: Pentecostal Forays in Science and Theology of Creation*. Eugene: Pickwick, 2009.

Yong, Amos, et al. ed. *Global Renewal Christianity: Spirit-Empowered Movements Past, Present, and Future*. 4 vols. Lake Mary: Charisma House, 2016–2017.

Part I

Scriptural Perspectives

1

The Apocalyptic Destruction of the Earth in Isaiah 24 and its Place in a Pentecostal Ecotheology

Anita Davis & Jacqueline N. Grey

The last decade has seen increasing concern among Pentecostal scholars to address issues of climate change and creation care. It has been commonly proposed that a significant doctrinal barrier for developing a Pentecostal ecotheology has been the pervasiveness of the pessimistic eschatological outlook of dispensational premillennialism. The doctrine anticipates an increased degradation of society leading up to the return of Christ. Readings of the apocalyptic literature of the Bible, particularly Revelation and Daniel, have been formative in fuelling the cataclysmic eschatological expectations of this doctrine. This has profound implications for community attitudes towards the environment.

In Pentecostal ecotheology considerations to date, this doctrinal barrier has primarily been addressed by drawing on the work undertaken in recent years by scholars to constructively revise Pentecostal eschatology. However, in hermeneutical approaches to an emerging Pentecostal ecotheology, there is an evident lack of direct engagement with prophetic and apocalyptic texts, particularly those that speak of the degradation of the earth by the hand of YHWH. This is important because the way these apocalyptic texts are read can either reinforce the pessimistic perspective or provide resources to expand the horizon of Pentecostal understanding of the Creator's intent for creation.

This chapter addresses this gap in the literature through a close reading of Isaiah 24. First, a summary of how dispensational premillennialism became entrenched in Pentecostalism and its dissonance with Pentecostal spirituality is described. Second, approaches to the revisioning of Pentecostal eschatology and their contribution to the emerging Pentecostal ecotheology is discussed. This will highlight the relative lack of direct engagement with apocalyptic texts in the Pentecostal ecotheology. Third, this chapter will present a close reading of Isaiah 24. The envisions a cosmic judgement symbolized by terrestrial degradation. What might such an apocalyptic style of text offer a Pentecostal perspective on creation care? Therefore, fourth, the contribution of Isaiah 24 to ecotheology will be considered. This includes the implications of key themes such as: the human responsibility for the degradation of creation; the ecological implications of broken covenant; and the renewing of the earth. Finally, some considerations will be presented on how to integrate the contribution of the apocalyptic text of Isaiah 24 into the current eschatological frameworks that support Pentecostal ecotheology.

Apocalyptic Eschatology in Pentecostal Ecotheology

Pentecostal consideration of issues of climate change and creation care has generally focused on addressing doctrinal barriers and limitations, particularly leveraging the Pentecostal pneumatological distinctive of Spirit baptism to embrace these issues within the scope of Pentecostal concern.[1] The main doctrinal barrier commonly identified as significant is an apocalyptic eschatological narrative, primarily attributed to dispensational premillennialism, that emphasizes the salvation of individual souls who escape a world destined for annihilation. The practical consequence of this narrative is a general disregard for violence and neglect towards non-human creation by humanity. Put simply, if creation is going to be annihilated, why be concerned for its welfare?[2]

---

1. Anita Davis, "Pentecostal Approaches to Ecotheology: Reviewing the Literature," *Australasian Pentecostal Studies* 22, no. 1 (2021): 4–33; see A. J. Swoboda, *Tongues and Trees: Towards a Pentecostal Ecological Theology* (Blandford Forum: Deo, 2013) for a substantive pneumatological proposal.

2. See Andrew Ray Williams, "Greening the Apocalypse: A Pentecostal Eco-Eschatological Exploration," *PentecoStudies* 17, no. 2 (2018): 206; Robby Waddell, "Apocalyptic Sustainability: The Future of Pentecostal Ecology," in *Perspectives in Pentecostal Eschatologies: World Without End*, eds. Peter Althouse and Robby Waddell (Eugene: Pickwick, 2010), 98. Also see Snell in relation to the impact of premillennial dispensationalism on concern for social reform: Jeffrey T. Snell, "Beyond the Individual and Into the World: A Call to Participation in the Larger

The early Pentecostal community emerged at the beginning of the twentieth century in the context of millennial expectation. Prioritizing the narrative of Acts 2, Pentecostals sought the baptism of the Holy Spirit as experienced by the early church. This outpouring was seen as the "latter rain" and signpost of the end times, indicating the imminent return (*parousia*) of Christ, the soon coming king. Subsequently there was an expectation among these early Pentecostals that they were living in the last days of human history.[3] The empowerment of the Spirit was needed for this end-time harvest of souls to be reaped before the return of Christ.

Scholars note it was in second and third generation Pentecostalism as Pentecostal denominations aligned more with fundamentalist evangelical movements that the eschatological narrative of dispensational premillennialism became entrenched.[4] This alignment was further strengthened in the 1920s and 30s as Pentecostals turned to fundamentalism and its mode of biblical interpretation to address the issues presented by "the menace of evolutionism."[5]

By way of background, dispensational premillennialism, developed by John N. Darby and further promulgated by the Scofield Study Bible in 1909 marks out the Bible according to historical periods characterized by the way in which God engages with humanity and sin. These dispensations are mutually exclusive. Premillennial dispensationalism advocates for a rapture of the church to heaven followed by a seven-year period of tribulation where the world is ruled by the Antichrist. After this period, Christ returns with the church and defeats the Antichrist in the battle of Armageddon. There is then a thousand-year rule of Christ with Satan banished. At the end of this rule, Satan is thrown into the lake of fire and sulphur and the final judgement occurs with believers going to heaven and unbelievers to hell.

Purposes of the Spirit on the Basis of Pentecostal Theology," *Pneuma: The Journal of the Society for Pentecostal Studies* 14, no. 1 (1992): 53.

3. The Pentecostal Assemblies of Canada, *Essential Truths: The PAOC Statement of Essential Truths Commentary* (Mississauga: The Pentecostal Assemblies of Canada International Office, 2023), 46.

4. Frost points out this alignment was incentivized by seeking longer term religious respectability. Michael J. Frost, "Materiality or Materialism: Revising Pentecostal Eschatology, Renewing the Earth, and Saving the Planet from the Prosperity Gospel," *Australasian Pentecostal Studies* 22, no. 1 (2021): 108, fn 24. Althouse points out the alignment with fundamentalism may not be as rigid as often thought. See Peter Althouse, "'Left Behind' – Fact or Fiction: Ecumenical Dilemmas of the Fundamentalist Millenarian Tensions within Pentecostalism," *Journal of Pentecostal Theology* 13, no. 2 (2005): 198, fn. 33.

5. Gerald W. King, "Evolving Paradigms," in *The Spirit Renews the Face of the Earth: Pentecostal Forays in Science and Theology of Creation*, ed. Amos Yong (Eugene: Pickwick, 2009), 112–13.

The basis for this eschatology is a literalist approach to biblical interpretation.[6] This means that prophecies and apocalyptic texts are understood literally and can be read as predictive of current world events.[7] As Althouse has explained, millennial expectations and predictions about the end of the world based on this type of biblical interpretation have been a constant since the second century.[8] Over time, based on this literal reading of Scripture, premillennial dispensationalism developed into a coherent and complex interrelationship of creation doctrine, soteriology, and eschatology which was then enforced on the biblical data.[9]

McQueen has pointed out that there were a variety of perspectives within early Pentecostalism that underpinned their eschatological fervor prior to the subsequent alignment with evangelical fundamentalism, and that these were not simply modifications of premillennial dispensationalism.[10] McQueen also refers to Prosser who concluded that the premillennial dispensationalist eschatology eventually adopted by Pentecostals was "alien" to the original Pentecostal eschatology.[11] King notes its adoption by early Pentecostals was not foundational to the original eschatological passion of the movement for lost souls in the context of an imminent parousia.[12] Similarly, Sheppard observes that the eschatological fervor of early Pentecostals was not centred on escape from the impending catastrophe of the great tribulation but rather the latter rain outpouring of the Spirit and the coming of Christ.[13]

---

6. John A. Bertone, "Seven Dispensations or Two-Age View of History: A Pauline Perspective," in *Perspectives in Pentecostal Eschatologies: World Without End*, eds. Peter Althouse and Robby Waddell (Eugene: Pickwick, 2010), 61.

7. Frost, "Materiality or Materialism?," 106.

8. Peter Althouse, "Landscape of Pentecostal and Charismatic Eschatology: An Introduction," in *Perspectives in Pentecostal Eschatologies: World Without End*, eds. Peter Althouse and Robby Waddell (Eugene: Pickwick, 2010), 1.

9. Marius Nel, *African Pentecostalism and Eschatological Expectations: He Is Coming Back Again!* (Cambridge: Cambridge Scholars, 2019), 143.

10. Larry McQueen, *Toward a Pentecostal Eschatology: Discerning the Way Forward*, Journal of Pentecostal Theology Supplement Series 39 (Blandford Forum: Deo, 2012), 142; McQueen, "Early Pentecostal Eschatology," 152. See also Peter Althouse, *Spirit of the Last Days: Pentecostal Eschatology in Conversation with Jürgen Moltmann*, Journal of Pentecostal Theology Supplement Series 25 (London: T&T Clark, 2003), 234–35.

11. McQueen, *Toward a Pentecostal Eschatology*, 11.

12. King, "Evolving Paradigms," 112–13. See also McQueen, *Toward a Pentecostal Eschatology*, 34.

13. Gerald T. Sheppard, "Pentecostals and the Hermeneutics of Dispensationalism: The Anatomy of an Uneasy Relationship," *Pneuma: The Journal of the Society for Pentecostal Studies* 6, no. 2 (1984): 7–10.

Scholars have also identified significant inconsistencies between dispensational premillennialism and the foundational assumptions that underpin early Pentecostal spirituality and practice. The first is that dispensationalism has a cessationist position where charismata are only applicable to the dispensation of the revelation of Christ, and not for the church age; and that Old Testament promises were only for Israel, and not for the church.[14] In contrast, for Pentecostals, the Old Testament had current relevance for the spirituality of the believer. Pentecostal spirituality experienced the promise of the Old Testament as not just for Israel, due to the New Testament's "no distinction" between Jew and Gentile, with the promise of the outpouring of the Holy Spirit with miraculous signs, including glossolalia in the present. Another problematic aspect is that Pentecostals understood the kingdom of God to be present in the outpouring of the Spirit. However, a dispensationalist view categorizes the kingdom of God as entirely in the future. The mutually exclusivity of dispensationalism means the "future dispensation of kingdom [is] distinct from the present dispensation of grace."[15]

The maturing of Pentecostal theology in recent decades has also included a revisioning of Pentecostal eschatology given the doctrinal inadequacy of premillennial dispensationalism, including its hermeneutical basis, and its inconsistency with Pentecostal spirituality and practice. This has generally been along the lines of a proleptic eschatology that the ultimacy of new creation has been inaugurated in the risen and ascended Christ. That is, we live in this inaugurated new life, the kingdom of God, through the life of the outpoured Spirit of Christ, living a life where Christ is Lord, yet still yearning with faithful patience for the "not yet" of ultimate fulfilment where God will be all in all.[16] Jesus Christ is the inauguration of the kingdom of God on earth, where God's will, the reign of divine love, is ultimate.[17] This perspective aligns with the eschatological last days fervor of early Pentecostalism that was centred on the latter day outpouring of the Spirit and a passion for Christ's return. It also, as Macchia points out, defers to the timetable of God and his patience as set

---

14. Bertone, "Seven Dispensations," 61.

15. Bertone, "Seven Dispensations," 66.

16. Althouse, *Spirit of the Last Days,"* 188, 253–55; John Christopher Thomas and Frank D. Macchia, *Revelation*, The Two Horizons New Testament Commentary (Grand Rapids: Eerdmans, 2016), 504.

17. Frank D. Macchia, *Baptized in the Spirit: A Global Pentecostal Theology* (Grand Rapids: Zondervan, 2006), 96–97.

out in 2 Peter 3:8–10 – nobody knows when and how the ultimacy of the new creation will be realized.[18]

Because this renewal has been inaugurated by the Spirit in the incarnated, risen, and ascended Christ, "new creation" does not mean the annihilation of creation, but rather its transformation. It is not new creation out of nothing (*ex nihilo*) but out of old (*ex vetera*).[19] The outpoured Spirit is the Spirit of life who reaches in the here and now for the eschatological renewal of all creation.[20] It is an apocalyptic eschatology of revealed hope for all of creation grounded in Christ and Pentecost, rather than of apocalyptic destruction without hope for God's creation, grounded in a human interpretive schema.[21] The "former things" that have passed away (Rev 21:4 KJV) are the death, grief, crying and pain of the creation that groans for the liberation of ultimate redemption (Rom 8:20–21).[22]

From this perspective, the Spirit of Pentecost is the Spirit of the last days. The hope of the transformation of people, social interactions, and humanity's relations with creation by the eschatological Spirit has been inaugurated in the person of Jesus and Pentecost. It is being foreshadowed by believers' faithfulness to the lordship of Christ over the lordship of this world, to the new in Christ in contrast to the old of the world, in anticipation of the ultimate fulfilment of his will being done on earth as in heaven.[23] The charismata such as healing in the ministry of Christ and of the church can be considered the foretaste of the ultimate realization of the intention of God for creation and affirming of the materiality of ultimate redemption.[24] From a missional perspective, socially responsible engagement with the world then becomes faithful participation and witness to the mission of God, revealed in Christ, for the transformative renewal of the world.[25] As McQueen and Macchia both point out, this eschatological understanding of the work of Christ and Spirit provides hope for our commitment to participate in this ultimate hope for all creation, rather than escape from the despair of the annihilation of creation.[26]

---

18. Frank D. Macchia, "The Time Is Near! Or, Is It? Dare We Abandon Our Eschatological Expectation?," *Pneuma: The Journal of the Society for Pentecostal Studies* 25, no. 2 (2003): 162.

19. Nel, *African Pentecostalism and Eschatological Expectations*, 149.

20. Macchia, *Baptized in the Spirit*, 41.

21. Althouse, "'Left Behind' – Fact or Fiction," 191.

22. McQueen, *Toward a Pentecostal Eschatology*, 253–54.

23. Althouse, *Spirit of the Last Days*, 236.

24. McQueen, *Toward a Pentecostal Eschatology*, 254–57.

25. Althouse, *Spirit of the Last Days*, 236.

26. McQueen, *Toward a Pentecostal Eschatology*, 268; Macchia, *Baptized in the Spirit*, 275.

This revisioning of Pentecostal eschatology by theologians such as McQueen, Althouse, and Macchia that is inclusive of all creation has provided the main eschatological foundation for Pentecostal ecotheological consideration of the implications for Pentecostal mission. It also addresses the "why bother" implications of premillennial dispensationalism in relation to creation care. For example, Althouse has leveraged his work on Pentecostal eschatology to consider the implications for Pentecostal responsibility in relation to all of creation. He argues that these fundamentalist approaches to the creation narrative, soteriology, and eschatology have narrowed the gospel to the salvation of souls in contrast to the expansiveness of the gospel for all of creation.[27] He draws on his engagement with the kenotic eschatology of Jürgen Moltmann to propose the charismatic giftings of the Holy Spirit are not simply for personal benefit but are for the sake of the world.[28] The self-limiting Spirit who sustains and indwells creation and enabled the ultimate self-giving of Jesus Christ is the Spirit who sustains the church, drawing it into God's mission: for the new creation "at blissful rest in the transfigured cosmos."[29] On this basis, missional self-giving service, the outworking of God's love, is "service to God, service to others, and service to the creation itself."[30]

A range of scholars have utilized these Pentecostal eschatological developments to consider the implications of an inaugurated eschatology for Pentecostal mission in relation to all of creation. For example, Williams urges Pentecostals to reclaim the eschatological fervor of early Pentecostalism oriented towards this expanded vision of God's intent for all creation.[31] Empowered by the eschatological Spirit of life, we can serve as "priests of healing to God's creation, bearing the ministry of reconciliation that Christ bore to us (2 Cor 5:16–21)."[32] Nel proposes Pentecostals should not only be praying for the physically ill, but also for the healing of creation, given the eschatological work of

---

27. Peter Althouse, "Implications of the Kenosis of the Spirit for a Creational Eschatology," in *The Spirit Renews the Face of the Earth: Pentecostal Forays in Science and Theology of Creation*, ed. Amos Yong (Eugene: Pickwick, 2009), 155–72; Peter Althouse, "Pentecostal Eco-Transformation: Possibilities for a Pentecostal in Light of Moltmann's Green Theology," in *Blood Cries Out: Pentecostals, Ecology, and the Groans of Creation*, ed. A. J. Swoboda (Eugene: Pickwick, 2014), 126.

28. Althouse, "Implications of the Kenosis," 156.

29. Althouse, "Implications of the Kenosis," 168.

30. Althouse, "Implications of the Kenosis," 172.

31. Williams, "Greening the Apocalypse," 225.

32. A. J. Swoboda, "Posterity or Prosperity?: Critiquing and Refiguring Prosperity Theologies in an Ecological Age," *Pneuma: Journal for the Society for Pentecostal Studies* 37, no. 3 (2015): 410.

the Spirit to renew creation.[33] Good stewardship should be primarily "pneumatologically and eschatologically motivated" as responsible participants in the "already" of the kingdom.[34] Frost encourages a more expansive view of renewal that includes all of creation and challenges "unbridled consumer capitalism" within and without the church, given its implications for the environment.[35]

Where Are the Apocalyptic Texts in a Pentecostal Ecotheology?

To turn now to hermeneutical approaches to Pentecostal ecotheology, the main concern has been to consider the implications of the scriptural witness for all of creation, not just from the perspective of humanity.[36] As has been discussed, the eschatological considerations undertaken by Pentecostal theologians have made a significant contribution to Pentecostal ecotheological development to date. However, the intersection of apocalyptic texts and eschatology, and the subsequent implications regarding responsibility for the welfare of creation, have received less attention. Consideration of this intersection is critical as it is the literalist hermeneutic that underpins the interpretation of Scripture that results in the conclusion that the world will be annihilated. Addressing this issue also has broader benefits. The first is that it provides a basis for Pentecostal hermeneutics that addresses (and re-dresses) its common literalistic interpretation within Pentecostalism. The second is that, in addressing these problematic texts, it provides interpretive principles that strengthen Pentecostal biblical scholarship more broadly.

Lamp and Waddell have both made initial forays into this issue. Lamp draws on Chris E. W. Green's hermeneutical approach to confront the issue of difficult texts that depict God as "one who wreaks havoc on nature on behalf of human beings."[37] Green's hermeneutic emphasizes a sacramental approach to Scripture that concerns shaping the believer toward holiness. Even engaging uncomfortable texts can contribute to the sanctification of the believer

---

33. Nel, *African Pentecostalism and Eschatological Expectations*, 195.
34. Nel, *African Pentecostalism and Eschatological Expectations*, 195.
35. Frost, "Materiality or Materialism?," 118.
36. See for example, recent contributions by Jeffrey Lamp, "Grey into Green: A Pentecostal Contribution to Ecological Hermeneutics," *Australasian Pentecostal Studies* 22, no. 1 (2021): 71–86, and John Daniel Griffiths, "Spirit-Baptized Creation: Locating Pentecost in the Meta-Narrative of Creation and Its Implications for a Pentecostal Ecology," *Australasian Pentecostal Studies* 22, no. 1 (2021): 46–60.
37. Lamp, "Grey into Green," 76.

as they are changed through the wrestling.[38] Adopting this approach, Lamp proposes these ecologically troubling texts are there precisely to challenge us as human beings into greater awareness of the cries of the earth.[39] Similarly, Waddell has addressed 2 Peter 3:10–13, a "proof text" that has been utilized by dispensationalists to support the notion of the eschatological annihilation of the cosmos.[40] He points out Jewish and ancient Christian apocalyptic texts are not about predicting the future but rather discerning "the spiritual significance of the present."[41] In this case, the focus of the text is not about predicting the annihilation of the universe, but a coming judgement where all the deeds of humanity will be laid bare.[42] It is about urging believers to live pure lives so "let the reader beware to live at peace with God."[43] This focus of the text on judgement of human deeds rather than cosmic annihilation consequently subverts the implications for human engagement with all of creation. If the focus is on cosmic annihilation, the implications are "why bother?" If the focus is on judgement of human deeds, the implications are the acknowledgment of human responsibility.

Engaging the Apocalyptic: An Analysis of Isaiah 24

To contribute to strengthening an engagement with apocalyptic texts in a Pentecostal ecotheology, a close reading of Isaiah 24 is now explored. While both Pentecostal and non-Pentecostal scholarship on Isaiah is utilized to enrich this discussion, there is currently a paucity of exegetical engagement of Isaiah by Pentecostals.[44] Isaiah 24 begins the section of Isaiah often referred to as the "little apocalypse," which includes chapters 24 to 27. Typical characteristics of the apocalyptic genre noted by John J. Collins include: insight into a supernatural world, revelation mediated by a supernatural being, an eschato-

---

38. Green, *Sanctifying Interpretation*, 36, 158.
39. Lamp, "Grey into Green," 84.
40. Roddy Waddell, "Apocalyptic Sustainability: The Future of Pentecostal Ecology," in *Perspectives in Pentecostal Eschatologies: World Without End*, eds. Peter Althouse and Robby Waddell (Eugene: Pickwick, 2010), 104; also, Lamp, "Ecotheology: A People of the Spirit for Earth," in *The Routledge Handbook of Pentecostal Theology*, ed. Wolfgang Vondey (New York: Routledge, 2020), 363.
41. Waddell, "Apocalyptic Sustainability," 109.
42. Waddell, "Apocalyptic Sustainability," 108.
43. McQueen, "Early Pentecostal Eschatology," 108.
44. The beginnings of this shift towards exegetical engagement by Pentecostal biblical scholars is expected with the forthcoming commentary on Isaiah 1–39 by Jacqueline Grey in the Pentecostal Commentary Series.

logical outlook, symbolical and mythical allusions, reversal of oppression and "retribution beyond the bounds of history," origins of evil, the corruption of creation caused by human sin, the end as a cosmic catastrophe, and God's sovereign judgement over the living and the dead.[45] While many of these features are shared with prophetic texts generally, Collins suggests that to strictly be categorized within the genre of apocalyptic a text must feature the revelation transmitted by a supernatural being.[46] Therefore, as the message of Isaiah 24 is not structured on a message mediated by a supernatural being it may be considered "apocalyptic" in the extended sense[47] or "proto-apocalyptic" for it shares many other key features in common with the genre. Isaiah 24–27 fits within this category of an earlier form of apocalyptic style writing. Interestingly, Pentecostal scholar Wonsuk Ma observes that explicit references to the Spirit are absent in this section of Isaiah 24–27,[48] unlike other comparable apocalyptic-type texts such as Joel 2:28–32.[49] A rationale for the absence of the Spirit in Isaiah 24 will be proposed below.

One of the central themes of Isaiah 24 concerns God's sovereign judgement over the cosmos. It describes an undoing of creation. The chapter divides quite evenly into two major parts (verses 1–13 and 14–23); the first part announces the judgement while the second part pictures the devastating implications of the announcement. The chapter opens with a declaration to "See" (24:1 NIV): the prophet demands that the hearer see how the cosmos is about to unravel through YHWH's punishment. He declares that YHWH will bring destruction through the defacing of the earth and the scattering of its inhabitants (v. 1). This upheaval will equally impact every level of human social order regardless of their gender, status, or circumstance. Despite the emphasis on the role of the leaders of the community within the pairings of 24:2 (such as priest and people), their suffering is democratized.

The responsibility of humanity for creation is explored by Wonsuk Ma using an "elect" pattern. In this approach, Ma highlights the special status of humanity to perform their "God-given task" of stewardship. This same elect pattern is also given to the covenant community for the missional task of being a light to the nations and similarly given to the political leaders within

---

45. Collins, *Apocalyptic Imagination*, 10–15.
46. Collins, *Apocalyptic Imagination*, 7, 10.
47. Collins, *Apocalyptic Imagination*, 10.
48. Wonsuk Ma, *Until the Spirit Comes: The Spirit of God in the Book of Isaiah* (Sheffield: Sheffield Academic Press, 1999), 185.
49. Notably Joel 3:1–5 in the Hebrew text.

the covenant community to rule justly.⁵⁰ Yet, as Isaiah 24:1–3 describes, the elect (humanity, the covenant community, political leaders) failed their task resulting in the devastation of the creation (24:1), the scattering of inhabitants of the earth (24:1, 3), and the suffering of the non-elite within the covenant community (24:2). Rather than the earth flourishing under the human stewards (Gen 1:26), it is described as diminishing. Similarly, rather than humanity increasing and multiplying (Gen 1:28), the population is reducing. The future of creation is described, using present tense, through the imagery of the earth twisting, withering, and drying up, and the heavens fading (24:4). This description captures the reversal of a creational theology. However, the prophet makes clear that such a future is irresistible because it is the resolve and word of YHWH (24:1, 3).

The reason for this devastation is because the earth is polluted by its inhabitants. The judgement by YHWH is a consequence of humanity breaking God's "everlasting covenant" (24:5).⁵¹ There are two mythical allusions here to reinforce the rebelliousness of humanity: the scattering is reminiscent of the tower of Babel myth (Gen 11:1–8), while the "everlasting covenant" infers the Noahic covenant (Gen 9:8–17). The Noahic covenant was not unconditional; it required accountability for the shedding of human blood (Gen 9:6). These references infer an older, all-embracing covenant with humanity and the created world.⁵² Both these mythical allusions point to the universal guilt of humanity for "concrete acts of disregard for the creator's intention for creation,"⁵³ which unleashes a curse of overwhelming devastation leaving only a remnant of inhabitants (Isa 24:6). Therefore, the environmental crisis described in this passage is clearly the result of the moral degradation of humanity and their rejection of YHWH's guidance (*Torah*).

Yet, the reference to the Noahic covenant also ensures salvation for future generations (human and non-human) through the promise that creation will never be fully destroyed again (Gen 9:1–17). This covenant with all flesh points ultimately to the renewing and flourishing of all creation despite a temporary

---

50. Wonsuk Ma, "The Spirit in Isaiah: God's Might and His Charismatic Presence on the Elect," in *The Spirit Throughout the Canon: Pentecostal Pneumatology*, eds. Craig S. Keener and William Oliverio Jr (Leiden: Brill, 2022), 37.

51. Christopher R. Seitz, *Isaiah 1–39* (Louisville: Westminster John Knox, 1993), 179–80.

52. John Barton, "Reading the Prophets from an Environmental Perspective," in *Ecological Hermeneutics: Biblical, Historical and Theological Perspectives*, eds. David Horrell, Cherryl Hunt, Christopher Southgate, and Francesca Stravrakopoulou (London: T&T Clark, 2010), 48–49.

53. Walter Brueggemann, *Isaiah 1–39* (Louisville: Westminster John Knox, 1998), 192.

"fall from grace."[54] This intertextual reference gives hope that this devastation in Isaiah 24 is not the end. Instead, it follows a pattern found throughout the biblical text of judgement preceding resurrection, which offers a "second beginning."[55] So despite the destruction described in Isaiah 24, the reference to the Noahic covenant both identifies the human cause for the judgement but also provides hope that this plundering will not be the end for the creation. This has important implications for Pentecostal eschatology, as discussed above. The Noahic covenant ensures that the apocalyptic devastation does not result in the annihilation of creation, but points to the renewing of creation. This pattern of judgement preceding new creation is also shared with the message of the prophet Joel in which a new order is described in 2:28–32, a passage quoted by Peter on the day of Pentecost and dear to the heart of the Pentecostal. There are other parallels between the apocalyptic-type texts of Isaiah 24 and Joel 2, such as reference to the "day of the Lord" (Isa 24:21; Joel 2:31), signs and wonders in the heavens (Isa 24:21–3; Joel 2:30–1), and the focus on YHWH, in whom salvation is found, present on Mt Zion (Isa 24:23; Joel 2:32). However, unlike Isaiah 24, Joel 2 explicitly connects the Spirit poured out on "all flesh" to bring about this restoration. It is suggested that it is the absence of repentance by the people that the Spirit is not given in Isaiah 24, in contrast to the people's cry of lament and repentance in Joel 2:18 which instigates the promise of the Spirit.[56] As Larry McQueen writes, "Thus lament is prerequisite to salvation which includes the giving of the spirit [sic] to all who call on Yahweh."[57]

Isaiah 24:7–13 continues to describe a universal mourning and grief as the flourishing and productivity of vineyards shrivel and the joy of revellers resign from sighs to silence (24:7–8). As Roberts notes, "the party is over."[58] The unnamed city of chaos (*tohu*) is broken (24:10), resembling somewhat the primordial formlessness of creation in Genesis 1:2. However, in this case, the Spirit is absent from bringing life and form to the impenetrable city. There is no new beginning as in the time of Noah. Instead, it is the end of creation that is in sight. This section concludes by confirming that this future end is in

---

54. Amos Yong, *Mission After Pentecost. The Witness of the Spirit from Genesis to Revelation* (Grand Rapids: Baker Academic, 2019), 30.

55. Yong, *Mission After Pentecost*, 31.

56. Larry R. McQueen, *Joel and the Spirit: The Cry of a Prophetic Hermeneutic*, Journal of Pentecostal Theology Supplement series 8 (Sheffield: Sheffield Academic Press, 1995), 39.

57. McQueen, *Joel and the Spirit*, 40. McQueen notes the comparable promise of Yahweh's Spirit in the tradition of Isaiah, particularly Isa 32:15 and Isa 34:3.

58. J. J. M. Roberts, *First Isaiah* (Minneapolis: Fortress, 2015), 314.

present sight for the inhabitants of the earth, like the shaking of an olive tree at the end of a harvest (24:13).

The next portion of Isaiah 24 describes the implications of the YHWH's judgement (24:14–23), beginning with a disputation pattern.[59] The focus shifts suddenly to the exultant worship of YHWH. The silence of the previous section (24:8, 11) is replaced with the rejoicing of an unidentified community worshipping YHWH once more (24:14). The name of YHWH is glorified from sunrise in the east to the sunset across the coastlands.[60] However, the prophet disputes this joyous worship of the people. The prophet cannot join in these songs; instead he cries out an alternative utterance and accusation using the much-debated phrase *razi*, meaning "secret." This term is also used in the book of Daniel to refer to "information known only to God but revealed by God to chosen intermediaries, generally in a context of prayer, fasting, visions, and converse with angels."[61] This suggests that the prophet is interpreting the mystery of the events revealed through divine revelation; although the people think they are pleasing God by their disingenuous worship, they are instead under the judgement of God.[62] This term is also a cry of woe that resonates with the calling of Isaiah; when confronted with the vision of the Holy One of Israel, he sees his own depravity (6:5). It is the depravity of those praising YHWH that causes this bitter response from the prophet. Despite their lusty singing, the people continue in their treachery. Blenkinsopp highlights the "apocalyptic tone of the seer's utterance," which is the entrée to the next series of cosmic judgements directly addressing these duplicitous people.[63]

The floodgates of judgement are now opened as the prophet streams bitter invectives over the people of the earth. None will escape the coming judgement; all will inevitably be ensnared in the pit, even by their own cowardice (24:17–18). The result is cosmic upheaval and the undoing of creation. The earth shakes once more. It is broken, split, sways like a drunkard, and falls (24:19–20). The universal judgement will continue "on that day" to punish both the supernatural and human powers at work in the world who undermine the rule of YHWH (24:21). The terminology of "that day" is common apocalyptic language pointing to a future time beyond the strictures of history

---

59. Marvin A. Sweeney, *Isaiah 1–39: An Introduction to Prophetic Literature*, The Forms of the Old Testament Literature 16 (Grand Rapids: Eerdmans, 1996), 328.

60. Roberts, *First Isaiah*, 315.

61. Joseph Blenkinsopp, *Isaiah 1–39: A New Translation with Introduction and Commentary* (New York: Bantam Doubleday Dell, 2000), 355.

62. Blenkinsopp, *Isaiah 1–39*, 355.

63. Blenkinsopp, *Isaiah 1–39*, 355.

when YHWH will intervene on behalf of his people to bring retribution and restoration. These rebellious powers will be imprisoned and punished to await their forthcoming punishment (24:22). This imagery is recycled in the book of Revelation as the powers hostile to God are also imprisoned in a dark and bottomless pit (Rev 9:2, 11).[64] Yet, this eschatological outlook gives hope to the faithful who suffer in the present. Similarly, the celestial bodies that have been elevated to divine status by idolators are shamed and put in their rightful place as created objects (24:23). This exposes the divine aspirations of created objects and strips them of any god-like mystique to restore the proper order of creation once more. The final verse references YHWH's reign on Mt Zion (24:23). The continued existence of Zion suggests that while the earth has been shaken and terrorized, it has not been annihilated. Instead, this points to a new beginning of God's order and rulership established on a transformed earth aided by a redeemed human community.

The Contribution of Isaiah 24 to a Pentecostal Ecotheology

There are two significant ways that Isaiah 24 can contribute to a Pentecostal ecotheology. One is by focusing on the literary resonances of Isaiah 24 with the text of the day of Pentecost. Acts 2 is often considered a hermeneutical key for Pentecostals. Contributing to a reading of this central text can enhance Pentecostal theology more generally and ecotheology more specifically. The second significant way that a study of Isaiah 24 can enhance a Pentecostal ecotheology is to consider how some key themes of this passage can contribute to a developing Pentecostal ecotheology, particularly regarding the human responsibility for the degradation of creation, the ecological implications of broken covenant, and the renewing of the earth.

In many ways, the day of Pentecost is a reversal of the judgement of Isaiah 24. Pentecost is an undoing of this text. The Pentecost account refers to the blessing of the Spirit poured out on all flesh, rather than judgement. In Isaiah 24, the people will be scattered (24:1) alluding to the scattering of humanity in the tower of Babel myth (Gen 11:7–9), while the Pentecost event is often considered a reversal of the Babel story. As noted above, the Babel story describes how God descended to bring confusion and disunity to rebellious humanity (Gen 11:7), resulting in linguistic disarray and the scattering of the people. Instead, at Pentecost, the disciples were waiting in unity for the Holy Spirit promised by the ascended Christ to descend upon them. Similarly, while Isaiah

---

64. Blenkinsopp, *Isaiah 1–39*, 357.

24 also presents a democratization of experience as the categories of social and economic class are removed (24:2), it is an experience of punishment and suffering rather than for empowering mission as described in the Pentecost event. Instead of the fire of eschatological judgement that burns and devours the inhabitants of the earth (24:6), the tongues of fire at Pentecost fall on the disciples as evidence of divine favour and presence (Acts 2:3). Rather than the silence of the normally drunken revellers in Isaiah 24 stunned by the depletion of the wine reserves (24:7–9), Acts 2 describes a cacophony of Spirit-inspired languages that is mistaken for drunkenness by the pilgrims in Jerusalem. Peter makes a direct connection between this phenomenon and Joel 2, a passage in which the Spirit is explicitly involved in the pattern of restoration following judgement, unlike the lack of reference to the Spirit in Isaiah 24.

However, there are also various resonances and consistencies between Isaiah 24 and the Acts 2 narrative. As the floodgates of heaven are opened, the earth is shaken (24:18b–20). This has some echoes in the Acts 2 as suddenly the sound of violent wind comes from heaven and fills the house (Acts 2:2). The imagery in both texts suggest a theophanic experience. Similarly, both Peter's use of Joel in his speech on the day of Pentecost and Isaiah 24 describe the cosmos turned haywire. Both texts refer to or allude to the "day of the Lord" (Isa 24:21; Acts 2:17, 20). This is the cosmic end-event in which God's eschatological reign is manifested and justice activated. Both texts refer to wonders in heaven and signs on earth (Isa 24:18; Acts 2:19). Isaiah's moon is dismayed (24:23), while Joel's moon turns to blood (Acts 2:20). Creation cannot contain the presence of God, resulting in cosmic and terrestrial upheaval. This apocalyptic imagery in both texts points to a coming new age marked by the eschatological rule of Yahweh. Isaiah 24 describes a future time when all inhabitants of the earth (24:23) universally acknowledge Yahweh's glory and rule. Peter announces the salvation offered by the Lord resulting from the intervention of the Lord on that glorious day (Acts 2:20). The repentance Peter preaches is reflected in the picture of humanity humbly accepting their proper place in God's reign (24:23) as Yahweh reigns on Mount Zion and before its elders. God's rule results in order restored, creation made right, and a sustainable future.

These connections to Acts 2, arguably the central text of the Pentecostal community, are helpful for a developing Pentecostal theology. However, Isaiah 24 can also contribute to a developing Pentecostal ecotheology through the exploration of its key themes. First, Isaiah 24 makes clear that humans are responsible for the diminishing of the earth and degradation of creation. In fact, it cannot be clearer: "The earth is defiled by its people" (24:5). The pollution of the earth and the suffering of creation is the direct result of human greed and irresponsibly. Despite being given the mandate to be loving stewards of creation (Gen 1:28), humanity has exploited rather than nurtured this world. Yet, Isaiah 24 ends with the hope of restoration that can only be achieved by humanity finding their correct place in God's just rule (24:23).

Second, the underlying cause of humanity's negative impact on the environment is their rejection of God's ways. While Israel was responsible to uphold the Torah in the Old Testament, there is also an expectation voiced in Isaiah 24:5 that non-Israelites were responsible to uphold the "everlasting covenant." As noted above, this refers to the Noahic covenant (Gen 9:8–17). This is considered a universal covenant, not restricted to Israel but made with all humanity. This covenant required humanity to ensure the flourishing of human and non-human communities. Food sources for Noah's descendants would not be restricted to plants but would also include "everything," except meat with the lifeblood in it. Humanity was to respect the earth, animals, and the sanctity of life, recognizing the image of God in one another (Gen 9:1–7). However, according to Isaiah 24:6, humanity abused its role and has broken this covenant and therefore pays the penalty. This passage highlights that the degradation of the earth is a covenantal problem. There is a relational brokenness between God, humanity, and the non-human creation. Therefore, the healing of this fractured relationship requires the repentance of humanity.

Third, despite the ominous opening to the prophetic pronouncement, the creation is not annihilated but renewed. Isaiah 24:1 opens with the declaration that the earth will be damaged and devastated, seemingly beyond repair. This poetic device of hyperbole is used to emphasize the situation of extremity, as is consistent with apocalyptic and eschatology style language. However, the devastation it describes is not the end. Instead, the last picture given in Isaiah 24 is of Yahweh reigning "on Mount Zion and in Jerusalem" (24:23). While Zion is often evocative of the presence of God due to the location of the temple, Jerusalem often functions in parallel in the prophetic literature as representing the ethno-political centre of the nation. Therefore, in this transformed world, it continues to function as the operational hub of the ruler in charge, except now it is Yahweh that reigns from this location. This consistency and continuance of location suggests that the earth has not been annihilated but transformed in the new rulership of Yahweh. This has profound implications for a Pentecostal ecotheology.

Conclusion: Refiguring Pentecostal Ecotheology

This analysis of Isaiah 24 concluded that because YHWH is Lord his presence will not be removed from creation, regardless of the results of humanity's rejection of this lordship. Rather, YHWH's everlasting covenant with creation means it will be renewed and transformed, not annihilated. Humanity's vocation has always been to humbly accept their proper place in God's reign rather than placing themselves as gods, with the consequent results of the moral degradation of humanity and of the earth. It is the right ordering of the relation of YHWH and humanity that is the basis for the flourishing of human and non-human communities. From this perspective, references in Scripture to the passing away of the world can be understood as the passing away of a world where YHWH is not Lord, where there is the absence of right relation and its consequential impacts. The new heaven and earth are creation in right relation with the Creator – YHWH is all in all.

In light of Pentecostal eschatological considerations and their contribution to the emerging Pentecostal ecotheology, this covenantal commitment to realizing the lordship of YHWH in creation has been definitively revealed in Jesus Christ. He is the inauguration of this ultimate lordship of the kingdom of God. Christ put aside his entitlement to divinity and bore the consequences of humanity's self-positioning as God. The resurrected and ascended Christ poured out his Spirit to bring humanity and all of creation into this rightly ordered relation. The Spirit empowers and enables humanity to fulfil our vocation: to bear witness in the present to the future hope of the transformation of creation into the dwelling place of God, where he reigns in glory. As Althouse proposes, we can "interpret the Spirit of the last days as God's presence and action to transform . . . creation itself into the eschatological new creation."[65]

This hope revealed in Christ subverts the hopelessness for creation of premillennial dispensationalism. What is annihilated is not the whole of creation. It is the passing away of "the lust of the flesh, the lust of the eyes, and the pride of life" (1 John 2:16 NIV) in the "present form" of the world (1 Cor 7:31), that which results in death and destruction.[66] The ultimate rule and reign of Christ is transformative of creation such that it can be considered a new creation because it is where YHWH is Lord. Given the characteristics of the risen Christ, and the signs and wonders that exceed created limits, any proposal about what this looks like can only be speculation. However, what we do know is that our mission as those who are baptized in the Spirit is to

---

65. Althouse, *Spirit of the Last Days*, 236.
66. McQueen, *Toward a Pentecostal Eschatology*, 254.

participate in the inauguration of this new creation in the here and now, to live in the fullness of the Spirit as a testament to the excessive scope, almost beyond our imagination, of the Father's intent for creation.

So instead of an eschatology that is based on a particular reading of apocalyptic texts in Scripture in the context of current events, Pentecostal eschatological fervor should be grounded in the self-giving love of God and covenantal commitment for all of humanity and creation. This is an order that results in shalom rather than the disorder of creation subject to the reign of sin and death. The apocalyptic imagery of Pentecost is a subversion of apocalyptic imagery as catastrophe. It is about restoration and renewal into the self-giving love of God revealed in Christ and through the outpoured Spirit, not the annihilation and chaos caused by human self-aggrandizement.

The implication for Pentecostal ecotheology is that Pentecostal mission is more expansive than the saving of souls to escape a world destined for destruction. It will be manifested as a responsible witness to the "already" of the kingdom through transformative rightly ordered relations with all of creation. As Nel concludes, "while secular people preserve nature because it is their present home, believers understand the world to be their present and future home."[67] Our mission then is pneumatologically and eschatologically motivated. It is a witness to the vision of hope grounded in Jesus Christ who has defeated sin and death and offers new life, not just for humanity, but for all of creation. It is this eschatological hope – the ultimate lordship of YHWH inaugurated in Christ – that we eagerly anticipate through our participation with the poured-out Spirit in the here and now.

Bibliography

Althouse, Peter. "Implications of the Kenosis of the Spirit for a Creational Eschatology." In *The Spirit Renews the Face of the Earth: Pentecostal Forays in Science and Theology of Creation*, edited by Amos Yong, 155–72. Eugene: Pickwick, 2009.

———. "The Landscape of Pentecostal and Charismatic Eschatology: An Introduction." In *Perspectives in Pentecostal Eschatologies: World Without End*, edited by Peter Althouse and Robby Waddell, 1–21. Eugene: Pickwick, 2010.

———. "'Left Behind' – Fact or Fiction: Ecumenical Dilemmas of the Fundamentalist Millenarian Tensions within Pentecostalism." *Journal of Pentecostal Theology* 13, no. 2 (2005): 187–207.

---

67. Nel, *African Pentecostalism and Eschatological Expectations*, 195.

———. "Pentecostal Eco-Transformation: Possibilities for a Pentecostal Ecotheology in Light of Moltmann's Green Theology." In *Blood Cries Out: Pentecostals, Ecology, and the Groans of Creation*, edited by A. J. Swoboda, 116–33. Eugene: Pickwick, 2014.

Barton, John. "Reading the Prophets from an Environmental Perspective." In *Ecological Hermeneutics: Biblical, Historical and Theological Perspectives*, eds. David Horrell, Cherryl Hunt, Christopher Southgate, and Francesca Stravrakopoulou, 46–55. London: T&T Clark, 2010.

Bertone, John A. "Seven Dispensations or Two-Age View of History: A Pauline Perspective." In *Perspectives in Pentecostal Eschatologies: World Without End*, edited by Peter Althouse and Robby Waddell, 61–94. Eugene: Pickwick, 2010.

Blenkinsopp, Joseph. *Isaiah 1–39. A New Translation with Introduction and Commentary*. New York: Bantam Doubleday Dell, 2000.

Brueggemann, Walter. *Isaiah 1–39*. Louisville: Westminster John Knox, 1998.

Collins, John J. *The Apocalyptic Imagination: An Introduction to Jewish Apocalyptic Literature*. 3rd edition. Grand Rapids: Eerdmans, 2016.

Davis, Anita. "Pentecostal Approaches to Ecotheology: Reviewing the Literature." *Australasian Pentecostal Studies* 22, no. 1 (2021): 4–33.

Frost, Michael J. "Materiality or Materialism?: Revising Pentecostal Eschatology, Renewing the Earth, and Saving the Planet from the Prosperity Gospel." *Australasian Pentecostal Studies* 22, no. 1 (2021): 104–21.

Green, Chris E. W. *Sanctifying Interpretation: Vocation, Holiness, and Scripture*. 2nd edition. Cleveland: CPT, 2020.

Griffiths, John Daniel. "Spirit-Baptised Creation: Locating Pentecost in the Meta-Narrative of Creation and Its Implications for a Pentecostal Ecology." *Australasian Pentecostal Studies* 22, no. 1 (2021): 46–60.

King, Gerald W. "Evolving Paradigms." In *The Spirit Renews the Face of the Earth: Pentecostal Forays in Science and Theology of Creation*, edited by Amos Yong, 93–114. Eugene: Pickwick, 2009.

Lamp, Jeffrey S. "Ecotheology: A People of the Spirit for Earth." In *The Routledge Handbook of Pentecostal Theology*, edited by Wolfgang Vondey, 357–66. New York: Routledge, 2020.

———. "Grey into Green: A Pentecostal Contribution to Ecological Hermeneutics." *Australasian Pentecostal Studies* 22, no. 1 (2021): 71–86.

Ma, Wonsuk. "The Spirit in Isaiah: God's Might and His Charismatic Presence on the Elect." In *The Spirit Throughout the Canon: Pentecostal Pneumatology*, edited by Craig S. Keener and L. William Oliverio Jr., 37–44. Leiden: Brill, 2022.

———. *Until the Spirit Comes: The Spirit of God in the Book of Isaiah*. Sheffield: Sheffield Academic Press, 1999.

Macchia, Frank D. *Baptized in the Spirit: A Global Pentecostal Theology*. Grand Rapids: Zondervan, 2006.

———. "The Time Is Near! Or, Is It? Dare We Abandon Our Eschatological Expectation?" *Pneuma: The Journal of the Society for Pentecostal Studies* 25, no. 2 (2003): 161–63. https://doi.org/10.1163/157007403776113215.

McQueen, Larry. "Early Pentecostal Eschatology in the Light of The Apostolic Faith, 1906–1908." In *Perspectives in Pentecostal Eschatologies: World Without End*, edited by Peter Althouse and Robby Waddell, 139–54. Eugene: Pickwick, 2010.

———. *Toward a Pentecostal Eschatology: Discerning the Way Forward*. Journal of Pentecostal Theology Supplement Series 39. Blandford Forum: Deo, 2012.

———. *Joel and the Spirit: The Cry of a Prophetic Hermeneutic*. Journal of Pentecostal Theology Supplement Series 8. Sheffield: Sheffield Academic Press, 1995.

Nel, Marius. *African Pentecostalism and Eschatological Expectations: He Is Coming Back Again!* Cambridge: Cambridge Scholars, 2019.

Roberts, J. J. M. *First Isaiah*. Minneapolis: Fortress, 2015.

Seitz, Christopher R. *Isaiah 1–39*. Louisville: Westminster John Knox, 1993.

Sheppard, Gerald T. "Pentecostals and the Hermeneutics of Dispensationalism: The Anatomy of an Uneasy Relationship." *Pneuma: The Journal of the Society for Pentecostal Studies* 6, no. 2 (1984): 5–33.

Snell, Jeffrey T. "Beyond the Individual and Into the World: A Call to Participation in the Larger Purposes of the Spirit on the Basis of Pentecostal Theology." *Pneuma: The Journal of the Society for Pentecostal Studies* 14, no. 1 (1992): 43–57.

Sweeney, Marvin A. *Isaiah 1–39: An Introduction to Prophetic Literature*. The Forms of the Old Testament Literature 16. Grand Rapids: Eerdmans, 1996.

Swoboda, A. J. "Posterity or Prosperity?: Critiquing and Refiguring Prosperity Theologies in an Ecological Age." *Pneuma: Journal for the Society for Pentecostal Studies* 37, no. 3 (2015): 394–411.

———. *Tongues and Trees: Towards a Pentecostal Ecological Theology*. Blandford Forum: Deo, 2013.

The Pentecostal Assemblies of Canada. *Essential Truths: The PAOC Statement of Essential Truths Commentary*. Mississauga: The Pentecostal Assemblies of Canada International Office, 2023.

Thomas, John Christopher, and Frank D. Macchia. *Revelation*. The Two Horizons New Testament Commentary. Grand Rapids: Eerdmans, 2016.

Waddell, Robby. "Apocalyptic Sustainability: The Future of Pentecostal Ecology." In *Perspectives in Pentecostal Eschatologies: World Without End*, edited by Peter Althouse and Robby Waddell, 95–110. Eugene: Pickwick, 2010.

Williams, Andrew Ray. "Greening the Apocalypse: A Pentecostal Eco-Eschatological Exploration," *PentecoStudies* 17, no. 2 (2018): 205–29.

2

The Sending and Groaning Spirit

An Eco-Pneumatological Reading of Mark's Temptation Narrative and Romans 8:18–27

Jeffrey Lamp

Among New Testament passages examined for their contributions to eco-theology is Romans 8:18–25, where the apostle Paul speaks of the liberation of the created order, subjected to corruption, finding its liberation with the liberation of the children of God.[1] Most such discussions find in the passage an affirmation that all of creation, human and other-than-human, is the object of God's salvation in Christ. Thus, discussions typically derive from this eschatological hope for creation an impetus to engage in creation care in the present.[2] The point of departure for this chapter is the inclusion of verses 26–27 in the discussion. The theme of "groaning" will be used to bring together creation, the children of God, and the Spirit to argue that the Spirit empowers the mission of believers in the world to engage in the care of creation to assist creation to anticipate its eschatological destiny.

Foundational to this understanding of Romans 8:18–27 is an examination of Mark's brief narrative of the temptation of Jesus in Mark 1:12–13. In this narrative, the Spirit drives Jesus into the wilderness where he is tested by Satan,

---

1. Sigve K. Tonstad, *The Letter to the Romans: Paul Among the Ecologists* (Sheffield: Sheffield Phoenix, 2016).

2. David G. Horrell, Cherryl Hunt, and Christopher Southgate, *Greening Paul: Rereading the Apostle in an Age of Ecological Crisis* (Waco: Baylor University Press, 2010).

but unique to this abbreviated telling is that upon completion of the testing, Jesus is attended by the wild animals and the angels. An ecological reading of this narrative shows that Jesus is here depicted in terms reminiscent of Adam in Eden, with the difference that Jesus resists the testing of Satan. Jesus reclaims the Adamic vocation to co-rule creation (Gen 1:26–28) in order to spread God's benevolence throughout creation and to lead creation to realize its destiny to become the dwelling place of God. Moreover, Jesus, the Second Adam, entrusts this reclaimed Adamic vocation to his followers.[3]

In bringing these two passages together, this chapter will argue that the same Spirit that drove Jesus into the wilderness to reclaim the Adamic vocation drives, accompanies, and empowers believers in the present in mission to extend God's benevolent rule for creation in anticipation of their joint eschatological destiny of liberation from corruption. The groaning Spirit facilitates an empathetic identification of the groaning children of God with the groaning creation as the life-giving Spirit leads both to their liberation, evidenced in the care for creation exercised by the children of God.

A note regarding method. The examination of these two passages is not primarily an exegetical analysis of the passages, if by that is meant discerning the intention of the biblical writers as they wrote. Rather, it is an ecological reading of these passages.[4] While traditional exegesis is certainly a part of an ecological reading, the primary emphasis of an ecological reading is to read the Bible in light of the current ecological crises plaguing the world. Pride of place is not given to the biblical text, for at the times of the composition of the Bible there simply was no such ecological crisis that would have served as the authors' intent for writing the passages as we now have them. Rather, an ecological reading interrogates the Bible for a contribution to addressing ecological crises in light of the fact that the authors did not have an ecological motivation for writing. The passages under examination here are examined to see how they might contribute to addressing ecological crises without arguing that this is the only, or original, meaning of the passages. This chapter proceeds from such an approach.

---

3. This theme is developed in Jeffrey S. Lamp, *Hebrews: An Earth Bible Commentary: A City That Cannot Be Shaken* (New York: T&T Clark, 2020).

4. A discussion of the aims and methods of ecological hermeneutics, see Jeffrey S. Lamp, *Reading Green: Tactical Considerations for Reading the Bible Ecologically* (New York: Peter Lang, 2017).

Pentecostals and Ecological Engagement

Pentecostals have been rather late to engage in efforts to care for creation. In my entry in the *Routledge Handbook of Pentecostal Theology*, I survey the reasons for this tendency.[5] Two reasons bear mention here. First, in North America, in the 1960s the environmental movement was initially associated with the political left, a position at odds with many Pentecostals who identified politically as conservative in light of the economic advancement of many Pentecostals in the latter half of the twentieth century. Second, Pentecostal eschatology influenced the lack of interest in ecological engagement. Widespread belief in a dispensational eschatology that frequently believed in the annihilation of the cosmos in the end favoured a missional emphasis on evangelism due to the imminence of the end of the age. However, recent decades have seen a proliferation of interest among Pentecostal thinkers who have persuasively argued that ecological engagement is a vital part of Pentecostal mission.[6] This shift was influenced by a growing interest in social issues among North American Pentecostals, which mirrored a more prominent interest in social issues among Pentecostals in the global South.

The tack taken by Pentecostals in this effort has been to re-vision pneumatology and eschatology such that ecological engagement is positioned as an appropriate response to such Pentecostal distinctives as Spirit baptism in light of the view that all of creation, human and other-than-human alike, will share in God's redemptive work in the eschaton. The following discussion will attempt to add to this effort via an ecological reading of Mark's temptation narrative and Romans 8:18–27. The result will be more than just another plank in the theological platform of Pentecostal ecological engagement. It will also argue that ecological engagement is a vital aspect of Pentecostal mission in the world, one that seeks the healing of all that God has created in anticipation of God's eschatological redemption of all things.

Mark's Temptation Narrative (Mark 1:12–13)

Mark's account of the temptation of Jesus is terse.

> And the Spirit immediately drove him out into the wilderness. He was in the wilderness forty days, tested by Satan, and he was with the wild beasts, and the angels waited on him.

---

5. Jeffrey S. Lamp, "Ecotheology: A People of the Spirit for Earth," in *The Routledge Handbook of Pentecostal Theology*, ed. Wolfgang Vondey (New York: Routledge, 2020), 358–59.

6. Lamp, "Ecotheology: A People of the Spirit for Earth," 361–64.

There are similarities between Mark's short account and those of Matthew (4:1–11) and Luke (4:1–13). In each account, it is the impetus of the Spirit that sends Jesus into the wilderness. There, Jesus is tempted by the devil for a period of forty days. In Matthew's account, there is mention of the angels attending to Jesus at the conclusion of the temptations (v. 11), a detail missing in Luke's version. Moreover, the temptation narratives in all three Gospels follow Jesus's baptism in the Jordan and precede Jesus's return to Galilee and the beginning of his public ministry.

Apart from these details, Mark's version varies significantly from those of the other synoptists. Of particular interest to both Matthew and Luke is the confrontation between Jesus and Satan. In each, Jesus is faced with a series of three temptations (though the sequence of the temptations differs) that Jesus effectively resists through quotations from Scripture. Mark simply notes that temptation occurred. While Matthew and Luke bring their accounts to an end by noting Jesus's victory, Mark, at best, implies that Jesus was victorious.

At a more detailed level, Mark uses the verb ἐκβάλλω (*ekballō*, "drove out") to describe the Spirit's direction of Jesus to the wilderness. This verb indicates a more forceful action in comparison to Matthew's and Luke's use of ἀνάγω (*anagō*, "led up") and ἄγω (*agō*, "led"), respectively. And at the conclusion of the temptations, Mark makes note that Jesus was "with the wild animals," a detail missing from the other accounts. Rather than view these details as mere curiosities, we will take the tack that they are indicative of a different purpose in Mark's telling than is present in the longer accounts of Matthew and Luke.

If Matthew and Luke focus more on the specifics of the temptations Jesus faced, what then is Mark's interest in shaping his temptation narrative as he did? If the showdown between Jesus and Satan is not Mark's primary concern, what is Mark's intent in depicting Jesus in this way? Perhaps a way forward is to go back to the beginning, so to speak, and look at God's intention with Adam and how that went astray. In looking at how the Adamic vocation in creation was framed and went astray, the narrative logic of Mark's temptation narrative becomes clearer, and in turn, informs a Spirit-empowered ecological engagement with the world.

Though the introduction of human beings into the creation story of Genesis 1 begins with verse 26, the context begins with verse 2: "The earth was without form and void, and darkness was over the face of the deep. And the Spirit of God was hovering over the face of the waters." God's creation of the cosmos, announced in the opening words of the Bible, is a pneumatological process. The unformed creation is brought into order in connection with the Spirit of God (רוח אלוהים, *ruah Elohim*), who hovers over the primordial chaos as a hen hovers over her chicks.⁷ The remainder of the account (vv. 3–31) unfolds the ordering work of God begun with the hovering Spirit.

Culminating this ordering is the creation of human beings (vv. 26–30). The crucial text for our purposes is verses 26–28, in which not only is it stated that God created human beings but also conferred upon them a vocation. The text reads

> Then God said, "Let us make humans in our image, according to our likeness, and let them have dominion over the fish of the sea and over the birds of the air and over the cattle and over all the wild animals of the earth and over every creeping thing that creeps upon the earth."
>
> So God created humans in his image,
> in the image of God he created them;
> male and female he created them.
>
> God blessed them, and God said to them, "Be fruitful and multiply and fill the earth and subdue it and have dominion over the fish of the sea and over the birds of the air and over every living thing that moves upon the earth."

Crucial to our understanding of the place of human beings in God's creation is the word "image" (צלם, *tsalam*). Middleton's seminal study on the significance of an "image" in the Ancient Near East indicates that an image stands in place of a ruler who has authority over a place but is physically absent.⁸ In the context of Genesis 1:26–28, it suggests that human beings were given a vocational mandate to exercise dominion over the creatures of the world in a way that demonstrates God's benevolent rule of creation. Human beings are thus coregents with God in the world. We must stress that this picture is given prior to the "fall" of Genesis 3, so the sense of dominion exercised by human beings with God is one that continues the ordering work of God. Genesis 2:15 provides further elaboration: "And the Lord God commanded the man to serve and to protect it."⁹ The picture is one of human beings extending God's benevolent care of the world from the garden of Eden into all creation.

---

7. St. Basil the Great, *Exegetical Homilies* 2:6. In the piel stem, the verb has the sense of a bird with wings fluttering and hovering in the air. See Ludwig Koehler and Walter Baumgartner, *The Hebrew and Aramaic Lexicon of the Old Testament*, rev. by Walter Baumgartner and Johann Jakob Stamm (Leiden: Brill, 2000), 1220.

8. Richard Middleton, *The Liberating Image: The Imago Dei in Genesis 1* (Grand Rapids: Brazos, 2005), ch. 3.

9. Translation mine.

It is interesting to note that in Jewish tradition human beings were in the garden of Eden not only with animals and plants, but also angelic beings.[10] While Genesis does not indicate such explicitly, it does provide indications that God's intention was to inhabit creation with both God's human and other-than-human creatures. One such indication is in Genesis 3:8 where God is shown walking in the garden in the "evening breeze." But a more significant reference is found in the establishment of the Sabbath (Gen 2:1–3).

Many scholars have noted the similarity of the pattern of the tabernacle in Exodus 25–40 with that of the ordering of creation in Genesis 1:3–31.[11] This suggests that creation itself was designed to be the dwelling place of God.[12] If so, this in turn suggests that the Adamic vocation in the world is to serve as a priestly intercessor between God and the other-than-human creation, a role evident in human beings created with both earthly and heavenly characteristics.[13] They would offer creation in priestly service to God who in turn blesses creation through human beings.

Of course, the story takes a tragic turn when human beings violate God's command not to eat of the tree of the knowledge of good and evil (Gen 2:17). If, as Terence Fretheim suggests, the serpent here is not viewed primarily as a satanic entity but rather as a simple creature of the garden over which human beings were to exercise God's benevolent care, then the fall may be seen as human abdication of their divine vocational mandate in subordinating themselves to the influence of a creature.[14] The resulting expulsion of human

---

10. For a detailed ecological reading of this passage, see Richard Bauckham, *Living with Other Creatures: Green Exegesis and Theology* (Waco: Baylor University Press, 2011), 111–32.

11. Margaret Barker, *Creation: A Biblical Vision for the Environment* (New York: T&T Clark, 2010), 38–49; Gregory K. Beale, *The Temple and the Church's Mission: A Biblical Theology of the Dwelling Place of God* (Downers Grove: InterVarsity 2004), 29–167; Jonathan Huddleston, *Eschatology in Genesis*, Forschungen zum Alten Testament 2 Reihe 57 (Tübingen: Mohr Siebeck, 2012), 157; Joe Laansma, "Hidden Stories in Hebrews," in *A Cloud of Witnesses: The Theology of Hebrews in Its Ancient Contexts*, eds. Richard Bauckham, Daniel Driver, Trevor Hart, and Nathan MacDonald (London: T&T Clark, 2008), 9–18; John H. Walton, *Ancient Near Eastern Thought and the Old Testament: Introducing the Conceptual World of the Hebrew Bible* (Grand Rapids: Baker, 2006), 113–34.

12. N. T. Wright, *Paul and the Faithfulness of God* (Minneapolis: Fortress, 2013), 102, 560.

13. For a discussion of St. Maximus the Confessor's thought in this regard, see Radu Bordeianu, "Maximus and Ecology: The Relevance of Maximus the Confessor's Theology of Creation for the Present Ecological Crisis," *The Downside Review* 127 (2009): 111–14; Andrew Louth, "Man and Cosmos in St. Maximus the Confessor," in *Toward an Ecology of Transfiguration: Orthodox Christian Perspectives on Environment, Nature, and Creation*, eds. John Chryssavgis and Bruce V. Foltz (New York: Fordham University Press, 2013), 59–71.

14. Terence Freitheim, *Book of Genesis*, New Interpreter's Bible (Nashville: Abingdon, 1994), 59–60; Norman C. Habel, *The Birth, the Curse and the Greening of Earth: An Ecological Reading of Genesis 1–11*, The Earth Bible Commentary (Sheffield: Sheffield Phoenix, 2011), 57.

beings from the garden is then a matter of God turning human beings over to the consequences of the forfeiture of their vocational mandate to survive in a creation that is at odds with human thriving.

Against this backdrop Mark's temptation narrative begins to take shape. The Spirit driving Jesus into the wilderness mirrors the expulsion of the first humans from the garden. Whereas the expulsion from the garden represents human forfeiture of their place in the created order, Jesus enters the wilderness with the intention to reclaim the Adamic vocation for human beings. Here Jesus faces an unspecified temptation from Satan to take the same path as Adam. Adam, situated in paradise, succumbs to the temptation to take another path to maturity than the path designed by God.[15] Jesus, situated in a wilderness that reflects the consequences of Adam's failure, triumphs against temptation and, in the process, begins the reclamation project of restoring the vocational mandate of the first Adam. In the way the Spirit was instrumental in bringing order out of chaos at the beginning of creation, the Spirit similarly drives Jesus into the wilderness to reorder corrupted creation.

It remains to show how this reclamation is indicated in Mark's narrative. Mark states that Jesus, upon his victory over temptation, was attended by the wild animals and the angels, though in the wilderness, the wild animals evidence a rapprochement with the man Jesus, a condition that prevailed in the garden with the first Adam. The presence of the angels with Jesus demonstrates the divine intention to have creation be the place where the human and the heavenly dwell together. Jesus, effectively, reverses the condition introduced by the failure of the first Adam. In the midst of a world that shows the effects of the Adamic failure, a beach head of the restored mission of God to dwell with God's creation is established. Coming as it does at the beginning of Jesus's ministry, it establishes as one of the themes of Jesus's ministry the re-ordering of creation to its original design. Against Mark's temptation narrative, the so-called "nature miracles" of Jesus in the Gospel, especially the calming of the sea (Mark 4:35–41),[16] find poignant expression. The concluding question in this narrative, "Who then is this, that even the wind and the sea obey him?" is dramatically answered. This man is the one who demonstrates what the first Adam was to have been – the one who brings order to creation.

If the full weight of Mark's temptation narrative is recognized, as argued here, it provides a key element of the mission of Jesus's disciples as expressed

---

15. For example, Gregory of Nazianzus, *Second Oration on Easter*, 8.
16. Lamp, *Reading Green*, 126–29.

in the various "great commission" passages at the conclusions of the synoptic Gospels.[17] Jesus's followers would also continue to fulfill what Jesus began.

In light of the current ecological crises facing the world at present, a valid expression of reclaiming the Adamic vocation for Jesus's disciples would arguably entail concern for the ecological care of creation. How this is expressed in the New Testament is found in an ecological-pneumatological reading of Romans 8:18–27, to which we now turn.

Romans 8:18–27 and the Care of Creation

As noted above, Romans 8:18–25 is one of the seminal New Testament passages cited as a foundation for Christian responses to current environmental crises. The passage draws on apocalyptic imagery[18] to describe the eschatological longing of creation for redemption from corruption.[19] For our purposes, we will extend the scope of the passage to include verses 26–27. As we will see, there are both contextual and lexical grounds for this inclusion.

The passage reads as follows.

> I consider that the sufferings of this present time are not worth comparing with the glory about to be revealed to us. For the creation waits with eager longing for the revealing of the children of God, for the creation was subjected to futility, not of its own will, but by the will of the one who subjected it, in hope that the creation itself will be set free from its enslavement to decay and will

---

17. Of course, there is the textual question of the authenticity of the so-called "longer ending" of Mark. If what is argued here is valid, then it is tempting to speculate that, if this ending is not original to Mark's gospel, its eventual inclusion is necessary. The commissioning of the disciples to spread the gospel into all creation may be seen as the counterpart to the Adamic vocation to spread God's benevolent care into all the world. This would include the project to make all creation into the dwelling place of God. This would, then, bring Mark's gospel full circle back to the temptation narrative.

18. Harry A. Hahne, *The Corruption and Redemption of Creation: Nature in Romans 8:19–22 and Jewish Apocalyptic Literature*, Library of New Testament Studies 336 (London: T & T Clark, 2006).

19. The reception history of the passage tilts decidedly in favour of seeing the four occurrences of "creation" (κτίσις, *ktisis*) in the passage as referring to the whole of creation, or at least the other-than-human creation. Some have argued that the term should be restricted to human beings. See Gregory P. Fewster, *Creation Language in Romans 8: A Study in Monosemy*, Linguistic Biblical Studies 8 (Leiden: Brill, 2013); J. Ramsey Michaels, "The Redemption of Our Body: The Riddle of Romans 8:19–22," in *Romans and the People of God: Essays in Honor of Gordon D. Fee on the Occasion of his 65th Birthday*, eds. Sven K. Soderlund and N. T. Wright (Grand Rapids: Eerdmans, 1999), 92–114. We will proceed with the understanding that the referent extends beyond human beings to include the other-than-human creation.

obtain the freedom of the glory of the children of God. We know that the whole creation has been groaning together as it suffers together the pains of labor, and not only the creation, but we ourselves, who have the first fruits of the Spirit, groan inwardly while we wait for adoption, the redemption of our bodies. For in hope we were saved. Now hope that is seen is not hope, for who hopes for what one already sees? But if we hope for what we do not see, we wait for it with patience.

Likewise the Spirit helps us in our weakness, for we do not know how to pray as we ought, but that very Spirit intercedes with groanings too deep for words. And God, who searches hearts, knows what is the mind of the Spirit, because the Spirit intercedes for the saints according to the will of God.

In the preceding paragraph (vv. 12–17), Paul speaks of those who have received the Spirit of adoption that allows them to cry out to God, "Abba! Father!" (v. 15). There is an interplay of three closely related terms that underscore the familial context that will be repeated in verses 18–25: "sons" (υἱοί, *huioi*, v. 14), "children" (τέκνα, *tekna*, vv. 16, 17), and "adoption" (υἱοθεσία, *huiothesia*, v. 15). Taken together, the terms contribute to the sense that those who have received the Spirit of adoption are those who also walk according to the Spirit (v. 13), those whose spirits bear witness with the Spirit that they are indeed the children of God (v. 16). Via this adoption into God's family these children of God are heirs of God and joint heirs with Christ (v. 17). Yet Paul raises a sobering counterpoint as he concludes the paragraph. With the particle εἴπερ (*eiper*) Paul introduces a conditional promise for those who have been united with God through the Spirit. To be glorified with the joint heir Christ, they must also suffer with him.

This point of departure introduces the paragraph of our concern. Paul reasons that whatever suffering the children of God experience in this life, it is of no comparison with the glory that will be revealed to us (v. 18). Here Paul brings the creation into the calculus. The creation awaits with eager expectation the revelation of the sons of God (v. 19). Here the "revelation" (ἀποκάλυψις, *apokalypsis*) of the sons of God, linked through the verbal cognate infinitive ἀποκαλυφθῆναι (*apokalyfthênai*, "to be revealed") in verse 18, indicates that the revelation for which the creation awaits is the eschatological glorification of the sons of God. With verses 20–21 Paul provides the reason creation thus awaits the revelation of the sons of God: creation was subjected to futility, not of its own accord, but "because of the one who subjected it."

Exegetes have puzzled over the referent of the subjecting agent here. The choices seem reduced to two: God or Adam.[20] On the one hand, it was God who pronounced the so-called "curse" on both human beings and creation in Genesis 3. The harmonious relationship between Adam and the other-than-human creation was severed and the resulting relationship would thereafter be contentious. Adam would have to contend with creation to secure his survival in the world, and this was at the decree of God. On the other hand, it was the first Adam, through his and his wife's disobedience, who forsook the divine mandate to co-rule creation with God, subjecting himself to creation. When human beings forfeited their vocation to spread God's benevolence throughout creation, it did not sever the connection between human beings and other-than-human creation. Human beings would still go into the world, but their influence over creation became adversarial, and human attempts to survive in a hostile world would nevertheless result in a perverted attempt to establish dominion over creation. As human beings acquired evermore powerful and destructive technologies to assert dominance over creation, creation itself suffered corruption.

What the creation awaits is a state of restored relationship between itself and its human caretakers. Creation's liberation from "its bondage to corruption" (v. 21) comes when the children of God come into their own glorious liberation. Paul likens creation's current state of corruption to a woman suffering the "pains of childbirth" (v. 22). Of course, with a woman, the eventual result of the pains of childbirth is birth, the bringing forth of new life. At the same time, human beings themselves also suffer in the present as they await their own salvation, which, as Paul stated in verse 17, is co-glorification with Christ. The outcome of the suffering of both is liberation from corruption.

Having sketched the connection between human beings and other-than-human creation in this section, Paul has provided us with the contours for human care of creation in the present. Both human beings and creation, their destinies inextricably joined in God's original acts of creation, now find themselves in a relationship of corruption. The culpability of Christianity for the current ecological crises has been argued perhaps most notably by Lynn White

---

20. N. T. Wright, *Romans*, New Interpreter's Bible (Nashville: Abingdon, 2020), 596. Douglas J. Moo, *Epistle to the Romans*, New International Commentary on the New Testament (Grand Rapids: Eerdmans Publishing, 1996), 515–16, and James D. G. Dunn, *Romans 1–8*, Word Biblical Commentary (Nashville: Thomas Nelson, 1988), 487–88, suggest that it was God who subjected creation to futility in response to human disobedience, while Robert Jewett, *Romans*, Hermeneia (Minneapolis: Fortress, 2007), 514, argues that it was human beings who subjected it via their disobedience.

Jr., who has cited the mandate for human beings to exercise dominion over the world (Gen 1:26–28) as a mandate to exploit the natural world for the flourishing of human beings.[21] Though many of White's assertions have been addressed by Christian theologians in recent decades,[22] it was White's article that provided the impetus for Christians to reassess their place in the world with respect to the wellbeing of creation.

As noted earlier, Romans 8:18–25 is a foundational passage for justifying Christian engagement in ecological issues. An ecological reading of the passage sees Paul's portrayal here as aptly characterizing the current ecological plight in which human beings find themselves. Creation suffers corruption precisely because it has been subjected to a corrupt expression of dominion by human beings. It suffers at the hands of human overseers who seek primarily their own thriving, not that of creation. But Paul's vivid language here indicates that creation has a sense of its own destiny in God's program. And it waits in hope, as do human beings, for the day that corruption ceases and God's glorious redemption is shared by all that God has created. All of creation, human and other-than-human alike, has a place in God's eschatological future. The God/human/other-than-human triad of harmony envisioned in the Genesis creation accounts will be re-established when God finally comes to indwell God's creation (cf. Rev 21–22).

The contention of this chapter is that Romans 8:26–27 help make more firm the ecological foundation provided in verses 18–25. The mention of the Spirit here states that the Spirit assists us in our weaknesses when we do not know how we should pray. Of course, many Pentecostals find here a reference to glossolalia. But that is not the only issue addressed in these verses. The key is found in the description of the Spirit's intercession as "groanings" (στεναγμός, *stenagmos*, v. 26). But the Spirit is not the only party groaning in the context. In verse 23, human beings are said to "groan" (στενάζω, *stenazō*) as they await their redemption. So, as human beings suffer in the present the indwelling Spirit groans along with them in their pursuit of liberation from present corruption. Peter Althouse has characterized the Spirit's role in this respect as a "kenosis" of the Spirit.[23] Not only this, but the whole creation itself

---

21. Lynn White Jr., "The Historical Roots of Our Ecologic Crisis," *Science* 155 (1967): 1203–7.

22. Francis A. Schaeffer's *Pollution and the Death of Man: The Christian View of Ecology* (Wheaton: Tyndale, 1970) provides the first substantive rejoinder to White's thesis. Bauckham, *Living with Other Creatures*, 15–19, provides a more recent rebuttal to White.

23. Peter Althouse, "Implications of the Kenosis of the Spirit for a Creational Eschatology," in *The Spirit Renews the Face of the Earth: Pentecostal Forays in Science and Theology of Creation*, ed. Amos Yong (Eugene: Pickwick, 2009), 155–72.

is "groaning together" (συστενάζω, *sustenazō*) as it currently experiences the "pains of childbirth" (v. 22). The Spirit, then, may be seen as a partner along with human beings and other-than-human creation as they proceed toward liberation from corruption and redemption.

Put in ecological terms, what is in view here is a picture of human beings led by the indwelling Spirit of God (v. 14) moving towards redemption in their suffering of corruption alongside the creation. Since Adam was a part of the subjection of creation to futility (that is, creation's inability to aspire to its destiny in God's creative plan), Adam's redemption entails bringing creation to its eschatological destiny. Stated another way, the partnership of a groaning creation, a groaning humanity, and a groaning Spirit entails the alleviation of the present suffering of creation as part of the Spirit-directed movement of human beings toward their eschatological glory. In an age of ecological degradation, that would itself entail an anticipatory reclamation of the original Adamic vocation to spread God's benevolence into all creation, and that would be expressed in ecological actions that help alleviate the suffering of creation in the present.

The final section of this chapter pulls together the strands of this discussion and describes how Pentecostals might respond in light of the two passages addressed above.

A Way Forward for Pentecostals

The two passages addressed in this discussion were chosen on the basis of their use of Adamic traditions and how the figure of Adam, particularly in the creation and fall narratives of Genesis, is connected with the destiny of the other-than-human creation. Our self-consciously ecological reading of these passages has plumbed their depths in light of an ecological assessment of Adam in the creation and fall narratives of Genesis 1–3. Reading the passages ecologically through the prism of Adam has led to the suggestion that Mark's portrayal of the temptation narrative depicts Jesus as the Second Adam who comes to recapitulate Adam's mission in the world to protect the garden and to extend its Paradisiacal state into all the world. We followed the same tack with respect to Paul's discussion of the groaning creation, reading Romans 8:18–27 through the prism of an ecological assessment of Adam to frame the corruption plaguing creation in terms of ecological degradation resulting from the first human beings' forfeiture of their original mission. Paul shows that the current and future states of the other-than-human creation are bound together with the suffering and anticipated redemption of human beings. Both groan in hope for liberation from corruption and fulfillment of the glorious destiny God had intended for the whole of creation. We have suggested that Paul draws the Spirit into the calculus by portraying him as groaning as he guides human beings, and by extension the other-than-human creation, toward their redemption.

By bringing these two passages into conversation via an ecological reading, we find a rather concise yet robust picture of how it is that human beings, empowered by the Spirit, may work in the present to fulfill their original vocational mandate in the world as anticipatory of the future glory that awaits all that God has created.

The presupposition of both passages is that, in some sense, the world as it currently is has been and remains corrupted by virtue of human action, both in the garden and in subsequent history. This seems to be in view in Mark's identification of the location of Jesus's temptation in the wilderness. As noted earlier, the first Adam faced temptation in paradise and yet failed to prevail. However, Jesus goes into the hostile world of the fall and emerges victorious. His victory unites heaven and earth as it was in the beginning, though in a proleptic sense. The victory is won in the temptation, confirmed in the death and resurrection of Jesus, and guaranteed for the future. Equally as important, though not explicit in Mark's gospel, is the role that the ascension of Jesus into heaven and Pentecost play in the present reclamation of the vocational mandate for human beings.

By virtue of his ascension into heaven, Jesus is enthroned as the Lord of all creation. All is subject to his rulership and human beings are established as co-rulers with him, seated with him in heavenly places and sent into the world to spread the kingdom of God. The outpouring of the Spirit on the day of Pentecost empowers Jesus's followers to spread God's kingdom into the world in a mission that entails serving and protecting creation in fulfillment of their original and now reclaimed vocational mandate.

Of course, human experience in the world is one of frequent hardship with respect to the rest of creation. Human beings suffer calamities from natural disasters and the natural world suffers from ever-expanding human technological prowess. In a tragic feedback loop, now many of humanity's attempts to dominate and exploit creation produce effects that cause damage to the environment and to human beings. Such effects as climate change, ocean acidification, and microplastic and "forever chemicals" pollution, to name but a few, threaten to make the world uninhabitable for human beings.

Seen from an ecological perspective, this is a fair interpretation of what Paul may have meant by the corruption rendering the creation futile. Creation groans, human beings groan. But the good news is that we have received the

Spirit of God, and when we find ourselves overwhelmed by the magnitude of the ecological degradation caused by human beings and now entrusted back to us for the exercise of our creational vocational mandate, the Spirit intercedes on our behalf and guides us as we exercise the new dominion granted us by Jesus to assist creation to attain to its eschatological destiny.

It is noteworthy that it was the Spirit who emphatically drove Jesus into the wilderness to face the temptation that Adam failed. Emerging victorious, Jesus showed us a glimpse of what the world will look like in the future. Not only that but, given that this vision was delivered in a world still experiencing corruption, it is a picture of what might be attained along the way to the redemption and liberation of all of God's creation. In the way that the Spirit drove Jesus into the wilderness to re-establish order to creation, the Spirit, too, drives us into the wilderness of a world marred by environmental degradation to continue to establish this new order in anticipation of the day that it will find ultimate fulfillment.

Perhaps the best way forward for Pentecostals in the care of creation is through Frank Macchia's reformulation of the doctrine of Spirit baptism.[24] Macchia argues that the scope of the baptism of the Spirit extends beyond human beings and the experience of glossolalia to encompass the whole of God's creation. In this reformulation, Macchia sees Jesus the Spirit baptizer as pouring out the Spirit on all creation, saturating creation with the presence of the Spirit, "liberat[ing] creation from within history toward new possibilities for free, eschatological existence."[25] The crucial element here is that the Spirit, who infills all creation, works with Spirit-baptized human beings to assist creation to realize proleptically the liberation that awaits all of God's creation, human and other-than-human alike. In ecological terms, this might be characterized as the groaning Spirit working through groaning Spirit-baptized human beings to alleviate the environmental suffering of the groaning creation, a creation that already shares the experience of Spirit baptism with those originally and newly commissioned to care for creation. Macchia's reformulation of Spirit baptism provides the infrastructural context for Pentecostals to engage in mission that frames Pentecostal pursuits of sanctification and spiritual formation in terms of concrete actions of compassion performed by

---

24. Frank D. Macchia, *Baptized in the Spirit: A Global Pentecostal Theology* (Grand Rapids: Zondervan, 2006).

25. Macchia, *Baptized in the Spirit*, 97.

Pentecostals on behalf of creation.²⁶ Our survey of Mark's temptation narrative and Romans 8:18–27, then, provides an ecologically-framed biblical rationale for those empowered by the Spirit to go forth in mission to reclaim the vocational mandate originally entrusted to human beings to care for creation.

Conclusion

Ecological crises are a rather recent phenomenon in human history, with concerted efforts to address these crises really only beginning to emerge in the mid-twentieth century. It was with responses to Lynn White's article, mentioned earlier, that Christians began to become involved with biblical and theological explorations that would come to provide justification for Christian involvement in ecological engagement in the world. Pentecostals, for a variety of reasons, have come to the party somewhat late. Our discussion here is an example of how reading the New Testament from an ecological point of view, and moreover from a pneumatological point of view, demonstrates that life in the Spirit entails living in the world in an ecologically responsible way, as the other entries in this volume also testify. It also demonstrates that the Spirit drives us headlong into a suffering world to bring ecological healing to the world in anticipation of the future glory in which God comes to dwell in our midst in a renewed creation.

Bibliography

Althouse, Peter. "Implications of the Kenosis of the Spirit for a Creational Eschatology." In *The Spirit Renews the Face of the Earth*, edited by Amos Yong, 155–72. Eugene: Pickwick, 2009.

Barker, Margaret. *Creation: A Biblical Vision for the Environment*. New York: T&T Clark, 2010.

Bauckham, Richard. *Living with Other Creatures: Green Exegesis and Theology*. Waco: Baylor University Press, 2011.

Beale, Gregory K. *The Temple and the Church's Mission: A Biblical Theology of the Dwelling Place of God*. Downers Grove: InterVarsity 2004.

---

26. Steven M. Studebaker, "The Spirit in Creation: A Unified Theology of Grace and Creation Care," *Zygon: Journal of Religion and Science* 43, no. 4 (2008): 943–59; Steven M. Studebaker, "Creation Care as 'Keeping in Step with the Spirit,'" in *The Liberating Spirit: Pentecostals and Social Action in North America*, eds. Michael Wilkinson and Steven M. Studebaker (Eugene: Pickwick, 2010), 248–63.

Bordeianu, Radu. "Maximus and Ecology: The Relevance of Maximus the Confessor's Theology of Creation for the Present Ecological Crisis." *The Downside Review* 127 (2009): 103–26.

Dunn, James D. G. *Romans 1–8*. Word Biblical Commentary. Nashville: Thomas Nelson, 1988.

Fewster, Gregory P. *Creation Language in Romans 8: A Study in Monosemy*. Linguistic Biblical Studies 8. Leiden: Brill, 2013.

Freitheim, Terence. *The Book of Genesis*. New Interpreter's Bible. Nashville: Abingdon, 1994.

Habel, Norman C. *The Birth, the Curse and the Greening of Earth: An Ecological Reading of Genesis 1–11*. The Earth Bible Commentary. Sheffield: Sheffield Phoenix, 2011.

Hahne, Harry A. *The Corruption and Redemption of Creation: Nature in Romans 8:19–22 and Jewish Apocalyptic Literature*. Library of New Testament Studies 336. London: T&T Clark, 2006.

Horrell, David G., Cherryl Hunt, and Christopher Southgate. *Greening Paul: Rereading the Apostle in an Age of Ecological Crisis*. Waco: Baylor University Press, 2010.

Huddleston, Jonathan. *Eschatology in Genesis*. Forschungen zum Alten Testament 2. Reihe 57. Tübingen: Mohr Siebeck, 2012.

Jewett, Robert. *Romans*. Hermeneia. Minneapolis: Fortress, 2007.

Koehler, Ludwig, and Walter Baumgartner. *The Hebrew and Aramaic Lexicon of the Old Testament*. Revised by Walter Baumgartner and Johann Jakob Stamm. Leiden: Brill, 2000.

Laansma, Jon. "Hidden Stories in Hebrews: Cosmology and Theology." In *A Cloud of Witnesses: The Theology of Hebrews in Its Ancient Contexts*, edited by Richard Bauckham, Daniel Driver, Trevor Hart and Nathan MacDonald, 9–18. London: T&T Clark, 2008).

Lamp, Jeffrey S. "Ecotheology." In *The Routledge Handbook of Pentecostal Theology*, edited by Wolfgang Vondey, 357–66. Abingdon: Routledge, 2020.

———. *Hebrews: An Earth Bible Commentary: A City That Cannot Be Shaken*. New York: T&T Clark, 2020.

———. *Reading Green: Tactical Considerations for Reading the Bible Ecologically*. New York: Peter Lang, 2017.

Louth, Andrew. "Man and Cosmos in St. Maximus the Confessor." In *Toward an Ecology of Transfiguration: Orthodox Christian Perspectives on Environment, Nature, and Creation*, edited by John Chryssavgis and Bruce V. Foltz, 59–17. New York: Fordham University Press, 2013.

Macchia, Frank. *Baptized in the Spirit: A Global Pentecostal Theology*. Grand Rapids: Zondervan, 2006.

Michaels, J. Ramsey. "The Redemption of Our Body: The Riddle of Romans 8:19–22." In *Romans and the People of God: Essays in Honor of Gordon D. Fee on the Occasion of his 65th Birthday*, edited by Sven K. Soderlund and N. T. Wright, 92–114. Grand Rapids: Eerdmans, 1999.

Middleton, Richard. *The Liberating Image: The Imago Dei in Genesis 1*. Grand Rapids: Brazos, 2005.

Moo, Douglas J. *The Epistle to the Romans*. New International Commentary on the New Testament. Grand Rapids: Eerdmans, 1996.

Schaeffer, Francis A. *Pollution and the Death of Man: The Christian View of Ecology*. Wheaton: Tyndale, 1970.

Studebaker, Steven M. "Creation Care as 'Keeping in Step with the Spirit.'" In *The Liberating Spirit: Pentecostals and Social Action in North America*, edited by Michael Wilkinson and Steven M. Studebaker, 248–63. Eugene: Pickwick, 2010.

———. "The Spirit in Creation: A Unified Theology of Grace and Creation Care." *Zygon: Journal of Religion and Science* 43 (2008): 943–60.

Tonstad, Sigve K. *The Letter to the Romans: Paul among the Ecologists*. Sheffield: Sheffield Phoenix, 2016.

Walton, John H. *Ancient Near Eastern Thought and the Old Testament: Introducing the Conceptual World of the Hebrew Bible*. Grand Rapids: Baker, 2006.

White, Lynn, Jr. "The Historical Roots of Our Ecologic Crisis." *Science* 155 (1967): 1203–7.

Wright, N. T. *Paul and the Faithfulness of God*. Minneapolis: Fortress, 2013.

———. *Romans*. New Interpreter's Bible. Nashville: Abingdon, 2002.

3

Apocalyptic Ecotheology

A Pentecostal Contribution

Jon K. Newton

Ecotheology is one of the primary emerging forms of Christian theology in response to the ecological issues facing the world. Pentecostals, however, were latecomers to this field. Shane Clifton in 2009 lamented, "environmental concern has rarely if ever been an important element of the Pentecostal message,"[1] as illustrated by the lack of mention in the *Australian Evangel*,[2] though he points out that Walter Hollenweger challenged Pentecostals on this point as early as 1978.[3]

Peter Althouse wrote in 2014, "Pentecostalism as a whole has remained reticent on issues related to nature and ecology. To date, a Pentecostal ecological theology is underdeveloped."[4] But more recently, Pentecostals have energetically joined the ecotheological conversation. This conversation has been driven by a renewed, and pneumatological, emphasis on creation and providence,

---

1. Shane Clifton, "Preaching the 'Full Gospel' in the Context of the Global Environmental Crises," in *The Spirit Renews the Face of the Ground: Pentecostal Forays in Science and Theology of Creation*, ed. Amos Yong (Eugene: Pickwick, 2009), 117.

2. The official magazine of the Assemblies of God in Australia, now defunct.

3. Clifton, "Preaching the 'Full Gospel,'"118, n. 3.

4. Peter Althouse, "Pentecostal Eco-Transformation: Possibilities for a Pentecostal Ecotheology in Light of Moltmann's Green Theology," in *Blood Cries Out: Pentecostals, Ecology, and the Groans of Creation*, ed. A. J. Swoboda (Eugene: Pickwick, 2014), 117. In a similar way, Swoboda commented in 2011 that "Within Pentecostal and Charismatic communities, ecotheological efforts are often viewed with suspicion." See A. J. Swoboda, "Eco-Glossolalia: Emerging Twenty-First Century Pentecostal and Charismatic Ecotheology," *Rural Theology* 9, no. 2 (2011): 103.

on the God-given responsibility of creation care to humanity, and the hope of renewal of all creation. It has been hindered by dispensationalist expectations of a destroyed earth[5] and fears of anti-Christian internationalism. So, where is the conversation up to, at least in its Pentecostal form? What is God calling us as Pentecostals to do about it? And what can the book of Revelation add to this?

Pentecostal Voices: An Update

One of the earlier articles to touch on ecology in a Pentecostal journal was Andrew Gabriel's 2007 "Pneumatological Perspectives for a Theology of Nature."[6] Gabriel explored a number of themes related to a theology of nature and argued for a "kinship model of our relationship to nature," which focuses on "our interconnection with other creatures."[7] He viewed the Spirit as the Life-Giver who also suffers when "the actions of humanity . . . work in opposition to the Spirit's own creative actions,"[8] and proposed that the Spirit may even lead humans to creatively modify and enhance nature through technology.

Perhaps the first collection of Pentecostal thoughts on ecotheology appeared in *The Spirit Renews the Face of the Earth*, edited by Amos Yong in 2009.[9] While many of the essays focused on Pentecostal attitudes to science in general, and evolution in particular, several focused more on ecological questions. Jerome Boone presented a stimulating biblical discussion of *shalom* in relation to the roles of humankind, Israel, and the church.[10] Peter Althouse, exploring Moltmann's concept of "the "kenosis of the Spirit," suggested that creation has "an ecological side as the dwelling place of the Spirit in the bio-

---

5. Cf. Clifton, "Preaching the 'Full Gospel,'" 118–20. Such fears are mirrored in some popular science fiction and secular apocalyptic scenarios, though some of them end optimistically in "the renewal of creation rather than its annihilation." See Robby Waddell, "A Green Apocalypse: Comparing Secular and Religious Eschatological Visions of Earth," in *Blood Cries Out: Pentecostals, Ecology, and the Groans of Creation*, ed. A. J. Swoboda (Eugene: Pickwick, 2014), 133–36.

6. Andrew Gabriel, "Pneumatological Perspectives for a Theology of Nature: The Holy Spirit in Relation to Ecology and Technology," *Journal of Pentecostal Theology* 15, no. 2 (2007): 195–212.

7. Gabriel, "Theology of Nature," 212.

8. Gabriel, "Theology of Nature," 205.

9. Amos Yong, ed. *Spirit Renews the Face of the Earth: Pentecostal Forays in Science and Theology of Creation* (Eugene: Pickwick, 2009). Yong also raised some of these issues in *Spirit Poured Out on All Flesh: Pentecostalism and the Possibility of a Global Theology* (Grand Rapids: Baker Academic, 2005), 280–82, 299–301.

10. R. Jerome Boone, "Created for Shalom: Human Agency and Responsibility in the World," in *The Spirit Renews the Face of the Earth: Pentecostal Forays in Science and Theology of Creation*, ed. Amos Yong (Eugene: Pickwick, 2009), 17–29.

ecological and cosmic systems of creation" and therefore "the world is not ours to use as we please, but we are servants to creation because God has entrusted us with it."[11] J. Kwabena Asamoah-Gyadu wrote of the African primal worldview in which "the earth is sacred *because it originates from the Supreme Being*."[12]

Robby Waddell challenged "a fixation on an anthropocentric eschatology,"[13] that is, an eschatology based on dispensationalism[14] and annihilationist readings of the book of Revelation, in particular. He argued instead for a transformationist reading of "the end" in Revelation based on comparisons with Isaiah 65, the paradigm of the resurrected Jesus, and the language of Revelation 21, as interpreted also by patristic writers like Irenaeus and Andrew of Caesarea.[15] Thus, he refuted those types of readings that make any kind of creation care irrelevant. In a similar article about eschatology, Waddell also argued for a non-annihilationist reading of 2 Peter 3.[16]

Shane Clifton's article analysed the factors holding back a Pentecostal contribution to environmental issues, including premillennialism, young Earth creationism, prosperity theologies, and a general dualistic truncated view of the church's mission.[17] He then argued that "core Pentecostal symbols are capable of generating and sustaining strong earthkeeping praxis" if there is "a thorough revisioning of Pentecostal worldview, one that encompasses an Earth affirming theology of creation."[18] Specifically, he advocated "a pneumatological theology of creation" and a "reframing" and expanding of the Pentecostal "full gospel" narrative to include an ecological perspective (for example, Jesus as healer of a sick creation, not just sick bodies).[19]

---

11. Peter Althouse, "Implications of the Kenosis of the Spirit for a Creational Eschatology: A Pentecostal Engagement with Jurgen Moltmann," in *The Spirit Renews the Face of the Earth: Pentecostal Forays in Science and Theology of Creation*, ed. Amos Yong (Eugene: Pickwick, 2009), 169.

12. J. Kwabena Asamoah-Gyadu, "God's Laws of Productivity: Creation in African Pentecostal Hermeneutics," in *The Spirit Renews the Face of the Earth: Pentecostal Forays in Science and Theology of Creation*, ed. Amos Yong (Eugene: Pickwick, 2009), 180; emphasis is in the original text.

13. Robby Waddell, "Revelation and the (New) Creation: A Prolegomenon on the Apocalypse, Science, and Creation," in *The Spirit Renews the Face of the Earth*, ed. Amos Yong (Eugene: Wipf & Stock, 2009), 32.

14. Waddell, "Revelation and the (New) Creation," 35.

15. Waddell, "Revelation and the (New) Creation," 39–50.

16. Waddell, "Apocalyptic Sustainability," 105–7.

17. Clifton, "Preaching the 'Full Gospel,'" 119–25.

18. Clifton, "Preaching the 'Full Gospel,'" 126.

19. Clifton, "Preaching the 'Full Gospel,'" 126–33.

Matthew Tallman also took the fourfold Pentecostal gospel as a useful framework for building a Pentecostal ecotheology.[20] Like many ecotheologians, he attacked anthropocentrism.[21] He called for a wider view of healing; praised Christian groups who try to help repair environmental degradation;[22] suggested that "a Pentecostal praxis of healing extended to all of creation can extend hope to a hopeless and nihilistic generation of postmoderns";[23] called for dialogue with other Christians who have pioneered ecotheology, while not ignoring the theological problems here; and suggested a reinterpretation of Pentecostal eschatology with input from Moltmann.[24]

One of the most substantial Pentecostal contributions came from A. J. Swoboda in *Trees and Tongues*, published in 2013.[25] Swoboda built on an extensive survey and analysis of ecotheologies in Roman Catholic, Orthodox, Protestant, and eco-feminist traditions; those of earlier Pentecostal authors; and followed these with an in-depth analysis of Denis Edwards's, Sallie McFague's, and Mark Wallace's contributions. He then put forward Pentecostal pneumatological ideas on which he built an incipient "green Pentecostal pneumatology." This featured the themes of "Spirit-baptized creation," "the charismatic community of creation," "the holistic Spirit of creation," and "the eschatological Spirit of ecological mission." He claimed to offer "a new awareness of the Spirit in the world, in all of creation, who seeks to free it from bondage and decay"[26] and concluded that "*all* of God's gifts must be stewarded, whether those gifts be tongues or trees."[27]

Drawing on the work of Jürgen Moltmann, his own earlier book on Pentecostal eschatology,[28] and the idea of the kenosis of the Spirit, Peter Althouse asserts,

---

20. Matthew Tallman, "Pentecostal Ecology: A Theological Paradigm for Pentecostal Environmentalism," in *The Spirit Renews the Face of the Earth*, ed. Amos Yong (Eugene: Wipf & Stock, 2009), 135–54.

21. Tallman, "Pentecostal Ecology," 136–37.

22. As in the example of African churches in Zimbabwe, see Tallman, "Pentecostal Ecology," 144.

23. Tallman, "Pentecostal Ecology," 144.

24. Tallman, "Pentecostal Ecology," 146–52.

25. A. J. Swoboda, *Tongues and Trees: Towards a Pentecostal Ecological Theology* (Blandford Forum: Deo, 2013). Much of this argument is summed up in his 2011 "Eco-Glossolalia" article.

26. Swoboda, *Tongues and Trees*, 247–48.

27. Swoboda, *Tongues and Trees*, 248; emphasis in original.

28. Peter Althouse, *Spirit of the Last Days: Pentecostal Eschatology in Conversation with Jürgen Moltmann* (London: A&C Black, 2003).

The violence that the human species unleashes on creation through national and global wars, economic privilege, and technological prowess, oppresses the ecological order of nature and must be labeled as sin. The Spirit's presence vitiates the world in order to overcome the violence rained down on what God has pronounced "good."[29]

This Althouse essay is one of the collected essays edited by Swoboda and Bouma-Prediger in 2014, *Blood Cries Out: Pentecostals, Ecology and the Groans of Creation*. Two of these specifically refer to the book of the Revelation. Robby Waddell built on Norman Habel's ecological hermeneutics, including a hermeneutic of suspicion, a hermeneutics of identification, and one of retrieval, to offer an ecotheological approach to *1 Enoch* and *Revelation*.[30] Paul Ede drew on several biblical passages related to the destruction and renewal of cities, especially the vison of the New Jerusalem (Revelation 21–22), to draw a vision of "a city . . . that is integrated with nature rather than being parasitic upon it."[31]

More recently, Andrew Ray Williams reviewed contributions to Pentecostal ecotheology and related eschatology in an article published in 2018.[32] He began by observing that "living in light of the end is natural for humans, thus one's eschatology will majorly impact one's present day decisions."[33] He then dialogued with three eminent Pentecostal scholars. He argued that "Althouse's eschatology can be exceptionally useful in maturing Pentecostal ecotheology" because it "helps in establishing that there is both *continuity* and *discontinuity* between the old creation and new creation."[34] Frank Macchia's "vision for God's final justification to include all of creation has clear eco-ethical implications"[35] and his understanding of praying in tongues as "an act of yearning for deliverance for the suffering creation"[36] should inspire not just prayer but action

---

29. Althouse, "Pentecostal Eco-Transformation," 126.

30. Waddell, "Green Apocalypse."

31. Paul Ede, "River from the Temple: The Spirit, City Earthkeeping and Healing Urban Land," in *Blood Cries Out: Pentecostals, Ecology and the Groans of Creation*, eds. A. J. Swoboda and Steven Bouma-Prediger (Eugene: Pickwick, 2014), 216.

32. Andrew Ray Williams, "Greening the Apocalypse: A Pentecostal Eco-Eschatological Exploration," *PentecoStudies* 17, no. 2 (2018): 69.

33. Williams, "Greening the Apocalypse," 206.

34. Williams, "Greening the Apocalypse," 209; emphasis in original.

35. Williams, "Greening the Apocalypse," 211.

36. Williams, "Greening the Apocalypse," 211, referring to Frank D. Macchia, "Justification through New Creation: The Holy Spirit and the Doctrine by Which the Church Stands or Falls," *Theology Today*, 58, no. 2 (2001): 202–17.

as part of the Spirit's work "within history."[37] Larry McQueen's revisioning of Pentecostal eschatology focuses on the final new creation (Rev 21–22), summoning "believers now to see themselves as God's participants in renewing the cosmos," including ecological issues,[38] while rejecting "eschatological anthropocentrism."[39] Williams concludes with a call for a pneumatological eco-eschatology that includes "partnering with God in renewing creation in the 'already' in anticipation of the 'not yet' of God's kingdom"[40] as the Spirit guides us.[41]

In conclusion, Pentecostals are thinking hard about ecology and the environment, at least at the scholarly level, and building bridges between Pentecostal theology and creation care. Some of the theological work is impressive, especially on the work of the Spirit in creation and seeing the journey to new creation as transformative, not annihilationist. However, I see three deficiencies with these otherwise laudable efforts. First, with some exceptions, such as Waddell and parts of Amos Yong's *Belief* commentary,[42] there is a deficiency on the biblical side: few of the articles and books engage much with Scripture or they only discuss it superficially. Second, there is a deficiency on the practical side: there are few suggestions about what Pentecostals (in particular) should be *doing* about the environmental issues discussed, and in my view the suggestions made are often rather trivial[43] or highly general; exceptions are the case study in Zimbabwe in Tallman's article,[44] the account of efforts at environmental repair in the Glasgow suburb of Possilpark in Ede's article,[45] and the joint book-length study by Swoboda and two non-Pentecostal authors, *Introducing Evangelical Ecotheology*,[46] which includes a lengthy section on praxis. And this leads to the third deficiency which is on the social or political side: these articles fail to grapple with the political and ethical issues (or dilemmas) for Pentecostals

---

37. Williams, "Greening the Apocalypse," 212.
38. Williams, "Greening the Apocalypse," 214.
39. Williams, "Greening the Apocalypse," 216.
40. Williams, "Greening the Apocalypse," 219.
41. Williams, "Greening the Apocalypse," 220.
42. Yong, *Revelation,* Belief: Theological Commentary on the Bible Series (Louisville: Westminster John Knox, 2021), 121–24.
43. For example, see the suggestions in Williams, "Greening the Apocalypse," 221.
44. Tallman, "Pentecostal Ecology," 144. See also Asamoah-Gyadu, "God's Laws of Productivity," 180.
45. Ede, "River from the Temple," 205–9.
46. Daniel L. Brunner, Jennifer L. Butler, and A. J. Swoboda, *Introducing Evangelical Ecotheology: Foundations in Scripture, Theology, History, and Praxis* (Grand Rapids: Baker Academic, 2014).

taking part (or not) in action to change government policies and the like.[47] For example, Shane Clifton (justifiably) faults Australian Pentecostals for "aggressive criticism of 'greenies'" and unwillingness to work with scientists,[48] but does not consider the difficulties Pentecostals would face in allying themselves with forces in society that are often hostile to Christian faith.[49]

Revelation Voices: A Survey and Analysis

Revelation is arguably the most creation-conscious and environmentally aware book in the Bible alongside Genesis. This contention is based on Revelation's emphasis on God as creator and sustainer of creation, its language of creation worshiping God and the Lamb, its imagery of environmental disaster, its personification of Earth, its critique of an all-consuming empire, its promise of a new/renewed heavens and Earth, and its specific warning to destroyers of the Earth (Rev 11:18).

Worshipping the Creator and Sustainer of Creation

The first portrayal of God in Revelation 4 focuses on two main points: God as the sovereign ruler seated on his heavenly throne (Rev 4:3–6) and being worshiped by the heavenly beings (Rev 4:6–11), and God as creator as the grounds of that worship:

> You are worthy, our Lord and God,
> to receive glory and honor and power,
> for you *created* all things,
> and by your will they existed and were *created*.[50] (Rev 4:11)

This affirmation takes the readers/hearers back to Genesis 1 and other creation passages in the Old Testament. The Pentecostal commentator John Christopher Thomas observes here that "This emphasis upon God as creator is not only foundational in terms of God's identity, but . . . it will leave

---

47. *Introducing Evangelical Ecotheology* makes some effort to address this but by their own admission the authors had trouble coming to a consensus here. See Brunner, Butler and Swoboda, *Introducing Evangelical Ecotheology*, 220.

48. Clifton, "Preaching the 'Full Gospel,'" 121.

49. Robby Waddell pointed me to an article in *Assemblies of God Heritage* about a maverick Pentecostal who initiated the idea of Earth Day, only to see it captured by political agendas. See Nicole Sparks and Darrin J. Rodgers, "John McConnell Jr. and the Pentecostal Origins of Earth Day," *Assemblies of God Heritage* (2010): 26–33.

50. Using forms of the Greek *ktizō*, "create"; emphasis added.

no doubt as to who is responsible for the creation of the new heaven and the new earth."[51] Moreover God "has created all things – even those things, as it turns out, that will rebel against him and refuse to repent."[52] It is followed by a universal response when the Lamb is revealed, aptly called the "Song from the Universe,"[53]

> Then I heard every creature[54] in heaven and on earth and under the earth and in the sea, and all that is in them [a comprehensive cosmos], singing
>
> "To the one seated on the throne and to the Lamb
> be blessing and honor and glory and might
> forever and ever!" (Rev 5:13, bracketed comment added)

In a similar way, in Revelation 14 we read,

> Then I saw another angel flying in midheaven, with an eternal gospel to proclaim to those who live on the earth – to every nation and tribe and language and people. He said in a loud voice, "Fear God and give him glory, for the hour of his judgment has come; and worship him who made[55] heaven and earth, the sea and the springs of water." (Rev 14:6–7)

David Aune notes, this language about God "is a frequent designation for God in the OT."[56] Note that this message is described as a "gospel" and it focuses on giving God fear, glory and worship because of his role as creator.

Environmental Disaster

Environmental disasters are a prominent feature of the Revelation narrative. The seal openings lead to food shortages that are likely caused by war or drought (Rev 6:4–8). David J. Hawkin argues that "the fourth horseman symbolizes ecological catastrophe . . . Plagues and roaming wild animals are

---

51. John Christopher Thomas, *The Apocalypse: A Literary and Theological Commentary* (Cleveland: CPT, 2012), 218.

52. Thomas, *The Apocalypse*, 218.

53. Kendell Easley, *Holman New Testament Commentary: Revelation* (Nashville: Broadman & Holman, 1998), 96–97, as quoted in Lichtenwalter, "Creation and Apocalypse," *Journal of the Adventist Theological Society* 15, no. 1 (2004): 126.

54. Greek *ktisma*, "creature."

55. Greek *poiēsanti*, from *poieō*, the more general word for "make" or "do."

56. David E. Aune, *Revelation 6–16*, Word Biblical Commentary 52B (Nashville: Thomas Nelson, 1998), 828.

symbols of the lethal forces of nature which are unleashed by the empire's repression and oppression."[57] Then comes a major earthquake affecting the heavens and the earth (Rev 6:12–14), perhaps a result of a cosmic collision, such as a comet hitting the earth.

The trumpets series carries an intensified litany of disasters with language possibly derived from the eruption of Mount Vesuvius in AD 79: the second trumpet blast especially suggests this as it is evocative of Pliny's account of this event,[58] "The second angel blew his trumpet, and something like a great mountain, burning with fire, was thrown into the sea. A third of the sea became blood, a third of the living creatures in the sea died, and a third of the ships were destroyed." (Rev 8:8–9)

The range of environmental events in this series is huge:

> hail and fire, mixed with blood . . . hurled to the earth; and a third of the earth was burned up, a third of the trees were burned up, and all green grass was burned up. (Rev 8:7)
>
> a great star fell from heaven, blazing like a torch, and it fell on a third of the rivers and on the springs of water . . . A third of the waters became wormwood, and many died from the water, because it was made bitter. (Rev 8:10–11)
>
> a third of the sun was struck, and a third of the moon, and a third of the stars, so that a third of their light was darkened; a third of the day was kept from shining, and likewise the night.[59] (Rev 8:12)
>
> from the shaft rose smoke like the smoke of a great furnace, and the sun and the air were darkened with the smoke (Rev 9:2).[60]

Then it all goes to another level with the bowl plagues described as "the last, for with them the wrath of God is ended" (Rev 15:1):

> The second angel poured his bowl into the sea, and it became like the blood of a corpse, and every living thing in the sea died. (Rev 16:3)
>
> the springs of water . . . became blood. (Rev 16:4)

---

57. David J. Hawkin, "Critique of Ideology in the Book of Revelation and its Implications for Ecology," *Ecotheology* 8, no. 2 (2003): 165.

58. Cf. Aune, *Revelation 6–16*, 519–20.

59. This might also be an allusion to the eruption of Vesuvius, as a result of which the sun was darkened for several days, according to ancient sources. See Aune, *Revelation 6–16*, 523.

60. Again, possibly due to volcanic activity. See Aune, *Revelation 6–16*, 527.

> The fourth angel poured his bowl on the sun, and it was allowed to scorch people with fire; they were scorched by the fierce heat. (Rev 16:8–9)
>
> the great river Euphrates . . . was dried up, (Rev 16:12)
>
> flashes of lightning, peals of thunder, and a violent earthquake, such as had not occurred since people were upon the earth, so violent was that earthquake . . . (Rev 16:18)
>
> huge hailstones, each weighing about a hundred pounds, dropped from heaven . . . (Rev 16:21)

These disasters, to some degree, are modelled on the plague accounts in Exodus and may not be meant literally. However, Sean McDonough observes that "de-creation pervades the book."[61] Scott Dunham also suggests that "certain language [in Revelation] seems to indicate a judgment of nature . . . God is not simply executing judgment by means of a natural disaster, but is actually damaging the earth."[62] However, in this way, the book of Revelation demonstrates a strong awareness of the dependence of humanity on a stable and favourable environment. As Richard Woods argues, the plagues in Revelation "evince a sophisticated insight into the organic connection that exists among biological and geological systems, the consequences of disrupting this balance through human greed, oppression, and malice, and, finally, the compensating divine response to ecocatastrophe."[63]

Earth as an Active Agent

Waddell emphasizes the need to give earth agency as a subject in an ecological hermeneutics.[64] Revelation contains one of the few biblical passages where this happens. The dragon is pursuing the woman (the Messiah's mother) and "from his mouth the serpent poured water like a river after the woman, to sweep her away with the flood. But the earth (Greek *gē*) came to the help of the

---

61. Sean McDonough, "Paradise by the Desolation Trail: De-Creation and the New Testament," in *As Long as The Earth Endures: The Bible, Creation and the Environment*, eds. Jonathan Moo and Robin Routledge (Nottingham: Apollos, 2014), 179.

62. Scott A. Dunham, "Ecological Violence of Apocalyptic Eschatology," *Studies in Religion* 32, no. 1–2 (2003): 103.

63. Richard Wood, "Seven Bowls of Wrath: The Ecological Relevance of Revelation," *Biblical Theology Bulletin* 38 (2008): 65. Wood applies the details of the bowl plagues of Revelation 16 to current climate change threats in this article.

64. Waddell, "Green Apocalypse," 138.

woman; it opened its mouth and swallowed the river" (Rev 12:15–16). What the passage really envisages here is unclear. In the OT, waters and seas can be seen as God's enemies (Pss 29:3; 74:15; 93:3–4; Hab 3:8) or symbols of nations hostile to Israel (Pss 46:2–4; 144:7; Hab 3:13–15). At least Earth here is not just an "it" but has agency.[65] This is an idea with OT roots too, such as the earth swallowing both the Egyptian army (Exod 15:12) and the rebel Israelites led by Korah, Dathan, and Abiram (Num 16:30–33). In fact, as John Christopher Thomas points out, there is an emphasis here on "the strength of the mouth of the earth, which is able to open and drink up the entire river."[66]

The All-Consuming Empire

Three sections of Revelation are specifically targeted at an anti-God empire. Most likely, John had the Roman Empire in mind, but the message cannot be confined to a specific place or time. Revelation 13 uses the imagery of two beasts to expose authoritarian oppression, especially of Christians. Revelation 17 uses the image of a high-class prostitute to expose the seductive nature of empire and its violent end. But Revelation 18, which contains a dirge celebrating or bemoaning the fall of the empire, is more economically and ecologically focused, depicting the empire as "as a powerful market economy."[67] A long section has the kings, merchants, shipowners, and sailors crying out in pain and sorrow at the loss of income that the fall of the empire would mean for them. Clearly John is describing the reach of a wide-ranging political and economic system.

As John portrays it, the empire devours the produce of the world as seen in the list of items imported to the capital city – all of them, in Aune's words, "luxury trade goods primarily for the consumption of the very wealthy"[68] (Rev 18:11–13). An ancient writer, Aelius Aristides, wrote of how produce from all over the world was brought to Rome, "It cannot be otherwise than that there always be here an abundance of all that grows and is manufactured among

---

65. Waddell, "Green Apocalypse," 149.
66. Thomas, *Apocalypse*, 379.
67. Barbara R. Rossing, "For the Healing of the World: Reading Revelation Ecologically," in *From Every People and Nation: The Book of Revelation in Intercultural Perspective*, ed. David Rhoads (Minneapolis: Fortress, 2005), 177.
68. David E. Aune, *Revelation 17–22*, Word Biblical Commentary 52C (Nashville: Thomas Nelson, 1998), 998; see 998–1003 for more details.

each people."⁶⁹ This was not fair trade. Only a minority profited by the sale of these goods, and the system was particularly grounded in slave labour (Rev 18:13) and violence (Rev 18:24). The environmental effects are not spelled out here but can be imagined with hindsight: ivory trade involves animal slaughter (Rev 18:12); "flour and wheat" were plundered from the Roman provinces.⁷⁰ As Hawkin comments, "Almost all of them would involve not only economic exploitation but also some ecological damage."⁷¹ Aristides himself commented, "one imagines that for the future the trees are left bare for the people there and that they must come here to beg for their own produce if they need anything."⁷²

This system of economic exploitation is denounced as "fornication" (Rev 18:3, 9), "sins" and "iniquities" (Rev 18:5), and "sorcery" (Rev 18:23). John prophesies of a just repayment following the principle of *lex talionis* ("proportional retribution" as in Exod 21:23–25):⁷³

> Render to her as she herself has rendered,
> and repay her double for her deeds;
> mix a double dose for her in the cup she mixed.
> As she glorified herself and lived luxuriously,
> so give her a like measure of torment and grief. (Rev 18:6–7)

The Promise of a Renewed Earth

After all the political, spiritual, economic, and ecological struggles in the narrative, there is hope at the end. God promises to dwell with all the peoples of the world and declares, "I am making all things new" (Rev 21:5). As Lichtenwalter asserts, "God is the ground of ultimate hope for the future creation of the world."⁷⁴

John then gives us an inspiring picture of a New Jerusalem surrounded by subservient nations whose kings "bring their glory into it" (Rev 21:24). It is a radically different world with no sea (Rev 21:1), apparently no sun or moon (Rev 21:23; 22:5), and no night (Rev 21:25; 22:5). The "river of the water of

---

69. Aelius Aristides, 26:11–13, as quoted in Aune, *Revelation 17–22*, 980; see 980–82 for other ancient evidence.

70. Cf. Barbara Rossing and Johan Buitendag, "Life in its Fullness: Ecology, Eschatology and Economy in a Time of Climate Change," *HTS Teologiese Theological Studies* 76, no. 1 (2020): 4.

71. Hawkin, "Critique of Ideology," 167.

72. Aune, *Revelation 17–22*, 980. For a fuller quote, see Hawkin, "Critique of Ideology," 166–67.

73. Cf. Aune, *Revelation 17–22*, 993.

74. Lichtenwalter, "Creation and Apocalypse," 129.

life" flows from God's earthly throne through the city and "on either side of the river is the tree of life . . . producing its fruit each month; and the leaves of the tree are for the healing of the nations" (Rev 22:1–2). This scene recalls the original garden of Genesis 2 and conveys a picture of environmental plenty. Such a radical change is reflected in John's declaration that "the first heaven and the first earth had passed away" (Rev 21:1) and "the first things have passed away" (Rev 21:4). Rossing and Buitendag claim that all this "offers the most earth-centred eschatological picture of the whole Bible."[75]

How are we to interpret all this? Is God going to destroy the planet earth and make a totally new one? If so, are we wasting our time looking after the present earth?[76]

Before rushing to these conclusions, let's consider what such an interpretation might imply. Is the idea of an earth with no sea, no sun, and no moon coherent? What changes would be needed to the solar system we live in and to the physical laws and conditions needed for human life? What would completely new heavens look like?

There are also hints in the passage that total destruction and new creation may not be intended. For example, God says, "I am making all things new" (Rev 21:5), not all new things.[77] The "nations" seem to be still there since "the nations will walk by its light" (Rev 21:24) and "the leaves of the tree are for the *healing* of the nations" (Rev 22:2, emphasis added), not their destruction. Moreover, their kings "bring their glory into" the New Jerusalem (Rev 21:24), and so do the people at large (Rev 21:26). Perhaps, as Rossing and Buitendag claim, "it is the Roman imperial world and the world of sin that must be replaced,"[78] not the planet. Or as Matthew Tallman remarks, "God is in the 'recycling' business."[79]

Warning to Earth's Destroyers

The final judgement that is envisaged in Revelation is grounded in the behaviour of people: "the dead were judged according to their works, as recorded

---

75. Rossing and Buitendag, "Life in its Fullness," 6; cf. Barbara Rossing, "God Laments with Us: Climate Change, Apocalypse and the Urgent Kairos Moment," *The Ecumenical Review* 62, no. 2 (2010): 128.

76. This is a common objection from some fundamentalist Christians (cf. Waddell, "Green Apocalypse," 136).

77. As pointed out by Waddell, "Green Apocalypse," 148.

78. Rossing and Buitendag "Life in its Fullness," 6.

79. Tallman, "Pentecostal Ecology," 50.

in the books" (Rev 20:12), a basic principle of justice in God's order as seen throughout the Bible.[80] There is a specific warning to one group of people:

> The nations raged,
> but your wrath has come, and the time for judging the dead . . .
> and for destroying *those who destroy the earth*. (Rev 11:18, emphasis added)

Who is this aimed at and what specifically are they guilty of? The passage does not spell it out. But we can get some light from the language used: first, it is the earth (Greek *gē*) that they are said to destroy,[81] not *kosmos* (world or universe) or *oikoumene* (inhabited earth). John seems to be referring to the physical world: *gē* is used always of dry ground in some form. Second, these people are said to "destroy it." The Greek verb is *diaphtheirō*, meaning "destroy" or "ruin" or in the passive, "wear away" or "decay." Third, the identity of the destroyers is revealed in other places in the text. They include human armies (Rev 6:3–8), hybrid "locusts" emerging from the abyss, possibly referring to demonic forces (Rev 9:1–11) (though their main target is unbelieving humans, not the environment [Rev 9:4]), and the all-consuming imperial economy discussed above (Rev 18).[82] They also include the devil:

> But woe to the earth and the sea,
> for the devil has come down to you
> with great wrath. (Rev 12:12)

How could John's hearers have understood this? What experience did they have to make sense of such language? They had no experience of a total destruction of the planet and it is not likely that this is meant in view of the language of the new earth, especially as people and the devil are blamed for the destruction here. But their experience of the Roman Empire with its all-consuming economic system, its violence, and its wars would give them a picture of the earth being ruined. They might, for example, remember the destruction of the trees around Jerusalem during the siege of AD 70[83] or the

---

80. Cf. Thomas, *Apocalypse*, 350.

81. Aune contends that "Here 'earth' is metonymy for the 'people of the earth'" (*Revelation 6–16*, 645). He gives no reasons. Amos Yong in his theological commentary on Revelation argues, correctly I think, that "the material world" is included (Yong, *Revelation*, 148).

82. Specifically, "the Devil, the Beast, the False Prophet, and those who had sided with them" and are therefore thrown into the lake of fire" (Waddell, "Green Apocalypse," 148).

83. Josephus, "The Wars of the Jews," in *The Works of Josephus*, trans. William Whiston (Peabody: Hendrickson, 1987), 5.6.3 (264), 6.1.1 (5).

salting of the fields around defeated Carthage so that "nothing would grow there again."[84] As Hawkin comments,

> The ecological disasters which were caused by the rapacity of the Roman Empire are . . . well documented. Whole forests disappeared, countless species of animals were wiped out, large areas were devastated by mining, the air was polluted and the water made unsafe for drinking. Rome itself was a terrible place to live. It was overcrowded, polluted and unsafe.[85]

And they would recall the earlier language of humanly-caused devastation in Revelation 6:4–8. As they read on, the portrayals of empire in Revelation 13, 17 and 18 would resonate with their experience of living under such a rapacious and unjust system.

But fourth, there comes "the time (Greek *kairos*) for judging the dead . . . and for destroying those who destroy the earth" (Rev 11:18). This is normally read as anticipating the final judgement of Rev 20:11–15, but Barbara Rossing suggests it is pointing to the fall of Rome: "Revelation's insistence on the imminent 'end' assures its audience that Rome will not rule the earth forever."[86] Thus "the tragic rape of the earth is the result of unjust imperial exploitation and conquest and that such abuse will soon be judged by God – who will destroy 'the *destroyers* of the earth' (11:18), not the earth itself."[87]

Implications

But let's pause and ask, what was John's (or the Spirit's) purpose in all this? And what did John or the Spirit want the audience to do in response?

First, he seems to be creating a kind of theodicy to justify God's judgements due to human sinfulness. The twofold use of *diaphtheirō* in Rev 11:18 implies a sense of justice; the human destroyers suffer the same fate by themselves being destroyed.[88] There is a similar thought in Rev 16:5–6:

> You are just, O Holy One, who are and were,
> for you have judged these things;

---

84. Hawkin, "Critique of Ideology," 170.

85. Hawkin, "Critique of Ideology," 170. Bredin comments, "Rome's deforestation of conquered lands was notorious." See Mark Bredin, "Ecological Crisis and Plagues (Revelation 11:6)," *Biblical Theology Bulletin* 39 (2009): 33.

86. Rossing, "God Laments with Us," 123–24.

87. Rossing, "For the Healing of the World," 170 (emphasis in original text), see also 173.

88. Cf. Aune, *Revelation 6–16*, 646.

> because they shed the blood of saints and prophets,
> you have given them blood to drink.
> It is what they deserve!

God in some way "punishes" the ungodly for their unjust ways by releasing environmental disasters on them, a theme prominent in the lament passage of Revelation 18 (especially verses 5–8), as I mentioned earlier.[89] If we apply that line of thinking to today's situation, perhaps climate change and other environmental degradations function as God's judgement on our civilization. On the other hand, Barbara Rossing is surely right to claim, "Revelation's primary polemic is not against the earth as such, but rather against the exploitation of the earth and its peoples."[90]

Second, John's language also seems to function as a call to repentance. Readers are warned that earth destroyers will themselves be destroyed hence they should engage in self-assessment and change their ways if they are guilty of such destruction. As Dunham suggests, "those who do not fear the Lord have lived destructive lifestyles – ones that destroy the earth" but this implies that the godly "treat the earth with love and respect."[91] The disasters of the trumpet series appear to be aimed at repentance, judging from the author's disappointment that "The rest of humankind, who were not killed by these plagues, did not repent of the works of their hands" (Rev 9:20). As Rossing claims, "The plagues serve as wake-up calls, warning of the consequences of Rome's unjust actions" and "issue dire threats of consequences if oppressors continue on their current path. But they also make clear that there is still time for change."[92] A similar thought is perhaps implied by the call in Rev 18:4:

> Come out of her, my people,
> so that you do not take part in her sins
> and so that you do not share in her plagues.

---

89. Perhaps a similar thought comes out of Rev 11:3–6. The witnesses are advocating repentance, being dressed in sackcloth, but have authority to "strike the earth with every kind of plague" (v. 6), presumably as a response to unrepentant attitudes. However, Mark Bredin resists the idea that the witnesses were vindictive or anti-creation and argues that this "striking" was actually what their enemies accused the witnesses of doing, not what they were actually doing ("Ecological Crisis," 27, 30–31).

90. Rossing, "God Laments with Us," 123. Rossing asserts that "Global warming is not punishment from God, but rather a consequence of the physical fact that in this universe created by God, with its finely-tuned atmosphere, certain actions cause other things to happen." See Rossing, "God Laments with Us," 125.

91. Dunham, "Ecological Violence," 105.

92. Rossing, "God Laments with Us," 125. Compare Rossing, "For the Healing of the World," 175–76.

So, God's people, that is, the readers and hearers of Revelation, are challenged to disassociate themselves in some radical way from that all-consuming imperial economy. As Aune argues, "the summons to flight refers to the necessity of Christians disentangling themselves and distancing themselves morally, and perhaps even socially, from the corrupt and seductive influences of Roman rule."[93] Waddell suggests, "it is our responsibility to resist along with Earth the evil that will eventually be judged."[94] And Ede argues that "The Spirit acts to arrest and judge anti-creational practices . . . and calls us to pro-creational action with regards to the land."[95] Applying that logic to today's situation, Christians are thus being called to disassociate themselves from the environmentally destructive habits and industries of our time and adopt a lifestyle of simplicity, which is closer to what most Pentecostal ecotheology advocates.[96]

But is John asking his audience to engage in political action or to support the empire to the extent it may want to act justly in this area? For example, we read of Domitian issuing a decree to limit the more profitable growth of grapes and olive trees because it limited the food supply for the empire,[97] which may be referred to in Revelation 6:6b. Obviously, first century Christians had no political clout. But it stands to reason that Christians would not resist such efforts that would help the more vulnerable people in the world; on the other hand, the command *not* to damage the olive oil and wine seems to come from God.[98]

There are also aspects of the book of Revelation that may be in tension with ecotheology. Much of the critique of premillennialism, for example, accuses it of dualism: dualism of body-soul, present-future, creation-new creation, and matter-spirit. This is seen in the idea of Christians just "going to heaven" when they die or the destruction of the present earth to make way for a new one. It is a fair criticism. But Revelation itself embraces a form of dualism, not an ontological dualism of matter-spirit, for example, but an ethical and spiritual dualism of good-evil, saved-lost, and even present-future. Thus, while

---

93. Aune, *Revelation 17–22*, 991. Or, as Rossing comments, the contrasting images of Babylon and the New Jerusalem "call on us to make an ethical choice between two citizenships. God's people must 'come out' of Babylon in order to enter into the blessing of the New Jerusalem." See "For the Healing of the World," 167.

94. Waddell, "Green Apocalypse," 149.

95. Ede, "River from the Temple," 222. See also Brunner, Butler and Swoboda, *Introducing Evangelical Ecotheology*, 157–59.

96. Cf. Brunner, Butler, and Swoboda, *Introducing Evangelical Ecotheology*, 177–216.

97. Cf. Aune, *Revelation 6–16*, 399–400.

98. Cf. Aune, *Revelation 6–16*, 400.

Waddell and others convincingly argue that the new earth is the current earth transformed, not replaced, that transformation is radical.

Related to this is the spiritual dualism or binary thinking throughout the book. This lies behind the call to John's readers to "come out" from Babylon (Rev 18:4), for example, and the constant call to the seven churches to disassociate themselves from Greco-Roman culture. This note in Revelation problematizes some recent ecotheology. Many authors write about what "we" (that is, human beings as a whole, or especially Westerners) have done to damage the ecosystems of the planet and what "we" should be doing to address environmental issues such as climate change. But the idea of Christians joining with unbelievers in taking actions like this is in tension with Revelation's call to Christians to keep away from Greco-Roman cultural practices (Rev 2:14–16, 20–23) and to "Come out of her, my people" (Rev 18:4).

In Revelation, Christians are separated from the rest of the (human) world by the mark of the beast, which they will not accept (Rev 13:16–18; 14:9–10; 20:4), and the mark of God and Christ which they alone receive (Rev 14:1; 7:7; 9:4). This implies that Christians should "keep a distance" between themselves and unbelievers, not following the example of unbelievers, and not joining with unbelievers in social or political actions they may initiate. Does this therefore imply that Christians today should avoid involvement with ecological activists, many of whom are atheists, pantheists, and humanists?

Certainly, such entanglements are problematic. But perhaps there is a better way of looking at this. Until recently, Christians have lagged behind others in recognizing and responding to ecological issues, though one of the first climate change scientists, John Houghton, was a believer.[99] But perhaps God is challenging us to set the pace, to take the lead, to show what God's charter to humanity in Genesis 1:26–28 really means and how humans ought to respond. After all, Revelation is arguably calling on its readers to take the lead in repudiating idolatry and sexual immorality and other Greco-Roman sins (Rev 9:20–21; 18:4; 22:15). The call to repentance is addressed first to the churches, who will actually hear the voice of the Spirit through John (Rev 2:5, 16, 21–22; 3:3, 19). They might be inspired to repent by the vision of the New Jerusalem.[100]

---

99. Andrew Freedman, "John Houghton, Renowned Climate Scientist Who Led IPCC Reports, Dies of Coronavirus at 88." *Washington Post*, April 20, 2020; Fred Taylor, "Obituary: John T. Houghton," *Nature Climate Change* 10, no. 491 (2020); Michael Bones, "RIP God's Scientist: The Faith and Reason of Climate Change Expert Sir John Houghton," *Eternity*, 21 April 2020, eternitynews.com.au.

100. Cf. Rossing, "God Laments with Us," 128.

And historically, Christians did repudiate idolatry and immorality and injustice, so effectively that the Roman emperor was converted and Roman culture was at least superficially reformed. Could such a possibility be there for believers today? If so, it would probably take the form of locally driven action rather than large-scale political campaigning, as in the Possilpark project or the Mozambique activities highlighted in *Introducing Evangelical Ecotheology*.[101] But if so, perhaps we need a reformed eschatology to help us think our way more clearly.

Eschatological Voices: Does Postmillennialism Have Something to Offer?

A number of Pentecostal and other authors have identified premillennialism as an important factor hindering the development of a vibrant Pentecostal ecotheology. For example, Dwight Wilson argued that Pentecostals "have rejected the reformist methods of the optimistic postmillennialists and have concentrated on 'snatching brands from the fire' and letting social reforms result from humankind being born again."[102] If so, maybe postmillennialism has something to offer here as an alternative eschatology.[103]

Premillennialism encourages the idea that Jesus's coming is imminent, which means that world-shaking disasters are about to come on the unbelieving world, that Jesus will sort out the environment in the millennium, and that ultimately he will build an entirely new planet. There is some truth here: in Revelation the huge ecological disasters are seen as part of God's judgements more than directly the result of human error. But if these themes in Revelation are pushed too far, so as to overwhelm the other themes we have been discussing, we end up with a distorted eschatology that negates all human involvement in God's mission of saving humanity and the planet.

Postmillennialism is controversial and takes many different forms, but it has two significant advantages as an eschatological framework for ecotheology. It makes space for the Spirit-filled church to advance the kingdom of God without depending exclusively on Jesus's parousia as a dramatic intervention. And second, it allows for the possibility that Jesus's coming may be still some

---

101. Cf. Brunner, Butler, and Swoboda, *Introducing Evangelical Ecotheology*, 3–4, 250–51.

102. Dwight J. Wilson, "Pentecostal Perspectives on Eschatology," in *The New International Dictionary of Pentecostal and Charismatic Movements*, eds. Stanley M. Burgess and Eduard Van Der Maas (Grand Rapids: Zondervan, 2002), 601–5.

103. For a more biblical consideration of the millennium, see Jon K. Newton, "Time Language and the Purpose of the Millennium," *Colloquium* 43, no. 2 (2011): 147–68.

distance away in time. Putting these two points together, a postmillennial approach makes ecotheology more imperative and more credible in the twenty-first century. But that is a topic for another time.

Bibliography

Althouse, Peter. "Implications of the Kenosis of the Spirit for a Creational Eschatology: A Pentecostal Engagement with Jürgen Moltmann." In *The Spirit Renews the Face of the Earth: Pentecostal Forays in Science and Theology of Creation*, edited by Amos Yong, 155–72. Eugene: Pickwick, 2009.

———. "Pentecostal Eco-Transformation: Possibilities for a Pentecostal Ecotheology in Light of Moltmann's Green Theology." In *Blood Cries Out: Pentecostals, Ecology and the Groans of Creation*, edited by A. J. Swoboda and Steven Bouma-Prediger, 116–32. Eugene: Pickwick, 2014.

———. *Spirit of the Last Days: Pentecostal Eschatology in Conversation with Jürgen Moltmann*. Journal of Pentecostal Theology Supplement Series 25. London: T&T Clark, 2003.

Asamoah-Gyadu, J. Kwabena. "'God's Laws of Productivity': Creation in African Pentecostal Hermeneutics." In *The Spirit Renews the Face of the Earth: Pentecostal Forays in Science and Theology of Creation*, edited by Amos Yong, 175–90. Eugene: Pickwick, 2009.

Aune, David E. *Revelation 6–16*. Word Biblical Commentary 52B. Nashville: Thomas Nelson, 1998.

———. *Revelation 17–22*. Word Biblical Commentary 52C. Nashville: Thomas Nelson, 1998.

Bauckham, Richard. *The Bible and Ecology: Rediscovering the Community of Creation*. Waco: Baylor University Press, 2010.

Baudin, Frederic. *Ecology and the Bible*. Translated by David Dimauro. Peabody: Hendrickson, 2020.

Boone, R. Jerome. "Created for Shalom: Human Agency and Responsibility in the World." In *The Spirit Renews the Face of the Earth: Pentecostal Forays in Science and Theology of Creation*, edited by Amos Yong, 17–29. Eugene: Pickwick, 2009.

Bredin, Mark. "Ecological Crisis and Plagues (Revelation 11:6)." *Biblical Theology Bulletin* 39 (2009): 26–38.

Brunner, Daniel L., Jennifer L. Butler, and A. J. Swoboda, *Introducing Evangelical Ecotheology: Foundations in Scripture, Theology and Praxis*. Grand Rapids: Baker Academic, 2014.

Clifton, Shane. "Preaching the 'Full Gospel' in the Context of Global Environmental Crises." In *The Spirit Renews the Face of the Earth: Pentecostal Forays in Science and Theology of Creation*, edited by Amos Yong, 117–34. Eugene: Pickwick, 2009.

Dunham, Scott A. "The Ecological Violence of Apocalyptic Eschatology." *Studies in Religion* 32, no. 1–2 (2003): 101–12.

Easley, Kendell. *Holman New Testament Commentary: Revelation*. Nashville: Broadman & Holman, 1998.

Ede, Paul. "River from the Temple: The Spirit, City Earthkeeping and Healing Urban Land." In *Blood Cries Out: Pentecostals, Ecology and the Groans of Creation*, edited by A. J. Swoboda and Steven Bouma-Prediger, 205–24. Eugene: Pickwick, 2014.

Freedman, Andrew. "John Houghton, Renowned Climate Scientist Who Led IPCC Reports, Dies of Coronavirus at 88," *Washington Post*, Obituary, April 20, 2020.

Gabriel, Andrew. "Pneumatological Perspectives for a Theology of Nature: The Holy Spirit in Relation to Ecology and Technology." *Journal of Pentecostal Theology* 15, no. 2 (2007): 195–212.

Hawkin, David J. "The Critique of Ideology in the Book of Revelation and its Implications for Ecology." *Ecotheology* 8, no. 2 (2003): 161–72.

Josephus. "The Wars of the Jews." In *The Works of Josephus*. Translated by William Whiston. Peabody: Hendrickson, 1987.

Lichtenwalter, Larry L. "Creation and Apocalypse." *Journal of the Adventist Theological Society* 15, no. 1 (2004): 125–37.

Macchia, F. D. "Justification Through New Creation: The Holy Spirit and the Doctrine by Which the Church Stands or Falls." *Theology Today* 58, no. 2 (2001): 202–17. https://doi.org/10.1177/004057360105800207.

McDonough, Sean. "Paradise by the Desolation Trail: De-Creation and the New Testament." In *As Long as The Earth Endures: The Bible, Creation and the Environment*, edited by Jonathan Moo and Robin Routledge, 169–85. Nottingham: Apollos, 2014.

Newton, Jon K. "Time Language and the Purpose of the Millennium." *Colloquium* 43, no. 2 (2011): 147–68.

Rossing, Barbara R. "For the Healing of the World: Reading Revelation Ecologically." In *From Every People and Nation: The Book of Revelation in Intercultural Perspective*, edited by David Rhoads, 165–82. Minneapolis: Fortress, 2005.

———. "God Laments with Us: Climate Change, Apocalypse and the Urgent Kairos Moment." *The Ecumenical Review* 62, no. 2 (2010): 119–30.

Rossing, Barbara R., and Johan Buitendag, "Life in its Fullness: Ecology, Eschatology and Economy in a Time of Climate Change." *HTS Teologiese/Theological Studies* 76, no. 1 (2020): 1–9.

Sparks, Nicole, and Darrin J. Rodgers. "John McConnell, Jr. and the Pentecostal Origins of Earth Day." *Assemblies of God Heritage* (2010): 26–33.

Swoboda, A. J. "Eco-Glossolalia: Emerging Twenty-First Century Pentecostal and Charismatic Ecotheology." *Rural Theology* 9, no. 2 (2011): 101–16.

———. *Tongues and Trees: Toward a Pentecostal Ecological Theology*. Blandford Forum: Deo, 2013.

Tallman, Matthew. "Pentecostal Ecology: A Theological Paradigm for Pentecostal Environmentalism." In *The Spirit Renews the Face of the Earth: Pentecostal Forays in Science and Theology of Creation*, edited by Amos Yong, 135–54. Eugene: Pickwick, 2009.

Taylor, Fred. "Obituary: John T. Houghton." *Nature Climate Change* 10, no. 491 (2020). https://doi.org/10.1038/s41558-020-0801-5.

Thomas, John Christopher. *The Apocalypse: A Literary and Theological Commentary*. Cleveland: CPT, 2012.

Waddell, Robby. "Apocalyptic Sustainability: The Future of Pentecostal Ecology." In *Perspectives in Pentecostal Eschatologies: World Without End*, edited by Peter Althouse and Robby Waddell, 95–110. Eugene: Pickwick, 2010.

———."A Green Apocalypse: Comparing Secular and Religious Eschatological Visions of Earth." In *Blood Cries Out: Pentecostals, Ecology and the Groans of Creation*, edited by A. J. Swoboda and Steven Bouma-Prediger, 133–51. Eugene: Pickwick, 2014.

———. "Revelation and the (New) Creation." In *The Spirit Renews the Face of the Earth: Pentecostal Forays in Science and Theology of Creation*, edited by Amos Yong, 30–50. Eugene: Pickwick, 2009.

Williams, Andrew Ray. "Greening the Apocalypse: A Pentecostal Eco-Eschatological Exploration." *PentecoStudies* 17, no. 2 (2018): 205–25.

Wilson, Dwight J. "Pentecostal Perspectives on Eschatology." In *The New International Dictionary of Pentecostal and Charismatic Movements*, edited by Stanley M. Burgess and Eduard Van Der Maas, 601–5. Grand Rapids: Zondervan, 2002.

Wood, Richard. "Seven Bowls of Wrath: The Ecological Relevance of Revelation." *Biblical Theology Bulletin* 38 (2008): 64–75.

Yong, Amos. *Revelation*. Belief: Theological Commentary on the Bible Series. Louisville: Westminster John Knox, 2021.

———. *The Spirit Poured Out on All Flesh: Pentecostalism and the Possibility of Global Theology*. Grand Rapids: Baker Academic, 2005.

Yong, Amos, ed. *The Spirit Renews the Face of the Earth: Pentecostal Forays in Science and Theology of Creation*. Eugene: Pickwick, 2009.

4

Many Tongues, Many Biocultural Niches

A Pentecostal Missiological Response to Language Endangerment and Environmental Degradation

Amos Yong

This chapter reconsiders the missiological implications of the Pentecost narrative in the contemporary context of environmental degradation. In light of the growing literature on biolinguistic diversity that connects the relationship between endangered languages (and their ethnic-cultural communities) and ecological destruction to and from the ends of the earth (first section), the essay explores how we might realize the Pentecost outpouring of the Spirit on all flesh enabling messianic witness in many languages amid environmentally apocalyptic conditions (second section). In response, consistent with and seeking fulfillment of the creational mandate (third section), fuelled by the Spirit's creative-redemptive work populating those from many nations, tribes, and languages imaged before the great throne and amid the healing potencies of the new creation (fourth section), a missiological program for cultural-linguistic revitalization is sketched (final section). At the heart of the following is a theology of witness in many tongues and languages[1] derived from reconsidering the Pentecost narrative against the backdrop of the creational invitation for filling the earth. The results include a bolstered missiology of cultural-linguistic revitalization and ecological renewal.

Language Endangerment and Environmental Degradation: Some Correlations

We begin by going back to the early 1990s when the clarion call about endangered languages was first sounded. Given the approximately 7,000 languages found around the world then, it was estimated that up to 50 percent of these were threatened with extinction within the next century.[2] With this alarm sounded, a great deal of effort has been invested in grasping more accurately what was happening. Leading the way in this regard (among various scholarly and research initiatives) has been the *Ethnologue* database – an annual reference published on the world's languages by SIL International (an organization devoted to linguistic study/documentation, literacy promotion/development, and biblical translation into local languages). More recent *Ethnologue* projections are both more precise and less dire – only one-third of known languages are "currently at some stage in the process of language loss"[3] (by which is meant: being recorded at least as declining in the number of users, if not also not being transmitted to the younger generation; being more and more limited to the oldest generations; or being extant in the community only symbolically,

---

1. Consider this chapter to be an extension of my theology of many tongues at Pentecost brought to the theology of the environment arena from its prior explorations in many other venues and most recently in Amos Yong, "Many Tongues, Many Formational Practices: Christian Spirituality/Formation Across Global Christian Contexts," *Spiritus: A Journal of Christian Spirituality* 22, no. 1 (2022): 59–70, and Amos Yong, "Pentecostal Christianities and Their Political Lives: Many Tongues, Many Political Practices," in *Politischer Pentekostalismus: Transformation des Globalen Christentums im Spiegel Theologischer Motive und Pluraler Normativität*, Weltkirche & Mission 18, eds. Leandro L. B. Fontana and Markus Luber (Regensburg: Friedrich Pustet, 2023), 183–96.

2. See Michael Krause, "The World's Languages in Crisis," *Language* 68, no. 1 (1992): 4–10; cf. David Harmon, *In Light of Our Differences: How Diversity in Nature and Culture Makes Us Human* (Washington, DC: Smithsonian Institution Press, 2002), 68–69.

3. Gary F. Simons and F. Paul Lewis, "The World's Languages in Crisis: A 20-Year Update," in *Responses to Language Endangerment: In Honor of Mickey Noonan: New Directions in Language Documentation and Language Revitalization*, eds. Elena Mihas, Kathleen Wheatley, Bernard Perley, and Gabriel Rei-Doval (Philadelphia: John Benjamins, 2013), 3–19.

not functionally).⁴ From this perspective, it takes a lifetime or three generations for a language to vanish, when the adult generation ceases to pass the language onto their children, and then that generation passes away and their language with them. Within this framework, our *Ethnologue* colleagues have determined that since about the end of the eighteenth century, which is as far back as tracking data can reliably reach, there has been "an accelerating rate of language loss over the past ten generations," deducing that, on average, by around 2000 AD approximately nine languages a year had ceased to be used: the rate of loss was expected to increase to twelve per annum by around 2025, fourteen per year by the mid-century, and sixteen per annum by 2075.⁵

While having only a third of our languages being endangered is much better than half, these figures have been and will continue to be contested. Amid these disputes, the rate of acceleration ought to raise other concerns specifically related to the reasons for linguistic imperilment. Whereas by some estimates we have averaged the loss of one language per year since the dawn of agricultural humanity 10,000 years ago,⁶ the increased rapidity of language loss more recently and its anticipated intensification into the future is related to our politics and economics. For instance, since the early modern period, more than 60 percent of the 1500 plus languages across the colonized Americas and Australia "have now become dead or [are] doomed."⁷ This much higher rate of loss can be attributed to the practices of what scholars call settler colonization, wherein indigenous groups are assimilated into the cultures and languages of the colonizing European countries.⁸ So, if for much of recorded human history (since the advent of the agricultural period) it has been the gathering of people around agrarian sites and the accompanying (mostly very gradual)

---

4. These would be levels 6b–9 on the Ethnologue Expanded Graded Intergenerational Disruption Scale (EGIDS); see Table 1 of the "Methodology" section at https://www.ethnologue.com/methodology/.

5. Gary F. Simons, "Two Centuries of Spreading Language Loss," *Proceedings of the Linguistic Society of America* 27, no. 4 (2019): 9.

6. Harmon, *In Light of Our Differences*, 58–59, speculates as follows: that in hunter-gatherer and emerging agricultural contexts, 500–1,000 speakers per language is the best guess, and if there were between five and ten million inhabitants, then we would have between 5,000–20,000 languages mathematically speaking, or perhaps between 10,000–15,000 languages (if we split the mathematical differences for historical projections), or even higher if there were more people (some estimates are twenty million). So, if we are down to about 7,000 languages now, this suggests "a net loss of 3,200–18,200 languages over 10,000 years or an average background extinction rate of 0.32–1.82 languages over 10,000 years."

7. Simons, "Two Centuries of Spreading Language Loss," 10.

8. See Salikoko S. Mufwene, *The Ecology of Language Evolution* (New York: Cambridge University Press, 2001), ch. 6.

growth of towns, cities, and urban areas that has in turn led to the enervation of languages, then it makes sense that the urbanization and globalization that is now fully upon us and expected to surge in our present century further hastens the decline of languages, particularly in minority and indigenous communities.

There is one more constellation of variables that connects these trends to the theme of this volume: the documented association between the endangerment of languages and of biological species. Here are some correlative perspectives that have been around for over two decades. First, equatorial regions of the world with relative annual climate stability have cultivated a much greater diversity of environmental habitats that have in turn been more generative of biological species diversification and of human cultural-linguistic differentiation. So, for example, New Guinea, which at 312,000 square miles is about half a percent of the world's surface, has 8 percent of the world's recognized vertebrates (i.e. mammals, reptiles, and amphibians) and 15 percent of the world's number of different languages.[9] Thus, as "the density of animal species is highest in equatorial regions and declines steadily towards the poles,"[10] so also has species diversity corresponded with linguistic plurality.

New Guinea is simply the most profligate case of the many other equatorial regions around the world. Studies before the turn of the millennium were already then documenting that "Of the twenty-five countries with the greatest number of endemic higher vertebrate species, sixteen are also among the top twenty-five in endemic languages," meaning 64 percent of countries with the most languages found uniquely therein also have the highest vertebrate species.[11] Further, with regard to endemic bird areas, "the concurrence is 12 of 19, or 63%."[12] And this extends beyond the biological realm: "13 out of the 17 megadiversity [defined as having the most plant species] countries (76%) are also among the top 25 in endemic languages . . . the pattern carries over to a comparison of endemic languages with flowering plant species, where the

---

9. And because New Guinea languages are also the least documented in the world, not only in terms of absolute numbers but also proportionately to the documented languages, new languages continue to emerge, although most are severely endangered (for example, with a handful of elderly speakers). See Bill Palmer, "Language Families in the New Guinea Area," in *The Languages and Linguistics of the New Guinea Area: A Comprehensive Account*, ed. Bill Palmer (Berlin: De Gruyter Mouton, 2017), 12, 15.

10. Mark Pagel and Ruth Mace, "The Cultural Wealth of Nations," *Nature* 428 (2004): 275.

11. Harmon, *In Light of Our Differences*, 87.

12. Harmon, *In Light of Our Differences*, 91.

concurrence between the top-25 lists is 17 of 26, or 68%."[13] Put otherwise, "Of the more than 6,900 languages currently spoken on Earth, more than 4,800 occur in regions containing high biodiversity,"[14] which includes both animal and plant realms.

Here is the difficulty: the biodiversity of these regions of the world is also being threatened. For another instance, and to concretize a global reality: "it is likely that the Pacific islands alone have lost 2,000 species of birds in the past 1,000 to 2,000 years, meaning that about 20 percent of all bird species on Earth have already gone extinct. A conservative estimate of global extinction rate over the past 500 years is about 1,000 species per year. The current global extinction rate for all species is likely 15,000 to 50,000 extinctions per year."[15] More problematic is that species endangerment, however, is directly correlated with human presence: "The numbers of endangered birds and mammals increase with human density (presumably because of greater habitat loss). There are more endangered birds and mammals in mountainous countries but fewer on islands,"[16] especially those less occupied by humans. With human presence comes not only destruction of natural surroundings and shrinking of wildlands (because of human farming, logging, mining, building, railroading, pollution/waste management, etc) but also expansion of non-native species like domesticated plants and animals introduced by agricultural and other human initiatives into regions that push out indigenous species. Then there are other environmental effects related to human activities such as climate changes related to global warming that lead to soil erosion and more rapid devastation of natural environments, more intensely raging and more extended fire seasons (exacerbating incidental human or arson activity), more extreme weather conditions and fluctuations, greater and more swift deforestation (besides human neglect of reforestation), and rising ocean levels from melting Arctic and Antarctic regions (that impact coastal environments and their capacities to support plant and species diversity), among other impacts. As

---

13. Harmon, *In Light of Our Differences*, 91. See also David Harmon, "Losing Species, Losing Languages: Connections between Biological and Linguistic Diversity," *Southwest Journal of Linguistics* 15, no. 1–2 (1996): 89–109.

14. L. J. Gorenflo, Suzanne Romaine, Russell A. Mittermeier, and Kristen Walker-Painemilla, "Co-Occurrence of Linguistic and Biological Diversity in Biodiversity Hotspots and High Biodiversity Wilderness Areas," *Proceedings of the National Academy of Sciences* 109, no. 21 (2012): 8035.

15. Keiran Suckling, "House on Fire: Connecting the Biological and Linguistic Diversity Cases," *Earth First!* 21, no. 5 (2001): 40–41.

16. William J. Sutherland, "Parallel Extinction Risk and Global Distribution of Languages and Species," *Nature* 423 (2003): 279.

our geophysical and oceanic environments are depleted, the biological niches sustained therein degenerate, leading to the strangulation of plant and animal life and, eventually, loss of species.

Now, while we may be unable to directly control how long droughts prolong, where storms happen, or when hurricanes hit and how strong they are – and this is not to deny that our ongoing emissions of carbon exaggerates global warming and forthrightly impacts our weather patterns – the reality is that globalization pressures continue to perpetuate modernist, meaning Euro-American-centric, economic and social policies that undergird the commercialization of our rural environments and ongoing urbanization. This means that bioculturally diverse regions of the world will be increasingly assimilated into the neoliberal capitalist economic mainstream with negative repercussions for indigenous cultural groups and further and deeper threats to the survivability of their languages in the longer run as regional and global languages carried by socioeconomic forces increasingly encroach. The point is that our failure to attend to and/or work intentionally to preserve environmental diversity has a direct correlation with both species (animal) diversity and human cultural-linguistic diversity.[17]

Don't forget that we began with concerns that our languages were disappearing at what I hope we can all agree is an alarming rate. We have seen now that the many languages we have are embedded in and spring from environmental niches that have been rich enough to promote a diversity of plant and biological species,[18] and these, in turn, have allowed for more local prosperity and related linguistic flourishing over millennia, especially among human groups less dominated by agricultural endeavours. All of these are now becoming steadily susceptible to humanly-induced developments, resulting in the demise – at ever increasing rates given the forces of late modern capitalism

---

17. Documented now in research extending over three decades and beginning with conservationists like David Harmon, whose work I have already been citing, and also, most substantively, by linguistic anthropologists like Luisa Maffi. See, for example, Luisa Maffi, "Linguistic, Cultural, and Biological Diversity," *Annual Review of Anthropology* 29 (2005): 599–617; Luisa Maffi, ed., *On Biocultural Diversity: A Global Sourcebook* (Washington, DC: Earthscan, 2010); and Tove Skutnabb-Kangas, Luisa Maffi, and David Harmon, *Sharing a World of Difference: The Earth's Linguistic, Cultural, and Biological Diversity*, ed. Linda King (Paris: UNESCO/Terralingua, 2003).

18. See also, for a more recent account, David Harmon and Jonathan Loh, "Congruence between Species and Language Diversity and Jonathan Loh," in *The Oxford Handbook of Endangered Languages*, eds. Kenneth L. Rehg and Lyle Campbell (Oxford: Oxford University Press, 2018), 659–82, and André Frainer, Tero Mustonen, and Sutej Hugu, "Cultural and Linguistic Diversities are Underappreciated Pillars of Biodiversity," *Proceedings of the National Academy of Sciences* 117, no. 43 (2020): 26539–43.

and globalization – of not only our natural haunts but also the cultural and linguistic resources that have served well our ancestral navigation with these various parts of our world. Hence, addressing our linguistic situation is tied in with engaging our environmental realities, even as prioritizing the latter leads straightforwardly to concerns regarding the viability of the very languages through which we *homo sapiens* have perennially found meaning in our worlds and given meaning to our lives.

Pentecost's Intervention: Many Tongues amid Apocalyptic Times

In a book on Pentecostal missiology, then, it should not be unforeseen that we will turn next to the Pentecost narrative of Acts 2. I zero in initially, however, on the Petrine retrieval of the Joel prophecy to make sense of the crowd's wondering regarding the many languages heard on the streets of Jerusalem that day: "What does this mean?" (Acts 2:12b).[19] What Luke, the author of the book of Acts, does is connect the linguistic sounds of his day with the outpouring of the divine Spirit promised by the ancient prophet to provide relief from a damaging plague of swarming locusts that had visited the people.[20] Thus, Israel's suffering prompted these cries:

> Is not the food cut off before our eyes, joy and gladness from the house of our God? The seed shrivels under the clods, the storehouses are desolate; the granaries are ruined because the grain has failed. How the animals groan! The herds of cattle wander about because there is no pasture for them; even the flocks of sheep are dazed. To you, O LORD, I cry. For fire has devoured the pastures of the wilderness, and flames have burned all the trees of the field. Even the wild animals cry to you because the watercourses are dried up, and fire has devoured the pastures of the wilderness. Blow the trumpet in Zion; sound the alarm on my holy mountain! Let all the inhabitants of the land tremble, for the day of the LORD

---

19. Unless otherwise noted, all biblical quotations will be from the New Revised Standard Version. In various other places I have read Acts 2 vis-à-vis the Christian doctrine of creation, for example, in my *The Spirit Poured Out in the Last Days: Pentecostalism and the Possibility of a Global Theology* (Grand Rapids: Baker Academic, 2005). The following elaborates on the linguistic aspects of this narrative.

20. The most substantive analysis of Acts 2 in relationship to the Joel prophecy is Larry R. McQueen, *Joel and the Spirit: The Cry of a Prophetic Hermeneutic*, Journal of Pentecostal Theology Supplement Series 8 (Sheffield: Sheffield Academic Press, 1995); see also Martin C. Salter, *The Power of Pentecost: An Examination of Acts 2:17–21* (Eugene: Resource, 2012).

> is coming, it is near – a day of darkness and gloom, a day of clouds and thick darkness! Like blackness spread upon the mountains a great and powerful army comes; their like has never been from of old, nor will be again after them in ages to come. Fire devours in front of them, and behind them a flame burns. Before them the land is like the garden of Eden, but after them a desolate wilderness, and nothing escapes them. The earth quakes before them, the heavens tremble. The sun and the moon are darkened, and the stars withdraw their shining. (Joel 1:16–2:3, 10)

One might easily think this was written about our present experiences of weather convulsions precipitating species suffering in the 2020s, but that would be to jump too far ahead. For the moment, we can appreciate that truly, then, the divine breath's appearance was needed in and for such apocalyptic times.[21]

And the Lukan account preserves exactly this calamitous and cataclysmic sentiment. Whereas Joel said that the divine wind would be blown in the wake of the catastrophic plague (Joel 2:28a), its reappropriation was considered as an eschatological fulfillment, indeed, through which God intended to meet human needs "in the last days" (Acts 2:17a). In Joel's context, the tumultuous environmental conditions might not even fully dissipate at or with the giving of the divine wind (Joel 2:30–31), yet "everyone who calls on the name of the Lord shall be saved," almost as if the divine breath preserves a remnant from out of the widespread death and annihilation: "for in Mount Zion and in Jerusalem there shall be those who escape, as the Lord has said, and among the survivors shall be those whom the Lord calls" (2:32). Similarly, in the Petrine proclamation, the Spirit's arrival occurs amid "portents in the heaven above and signs on the earth below, blood, and fire, and smoky mist. The sun shall be turned to darkness and the moon to blood" (Acts 2:19–20a); but these displays both announce "the coming of the Lord's great and glorious day" and enable also then that, "everyone who calls on the name of the Lord shall be saved" (2:20b–21). In other words, the Pentecost deluge both overlays upon and answers to the environmental spasms, without necessarily eliminating them. Apocalyptic tremors are felt in and through the Earth's shaking, quavering, and shuddering, and in the midst of this is the gift of the Holy Spirit that makes possible human salvation.

---

21. In the Hebrew and Greek, the word for *spirit* means also breath or wind; see my *Mission after Pentecost: The Witness of the Spirit from Genesis to Revelation* (Grand Rapids: Baker Academic, 2019).

It is in this context that I want to observe again what Luke records as part of the Pentecost manifestations

> at this sound [of "the rush of a violent wind" mentioned in Acts 2:2a] the crowd gathered and was bewildered, because each one heard them speaking in the native language of each. Amazed and astonished, they asked, "Are not all these who are speaking Galileans? And how is it that we hear, each of us, in our own native language? Parthians, Medes, Elamites, and residents of Mesopotamia, Judea and Cappadocia, Pontus and Asia, Phrygia and Pamphylia, Egypt and the parts of Libya belonging to Cyrene, and visitors from Rome, both Jews and proselytes, Cretans and Arabs – in our own languages we hear them speaking about God's deeds of power." (Acts 2:6–11)

To cut to the chase: the gift of the Holy Spirit (Acts 2:1–4) reauthorizes the many languages of the (Mediterranean) world for the missiological purposes of being witnesses of the gospel "in Jerusalem, in all Judea and Samaria, and to the ends of the earth" (1:8b). The sixteen proper names are not intended to be an exhaustive catalogue but function as a representative indicator of divergent people groups and those gathered from disparate regions of the world, indeed, "from every nation [Greek: *ethnos*] under heaven" (2:5). Missionary tongues, from a Pentecostal perspective, are no respecter of ethnic or cultural groups, even in the face of hegemonistic imperial forces: the many local languages then, and every language today – the 7,000 or so in existence – has the capacity to capably declare God's deeds of power.

It is important here to press further into the point that the many local languages in Acts 2 all operated under the sway of the imperial Greek language spread out across the *Pax Romana*.[22] While Rome provides the geographic horizon that encapsulates the extent of the gospel's relevance – "to the ends of the earth" which are reached in Acts 28 when Paul arrives at the imperial capital – its language, even if the medium through which the book of Acts and the rest of the New Testament is written, has no privileged status. That "visitors from Rome" are included as part of the list means that Latin, perhaps even in its various dialects (not to mention vernaculars and idioms of the other

---

22. See Gary Gilbert, "The List of Nations in Acts 22: Roman Propaganda and the Lukan Response," *Journal of Biblical Literature* 121 (2002): 497–529.

heard languages), was resounded on the streets of Jerusalem.[23] Even amid imperial policy and pressures, the crowd heard the local or native languages of their various indigenously identified groups[24]: whether Hebrew or Aramaic as might have been relevant for Galileans or Judeans; Babylonian or remnants of Assyrian for Mesopotamians; Lydian, Pisidian, Phrygian, or Lycaonian (see Acts 14:11), among the many other possible ancient languages of Asia Minor; Hieratic, Demotic, or Coptic, besides the dominant Egyptian, in Egypt; or Thamudic, Safaitic, or Sabaic as antecedents of what is later recognized as linguistic Arabic, etc. Some of the languages spoken then remain today, even if in different forms (for instance Koine Greek is the ancestor of modern Greek even as biblical Hebrew is related to but yet, in fundamental respects, is a different linguistic system compared with its contemporary counterpart), but each one then was en-spirited, that is, inspired to announce the gospel. In that respect, it is neither the widespread usage nor the number of speakers that is of import, since in that case, Greek would have been of higher theological or missiological value. Rather, each language was embraced as a medium for expressing God's word in the world, regardless of whether or to what extent any one or a few languages might predominate over all of the others.[25]

From this perspective, the long-observed parallels between what happened at the tower of Babel and on the day of Pentecost are illuminating. As there is some indication in the former that the many languages are punitively imposed on the Babelites (or Shinarians, the residents of Shinar where Babel was purportedly located), a growing number of interpreters thereby see the sin at the tower concerns that of bucking dispersal to the ends of the earth and, in that respect, understand Pentecost to be a positive mechanism through which

---

23. See David Crystal, "Why Did the Crowd Think St Peter Was Drunk?: An Exercise in Applied Sociolinguistics," *New Blackfriars* 79 (1998): 72–76; cf. Bob Zerhusen, "An Overlooked Judean Diglossia in Acts 2?," *Biblical Theology Bulletin* 25, no. 3 (1995): 118–30.

24. Note that the Lukan description of the derivation of these languages was delineated under three categories: first, related to three ethnic groups, e.g., "Parthians, Medes, Elamites"; second, as spoken by residents of ten distinct regions or nations (thus denoting what we might imagine as mother-tongues vis-à-vis those raised in these places); and third, those spoken by four sets of visitors from Rome (these sojourners would have been presumed to be at least bilingual, if not even more linguistically adept in three or more languages). For a broader discussion, see Eric R. Dursteler, "Speaking in Tongues: Language and Communication in the Early Modern Mediterranean," *Past & Present* 217 (2012): 47–77.

25. Language as creaturely and also fallen may not be world-creating but is at least "world-disclosing and world-constituting" and can be redemptive. See Craig G. Bartholomew, "Before Babel and After Pentecost: Language, Literature and Biblical Interpretation," in *After Pentecost: Language and Biblical Interpretation*, The Scripture and Hermeneutics Series 2, eds. Craig Bartholomew, Colin Greene, and Karl Möller, 131–70 (Grand Rapids: Zondervan, 2001), 150–51.

such diffusion is further invigorated.[26] Intriguingly, if the tower of Babel was erected as a sign of Neo-Assyrian imperial power, as many scholars believe (see next section), then, for our own revisitation of the day of Pentecost, we can comprehend how the people of God "received power not to build nations [or empires, as national languages are often deployed to secure] but the power to heal nations."[27] Even more pointedly, the dispersal of the descendants of Shem, Ham, and Japheth in Genesis 10 is represented in the Pentecost account, with the first three names in Acts 2:9–11 being Shemitic nations, "the last three names represent[ing] all three sons of Noah," and the nine countries in the middle inclusive of various pairings.[28] I am here making not an exegetical argument regarding Luke intending to reverse the Babel motif – about which there is no consensus in the commentarial literature – but a theological connection: the many languages of Pentecost register the cultural-linguistic diversity of the first century Mediterranean world navigating Roman imperial pressures and extend an important theme from the primeval history of the biblical record, one that affirms the worldwide distribution of human ethnicities and nations in the face of even more ancient imperial forces encompassing God's people.

The Creational Mandate: Many Languages Filling the Earth

The foregoing warrants further review of the relevant Genesis passages. Beginning with the tower story, the following observations are noteworthy. First, the "one language" in Genesis 11:1 and 6 has a broad semantic range and can/should be appropriately translated "one lip" or, even more suitably, "one unified

---

26. Pentecostal theologians have argued this point. See Frank D. Macchia, "Babel and the Tongues of Pentecost: Reversal or Fulfilment? A Theological Perspective," in *Speaking in Tongues: Multi-Disciplinary Perspectives*, ed. Mark J. Cartledge (Waynesboro: Paternoster, 2006), 34–51 and L. Jose, *A Postcolonial Reading of the Acts of the Apostles: Apostles: Implications for Theological Education in India*. Biblical Hermeneutics Rediscovered 12 (New Delhi: Christian World Imprints, 2018), 135–37. See also Joel B. Green, "In Our Own Languages: Pentecost, Babel, and the Shaping of Christian Community in Acts 2:1–13," in *The Word Leaps the Gap: Essays on Scripture and Theology in Honor of Richard B. Hays*, eds. J. Ross Wagner, C. Kavin Rowe, and A. Katherine Grieb (Grand Rapids: Eerdmans, 2008), 198–213.

27. Willie James Jennings, "Speaking in Tongues: Language, Nationalism, and the Formation of Church Life," in *On Being Christian . . . and Human: Essays in Celebration of Ray S. Anderson*, ed. Todd H. Speidell (Eugene: Wipf & Stock, 2002), 229.

28. James M. Scott, *Geography in Early Judaism and Christianity: The Book of Jubilees* (Cambridge: Cambridge University Press, 2002), 82; see also Scott's "Luke's Geographical Horizon," in *The Book of Acts in Its First Century Setting*, vol. II: *The Book of Acts in Its Graeco-Roman Setting*, eds. David W. J. Gill and Conrad Gempf (Grand Rapids: Eerdmans, 1994), 483–544.

plan."²⁹ In fact, "The last two words of v. 1 reiterate the unity of the people's speech by noting that they had the 'same words.'"³⁰ Thus, however many words or dialects or languages may have been in play, efforts were made to unify the community around a common objective. Their plan came to revolve around building their city (11:4a) – which in the ancient historical account has so far been only negatively associated, namely, with Cain's exile (4:17) and Nineveh (10:12), the capital city of the Assyrian empire³¹ – and making a name for themselves (11:4b), rather than, more appropriately, receiving names from their deity (cf. 5:2).³² These motivations were propelled, it appears, by certain anxieties: "otherwise we shall be scattered abroad upon the face of the whole earth" (11:4c). In this case, the "one lip" or "one plan" in 11:6 concerns not their linguistic homogeneity but signals both their aspirations and worries; as YHWH comes down to observe and then summarize: "this is only the beginning of what they will do; nothing that they propose to do will now be impossible for them," the latter projected organization is then also understandable in "the sense of plotting, scheming . . . with hubristic ambition."³³ This translation is even more persuasive when we recognize, at its earliest, an eighth century BCE Neo-Assyrian imperial background or provenance behind this passage – given that Shinar always appears in the Hebrew Bible with reference to Babylon and also since Genesis 2:13–14 clarifies ancient geography in relationship to

---

29. See Samuel L. Boyd, *Babel: Political Rhetoric of a Confused Legacy* (Minneapolis: Fortress, 2023), 112–23. Christof Uehlinger made a similar argument earlier in *Weltreich und 'Eine Rede': Eine Neue Deutung der Sogenannten Turmbauersählung (Gen. 11:1–9)* (Freiburg: Universitätsverlag, 1990).

30. Brian Neil Peterson, *Genesis: A Pentecostal Commentary*, Pentecostal Commentary Series 8 (Leiden: Brill, 2022), 115.

31. Andrew Dominic Giorgetti, "Building a Parody: Genesis 11:1–9, Ancient Near Eastern Building Accounts, and Production-Oriented Intertextuality" (PhD diss., Fuller Theological Seminary, 2017), 454.

32. On this latter naming front, see John T. Strong, "Shattering the Image of God: A Response to Theodore Hiebert's Interpretation of the Story of the Tower of Babel," *Journal of Biblical Literature* 127, no. 4 (2008): 625–34. Strong is, like LaCocque in the next reference, responding to Theodore Hiebert, ed., *Toppling the Tower: Essays on Babel and Diversity* (Chicago: McCormick Theological Seminary, 2004), particularly the latter's claims that Genesis 11:1–9 should not be read in any punitive sense (which in my understanding is present albeit, as at best, a secondary dimension of the tower account).

33. André LaCocque, "Whatever Happened in the Valley of Shinar? A Response to Theodore Hiebert," *Journal of Biblical Literature* 128, no. 1 (2009): 35.

Assyrian regions – and, at latest, a post-exilic context for the final form of the text and the book of Genesis as a whole.[34]

In this reading, the purpose of the passage is not to provide an etiology of linguistic diversification but, even if indirectly, to resist imperial hegemony – either Assyrian or Babylonian, or both, depending on when the various forms of the text and their redactions and final form was established – enforced by linguistic conformity.[35] While the confusion of languages here might suggest linguistic bourgeoning, local dialectic or vernacular impenetrability sufficiently explains the ensuing communicative bafflement. More accurately, the divine goal is to disrupt imperial building and, in that respect, even if the tower might have been (somewhat) completed, as 11:5 suggests, mission was accomplished: "So the LORD scattered them abroad from there over the face of all the earth, and they left off building the city" (11:8). And in case this was missed, the linguistic mix-up is subordinated to the explicitly divinely intended result, repeated again: "from there the LORD scattered them abroad over the face of all the earth" (11:9b). Hence, it is not the unified language but the collusion of humans conspiring quite apart from divinity that YHWH suspends; it is not the *unity* of language but the *imperiality* of fallen human collective arrogance that is broken up.

Backtracking then into Genesis 10, the tower story thus documents efforts to decelerate or even altogether impede and stop human diffusion. The preceding consideration of Babel minimizes the incoherence of Genesis 11:1–9 being read as a divinely-orchestrated etiology of the plurality of languages following the tenth chapter's account of the many languages distending in an apparently organic manner. In our proposed approach, the Hebrew original of 11:1 hearkens back to Genesis 10: "'and all of the land existed as one lip and units [of] words.' The plural number of 'units [of] words' in the second part of the phrase may be, and occasionally was, taken as a reference to the story about Noah's sons in Genesis 10 and as implying that many languages had already

---

34. Also, Angelika Berlejung, "Living in the Land of Shinar: Reflections on Exile in Genesis 11:1–9?," in *The Fall of Jerusalem and the Rise of the Torah*, Die Zerstörung Jerusalems und die Entstehung der Torah 107, eds. Peter Dubovak, Dominik Markl, and Jean-Pierre Sonnet (Tübingen: Mohr Siebeck, 2016), 89–111.

35. Besides some of the sources referred to above (esp. Boyd, Giorgetti, and Uehlinger), see also Pablo Andiñach, "Denouncing Imperialism: An Argentine Rereading of the Tower of Babel (Gen 11:1–9)," in *La Violencia and the Hebrew Bible: The Politics and Histories of Biblical Hermeneutics on the American Continent*, ed. Susanne Scholz (Atlanta: Scholars, 2016), 105–19; also Bobby Kurnia Putrawan, Ludwig Beethoven J. Noya, and Alisaid Prawiro Negoro, "Centripetal–Centrifugal Forces in the Tower of Babel Narrative (Gen 11:1–9)," *Old Testament Essays* 35, no. 2 (2022): 192–210.

existed."[36] And, that was the communicative intent of the antecedent chapter, recapitulated at the end as a record of "the families of Noah's sons, according to their genealogies, in their nations; and from these the nations spread abroad on the earth after the flood" (10:32). The chapter itself delineates how the descendants of Japheth, Ham, and Shem were so circulated, concluding each group thus:

- "From these the coastland peoples spread. These are the descendants of Japheth in their lands, with their own language, by their families, in their nations" (10:5).
- "These are the descendants of Ham, by their families, their languages, their lands, and their nations" (10:20).
- "These are the descendants of Shem, by their families, their languages, their lands, and their nations" (10:31).

While there is a great deal of scholarship that could be brought to bear on these summary statements and the details regarding the various names (of individuals, founding ancestors, and their tribes, and of cities and other locations[37]), two observations are pertinent for our immediate purposes. First, there are interconnections between families, languages, lands, and nations, to follow the reiterated order of the Ham and Shem lineages and these connote anthropological-communicative-geographical-and-national matrices of relationality. The Japheth summation does not appear in the same order, even as its distinctive sequence fore-fronting "land" may be related to the also uniquely qualifying phrase regarding these groups settling in "coastland" areas,[38] with linguistics in a secondary place to geography even prior to familial/tribal associations, and long before national identities emerge. Either way, languages follow people groups (families) and environmental niches (coastlands, which includes aquatic ecologies). Altogether, Genesis 10 bears witness to the inter-

---

36. Yuliya Minets, *That Slow Fall of Babel: Language and Identity in Late Antique Christianity* (Cambridge: Cambridge University Press, 2023), 101. The italicized "s" and brackets of this Gen 11:1 translation are both Minets's.

37. Allen P. Ross, *Creation and Blessing: A Guide to the Study and Exposition of the Book of Genesis* (Grand Rapids: Baker, 1988), 224.

38. "Coastlands" may also indicate that "all the nations descending from Japheth were believed to live across the sea from ancient Israel's continental homeland." See Wayne Horowitz, "The Isles of the Nations: Genesis X and Babylonian Geography, in *Studies in the Pentateuch*, Vetus Testamentum Supplements 41, ed. J. A. Emerton (Leiden: Brill, 1990), 43. For other explanations that have been floated (and contested) regarding the triadic organization, including one suggesting what we see are nomadic Shemites, agricultural Hamites, and seafaring Japhethites or Gentiles, see the discussion in B. Oded, "The Table of Nations (Genesis 10) – A Socio-Cultural Approach," *Zeitschrift für die Alttestamentliche Wissenschaft* 98 (1986): 14–31.

relationality of biological-cultural-linguistic-and-geographic diversity we have already seen.

Second, and extending the prior point, an argument can be made that, in the final form of the creation account as we have it, "The function of this genealogy isn't temporal; it is geographical. This genealogy traces the descendants of Noah as they repopulate and fill the various parts of the earth."[39] The narrative brings to culmination (e.g. 10:1, 18, 32) the migratory movements across the earth of humankind, represented in the sons of Noah and their families, filling in the details of what was even earlier forecasted: both "Be fruitful and multiply, and fill the earth," and, repeated, "These three were the sons of Noah; and from these the whole earth was peopled" (9:1, 19).[40] While the Babelites were, as we saw, concerned about being scattered (11:4), bringing to the surface that people/group movement is never without trepidation,[41] not only did that process unfold progressively after the flood, but it was also consistent with (and effectively) an exact reiteration of the creational mandate: that human beings should "Be fruitful and multiply, and fill the earth" (1:28a).

Yet creationally speaking, beyond *homo sapiens*, the living creatures were also instructed to "Be fruitful and multiply and fill the waters in the seas, and let birds multiply on the earth" (1:22) and the earth was also commanded to produce land creatures.

> "Let the earth bring forth living creatures of every kind: cattle and creeping things and wild animals of the earth of every kind." And it was so. God made the wild animals of the earth of every kind, and the cattle of every kind, and everything that creeps upon the ground of every kind. And God saw that it was good. (1:24–25)[42]

So much so that in disembarking from the ark, Noah was divinely instructed: "Bring out with you every living thing that is with you of all flesh – birds and animals and every creeping thing that creeps on the earth – so that

---

39. Liane M. Feldman, *The Consuming Fire: The Complete Priestly Source, from Creation to the Promised Land* (Berkeley: University of California Press, 2023), 61.

40. See John Day, *From Creation to Abraham: Further Studies in Genesis 1–11* (London: T&T Clark, 2022), ch. 9 on the Table of Nations.

41. Carol M. Kaminski, *From Noah to Israel: Realization of the Primaeval Blessing after the Flood* (London: T&T Clark, 2004), ch. 2 explores this point.

42. Elsewhere I have provided a pneumatological/ruahological reading of the creation narratives that accentuates the earth's responsive participation in the divine creational activity; see Yong, "Ruach, the Primordial Waters, and the Breath of Life: Emergence Theory and the Creation Narratives in Pneumatological Perspective," in *The Work of the Spirit: Pneumatology and Pentecostalism*, ed. Michael Welker (Grand Rapids: Eerdmans, 2006), 183–204.

they may abound on the earth, and be fruitful and multiply on the earth" (8:17). The Genesis narrative makes clear that the circulation of human families across the earth was interwoven with creaturely diversification across its various terrestrial and marine environments, and this is accomplished over time. "The Table of Nations thus allows us to set aside concern for other nations, so we may focus on the next part of the story – Israel,"[43] which picks up after the Babel interlude with further development of Shem's line in 11:10, leading up to Abraham in Genesis 12.

Reading Genesis 10–11 together, then, leads us to two preliminary conclusions at this juncture. First, the plurality of languages is not an obstacle to be overcome but part of the overall diversity of God's creation. The Babel story read this way can acknowledge the negative connotations of "confuse" and "scatter" but also grant that they are "not an isolated act of punishment but rather a calculated act of discipline with both an immediate intent to intervene and an ultimate intent to restore and bless."[44] Divine intrusion at Shinar was needed to ensure that the peopling of the earth was not interrupted by centripetal and (linguistically) hegemonistic or imperialistic forces.[45] Second, the proliferation of languages contesting imperial hegemony is also situated against the backdrop of a multi-dimensional creation intended to fully flourish precisely in its own multiplicative and diversifying potencies. The fortunes of families and nations, in other words, are intimately interrelated not with top-down injunctions as if from a centralized tower (e.g. of the United Nations, the so-called *Pax America* or the Chinese Belt & Road Initiative!), but bottom-up, effectively, with the thriving of languages amid the blooming of environmental abodes. As one biblical scholar urges in light of the primeval account: "God's will for his creation is diversity rather than homogeneity."[46]

---

43. Matthew A. Thomas, *These are the Generations: Identity, Covenant, and the Toledot Formula*. Library of Hebrew Bible/Old Testament Studies 551 (New York: T&T Clark, 2011), 92.

44. Larry S. Hayashi, "The Blessing of Babel: A Theology of Languages," *CanIL Electronic Working Papers* 3 (2017): 70.

45. See Gary F. Simons, "Language Diversity: Curse or Blessing?" In *God and Language: Exploring the Role of Language in the Mission of God*, eds. Michael Greed and Dawn Kruger (Dallas: Summer Linguistic Institute, 2022), 27–46, including his drawing the notion of "linguistic hegemony" from W. Creighton Marlowe, "The Sin of Shinar (Genesis 11:4)," *European Journal of Theology* 20, no. 1 (2001): 29–39.

46. Bernhard W. Anderson, *From Creation to New Creation: Old Testament Perspectives* (Minneapolis: Augsburg Fortress, 1994).

The Vision of the New Earth/Jerusalem: Many Languages, Many Witnesses

Where are we at on our journey? We began by observing how the phenomenon of language endangerment is intertwined with that of species and environmental flourishing. From our Pentecostal perspective, it then made sense to return to the Acts 2 narrative to observe how we might think more substantively about a theology of languages, realizing along the way that the Spirit of Pentecost is more concerned with galvanizing the multitude of languages for missional purposes than being subservient to any imperial discourse. If the plurality of languages is missiologically less a problem than it is a solution, then we needed to reconsider the tower of Babel narrative, and there we not only confirmed its consistency with the day of Pentecost account but also became able to appreciate a more creational matrix for our theology of languages. What then are next steps for missiological praxis?

Missionally, our beliefs and practices are guided both by foundational theological commitments, precisely what we have focused our energies on so far, and by a vision that draws us forward. For Pentecostal Christians, this returns us also to the person and message of Jesus Christ, sent by and also sender of his Spirit, to enable our participation in God's redemptive efforts. As the arc of this missional vision reaches its further horizons in the Apocalypse, I am stirred to follow out the intuitions of our incipient theology of language to see if and how the book of Revelation might further animate our missiological imagination. While much can be said given how this final book of the biblical canon has had environmental purchase, we will be trained on the missiological implications of the many-ness of language in John's visions.[47]

Foregrounding languages leads us immediately to the great throne scene where the seer of Patmos looks and sees "a great multitude that no one could count, from every nation, from all tribes and peoples and languages, standing before the throne and before the Lamb, robed in white, with palm branches in their hands" (Rev 7:9). While this combination is repeated thrice more across the visions and on each occasion in a different sequence (10:11; 11:9; 17:15),[48] together they hearken back toward the families, languages, lands, and nations in Genesis 10, albeit with "lands" missing. What is not ambivalent is that the diversity of Noah's sons' families which reverberates through the Pentecost

---

47. I have provided a missiological reading of Revelation in my *Mission after Pentecost, The Witness of the Spirit from Genesis to Revelation* (Grand Rapids: Baker Academic, 2019), §§8.4–8.5.

48. For more on this, see my *Revelation*, Belief: A Theological Commentary on the Bible (Louisville: Westminster John Knox Press, 2021), 138.

narrative finds its full realization in this eschatological moment and site. And while the nations do collectively "drink of the wine of the wrath of [Babylon's] fornication" (14:8), are "deceived by [her] sorcery" (18:23), and are deceived by Satan (20:7–8), they will also worship the Lamb (15:4) even as they will walk in the Lamb's light (21:24), and their glory and honour will be brought by the peoples of the earth into the New Jerusalem (21:26).[49]

The New Jerusalem, further, has as its vital artery "the river of the water of life, bright as crystal, flowing from the throne of God and of the Lamb through the middle of the street of the city. On either side of the river is the tree of life with its twelve kinds of fruit, producing its fruit each month; and the leaves of the tree are for the healing of the nations" (Rev 22:1–2). Here we find a renewal of the primordial river of Eden that not only nurtured the garden's vegetation but also, with its quadruple branches, flowed out into and nourished the earth in four directions (Gen 2:8–14). In both instances, land and water not only resource the plants of the ground but sustain creaturely life and wellbeing. The garden's trees (except one!) and vegetation were initially given to nourish *ha adam* and sustain the other named creaturely partners in the Edenic environment (Gen 2:16–20), however they were also drawn by the nascent couple to cover their recognized nakedness and shield them from the deity's glorious gaze (3:7n–8). Likewise, New Jerusalem's crops not only suckle the city's denizens but also provide therapeutic leaves for the full scope of national collectivities that Noah's sons and their families have grown eschatologically into.[50] The salvation and shalom of human creatures, then, involves not only their socially gathered wellbeing but also the full regeneration of their biosphere (the new heavens [Rev 12:12]) and the replenishment of their terrestrial homes (the new earth [Rev 21:1]).[51]

If Christian witness and missional practice is predicated on a concrete vision of what it is we are partnering with the Holy Spirit to herald and embody, then these are unveiled in the book of Revelation. The gospel of Jesus Christ is good news for the poor, for their communities, and for the lands (and seas) that bear them. Put more Pentecostally, the good news of God in Christ is professed

---

49. See Alan J. McNicol, *The Conversion of the Nations in Revelation*, Library of New Testament Studies 438 (New York: T&T Clark, 2011).

50. See Amos Yong, "Kings, Nations, and Cultures on the Way to the New Jerusalem: A Pentecostal Witness to an Apocalyptic Vision," in *The Pastor & the Kingdom: Essays Honoring Jack W. Hayford*, eds. S. David Moore and Jonathan Huntzinger (Southlake: TKU & Gateway Academic, 2017), 231–51.

51. For example, Michael D. Kiel, *Apocalyptic Ecology: The Book of Revelation, the Earth, and the Future* (Collegeville: Liturgical/Michael Glazier, 2017).

by those from every nation under heaven in and through the particularities of their multiple dialects and languages, which are themselves from out of those families, tribes, communities, and cultural groups' navigation of their geographic and aquatic environments.[52] To be filled with the Spirit of Pentecost is thus to preserve, deepen, and retrieve the languages of the world so that we can once again amplify God's powerful deeds, even in apocalyptic times.

Instead of a Conclusion: Environmental Engagement and Linguistic Revitalization in Pentecostal Missiological Perspective

This chapter argues that environmental missiology in Pentecostal perspective is or should be intimately interwoven with the movement's theology of languages, particularly the multiplicity and diversity of tongues as pronounced at Pentecost. I conclude with some calls to action in at least three venues that constitute, as sketched, no more than placeholders for more robustly articulated initiatives as part of the fabric of contemporary Pentecostal missiological praxis.

1. The growing levels of environmental degradation invite every one of us to take personal responsibility for "going green" across the various domains of our personal lives, from our consumer habits to our travel mechanisms to our recycling practices, etc; collectively, we also support local, regional, national, and, where possible, international efforts to live in harmony with the earth and its resources.

2. More concretely, we can look to come alongside and support local and regional development initiatives aimed at preserving, conserving, and renewing environmental regions, both securing those under more direly threatened conditions and expanding and growing the scope and range of others;[53] strategically, as part of this realm of activism, we should always prioritize indigenous, minoritized communities and their cultural and spiritual values, knowledge, and commitments, seeking to be in solidarity with their efforts to secure shalom for all biological life and environmental wellbeing in their

---

52. Intriguingly, it is likely that the author of the Apocalypse was bi- or even tri- lingual, with familiarity also with Hebrew and Aramaic, being so well versed in various Old Testament texts available in these languages; see G. Mussies, *The Morphology of Koine Greek as Used in the Apocalypse of John: A Study in Bilingualism*, Supplements to Novum Testamentum 27 (Leiden: Brill, 1971), 352–53.

53. See also Luisa Maffi and Ellen Woodley, *Biocultural Diversity Conservation: A Global Sourcebook* (Washington, DC: Earthscan, 2010).

habitation in ways that nevertheless remain in relationship with their neighbours and interact integratively and sustainably with broader (global) economic developments.[54]

3. Linguistically, speaking in other languages as the Spirit enables means also discerning how the task of community development (immediately above) is intimately interdependent with the preserving and reviving of endangered languages (even resurrecting those that may no longer be in use), which could happen with biblical translation projects (for instance as documented by Lamin Sanneh).[55] It also means developing collaborative partnerships with many others to defend and promote what some call the linguistic rights of peoples around the world: the right to fortify indigenous communities navigating environmental and socio-political pressures in ways that recognize the unique and distinctive linguistic contributions from the perspectives and experiences of peoples rooted in and derived from specific places for our local, regional, and collective cultural lives, communal health, and spiritual vibrancy.[56] As part of this level of linguistic missiology, we must be attentive to language education policies and practices, especially as they catalyze intergenerational transmission linkages, and to strengthening overall educational programs across the life-span in relationship to ethnic and indigenous cultural revitalization strategies that interface with other spheres of life (home, market, work, religion, government, etc). This includes cultural revitalization strategies related to documentation, preservation, and celebration of local cultural heritages in relationship to broader regional and national communication initiatives (e.g. in social media, music, literature, and the arts).[57]

---

54. For example, Darrell Addison Posey, ed., *Cultural and Spiritual Values of Biodiversity* (London: United Nations Environment Programme and Intermediate Technology Publications, 1999) and Gary Paul Nabhan, ed. *Ethnobiology for the Future: Linking Cultural and Ecological Diversity* (Tucson: The University of Arizona Press, 2016).

55. See Lamin Sanneh, *Translating the Message: The Missionary Impact on Culture*, rev. ed. (Maryknoll: Orbis, 2009).

56. See Tove Skutnabb-Kangas, *Linguistic Genocide in Education – Or Worldwide Diversity and Human Rights* (Mahwah: Lawrence Erlbaum Associates, 2000). Also, Kendall A. King, et al., eds. *Sustaining Linguistic Diversity: Endangered and Minority Languages and Language Varieties* (Washington, DC: Georgetown University Press, 2008).

57. Lenore A. Grenoble and Lindsay J. Whaley, *Saving Languages: An Introduction to Language Revitalization* (Cambridge: Cambridge University Press, 2006) and M. Paul Lewis and Gary F. Simons, *Sustaining Language Use: Perspectives on Community-Based Language Development*

For those with eyes to see and ears to hear, may we respond and live into what the Spirit is saying to the churches in our time of climate change and environmental degradation.[58]

Bibliography

Anderson, Bernhard W. *From Creation to New Creation: Old Testament Perspectives*. Minneapolis: Augsburg Fortress, 1994.

Andiñach, Pablo R. "Denouncing Imperialism: An Argentine Rereading of the Tower of Babel (Gen 11:1–9)." In *La Violencia and the Hebrew Bible: The Politics and Histories of Biblical Hermeneutics on the American Continent*, edited by Susanne Scholz, 105–19. Atlanta: Scholars, 2016.

Bartholomew, Craig G. "Before Babel and After Pentecost: Language, Literature and Biblical Interpretation." In *After Pentecost: Language and Biblical Interpretation*, edited by Craig Bartholomew, Colin Greene, and Karl Möller, 131–70. The Scripture and Hermeneutics Series 2. Grand Rapids: Zondervan, 2001.

Berlejung, Angelika. "Living in the Land of Shinar: Reflections on Exile in Genesis 11:1–9?" In *The Fall of Jerusalem and the Rise of the Torah*, edited by Peter Dubovak, Dominik Markl, and Jean-Pierre Sonnet, 89–111. Die Zerstörung Jerusalems und die Entstehung der Torah 107. Tübingen: Mohr Siebeck, 2016.

Boyd, Samuel L. *Babel: Political Rhetoric of a Confused Legacy*. Minneapolis: Fortress, 2023.

Crystal, David. "Why Did the Crowd Think St Peter Was Drunk? An Exercise in Applied Sociolinguistics." *New Blackfriars* 79 (1998): 72–76.

Day, John. *From Creation to Abraham: Further Studies in Genesis 1–11*. London: T&T Clark, 2022.

Dursteler, Eric R. "Speaking in Tongues: Language and Communication in the Early Modern Mediterranean." *Past & Present* 217 (2012): 47–77.

Ethnologue. Expanded Graded Intergenerational Disruption Scale. Online Database. See https://www.ethnosproject.org/expanded-graded-intergenerational-disruption-scale/.

Feldman, Liane M. *The Consuming Fire: The Complete Priestly Source, from Creation to the Promised Land*. Berkeley: University of California Press, 2023.

(Dallas: SIL International, 2016); cf. Leeanne Hinton, Leena Huss, and Gerald Roche, eds., *The Routledge Handbook of Language Revitalization* (New York: Routledge, 2018).

58. Thanks to Rick Wadholm and Don Daniels (mediated by Steve Overman) for feedback on an initial draft of this paper, especially (but not only) their help with some of the languages related to the Acts 2 passage, and for the latter's additional comments on the biolinguistic first section. All errors of fact or interpretation remain my own.

Frainer, Andre, Tero Mustonen, and Sutej Hugu. "Cultural and Linguistic Diversities are Underappreciated Pillars of Biodiversity." *Proceedings of the National Academy of Sciences* 117, no. 43 (2020): 26539–43.

Gilbert, Gary. "The List of Nations in Acts 2: Roman Propaganda and the Lukan Response." *Journal of Biblical Literature* 121 (2002): 497–529.

Giorgetti, Andrew Dominic. "Building a Parody: Genesis 11:1–9, Ancient Near Eastern Building Accounts, and Production-Oriented Intertextuality." PhD diss., Fuller Theological Seminary, 2017.

Gorenflo, L. J., Suzanne Romaine, Russell A. Mittermeier, and Kristen Walker-Painemilla. "Co-occurrence of Linguistic and Biological Diversity in Biodiversity Hotspots and High Biodiversity Wilderness Areas." *Proceedings of the National Academy of Sciences* 109, no. 21 (2012): 8032–37.

Green, Joel B. "'In Our Own Languages': Pentecost, Babel, and the Shaping of Christian Community in Acts 2:1–13." In *The Word Leaps the Gap: Essays on Scripture and Theology in Honor of Richard B. Hays*, edited by J. Ross Wagner, C. Kavin Rowe, and A. Katherine Grieb, 198–213. Grand Rapids: Eerdmans, 2008.

Grenoble, Lenore A., and Lindsay J. Whaley. *Saving Languages: An Introduction to Language Revitalization.* Cambridge: Cambridge University Press, 2006.

Harmon, David. *In Light of Our Differences: How Diversity in Nature and Culture Makes Us Human.* Washington, DC: Smithsonian Institution Press, 2002.

———. "Losing Species, Losing Languages: Connections between Biological and Linguistic Diversity." *Southwest Journal of Linguistics* 15, no. 1–2 (1996): 89–109.

Harmon, David, and Jonathan Loh. "Congruence between Species and Language Diversity." In *The Oxford Handbook of Endangered Languages*, edited by Kenneth L. Rehg and Lyle Campbell, 659–82. Oxford: Oxford University Press, 2018.

Hayashi, Larry S. "The Blessing of Babel: A Theology of Languages." *CanIL Electronic Working Papers* 3 (2017): 64–76.

Hiebert, Theodore, ed. *Toppling the Tower: Essays on Babel and Diversity.* Chicago: McCormick Theological Seminary, 2004.

Hinton, Leeanne, Leena Huss, and Gerald Roche, eds. *The Routledge Handbook of Language Revitalization.* New York: Routledge, 2018.

Horowitz, Wayne. "The Isles of the Nations: Genesis X and Babylonian Geography." In *Studies in the Pentateuch*, edited by J. A. Emerton, 35–43. Vetus Testamentum Supplements 41. Leiden: Brill, 1990.

Jennings, Willie James. "Speaking in Tongues: Language, Nationalism, and the Formation of Church Life." In *On Being Christian . . . and Human: Essays in Celebration of Ray S. Anderson*, edited by Todd H. Speidell, 224–35. Eugene: Wipf & Stock, 2002.

Kaminski, Carol M. *From Noah to Israel: Realization of the Primaeval Blessing after the Flood.* London: T&T Clark, 2004.

Kiel, Micah D. *Apocalyptic Ecology: The Book of Revelation, the Earth, and the Future.* Collegeville: Liturgical/Michael Glazier, 2017.

King, Kendall A., Natalie Schilling-Este, Jia Jackie Lou, Lyn Wright Fogle, and Barbara Soukup. *Sustaining Linguistic Diversity: Endangered and Minority Languages and Language Varieties*. Washington, DC: Georgetown University Press, 2008.
Krause, Michael. "The World's Languages in Crisis." *Language* 68, no. 1 (1992): 4–10.
L, Jose. *A Postcolonial Reading of the Acts of the Apostles: Implications for Theological Education in India*. Biblical Hermeneutics Rediscovered 12. New Delhi: Christian World Imprints, 2018.
LaCocque, André. "Whatever Happened in the Valley of Shinar? A Response to Theodore Hiebert." *Journal of Biblical Literature* 128, no. 1 (2009): 29–41.
Lewis, M. Paul, and Gary F. Simon. *Sustaining Language Use: Perspectives on Community-Based Language Development*. Dallas: SIL International, 2016.
Macchia, Frank D. "Babel and the Tongues of Pentecost: Reversal or Fulfilment? A Theological Perspective." In *Speaking in Tongues: Multi-Disciplinary Perspectives*, edited by Mark J. Cartledge, 34–51. Waynesboro: Paternoster, 2006.
Maffi, Luisa. "Linguistic, Cultural, and Biological Diversity." *Annual Review of Anthropology* 29 (2005): 599–617.
Maffi, Luisa, ed. *On Biocultural Diversity: Linking Language, Knowledge, and the Environment*. Washington, DC: Smithsonian Institution Press, 2001.
Maffi, Luisa, and Ellen Woodley. *Biocultural Diversity Conservation: A Global Sourcebook*. Washington, DC: Earthscan, 2010.
Marlowe, W. Creighton. "The Sin of Shinar (Genesis 11:4)." *European Journal of Theology* 20, no. 1 (2001): 29–39.
McNicol, Alan J. *The Conversion of the Nations in Revelation*. Library of New Testament Studies 438. New York: T&T Clark, 2011.
McQueen, Larry R. *Joel and the Spirit: The Cry of a Prophetic Hermeneutic*. Journal of Pentecostal Theology Supplement Series 8. Sheffield: Sheffield Academic Press, 1995.
Minets, Yuliya. *That Slow Fall of Babel: Language and Identity in Late Antique Christianity*. Cambridge: Cambridge University Press, 2023.
Mufwene, Salikoko S. *The Ecology of Language Evolution*. New York: Cambridge University Press, 2001.
Mussies, G. *The Morphology of Koine Greek as Used in the Apocalypse of John: A Study in Bilingualism*. Supplements to Novum Testamentum 27. Leiden: Brill, 1971.
Nabhan, Gary Paul, ed. *Ethnobiology for the Future: Linking Cultural and Ecological Diversity*. Tucson: The University of Arizona Press, 2016.
Oded, B. "The Table of Nations (Genesis 10) – A Socio-Cultural Approach." *Zeitschrift für die Alttestamentliche Wissenschaft* 98 (1986): 14–31.
Pagel, Mark, and Ruth Mace. "The Cultural Wealth of Nations." *Nature* 428 (2004): 275–78.
Palmer, Bill. "Language Families in the New Guinea Area." In *The Languages and Linguistics of the New Guinea Area: A Comprehensive Account*, edited by Bill Palmer, 1–19. Berlin: De Gruyter Mouton, 2017.

Peterson, Brian Neil. *Genesis: A Pentecostal Commentary*. Pentecostal Commentary Series 8. Leiden: Brill, 2022.

Posey, Darrell Addison, ed. *Cultural and Spiritual Values of Biodiversity*. London: United Nations Environment Programme and Intermediate Technology Publications, 1999.

Putrawan, Bobby Kurnia, Ludwig Beethoven J. Noya, and Alisaid Prawiro Negoro. "Centripetal–Centrifugal Forces in the tower of Babel Narrative (Gen 11:1–9)." *Old Testament Essays* 35, no. 2 (2022): 192–210.

Ross, Allen P. *Creation and Blessing: A Guide to the Study and Exposition of the Book of Genesis*. Grand Rapids: Baker, 1988.

Salter, Martin C. *The Power of Pentecost: An Examination of Acts 2:17–21*. Eugene: Resource, 2012.

Sanneh, Lamin. *Translating the Message: The Missionary Impact on Culture*. Revised edition. Maryknoll: Orbis, 2009.

Scott, James M. *Geography in Early Judaism and Christianity: The Book of Jubilees*. Cambridge: Cambridge University Press, 2002.

———. "Luke's Geographical Horizon." In *The Book of Acts in Its First Century Setting*, Vol. II: *The Book of Acts in Its Graeco-Roman Setting*, edited by David W. J. Gill and Conrad Gempf, 483–544. Grand Rapids: Eerdmans, 1994.

Simons, Gary F. "Language Diversity: Curse of Blessing?" In *God and Language: Exploring the Role of Language in the Mission of God*, edited by Michael Greed and Dawn Kruger, 27–46. Dallas: Summer Linguistic Institute, 2022.

———. "Two Centuries of Spreading Language Loss." *Proceedings of the Linguistic Society of America* 27, no. 4 (2019): 1–12.

Simons, Gary F., and F. Paul Lewis. "The World's Languages in Crisis: A 20-Year Update." In *Responses to Language Endangerment: In Honor of Mickey Noonan: New Directions in Language Documentation and Language Revitalization*, edited by Elena Mihas, Kathleen Wheatley, Bernard Perley, and Gabriel Rei-Doval, 3–19. Philadelphia: John Benjamins, 2013.

Skutnabb-Kangas, Tove. *Linguistic Genocide in Education – Or Worldwide Diversity and Human Rights*. Mahwah: Lawrence Erlbaum Associates, 2000.

Skutnabb-Kangas, Tove, Luisa Maffi, and David Harmon. *Sharing a World of Difference: The Earth's Linguistic, Cultural, and Biological Diversity*, edited by Linda King. Paris: UNESCO/Terralingua, 2003.

Strong, John T. "Shattering the Image of God: A Response to Theodore Hiebert's Interpretation of the Story of the Tower of Babel." *Journal of Biblical Literature* 127, no. 4 (2008): 625–34.

Suckling, Kieran. "A House on Fire: Connecting the Biological and Linguistic Diversity Cases." *Earth First!* 21, no. 5 (2001): 40–41.

Sutherland, William J. "Parallel Extinction Risk and Global Distribution of Languages and Species." *Nature* 423 (2003): 276–79.

Thomas, Matthew A. *These are the Generations: Identity, Covenant, and the Toledot Formula*. Library of Hebrew Bible/Old Testament Studies 551. New York: T&T Clark, 2011.

Uehlinger, Christoph. *Weltreich und 'Eine Rede': Eine Neue Deutung der Sogenannten Turmbauersählung (Gen. 11:1–9)*. Freiburg: Universitätsverlag, 1990.

Yong, Amos. "Kings, Nations, and Cultures on the Way to the New Jerusalem: A Pentecostal Witness to an Apocalyptic Vision." In *The Pastor & the Kingdom: Essays Honoring Jack W. Hayford*, edited by S. David Moore and Jonathan Huntzinger, 231–51. Southlake: TKU & Gateway Academic, 2017.

———. "Many Tongues, Many Formational Practices: Christian Spirituality/Formation Across Global Christian Contexts." *Spiritus: A Journal of Christian Spirituality* 22, no. 1 (2022): 59–70.

———. *Mission after Pentecost: The Witness of the Spirit from Genesis to Revelation*. Mission in Global Community. Grand Rapids: Baker Academic, 2019.

———. "Pentecostal Christianities and Their Political Lives: Many Tongues, Many Political Practices." In *Politischer Pentekostalismus: Transformation des Globalen Christentums im Spiegel Theologischer Motive und Pluraler Normativität*, edited by Leandro L. B. Fontana and Markus Luber, 183–96. Weltkirche & Mission 18. Regensburg: Friedrich Pustet, 2023.

———. *Revelation*. Belief: A Theological Commentary on the Bible. Westminster: John Knox Press, 2021.

———. "*Ruach*, the Primordial Waters, and the Breath of Life: Emergence Theory and the Creation Narratives in Pneumatological Perspective." In *The Work of the Spirit: Pneumatology and Pentecostalism*, edited by Michael Welker, 183–204. Grand Rapids: Eerdmans, 2006.

———. *The Spirit Poured Out on All Flesh: Pentecostalism and the Possibility of Global Theology*. Grand Rapids: Baker Academic, 2005.

———. "The Spirit Poured Out in the Last Days: Toward a Pneumatology of Final Creation." In *The Spirit of Prophecy and Reconciliation: Essays in Honor of Rickie D. Moore*, edited by Robby Waddell and Chris E. W. Green, 151–66. Sheffield: Sheffield Phoenix, 2023.

Zerhusen, Bob. "An Overlooked Judean Diglossia in Acts 2?" *Biblical Theology Bulletin* 25, no. 3 (1995): 118–30.

Part II

Theological Perspectives

5

Greening Hollenweger

Retrieving Ecological Dimensions from the Dean of Pentecostal Studies

A. J. Swoboda

This chapter engages the ecological thinking of Walter Hollenweger (1927–2016). While contributions have been made in recent years to the ecological theology of Pentecostal and charismatic theology, much has yet to be done to understand some of the more formative voices in and around the movement. As such, we will attempt a full examination of Hollenweger's writing and thoughts to mine some of the key contributions to his life's work for the purpose of further construction and implementation of ecological theology and practice among Pentecostal and charismatic movements in the twenty-first century.

Retrieving Hollenweger

The lasting theological and ecumenical legacy of Walter J. Hollenweger continues to be felt fifty years on from the 1972 first edition publication of his *The Pentecostals*.[1] Widely recognized for his tireless work of shedding light on

---

1. Walter J. Hollenweger, *The Pentecostals: The Charismatic Movement in the Churches* (Minneapolis: Augsburg, 1972). This would later be followed up by Hollenweger, *Pentecostalism: Origins and Developments Worldwide* (Peabody: Hendrickson, 1997). For a biographical sketch of Hollenweger's life, see D. D. Bundy, "Hollenweger, Walter Jacob," in *The New Dictionary of*

global Pentecostalism for a largely sceptical and uninformed Western academic environment, Hollenweger's vast interests were by no means limited to these seemingly exotic outpourings of charismatic Christianity. A perusal of Hollenweger's bibliography exposes a legion of interests (and publications) spanning topics such as intercultural theology, narrative exegesis, drama, evangelism, missiology, Dietrich Bonhoeffer, and a life-long interest in the life and theology of Ulrich Zwingli.[2] But it was unquestionably his work on Pentecostalism that put him on the map. In the decades following the Azusa Street revival of the early 1900s, Hollenweger played a trusted role in providing clarity to the broader world exactly how these emerging Pentecostal and charismatic movements were shaping global Christianity, reframing ecumenical conversations, and renewing premodern forms of oral theological reflection.[3]

An ongoing reckoning with the vast contributions of Hollenweger – who Amos Yong calls the "recognized dean of Pentecostal studies" – has spurred on a cottage industry of fruitful scholarly contributions.[4] The ethics and theology of Dietrich Bonhoeffer,[5] intercultural studies,[6] and evangelism/missiology,[7] to name just a few, have proven stable foundations from which scholars have built on Hollenweger's thought. And one can only imagine a perennial retrieval of his thinking will not slow down any time soon. Nor should it. Pentecostalism shows little sign of slowing down or going away so, as Pentecostal scholarship enters its second and third generation, returning to its most generative foundational voices will be paramount to grounding its future. Still, many facets of Hollenweger's work have yet to be retrieved. As theological biographer Lynn

---

Pentecostal and Charismatic Movements, eds. Stanley M. Burgess and Eduard M. van der Maas (Grand Rapids: Zondervan, 2002), 729.

2. An exhaustive bibliography of Hollenweger's work can be found at Paul van der Laan and Peter Versteeg, "Bibliography of Walter J. Hollenweger," *PentecoStudies* 4, no. 1 (2005): 1–47.

3. For a comprehensive overview of Hollenweger's theological endeavours, see Lynne Price, *Theology Out of Place: A Theological Biography of Walter J. Hollenweger*, Journal of Pentecostal Theology Supplement Series 23 (Sheffield: Continuum, 2002).

4. Amos Yong, "Spirit and Proclamation: A Pneumatological Theology of Preaching. Part 1," *The Living Pulpit*, May 2015; https://www.pulpit.org/2015/05/.

5. Nikolaj Christensen, "Pentecost for Others: Dietrich Bonhoeffer According to Walter Hollenweger," *PentecoStudies* 15, no. 1 (2016): 25–45.

6. William Sweet, "Bridging Divides, Building Relations, and the Proposal for Intercultural Theology," *Toronto Journal of Theology* 38, no. 1 (2022): 81–100; Allen H. Anderson, "The Intercultural Theology of Walter J. Hollenweger," *Journal of the European Pentecostal Theological Association* 41, no. 1 (2021): 35–51.

7. Tony Richie, "'Infectious as the Flu': Evangelization and Mission in the Work of Walter J. Hollenweger," *Journal of the European Pentecostal Theological Association* 41, no. 1 (2021): 52–67; Tony Richie, "Revamping Pentecostal Evangelism: Appropriating Walter J. Hollenweger's Radical Proposal," *International Review of Mission* 96, no. 382–83 (2007): 343–54.

Price points out, Hollenweger's work was broadly effective at addressing the three "publics" of theology (academy, church, and society).[8] But this chapter takes Hollenweger in a different direction. What of the ecological, non-human, and cosmological notes of his thought? Given the voluminous contributions Hollenweger made, what might he theologically contribute regarding the ecological crisis we find ourselves in?

Greening Hollenweger is no easy task. On the one hand, any intercultural and interdisciplinary engagement of his work is likely to have made him proud. One clear motivation propelling Hollenweger was a clear desire to nudge Pentecostals toward embodying a witness interculturally in whatever context they found themselves. In so doing, they might develop a kind of "bilingual" missional tongue and bear witness to the Spirit in every domain of life and society.[9] Given his own efforts at forging the path for non-Western Pentecostals to enter European academic settings, Hollenweger could not help but celebrate that there were more and more Pentecostals becoming theologians, biblical scholars, and historians in prestigious academic programs – something Hollenweger foreknew would "change the breadth and depth of Pentecostalism."[10] Bridging Pentecostal theology to ecological studies is, no doubt, part of the kind of missional bilingualism Hollenweger desired. Yet, on the other hand, such an examination is fraught with difficulty. Nowhere does Hollenweger directly offer a full-length engagement of the ecological conversation or environmental degradation. Nor did he engage extensively with the ecotheological thought that was beginning to mature during his career. An engagement of this sort, as such, requires a reconstruction of Hollenweger's thought by a full reading of his corpus with an eye toward momentary nods he lent to the topic.

Still, we know Hollenweger deeply cared about the earth. His writings, thinking, and even prayer life were baptized in ecological landscapes. In one prayer, he tells of a mosquito in the kingdom of God, a caterpillar eschatologically longing to be a butterfly, a turtle who (in its shell) cannot break through to people, a singing bird that is not listened to, and a dirt-eating earthworm being eaten by magpies to whom God says, "no life, no plants, no vegetables, no animals, no people, no university, no government, no science and art and no magpies in all their academic glory . . . but, dear God, I wonder whether

---

8. As pointed out in Price, *Theology Out of Place*, 23, 26. Here, Price references the "three publics" of David Tracy, *The Analogical Imagination* (London: SCM, 1981), 51.

9. Walter J. Hollenweger, "Pentecostalism's Global Language," *Renewal Journals* 3, nos. 11–15 (2012): 206.

10. Hollenweger, "Pentecostalism's Global Language," 206.

you couldn't tell that to the magpies too."[11] Another – the "prayer of the singing bird" – tells of a bird finding encouragement in the Holy Spirit as people walk by with music playing in their ears.[12] In another meditation, Hollenweger confesses to God: "Dear God, Sometimes I feel like a frog . . . Why must I be such an in-between creature, neither fish nor bird, not quite at home in the water or on the air?"[13] There can be no doubt that the Swiss countryside of Hollenweger's childhood remained a part of his adult theological imagination.

At the same time, Hollenweger's interest in creation was by no means relegated to homely meditations. In one interview, he is prodded as to what concerned him most about the future of Pentecostalism. Two issues rise to the surface. First, Hollenweger fears a Pentecotalism that tends toward sectarianism and separation from worldly affairs. And, second, how Pentecostalism (and all Christians) would engage the ecological crisis. "What do we do with the ecological threat to the world?" Hollenweger reflects. "What do we do with the threat of hunger and the plight of refugees?"[14]

Hollenweger was quiet about creation. But not silent. What follows is a theological retrieval of Hollenweger for our present ecological moment. Price notes in her biography that Hollenweger is important for a postmodern era torn between "unity and diversity, particularism and universalism, [which are] the polarities on which we hang the question marks at the beginning of the millennium."[15] But, in a way, I suspect Hollenweger is and always will be timely for Pentecostals. In this chapter, I would like to suggest that he is as important for our ecological age. In due course, we will explore Hollenweger's thought with an eye toward his ecological pneumatology, ecclesiology, and soteriology.

Ecological Pneumatology

How did Hollenweger envision the work of the Spirit in the context of creation? There are two dimensions worth noting: his broadening of Pentecostal

---

11. Hollenweger, *Pentecostalism*, 180, 80, 199–200, 286–87, and 40, respectively. Price points these out and acknowledges that the earthworm prayer was often utilized by Hollenweger in public settings. See Price, *Theology Out of Place*, 40–41.

12. Walter Hollenweger, "Evangelism: A Non-Colonial Model," *Journal of Pentecostal Theology* 3, no. 7 (1995): 128.

13. Quoted in Richard Friedli, "Hollenweger Als Theologe," in *Pentecost, Mission and Ecumenism: Essays on Intercultural Theology*, ed. J. A. B. Jongeneel (Frankfurt: Peter Lang, 1992), 22–23.

14. Hollenweger, "Pentecostalism's Global Language," 209.

15. Price, *Theology Out of Place*, 2.

pneumatology and his doctrine of glossolalia. As mentioned, Hollenweger took great interest in Christian history. For example, he nurtured a life-long passion for the works of Zwingli about whom he often comments in his writings.[16] Hollenweger's interest in Christian history is fully displayed in a chapter entitled "All Creatures Great and Small" as he reflects on the 11th-century *filioque* controversy of the Eastern and Western churches. By adding "and the son" to the Nicene Creed, he contends, the Western churches rightly attempted to guard against what he calls a "free-floating spiritualism."[17] In so doing, however, the Western pneumatological tradition – shared by the Western fathers, Augustine, and, eventually, the Reformed fathers in Calvin and Luther – would be unintentionally hamstrung. By subsuming pneumatology under Christology, Hollenweger believed the Spirit's work was minimized as a mere function of Christ and the church. Hollenweger traces why and how much of Pentecostalism eventually embraced the Western formula uncritically. His most stringent critique of this embrace is found in *Pentecostalism*.

> In the West, what is spiritual is determined exclusively by Christology. In turn, proper Christology is determined in the Catholic Church by the *curia*, and in the Protestant and Pentecostal churches by the confessional declarations and the local pastors. The Eastern Orthodox churches complain bitterly, saying that this is not a doctrine of the Spirit but [an attempt to] control and domesticate the Spirit in Pentecostal, Catholic, and Protestant churches.[18]

Hollenweger believed this ultimately undermined the potential of Pentecostalism and limited its capacity to envision the Spirit's activity outside the church. Drawing on theologians like Karlstadt, Schwenkfeld, and Zwingli, Hollenweger attempts a reconstruction of Pentecostal pneumatology with an eye to Eastern theologies of the Spirit finding inspiration in Zwingli: "For [Zwingli] the Spirit is not confined to the Church or to the preaching of the gospel. [Zwingli] expects to find pagans in heaven."[19] It is important to note

---

16. Many of which are written in German. For a helpful English entree into his thought on Zwingli, see Walter Hollenweger, "Zwingli Writes the World into His World's Agenda," *The Mennonite Quarterly Review* 43, no. 1 (1969): 70–94. For the rest of his published works on Zwingli, see van der Laan and Versteeg, "Bibliography Walter J. Hollenweger," 1–47.

17. Walter J. Hollenweger, "All Creatures Great and Small: Towards a Pneumatology of Life," in *Strange Gifts?: A Guide to Charismatic Renewal*, eds. David Martin and Peter Mullen (Oxford: Basil Blackwell, 1984), 43.

18. Hollenweger, *Pentecostalism*, 218–19.

19. Hollenweger, "All Creatures Great and Small," 44.

his broadening of pneumatology. If Pentecostals leaned in a more Eastern direction – where Hollenweger believes the Spirit has not been relegated as a footnote to Christology – then they could more readily envision the vivifying work of the Spirit in *all* of creation, society, and life. By subsuming the Western formula, Pentecostals have, sadly,

> [R]estricted its doctrine of the Holy Spirit to the realization of a Christ-centred theology and the doctrine of salvation. The *creator spiritus*, the life-giving *ruach Yahweh* is a perplexing "lost" entity for the west. In other words, the pneumatology of Pentecostals and Charismatic Movements share the deficiencies of the pneumatologies of western tradition.[20]

Forging a theological imagination that envisioned the work of the Spirit in the whole world was a regular theme in Hollenweger's theological agenda. His desire to see the Spirit's work in broader creational terms is part of what he would later call a "charismatic theology of the world."[21] Hollenweger long believed that Pentecostals – in walking side-by-side with the Western tradition – were prone to simply rearticulating others' theological agendas. He saw this in its uncritical acceptance of the holiness doctrine of the nineteenth century "dressed up with the doctrine of 'initial sign' (speaking in tongues)."[22]

Hollenweger's doctrine of glossolalia played a key role in his thinking about creation. In his article "Creator Spiritus," Hollenweger explores how Pentecostal pneumatology must be reconsidered as it enters every new context it finds itself in. He begins by exploring New Testament language around "gifts" (Gr. *charismata*) and then attempts a broad pneumatology for the whole world. "A rethinking of the theology of the world would have to start from the following," writes Hollenweger, "If we take seriously the understanding of the Spirit in the Old Testament and the experience of the Spirit in the Third Church, then we have to reckon with the Holy Spirit not only in the church but also in the world."[23] This broadening, no doubt, put Hollenweger at odds with much Pentecostal thinking on the topic. Tongues, he contended, were not given by

---

20. Hollenweger, "All Creatures Great and Small," 44. Richie summarizes what Hollenweger is doing here, saying that "Western pneumatology is weak, including Pentecostal/charismatic varieties, because it is not based on an adequate doctrine of creation that allows and invites the Spirit's presence and influence to be active everywhere." Richie, "Revamping Pentecostal Evangelism," 345.

21. Walter Hollenweger, "Creator Spiritus: The Challenge of Pentecostal Experience to Pentecostal Theology," *Theology* 81, no. 679 (1978): 35.

22. Hollenweger, "Creator Spiritus," 34.

23. Hollenweger, "Creator Spiritus," 36.

the Spirit upon Spirit baptism only but should be seen as a gift of the natural man – "speaking in tongues is a natural gift, which some people have and some people have not."[24] This helped Hollenweger explain the phenomena of tongues outside non-Christian traditions among the indigenous, African, and Indian communities. Just as a secular doctor could heal without Spirit baptism, so could the unregenerated speak in glossolalia. He writes,

> If we understand the Holy Spirit as part of God's creation then he does not become a stop-gap explanation for things not or not yet explained, but rather the root and fountain of everything, whether explainable or not explainable.[25]

A similar point is echoed in his entry in *The International Dictionary of Pentecostal and Charismatic Movements* entitled "Gifts of the Spirit, Natural and Supernatural." Here Hollenweger takes a similar aim at an ecclesial-centric vision of the Spirit common to Pentecostals. Taking his cues from Russell Spittler, he suggests tongues are not "supernatural" but "natural" – part of the created human person. He believes that the lists of the gifts of the Spirit are lists of extraordinary (healing, prophesy, glossolalia) and ordinary (management, teaching, caring for the poor). There is no distinguishing between them. What is different is *how* they function. "A charism is a natural gift that is given for the common good . . . operations in an ecclesiological and Christological context and is open to judgment by the ecumenical community."[26] He continues:

> Just as music, normal speech, and the bread in Eucharist are common gifts of creation and may be transformed in the liturgical context, so speaking in tongues and other gifts are natural gifts that many human beings may possess. Just as a cathedral is built of ordinary stones, so glossolalia and other gifts are ontologically natural and ordinary phenomena. And just as, when put together in a masterpiece, the stones in a cathedral do not change ontologically but functionally, so speaking in tongues and other gifts can become something that, like a cathedral, proclaims, "God is here."[27]

---

24. Hollenweger, "Creator Spiritus," 37.
25. Hollenweger, "Creator Spiritus," 36–37.
26. Walter Hollenweger, "Gifts of the Spirit: Natural and Supernatural," in *The New International Dictionary of Pentecostal-Charismatic Movements*, eds. Stanley M. Burgess and Eduard M. van der Maas (Grand Rapids: Zondervan, 2002), 667.
27. Hollenweger, "Gifts of the Spirit," 667.

The invitation, then, for Pentecostals would be a return to a theology of *ruach Yahweh* that gives sustaining life to all of creation – the *spiritus creator*.[28] This opening would create so much potential for renewed reflection. For Hollenweger, this included a greater grasp on the topics of parapsychology and physics[29] as well as social reconciliation and inter-religious dialogue.[30] Hollenweger, in part, seems to appropriate what we might call a transubstantiated view of glossolalia. As a priest holds the bread and the wine that are already present, the elements are transformed into the body and blood of Christ. Similarly, when a Spirit-baptized Christian speaks in tongues, a capacity they already had in their natural selves is being lifted to God and given new power and transformation.

Certainly, Hollenweger's panentheistic (God *in* all things) pneumatology – aligning with Protestants like Moltmann – would be a challenge for many Pentecostals.[31] On many levels, it is for me. But it does show an important opening for Pentecostals to reconsider both their theological alliances and their tendency toward church-centric pneumatology. And such an opening is needed particularly in an ecological age. For Hollenweger, the Spirit cannot be limited only to the realm of the church because the Spirit does not belong to the church. The Spirit hovered over the chaos of all of creation in Genesis 1. And the Spirit continues to do so today.

Ecological Ecclesiology

Ecclesiology, alongside pneumatology, was a recurring theme in Hollenweger's work. Two dimensions of his theology of the church offer ecological nods: intercultural theology and the healing motif within Pentecostal ecclesiology. Intercultural theology remains one of Hollenweger's most lasting contributions. By the end of the 1980s, his most formative thoughts on the topic had come to maturity, including seven core movements: (1) theology is perennially in a culturally-conditioned form; (2) contextual theologies are not problematic; (3) cross-cultural engagement allows us to see how culturally-conditioned one's theology is; (4) culturally-conditioned voices are ignored to our own detriment;

---

28. Language used in Walter Hollenweger, "After Twenty Years' Research on Pentecostalism," *Theology* 87, no. 720 (1984): 407.

29. A common theme throughout his *Spirit and Matter*, published in German as Hollenweger, *Geist Und Materie: Interkulturelle Theologie 3* (Munich: Chr. Kaiser, 1988).

30. Walter Hollenweger, "Towards a Church Renewed and United in the Spirit," *Ecumenical Review* 31, no. 3 (1979): 305–9.

31. Hollenweger, *Pentecostalism*, 219.

(5) Scripture is the shared point of contact between these expressions; (6) such tension helps theology flourish; (7) and only through hearing the reflection of global Christian voices can the task of theology be appropriately undertaken.[32] Central to Hollenweger's method was a conviction that the means and methods of Western academic theology – in its technical, rational, and literary forms – tend to minimize and obfuscate non-Western, oral contributors. Building on Bonhoeffer's ecclesiology in *The Church for Others*, intercultural theology has at its heart the simple conviction that "the church transcends the boundaries of class, race, and nation."[33] In this framework, intercultural theology provokes a method of theological reflection both recognizing *and* involving the global church – not merely its Western, literary, affluent voices. A Pentecostal theology should be one of the *entire* global Pentecostal community.

Any reader of Hollenweger continually finds him fixated on a nagging reality: namely, that Pentecostalism had wrongly come to be viewed as a distinctly American array of social and denominational phenomena. As he often points out, Pentecostalism has the rich heritage of being but one of two global Christian movements started by people of colour: Pentecostalism and Christianity. The movement has been (and continues to be) most capable of crossing boundaries, ethnic, cultural, and national. In so doing, it has found a welcome home among countless non-Western, non-literary, and non-Enlightenment cultures. But where are these voices in theological dialogue? As the Spaniards conquered the Mexicans, Hollenweger would reflect, literate Pentecostalism has quietly colonized oral Pentecostalism. With it, "the songs died away, the flowers were trampled underfoot."[34] The form of middle-class, populist, and Republican Pentecostalism popular in America has not reflected the theology of Pentecostalism that has grown throughout the world.[35]

---

32. I've summarized these seven points in my own language. But I do so with gratitude for the synthesizing work around Hollenweger's intercultural theology in Mark J. Cartledge, "Pentecostal Theological Method and Intercultural Theology," *Transformation* 25, nos. 2–3 (2008): 92–102.

33. Walter Hollenweger, "Intercultural Theology," *Theology Today* 43, no. 1 (1986): 29. For a helpful overview of Holleweger's intercultural theology, see both Werner Ustorf, "The Cultural Origins of Intercultural Theology," *Mission Studies* 25, no. 2 (2008): 229–51 and Anderson, "The Intercultural Theology of Walter J. Hollenweger." A summative exploration of Hollenweger's use of Bonhoeffer can be found in Christensen, "Pentecost for Others," 25–45.

34. Walter J. Hollenweger, "Flowers and Songs: A Mexican Contribution to Theological Hermeneutics," *International Review of Mission* 60, no. 238 (1971): 239.

35. One can see his passionate frustration in a foreword written for Charles Jones, *A Guide to the Study of the Pentecostal Movement*, vol. 1 (Metuchen: Scarecrow, 1983), vii–ix. Hollenweger leverages a critique of middle-class Pentecostalism in the context of this "prophetic orality" in his "Pentecostalism and Black Power," *Theology Today* 30, no. 3 (1973): 228–38.

To remedy this, Hollenweger commended a return to the "oral root" of Pentecostalism.[36] For Hollenweger, the poor who have most often been excluded from the theological table should be at its centre. Undoubtedly, as it relates to ecological concerns, listening to the voices of the global poor is not only necessary; it is paramount. Hollenweger knew this. Noteworthy is the fact that as Hollenweger is asked about what most concerns him regarding Pentecostalism in the introduction, he offers two answers. The first is the concern about Pentecostal sectarian tendencies. The second is about eco-crisis and poverty – "What do we do with the ecological threat to the world? What do we do with the threat of hunger and plight of refugees?"[37] Interestingly, Hollenweger connects ecological concerns with humanitarian concerns for the poor. There remains no shortage of work exploring how the poor are often most impacted by ecological degradation.[38] But adding global Pentecostals into the mix adds a fascinating dimension to the conversation. Given the meteoric rise of Pentecostalism among the poor of the global South, one could say that Pentecostal concern for the environment should be all the more heightened given that Pentecostal churches are – in Hollenweger's words – "not churches *for* the poor but churches *of* the poor."[39]

If Hollenweger's intercultural theology were applied in an ecological age, then the poor – with their oral testimonies of seeing their lands ruined, the crops decimated, and the minerals stolen – would be at the forefront of theological dialogue. While Western Pentecostals argue over the nuances of theology and practice of glossolalia, Pentecostals in the South die of floods and famine. An intercultural theology applied ecologically would demand that we listen carefully to the voices of those who do not write in our academic journals, to stories that are often never heard in the West. So long as Pentecostalism is purported to be the religion of the middle-class and "prosperous," then these

---

36. Hollenweger's five roots were the Catholic, evangelical, critical, ecumenical, and oral. The black oral root tradition was exceedingly important for Hollenweger, occupying up to 85 percent of the first 145 pages of his *Pentecostalism* (as pointed out in Yong, "Spirit and Proclamation," n. 10).

37. Hollenweger, "Pentecostalism's Global Language," 209. He would later write about the intersection of Pentecostalism and the poor in his chapter, "The Pentecostal Elites and the Pentecostal Poor: A Missed Dialogue?" in *Charismatic Christianity as a Global Culture*, ed. Karla Poewe (Columbia: University of South Carolina Press, 1994), 200–216.

38. On the intersection of poverty and the ecological crisis, see Philani Moyo, *Architects of Poverty: Why African Capitalism Needs Changing* (Oxfordshire: Taylor & Francis, 2012); Leonardo Boff, *Cry of the Earth, Cry of the Poor* (Maryknoll: Orbis, 2002).

39. Italics in the original. Walter Hollenweger, "An Introduction to Pentecostalisms," *Journal of Beliefs & Values* 25, no. 2 (2004): 133.

voices will not (and cannot) be heard as they should.[40] By listening to the testimonies and experiences of impoverished Pentecostals who experience the brunt of the ecological travesty, the Western church is doing what Hollenweger wished: it is being "re-oralized."[41]

In addition, Hollenweger's ecclesiology envisioned the church as a covenant people who have the power to bring healing to a fractured world. In one article "Towards a Church Renewed and United in the Spirit," he frames the church as "a social experience of God, not in isolation from or at the expense of others."[42] This social context can only be possible through the work of the "Go-Between God" who mitigates fractured and unjust relationships. Certainly, this was not new to Hollenweger. He is tapping into some deep historical roots that go back to the racial divides of the twentieth century in which Pentecostalism was born. Under the leadership of William Seymour, the Azusa Street revival brought about the first interracial worship gatherings in Los Angeles and gave rise to a movement that has seen many reconciliation movements birthed. Azusa was merely another Pentecost. This new Pentecost, in Hollenweger's words,

> Broke down the walls of the nations, colour, language, sex, and social class . . . The body of Christ can only come to its full maturity when all the gifts of all its members reach full interplay with each other.[43]

As a new Pentecost, the church existed as a dynamic space of healing and reconciliation. One so powerful, he asides, that even Aryans may be surprised to meet their Jewish Christ.[44] Pentecostal gatherings are where this radical healing and reconciliation can best be seen. In Pentecostal liturgy, the emphasis is not on the sermon, readings, or rigid practice of sacraments. The emphasis is

---

40. On an ecological critique of the Pentecostal prosperity gospels that robs the poor, see my "Posterity or Prosperity?: Critiquing and Refiguring Prosperity Theologies in an Ecological Age," *Pneuma: The Journal of the Society for Pentecostal Studies* 37, no. 3 (2015): 394–411.

41. Walter Hollenweger, "The Ecumenical Significance of Oral Christianity," *The Ecumenical Review* 41, no. 2 (1989): 264. In one article, Hollenweger recalls his earliest years as a Swiss Pentecostal where Bible teachers would "use their Bible to understand what happened to them in the factory, when they were injured or lost their jobs, or when they had no food for their children." This oral tendency for testimony was what he called "the most important contribution of Pentecostalism." See Walter Hollenweger, "An Irresponsible Silence," *Asian Journal of Pentecostal Studies* 7, no. 2 (2004): 219.

42. Hollenweger, "Towards a Church Renewed and United in the Spirit," 23.

43. Walter Hollenweger, *Pentecost between Black and White: Five Case Studies on Pentecost and Politics* (Belfast: Christian Journals, 1974), 10.

44. Hollenweger, "Intercultural Theology," 32.

on the experience and real presence of God. To that end, Hollenweger ended up writing a good deal on the nature of Pentecostal liturgy as the cultivation of the abiding and immediate presence and work of the Holy Spirit.[45] Such an immediate presence – like that reported at Azusa Street and across the globe – had the dual power of creating a space for the healing of bodies and the reconciling of fractured relationships. The presence of God breaks down walls and makes bodies well. Writing about the salvation experience in an African Pentecostal context, Hollenweger writes,

> Therefore – as in the healing ministry of Jesus – these churches deal also with the bodies of their clients. In a survey of the reasons for conversion, we found that in the Third World – but perhaps not only there – people either get converted because of a healing (of themselves or of a friend or a member of the family), because of a dream or a vision, or because they have a friend who is a Christian. We have not found one single instance where somebody was saved on the basis of arguments, or on the basis of a sermon, and certainly not on the basis of a hell-fire sermon. The sermon seems to have other functions.[46]

In many parts of the world, he believed, healing was *the* Pentecostal liturgy. Still, much work has to be done on the role of Pentecostal theologies of healing, reconciliation, and creation.[47] But his thought here most certainly lends itself to providing a means through which we might imagine the healing of the fragmented relationships between humans and non-human creation. Paul, in his letter to the Romans, speaks to "creation groaning" as it awaits the "sons of God to be revealed" (Rom 8:19). No doubt Paul is speaking to the fractures resulting from the human rebellion in the garden: fractures within the self, between humans, and between humans and creation. There is strife between humans and their world. For Hollenweger, the church becomes not only a space for healing, but the reason for it. The church does not just heal. It incorporates what it heals. And so, in being a people of healing, it begins to take more seriously the call of salvation to address creation that groans as well as to begin to make room in its midst for creation.

---

45. Walter Hollenweger, "The Social and Ecumenical Significance of Pentecostal Liturgy," *Studia Liturgica* 8, no. 4 (1971): 207–15.

46. Walter Hollenweger, "Salvation in Pentecostalism," in *For Us and For Our Salvation: Seven Perspectives on Christian Soteriology*, ed. Rienk Lanooy (Utrecht: IIMO, 1994), 12.

47. See my initial foray into the topic at A. J. Swoboda, "Reconciling Creation: Spirit, Salvation, and Ecological Degradation," *Australasian Pentecostal Studies* 22, no. 1 (2021): 87–103.

Ecological Soteriology

Last, and finally, Hollenweger's soteriology. Hollenweger saw himself as an evangelist. A good deal of his work can be seen through this lens.[48] His plays and dramas were attempts to give voice to the Scripture and the gospel from the backside – through story, sets, and creativity. But much of his approach toward mission and evangelism must be set in the Western reaction against its most recent colonial memory. Setting a trajectory that runs counter to any sort of one-way, top-down approach toward evangelism was an approach he called "evangelism as dialogue."[49] His point of departure was Acts 10. As Peter goes to preach the gospel to Cornelius's family, he bears the gospel. But Peter was also transformed by the experience and reported to the Jerusalem church all that God was doing.[50] All evangelistic encounters, Hollenweger believed, should be marked by mutuality. Overviewing Hollenweger's missiology, Tony Richie suggests there are four core themes to his thinking: (1) the investment of resources in indigenous evangelists, pastors, and theologians; (2) the concern for theological education; (3) a confrontation with systemic realities that impoverish and harm people; (4) an ecumenical renewal.[51] In this schema, salvation is a reality that touches every element of creation.

Surveying this schema, Hollenweger's soteriology was comprehensive and holistic. For one, he envisioned robust evangelism as embracing social care and concern for the other. Indeed, confronting systemic evils such as racism, inequality, and unjust war were initial themes that consistently weave themselves through the early Pentecostal ministries of Frank Bartleman and William Seymour. And, Hollenweger believed, they should continue to play themselves out in contemporary Pentecostal practice. As Richie has shown, this Pentecostal vision for social concern has been far quieter in modern times than it was originally. But he sees a return to Hollenweger as a step in the right direction. "Hollenweger was convinced," writes Richie, "that poverty, racism, sexism, inequality, oppression, the defenselessness of vulnerable populations caught in the vicelike grip of situations of war and violence, and creation care

---

48. See Walter Hollenweger, *Evangelism Today: Good News or Bone of Contention?* (Belfast: Christian Journals, 1976).

49. Walter Hollenweger, "Evangelisation Als Dialog," *Leben Und Glauben* 48 (November 1973): 9–10.

50. Allen Anderson and Walter Hollenweger, eds., *Pentecostals after a Century: Global Perspectives on a Movement in Transition* (Sheffield: Sheffield Academic Press, 1999), 178, 183–88, and 190–91.

51. Richie, "Infectious as the Flu," 57.

impact the way Christians ought to present the gospel."[52] Pentecostals are not only called to share the gospel of the good news, they are called to embody the gospel of the good news for a suffering world. In what he called the "Zaccheus mission," he advocated for not only an encounter with Jesus; Hollenweger wanted those who had been doing injustice to make right their wrongs.[53] This was what he called the "critical root" of Pentecostalism.

But a Pentecostal way of doing social justice is abnormal. Again, Hollenweger located the work of justice in the very liturgies of Pentecostals. Pentecostals "do not act from a concept of social justice." Rather, he writes, "they act through liturgical responses which welcome the outcasts of this world within their oral and communitarian worship."[54] Social concern for the poor is embodied in Pentecostal healing gatherings. Salvation, for Pentecostals, is not escaping to heaven. It includes the healing of the body in the here and now.[55] Healing fascinated Hollenweger – likely due to the fact of his own healing as a child from a skin disease. One such exploration Hollenweger undertook examines the healing practices of the Brazilian Pentecostal church.[56] He was also drawn to the black Pentecostal tradition which he saw as being embodied, healing-centred, and rhythmic.[57] And these expressions, he believed, showed that Pentecostalism was a movement of the body. And this is underscored by the fact that the black Pentecostal traditions do not separate the healing of the body from the healing of the soul. Healing is a package deal. Being healed in part is to be healed in sum. Unlike many forms of revivalist dispensationalism, Pentecostalism did not limit soteriology to the "by and by." Rather, it offered an embodied kind of Christianity for people in the immediate present.

Both of these dimensions of Hollenweger's thought have ecological dimensions to them. Again, Richie, in summarizing Hollenweger's missiology, contends that bodily healing has a hidden creational dynamic embedded within it.

---

52. Richie, "Infectious as the Flu," 63.

53. See Walter Hollenweger, "My Pilgrimage in Mission," *International Bulletin of Missionary Research* 29, no. 2 (2005), 85–88.

54. Walter Hollenweger, "Thirteen Responses to Evangelization, Proselytism and Common Witness," *Pneuma: The Journal of the Society for Pentecostal Studies* 21, no. 1 (1999): 64.

55. As best discussed in Miroslav Volf, "Materiality of Salvation: An Investigation in the Soteriologies of Liberation and Pentecostal Theologies," *Journal of Ecumenical Studies* 26, no. 3 (1989): 447–67.

56. Walter Hollenweger, "Evangelism and Brazilian Pentecostals," *The Ecumenical Review* 20, no. 2 (1968): 163–70.

57. Walter Hollenweger, "The Black Roots of Pentecostalism," in *Pentecostals after a Century*, eds. Walter Hollenweger and Allan Anderson (Sheffield: Sheffield Academic Press, 1999), 33–44.

He writes that Pentecostals "affirm the healing of the body along with the saving of the soul similarly compels them to appreciate the physical world as objects of divine care and concern – and therefore, of significance to human care and concerns as well."[58] That God can (and does heal) the body in the salvific process reveals a matter-affirming practice and theology. In fact, Hollenweger consistently offered strong critiques of Western medicine and its false promise of providing true healing through technique alone. In the end, medicine can only heal; it cannot bring health.[59] What is needed for restoration is a holistic experience of Christ and the power of the Holy Spirit. Hollenweger's penchant for appreciating the healing ministry of Pentecostalism – along with a critique of Western medical pragmatism – reminds us that most global Pentecostals are people who are in touch with creation by being in touch with their bodies. Therefore, that part of our own healing process is to become more and more at home in the bodies God has placed us. This is a welcome critique for much of Pentecostal contemporary spirituality can succumb to a "pie-in-the-sky" soteriology that sees the good world God has made as an afterthought. But it is no afterthought. God would not heal matter if it did not matter.

As Hollenweger surveyed the black churches, he found something interesting. They spoke often of the *charismata*. And they practiced the *charismata*. But he discovered that their lists of gifts did not merely include tongues and healing and ecstatic praise – they also included political demonstrations as gifts of the Spirit.[60] Given how much he wrote about race at his moment in time, it is clear that these churches had a profound influence on his life. This retrieval reminds us that the work of the Spirit can (and does) propel the Christian to speak and act on behalf of the broken and destitute. Salvation is not only the salvation of our spirit. It is the salvation of our bodies, our relationships, our families, our mental health, and our societies and institutions. While it may seem uncomfortable to many contemporary Pentecostals, the "critical tradition" of challenging the status quo is at the bedrock of Pentecostal spirituality. From racial reconciliation to pacifism to feeding programs, Pentecostals set a foundation of care for the world on the basis of their gospel. In our ecological age, we must not just resort to easy actions like recycling and driving less to quell our guilty conscience. There is a deeper need – a Zaccheaus mission.

---

58. Richie, "Infectious as the Flu," 64.

59. Walter Hollenweger, "Theology of the New World," *The Expository Times* 87, no. 8 (1976): 230.

60. Hollenweger, *Pentecost between Black and White*.

What would it look like not only to encounter Jesus but begin to live so as to right the wrongs we have done?

In his chapter "Salvation and Pentecostalism," Hollenweger points out that when someone says they are "saved" in two very different cultures, these can come to mean very different things. When a middle-class person says they are saved, they usually mean they have believed in Jesus and are now going to heaven. But when a black person says they are saved, "he means that he has literally been saved . . . He owes his physical, psychological, cultural, and spiritual existence to the saving power of Jesus Christ and his saving community."[61] Salvation can have multiple meanings given the time, place, and culture. No doubt, in our moment, the issue of caring for creation is an issue of physical salvation for many. And as we continue to move into the new world we find ourselves in, it would be appropriate to begin to better explore how Pentecostal understandings of salvation can help to mitigate issues around the eco-crisis rather than exasperate them. Because, likely, a time is coming when someone will say they have been "saved." And by that, they mean they have been rescued from a flood, from the death of their crops, and endless drought.

Conclusion

Hollenweger's theology provides countless launching points to think about creation. And I believe that his theology creates some rich space for ecotheological imagination for Pentecostals. Still, it is not without some critique. The blurring of the lines between the church-centred and natural *charismata* is, in my opinion, not as clearly considered as it should be. It would be interesting to hear his reflections on the gifts in a graduate seminar with Pauline scholars. It is possible to see the work of the Spirit in creation without minimizing the sanctifying work of the Spirit in the church. Indeed, the Spirit has two very powerful hands. As well, while making brief mention from time to time, he never fully dealt with the ecological crisis of his own time. True, it would be anachronistic to hold him to account for what we know now. But by the 1980s and 90s – the peak of his writing career – he spent noticeably scant attention directly addressing it. But this largely reflects Pentecostalism as a whole than it is of Hollenweger directly.[62]

---

61. Hollenweger, "Salvation in Pentecostalism," 1.

62. For an overview of how Pentecostals have traditionally thought about creation, see my *Tongues and Trees: Towards a Pentecostal Ecological Theology* (Blandford Forum: Deo, 2013).

Hollenweger was a realistic thinker. He did not sway toward an over-spiritualization of complex worldly dynamics. Nor did he under-spiritualize them. In commenting about the ministry of healing, he makes an arresting statement in his magnum opus, *Pentecostalism*.

> A causal connection between the sin of a patient (or the sin of his ancestors) and his or her illness is *expressis verbis* rejected by the gospel. Of course, the Bible knows that there might be a connection. After all, if we persist in poisoning our food, our air, and our water, then it is not surprising that we become sick. But – and this is the difference – it is not necessarily those who sin who become sick. It is often the innocent who are affected.[63]

Hollenweger is realistic about the fact that creation was experiencing great travail as a result of the human rebellion against God. When we eat poisoned food and drink contaminated water, we get sick for a reason. Not everything is the devil's fault – even if the world is broken because of sin; Hollenweger is also keenly aware that the decisions of some people impact others. As he writes, "It is not necessarily those who sin who become sick. It is often the innocent who are affected." In one fell swoop, he affirms healing, systemic evil, and the ecological crisis. Elsewhere, he reflects, "What is the use in treating infectious diseases when the water we drink and the air we breathe become more and more polluted?"[64] Hollenweger, here, speaks as someone who has a deep grasp of our interconnected world. He sounds like an ecologist. And, for our sake, it is greatly helpful that he tackled the world's issues realistically with a deep hope in God and the power of the Spirit.

Hollenweger was a generative, critical, compassionate, and foundational thinker for Pentecostals and Pentecostal scholarship. And we must continue to engage his important contributions. As the church fully begins to understand its responsibility in a world that is "groaning," perhaps we can, once again, be willing to hear the voices of our forebears for the faint echoes of the Spirit's heart. He certainly made himself loud in Hollenweger's. He was no ecologist or eco-theologian. But he made their task a lot easier by laying a pathway for imagining the work of the Spirit not only in the church, but in the whole world.

---

63. Hollenweger, *Pentecostalism*, 244.
64. Walter Hollenweger, "Charismatic Renewal in the Third World: Implications for Mission," *Occasional Bulletin of Missionary Research* 4, no. 2 (1980): 71.

Bibliography

Anderson, Allan H. "The Intercultural Theology of Walter J. Hollenweger." *Journal of the European Pentecostal Theological Association* 41, no. 1 (2021): 35–51.

Anderson, Allan, and Walter Hollenweger. *Pentecostals after a Century: Global Perspectives on a Movement in Transition.* Sheffield: Sheffield Academic Press, 1999.

Boff, Leonardo. *Cry of the Earth, Cry of the Poor.* Maryknoll: Orbis, 1997.

Bundy, D. D. "Hollenweger, Walter Jacob." In *The New Dictionary of Pentecostal and Charismatic Movements*, edited by Stanley M. Burgess and Eduard M. van der Maas, 729. Grand Rapids: Zondervan, 2002.

Cartledge, Mark. "Pentecostal Theological Method and Intercultural Theology." *Transformation* 25, nos. 2–3 (2008): 92–102.

Christensen, Nikolaj. "Pentecost for Others: Dietrich Bonhoeffer According to Walter Hollenweger." *PentecoStudies* 15, no. 1 (2016): 25–45.

Friedli, Richard. "Hollenweger Als Theologe." In *Pentecost, Mission and Ecumenism: Essays on Intercultural Theology*, edited by J. A. B. Jongeneel, 15–26. Frankfurt: Peter Lang, 1992.

Hollenweger, Walter. "After Twenty Years' Research on Pentecostalism." *Theology* 87, no. 720 (1984): 403–12.

———. "All Creatures Great and Small: Towards a Pneumatology of Life." In *Strange Gifts?: A Guide to Charismatic Renewal*, edited by David Martin and Peter Mullen, 41–53. Oxford: Basil Blackwell, 1984.

———. "An Introduction to Pentecostalisms." *Journal of Beliefs & Values* 25, no. 2 (2004): 125–37.

———. "An Irresponsible Silence." *Asian Journal of Pentecostal Studies* 7, no. 2 (2004): 219–24.

———. "Charismatic Renewal in the Third World: Implications for Mission." *Occasional Bulletin of Missionary Research* 4, no. 2 (1980): 68–75.

———. "Creator Spiritus: The Challenge of Pentecostal Experience to Pentecostal Theology." *Theology* 81, no. 679 (1978): 32–40.

———. "Evangelisation Als Dialog." *Leben Und Glauben* 48 (November 1973): 9–10.

———. "Evangelism: A Non-Colonial Model." *Journal of Pentecostal Theology* 3, no. 7 (1995): 107–28.

———. "Evangelism and Brazilian Pentecostals." *The Ecumenical Review* 20, no. 2 (1968): 163–70.

———. *Evangelism Today: Good News or Bone of Contention?* Belfast: Christian Journals, 1976.

———. "Flowers and Songs: A Mexican Contribution to Theological Hermeneutics." *International Review of Mission* 60, no. 238 (1971): 232–44.

———. *Geist und Materie: Interkulturelle Theologie 3.* Munich: Chr. Kaiser, 1988.

———. "Gifts of the Spirit: Natural and Supernatural." In *The New International Dictionary of Pentecostal-Charismatic Movements*, edited by Stanley M. Burgess and Eduard M. van der Maas, 667–68. Grand Rapids: Zondervan, 2002.

———. "Intercultural Theology." *Theology Today* 43, no. 1 (1986): 28–35.

———. "My Pilgrimage in Mission." *International Bulletin of Missionary Research* 29, no. 2 (2005): 85–88.

———. *Pentecost between Black and White: Five Case Studies on Pentecost and Politics*. Belfast: Christian Journals, 1974.

———. "Pentecostalism and Black Power." *Theology Today* 30, no. 3 (1973): 228–38.

———. *Pentecostalism: Origins and Developments Worldwide*. Peabody: Hendrickson, 1997.

———. "Pentecostalism's Global Language." *Renewal Journals* 3, nos. 11–15 (2012): 205–10.

———. "Salvation in Pentecostalism." In *For Us and For Our Salvation: Seven Perspectives on Christian Soteriology*, edited by Rienk Lanooy, 1–13. Utrecht: IIMO, 1994.

———. "The Black Roots of Pentecostalism." In *Pentecostals after a Century*, edited by Walter Hollenweger and Allan Anderson, 33–44. Sheffield: Sheffield Academic Press, 1999.

———. "The Ecumenical Significance of Oral Christianity." *The Ecumenical Review* 41, no. 2 (1989): 259–65.

———. "The Pentecostal Elites and the Pentecostal Poor: A Missed Dialogue?" In *Charismatic Christianity as a Global Culture*, edited by Karla Poewe, 200–216. Columbia: University of South Carolina Press, 1994.

———. *The Pentecostals: The Charismatic Movement in the Churches*. Minneapolis: Augsburg, 1972.

———. "The Social and Ecumenical Significance of Pentecostal Liturgy." *Studia Liturgica* 8, no. 4 (1971): 207–15.

———. "Theology of the New World." *The Expository Times* 87, no. 8 (1976): 228–32.

———. "Thirteen Responses to Evangelization, Proselytism and Common Witness." *Pneuma: The Journal of the Society for Pentecostal Studies* 21, no. 1 (1999): 63–67.

———. "Towards a Church Renewed and United in the Spirit." *Ecumenical Review* 31, no. 3 (1979): 305–9.

———. "Zwingli Writes the World into His World's Agenda." *The Mennonite Quarterly Review* 43, no. 1 (1969): 70–94.

Jones, Charles. *A Guide to the Study of the Pentecostal Movement*, Vol. 1. Metuchen: Scarecrow, 1983.

Moyo, Philani. *Architects of Poverty: Why African Capitalism Needs Changing*. Oxfordshire: Taylor & Francis, 2012.

Price, Lynne. *Theology Out of Place: A Theological Biography of Walter J. Hollenweger*. Journal of Pentecostal Theology Supplement Series 23. Sheffield: Continuum, 2002.

Richie, Tony. "'Infectious as the Flu': Evangelization and Mission in the Work of Walter J. Hollenweger." *Journal of the European Pentecostal Theological Association* 41, no. 1 (2021): 52–67.

———. "Revamping Pentecostal Evangelism: Appropriating Walter J. Hollenweger's Radical Proposal." *International Review of Mission* 96, no. 382–83 (2007): 343–54.

Sweet, William. "Bridging Divides, Building Relations, and the Proposal for Intercultural Theology." *Toronto Journal of Theology* 38, no. 1 (2022): 81–100.

Swoboda, A. J. "Reconciling Creation: Spirit, Salvation, and Ecological Degradation." *Australasian Pentecostal Studies* 22, no. 1 (2021): 87–103.

———. "Posterity or Prosperity?: Critiquing and Refiguring Prosperity Theologies in an Ecological Age." *Pneuma: The Journal of the Society for Pentecostal Studies* 37, no. 3 (2015): 394–411.

———. *Tongues and Trees: Toward a Pentecostal Ecological Theology*. Journal of Pentecostal Theology Supplement Series 40. Blandford Forum: Deo, 2013.

Tracy, David. *The Analogical Imagination*. London: SCM, 1981.

Ustorf, Werner. "The Cultural Origins of Intercultural Theology." *Mission Studies* 25, no. 2 (2008): 229–51.

van der Laan, Paul, and Peter Versteeg. "Bibliography of Walter J. Hollenweger." *PentecoStudies* 4, no. 1 (2005): 1–47.

Volf, Miroslav. "Materiality of Salvation: An Investigation in the Soteriologies of Liberation and Pentecostal Theologies." *Journal of Ecumenical Studies* 26, no. 3 (1989): 447–67.

Yong, Amos. "The Spirit and Proclamation: A Pneumatological Theology of Preaching. Part 1." *The Living Pulpit* (May 2015). https://www.pulpit.org/2015/05/.

6

Missio Dei, Imago Dei and the *Spiritus Dei*

Oneness Pentecostals and Creation Care

Joey Peyton

The ironic statistical and factual connections often made during research leave one astonished and questioning the presumed ongoing blindness to many things, including the environmental destruction of creation in the world around us that is needed for human life to continue. This author is no different. Having completed my PhD in Intercultural Studies at the Assembly of God Theological Seminary in 2022 and having written my dissertation on the pastoral care of diaspora populations (specifically Central and South American diaspora), I, with other Pentecostals, rejoice at the explosion of Pentecostalism in the global South. Todd Johnson of Gordon Conwell University named Brazil as the country with the highest percentage of Pentecostals (greater than 50 percent), both currently and historically.[1] This phenomenal growth is noteworthy and equally true for both Oneness and Trinitarian Pentecostals. Yet, at the same time and in the same place, and at the risk of destroying the world, political and industrial forces are burning more than 72,000 acres of the

---

1. Todd M. Johnson, "Pentecostal/Charismatic," *Christianity World Christian Encyclopedia*, 3rd ed., 27 May 2020, https://www.gordonconwell.edu/blog/pentecostal-charismatic-christianity/.

Amazon rainforest every day (for a total of 26.4 million acres in 2023 alone – 5 percent of the entire South American rainforest).[2]

Having seen such news articles in my research for my dissertation, I, like most Pentecostals, continue with the more "relevant and important" research at hand (salvation, pastoral care, injustice, etc.) However, after the invitation to write this chapter and after extensive research online, this researcher could not find a single statement, website, blog, agency, or other concern from a single North or South American Pentecostal (person or group) about the burning of the rainforest or any other environmental issue. Mentally, spiritually, and emotionally, how do Pentecostals stay disconnected from such physically and socially destructive behaviour, especially when, in this author's experience, Pentecostals are generally passionate and sacrificial people? While I can't speak for all Pentecostals, perhaps not even for all Oneness Pentecostals (I am a Oneness Pentecostal, third generation United Pentecostal Church, International [UPCI] preacher/pastor/teacher, ordained thirty-plus years, and in ministry over forty-five years, mainly among Oneness Pentecostals), I can clearly speak as a classical Oneness Pentecostal and will consider this dichotomy in theological foci with a Oneness Pentecostal lens.

What is problematic in our theological understanding (or misunderstanding) that contributes to the ongoing degradation of the environment? What is lacking in our understanding of the missional impulses of the biblical text, e.g. the *missio Dei*, the *missio spiritus*, and the *missio iglesias*? What is missing in our understanding of the environment, of human biology, and the symbiotic nature between the two? In this brief chapter, these are the questions that lie at the foundation of this effort. First, I want to define the problem while considering both the evidence and the consequences of continuing in our present predilection. Second, while coming to grips with the problem, an attempt will be made to understand the historic worldview of classical Pentecostals that impact this dichotomy, a worldview that many Oneness Pentecostals still possess. Our historic lack of formal theological and scientific educational foundations, along with the limited/narrow theological foci of many Oneness Pentecostal ministers, exacerbates the problem. Finally, this writer will suggest course corrections from the conclusions made and lessons learned – course corrections that should situate the *missio Dei*, the *imago Dei*, and the spiritus Dei within the overt theology and worldview of Oneness Pentecostals, or maybe conversely, to situate the theology and worldview of Oneness Pentecostals within the

---

2. Suzanne Pelletier et al., "Amazon Rainforest Fires," Rainforest Foundations US, online article, 18 May 2024. https://rainforestfoundation.org/engage/brazil-amazon-fires/.

greater *missio Dei*. These corrections should compel us, filled with the *spiritus Dei*, to live as the *imago Dei*, embracing God's nature and mission to care for the whole of his creation, as well as our unmatched commitment to his name.

The Problem

Recent Oneness Pentecostal news sources are flush with reports of revival, numbers of water/Spirit baptisms, new church plants, construction projects, mission trips, missionaries, and even humanitarian aid efforts in disaster spots around the world. However, there is no report or even a hint of a single environmental concern coming from Oneness preachers, scholars, and/or writers. This author maintains a growing email database of Oneness scholars in the areas of theology, ecclesiology, missiology, and pastoral care (currently 108 are defined as having a graduate-level degree or higher). In an effort to gather information about environmental research, papers, articles, presentations, sermons, podcasts, and/or thoughts and attitudes, among Oneness Pentecostals on 1 Dec 2023 an email was sent to these scholars. Of the 108, 83 percent of the emails were opened and read, 5 percent bounced and returned, 12 percent remained unopened at the writing of this article. In the sixteen responses (15 percent of addressees), there were two noted commonalities.

The first commonality was an overwhelming feeling that no such writing/speaking/research existed: five specifically stated that there were none (or almost none); four sent me papers from students concerned about the environment who had pursued graduate degrees at Urshan Graduate School of Theology and had written papers on the topic (one each in 2014, 2019, 2020, 2023); two sent me excerpts from books they had written that included a few paragraphs they perceived to address environmental concerns; and seven said they didn't know of any but would look and see what they could find and get back to me (four months later none have done so). The second commonality was that the majority (greater than 60 percent of the respondents) specifically requested, "Please don't quote me!" or "Please don't identify me in your article!" One student's paper was shared with the specific request that I didn't use any of the information in the paper in connection with his name.

David K. Bernard, General Superintendent of the UPCI and the uncontested academic leader/head of all Oneness Pentecostals, regardless of organizational affiliation, did respond and sent several paragraphs (mentioned above) from his 2019 book, *Apostolic Identity in a Postmodern World*,[3] and a four-minute UPCI video blog, *Apostolic Life in the Twenty-First Century, Episode 48*, titled, "Should Christians Be Concerned about Climate Change?" Bernard admits in the email, "I don't have much" and acknowledges in the video blog that "Christians should be interested in the care of the earth."[4]

Others who responded to my request for information (but would not give their consent to be identified) stated: "I have a feeling that respecting the church building may be the limit of 'our' (Oneness) published material in the realm of missiology and ecology." "Sadly, I know of no scholar in our movement who researches (or even cares about) ecology (except you)." [parentheses were included in the original messages] "I highly doubt any Oneness Pentecostal has done any work on this subject, especially with an escapist theology so prevalent among our ranks." "I . . . do not have anything to contribute towards this area of study at this time."

Further, after extensively searching through the social media accounts of Oneness Pentecostal churches and individuals, I could not find a single concern, involvement, warning, postulation, effort, meme, reel, video, sermon, book, blog, archive, etc. that even remotely seemed to encourage one another to be mindful of the environment or see creation care as part of the church's mission (this included review of my own personal and ministry social media accounts).

David Norris, another prominent Oneness Pentecostal scholar and professor at UGST, acknowledges in his article, "Creation Revealed: An Early Pentecostal Hermeneutic," that was published in a book edited by Amos Yong, *The Spirit Renews the Face of the Earth: Pentecostal Forays in Science and Theology of Creation*, that early modern Oneness Pentecostals "had little or nothing to say on the subject" and characterizes early Pentecostals' view of creation as, "The Bible is true. Evolution is wrong. End of discussion."[5] Mitch McQuinn wrote in response to Norris's assertions in his master's thesis, "Apostolic Creationism: Why Young Earth Creationism is the Only Position Consistent with an Apostolic Hermeneutic," concerning creation, "The overriding attitude

---

3. David K. Bernard, *Apostolic Identity in a Postmodern World* (Weldon Springs: Word Aflame, 2019), 175–76.

4. David K. Bernard, "Should Christians Be Concerned about Climate Change?," *Apostolic Life in the Twenty-First Century Podcast*, episode 48, YouTube, 12 minutes, 49 seconds, 28 May 2022, https://www.youtube.com/watch?v=tZkNUYV2YOg.Episode 48.

5. David S. Norris, "Creation Revealed: An Early Pentecostal Hermeneutic," in *The Spirit Renews the Face of the Earth: Pentecostal Forays in Science and Theology of Creation*, ed. Amos Yong (Eugene: Pickwick, 2009), 74.

appears to have been one of indifference or scorn toward evolution, with few attempts to address it academically."[6]

While the unfortunate truth is that not only are Oneness scholars not writing or researching about caring for creation, and Oneness preachers are not preaching or teaching about ecological responsibility, there is ultimately very little, if anything, being practically done by Oneness Pentecostals, individually or collectively, to overtly improve or repair the whole of God's creation (sans ultimate salvation of humanity). Consequently, because little to nothing is being done, "revival" continues while the Brazilian rainforest burns, the polar ice caps melt, the oceans rise, and severe weather devastates the world. One could (and some may) argue that there is nothing that can be (or could be) done to change the course of the world and/or, "We didn't cause the problem!" However, with this collective inactivity, ecological degradation continues. If such an argument was made by Noah (Gen 5 and 6) as the world ignored his warnings (Heb 11:7), the ark would have never been built; if such an argument was made by Stephen as the rocks took his life (Acts 7:54–60), Paul may have never been converted. However, the question that this essay will try to answer is: Why are Oneness Pentecostals ecologically inactive, environmentally uninvolved, and/or foundationally naïve to what is happening in the world God created?

The unfortunate truth is that most Oneness Pentecostals don't have a position, and those that may have an opinion are passive, yet inactive, at best. Not only did this researcher not find anything that specifically and/or intentionally promoted the care of the environment, I also did not find anything that seemed to be *against* caring for the environment, unless you consider a resignation for the inevitable end of the planet (destroyed by fire) or the general unwillingness to be identified with the subject matter to be pejorative. The truth be told, many, if not most, Oneness Pentecostals isolate interests and efforts to the repetitious outpouring of the *spiritus Dei* with little regards to, or understanding of, how being Spirit-filled fits into the larger *missio Dei*, or our own existence in God's present world as the *imago Dei*. Often the excitement created while counting the "saved" and "baptized" supersedes instruction on salvation's purpose in God's mission or our role as God's image on earth, as newly in Christ and the kingdom of God.

---

6. Mitchell McQuinn, "Apostolic Creationism: Why Young Earth Creationism is the Only Position Consistent with an Apostolic Hermeneutic" (Master's Thesis, Urshan Graduate School of Theology, 2019), 20.

Consequently, discipleship often grounds new converts in a formulaic approach to "initial salvation" and/or the "end-time" as the destination and not how to live as God's image in the kingdom of God every day in the time between one's *soteria* and the *eschaton*. This lack of a comprehensive theological understanding for who we are as Spirit-filled *imago Dei* and what our role is in the overarching *missio Dei*, in which we are called to participate, has existed since the beginning of the movement. Further, not only do the majority of Oneness Pentecostals, like most Pentecostal groups, generally lack foundational theological education, but many of us also lack the foundational biological and ecological education that establish the symbiotic nature of all of God's creation. The result is often a general lack of care for (or the ignoring of) any part of creation, be it the burning of the Amazon rainforest or the homeless living on the sidewalks of American cities, both of which endangers the whole of creation. For me, the absence of any effort to care for the environment and the absence of care for one's community are one and the same problem: a profound failure to understand the role of the *imago Dei* in the *missio Dei* outlined in Genesis 1:28, 2:15, 12:1–3, 9:9–10; Leviticus 19:18–19; Matthew 28:19–20; and Mark 12:29–31. Before I dare to suggest that Oneness Pentecostal discipleship should refocus on "being" God's image and living/serving in God's mission for/to the whole of creation, I want to take a closer look at the historic reasons for this lack of a comprehensive understanding, acceptance, and/or pursuit of *missio Dei* theology that includes caring for the symbiotic existence of all creation.

Oneness Pentecostal Identity

Oneness Pentecostals, not unlike "other" classical Pentecostals, derive theological foundations from the nineteenth-century Wesleyan-holiness movement that was amalgamated around a "fourfold gospel." Donald Dayton, in his book, *Roots of Pentecost*, identified these foundations as saviour, sanctifier, healer, and soon coming king,[7] which among classical Pentecostals would become the doctrines of salvation by Christ alone; baptism of the Holy Spirit (for many early classical Pentecostals this would include initial evidence by speaking in tongues); divine healing/deliverance; and the return of Christ or the Rapture. While many Pentecostal groups moved on, matured, expanded, changed, or abandoned these theological roots, this author would argue that many, if not most (me included), Oneness Pentecostals still identify with these foundations

---

7. Donald W. Dayton, *Theological Roots of Pentecostalism* (Peabody: Hendrickson, 1987), 15–28.

today. Because of Oneness Pentecostals' historic resistance to liberal influence and/or a consuming concern about losing the "old paths," for many, this insistence on standing firm on the foundations of the apostles has become, without deliberative intent, holding onto what the early modern Oneness Pentecostal preachers believed/preached/taught (the Godhead in Jesus, tongues as evidence of the Spirit, divine healing, and the imminent rapture of the church).

Clara Burton, a graduate student at UGST, in her 2023 paper, "Climate Change and the Christian: An Ecclesiology of the Earth from an Apostolic Perspective," takes a slightly different view (though similar to Dayton's above) on the "distinct lack of ecclesiology regarding the topic of climate change within the church, specifically within the [Oneness Pentecostal] movement."[8] She identifies three factors that contribute to our resistance to concerns for the environment: the perception that ecological ideology is a product of liberal theology; Greek dualistic notions that bifurcate theologically the overarching missiological impulse of the Old and New Testament; and the multiplicity of eschatological views.[9] Bernard, in the brief video blog mentioned above, also acknowledges some of Dayton's Quadrilateral, "Many times [Oneness Pentecostals] think the Lord is coming and we're going to the millennial kingdom . . . so we don't care about present earth!" However, he also admonishes "that shouldn't be the way we treat the earth."[10] Finally, both Bernard and Barton attribute some of the resistance to liberal theology's promotion of climate care to its presumed connection to a liberal political agenda, "It is hard to trust information from sources we feel might manipulate facts to suit their political agenda."[11]

In many ways, Oneness Pentecostals' determination to hold fast to historic "truth" and remain untainted with liberal agendas has limited further exploration of missiological subjects. This limited investigation of the *missio Dei*, and/or one's behaviour as the *imago Dei* within the *missio Dei*, has focused our energies on the conversion experiences that have produced great "revivals." For example, an early twenty-first century Oneness Pentecostal slogan that was printed on a large banner and hung in a church I pastored was, "If we don't have revival, nothing else matters! If we do have revival, nothing else matters!" Of course, "revival" was defined by, and limited to, the number of those who

---

8. Carla Burton, "Climate Change and The Christian: An Ecclesiology of the Earth from an Apostolic Perspective," paper written at Urshan Graduate School of Theology, 2023.

9. Burton, "Climate Change and The Christian," 1.

10. Bernard, Episode 48.

11. Burton, "Climate Change," 1.

were Spirit-filled and/or water baptized (what Oneness Pentecostals consider to be part of salvation). As McQuinn succinctly states, "Oneness Pentecostals have tended to be indifferent, dismissive, or narrowly focused upon other, arguably more important doctrines pertaining to apostolic distinctives, such as the new birth, holiness, and the Oneness of God."[12]

While such a narrow focus determines the efforts, the funds, and the results in a very restricted soteriological and eschatological fashion, it also limited theological exploration by Oneness academics in other areas of biblical importance. Any efforts to redirect organizational energies to something besides the adopted foundations of the oneness of God, evidential glossolalia, divine healing, or an impending eschatology are extremely uncomfortable and can be met with suspicions at best and ostracization at worst (which became painfully obvious in the return emails searching for Oneness Pentecostal contributions for this article). This becomes even more true when such exploration comes with Latin or Greek words and/or sounds a lot like something being preached down the street at liberal churches without the "whole" gospel. Historic resistance to any recognition of non-Oneness, non-Pentecostal, and non-holiness theology has created for some a spontaneous, negative reaction to the consideration or the research of all theology but our own.

Not only are many Oneness Pentecostals resistant to theology that is taught by *others*, but we have historically been resistant to all formal education (religious and non-religious) and often find affinity with the "unlearned and ignorant men" of the early church (Acts 4:13 KJV). While experientially we know that we, like the disciples, have been with Jesus, resistance to educational efforts has impeded growth in the church's theological understanding of our personal and present role in the larger biblical theme of the *missio Dei*. While theological education has changed drastically over the last twenty years, with the creation and accreditation of UGST (now Urshan University) in Missouri and Wilson University in California, the number of Oneness people with formal and accredited graduate-level theological education is still numbered in the hundreds, while the Oneness constituents are in the tens of millions (or more). Consequently, beyond a Oneness adaptation of Dayton's classical Pentecostal quadrilateral (the godhead, evidential tongues, divine healing, and the imminent rapture of the church), this opposition often trickles down to a lack of missiological depth by the person in the pulpit and/or pew.

As well, this historic resistance to education is compounded in other areas of education; apropos to our topic here is ecological and/or biological educa-

---

12. McQuinn, "Apostolic Creationism," 7.

tion. Very few understand the symbiotic interdependence between the decline of the earth's forests and the quality of the air one breathes, or the connection between the oceanic garbage dumps off the coasts of the world's larger cities and the quality of the water we drink or the crops we grow. This lack of knowing is further complicated by an expectation that an impending rapture includes the eminent destruction of the world. Lack of knowing, coupled with the expectation of the inevitable obliteration of life on Earth, often discourages educational pursuits of knowledge and/or a passionate outcry against pollution, for conservation, and/or any other response to ecological degradation. The ignorance towards creation's need of care (to dress it and keep it, Gen 1:15) by humans, combined with the absence of seeing the church and/or individual as having an active and practical place in the *missio Dei* makes me, along with many other Oneness Pentecostals, ignorantly complicit in the current, ongoing degradation of God's creation.

Suggested Course Corrections Towards a Creational Oneness Pentecostal Missiology

So far, this research can only conclude that the majority of Oneness Pentecostals fall into one or more of the following reasons for not being involved in creation care: we are not aware of the need for creation care; we do not believe creation care is needed; we do not believe creation care will impact the outcome; and/or we do not see creation care as being theologically part of what God has called the church to be. For Oneness Pentecostals, me included, the first three reasons are secondary, for some completely irrelevant, if we do not believe the fourth reason: to see creation care as part of what God has called the church to be and do (the *missio Dei*). Unfortunately, one must also conclude that embracing creation care as part of the *missio Dei* is obstructed by Oneness Pentecostals' resistance to exploration of the biblical text beyond the accepted historic landmarks (the godhead, evidential tongues, divine healing, and the imminent rapture of the church) for fear of liberal encroachment and/or loss of "apostolic identity." Therefore, if course correction is needed (something this writer feels strongly about), it will be needed in: first, expanding Oneness Pentecostals' biblical/theological understanding of God's overarching mission (a single *missio Dei* from "In the beginning . . ." to this present moment); second, establishing how the mission of the church today must be part of God's mission, *missio iglesias*; and third, how we personally, as the Spirit-filled *imago Dei*, must be part of this same mission, *missio spiritus*.

Ever since Christopher Wright first wrote, "Mission is what the Bible is all about" in 2006, in his *The Mission of God* that established the *missio Dei* as the biblical hermeneutic,[13] the *missio iglesias,* desiring to be on task as God's mission, has struggled to amalgamate the *missio Dei* as the prevailing "biblical test" for legitimacy and authenticity for the praxis of the church. Wright centred his explanation of God's mission in the Abrahamic covenant:[14]

> Go from your country, and from your relatives and from your father's house, to the land which I will show you; and I will make you into a great nation, and I will bless you, and make your name great; and you shall be a blessing; and I will bless those who bless you, and the one who curses you I will curse. And in you all the families of the earth will be blessed. (Gen 12:1–3)

Wright connected the Abrahamic covenant's call to "be a blessing" to the creation imperative given to the first of humanity, "And God blessed them, and God said unto them, Be fruitful, and multiply, and replenish the earth, and subdue it: and have dominion over the fish of the sea, and over the fowl of the air, and over every living thing that moveth upon the earth" (Gen 1:28).

As well, Wright connected the blessings to the overarching twin imperatives of both testaments, loving God and loving neighbor (Lev 19:18; Luke 10:27), and to the great commission itself, go make disciples (Matt 28:19). Such an all-inclusive understanding of the *missio Dei* "provides a place to begin our consideration of the church's responsibility to provide care in the modern era."[15] In my book, *The Second Commandment: Loving Your Neighbor in Today's Changing World*, I argue that this missional concept is the foundation of all care:

> Such threads, seen throughout the biblical record, contain the core of God's mission – the restoration/redemption of humans as the image of God in the world. The Bible's command to "be a blessing" cannot be separated from the Great Commission – go and teach all nations – or from the great commandments: love God, love your neighbor. Ancient caregivers provided care in emulation of God's nature that was founded upon this foundation (be

---

13. Christopher J. H. Wright, *The Mission of God: Unlocking the Bible's Grand Narrative* (Downer Grove: IVP Academic, 2018), 17, 29.

14. Wright, *The Mission of God*, 60.

15. Joey Peyton, *The Second Commandment: Loving Your Neighbor in Today's Changing World* (Eugene: Wipf & Stock, 2024), 203.

a blessing to all nations, go and teach all nations, and do so while loving God/loving others).[16]

Neither can care for humanity be separated from caring for all God's creation, a creation that is imperative to the health of us all. To bifurcate the *imago Dei* (especially we who are filled with the *spirito Dei*) from a single, comprehensive *missio Dei*, is a denial of God's ongoing nature in his image that cares for the whole of creation and promotes selfishly motivated dualism.

Clearly, creation's call/command for the first people of God to be fruitful, multiply, and replenish the earth, mirrors the call/command for all future peoples of God to bless, love, and make disciples among the nations and is the totem of the *missio Dei*, and ultimately the *iglesias missio*. Wright's description of the ancient Abrahamic covenant to bless, as the summary of the *missio Dei*,[17] demands that the modern church's mission to communal blessing includes creational, relational, missional, historical, covenantal, ethical, multinational, and incarnational elements. If the Bible is about God's mission, and God's mission is about blessing the nations, then the Bible is a book about the people of God being called to be and live that blessing.[18] Therefore, one can only conclude that God's mission in the world includes, and possibly equates, the church's call to be a blessing to the nations/neighbors. Further, it should also be understood that the church, as God's intended blessing to the nations, must not limit that blessing to the Oneness Pentecostal quadrilateral (the godhead, evidential tongues, divine healing, and the imminent rapture of the church). While one may correctly argue that each leg of this quadrilateral is firmly within the church's mandate to be a blessing, limiting God's blessing in such a manner negatively impacts the church's role when caring for the created world, for our neighbors, and ultimately for living as God's unchanging mission on earth.

While many modern Oneness Pentecostals may have "little or nothing to say on the subject,"[19] seem indifferent to the subject matter, and/or make "few attempt to address it academically,"[20] efforts within the movement are beginning to expand upon these limited historic positions. Bernard's 2019 book, *Apostolic Identity in a Postmodern World*, includes a greatly expanded list of what Apostolics (Oneness Pentecostals) believe and contains an entire chapter, "God's Purpose in Creation," that identifies fourteen "creation purposes

---

16. Peyton, *The Second Commandment*, 223–24.
17. Wright, *Mission of God*, 208–16.
18. Wright, *Mission of God*, 29.
19. Norris, "Creation Revealed," 74.
20. McQuinn, "Apostolic Creationism," 20.

of God for the human race." Apropos to our conversation are the purposes: to bear God's image, to be fruitful and multiply, to have dominion over the earth, to work in God's creation, and to enjoy God's creation.[21] While Bernard's own words, "I don't have much!" is certainly true (he only includes a single-sentence explanation for each purpose); however, the inclusion of creation principles/purposes among Apostolic identity markers opens the door for others to research and explore what they mean for the church today.

In the UPCI video blog, *Apostolic Identity in the Twenty-First Century*, often used to clarify misunderstanding or confusion within segments of the church, however brief, Bernard is very clear that from the garden of Eden "taking care of God's creation and being a steward of God's creation and working to tend it is biblical . . . that is God's plan."[22] Confessionally, he admonishes that the involvement of the church in caring for creation should be "much more than . . . we have been in the past." And, "We should be good stewards . . . we have oversight of God's natural creation here on earth, of the plants and animals, so we should do our part to treat them . . . humanely . . . in a responsible way, a caring way." Unfortunately, even though this author greatly appreciates the clarity (and permission) offered/granted in this video blog and book, these statements lack the strength that would come with an understanding from teaching and preaching that fully establishes creation care within the *iglesias missio* fulfilling the *missio Dei*.

To make this change, from an isolated missiology that solely includes soteriology motivated by the eschaton to a people fully and completely living as God's blessing to the nations, Oneness Pentecostals (in general) will have to revisit the whole idea of what it means to make disciples. This is not saying the church should eliminate or minimize Dayton's Quadrilateral but expand discipleship to encompass the full breadth of the *missio Dei* and understand care and blessing as the core of the *missio iglesias*. Consequently, when making disciples throughout the world (Matt 28:19) we should also be concerned about dressing and keeping all of creation, as concerned as we are with the single act of spiritual reproduction/soteriology. Thus, we must produce disciples who live every moment filled with his Spirit as the *imago Dei* (using our God-given dominion, infused with his very nature as a blessing to our neighbors). Each day these new disciples must focus on being part of the ongoing *missio Dei*: dressing and keeping the whole of creation (Gen 1:15) in preparation for his soon return. Further, new disciples must strive to be a blessing to others (Gen

---

21. Bernard, *Apostolic Identity*, 135–37.
22. All of the quotations in this paragraph are from the Bernard video, episode 48.

12:1–3), the neighbor, the least, and the stranger, thereby jointly loving God and loving neighbor (Lev 19:18; Luke 10:27). And finally, disciple-makers fulfill the breadth of the great commission by making disciples that understand that they too are part of the eternal *missio Dei* (Matt 28:19).

David Bernard, David Norris, Clara Barton, Mitch McQuinn, and others unnamed, thankfully have exposed the theological tip of the disastrous ecological iceberg (Oneness Pentecostals' lack of concern and care for God's creation, due to our limited view of God's *missio Dei*). With Bernard, this author echoes that we Oneness Pentecostals must do more than we have in the past. Expanding on the church's understanding of the *missio Dei* as we make disciples is the place to begin. As new disciples begin to appreciate today's *iglesias missio* within the entirety of *missio Dei*, one can only pray that we will comprehend the vast need for creation care, that we will believe that creation care done by those filled with the *spirito Dei* can make a difference, and that we will impactfully participate as the *imago Dei* in the same creation care ordained in the garden at the beginning. Finally, establishing the ever-reaching *missio Dei* as the foundation (the covenant) for all theology, not only for humanity and her offspring, but "with every living creature that is with you, of the fowl, of the cattle, and of every beast of the earth with you; from all that go out of the ark, to every beast of the earth" (Gen 9:9–10).

Bibliography

Bernard, David K. *Apostolic Identity in a Postmodern World*. Weldon Springs: Word Aflame, 2019.

——— "Should Christians Be Concerned about Climate Change?" *Apostolic Life in the Twenty-First Century Podcast*. Episode 48, YouTube, 12 minutes, 49 seconds, 28 May 2022. https://www.youtube.com/watch?v=tZkNUYV2YOg.

Burton, Carla. "Climate Change and The Christian: An Ecclesiology of the Earth from an Apostolic Perspective." Paper written at Urshan Graduate School of Theology, 2023.

Dayton, Donald W. *Theological Roots of Pentecostalism*. Peabody: Hendrickson, 1987.

Johnson, Todd M. "Pentecostal/Charismatic Christianity," *World Christian Encyclopedia* 3rd ed., 27 May 2020. https://www.gordonconwell.edu/blog/pentecostal-charismatic-christianity/.

McQuinn, Mitchell. "Apostolic Creationism: Why Young Earth Creationism is the Only Position Consistent with an Apostolic Hermeneutic." Master's Thesis, Urshan Graduate School of Theology, 2019.

Norris, David S. "Creation Revealed: An Early Pentecostal Hermeneutic," In *The Spirit Renews the Face of the Earth: Pentecostal Forays in Science and Theology of Creation*, edited by Amos Yong, 74–92. Eugene: Pickwick, 2009.

Pelletier, Suzanne, et al. "Amazon Rainforest Fires," Rainforest Foundations US. Online article, 18 May 2024. https://rainforestfoundation.org/engage/brazil-amazon-fires/.

Peyton, Joey R. *The Second Commandment: Loving Your Neighbor in Today's Changing World*. Eugene: Wipf & Stock, 2024.

Wright, Christopher J. H. *The Mission of God: Unlocking the Bible's Grand Narrative*. Downer Grove: IVP Academic, 2018.

7

Materiality, Interdependence and Participation

Viewing the Renewal of Creation Through the Lens of Pentecostal Experience

Michael J. Frost

Ecological crisis is one of the most pressing issues of our time. Human culpability in the degrading of ecosystems, toxic pollution, and the extinction of species is self-evident. Moreover, the scientific consensus is that climate change – despite the ideological battles of political tribalism that muddy the waters – is also largely attributable to human action (and inaction).[1] The ecological crisis raises important questions for the Christian church and for the Pentecostal movements that have grown rapidly in the past century. Pentecostals have been criticized in some quarters for a lack of ecological consciousness in their theology and conceptions of salvation, as well as in their beliefs and practices surrounding the work of the Spirit.[2] While Pentecostal theologians have increasingly developed more socially minded Pentecostal theologies,

---

1. See Thomas Dietz, "Political Events and Public Views on Climate Change," *Climatic Change* 161, no. 1 (2020): 1–8 and Dana Nuccitelli, "How We Know the Earth Is Warming and Humans Are Responsible," *Bulletin of the Atomic Scientists* 76, no. 3 (2020): 140–44.

2. Anita Davis, "Pentecostal Approaches to Ecotheology: Reviewing the Literature," *Australasian Pentecostal Studies* 22, no. 1 (2021): 4–33, 5.

Pentecostal ecotheology remains in its infancy.[3] Pentecostal ecotheology is important for at least two important reasons. First, as a now significant global Christian movement, Pentecostal responsiveness to the climate crisis and other ecological concerns have the potential to impact the wider Christian community and global society. Secondly, much of the growth of Pentecostal spirituality has been among the poor, the Majority World, and other marginalized communities; communities who are likely to experience the harsh edge of the climate crisis, at least in the first instance.[4] The ecological crisis is not only an important issue for the global community and the future of all human life, but also an urgently looming crisis for the communities of people who make up much of the modern Pentecostal movement.

To this point, Pentecostal ecotheologies remain underdeveloped although some important work has been done to argue for the cosmic scope of the Spirit's presence and work, and to see Pentecostal distinctives such as Spirit baptism within the context of an eschatologically informed, holistic, and cosmic indwelling of all things by the Spirit. My aim here is to further interrogate the meaning of Pentecostal experiences of the Spirit by focusing on the materiality, interdependence, and participatory nature of these experiences. These features of Pentecostal experience will be taken as an insight into understanding how the Spirit acts to bring renewal and so will have implications for Pentecostal ecotheology.

Pentecostal Experience

Rather than being defined as a movement that is "Evangelicalism plus tongues" global Pentecostalism is more helpfully defined in a phenomenological sense by the centrality of pneumatic experience in the life of Pentecostal believers and the activity of the spiritual gifts.[5] This does not mean that Pentecostalism lacks theological and historical distinctions (some of those distinctions can be important in adequately understanding the various contextual forms of the movement) but rather that the diverse origins and contextual forms of Pentecostal spirituality worldwide problematize any attempt to define the move-

---

3. Andrew Ray Williams, "Flame of Creation: Pentecostal Ecotheology in Dialogue with Clark Pinnock's Pneumatology," *Journal of Pentecostal Theology* 26, no. 2 (2017): 273.

4. Edward B. Barbier and Jacob P. Hochard, "The Impacts of Climate Change on the Poor in Disadvantaged Regions," *Review of Environmental Economics and Policy* 12, no. 1 (2018): 26–47.

5. Allan Anderson, *An Introduction to Pentecostalism* (New York: Cambridge University Press, 2004).

ment in purely theological or historical terms.⁶ In fact, even what distinguishes Pentecostalism in a theological sense is not distinctive doctrinal content but rather that the task of Pentecostal theology itself is shaped by experientialist spirituality. As Peter Neumann explains, "if experience is explicitly granted such a central place in Pentecostal self-understanding, this implies experience does (and should) occupy a fundamental role in Pentecostal theological construction."⁷

When we speak of Pentecostal experience in this way we are not speaking of unmediated encounters with God that should be taken as direct revelation. Rather, Frank Macchia highlights that we are speaking of experiences that are mediated by the system of symbols (or, put differently, the cultural-linguistic framework) that shape Pentecostal experience.⁸ This requires that we pay theological attention to the beliefs and practices that give rise to this form of experientialism. Simultaneously, however, a Pentecostal view of these experiences is to see them not only as the products of beliefs and practices, but rather that the genuine presence and work of the Spirit in those experiences can consequently reshape the system of symbols, the beliefs, and practices of Pentecostal spirituality. All of this means that any attempt to incorporate Pentecostal experience into the task of theology should reflect on the dialectical relationship between the system of symbols that shape Pentecostal experiences of the Spirit, and the way those experiences can concurrently act to reshape that same system of symbols.⁹

Pentecostal Experience and Mission

If Pentecostalism is an experientialist form of Christian spirituality, it has also been characterized as an inherently missionary movement.¹⁰ In early Pentecostalism an eschatological fervor, fuelled by the belief in Christ's imminent return, provided a strong impetus for missionary endeavours. The outpour-

---

6. Michael J. Frost, *The Spirit, Indigenous Peoples and Social Change: Māori and a Pentecostal Theology of Social Engagement*, Global Pentecostal and Charismatic Studies 30 (Leiden: Brill, 2018), 25.

7. Peter D. Neumann, *Pentecostal Experience: An Ecumenical Encounter* (Eugene: Wipf & Stock, 2012), 7.

8. Frank D. Macchia, "Christian Experience in the World," *Ecumenical Trends* 31, no. 8 (2002): 10–14.

9. Macchia, "Christian Experience," 12.

10. Allen Anderson, *To the Ends of the Earth: Pentecostalism and the Transformation of World Christianity* (New York: Oxford University Press, 2013), 63.

ing of the Spirit was understood in some quarters as the "latter rain," renewing and empowering the church to usher in the salvation of souls before the *parousia*.[11] As eschatological urgency has waned in many streams of contemporary Pentecostalism however, missionary motivation has not necessarily subsided. Instead, what seems apparent is that experience of the Spirit itself is one of the primary motivators of Pentecostal mission.[12] Empowerment for mission has been connected to the infilling of the Spirit from the very early years of Pentecostalism.[13] In many respects, sanctification, glossolalia, and the spiritual gifts, eschatologically informed as they were, were not ends in themselves but were connected to the renewal of the individual and the church for the proclamation of the gospel to all nations.

While much of Pentecostalism has integrated a sense of missional urgency into its spirituality, this missional call has often been narrow in focus and intent. Pentecostals – like many evangelicals – have focused largely on the saving of souls for heaven rather than the transformation of socio-political realities on earth.[14] As A. J. Swoboda notes, "the larger Pentecostal community has struggled to face other social evils of our day such as gender inequality, political and economic corruption, and the ecological crisis."[15] Many Pentecostals have been wary of the distractions of a "social gospel," intentionally steering away from an understanding of mission that encompasses social, economic and political transformation.[16] As Keith Warrington observes, "Pentecostals have tended to view the work of the Spirit in empowering the Church to evangelise the world and not considered his role in socially transforming it."[17] Despite the reticence to focus on social programs, both local and global Pentecostal missions have consistently led to the formation of ministries of social concern and it has been the nature of Pentecostal experience itself (rather than Pentecostal

---

11. Steven Land, *Pentecostal Spirituality: A Passion for the Kingdom* (Cleveland: CPT, 2010) 75.

12. David Perry, "Spirit Baptism and Social Action: The Pentecostal Experience of Spirit Baptism as a Rationale for Social Action and Mission," *Australasian Pentecostal Studies* 16 (2014), https://aps-journal.com/index.php/APS/article/view/138.

13. Frost, *The Spirit, Indigenous Peoples and Social Change*, 26–31.

14. Gary B. McGee, "The Lord's Pentecostal Missionary Movement: The Restorationist Impulse of a Modern Mission Movement," *Asian Journal of Pentecostal Studies* 8, no. 1 (2005): 49–65.

15. A. J. Swoboda, *Tongues and Trees: Towards a Pentecostal Ecological Theology* (Blandford Forum: Deo, 2013), 12.

16. Keith Warrington, "Social Transformation in the Missions of Pentecostals: A Priority or a Bonus?" *Journal of the European Pentecostal Theological Association* 1 (2011): 20.

17. Warrington, "Social Transformation," 21.

theology) that has played a role in orienting Pentecostals toward socio-political concerns.[18] The notion of personal empowerment and of being commissioned by God for missional purpose appears to have inspired a range of missional programs aimed not only at evangelistic goals but with wider socio-political concerns in mind. Realities "on the ground" in Pentecostal communities suggest that ministries of social concern are continuing to emerge and flourish.[19]

If this is the case at the grassroots level, there are theologies of Pentecostal experience that are also seeking to explore this connection between experience and a more holistic understanding of mission. These theologies are important given our earlier claim that the meaning of experience is itself connected to the pre-existing system of symbols from which such experiences emerge. As Dhan Prakash states, "Experience in itself cannot equip one for the task of mission, it has its own limitations . . . One of the tasks of theology would be to provide a theological framework that will help Pentecostals to interpret their experience in relation with the world."[20]

Murray Dempster has argued that the mission of Jesus, as the one uniquely anointed by the Spirit, is connected to an ethic of the kingdom of God.[21] Jesus identified with the statement of Isaiah in his understanding of the coming kingdom: good news for the poor, the imprisoned, and the blind. Not only is this kingdom ethic central to the mission of Jesus, but Dempster argues that this same mission was given to the church when the Spirit who anointed Jesus was "transferred" to the church at Pentecost.[22] This charismatic transfer is not simply about power or evangelism, but about the much wider scope of the social ethic of the coming kingdom of God as embodied in the life and ministry of Jesus.

---

18. In the first instance, Douglas Petersen argues that social ministries featured a pragmatic kind of compassion that came out of a "rather vague and charitable concern toward persons who needed evangelization," but Albrecht argues for a clearer connection between the impact of Pentecostal experience and the impetus for a more socially-minded mission. Douglas Petersen, *Not by Might, Nor by Power: A Pentecostal Theology of Social Concern in Latin America* (Eugene: Wipf & Stock, 1996), 147–48; Daniel E. Albrecht, *Rites in the Spirit: A Ritual Approach to Pentecostal/Charismatic Spirituality* (Sheffield: Sheffield Academic Press, 1999), 248.

19. Donald E. Miller and Tetsunao Yamamori, *Global Pentecostalism: The New Face of Christian Social Engagement* (Berkeley: University of California Press, 2007).

20. Dhan Prakash, "Toward a Theology of Social Concern: A Pentecostal Perspective," *Asian Journal of Pentecostal Studies* 13, no. 1 (2010): 71.

21. Murray W. Dempster, "Evangelism, Social Concern and the Kingdom of God," in *Called and Empowered: Global Mission in Pentecostal Perspective*, eds. Murray W. Dempster, Byron D. Klaus, and Douglas Petersen (Peabody: Hendrickson, 1991), 22–43.

22. Dempster, "Evangelism, Social Concern and the Kingdom of God," 23.

While this connects Pentecostal experience of the Spirit to a more holistic sense of mission, it is still broadly anthropocentric. We do find, however, within the work of Frank Macchia and A. J. Swoboda, reflections on the cosmic implications of both Pentecostal experience and mission. Macchia claims that Spirit baptism is not confined to individual experience.[23] Rather, he argues that the individual experience of Spirit baptism is participation in a cosmic Spirit baptism through which all of creation is being transformed until God inhabits all things.[24] This eschatologically and cosmically informed view of Spirit baptism invites the Pentecostal to see their personal experience of Spirit baptism – and consequently, their ongoing experience of the Spirit – as a kind of "entering in" to the process of the infilling of all of creation with the Spirit of God. Swoboda takes this kind of thinking a step further to make explicit the idea that if all of creation comes to be filled with the Spirit as the *telos* of the Spirit's work, then "based on a holistic pneumatology of the church and creation, the wall of separation between human and nonhuman creation is in some way lessened by means of the Spirit who has empowered the church, and the Spirit who has 'filled the universe' (Eph 4:10)."[25] Thus, we can connect the holistic missional pneumatology of Dempster, who suggests that the mission of the Spirit is about more than evangelism but is also about socio-political concerns, with a cosmic theology of Spirit baptism and its consequent ecological implications. As Peter Althouse asserts,

> Because Pentecostals view Spirit-baptism as empowerment for mission (however limiting empowerment is for a full understanding of the doctrine), by implication the baptism of the Spirit also empowers for the care of creation. Those who have been baptized in the Spirit are representatives of the renewal of creation as God's mission in the world and are therefore called to care for creation.[26]

If there are continuities between personal experience and cosmic renewal, then we can reflect on experience as a lens for understanding the Spirit's work in renewing all things. In the remainder of this chapter, we will focus on three

---

23. Frank D. Macchia, *Baptized in the Spirit: A Global Pentecostal Theology* (Grand Rapids: Zondervan, 2006).

24. Macchia, *Baptized in the Spirit*, 93–94.

25. Swoboda, *Tongues and Trees*, 208.

26. Althouse, "Pentecostal Eco-Transformation: Possibilities for a Pentecostal Ecotheology in Light of Moltmann's Green Theology," in *Blood Cries Out: Pentecostals, Ecology, and the Groans of Creation*, ed. A. J. Swoboda (Eugene: Pickwick, 2014), 127.

further aspects of Pentecostal experience with a view toward the ecological implications therein: materiality, interdependence, and participation.

The Materiality of Pentecostal Experience

At first glance, Pentecostal experience can appear to be otherworldly.[27] First, at its worst, the urgent premillennial eschatology of early Pentecostals fostered an escapist view of human destiny in which Pentecostal mission was defined by the rescuing of souls from hell.[28] This necessarily entailed a focus on the "next life" in a way that could be described as "otherworldly." Second, otherworldliness can be seen in the centring of non-physical, spiritual experiences that are by their very nature occurring in the unseen and immaterial dimension.[29] This form of spirituality implies a kind of dualism in which spiritual and material realities are separate from one another, and in which the spiritual is of much greater importance than the material.[30]

While this way of understanding Pentecostal experience does appear to substantiate criticisms of the movement as "otherworldly," this apparent dualism of Pentecostal spirituality is not always consistent with Pentecostalism on the ground, nor is it the only way to understand the meaning and implications of Pentecostal experience. In many respects, Pentecostal experience is connected to a striking emphasis on the materiality of life in the present and to the transformation of material realities. For example, the work of scholars across global Pentecostal movements demonstrate that Pentecostalism can contribute to social uplift among the poor.[31] The experience of the Spirit is connected to a transformed view of self with an accompanying sense of boldness and courage to transform one's own social, economic, and political situation.[32] Understanding these material implications of Pentecostal spirituality and experience has the potential to foster a holistic spirituality that sees the Spirit at work in every aspect of human life.

---

27. Russell Paul Spittler, "Spirituality, Pentecostal and Charismatic," in *Dictionary of Pentecostal and Charismatic Movements*, eds. Stanley M. Burgess, Gary B. McGee, and Patrick H. Alexander (Grand Rapids: Zondervan, 1988), 805.

28. D. William Faupel, *The Everlasting Gospel: The Significance of Eschatology in the Development of Pentecostal Thought* (Sheffield: Sheffield Academic Press, 1996), 33.

29. Amos Yong, *In the Days of Caesar: Pentecostalism and Political Theology* (Grand Rapids: Eerdmans, 2010), 47.

30. Frost, *The Spirit, Indigenous Peoples and Social Change*, 267.

31. Miller and Yamamori, *Global Pentecostalism*.

32. Petersen, *Not by Might*, 43.

Perhaps this is most prominently demonstrated in the Pentecostal emphasis on healing.[33] Divine healing has been a constant emphasis within Pentecostalism since the movement's inception and, in many parts of the world, it has been healing, rather than an emphasis on glossolalia, that has been central to the growth of the movement. That certainly seems to be the case in my own context. New Zealand Pentecostalism emerged in the 1920s due to the healing ministry of the British evangelist Smith Wigglesworth, as well as the Christian Māori healer and prophet, Tahupōtiki Wiremu Rātana.[34] Moreover, Brett Knowles argues that it was the emphasis on healing that largely contributed to the rapid growth of the movement in the 1960s.[35]

While healing may be viewed as a supernatural miracle, it is also unavoidably physical and material. As James K. A. Smith argues,

> even though Pentecostals have often accepted such dualistic rejections of "the world," a core element of a Pentecostal worldview – the affirmation of bodily healing – actually deconstructs such dualism. One of the concomitant effects of this should be a broader affirmation of the goodness of embodiment and materiality, and therefore an affirmation of the fundamental goodness of spheres of culture related to embodiment.[36]

This suggests that experience of the Spirit's presence and activity is not related solely to an immaterial spiritual realm but is experienced in the material body with the resultant material transformation. As Daniel Albrecht notes, healing "has a sacramental quality for Pentecostals. In the manifestations of power God proves God's interest in the affairs of humankind in specific ways."[37] In Pentecostalism, this emphasis on healing has also been extended into other material dimensions of life including the belief that the Spirit empowers believers to overcome circumstances of poverty and, in more extreme examples of the prosperity gospel, that the Spirit empowers believers to become assured of both

---

33. More than thirty years ago Miroslav Volf highlighted the way Pentecostals incorporate divine healing into the atonement as an example of the "materiality of salvation." Miroslav Volf, "Materiality of Salvation: An Investigation in the Soteriologies of Liberation and Pentecostal Theologies," *Journal of Ecumenical Studies* 26, no. 3 (1989): 448.

34. Michael J. Frost, "Pentecostalism in Aotearoa–New Zealand," in *Asia Pacific Pentecostalism*, eds. Denise Austin, Jacqueline Grey, and Paul W. Lewis (Leiden: Brill, 2019), 347–71.

35. Brett Knowles, *Transforming Pentecostalism: The Changing Face of New Zealand Pentecostalism, 1920–2010* (Lexington: Emeth, 2014), 98, 115.

36. James K. A. Smith, *Thinking in Tongues: Pentecostal Contributions to Christian Philosophy* (Grand Rapids: Eerdmans, 2020), 42.

37. Albrecht, *Rites in the Spirit*, 247.

health and wealth.[38] While the excesses of the prosperity gospel are deserving of considerable critique, the belief that the presence and activity of the Spirit might contribute to the transformation of material realities (rather than simply some kind of otherworldly spiritual experience) is worth reflecting on.[39]

In addition to the material implications of Pentecostal experience, it is also important to consider the embodied nature of Pentecostal experience itself. In experiencing the Spirit, Pentecostals speak of various phenomena including shaking, heat or warmth, internal and external bodily sensations associated with love and power, and being "slain in the Spirit" in which one's body may fall to the floor.[40] Moreover, the spiritual gift of speaking in tongues, so often the core of Pentecostal self-identity, is unavoidably an embodied experience. When we consider this in combination with the emphasis on bodily healing that we examined earlier, what we find is not an immaterial or otherworldly set of experiences, but highly embodied experiences occurring quite distinctly in the materiality of human life. Thus, it is not only the "outcomes" of experience that may lead to transformed material circumstances, but also the very nature of those experiences themselves that highlight the presence of the Spirit in the body, in the very physicality of humanness, in the materiality of existence.

In summary, Pentecostal experience is highly embodied, involving and affecting the physicality of a person in the dimension of the Spirit's presence and activity. Moreover, these embodied (material) experiences of the Spirit often lead to what I have elsewhere called the materiality of the Spirit's work.[41] If this is the case, then Pentecostal experience is deeply connected to the transformation and renewal of materiality and this experience is "evidence" (to use classical Pentecostal language) that the Spirit vivifies and renews physical creation. This coheres well with Veli-Matti Kärkkäinen's claim that "'spirit' (*ruach, pneuma*) in the biblical understanding is not something opposed to 'earthly' or 'bodily,' but rather the divine life-energy penetrating and permeating all created reality."[42] Similarly, Swoboda argues that Pentecostal experience

---

38. Frost, *The Spirit, Indigenous Peoples and Social Change*, 30, 119.

39. Michael J. Frost, "Materiality or Materialism: Revising Pentecostal Eschatology, Renewing the Earth, and Saving the Planet from the Prosperity Gospel," *Australasian Pentecostal Studies* 22, no. 1 (2021): 104–21.

40. Michael Wilkinson, "Pentecostalism, the Body, and Embodiment," *Annual Review of the Sociology of Religion* 8 (2017): 15–35.

41. Frost, "Materiality or Materialism?"

42. Veli-Matti Kärkkäinen, "The Greening of the Spirit: Towards a Pneumatological Theology of the Flourishing of Nature," in *Blood Cries Out: Pentecostals, Ecology, and the Groans of Creation*, ed. A. J. Swoboda (Eugene: Pickwick, 2014), 91.

of the Spirit is "a renewed experience of all of creation made alive once again where 'all flesh' is endowed with God's Spirit."[43] If Pentecostals can see their own experience as connected to, rather than distinct from, the presence of the Spirit in the materiality of all creation, it is possible that Pentecostals have within their own spirituality the resources to view creation care as an entirely logical – and even necessary – part of the Spirit-filled life.

Pentecostal Experience and Interdependence

Pentecostalism is often thought of as an individualist spirituality, a spirituality perfectly designed for the modern individualist world. Swoboda argues that this is especially the case in Western forms of Pentecostalism where, "Pentecostal spiritual identity remains virtually an individualistic affair that has yet to fully incorporate communal and creational dimensions."[44] This individualism escalates further in forms of Pentecostalism that have been captured by the prosperity gospel – a modern, individualist gospel emphasizing the acquiring of personal wealth. As Gerardo Marti states, "prosperity theology empowers individuals to exercise their individuality in exactly those ways that are required by our new societal systems."[45] If this is the case in Pentecostal spirituality more broadly, these individualist descriptors can also be applied to notions of Pentecostal experience itself. John D. Griffiths states, "The Pentecostal understanding of the baptism of the Spirit has traditionally been understood in relation to the individual believer and their salvation."[46] And, as Harvey Cox states, "The core of all Pentecostal conviction [is] that the Spirit of God needs no mediators but is available to anyone in an intense, immediate, indeed interior way."[47] While experience of the Spirit is often described in personal and individualist terms, the reality of Pentecostal experience is often far more communal and interdependent, something which I argue has ecological implications for, as Davis points out, "An anthropocentric and individualistic understanding of

---

43. Swoboda, *Tongues and Trees*, 14.

44. Swoboda, *Tongues and Trees*, 13.

45. Gerardo Marti, "The Adaptability of Pentecostalism Gerardo: The Fit Between Prosperity Theology and Globalized Individualization in a Los Angeles Church," *Pneuma: The Journal of the Society for Pentecostal Studies* 34, no. 1 (2012): 24.

46. John Daniel Griffiths, "Spirit-Baptised Creation: Locating Pentecost in the Meta-Narrative of Creation and Its Implications for a Pentecostal Ecology," *Australasian Pentecostal Studies* 22, no. 1 (2021): 46.

47. Harvey G. Cox, *Fire from Heaven: The Rise of Pentecostal Spirituality and the Reshaping of Religion in the Twenty-First Century* (Reading: Addison-Wesley, 1995), 87.

the scope of salvation by Pentecostals is commonly identified as a key inhibitor to Pentecostal interest and attention to matters of ecology."[48]

Pentecostal experiences of the Spirit are not typically experienced in isolation from the gathering of church community and the rituals of Pentecostal practice. In fact, it is the communal rituals and rites of Pentecostal gatherings that often facilitate, shape, and give meaning to the experiences of individual believers. Daniel Albrecht (1999) notes the range of rituals and practices within church meetings that emphasize and facilitate the presence and activity of the Spirit.[49] This takes place, for example, within worship practices in which Albrecht observes that "during 'the worship' they [Pentecostals] sense the proximity of the Holy Spirit and the reality of close communion with the divine heightened during their singing, listening and participating in the music and the other sounds of worship."[50] Other features of the church gathering similarly emphasize God's presence and activity, whether it be through the altar call, the prayer ministry, the intention of the Pentecostal preacher for the Spirit to be heard and encountered, and so on. This means that Pentecostal experience, even when experienced by individuals, cannot be adequately understood in isolation from the wider Pentecostal community; there is an important interdependence at play here.

We often see the embodied nature of experience combined with this communal and interdependent practice of experience. One example of this can be seen in Pentecostal practice of the laying on of hands during prayer. This practice occurs during prayer ministry of many types including prayers for salvation, healing, deliverance, blessing, the infilling of the Spirit, spiritual gifts and so on.[51] This laying on of hands is not merely symbolic in the Pentecostal tradition; rather, it is often understood as a means of "impartation." Scott Lewis Adams suggests that in Acts 8:4–25 Peter and John were sent to the Samaritans to lay hands on them to transfer blessing and to dispense the Spirit (as well as to symbolize ethnic solidarity).[52] In Acts 9 we also see Paul's infilling of the Spirit (as well as the healing of his blindness) takes place via the laying on of hands by Ananias. Despite Paul's personal conversion on the road to Damascus, his embodied Pentecostal experience (so to speak) was dependent on the

---

48. Davis, "Pentecostal Approaches to Ecotheology," 5.

49. Albrecht, *Rites in the Spirit*.

50. Albrecht, *Rites in the Spirit*, 143.

51. Wolfgang Vondey, *Pentecostal Theology: A Guide for the Perplexed* (London: T&T Clark, 2012), 90.

52. Scott Lewis Adams, "The Coming of the Spirit and the Laying on of Hands: A Paradigm for Ethnic Reconciliation," *Journal of Pentecostal Theology* 29, no. 1 (2020): 128.

body of another. This is not to be confused with a priestly mediation of God's presence but that all Pentecostal believers can join with one another, helping to facilitate one another's experience of the Spirit through prayer, worship, laying on of hands, and other communal rites and rituals.[53] The experience of the Spirit is a personal experience *and* an interdependent and communal affair. As Vondey states, "This relational dimension of the transforming power of the Spirit runs against much of Western individualistic, spiritualized, and internalized ideas of the charismatic life."[54]

Not only is the Spirit experienced in community, the depth of meaning to these experiences is also predicated on their embodiment within charismatic communities. For example, the idea that all participants within a community have access to the Spirit's power and the spiritual gifts means that the democratization of the charismata can be a profound social statement, only discovered in communal contexts.[55] This observation can be made in various forms of Pentecostal communities, especially among those who are constituted by otherwise marginalized or disempowered figures.[56] The "pouring out on all flesh" of the Spirit at Pentecost is an egalitarian empowerment that should be borne out in the social realities of church communities. Pentecostal experience, available to all, can be seen as a force for overcoming systems of racial prejudice, gendered hierarchies, the marginalization of the poor, and other socio-political divisions.[57] For the purposes of our discussion here, what this means is that both the experience of the Spirit and the meaning of those experiences is reliant on the interdependence of believers in community with one another. In reflecting on the social and communal implications of the Spirit's indwelling, Swoboda[58] suggests that "In all of these contexts regarding creation, gender, and race, the Spirit-baptized creation recaptures the call to a garden where the interconnected creation lives in harmony based on the Spirit's presence."

---

53. Vondey, *Pentecostal Theology*, 90.
54. Vondey, *Pentecostal Theology*, 188.
55. Frost, *The Spirit, Indigenous Peoples and Social Change*, 125.
56. For example, Samuel Solivan claims that in Hispanic Pentecostalism the church is "a community where the dispossessed become leaders, where the voiceless are empowered by the Holy Spirit to speak not only for themselves but also for God. The non-persons, the invisible ones, become visible; the non-person is accepted as a full person, respected and loved." Samuel Solivan, *Spirit, Pathos and Liberation: Toward an Hispanic Pentecostal Theology* (New York: Continuum, 1998), 31.
57. Dempster, "Evangelism, Social Concern and the Kingdom of God," 28.
58. Swaboda, *Tongues and Trees*, 201.

Seeing interdependence at the very heart of personal experience should prompt reflection on the wider dependence of human communities not only on one another, but on the natural world and ecosystem of which they are a part and upon which they are reliant. If our experiences of the Spirit are embedded within our interdependent social relations, then those same social relations are dependent on the wider ecosystem we inhabit.[59] As Robby Waddell argues, "Put bluntly, humans simply cannot have God as their Father unless they also have Earth as their mother. The hermeneutic of identification correlates with the principle of interconnectedness. In other words, not only are humans from Earth but they are also dependent on it."[60] Human beings are of the earth, are sustained by it. This has ecological implications, and as Davis puts it, "human beings' responsibilities in relation to neighbour should be expanded to encompass the whole of the created order as neighbour; and not to do so is a sin against creation and God."[61]

Pentecostal Experience as Participatory

There has been a tendency by some to characterize the outpouring of the Spirit in Pentecostalism as spontaneous or as "suddenly from heaven," yet once again the reality of Pentecostalism does not always match the perception.[62] The ritual of the altar call, for example, asks the Pentecostal to get out of their seat and "come to the front" for an encounter with God.[63] The lifting of hands in worship is a sign of surrender to God and an openness to the Spirit. Even the early Pentecostal practice of "tarrying," in which believers would pray and wait in persistence until they experienced Spirit baptism and speaking in tongues demonstrates a thoroughgoing belief that human participation is vital to experience of the Spirit.[64] This is no kind of charismatic monergism, but rather sees the human element of participation as vital to experiences of the Spirit. As Dale Coulter suggests, "Rather than degrees of measurement, as

---

59. Amos Yong, *The Spirit of Creation: Modern Science and Divine Action in the Pentecostal-Charismatic Imagination* (Grand Rapids: Eerdmans, 2011), 61–62.
60. Waddell, "A Green Apocalypse," 139.
61. Davis, "Pentecostal Approaches to Ecotheology," 13.
62. Cox, *Fire from Heaven*.
63. Vondey, *Pentecostal Theology*, 41.
64. Vondey, *Pentecostal Theology*, 41.

though the Spirit's presence was akin to more or less water, it may be that Spirit fullness is a condition achieved by increasing cooperation with the Spirit."[65]

At times, Pentecostals can mistake this synergism for a kind of instrumentalism, in which the Spirit's power can be "used" at the beck and call of the one with sufficient faith.[66] But participation does not need to mean instrumentalism. As Chris Green explains, "Certainly, we cannot use God. Instead, we should shift to metaphors of intimacy: God collaborates with us as friends, and more than friends. In truth, even those metaphors remain too instrumentalist, because God's work is simply our work brought about from and into a fullness that both is and is not our own."[67] What we see here is genuine participation in collaborative relationship between the human and divine. Green goes on to say that "Of course, God does not need our help, our contributions," a statement that I think overdoes the distinction between creator and creaturely actions in an effort to maintain God's otherness.[68] But whether God can or cannot choose to act without our help or contribution, the fact remains that God does not appear to act this way in Pentecostal experiences of the Spirit. God's actions in the world are more helpfully understood as necessarily requiring the participation of creation, including humankind, in those actions. This is true of Pentecostal experience, and I think it is true of a Pentecostal way of seeing divine agency in the world to bring about renewal in every material dimension.

This has profound implications for a Pentecostal ecotheology in that any abdication of responsibility due to an expectation of direct divine intervention at some point in the future is misguided and even negligent. Rather than waiting for God to renew creation by Godself, the participatory nature of Pentecostal experience suggests that human agents must also play their role in the renewal of the cosmos.[69] Increased agency and an assurance of their valid place in God's world and God's mission, put alongside a theological paradigm that includes creation care and cosmic renewal, can provide Pentecostals with

---

65. Dale Coulter, "Delivered by the Power of God: Toward a Pentecostal Understanding of Salvation," *International Journal of Systematic Theology* 10, no. 4 (2008): 465.

66. We see this in the extremes of the faith movement, for example, Frost, *The Spirit, Indigenous Peoples and Social Change*, 59.

67. Chris E. W. Green, "If I Could Just Touch the Hem of His Garment: Mediation in Pentecostal Spirituality and Theology," *Journal of Pentecostal Theology* 30, no. 1 (2021): 28.

68. Green, "If I Could Just Touch," 28.

69. Indeed, the enhanced sense of confidence, self-worth and personal agency that we see among Pentecostals, especially those at the margins, supports this perspective. See Eugene Baron, "Protecting Our Environment: The Need for South African Youth with a Mission and Black Consciousness," *HTS Teologiese Studies/Theological Studies* 77, no. 2 (2021): e1–e9.

the belief that they have a genuine role to play in ecological transformation. Further, as Swoboda claims, a Pentecostal theology that takes seriously human participation in the renewal of all things will require "a more process-oriented understanding of healing where laying of hands is equally as important. As we lovingly lay our hands on the soil, the tree, and the animal to care, healing is possible. And creation can, through God's Spirit, heal creation over years, decades, and generations."[70]

What may require a more thorough interrogation at some point is how Pentecostals anticipate the final eschatological making of all things new. While this is in the realm of speculation, I think there is little to be gained from anticipating some momentous and interruptive divine action in the future that does not in some way rely on human participation and collaboration in making all things new. In fact, despite the attempts of contemporary eschatology to emphasize the "this-worldly" nature of the coming renewal, if God is nevertheless seen to ultimately act independently of human and creaturely action, or if human action is ultimately unnecessary, then of what real importance is human participation in creation care? Instead, taking Pentecostal experience of the Spirit as a model for divine action, perhaps human participation is vital to the work of renewal, both now and in the eschatological future.

Conclusion

Altogether, my suggestion is that the nature and meaning of Pentecostal experience can offer a richness of resources for a missiological response to ecological degradation. If Pentecostal experience informs and empowers Pentecostal mission, and if that mission extends from the personal, to the communal, to the cosmic, then the meaning of Pentecostal experience can be brought to bear on our understanding of the ecological dimensions of the Spirit's work in the coming kingdom of God.

Rather than an otherworldly, immaterial, and individualist faith in which God's actions are spontaneous and unidirectional, Pentecostal experience offers us a different framework for spirituality and for understanding divine agency; one which has direct ecological implications. First, the embodied nature of Pentecostal experience – along with the material implications of the Spirit's presence and work – suggest to us that the work of renewal (and thus of mission) is not limited to immaterial dimensions of an interior spiritual life. Rather, the Spirit is at work in the very materiality of creation itself, from the personal

---

70. Swoboda, *Tongues and Trees*, 224.

and communal to the political, ecological, and cosmic domains of existence. The renewal of one's own body is but a microcosm of, and participation in, the renewal of the earth's body. This means that Pentecostal experience, inasmuch as it has propelled ministries of evangelism and even of social concern, could also be understood as empowerment for ecological action. Second, it challenges any individualist tendencies by relying on interdependence and interconnection in the very dynamic of Pentecostal experience itself. This challenges us to see the work of the Spirit as being present not within independent entities but within interconnections in which the whole of creation is our neighbour, to be loved and cared for as we love God and ourselves. Lastly, the participatory nature of Pentecostal experience suggests that if the Spirit's goal is to renew all of material creation, this too is dependent not just on God's actions but on creaturely collaboration with God. As those entrusted with stewardship of creation, and who are contributing significantly to ecological degradation, humankind must be at the forefront of creaturely responsiveness to the Spirit's action to renew all of creation and make it the dwelling place of God.

The beliefs and practices of Pentecostalism necessarily inform the meaning of Pentecostal experience for believers and so this is an invitation to broaden the theology and rituals that both foster and interpret these experiences. Perhaps we could envisage a Pentecostal altar call whereupon believers are called forward to receive prayer and the laying on of hands so that they might be empowered by the Spirit toward ecologically mindful actions? Or we could imagine a gathering in which Pentecostals who desire a holistic gift of healing might be anointed with oil and sent out into the world to plant trees and clean up rivers? Could the infilling of the Spirit be understood to provide the empowerment, boldness, and confidence needed for believers to protest against climate injustice? This requires a missiology that can shape ecological interpretations of experiencing the Spirit; one that connects personal experience with cosmic renewal, and – which I have argued here – sees the Spirit's presence and work as oriented toward materiality interdependence and participation.

Bibliography

Adams, Scott Lewis. "The Coming of the Spirit and the Laying on of Hands: A Paradigm for Ethnic Reconciliation." *Journal of Pentecostal Theology* 29, no. 1 (2020): 113–32.

Albrecht, Daniel E. *Rites in the Spirit: A Ritual Approach to Pentecostal/Charismatic Spirituality*. Sheffield: Sheffield Academic Press, 1999.

Althouse, Peter. "Pentecostal Eco-Transformation: Possibilities for a Pentecostal Eco-theology in Light of Moltmann's Green Theology." In *Blood Cries Out: Pentecostals,*

Ecology, and the Groans of Creation, edited by A. J. Swoboda, 116–32. Eugene: Pickwick, 2014.

Anderson, Allan. *An Introduction to Pentecostalism*. Cambridge University Press, 2004.

———. *To the Ends of the Earth: Pentecostalism and the Transformation of World Christianity*. New York: Oxford University Press, 2013.

Barbier, Edward B., and Jacob P. Hochard. "The Impacts of Climate Change on the Poor in Disadvantaged Regions." *Review of Environmental Economics and Policy* 12, no. 1 (2018): 26–47.

Baron, Eugene. "Protecting Our Environment: The Need for South African Youth with a Mission and Black Consciousness." *HTS Teologiese Studies/Theological Studies* 77, no. 2 (2021): e1–e9.

Coulter, Dale. "'Delivered by the Power of God': Toward a Pentecostal Understanding of Salvation." *International Journal of Systematic Theology* 10, no. 4 (2008): 447–67.

Davis, Anita. "Pentecostal Approaches to Ecotheology: Reviewing the Literature." *Australasian Pentecostal Studies* 22, no. 1 (2021): 4–33.

Dempster, Murray W. "Evangelism, Social Concern and the Kingdom of God," In *Called and Empowered: Global Mission in Pentecostal Perspective*, edited by Murray W. Dempster, Byron D. Klaus and Douglas Petersen, 22–43. Peabody: Hendrickson, 1991.

Dietz, Thomas. "Political Events and Public Views on Climate Change." *Climatic Change* 161, no. 1 (2020): 1–8.

Faupel, D. William. *The Everlasting Gospel: The Significance of Eschatology in the Development of Pentecostal Thought*. Sheffield: Sheffield Academic Press, 1996.

Frost, Michael J. "Materiality or Materialism?: Revising Pentecostal Eschatology, Renewing the Earth, and Saving the Planet from the Prosperity Gospel." *Australasian Pentecostal Studies* 22, no. 1 (2021): 104–21.

———. "Pentecostalism in Aotearoa–New Zealand." In *Asia Pacific Pentecostalism*, edited by Denise Austin, Jacqueline Grey, and Paul W. Lewis, 347–71. Leiden: Brill, 2019.

———. *The Spirit, Indigenous Peoples and Social Change: Māori and a Pentecostal Theology of Social Engagement*. Global Pentecostal and Charismatic Studies 30. Leiden: Brill, 2018.

Green, Chris E. W. "'If I Could Just Touch the Hem of His Garment': Mediation in Pentecostal Spirituality and Theology." *Journal of Pentecostal Theology* 30, no. 1 (2021): 20–29.

Griffiths, John Daniel. "Spirit-Baptised Creation: Locating Pentecost in the Meta-Narrative of Creation and its Implications for a Pentecostal Ecology." *Australasian Pentecostal Studies* 22, no. 1 (2021): 46–60.

Kärkkäinen, Veli-Matti. "The Greening of the Spirit: Towards a Pneumatological Theology of the Flourishing of Nature." In *Blood Cries Out: Pentecostals, Ecology, and the Groans of Creation*, edited by A. J. Swoboda, 41–57. Eugene: Pickwick, 2014.

Knowles, Brett. *Transforming Pentecostalism: The Changing Face of New Zealand Pentecostalism, 1920–2010*. Lexington: Emeth, 2014.

Land, Steven Jack. *Pentecostal Spirituality: A Passion for the Kingdom*. Cleveland: CPT, 2010.

Macchia, Frank D. *Baptized in the Spirit: A Global Pentecostal Theology*. Grand Rapids: Zondervan, 2006.

———. "Christian Experience and Authority in the World." *Ecumenical Trends* 31, no. 8 (2002): 10–14.

Marti, Gerardo. "The Adaptability of Pentecostalism: The Fit Between Prosperity Theology and Globalized Individualization in a Los Angeles Church." *Pneuma: The Journal of the Society for Pentecostal Studies* 34, no. 1 (2012): 5–25.

McGee, Gary B. "The Lord's Pentecostal Missionary Movement: The Restorationist Impulse of a Modern Mission Movement." *Asian Journal of Pentecostal Studies* 8, no. 1 (2005): 49–65.

Miller, Donald E., and Tetsunao Yamamori. *Global Pentecostalism: The New Face of Christian Social Engagement*. Berkeley: University of California Press, 2007.

Neumann, Peter D. *Pentecostal Experience: An Ecumenical Encounter*. Eugene: Wipf & Stock, 2012.

Nuccitelli, Dana. "How we Know the Earth is Warming and Humans are Responsible." *Bulletin of the Atomic Scientists* 76, no. 3 (2020): 140–44.

Perry, David. "Spirit Baptism and Social Action: The Pentecostal Experience of Spirit Baptism as a Rationale for Social Action and Mission." *Australasian Pentecostal Studies* 16 (2014). https://aps-journal.com/index.php/APS/article/view/138.

Petersen, Douglas. *Not by Might, Nor by Power: A Pentecostal Theology of Social Concern in Latin America*. Eugene: Wipf & Stock, 1996.

Prakash, Dhan. "Toward a Theology of Social Concern: A Pentecostal Perspective." *Asian Journal of Pentecostal Studies* 13, no. 1 (2010): 65–97.

Smith, James K. A. *Thinking in Tongues: Pentecostal Contributions to Christian Philosophy*. Grand Rapids: Eerdmans, 2010.

Solivan, Samuel. *Spirit, Pathos and Liberation: Toward an Hispanic Pentecostal Theology*. New York: Continuum, 1998.

Spittler, Russell Paul. "Spirituality, Pentecostal and Charismatic." In *Dictionary of Pentecostal and Charismatic Movements*, edited by Stanley M. Burgess, Gary B. McGee, and Patrick H. Alexander, 804–9. Grand Rapids: Zondervan, 1988.

Studebaker, Steven M. "The Spirit in Creation: A Unified Theology of Grace and Creation Care." *Zygon: Journal of Religion and Science* 43, no. 4 (2008): 943–60.

Swoboda, A. J. "Eco-Glossolalia: Emerging Twenty-First Century Pentecostal and Charismatic Ecotheology." *Rural Theology* 9, no. 2 (2011): 101–16.

———. *Tongues and Trees: Towards a Pentecostal Ecological Theology*. Blandford Forum: Deo, 2013.

Volf, Miroslav. "Materiality of Salvation: An Investigation in the Soteriologies of Liberation and Pentecostal Theologies." *Journal of Ecumenical Studies* 26, no. 3 (1989): 447–67.

Vondey, Wolfgang. *Pentecostal Theology: Living the Full Gospel*. New York: Bloomsbury, 2017.

Waddell, Robby. "A Green Apocalypse: Comparing Secular and Religious Eschatological Visions of Earth." In *Blood Cries Out: Pentecostals, Ecology, and the Groans of Creation*, edited by A. J. Swoboda, 133–51. Eugene: Pickwick, 2014.

Warrington, Keith. "Social Transformation in the Missions of Pentecostals: A Priority or a Bonus?" *Journal of the European Pentecostal Theological Association* 1 (2011): 17–35.

Wilkinson, Michael. "Pentecostalism, the Body, and Embodiment." *Annual Review of the Sociology of Religion* 8 (2017): 15–35.

Williams, Andrew Ray. "Flame of Creation: Pentecostal Ecotheology in Dialogue with Clark Pinnock's Pneumatology." *Journal of Pentecostal Theology* 26, no. 2 (2017): 272–85.

Yong, Amos. *In the Days of Caesar: Pentecostalism and Political Theology*. Grand Rapids: Eerdmans, 2010.

———. *The Spirit of Creation: Modern Science and Divine Action in the Pentecostal-Charismatic Imagination*. Grand Rapids: Eerdmans, 2011.

8

Beyond Eco-Mission

Toward a Zoological Imperative in Theological Discourse

Daniela Rizzo

The contemporary ecological dilemma poses a global ethical challenge for humanity, inviting a comprehensive response that draws from various ethical perspectives, including Christian theology. Moreover, extinction and consequent nonhuman suffering prompt inquiries into the nature of the role and extent of Christian mission. Today, we are confronted with rapid shifts in atmospheric conditions, leading to temperatures exceeding typical interglacial levels due to escalating CO_2 levels. This, coupled with a myriad of ecological stressors such as habitat fragmentation, pollution, overfishing, overhunting, invasive species, and pathogens, presents unprecedented challenges for countless species. Furthermore, the expansion of human biomass adds additional strain to our ecosystems. Without concerted efforts to address these pressing issues, they are poised to worsen over time, exacerbating the extinction crisis, particularly given the complex intersection between these stressors.[1] A staggering statistic reveals that more than 99.9 percent of all species that have ever existed on Earth are now extinct, underscoring a pattern of significant species

---

1. Anthony D. Barnosky, et al., "Has the Earth's Sixth Mass Extinction Already Arrived?," *Nature* 471, no. 7336 (March 3, 2011): 56. While recognizing anthropocentrism and human-induced violence beyond colonial and capitalist realms, we must address the specific nature of today's climate change and violence against non-human animals.

disappearance across Earth's history, often within relatively brief geological periods.[2] Current assessments of extinction rates, though varied, suggest a rate at least 100 times higher than the natural background extinction rate over the long term. Current data paints a concerning picture, revealing an average decline of 69 percent in species abundance between 1970 and 2018, with wild animals now constituting only a mere 4 percent of the total global biomass.[3] Consequently, the ongoing ecological crisis has been labelled as the sixth mass extinction event.

Practical theology operates at the intersection of crisis and opportunity, navigating the delicate balance between present realities and potential futures. In the Anthropocene era, where human actions significantly influence the planet's fate, crises manifest in various forms, from problematic circumstances to critical decision-making moments.[4] Practical theologians are tasked with delving deeper into these dynamics of change, addressing ingrained habits that contribute to ecological degradation alongside traditional human-focused crises. This expanded perspective calls for urgent reactive responses to immediate threats like the global climate crisis, while also emphasizing proactive and anticipatory actions to safeguard the planet's future.

From this premise, conservation transcends its practical dimensions to assume a theological significance, casting environmental stewardship as an integral facet of a mission known as eco-mission. Rooted in the ethos of eco-mission, a zoological focus amplifies the imperative to safeguard animal habitats, prevent species extinction, and foster biodiversity, thus championing the flourishing of non-human creatures. This approach aims to acknowledge the

---

2. Barnosky, et al., "Has the Earth's," 51.

3. Rosamunde Almond, M. Grooten, D. Juffe Bignoli, and T. Petersen, eds., *Living Planet Report 2022: Building a Nature-Positive Society* (Gland: WWF, 2022), 31.

4. The term "Anthropocene" combines anthropos (human) and kainos (new, recent), suggesting a geological epoch marked by humanity's significant influence on Earth's geological layers. It signifies the transition from the Holocene, characterized by agricultural and societal development, due to profound human impacts on planetary processes. In Craig Ritchie's dissertation, he makes note of indigenous and decolonial scholars who have critiqued the discourse surrounding the Anthropocene for its overarching "one world" framework and fatalistic undertones. Indigenous scholars argue that the notion of a singular future "end of the world" and the idea that "we are all in it together" amplify colonial narratives that portray extinction or eradication as inevitable for indigenous peoples and other marginalized communities. Additionally, they contend that this discourse obscures the underlying social conflicts of the Anthropocene, including the reality that the world currently facing its demise was only made possible by the destruction of numerous other worlds, the repercussions of which continue to be felt today. See Craig Ritchie, "Extinction in the Anthropocene: A Critical Analysis" (PhD diss., University of Kent, 2022), 137.

interdependence of all sentient creatures while underscoring humanity's sacred responsibility to nurture the earth.

By prioritizing the welfare of animals and their ecosystems, zoological mission embodies a holistic approach to stewardship that extends beyond anthropocentric concerns. It prompts a re-evaluation of existing missiological frameworks to embrace this expansive perspective and advocates for active involvement to safeguard sentient life on our planet.

Extinction as a Theological Problem

Anthropocentric perspectives prioritize the benefits nature provides to humans, often framed as ecosystem services or within planetary boundaries conducive to human flourishing. While this approach may inspire efforts to protect ecosystems, it can also lead to a bias towards human interests. From a theological standpoint, this perspective may be considered incomplete, as it fails to fully embrace the biblical depiction of God's concern for animals, exemplified in God's covenant with Noah and the animals (Gen 9:9–10) and passages like Psalm 104:17–22, which highlight God's care for all living creatures, irrespective of human involvement. The biblical text portrays animals as capable of expressions like praise and lament, suggesting that they live in relationship with God and respond to divine love according to their nature. While lacking apparent reflective consciousness like humans, animals still bear witness to the Creator's power, challenging the notion that divine relationship is exclusive to humans.[5] This expanded understanding of spirituality challenges anthropocentric perspectives and highlights animals' unique relationship with God as co-creatures enlivened by the life-giving Spirit. In this context, an eco-mission perspective deepens Christian concern for animals and our shared environments, recognizing the interdependence of all creation in the pursuit of flourishing lives. A zoological focus within our theology underscores the importance of stewardship practices that extend beyond human-centric concerns to encompass the wellbeing of all creatures. The scriptural expressions of creation as the fitting abode for creaturely existence is a fundamental feature of Abrahamic faiths, however, Christian theology has historically overlooked the significance of individual species' lives and deaths. While Christian environmental ethics often addresses extinctions as indicative of larger issues such

---

5. For a detailed theological discourse on animal sentience, see my article: D. Rizzo, "Animal Glossolalia: A Pneumatological Framework for Animal Theology," *Pneuma: Journal for the Society for Pentecostal Studies* 46, no. 1 (2024), 64.

as industrialism, modernity, or colonialism, specific attention to nonhuman lives and deaths remains minimal within Christian discourse.[6] Andrew Linzey echoes this sentiment and affirms that, "Christians entrusted with a ministry of reconciliation to the whole of creation need to be credible signs of the Gospel for which all creatures long."[7]

For Sigurd Bergmann, extinction (in the context of anthropogenic climatic change) can be regarded as human sin due to its connection to the broader human failing of fetishizing power. This mindset leads to the disenchantment of the sacredness inherent in earth and life, reducing them to mere instruments for dominance.[8] From a Christian ecological perspective, recognizing this distortion of power allows us to discern the Holy Spirit's presence in the struggles of all living creatures, including those facing extinction.

Pentecostal scholar Anita Davis offers a feminist perspective on sin concerning non-human creation. She suggests a relational interpretation of sin, viewing it as actions or attitudes that disrupt the intended harmony between creator and creation. Sin, according to Davis, opposes the transformative vision of Pentecost, which seeks to unite all of creation in divine communion. This understanding of sin goes beyond mere ethical wrongdoing; it encompasses a deeper alienation of creation from its source of life. From an eco-feminist standpoint, sin manifests as unjust oppression of both women and nonhuman creatures, stemming from a denial of their interconnectedness with God. Ultimately, sin against one another and against nonhuman creation is fundamentally a sin against God. The Pentecostal perspective highlights the relational dynamics between Creator and creation, underlining the disordered state of creation. That is, "the relational relativity of Creator and creation in Christ by the Spirit and the vocational call to humanity through Pentecost provides the basis for understanding the current state of creation."[9] Understanding extinction as a consequence of unjust fragmentation and exploitation of creaturely life underscores the need to view our neighbours, both human and nonhuman, as equals rather than commodities.

---

6. Willis Jenkins, "Loving Swarms: Religious Ethics amid Mass Extinction," in *Extinction and Religion*, Religion and the Human Series. eds. Jeremy H. Kidwell and Stefan Skrimshire (Bloomington: Indiana University Press, 2024), 20.

7. Andrew Linzey, *Animal Gospel* (Louisville: Westminster John Knox, 1998), 15.

8. Sigurd Bergmann, "Where on Earth Does the Spirit 'Take Place' Today? Considerations on Pneumatology in the Light of the Global Environmental Crisis," in *Christian Faith and the Earth: Current Paths and Emerging Horizons in Ecotheology*, ed. Ernst M. Conradie (New York: Bloomsbury, 2014), 62.

9. Anita Davis, "Pentecostal Theological Perspective: Reviewing the Literature," *Australasian Pentecostal Studies* 22, no. 1 (2021): 62–63.

The incarnate presence of Christ in the world signifies redemption and transformation, serving as the locus of God's definitive self-disclosure and the apex from which God's engagement with the created order is most fully realized. This pivotal moment embodies God's relationship with humanity and the material realm, marking a divine entry into the deepest dimensions of spatial and temporal existence. Historical accounts of Jesus depict him as intimately attuned to the natural world, finding communion with God not solely in conventional settings like temples or households, but also amidst the open expanse of hillsides, gardens, and wilderness. His seamless interaction with both urban and natural environments, coupled with his frequent use of natural imagery and metaphors, underscores a kinship with the created order.

While the historical Jesus offers a contextualized human expression of divine wisdom, it is imperative to transcend this limited framework and embrace the broader Christological significance inherent in his identity. The concept of the Word becoming flesh extends beyond the confines of Jesus of Nazareth, encompassing God's presence within all matter and the natural world itself. Within this expanded theological paradigm, the proximity of God to humanity becomes palpable, with divine presence permeating every aspect of existence. For Moltmann, the encounter with God, catalysed by the advent of the Spirit, transcends the limitations of particular individuals, groups, or even species. It extends its embrace to encompass the boundless breadth of creation, embracing "all flesh" in its expansive, creaturely entirety.[10] This expansive vision resonates with his understanding of the Spirit's work that extends beyond the human realm, resonating with every form of life. Pneumatology further enriches this perspective by revealing the Spirit's creative and sustaining presence within the fabric of creation, underscoring the inseparable bond between the Creator and his creatures.

Matthew Eaton rightly perceives extinction as a profound expression of eschatological tragedy and loss. For Eaton, extinction not only extinguishes specific forms of divine revelation but also reverberates within the divine essence indefinitely.[11] He suggests that extinction can be seen as a form of divine annihilation resulting from violence, proposing the term "ecocide" as a parallel to "deicide." He clarifies that ecocide does not imply the complete obliteration

---

10. Jürgen Moltmann, *The Spirit of Life: A Universal Affirmation*, trans. Margeret Kohl (London: SCM, 1999), 57.

11. Matthew Eaton, "Ecocide as Deicide: Eschatological Lamentation and the Possibility of Hope," in *Integral Ecology for a More Sustainable World: Dialogues with Laudato Si'*, eds. Dennis O'Hara, Matthew Eaton, and Michael T. Ross (London: Lexington, 2019), 363.

of earth but rather the temporary disruption of its creative harmony, where human actions subjugate planetary creativity to one species' dominance over others. This disruption, imbued with ecological cruciformity, will be lamented eschatologically. In Eaton's view, Christ's embodiment emphasizes the sanctity of physical existence, elevating creaturely concerns and experiences to the realm of the divine. A crucial aspect of this is the understanding of suffering, which plays a significant role in defining divine identity and experience. The pivotal event in shaping this understanding within Christian tradition is the crucifixion, where Jesus's death is interpreted as a rejection of the oppressive power and violence wielded by the Roman Empire. Jesus stands in opposition to the brutality used by the elite to maintain control over diverse communities, particularly the marginalized. Therefore, the cross is not seen as a passive acceptance of the fate of vulnerable bodies but rather as a divine protest against the sovereignty of the powerful at the expense of the weak. Jesus, embodying human vulnerability, becomes a champion for the oppressed, and his life and death follow a pattern of advocating for justice, especially when bodily integrity is violated. This concept, termed "cruciformity," suggests that God incorporates experiences of injustice, violence, and the subsequent ethical imperative for liberation into divine being. Cruciformity embodies a divine stance against violence, carrying forward into the divine essence in an eschatological sense. Eaton concludes with an ecological interpretation of Matthew 25, emphasizing that human actions toward earth and its creatures are inseparable from their actions toward God.[12]

Extinction, viewed through the lens of theology, is not merely a biological phenomenon but also a spiritual and ethical one. It represents a rupture in relationship beyond the human community into the creaturely. From a theological standpoint, extinction can be seen as a consequence of human sin and a distortion of power dynamics that prioritize human interests over the wellbeing of other creatures.[13] This perspective challenges us to confront

---

12. Eaton, "Ecocide as Deicide," 363.

13. Christopher Southgate's evolutionary-theodicy framework recognizes pre-human extinctions as integral components of the earth's evolutionary history, contributing to the diversity of life. He views them as part of the dynamic and often unpredictable nature of evolution, shaping the trajectory of life on earth. Similarly, human-induced extinctions represent a continuation of this process, albeit with a significant difference: they are driven by human activity rather than natural forces. While pre-human extinctions occur as a result of environmental change and competition, human-induced extinctions stem from factors such as habitat destruction, pollution, and overexploitation of resources. Southgate contends that these activities disrupt ecosystems and accelerate extinction rates beyond what would occur naturally. Unlike pre-human extinctions, which are part of the inherent dynamics of evolution, human-induced extinctions

the ways in which our actions, driven by greed, exploitation, and indifference, contribute to mass extinction. Extinction is not only a tragedy in itself but also a symptom of larger systemic injustices that perpetuate environmental degradation and social inequities.

Moreover, extinction raises theological questions about the nature of God's relationship with creation and the role of humanity as stewards of the earth. The biblical narrative of God's covenant with Noah and the animals highlights God's concern for all living creatures and underscores humanity's responsibility to care for and protect the diversity of life on earth.[14] Extinction, therefore, represents a failure of humanity to fulfill its sacred vocation as caretakers of creation.

In the face of extinction, eco-mission takes on renewed urgency, calling Christians to engage in acts of restoration, reconciliation, and redemption that seek to heal the wounds inflicted upon God's creation. Conservation efforts, grounded in theological principles of justice, compassion, and solidarity, become essential expressions of faith in action. Through eco-mission, Christians are called to work towards the restoration of ecosystems, the protection of endangered species, and the promotion of sustainable practices that honour the inherent value of all life forms.

---

reflect a deviation from ecological balance and pose a threat to the stability of ecosystems worldwide. In comparing pre-human and human-induced extinctions, Southgate underscores the ethical dimension of the latter. While both types of extinctions shape the evolutionary process, human-induced extinctions raise moral questions about humanity's stewardship of the earth and its responsibility to preserve biodiversity. From Southgate's perspective, addressing human-induced extinctions requires not only scientific understanding but also ethical reflection and concerted efforts to mitigate the impacts of human activity on the natural world. See Christopher Southgate, *The Groaning of Creation: God, Evolution and the Problem of Evil* (Louisville: Westminster John Knox, 2008), 124–33. See also Elizabeth A. Johnson, *Ask the Beasts: Darwin and the God of Love* (London: Bloomsbury Continuum, 2014), 248–53. Yong advances this perspective by contextualizing Romans 5 within the paradigm of evolutionary geology to account for animal death before the emergence of humans. See Amos Yong, *Renewing Christian Theology: Systematics for a Global Christianity* (Waco: Baylor University Press, 2014), 275–76.

14. I consider that amid destructive forces a remnant of animal life is saved alongside the human. The value of animal life is emphasized not just through preservation, but also through promise (covenant). For David Clough, the Noahic covenant demonstrates how "it is not only human animals that are addressed by God and called to live lives in response to God." See David L. Clough, *On Animals, Systematic Theology*, vol. 1 (London: T&T Clark, 2014), 41.

Eco-Mission: Rethinking Mission in the Context of Creation and Animal Care

A holistic response to mission involves adopting an eco-mission approach rooted in a comprehensive understanding of salvation across creation.[15] This approach transcends a narrow focus on human conversion, accenting the church's role in proclaiming God's reign and striving for inclusivity, service, and wholeness instead of dominance. Recognizing and responding to the yearnings of fellow creatures, be they animal or human, holds theological significance. It acknowledges that creation is not self-sustaining and that both animals and humans share in the burden of bondage and decay. Understanding this common struggle unites us in shared suffering and highlights the ongoing need for liberation and restoration.[16]

Eco-mission challenges us to expand our understanding of mission beyond human salvation to encompass the restoration of the entire created order. In contemplating the essence of creation, a divergence emerges from traditional perspectives that often elevate humanity to the pinnacle, whereas scholars like Woodley and Moltmann assert the Sabbath as the true crown of creation. The Sabbath, according to indigenous theologian Randy Woodley, is intertwined with the notion of rest on the seventh day and serves as a vital link to the entirety of creation. In a state where all aspects of creation are in harmony, God refrains from "labour" to delight in its perfection, as humanity, when rightly aligned with all creation, mirrors the Creator's original intentions for the world. Within the Sabbath lies the directive for all humans, as well as their working animals, to abstain from toil and instead embrace the day by acknowledging the holiness of God and the sacredness of creation. "Shalom," lived in its intended form, entails an acknowledgement that every element of

---

15. The thesis of the article is based on the notion that "mission" (as derived from Darrell L. Guder's definition) is the outcome of God's initiative, stemming from his intention to restore and heal creation. Brunner, Butler, and Swoboda draw from Guder's definition for an ecotheological context, noting that mission, meaning "sending," is a central biblical theme describing the purpose of God's action, which embraces all of creation where salvation, healing, and shalom are all part of God's mission, calling us to responsible partnership in that endeavour. See Daniel L. Brunner, Jennifer L. Butler, and A. J. Swoboda, *Introducing Evangelical Ecotheology: Foundations in Scripture, Theology, History, and Praxis* (Grand Rapids: Baker Academic, 2014), 33.

16. Andrew Linzey and Dan Cohn-Sherbok, *After Noah: Animals and the Liberation of Theology* (London: Mowbray, 1997), 84. In an ecological interpretation of Romans 8, creation's narrative unfolds as a journey from crisis to liberation. While the origins of this crisis remain unexplored, the spotlight is on God's intervention, guiding humanity and all creation towards freedom. David G. Horrell, Cherryl Hunt, and Christopher Southgate, *Greening Paul: Rereading the Apostle in a Time of Ecological Crisis* (Waco: Baylor University Press, 2010), 83.

existence is recognized as sacred.¹⁷ This perspective naturally fosters creation spirituality and care, making ecojustice, stewardship, and spirituality not just options but essential aspects. Soteriologically, it implies a theme of renewing creation, including both humanity and the environment, constituting human and eco-salvation.

In alignment with this indigenous vision, Moltmann underscores the Sabbath as the quintessential hallmark of biblical, Jewish, and Christian doctrines of creation, marking the culmination of creation through the peace it bestows. In contrast to nature's continual productivity, devoid of rest, the Sabbath bestows blessings and sacredness and unveils the world as God's creation. For humanity, recognizing the resting, celebrating, and rejoicing God on the Sabbath signifies that only through this divine rest does creation find its completion and fulfillment. It is in the Sabbath rest that the creative essence of God attains its ultimate purpose and glory. When humankind observes the Sabbath, we perceive the world as God's creation, as the Sabbath's peace allows the world to be as it was intended.¹⁸

The broader term of eco-missiology encompasses a vision of mission centred on reconciliation across all levels. In his considerations of eco-missiology, Mick Pope recognizes that the gospel extends beyond the individual relationship between oneself and Jesus, as God's involvement spans the entirety of creation, not solely human beings. Eco-missiology prioritizes the care for creation not only as an issue of ecojustice, considering that the most vulnerable, particularly the global poor, bear the brunt of environmental degradation, but

---

17. Randy Woodley, *Shalom and the Community of Creation: An Indigenous Vision* (Grand Rapids: Eerdmans, 2012), 28. For Woodley, Native American spirituality and shalom spirituality are both primarily concerned with maintaining harmony in cooperation with creation, the Creator and others.

18. Jürgen Moltmann, *God in Creation: An Ecological Doctrine of Creation*, trans. Margaret Kohl (London: SCM, 1985), 6. Moltmann emphasizes that the Sabbath carries an eschatological element, symbolizing the future.

Yong reflects on the pneumatological vision of the prophet Isaiah which illustrates messianic healing and reconciliation set in the backdrop of a peaceable kingdom, where "the Spirit is poured out upon all flesh, including the wolf and the lamb, the leopard and the kid." See Amos Yong, *The Spirit Poured Out on All Flesh: Pentecostalism and the Possibility of a Global Theology* (Grand Rapids: Baker Academic, 2005), 300. And, again, in another work, Yong emphasizes how "humans are pneumatologically interrelated not only with one another but also with non-human animals since all of life throbs with and through the breath given by the *ruach* of God." See Amos Yong, "Missio Spiritus: Towards a Pneumatological Missiology of Creation," in *Creation Care in Christian Mission*, ed. Kapya J. Kaoma, Regnum Edinburgh Centenary Series 29 (Oxford: Regnum, 2013), 127. Here, Yong suggests that the *ruach Elohim* creates, sustains, and therefore links all life together while maintaining levels of subordination dictated by relative sentience. The themes presented by Yong resonate with Moltmann's theology which underscores a pneumatologically based existence for all flesh.

also as an expression of eco-spirituality and a new perspective on stewardship. Viewing the nurturing of creation as a form of mission underscores the importance of eco-praxis, which is inherently communal rather than individualistic, thus challenging traditional notions of salvation.[19] An expanded perspective on mission emerges when we acknowledge that the church's role extends beyond human-centric conversion to proclaiming the reign of God. This vision seeks wholeness, inclusion, and service, prioritizing these over domination. As Linzey puts it, "human beings are to be stewards of God's right in creation, that is, they are to cooperate with the Spirit in actualising his right reign of peace and justice."[20]

Drawing upon Pentecostal earth-keeping practices, Paul Ede articulates that the Spirit is dynamically engaged in confronting and denouncing behaviours that run counter to the wellbeing of creation. This intervention is particularly significant in urban environments where self-centred attitudes often predominate. Ede highlights the Spirit's role in prompting us toward endeavours that foster the nurturing and responsible stewardship of the land. Reinterpreting scriptural passages traditionally embraced by the Pentecostal tradition (such as 2 Chr 7:14 and Ezek 16:47–48) challenges the anthropocentric interpretations they have often been subjected to, liberating them from alignment with anti-creational views of the end times. For Ede, the significant potential of a more expansive Pentecostal pneumatology to guide an eco-mission focused on caring for creation and fostering sustainable urban environments. Given that the most severe environmental impacts are expected to disproportionately affect urban areas, particularly the slums of the global South where Pentecostalism has a strong presence, it is imperative for Christian theology, and Pentecostal theology in particular, to actively engage with urban ecology.[21]

South African theologian, Ernst Conradie, challenges the view that Christian mission is primarily about caring for the earth, arguing that it is cosmologi-

---

19. Mick Pope, "Eco-Missiology and Narrative: A Study in Romans and Eco-Missiological Method," *Australian Journal of Mission Studies* 6, no. 2 (2012): 40–41.

20. Andrew Linzey, *Christianity and the Rights of Animals* (Eugene: Wipf & Stock, 2016), 88.

21. Paul Ede, "River from Temple: The Spirit, City Earthkeeping and Healing Urban Land," in *Blood Cries Out: Pentecostals, Ecology and the Groans of Creation*, eds. A. J. Swoboda and Steven Bouma-Prediger, 205–24 (Eugene: Pickwick, 2014), 224. The feminist theologian, Rosemary Radford Ruether, furthers that for the church to effectively engage in ecojustice ministry within its broader community, it must embody the vision of ecojustice in its teachings, worship, and actions. Ecojustice must be at the core of the church's mission as anything less would compromise its credibility. It can be argued that some communities would be unaccepting of missionaries who shared the gospel yet could not practically steward land and animals. See Evelyn Hibbert, Lance Williamson and Barbara Williamson, "Developing a Missiology for Ministry to Nomads," *Missiology: An International Review* 51, no. 2 (2023): 134.

cally illogical given humanity's recent emergence in the universe. He questions the dynamics of who is sending whom and for what purpose in this scenario, suggesting that reducing God's call to mission to the church's responsibility diminishes the richness of Christian theology. Instead of this reductionist view, Conradie proposes a deeper theological understanding by distinguishing between creation as an act (*creatio*) and as an outcome (*creatura*). He emphasizes that speaking of the world as God's creation requires a confessional kind of knowledge rooted in the historic Christian creeds, particularly in understanding the role of the Holy Spirit as the giver of life, where "Pneumatology is thus the deepest theological connection between God's creation and God's mission."[22] For Conradie, God's mission is for the flourishing of creation, with creation at its heart. Humans are not saved merely for the sake of salvation but to enable creation to flourish once again. He asserts that the church exists for the sake of the world, and humans should participate in communion with the rest of creation in celebrating the work of the Creator. Contemplating the world as God's cherished creation should ignite an ecological ethos, praxis, and spirituality. This Christian acknowledgement of the world as God's handiwork serves as the foundation for inspiring Christian mission, fostering a revitalized vision and moral impetus to confront environmental obstacles.

Linzey would be aligned with Conradie's call for a more inclusive and holistic approach to mission that embraces all creatures. When observing Christians portraying humanity as the favoured and privileged species, Linzey posits that our designation as "chosen" entails a role of service rather than mastery.[23] He argues that human "calling" is to employ our influence for the benefit of the weak, defenceless, vulnerable, unprotected, and innocent – those unable to advocate for themselves. This, he argues, embodies Christian ministry: a Christ-like service to all suffering creatures treating the other as an equal subject worthy of love, thereby fostering a more harmonious and respectful relationship with all creatures. He furthers that human distinctiveness can be characterized by the ability to serve and sacrifice for others, a standpoint

---

22. Ernst M. Conradie, "Creation and Mission," *International Review of Mission* 101, no. 2 (2012): 341. A response to Conradie's challenge in this instance is "How can the Pentecostal movement, characterized by its pragmatism, mobilize eco-mission?"

23. Linzey, *Creatures*, 104. In the Christian tradition, the ordering of human beings above other creatures has often been substantiated on the understanding that humans are uniquely created as the *imago Dei* (Gen 1:26–27). From at least Augustine onwards (particularly in the Western world), the location of human beings at the top of such hierarchy has been tied to the understanding that the divine likeness is found chiefly in human rationality. Creatures without such rationality were thus relegated to the category of "dumb beasts" (or creatures without sentience).

where humans are uniquely tasked with embodying a sacrificial priesthood, "not just for members of their same species, but for all sentient creatures."[24] These self-sacrificing actions claim that the Spirit longs for human creatures to transcend themselves, to find new ways of relating to their co-creatures.

Hence, in resonance with Linzey's perspective, I expand the concept of eco-mission to encompass a mission inclusive of all species. This expanded vision, which I refer to as "zoological mission," calls upon us to follow Christ's example by coexisting with and serving as representatives of the *imago Christi* among other creatures. Amidst the contemporary imperative for justice and peace, this mission becomes all the more crucial. To live in harmony with the Holy Spirit, the ultimate origin and sustainer of life, entails not only advocating for life, justice, and solidarity, but also extending these principles specifically to our non-human cohabitants.[25]

Zoological Mission and Animal Conservation

The convergence of conservation and eco-mission intertwines current eco- and animal theologies with tangible actions to preserve biodiversity and safeguard ecosystems. It underscores humanity's role as custodians of the earth, responsible for nurturing its flourishing. By integrating eco-mission with a specific emphasis on the wellbeing of animals, we pave the way for zoological mission. This approach extends the traditional notion of mission beyond human realms, embracing a holistic, yet specific vision that prioritizes the flourishing and protection of sentient animals.

It is important to acknowledge the distinction between ecotheology, which encompasses concerns for the entirety of creation, and animal theology, which focuses specifically on non-human creatures.[26] While both fields are significant

---

24. Linzey, *Animal Theology*, 45.

25. For Moltmann, God's profound love and care for his creation is affirmed in the existence of every creature with the Spirit actively engaging in bringing forth and sustaining life. A consequence is that God's presence is not distant but deeply embedded within every created being, immersing himself in their experiences and essence. God's love for his creatures is so powerful that it draws him out of his divine essence and into the lives of the creatures he adores, making him intimately connected to all aspects of creation. This portrayal of God as the "lover of life" and the innermost mystery of all living things underscores the active and involved role he plays in the ongoing existence and well-being of creation. Moltmann, *The Spirit of Life*, 50.

26. Linzey delineates these distinctions by offering three specific points. First, animal theologians perceive vegetarianism as the initial stride towards forging a world devoid of violence, presenting a contrasting vision of humanity's role within creation. Second, Linzey emphasizes the issue of suffering, particularly in the context of hunting (a practice that some ecotheologians do not oppose). Lastly, he examines human intervention in animal species management in

within theological discourse, recognizing this distinction becomes particularly relevant within a missiological context. When considering our obligations to animals, Linzey explains that it becomes evident that mere attempts to minimize suffering or prevent wanton destruction fall short of fulfilling our responsibilities. Instead, what is demanded is a more profound commitment – a generosity paradigm that entails generous, costly actions aimed at promoting the wellbeing of animals.[27] In examining human superiority, Linzey argues that we must move beyond a narrow conception of lordship to encompass the idea of Christ-like service. This entails understanding that true lordship inherently involves service, and genuine service implies a form of lordship.[28] Thus, recognizing our inherent value as human beings and our capacity to contribute to creation becomes integral within the framework of God's kingdom. Linzey augments this argument by underscoring that our interaction with animals highlights a unique moral obligation, reminiscent of the responsibilities parents have towards their children. Just as special relationships entail unique responsibilities, so too do our relationships with animals necessitate sacrificial, generous love as a daily moral imperative. Therefore, when advocating for animals, our actions should prioritize their individual interests rather than serving solely to advance our own agendas.[29]

While my intention here has not been to fully develop this theology, I have instead sought to propose that there exists a plausible alternative to conventional approaches to mission, which is often centred on human sinfulness and God's response to it. The essence of God's love is not merely a proclamation of

---

which conservationists may prioritize the preservation of endangered species by sacrificing or exterminating others. See Linzey's chapter on the conflict of ecotheology and animal theology. Linzey, *Creatures*, 29–44.

While I advocate for the conservation of endangered species, it is imperative to explore alternative management practices that mitigate the need for culling predatory species. Mobilizing compassionate conservation can replace killing *for* conservation. Compassionate conservation proposes an interdisciplinary approach that integrates conservation and animal protection ethics, aiming to achieve conservation outcomes while minimizing harm to the welfare of individual animals. See Ngaio J. Beausoleil, "I Am a Compassionate Conservation Welfare Scientist: Considering the Theoretical and Practical Differences Between Compassionate Conservation and Conservation Welfare," *Animals* 10, no. 2 (2020): 257. See also Arian D. Wallach, Marc Bekoff, Michael Paul Nelson, and Daniel Ramp, "Promoting Predators and Compassionate Conservation," *Conservation Biology* 29, no. 5 (2015): 1481–84.

27. Linzey, *Animal Theology*, 32. Yong concurs with Linzey on this point, noting in his reflection on Romans 5 that the redemption of the world is intricately linked to the renewal of our minds. This creaturely renewal will inspire loving behaviour, carry political significance, and advocate for the protection of the vulnerable. Yong, *Renewing Christian Theology*, 279.

28. Linzey, *Animal Theology*, 33.

29. Linzey, *Animal Theology*, 36–37.

future salvation from the earth's destructive forces but an invitation to engage in the healing process, both for ourselves and for non-human creatures, by participating in the Spirit's transforming and transformative work. This perspective necessitates a reorientation of our understanding, bridging the realms of mission, theology, and creation. A creaturely-conscious mission entails inviting fellow humans into authentic relationships with God, each other, and our co-creatures. Moreover, as the future kingdom envisions the eradication of grief and suffering, zoological mission entails alleviating such afflictions on sentient creatures in the here and now. Therefore, zoological mission serves as an act of worship, affirming the value of every creature and endorsing its flourishing as praise to God.

Zoological mission recognizes animals' vital roles in ecosystems and strives to protect their habitats, prevent species extinction, and foster biodiversity through conservation efforts. This approach emphasizes understanding and respecting the diverse needs and behaviours of different animal species, including habitat requirements, migration patterns, and social dynamics, all of which are essential for effective conservation strategies.[30] By prioritizing the flourishing of animals and their habitats, zoological mission embodies a holistic approach to stewardship that embraces the flourishing of all God's creatures while recognizing their sentience and creaturely value. Christians who actively engage in conservation both foster a connection with non-human creatures and their environments and have opportunities to encounter God's presence in the beauty and vitality of creation. These experiences, though perhaps not explicitly articulated in theological terms, cultivate a deep sense of connection, meaning, and fulfillment rooted in relationship with God. In God's garden, we discover glimpses of divine presence and purpose amidst the rhythms of nature.

---

30. According to ecologist Michael Rosenzweig, conservation efforts must be grounded in the recognition that the future of biodiversity hinges on self-sustaining ecosystems. Evidence suggests that the extent of habitat available directly correlates with species diversity. Therefore, if we desire to preserve more than a fraction of Earth's biodiversity, we must redesign our habitats to accommodate wildlife. While Rosenzweig acknowledges that this endeavour will require significant research and innovation, he suggests that reconciliation ecology offers a promising framework for achieving conservation success. Michael L. Rosenzweig, "Avoiding Mass Extinction: Basic and Applied Challenges," *The American Midland Naturalist* 153, no. 2 (2005): 200. Reconciliation ecology entails the science of devising, establishing, and maintaining new habitats to preserve species diversity in areas where humans live, work, or engage in leisure activities. This does not imply creating new habitats in reserves or restoration sites. Instead, it acknowledges that humans occupy the majority of the world's land surface and advocates for utilizing it more thoughtfully to accommodate both human needs and those of native wildlife. Michael L. Rosenzweig, *Win–Win Ecology: How the Earth's Species Can Survive in the Midst of Human Enterprise* (Oxford: Oxford University Press, 2003), 7.

Conclusion

In this chapter, I shaped the parameters of a zoological mission within an eco-missiological paradigm. Despite the absence of a specific missional approach to animals within existing Pentecostal and animal theologies, there exists considerable potential to further develop a creaturely missiology. By incorporating theological considerations of non-human creatures, tangible actions can be facilitated for environmental protection and the enhancement of biodiversity, specifically concerning animals, within the context of zoological mission.

This stress on the ontological worth of animals instigates a reassessment of anthropocentric beliefs, prompting a more conscientious approach to animal stewardship. Pentecostals can embrace and expand upon these ideals through the development of robust animal theologies, active advocacy, and collaborative efforts with like-minded individuals, scientists, communities, and organizations, thus paving the way for a more harmonious and inclusive relationship with all creatures.

Bibliography

Almond, Rosamunde, M. Grooten, D. Juffe Bignoli, and T. Petersen, eds. *Living Planet Report 2022: Building a Nature-Positive Society*. Gland: WWF, 2022.

Barnosky, Anthony D., Nicholas Matzke, Susumu Tomiya, et al. "Has the Earth's Sixth Mass Extinction Already Arrived?: Nature." *Nature* 471, no. 7336 (March 3, 2011): 51–57. https://doi.org/10.1038/nature09678.

Beausoleil, Ngaio J. "I am a Compassionate Conservation Welfare Scientist: Considering the Theoretical and Practical Differences Between Compassionate Conservation and Conservation Welfare." *Animals* 10, no. 2 (2020): 257. https://doi.org/10.3390/ani10020257.

Bergmann, Sigurd. "Where on Earth Does the Spirit 'Take Place' Today? Considerations on Pneumatology in the Light of the Global Environmental Crisis." In *Christian Faith and the Earth: Current Paths and Emerging Horizons in Ecotheology*, edited by Ernst M. Conradie, 51–64. New York: Bloomsbury, 2014.

Brunner, Daniel L., Jennifer L. Butler, and A. J. Swoboda. *Introducing Evangelical Ecotheology: Foundations in Scripture, Theology, History, and Praxis*. Grand Rapids: Baker Academic, 2014.

Clough, David L. *On Animals, Systematic Theology*. Vol. 1. London: T&T Clark, 2014.

Conradie, Ernst. "Creation and Mission." *International Review of Mission* 101, no. 2 (2012): 339–44. https://doi.org/10.1111/j.1758-6631.2012.00107.x.

———. *Secular Discourse on Sin in the Anthropocene: What's Wrong with the World?* Environment and Society Series. Lanham: Lexington, 2020.

Davis, Anita. "A Pentecostal Theological Perspective on Ecofeminism." *Journal of Pentecostal and Charismatic Christianity* 44, no. 1 (2024): 54–69.

Eaton, Matthew. "Ecocide as Deicide: Eschatological Lamentation and the Possibility of Hope." In *Integral Ecology for a More Sustainable World: Dialogues with Laudato Si'*, edited by Dennis O'Hara, Matthew Eaton, and Michael T. Ross, 359–72. London: Lexington, 2019.

Ede, Paul. "River from the Temple: The Spirit, Earthkeeping and Healing Urban Land." In *Blood Cries Out: Pentecostals, Ecology, and the Groans of Creation*, edited by A. J. Swoboda, 205–24. Eugene: Wipf & Stock, 2014.

Hibbert, Evelyn, Lance Williamson, and Barbara Williamson. "Developing a Missiology for Ministry to Nomads." *Missiology: An International Review* 51, no. 2 (2023): 123–38.

Horrell, David G, Cherryl Hunt, and Christopher Southgate. *Greening Paul: Rereading the Apostle in a Time of Ecological Crisis*. Waco: Baylor University Press, 2010.

Jenkins, Willis. "Loving Swarms: Religious Ethics amid Mass Extinction." In *Extinction and Religion*, edited by Jeremy H. Kidwell and Stefan Skrimshire, 16–59. Religion and the Human Series. Bloomington: Indiana University Press, 2024.

Johnson, Elizabeth A. *Ask the Beasts: Darwin and the God of Love*. London: Bloomsbury Continuum, 2014.

Linzey, Andrew. *Animal Gospel*. Louisville: Westminster John Knox, 1998.

———. *Animal Theology*. Champaign: University of Illinois Press, 1995.

———. *Christianity and the Rights of Animals*. Eugene: Wipf & Stock, 2016.

———. *Creatures of the Same God: Explorations in Animal Theology*. New York: Lantern, 2009.

Linzey, Andrew, and Dan Cohn-Sherbok. *After Noah: Animals and the Liberation of Theology*. London: Mowbray, 1997.

Moltmann, Jürgen. *God in Creation: A New Theology of Creation and the Spirit of God*. Translated by Margaret Kohl. Minneapolis: Fortress, 1993.

———. *The Spirit of Life: A Universal Affirmation*. Translated by Margaret Kohl. London: SCM, 1999.

Pope, Mick. "Eco-Missiology and Narrative: A Study in Romans and Eco-Missiological Method." *Australian Journal of Mission Studies* 6, no. 2 (2012): 40–47.

Radford Ruether, Rosemary. "Ecology and Theology: Ecojustice at the Centre of the Church's Mission: Creation Groaning." *Interpretation* 65, no. 4 (2011): 354–63.

Ritchie, Craig. "Extinction in the Anthropocene: A Critical Analysis." PhD diss., University of Kent, 2022. https://doi.org/10.22024/UniKent/01.02.99251.

Rizzo, Daniela. "Animal Glossolalia: A Pneumatological Framework for Animal Theology." *Pneuma: Journal for the Society for Pentecostal Studies* 46, no. 1 (2024): 60–79. https://doi.org/10.1163/15700747-bja10108.

Rosenzweig, Michael L. "Avoiding Mass Extinction: Basic and Applied Challenges." *The American Midland Naturalist* 153, no. 2 (2005): 195–208.

———. *Win-Win Ecology: How the Earth's Species Can Survive in the Midst of Human Enterprise*. Oxford: Oxford University Press, 2003.
Southgate, Christopher. *The Groaning of Creation: God, Evolution and the Problem of Evil*. Louisville: Westminster John Knox, 2008.
Wallach, Arian D., Marc Bekoff, Michael Paul Nelson, and Daniel Ramp. "Promoting Predators and Compassionate Conservation." *Conservation Biology* 29, no. 5 (2015): 1481–84.
Woodley, Randy S. *Shalom and the Community of Creation: An Indigenous Vision*. Grand Rapids: Eerdmans, 2012.
Yong, Amos. "The Missio Spiritus: Towards a Pneumatological Missiology of Creation." In *Creation Care in Christian Mission*, edited by Koama Kapya, 121–33. Regnum Edinburgh Centenary Series. Oxford: Regnum, 2015.
———. *Renewing Christian Theology: Systematics for a Global Christianity*. Waco: Baylor University Press, 2014.
———. *The Spirit Poured Out on All Flesh: Pentecostalism and the Possibility of Global Theology*. Grand Rapids: Baker Academic, 2005.

Part III

Global Perspectives

9

Pentecostals, Poverty and the Environmental Crisis

Recuperating an Ecotheology among Pentecostals in Central and Eastern Europe

Melody J. Wachsmuth & Adrian Ana

Southeastern and Eastern Europe is a complex geo-political region of interlapping and contrasting political, ethnic, and religious identities. Over the past forty years, the region has experienced drastic changes, including the fall of communism and new democratic governments, war, and entrance into the European Union. Pentecostalism is a minority Christian tradition in the region where the dominant religions in a given country are either Catholic, Orthodox, or Islam. According to the *World Christian Encyclopedia*, Croatia is 94.4 percent Christian and of that, 83.8 percent are Catholic. Protestants are 8 percent with Pentecostal believers only 3 percent of that eight.[1] Within Romania, Pentecostalism is one of the fastest growing evangelical movements. According to the 2021 national census, the total number of Pentecostals was estimated at approximately 404,475 believers (2.12 percent of the total population), growing approximately by 42,161 (11.64 percent) since the last census

---

1. Todd M. Johnson and Gina A. Zurlo, *Encyclopedia of World Christianity*, 3rd ed. (Edinburgh: Edinburgh University Press, 2020).

which was taken in 2011.[2] Pentecostalism represents the fourth largest religious affiliation after Eastern Orthodoxy, Roman-Catholicism, and the Reformed tradition which have dominated the historical religious landscapes of Romania for hundreds of years. In comparison to the other faith religions[3] and the general population demographic,[4] Romanian Pentecostalism is more evidently rural in nature and character. Out of the total number of adherents, 136,316 (33.7 percent) live in urban areas while 268,159 (66.3 percent) live in rural areas around the country.

Historically, Romanian Pentecostalism is a movement that was birthed in rural Romania, more precisely in the town of Paulis,[5] in 1922. Pentecostalism appeared in Romania during a historically complex and tumultuous time marked by the end of the First World War, in the midst of the poor peasantry. It continued to develop and grow in the context of Romania's political instability and experienced the unmeasurable repressions of diverse oppressive governments, such as monarchy, fascism, and communism.

In Croatia and Serbia, Pentecostalism stretches back to the beginning of the twentieth century, a revival first beginning among Germans in Lutheran and Reformed communities before spreading to others.[6] Among Roma communities, although revivals began in 1950s, 1960s, and 1970s – primarily in Western Europe although also in Bulgaria and Romania – Pentecostalism spread more rapidly in Central and Eastern Europe after 1989. In the mid-1990s, through a revival in Southern Serbia, hundreds were converted, and this momentum created a church-planting initiative in Serbia causing ripple effects throughout former Yugoslavia.

---

2. Institutul National de Statistică, *Recensământul Populatiei și Locuințelor 2021: Populatia Residentă după Religie.* 8 April 2024.

3. The exception being the Seventh-day Adventists, who also represent a rural religious movement.

4. The national population demographics show 9,939,102 (52.16%) live in urban areas while 9,114,713 (47.84%) live in rural areas.

5. Ciprian Balaban, *Istoria Bisericii Penticostale din Romania (1922–1989): Instituție și Harisme* (Oradea: Scriptum, 2016), 18–19; Ciprian Balaban, "Scurtă Istorie a Cultului Creștin Penticostal din Romania," in *Monografia Culutului Creștin Penticostal – Biserica lui Dumnezeu Apostolică din Romania 100 de ani de la Inființarea Primei Biserici Penticostale din Romania*, eds. Dragoș Ștefănică and Ioan Brie (Bucharest: Pleroma, 2022), 27–29.

6. Driton Krasniqi, "The Development of Pentecostalism in Southeastern European Nations: Albania, Bosnia and Herzegovina, Greece, Macedonia, Montenegro, Kosovo, Serbia," in *European Pentecostalism*, eds. William K. Kay and Anne E. Dyer (Leiden: Brill, 2011), 208; Stanko Jambrek, "Pentekostni Pokret u Hrvatskoj 1907–2007," *Kairos: Evanđeoski Teološki Časopis* 2 (2007): 210.

Within this historical context, Pentecostalism in Southeastern and Eastern Europe often displays a dualistic mentality between lived experience and espoused theology in regard to the environment. On the one hand, there is a predominant escapist theology manifesting in apathetic or dismissive attitudes toward the present environmental crisis. On the other hand, there is a long tradition of practical eco-stewardship of people in their natural environments, especially with respect to waste management, land, and animal care. In fact, in rural contexts, these communities are often dependent on the land for survival. To further complicate matters, research has often demonstrated that those in poor or marginalized communities can be disproportionately affected by the various environmental crises. This chapter will probe the diverse reasons – ranging from the effects of communism, poverty, and survival to the abundant flow of premillennial Western missionaries – for this dualism and discuss possible ways to bridge the gap between current Pentecostal theology in discrete contexts and lived experience. Given the diversity of contexts and peoples, this paper will focus primarily on Romania, Croatia, and Roma Pentecostals in Southeastern Europe.

Romania

Legacy of Communism: Living Memories of Persecution

The origin of Romanian Pentecostalism's escapist and dualistic mentality, which is deeply rooted in its theological consciousness and spirituality, can be identified in the legacy of communistic persecutions (which remain in living memory) as well as the theological inheritance of premillennial evangelical missionaries. The Communists saw Pentecostals, especially their supernatural spirituality (mysticism) and eschatology, as a potential threat to the regime, a virus that needed to be stopped. As such, the Communists took action to suppress, censor, and if possible, eliminate the Pentecostal movement altogether. This was most evident in the censorship of Pentecostal hymns,[7] the suppression of any Pentecostal publications deemed anti-communistic, such as the statements and articles of faith,[8] as well as the systematic infiltration of the agents in key positions of leadership.[9] Though many hymns were censored in

---
7. Balaban, *Istoria Bisericii Penticostale*, 114.
8. Balaban, *Istoria Bisericii Penticostale*, 148–49.
9. Balaban, *Istoria Bisericii Penticostale*, 101.

content, it is interesting to note that these hymns were generally characterized by lament and eschatological longing for liberation. This characteristic lament and eschatological longing tell in part of the brutal communistic persecutions that the Pentecostal Christian communities experienced. These persecutions entailed exorbitant fines, employment dismissals and bans, the seizure of all assets, arrests and imprisonments, physical beatings, and even martyrdom.[10]

Persecution and repression were not only limited to isolated individual incidences but were also felt holistically throughout the Pentecostal denomination. Though officially recognized by the Romanian government in 1951, the Pentecostal denomination in reality had very limited, if any, religious rights. The Communists forced the unification of all Pentecostal movements under one synchronized denomination with the scope of controlling and monitoring all religious activities.[11] They restricted the use of charismatic manifestations[12] as well as restricting the time and place where the believers could worship.[13] Preachers, pastors, and even entire communities lost their legal authorizations and rights if they did not align with the communist agenda.[14]

In this context, where lived experience and memory of the Pentecostal community was marked by inhumane persecution, physical reality became portrayed as bleak and dark. It came to be perceived as a place of evil and suffering, under the rule of Satan. As such, it is not shocking to understand why escapist theology bloomed, especially if these persecutions are placed within the wider apocalyptic context of the world wars. When physical life was threatened and physical escape seemed impossible, the only way forward for the believer was anticipating leaving the physical and escaping to the spiritual realm of existence where persecution no longer existed, to the place of true freedom where Christ is Lord and rules in supremacy. Ion-Emil Lungeanu, a representative of the Ministry of Religious Affairs, in his characterization of the Pentecostal denomination in 1974, interestingly identifies the presence of a visible and widespread escapist mentality within Pentecostalism. According to Lungeanu, due to the widespread religious Pentecostal message promoting worldly renunciation, "Christians became isolated from 'true life' and 'human happiness.' As a result of this type of life, the Pentecostals came to embrace

---

10. Balaban, *Istoria Bisericii Penticostale*, 153–56; Balaban, "Scurtă Istorie," 81–85; Ciprian Balaban, *Foc din Cer: Un Secol de Penticostalism Românesc* (Bucharest: Pleroma, 2022), 153–60.

11. Balaban, *Foc din Cer*, 111.

12. Balaban, *Istoria Bisericii Penticostale*, 145–48.

13. Balaban, *Istoria Bisericii Penticostale*, 143–44.

14. Balaban, *Istoria Bisericii Penticostale*, 143.

hopelessness and the belief that this world had no hope for redress nor salvation, but only in the world to come."[15]

Premillennial Evangelical Missionaries

The escapist mentality was not only fuelled and propelled by communistic persecution but, in a more fundamental way, was a result of the theological legacy left by premillennial evangelical missionaries, especially those tied to the Assemblies of God. Historically, the appearance and growth of Pentecostalism in Romania was, and is, largely indebted to the missionary work of the Assemblies of God, most evident through the person of Pavel Budeanu and the Danzig Biblical Institute.

Pavel Budeanu became an ordained minister of the Assemblies of God in October 1923 and actively collaborated with the Pentecostal organization until 1937.[16] During this time, Pavel Budeanu came into contact with the Bradin family, who later became the first Pentecostals in Romania. After communicating fervently with Budeanu about the Pentecostal faith, especially with respect to the baptism of the Holy Spirit and healing through faith, the Bradins were heavily influenced theologically by Budeanu's Pentecostalism which was rooted in the Assemblies of God's premillennialist rapture theology. Budeanu's influence stood not only in his communications with the Bradin family, but also his missionary visits to Romania, where in 1924, he officiated the first Pentecostal water baptism and drafted the first Pentecostal statement of faith.[17] This statement of faith, which was submitted to the Ministry of Religious Affairs for official state recognition, was a poorly translated copy of the Assemblies of God's Statements of Fundamental Truths[18] published in the weekly *Evangel* in 1916–1917 in which premillennial rapture theology is evident.[19]

The Assemblies of God's influence over Romanian Pentecostalism was not limited to the person of Pavel Budeanu, but was also visible through the influence of the Danzig Biblical Institute.[20] This biblical institute was the first Pentecostal Bible school in Eastern Europe, sponsored and established by the

---

15. Balaban, *Istoria Bisericii Penticostale*, 152.
16. Balaban, "Scurtă Istorie," 27–28.
17. Balaban, "Scurtă Istorie," 29.
18. Balaban, *Istoria Bisericii Penticostale*, 24; Valeriu Andreiescu, "Doctrinele Penticostalismului Românesc Românesc aşa cum Rezultă din Diferitele Sale Mărturisiri de Credinţă," *Pleroma* 1 (2005): 105.
19. J. W. Welch, "Statement of Fundamental Truths," *The Weekly Evangel* 172 (1917): 8.
20. Balaban, *Istoria Bisericii Penticostale*, 51; Balaban, "Scurtă Istorie," 43.

Pentecostal mission organization, the Russian and Eastern European Mission (REEM), which was affiliated with the Assemblies of God.[21] The purpose of this Bible school was to teach and grow Pentecostal ministers in Eastern Europe. One of the most prolific Romanian Pentecostals to study at this institute was Eugen Bodor, who was the leader of a major Pentecostal movement within Romania entitled, "The Christians Baptized with the Holy Spirit." Eugen Bodor, after converting to Pentecostalism, came into contact with and fell under the influence of Ianos Lerch, a REEM missionary, and Gustav H. Schmidt, the superintendent of REEM's mission.[22] Their influence over Bodor was most evident in but not restricted to the refusal of the feet washing at the eucharist and the acceptance of alcoholic drinks.[23] Bodor's ties with REEM's missionaries and its superintendent as well as his participation at the Danzig Biblical Institute led to the mass influence of the Assemblies of God over many Pentecostal communities especially during his presidency in 1932–1933.[24]

Although the Assemblies of God was not the only missionary organization active within Romania, it was by far the most influential for Romanian Pentecostalism. Other occidental missionary organizations that appeared during communist times and also held a significant impact were: Campus Crusade for Christ, Slavic Gospel Association, Operation Mobilization, European Christian Mission, The Navigators, East European Bible Mission, Open Doors, among others. These mission organizations joined together to create the Biblical Education by Extension organization through which many Bible study manuals were translated and published and then clandestinely introduced into communist countries.[25]

Exploring Attitudes Toward Creation in Evangelical Theological Journals and Pentecostal Publications

In the following section, we will describe attitudes toward creation among Romanian Pentecostal journals (including both theological and practical perspectives), Trandafir Sandru (the founder and director of the Pentecostal Theological Seminary in Bucharest, the General Secretary and Vice President

---

21. Tom Salzer, "The Danzig Gdanska Institute of the Bible," *Heritage* 8, no. 3 (1988): 9–10.
22. Balaban, *Istoria Bisericii Penticostale*, 51.
23. Balaban, *Istoria Bisericii Penticostale*, 51.
24. Balaban, "Scurtă Istorie," 38; Balaban, *Foc din Cer*, 40–41.
25. Balaban, *Istoria Bisericii Penticostale*, 168.

of the Romanian Pentecostal denomination, and the editor of Buletinul Crestin Penticostal), and the catechetic manual of the Romanian Pentecostal Church.

Romanian Pentecostal Journals (1929–1989)

The Pentecostal attitudes toward creation, presented and promoted in the Romanian Pentecostal journals (i.e. Cuvantul Adevatului, Vestitorul Evangheliei, Mangaietorul, Buletinul Crestin Penticostal, etc.) during 1929–1989, are composed of two parts: theological and practical. The theological perspective is based on the analysis of the biblical texts with respect to creation, the fall of humankind, and eschatology. The practical perspective applies the theology to agricultural practice. The former can be summarized in three points.

Nature was Created for the Happiness and Joy of Humankind

The idea that humankind represented the crown of creation was widespread throughout Romanian Pentecostalism since its early beginnings.[26] This identification of human superiority over against the rest of creation was perceived in the differences between the creative acts[27] as well as the progressive nature of the creation narrative.[28] Humankind was perceived not only as the crown of creation but also as its rulers, who represented the Creator and bore responsibility.[29] Though the Pentecostals perceived the creation narrative through an anthropocentric lens, they nonetheless understood the interconnectedness of humankind within the natural world. Most evident is the way they perceived the garden of Eden, in which humankind was placed. It was understood as the paradisiac place of blessedness where humankind could find happiness.[30]

---

26. Gheorghe Bradin, "Educația Noastră Duhovnicească," *Cuvântul Adevărului* 11 (1930): 3; Gheorghe Bradin, "Dreptarul Învățăturilor Sănătoase," *Cuvântul Adevărului* 7 (1932): 3–4; Maidan Ioachim Țunea, "Ascultați Cuvântul Domnului," *Cuvântul Adevărului* 6 (1933): 1; Gheorghe Bradin, "Calea Vieții și Calea Morții," *Cuvântul Adevărului* 8 (1935): 1; Gheorghe Bradin, "Studiu Biblic," *Vestitorul Evangheliei* 16 (1947): 3; [Unknown Author] "Dumnezeu – Creatorul," *Buletinul Cultului Penticostal* 4 (1953): 8.

27. Bradin, "Dreptarul Învățăturilor," 3–4; Bradin, "Calea Vieții," 1; [Unknown Author] "Lecțiuni Biblice," *Cuvântul Adevărului* 1 (1937): 10; Bradin "Studiu Biblic," 3; Trandafir Sandru, "Să Facem om după Chipul Nostru, după Asemănarea Noastră," *Buletinul Cultului Penticostal* 5–6 (1967): 8–9; [Unknown Author] "Indrumări," Buletinul *Cultului Penticostal* 11–12 (1973): 4.

28. [Unknown Author] "Geneza," *Buletinul Cultului Penticostal* 1–2 (1975): 7–8; Țunea, "Ascultați Cuvântul Domnului," 1.

29. [Unknown Author] "Lecțiuni Biblice," 10; Trandafir Sandru, "Să Facem om după Chipul Nostru, După Asemănarea Noastră," *Buletinul Cultului* Penticostal 5–6 (1967): 8.

30. Pavel Bochian, "Omul Vechi și Nașterea," *Buletinul Cultului Penticostal* 5–6 (1967): 2; Adam Marcu, "Căderea Omului în Păcat," *Vestitorul Evangheliei* 8 (1946): 7; Vasilie Rista, "Păcatul Venit în Lume," *Cuvântul Adevărului* 1 (1934): 8; I. D., "Creația și Nașterea din Nou," *Buletinul Cultului Penticostal* 5–6 (1962): 5.

They even go as far as stating that the garden of Eden was created solely for humankind, who were exclusively identified as the only beings able to perceive the majestic beauty and goodness of the created order and delight in it.[31] As such, creation in all its beauty and goodness was understood as the essential framework for the primordial happiness of humankind. This happiness lay in the untainted interrelationship between creation, humankind, and God.[32]

Nature's Paradigm Shift

A paradigmatic saw nature as both cursed and the theater of human salvation. Sadly, this interconnectedness between humans, nature, and God was destroyed when humankind fell into sin. Although in the Pentecostal consciousness, creation retains its beauty and goodness,[33] reflecting in itself the wisdom and glory of the Creator,[34] it is none the less branded as cursed. This cursedness is identified in the disconnected relationship between humans, animals, and the land, as well as the fundamental loss of the intended paradisiac happiness.[35] In their understanding, humankind lost its vocational role as rulers over creation,[36] and as such the appearance of disorder became evident in the form of animal aggressiveness and non-fruitful lands (thorns and thistles). It is here that the understanding of the role of creation was transformed: as it could no longer produce the happiness it was intended to produce, it became the place or theatre where humankind's salvation was to take place.[37] Founded on this theological premise, earthly life became regarded as but a transitory journey to eternal life.

---

31. Nicolae Zgârgea, "Păcatul lui Adam și Făgăduința Mântuiri," *Mângăietorul* 2 (1940): 4; Bradin, "Studiu Biblic," 2–3; Marcu, "Căderea Omului," 7.

32. Trandafir Sandru, "Noul Adam," *Vestitorul Evangheliei* 2 (1946): 5; Sandru, "Să Facem om," 8–9.

33. I. Stanciu, "Facerea Omului," *Cuvântul Adevărului* 10 (1933): 12; S. E. Miller, "Meşter Creator și Salvator," *Vestitorul Evangheliei* 18 (1947): 4–5; Zgârgea, "Păcatul lui Adam," 4; Pavel Bochian, "Să Trăim Frumos," *Buletinul Crestin Penticostal* 9–10 (1965): 4; Trandafir Sandru, "A Sosit Primăvara," *Buletinul Cultului Penticostal* 3–4 (1967): 1–2.

34. [Unknown Author] "Dumnezeu – Creatorul," 8.

35. [Unknown Author] "Lecțiuni Biblice," 11; Bradin, "Studiu Biblic," 2–3; Tandafir Sandru, "Noul Ierusalim," *Vestitorul Evangheliei* 3 (1948): 4–5; Bochian, "Omul Vechi," 2; [Unknown Author] "Căci Vremea este Aproape," *Mângăietorul* 5 (1940): 4.

36. I. D., "Creația și Nașterea," 5.

37. I. D., "Creația și Nașterea," 5; Sandru, "Noul Ierusalim," 4–5.

Nature's Eschatological Restoration and Destruction

Romanian Pentecostal eschatology was unanimously premillennial in thought. Creation, within this theological framework, was understood as being in a paradoxical eschatological tension between its future restoration and ultimate destruction. This future restoration of creation from its current futility and decay, which should reach its climax after the rapture of the church and the Holy Spirit,[38] would be fulfilled and realized in the millennial reign of Christ on earth.[39] This earthly restoration was seen as the return to the pre-fallen Edenic state of creation, where human and nature's relationships were to be restored.[40] Yet, paradoxically, after creation is restored to its primordial state of goodness, it will later be physically destroyed to make way for the new heavens and earth. This concept of the new heavens and new earth was almost unanimously understood in its literal sense meaning the total annihilation of the old created order with the scope of replacing it with a totally new physical creation.[41] As Gheorghe Bradin stated "if the fire is not literal but symbolic, then the waters that flooded the earth must also be understood as symbolic and not literal."[42]

Agrarian Agendas

The practical application of the theological Pentecostal mindset with respect to creation can be identified in the over forty agricultural articles written between 1953–1967. These articles, which contained diverse agricultural practices, tips, and calendars, followed a common theological thread in which agricultural work was identified as God-given and necessary.[43] Yet, after 1967 these agricultural essays suddenly disappeared almost indefinitely.[44] The appearance of

---

38. Trandfir Sandru, "A Doua Venire a Domnului Isus," *Vestitorul Evangheliei* 5 (1946): 5.

39. [Unknown Author] "Căci Vremea este Aproape," 4.

40. Bradin, "Educația Noastră Duhovnicească," 2; I. T., "Doamne Aduți Aminte de Mine Când Vei Veni ân Împărăția ta," *Mângâietorul* 2 (1939): 6–77; [Unknown Author] "Căci Vremea este Aproape," 4, 6.

41. Tr. C. Dincă, "Invățături despre Credința Apostolică," *Cuvântul Adevărului* 4 (1930): 5; Bradin, "Educația Noastră Duhovnicească," 2; Gheorghe Bradin, "Studiu in Apocalipsa," *Cuvântul Adevărului* 4 (1933): 6; [Unknown Author] "Căci Vremea este Aproape," 3–4; [Unknown Author] "Ce Predicăm Noi?," *Vestitorul Evangheliei* 1 (1945): 3; Aurelia Gavri, "Sună Trâmbița: Deșteptare," *Vestitorul Evangheliei* 4–5 (1945): 16.

42. Bradin, "Studiu in Apocalipsa," 6–7.

43. Unknown Author,"Ogorul Unui om Leneș," *Buletinul Cultului Penticostal* 7–8 (1963): 11; Bochian, "Să Trăim Frumos," 4; Pavel Bochian, "O Comoară Prețioasă," *Buletinul Cultului Penticostal* 5–6 (1967): 6.

44. Balaban, *Istoria Bisericii Penticostale*, 133.

these articles in the Pentecostal journals can be explained at least in part on the initial optimism of the Pentecostal community with respect to the Communists' political agrarian agenda. This is best exemplified in the apologetic works of Gheorghe Bradin, the leader of Romanian Pentecostalism (1922–1950) and the first president of the Romanian Pentecostal denomination (1950–1962). His positivity, as Ciprian Balaban states, "most likely stemmed from his poor familial village background."[45] Yet, Gheorghe Bradin was not alone. This optimistic sentiment captured the hearts of many Pentecostal believers, many of whom shared a similarly poor and agricultural background.

Trandafir Sandru

Trandafir Sandru's perspective regarding creation remained heavily rooted in the Romanian Pentecostal theological tradition. More precisely, Sandru continued to identify, anthropocentrically, that nature was ultimately created for the happiness and salvation of humankind.[46] This ultimate goal and purpose came to eclipse and overshadow creation's immediate goal, the glorification[47] and revelation of the Creator.[48] Though creation was understood as fundamentally good in its wholeness,[49] the author nonetheless continued to characterize it as something accursed.[50] According to Sandru, this state of cursedness will disappear during the millennial reign of Christ when creation will be liberated from its corruption and decay and "humankind will reclaim its lost position as the ruler of the world."[51] Though Sandru upheld a premillennialist theology, he interestingly argued against the dominant eschatological idea of a total cosmic annihilation of the created order, proposing instead the concept of its complete transformation and renewal.[52] He envisaged the cosmos as being regenerated and sanctified, ascending to a higher form of existence.

---

45. Balaban, *Istoria Bisericii Penticostale*, 149, 239–40; Balaban, *Foc din Cer*, 199–200.

46. Trandafir Sandru, *Doctrinele Biblice, ale Bisericii* (Oradea: Metanoia, 2013), 77; Trandafir Sandru, *Dogmatica Bisericii Lui Dumnezeu Apostolice Penticostale* (Oradea: Metanoia, 2017), 106.

47. Sandru, *Doctrinele Biblice*, 76; Sandru, *Dogmatica Bisericii*, 105.

48. Sandru, *Doctrinele Biblice*, 76–77; Sandru, *Dogmatica Bisericii*, 106.

49. Sandru, *Dogmatica Bisericii*, 370.

50. Sandru, *Dogmatica Bisericii*, 130.

51. Sandru, *Dogmatica Bisericii*, 350–51.

52. Sandru, *Dogmatica Bisericii*, 361–62.

Catechetic Manual of the Christian Pentecostal Denomination

The current catechism manual of the Pentecostal Church in Romania introduces and identifies creation in its wholeness as good and establishes this goodness on the basis of the divine creative act (Gen 1:31).[53] Though no explicit explanation is provided for the purpose of the visible creation, there exists none the less an implicit undertone in which, when referencing humankind's creation and their relationship to nature, humankind was created to "govern the visible creation, as a messenger of God (Gen 1:26–28; 2:19–20)."[54] In other words, creation's scope was to be governed by and subordinated to humankind, whose vocation was to be the messengers of God on earth. As such, in comparison to the Pentecostal literature presented above, the anthropocentric attitude and lens, through which Romanian Pentecostals previously viewed the created order in relation to the creation narrative, has started to change. Likewise, there exists an evident discontinuity in language with regards to the consequences of human fallenness and creation. It appears that the authors evidently avoided the use of any terminology of cursedness to describe the present creation, stating only its transitory nature.[55] Yet, from an eschatological perspective, the authors remain loyal to the premillennialist tradition and thought which they inherited, a paradoxical eschatological tension between regeneration[56] and physical annihilation.[57]

Lived Experience

At the heart of rural Romanian Pentecostalism exists an evident interconnectedness between land, animals, humans, and faith, expressed in the lived rural experiences embedded deep within nature. This interconnected relationship defines the Pentecostals' fundamental theological and practical understanding of humankind's role within and relationship with nature. Though the theological premise with regards to the environment in Romanian Pentecostalism remains largely anthropocentric and eschatological, the practical experience and ethic is paradoxically different. In the lived natural experience of Pentecostalism, believers come to perceive the beauty and goodness of creation as

---

53. Ioin Brie and Ciprian-Flavius Terinte, *Manualul Catehetic al Cultului Creștin Penticostal Biserica lui Dumnezeu Apostolică din Romania* (Bucharest: Pleroma, 2015), 25.
54. Brie and Terinte, *Manualul Catehetic*, 26.
55. Brie and Terinte, *Manualul Catehetic*, 27.
56. Brie and Terinte, *Manualul Catehetic*, 64.
57. Brie and Terinte, *Manualul Catehetic*, 65.

well as identify its divine gracious giftedness. Thus, they subconsciously offer more value and importance to the created order than their theological eschatology envisages, especially with regards to caring for the land and animals.

The land is perceived as a gift given by God. This giftedness had its roots not only in the theology of the creation narrative, but also in its sustainability in producing the fruits and vegetables necessary for life. As such, it was subconsciously and inseparably tied to the wellbeing and, ultimately, the happiness of the believer, especially in the historic context of economic impoverishment. This understanding of divine giftedness prompted and promoted the action of caring for the land and animals and identifying this care as a God-given human responsibility. As such, it is common for Pentecostal rural households to have self-sustenance family farms,[58] in which a family plants diverse fruit trees and grows vegetable gardens, utilizing organic agricultural methods. These self-sustenance farms are incomplete without the presence of diverse and essential animals such as (but not limited to) chickens, pigs, cows, and horses. It is important to note that these farms are part and parcel of the common rural family household unit. As such, the farm, land, and animals included are integral and inseparable parts of the families' everyday lived experience and livelihood. Another important aspect characteristic of the Pentecostal rural communities is waste management. Due to the history of economic instability as well as the idea of creation as a divine gift, the Pentecostals came to view any type of waste as sinful. As such, they would reuse and recycle everything in their power to eliminate the production of waste through its reutilization.

Croatia: Persistence of Dualism and the Sacred/Secular Split in Pentecostal Churches

In Croatia, in one sense, religion is everywhere as the Catholic Church is intertwined with Croatian national identity – from religious instruction in the schools, to numerous church holidays, to adherence to formal religious rituals, to the practice of religio-cultural traditions that are linked to Christianity. On the other hand, interesting discrepancies are apparent. Although Croatia has a high percentage of identification with Christianity, there is a much lower conformity with a morality linked to Catholic theology, corruption is still a big

---

58. Most Romanian farms (2.89 million farm holdings) are identified as family subsistence or semi-subsistence under two hectares. See Agatha Popescu, "Farm Structure and Farmland Concentration in Romania and in Other Selected EU's Countries with Large Utilized Agricultural Area," *Scientific Papers Series Management, Economic Engineering in Agriculture and Rural Development* 23 (2023): 604, 609.

factor in socio-political and economic spheres, and ethno-religious nationalism – which has been complicit in violence in the past – continues to manifest through story, memory, and rituals of remembrance.[59] In an essay from *Balkan Contextual Theology*, Davor Džalto discusses the difference between perception and reality in Croatia as a newer democracy – he argues that often religion is either instrumentalized or since "reduced to a symbolic enemy is excluded . . . from contributing to the common good."[60]

In this context, the Pentecostals and evangelical minorities in Southeastern Europe have been inclined – although certainly not exclusively – to privatize faith and thus there can be a dualism between "spiritual" activities and every day "secular" activities.[61] Although Croatian Pentecostals are explicitly connected to wider movements such as the Lausanne Movement and the European Evangelical Alliance, this spiritual/secular split often persists at the grassroots level. Evangelical and Pentecostal scholars have addressed this theological dualism from different spheres in scholarly articles, highlighting the necessity of a kingdom culture and the effects of a narrow concept of salvation.[62] Kerovec postulated that people lean toward a truncated view of salvation or a disembodied spirituality in Croatia because it is a kind of escapism from painful issues in one's context: "These dualistic divisions invest into the content and character of the message of the gospel so that Christians – who are characterized by the gospel itself find unexpected relief when they discover that it is 'spiritual' to keep away from the painful questions of politics, society and public life, and proclaim the establishment of a personal relationship with God."[63]

Thus, often "mission" meant a focus on individual evangelism; however, during the war in former Yugoslavia (1991–1995; 1998–1999) social action became part and parcel of church mission, providing shelter, food, and help to

---

59. Dinka Marinović Jerolimov and Siniša Zrinščak, "Religion Within and Beyond Borders: The Case of Croatia," *Social Compass* 53, no. 2 (2006): 281–82; Zoran Grozdanov and Stipe Odak, eds., *Balkan Contextual Theology: An Introduction, Routledge Studies in Religion* (London; Routledge, 2023), 5.

60. Davor Džalto, "'Democratic Jet Lag' and EUgoslav YUtopias," in *Balkan Contextual Theology: An Introduction*, eds. Zoran Grozdanov and Stipe Odak, Routledge Studies in Religion (London: Routledge, 2023), 7.

61. Although Pentecostal churches are differentiated from other neo-evangelical churches in Croatia (such as Baptist, Church of God, etc.) the neo-evangelical churches are such a small minority that denominations often cooperate and sometimes boundaries are porous.

62. Ervin Budiselić, "A Proper Understanding of the Gospel as the Key for Healthy Church Evangelism, Life and Ministry," *Kairos (Hrvatsko Izd.)* 7, no. 1 (2013): 10.

63. Roko Kerovec, "The Resurrection of Christ and the Eschatological Vision of the Kingdom of God as the Platform for Evangelistic Practice: The Challenges and Possibilities of the Evangelical Commission," *Kairos: Evangelical Journal of Theology* 11, no. 2 (2008): 206.

refugees and impoverished people.[64] Balog thoroughly analyzed holistic mission through the lens of the evangelical humanitarian organization *Agape*, in which Pentecostals were very active. In this, he explored how the war raised questions of justice, mercy and compassion in relation to the gospel and the church's action.[65]

Further, in 2017, Dražen Glavaš analyzed Christian dualism in regard to faith and the marketplace, pointing to the discrepancy between Christian confession and problems of corruption. He pointed to two primary factors: the specific influence of communism that contributed to the separation of public and private domains and the history of church-state relations in light of the dominant position of the Catholic Church.[66] In addition, Pentecostal and evangelical churches have legal rights, but because of their minority status, churches in the past felt defensive, persecuted, or misunderstood, and thus focused on either evangelism as an individualistic enterprise or church maintenance without engaging in society. This is also influenced by the lingering effects of communism where people feel helpless in the face of looming social or political problems and a low level of trust in institutions. As Glavaš noted: "The social situation is perceived as something unalterable. People often say; 'There is nothing we can do to change the situation.'"[67] This skepticism toward institutions and the state, as well as the Western Balkans' unique history, also contributes to a tendency towards dabbling in conspiracy theories and thus skepticism of climate change, both issues in certain circles.

Another influence has been missionaries from the West. Certain events – the fall of communism[68] and the wars in former Yugoslavia – precipitated a large movement of Western missionaries across borders, bringing both the

---

64. Stanko Jambrek, "The Great Commission in the Context of the Evangelical Churches of Croatia in the Second Part of the Twentieth Century," *Kairos: Evangelical Journal of Theology* 2, no. 2 (2008): 168–67.

65. Antal Balog, *Toward an Evangelical Missiology of Humanitarian Aid Ministry* (Osijek: Evangelical Theological Seminary), 300–301.

66. Dražen Glavaš, "Christian on Sunday and Atheist on Monday: Bridging the Faith and Work Gap in Croatian Culture Part 2," *Kairos (Hrvatsko Izd.)* 11, no. 1 (2017): 155–86 and "Christian on Sunday and Atheist on Monday: Bridging the Faith and Work Gap in Croatian Culture 1," *Kairos (Hrvatsko Izd.)* 11, no. 1 (2017): 168–70; Ankica Marinović and Dinka Marinkovć Jerolimov, "What about our Rights?" The State and Minority Religious Communities in Croatia: A Case Study," *Religion and Society in Central and Eastern Europe* 5, no. 1 (2012): 43.

67. Glavaš, "Christian on Sunday and Atheist Part 1," 46.

68. According to a 1996 article quoting a 1993 study, there were around 760 Western religious organizations, church, and parachurch groups working in former communist countries. See Miroslav Volf, "Fishing in the Neighbor's Pond: Mission and Proselytism in Eastern Europe," *International Bulletin of Missionary Research* 20, no. 1 (1996): 26.

best and worse the West had to offer in terms of theology, mission praxis, and various programs and initiatives.[69] In fact, Macelaru notes the significant sacred–secular split as a theological framework that many missionaries carried with them to Central and Eastern Europe.[70] There has been no systematic study in former Yugoslavia regarding the quality and impact of Western mission, although certainly there has been critique.[71] One can surmise, however, that the loss or minimizing of the doctrine of creation from Western evangelical theology would have influenced missionary contributions. Bookless notes, for example, the shift in American evangelicalism (particularly in the Bible belt) in the late nineteenth and early twentieth century that made it suspicious of science when environmentalism became a concern in the 1960s. Broadly speaking, dispensationalist leanings and an escapist eschatology meant that "Christian mission was popularly presented as saving souls from a planet destined for destruction."[72] Accompanied by this was a fear of environmentalism being linked to liberalism or New Age – thus this brand of evangelism, even with a fervor for mission, developed with anti-intellectual, anti-science, and anti-environmental tendencies.[73]

Roma Pentecostals, Social Uplift and Environmental Racism

The Roma people are Europe's largest minority, numbering about 10–12 million. However, they are not uniform in identity but live within a wide range of societies and cultures, diverse in terms of language, cultural practices and

---

69. Mark Elliott, "Western Ministries in East Central Europe and the Former Soviet Union: Cross-Purposes or the Purposes of the Cross?," *East-West Church & Ministry Report* 1 (1993): 16.

70. Marcel V. Macelaru, "Eastern Europe," in *Whole-Life Mission for the Whole Church: Overcoming the Sacred–Secular Divide through Theological Education*, eds. Mark Greene and Ian J. Shaw, ICETE Series (Carlisle: Langham Global Library, 2021), 80–83.

71. Melody J. Wachsmuth and Ksenija Magda, "'Discerning the Body,' in Cross-Cultural Relationships: A Critical Analysis of Missional Partnership in Southeastern Europe," *Kairos (Hrvatsko izd.)* 8, no. 1 (2014): 26; Davorin Peterlin, "The Wrong Kind of Missionary," *Mission Studies* 12, no. 1 (1995): 164–74.

72. Dave Bookless, "'Jesus Is Lord . . . of All?' Evangelicals, Earth Care and the Scope of the Gospel," in *Creation Care in Christian Mission*, ed. Kapya J. Kaoma, Regnum Edinburgh Centenary Series 29 (Oxford: Regnum, 2015), 111.

73. Dave Bookless, "Jesus Is Lord . . . of All?" only links this to mission influence into Africa and South America but, given the sizeable American missionary influx into the Western Balkans in the 1990s, one can make the same correlation.

religion.⁷⁴ By addressing them separately from Croatian Pentecostals, we do not intend to exoticize them as "separate" from other Pentecostals. Rather, although they were influenced and shaped by similar historical, cultural, and political forces, they simultaneously have a long, complicated, and often tragic relationship with the majority cultures around them ranging from banishment, forced assimilation, slavery, and even extermination in World War II. Today, in Central and Eastern Europe, the majority of Roma communities have higher rates of poverty, illiteracy, unemployment, sub-standard housing, and health problems. In addition, despite better transnational and national policies, they still experience severe social exclusion and anti-Gypsyism.⁷⁵

This reality interacts with environmental degradation in ways that are consistent with other marginalized communities around the globe in what has been termed "environmental racism."⁷⁶ One 2020 report published by the European Environmental Bureau and European Roma Grassroots Organizations described this in terms of less access to services, resources, and knowledge as well as participatory power in decisions, leading to more negative health outcomes and general wellbeing. The report, focusing on Roma communities in North Macedonia, Hungary, Slovakia, Bulgaria, and Romania found major issues were being cut off from clean water, trash, and sanitary services, living in hazardous areas, or forced out of communities for the sake of tourism or housing.⁷⁷ In addition, in some impoverished areas with proximity to a city

---

74. Martin Kovats, "Problems of Intellectual and Political Accountability in Respect of Emerging European Roma Policy," *JEMIE – Journal on Ethnopolitics and Minority Issues in Europe* (2001): 7. Roma identity and history is complex and beyond the scope of this chapter. For the sake of clarity, we are using the term "Roma" to encompass a wide umbrella of groups who self-identify as such or may self-identify differently but accept the term.

75. FRA, *Fundamental Rights Report 2017* (Luxembourg: European Union Agency for Fundamental Rights, 2017), 103–30, https://fra.europa.eu/sites/default/files/fra_uploads/fra-2017-fundamental-rights-report-2017_en.pdf; FRA, *Second European Union Minorities and Discrimination Survey–Main Results* (Luxemburg: European Union Agency for Fundamental Rights, 2017), https://fra.europa.eu/sites/default/files/fra_uploads/fra-2017-eu-midis-ii-main-results_en.pdf.

76. See, for example: Alice Bloch and Katharine Quarmby, "Environmental Racism, Segregation and Discrimination: Gypsy and Traveller Sites in Great Britain," *Critical Social Policy* 45, no. 1 (2024): 94–114.

77. Patrizia Heidegger and Katy Wiese, *Pushed to the Wastelands: Environmental Racism against Roma Communities in Central and Eastern Europe* (Brussels: European Environmental Bureau, 2020), 20. Wachsmuth also discusses this report in her 2021 article which highlights a story of displaced Roma, Ashkali, and Egyptians who were forced to be on a contaminated mine for eleven years in Kosovo and have experienced devastating long-lasting effects of lead poisoning as a result. See Melody J. Wachsmuth, "A Side Salad or Main Course? The Theological Importance of Creation Care in Central and Eastern Europe," *ACTA* 9 (2021): 21–36.

waste site, individuals sift through the waste looking for scrap metal to strip and sell – this exposes them to dangerous chemicals and other substances.[78]

In terms of the Roma Pentecostals in Southeastern Europe, a few contextual characteristics can be mentioned which are relevant to this chapter. First, the outpourings of the Spirit which Roma Pentecostals expect and pray for are often in marginalized communities. Second, prayer and expectation for healings in poor and marginalized communities frequently go hand and hand with how revivals began or spread or how Roma initially connect with the Pentecostal movement. Finally, the egalitarian nature of Pentecostalism in terms of access to the Spirit for all has allowed it to flourish in Roma communities, empowering the formation of local leadership.[79] In other words, they live in daily expectation of the Spirit's guidance and power, a lived theology that could perhaps be connected to the Spirit's role in sustaining creation in their local contexts.

Interestingly, in certain ways, Pentecostal Roma in Southeastern Europe are less dualistic than other Pentecostals in the region. They have a long history of being marginalized or persecuted by society and the state and, although mistrust of the state is a common theme in the Western Balkans, it is more poignant in this case. As one leader put it, "Who will [save] the Roma people besides the Roma people?"[80] Many see the church, fueled by the Spirit, as the only institutional hope for the Roma. Thus, Roma Pentecostals are not interested in a Pentecostalism that does not transform their communities and uplift the general status of their people. A prior survey of Roma Pentecostals illustrated their definition of human flourishing or "the good life." Answers covered spheres of socioeconomic (peaceful relations between Roma and non-Roma, skills to fully participate in modern life, better jobs, education), spiritual (personal growth, prayer, and mission), and family.[81] To this end, Pentecostals developed Roma kindergartens to prepare their children for school, job creation initiatives, emphasized educational, and numerous other endeavours intent on social transformation. Thus, their hope is fueled by the

---

78. For example, Wachsmuth encountered a Roma community living in dire poverty on a landfill outside of Tirana, Albania, in 2015. Individuals shared horror stories of being exposed to chemicals, rats and accidents on a daily basis.

79. Melody J. Wachsmuth, *Roma Pentecostals Narrating Identity, Trauma, and Renewal in Croatia and Serbia*, Global Pentecostal and Charismatic Studies 44 (Leiden: Brill, 2023), 196–201.

80. Melody J. Wachsmuth, "Roma Christianity in Central and Eastern Europe: Challenges, Opportunities for Mission, Modes of Significance," in *Mission in Central and Eastern Europe: Realities, Perspectives, Trends*, ed. Corneliu Constanteanu, et al. (Oxford: Regnum, 2017), 558.

81. Melody J. Wachsmuth, "The Good Life: Descriptors of Change in Roma Pentecostal Communities in Serbia and Croatia," *Spiritus: ORU Journal of Theology* 2, no. 2 (2017): 108.

Spirit who is active at transforming lives, communities, and the relationship between Roma and non-Roma.[82] Although in this way, their perspective tends to be more holistic than other Pentecostals in Croatia, there is still a tendency toward an "anthropocentric eschatology," or a focus on eternal life rather than new creation.[83] In poor and marginalized communities, a promise of escape from this world is an easier alternative rather than cultivating theological imagination to see how God could renew and refine creation around them. Daily life can be quite difficult. Thus, there is a tendency toward the focus on the miraculous separated from daily existence or only in individual healings as opposed to the possibility the Spirit could render something miraculous in their ecological spaces. In addition, the concept of sin, similar to Tallmann's observations, narrows on individual behaviour such as smoking, whilst not considering other harmful consequences to the body such as exposure through harmful chemicals in waste sites.[84]

Pentecostal Theologies of Place

Both Croatian and Roma Pentecostals, although continuing to be influenced by global Pentecostal theology, missionary groups and organizations through mission partnerships, media, and conferences, are also wrestling with their own contextual questions and approaches, some leaders becoming more nuanced and skeptical in what they accept from the West. For example, the traveling Roma Bible School, formed primarily by Roma leaders in 2022, is oriented towards applying a Pentecostal theology to the questions and issues emerging out of a Roma context.

Indeed, Pentecostalism, with its flexible, spirit-driven theology should be able to adapt and merge with the particular questions in a socio-cultural context. Although understanding of the gospel has been expanded to include social responsibility, justice, and mercy, as a result of socio-political realities, creation is still largely absent from local theologies. Despite people's depend-

---

82. Studies have shown that indeed Pentecostalism in discrete Roma communities is linked to social change. See, for example, Tatiana Zachar Podolinská and Tomáš Hrustič, "Religious Change and Its Effects on Social Change for Roma in Slovakia," *Acta Ethnographica Hungarica* 59, no. 1 (2014): 235–56.

83. Robby Waddell, "Revelation and the (New) Creation: A Prolegomenon on the Apocalypse, Science, and Creation," in *The Spirit Renews the Face of the Earth: Pentecostal Forays in Science and Theology of Creation*, ed. Amos Yong (Eugene: Wipf & Stock, 2009), 32.

84. Matthew Tallmann, "Pentecostal Ecology: A Theological Paradigm for Pentecostal Environmentalism," in *The Spirit Renews the Face of the Earth: Pentecostal Forays in Science and Theology of Creation*, ed. Amos Yong (Eugene: Wipf & Stock, 2009), 143.

ence on land in Southeastern and Eastern Europe, in terms of tourism, sustenance, and survival, rarely does the ecology of a specific geographic location enter the theological imaginary for reasons discussed above.

Developing a local theology of place, conceptually extending from the Spirit's role in creation, is a vital need for Pentecostal communities. As indigenous theologian Randy Woodley argues: "A local theology developed from within a local community and a local theology of place that considers the social history, the geologic factors, the seasons, and so on should be of primary importance to a creation theology, or any type of theology."[85] Further, Brueggemann places the question of "land" – both in a symbolic sense and literal sense – as of central importance to the Bible. The land is both physical dirt but also "is always physical dirt freighted with social meanings derived from historical experience."[86] This biblical perspective invites a Pentecostal contextual imagining of a land heavy with the remembrances of empires, wars, and persecutions, but also stunningly beautiful and rich in resources. In terms of Roma Pentecostalism, land and belonging have particular historical poignance given the history of rejection and marginalization – thus, "belonging" could be a key theme to reflect on in terms of socio-ecological relationships that foster peace and reconciliation. If it is the Spirit that brings about unity and reconciliation – how can a local theology reflect on the Spirit's role in peace and fruitfulness of the land? How can the concept of divine healing, so important in Roma Pentecostalism, be widened and deepened to extend to the land and human relationship to it?[87]

Additionally, a theology of place is intricately related to human dignity. Living sustainably in a thriving biodiverse context fosters a flourishing of humans as image bearers; conversely, dwelling in a place that is being degraded and exploited adversely affects human dignity. This is particularly noticeable, as mentioned above, in how often poor communities are living in environmentally problematic areas which are more susceptible to pollution and climate change. This connection between place, ecology, and image bearers must be overtly made to overcome the dualism.

---

85. Randy S. Woodley, *Indigenous Theology and the Western Worldview: A Decolonized Approach to Christian Doctrine* (Grand Rapids: Baker Academic, 2022), 66.

86. Walter Brueggemann, *The Land: Place as Gift, Promise, and Challenge in Biblical Faith.* Overtures to Biblical Theology (Philadelphia: Fortress, 1977), 2.

87. Shane Clifton, "Preaching the 'Full Gospel' in the Context of the Global Environmental Crises," in *The Spirit Renews the Face of the Ground: Pentecostal Forays in Science and Theology of Creation*, ed. Amos Yong (Eugene: Pickwick, 2009), 123.

If discussions regarding creation care or ecotheology are not rooted in a local theology of place, explicitly connected to the Spirit's presence in creation, they remain disembodied and abstract, merely an attempt at behaviour modification. This might explain, for example, some observations regarding student behaviours in the months after a unit on creation care was taught at the Roma Bible School. The lecturer grounded the lessons in biblical theology and later everyone participated in a trash clean-up as a class. However, in the succeeding months it was noticed – through conversations with the students and observed behaviours – that there was a certain ambivalence to this as something "other" that was either irrelevant or of lesser importance than evangelism or personal healing.[88] It seemed categorized as a vague task to "do" but still not connected with their everyday lived reality and theological praxis.

Concluding Thoughts

This chapter has postulated numerous reasons behind a sacred/secular and dualistic split that can be found in Pentecostal circles in Southeastern and Eastern Europe and suggested possible ways forward to bridging this gap between people's care of the land and their theological understanding. Given the lands' history with wars, communism, and corruption, but also as a region rich in natural beauty and resources, it would be helpful for Pentecostal theologians to postulate local theologies of place as an extension of their Spirit-empowered understanding of Christian praxis. The Spirit that hovered over the creation in the beginning and sustains creation now can also heal the deep wounds in the land as well as the relationship between people and the land. In a region which is largely collectivistic, prioritizing relationship over task, Pentecostal theologies of place must be rooted in this relational sphere of the Spirit.

Bibliography

Andreiescu, Valeriu. "Doctrinele Penticostalismului Românesc aşa cum Rezultă din Diferitele Sale Mărturisiri de Credinţă." *Pleroma* 1 (2005): 105–35.

Balaban, Ciprian. *Foc din Cer: Un Secol de Penticostalism Românesc*. Bucharest: Pleroma, 2022.

---

88. For example, after a student threw her trash on the street, I (Wachsmuth) questioned her about it, and I could see that she had made no connection between her action and her relationship with God. In a conversation with another student, he mentioned that the lecturer was "too extreme" in his ideas about creation care.

———. *Istoria Bisericii Penticostale din Romania (1922–1989): Instituție și Harisme.* Oradea: Scriptum, 2016.

———. "Scurtă Istorie a Cultului Creștin Penticostal din Romania." In *Monografia Culutului Creștin Penticostal – Biserica lui Dumnezeu Apostolică din Romania 100 de ani de la Înființarea Primei Biserici Penticostale din Romania,* edited by Dragoș Ștefănică and Ioan Brie, 27–110. Bucharest: Pleroma, 2022.

Balog, Antal. *Toward an Evangelical Missiology of Humanitarian Aid Ministry.* Osijek: Evangelical Theological Seminary, 2007.

Bauckham, Richard. *Living with Other Creatures: Green Exegesis and Theology.* London: Paternoster, 2012.

Bloch, Alice, and Katharine Quarmby. "Environmental Racism, Segregation and Discrimination: Gypsy and Traveller Sites in Great Britain." *Critical Social Policy* 45, no. 1 (2024): 94–114. https://doi.org/10.1177/02610183241229053.

Bochian, Pavel. "O Comoară Prețioasă." *Buletinul Cultului Penticostal* 5–6 (1967): 6.

———. "Omul Vechi și Nașterea la o Viață Nouă." *Buletinul Cultului Penticostal* 5–6 (1971): 2–4.

———. "Să Trăim Frumos." *Buletinul Crestin Penticostal* 9–10 (1965): 4–5.

Bookless, Dave. "Jesus Is Lord . . . of All? Evangelicals, Earth Care and the Scope of the Gospel." In *Creation Care in Christian Mission,* edited by Kapya J. Kaoma, 105–20. Regnum Edinburgh Centenary Series 29. Oxford: Regnum, 2015.

Bradin, Gheorghe. "Calea Vieții și Calea Morții." *Cuvântul Adevărului* 8 (1935): 1–4.

———. "Dreptarul Învățăturilor Sănătoase." *Cuvântul Adevărului* 7 (1932): 3–4.

———. "Educația Noastră Duhovnicească." *Cuvântul Adevărului* 8 (1930): 2–3.

———. "Educația Noastră Duhovnicească." *Cuvântul Adevărului* 11 (1930): 3.

———. "Educația Noastră Duhovnicească." *Cuvântul Adevărului* 12 (1930): 2–3.

———. "Studiu in Apocalipsa." *Cuvântul Adevărului* 4 (1933): 4–7.

———. "Studiu Biblic." *Vestitorul Evangheliei* 16 (1947): 2–3.

———. "Studiu Biblic." *Vestitorul Evangheliei* 17 (1947): 3.

Brie, Ioan, and Ciprian-Flavius Terinte. *Manualul Catehetic al Cultului Creștin Penticostal Biserica lui Dumnezeu Apostolică din Romania.* Bucharest: Pleroma, 2015.

Brueggemann, Walter. *The Land: Place as Gift, Promise, and Challenge in Biblical Faith.* Overtures to Biblical Theology. Philadelphia: Fortress, 1977.

Budiselić, Ervin. "A Proper Understanding of the Gospel as the Key for Healthy Church Evangelism, Life and Ministry." *Kairos (Hrvatsko Izd.)* 7, no. 1 (2013): 9–33.

Clifton, Shane. "Preaching the 'Full Gospel' in the Context of Global Environmental Crises." In *The Spirit Renews the Face of the Earth,* edited by Amos Yong, 117–34. Eugene: Wipf & Stock, 2009.

Dincă, Tr. C. "Învățături despre Credința Apostolică." *Cuvântul Adevărului* 4 (1930): 4–5.

Džalto, Davor. "'Democratic Jet Lag' and EUgoslav YUtopias." In *Balkan Contextual Theology: An Introduction,* edited by Zoran Grozdanov and Stipe Odak, 119–38. Routledge Studies in Religion. London: Routledge, 2023.

Elliott, Mark. "Western Ministries in East Central Europe and the Former Soviet Union: Cross-Purposes or the Purposes of the Cross?" *East–West Church & Ministry Report* 1 (1993): 16. https://www.eastwestreport.org/articles/ew01113.htm.

FRA. *Fundamental Rights Report*. Luxembourg: European Union Agency for Fundamental Rights, 2017. https://fra.europa.eu/sites/default/files/fra_uploads/fra-2017-fundamental-rights-report-2017_en.pdf.

———. *Second European Union Minorities and Discrimination Survey–Main Results*. Luxemburg: European Union Agency for Fundamental Rights, 2017. https://fra.europa.eu/sites/default/files/fra_uploads/fra-2017-eu-midis-ii-main-results_en.pdf.

Gavri, Aurelia. "Sună Trâmbița: Deșteptare." *Vestitorul Evangheliei* 4–5 (1945): 16.

Glavaš, Dražen. "Christian on Sunday and Atheist on Monday: Bridging the Faith and Work Gap in Croatian Culture 1." *Kairos (Hrvatsko Izd.)* 11, no. 1 (2017): 29–66.

———. "Christian on Sunday and Atheist on Monday: Bridging the Faith and Work Gap in Croatian Culture Part 2." *Kairos (Hrvatsko Izd.)* 11, no. 1 (2017): 155–86.

Grozdanov, Zoran, and Stipe Odak, eds. *Balkan Contextual Theology: An Introduction*. Routledge Studies in Religion. London: Routledge, 2023.

Heidegger, Patrizia, and Katy Wiese. *Pushed to the Wastelands: Environmental Racism against Roma Communities in Central and Eastern Europe*. Report. Brussels: European Environmental Bureau, 2020. www.eeb.org/library/pushed-to-the-wastelands.

I. D. "Creația și Nașterea din Nou." *Buletinul Cultului Penticostal* 5–6 (1962): 5–7.

I. T. "Doamne Aduți Aminte de Mine Când Vei Veni ân Împărăția ta." *Mângâietorul* 2 (1939): 6–7.

Institutul National de Statistică, *Recensământul Populatiei și Locuințelor 2021: Populatia Residentă după Religie*. April 8, 2024. https://www.recensamantromania.ro/rezultate-rpl-2021/rezultate-definitive-caracteristici-etno-culturale-demografice/.

Jambrek, Stanko. "Evangelism and Proselytism in Croatia." *Occasional Papers on Religion in Eastern Europe* 17, no. 5 (1997): 1–9.

———. "Pentekostni Pokret u Hrvatskoj 1907–2007." *Kairos: Evanđeoski Teološki Časopis* 2 (2007): 207–34.

———. "The Great Commission in the Context of the Evangelical Churches of Croatia in the Second Part of the Twentieth Century." *Kairos: Evangelical Journal of Theology* 2, no. 2 (2008): 153–79.

Jerolimov, Dinka Marinović, and Siniša Zrinščak. "Religion Within and Beyond Borders: The Case of Croatia." *Social Compass* 53, no. 2 (2006): 279–90. https://doi.org/10.1177/0037768606064340.

Johnson, Todd M., and Gina A. Zurlo, eds. *Encyclopedia of World Christianity*. 3rd ed. Edinburgh: Edinburgh University Press, 2020.

Kaoma, Kapya J., ed. *Creation Care in Christian Mission*. Regnum Edinburgh Centenary Series 29. Oxford: Regnum, 2015.

Kerovec, Roko. "The Resurrection of Christ and the Eschatological Vision of the Kingdom of God as the Platform for Evangelistic Practice: The Challenges and Possibilities of the Evangelical Commission." *Kairos: Evangelical Journal of Theology* 11, no. 2 (2008): 189–208.

Kovats, Martin. "Problems of Intellectual and Political Accountability in Respect of Emerging European Roma Policy." *JEMIE – Journal on Ethnopolitics and Minority Issues in Europe* (2001): 2–10.

Krasniqi, Driton. "The Development of Pentecostalism in Southeastern European Nations: Albania, Bosnia and Herzegovina, Greece, Macedonia, Montenegro, Kosovo, Serbia." In *European Pentecostalism*, edited by William K. Kay and Anne E. Dyer, 205–24. Leiden: Brill, 2011.

Macelaru, Marcel V. "Eastern Europe." In *Whole-Life Mission for the Whole Church: Overcoming the Sacred–Secular Divide through Theological Education*, edited by Mark Greene and Ian J. Shaw, 80–84. ICETE Series. Carlisle: Langham Global Library, 2021.

Marcu, Adam. "Căderea Omului în Păcat." *Vestitorul Evangheliei* 8 (1946): 7–8.

Marinović, Ankica, and Dinka Marinkovć Jerolimov. "What about Our Rights? The State and Minority Religious Communities in Croatia: A Case Study." *Religion and Society in Central and Eastern Europe* 5, no. 1 (2012): 39–53.

Miller, S. E. "Meşter Creator şi Salvator." *Vestitorul Evangheliei* 18 (1947): 4–5.

Peterlin, Davorin. "The Wrong Kind of Missionary." *Mission Studies* 12, no. 1 (1995): 164–74. https://doi.org/10.1163/157338395X00178.

Podolinská, Tatiana Zachar, and Tomáš Hrustič. "Religious Change and Its Effects on Social Change for Roma in Slovakia." *Acta Ethnographica Hungarica* 59, no. 1 (2014): 235–56. https://doi.org/10.1556/AEthn.59.2014.1.12.

Popescu, Agatha. "Farm Structure and Farmland Concentration in Romania and in Other Selected EU's Countries with Large Utilized Agricultural Area." *Scientific Papers Series Management, Economic Engineering in Agriculture and Rural Development* 23 (2023): 603–18.

Rista, Vasilie. "Păcatul Venit în Lume." *Cuvântul Adevărului* 1 (1934): 8.

Salzer, Tom. "The Danzig Gdanska Institute of the Bible." *Heritage* 8, no. 3 (1988): 8–19.

Sandru, Trandafir. *Doctrinele Biblice ale Bisericii*. Oradea: Metanoia, 2013.

———. *Dogmatica Bisericii Lui Dumnezeu Apostolice Penticostale*. Oradea: Metanoia, 2017.

———. "A Doua Venire a Domnului Isus." *Vestitorul Evangheliei* 5 (1946): 4–6.

———. "Noul Adam." *Vestitorul Evangheliei* 2 (1946): 5–6.

———. "Noul Ierusalim." *Vestitorul Evangheliei* 3 (1948): 4–5.

———. "Să facem om după chipul nostru, după asemănarea noastră." *Buletinul Cultului Penticostal* 5–6 (1967): 8–9.

———. "A Sosit Primăvara." *Buletinul Cultului Penticostal* 3–4 (1967): 1–2.

Stanciu, I. "Facerea Omului." *Cuvântul Adevărului* 10 (1933): 12.

Tallmann, Matthew. "Pentecostal Ecology: A Theological Paradigm for Pentecostal Environmentalism." In *The Spirit Renews the Face of the Earth*, edited by Amos Yong, 135–54. Eugene: Wipf & Stock, 2009.

Taylor, Dorceta. *Toxic Communities: Environmental Racism, Industrial Pollution, and Residential Mobility*. New York: New York University Press, 2014. https://doi.org/10.18574/9781479805150.

Țunea, Maidan Ioachim. "Ascultați Cuvântul Domnului." *Cuvântul Adevărului* 6 (1933): 1–3.

Volf, Miroslav. "Fishing in the Neighbor's Pond: Mission and Proselytism in Eastern Europe." *International Bulletin of Missionary Research* 20, no. 1 (1996): 26–31. https://doi.org/10.1177/239693939602000107.

Wachsmuth, Melody J. "A 'Religionless' Mission?: Reflecting on Creation's Place in Mission Theology with Reference to the Croatian Context." *Kairos (Zagreb, Croatia)* 17, no. 2 (2023): 163–77. https://doi.org/10.32862/k.17.2.4.

———. "A Side Salad or Main Course?: The Theological Importance of Creation Care in Central and Eastern Europe." *ACTA* 9 (2021): 21–36.

———. "Roma Christianity in Central and Eastern Europe: Challenges, Opportunities for Mission, Modes of Significance." In *Mission in Central and Eastern Europe: Realities, Perspectives, Trends*, edited by Corneliu Constanteanu, et al. 544–68. Oxford: Regnum, 2017.

———. *Roma Pentecostals Narrating Identity, Trauma, and Renewal in Croatia and Serbia*. Global Pentecostal and Charismatic Studies 44. Leiden: Brill, 2023. https://ezproxy-prd.bodleian.ox.ac.uk/login?url=http://dx.doi.org/10.1163/9789004518971.

———. "The Good Life: Descriptors of Change in Roma Pentecostal Communities in Serbia and Croatia." *Spiritus: ORU Journal of Theology* 2, no. 2 (2017): 99–118.

Wachsmuth, Melody J., and Ksenija Magda. "'Discerning the Body.' In Cross-Cultural Relationships: A Critical Analysis of Missional Partnership in Southeastern Europe." *Kairos (Hrvatsko izd.)* 8, no. 1 (2014): 23–40.

Waddell, Robby. "Revelation and the (New) Creation: A Prolegomenon on the Apocalypse, Science, and Creation." In *The Spirit Renews the Face of the Earth*, edited by Amos Yong, 30–52. Eugene: Wipf & Stock, 2009.

Welch, J. W. "A Statement of Fundamental Truths." *The Weekly Evangel* 172 (1917): 8.

Wilson, Jonathan R. *God's Good World: Reclaiming the Doctrine of Creation*. Grand Rapids: Baker Academic, 2013.

Wirzba, Norman. *The Paradise of God Renewing Religion in an Ecological Age*. Oxford: Oxford University Press, 2003.

Woodley, Randy S. *Indigenous Theology and the Western Worldview: A Decolonized Approach to Christian Doctrine*. Grand Rapids: Baker Academic, 2022.

Yong, Amos, ed. *The Spirit Renews the Face of the Earth: Pentecostal Forays in Science and Theology of Creation*. Eugene: Wipf & Stock, 2009.

Zgârgea, Nicolae. "Păcatul lui Adam și Făgăduința Mântuiri." *Mângăietorul* 2 (1940): 4–5.

[Unknown Author]. "Căci Vremea este Aproape." *Mângăietorul* 5 (1940): 2–7.

[Unknown Author]. "Ce Predicăm Noi?" *Vestitorul Evangheliei* 1 (1945): 2–3.

[Unknown Author]. "Dumnezeu – Creatorul." *Buletinul Cultului Penticostal* 4 (1953): 14–15.
[Unknown Author]. "Geneza." *Buletinul Cultului Penticostal* 1–2 (1975): 7–8.
[Unknown Author]. "Indrumări." *Buletinul Cultului Penticostal* 11–12 (1973): 4–8.
[Unknown Author]. "Lecțiuni Biblice." *Cuvântul Adevărului* 1 (1937): 9–12.
[Unknown Author]. "Ogorul Unui om Leneș." *Buletinul Cultului Penticostal* 7–8 (1963): 11.

10

Towards an African Pentecostal Ecotheology of the Forest

Ocen Walter Onen & Tanya Riches

Climate change has had a devastating impact across the continent of Africa. The sub-Saharan nation of Uganda, in particular, is already vulnerable to climate change due to poverty, land degradation, and unplanned rapid urbanization. The forest is crucial to Ugandan life as a key source of cultural, economic, and environmental sustenance. For example, it provides various foods and traditional medicines with historical and ancestral connections, as well as supporting agricultural activities by promoting rain, sequestrating carbon, increasing soil health, and reducing erosion. Additionally, the forest generates significant revenue annually to the government of Uganda from timber sales, tourism, and other forest-related activities. Recently, Uganda has suffered drought and erratic rainfall due to one of the highest deforestation rates in the world; yet, unfortunately, the poor are very often reliant upon the forest to survive. The central question of this chapter is, "How are African Pentecostal[1] churches and their development workers engaging in environmental issues? How does this interact with the forest?"

This theologically engaged development studies investigation adopts a grounded approach to investigate community and development activities. It centres on the case of one Eastern Ugandan Pentecostal congregation undertaking forest regeneration. The authors posit that it is the deep relationship

---

1. In this chapter "Pentecostal" represents the broad global Pentecostal-charismatic movement with its diverse theologies. See James K. A. Smith, *Thinking in Tongues: Pentecostal Contributions to Christian Philosophy* (Grand Rapids: Eerdmans, 2010), Kindle Loc 207.

between the two East African Pentecostal-charismatic practitioners pursuing a community-focused forest regeneration program that has drawn in the Pentecostal church and generated a uniquely African Pentecostal ecotheology capable of an ever-widening circle of influence, moving beyond the church to the community both local and international. We propose this as a nascent sustainable Pentecostal development approach with an active ecotheology that represents a flourishing relationship (or, friendship) between these practitioners, the church, community, and environment. Importantly, here love flows from action or practice. This case study provides tangible evidence of the Spirit's work within and upon Pentecostal believers as they act to liberate their forest and end poverty in their community. This missional movement encompassing creation extends outward towards other local, national, and global partnerships, and, accordingly, the mutuality of the friendship network grows.

Literature Review

To situate forest degradation as critical to Ugandan sustainable development practice, the authors first turned to development studies to assess the significance and current state of the forest locally and globally. Trajectories in African ecotheology are then outlined from the literature to contextualize the chapter.

The Importance of Forests in Uganda

The forest is undoubtedly culturally important to Ugandan life, particularly for indigenous communities. Forests were often considered sacred space, but have also structured the everyday lives of their inhabitants as ecosystems with boundless species of plants, animals, fungi and insects that provided food and medicine, contributed to the construction of homes, and formed the basis of various livelihoods. Importantly, some economists assess the forest's economic value as a vital force behind the growth of Uganda's economy.[2] Revenue accrues from export and domestic sales of products such as timbers, poles, and wood fuels. Additionally, Ugandan forests have become tourist destinations, bringing substantial amounts of income to the government. For instance, in 2004, the forest contributed approximately USD 304 million to the economy, roughly 5.2

---

2. G. Bush, et al., *The Value of Uganda's Forests: A Livelihoods and Ecosystems Approach* (Kampala: Wildlife Conservation Society, 2004), 9.

percent of the total Gross Domestic Product of that financial year.³ However, with an exponential decrease of forest cover in the country, this figure has gradually reduced. The forests continue to provide gainful employment to a considerable proportion of Uganda's population, for instance, as early as 2001, roughly 2.2 percent of its citizens were working in forest-backed industries.⁴ Most of these jobs are informal, attracting low salaries. However, for local Ugandans these roles are better than unemployment since the latter not only leads to poverty but other vices. The nature of such poverty is both extreme and multi-faceted.⁵ However, some scholars have identified that the financial benefits of the forest accrue largely to only a few forest-adjacent organized communities with well-defined structure and resilient members.⁶ This means the majority of Ugandans are left out, which is a grave injustice.

There are also many ecological benefits of forests, especially reduction of the amount of greenhouse gasses in Uganda through the process of photosynthesis. Forest landscapes are essential for carbon sequestration.⁷ Therefore, many reforestation projects, mainly funded by development agencies, are now emerging, for example, those in Bukaleba Central Forest Reserve, bordering Lake Victoria, and Lango Forestry.⁸ These programs aim towards carbon-offset, but with additional commercial benefit to the government and/or the communities involved in planting the trees. Without this restoration action, the current degradation of the forest will greatly affect the future livelihoods of Uganda's many inhabitants who depend upon the forests for survival. The seriousness of this forest degradation will be explored next in terms of its

---

3. J. Obua, J. G. Agea, and J. J. Ogwal, "Status of Forests in Uganda," *African Journal of Ecology* 48, no. 4 (2010): 854.

4. F. I. B. Kayanja and D. Byarugaba, "Disappearing Forests of Uganda: The Way Forward," *Current Science* 81, no. 8 (2001): 937.

5. O. W. Onen, "Poverty Eradication: Innovative Approach to Accelerate Poverty Alleviation in Uganda, Africa," in *SDGs in Africa and the Middle East Region*, eds. W. Leal Filho, Ismaila Rimi Abubakar and Izael da Silva (New York: Springer, 2023), 28.

6. C. Mawa, D. M. Tumusiime, and F. Babweteera, "Are Community Forests Delivering Livelihood Benefits?," *Trees and Livelihoods* 30, no. 2 (2021): 139.

7. V. Birungi, S. W. Dejene, M. S. Mbogga, and M. Dumas-Johansen, "Carbon Stock of Agoro Agu Central Forest Reserve in Lamwo District, Northern Uganda," *Heliyon* 9, no. 3 (2023): 1–10.

8. A. Nel and D. Hill, "Constructing Walls of Carbon: The Complexities of Community, Carbon Sequestration and Protected Areas in Uganda," *Journal of Contemporary African Studies* 31, no. 3 (2013): 25.

detriment to human flourishing and the threat to the entire ecosystem.[9] The cumulative effect of restoring both natural and artificial forests may enable Uganda to achieve its ambitious goal of lowering "greenhouse gas emission by 24.7% by 2030."[10] This is commendable, however, it is uncertain whether there is enough political will, financial resources, or citizen interest amongst local communities to ensure success.

Degradation of the Forest

Across the world, forest degradation is occurring at an unprecedented (and exponential) rate.[11] While the need for action is great, global citizens have lost their ecocentric moral authority to properly respond. When combined with other stressors such as poverty, natural disasters, and poor policies, this can lead to the depletion, degeneration, and even extinction of forests.

In Uganda, the rate of forest degradation is catastrophic. Since 1990, the country has lost approximately 12 percent of its forest cover.[12] Only 50 percent of what existed three decades ago remains. If this trend remains uninterrupted, it can be expected that the present and future thriving of forests will be under extreme threat. This is something the government of Uganda and her citizens must not take lightly. Furthermore, the increasing destruction of forests generates numerous other consequences; soil erosion, extinction of biological biodiversity, and an existential threat to wildlife.[13] This has impacted upon the productivity of the agricultural and tourism sectors of Uganda's economy, and its food security.

In Uganda, just as in many contexts where poverty exists, the increasing exploitation of the forest is reinforced by insensitivity to the discourse of its sustainable utilization.[14] The degradation of Ugandan forests is mainly orchestrated by over-dependence on subsistence and commercial agriculture[15] which

---

9. J. Ghazoul, et al., "Conceptualizing Forest Degradation," *Trends in Ecology & Evolution* 30, no. 10 (2015): 622; D. M. Lapola, et al., "The Drivers and Impacts of Amazon Forest Degradation," *Science* 379, no. 6630 (2023): 4.

10. Birungi, et al., "Carbon Stock of Agoro Agu Central Forest Reserve," 7.

11. Ghazoul, et al., "Conceptualizing Forest Degradation," 630.

12. D. Bamwesigye, "Willingness to Pay for Alternative Energies in Uganda: Energy Needs and Policy Instruments towards Zero Deforestation 2030 and Climate Change," *Energies* 16, no. 2 (2023): 2; Birungi et al., "Carbon Stock of Agoro Agu Central Forest Reserve," 2.

13. Kayanja and Byarugaba, "Disappearing Forests of Uganda," 936.

14. P. K. Kelly, "The Need for Ecojustice," *The Fletcher Forum of World Affairs* 14, no. 2 (1990): 329; Bamwesigye, "Willingness to Pay," 2.

15. Nel and Hill, "Constructing Walls of Carbon," 424.

have significant roles in the survival and wellbeing of Uganda's increasing population. Increasingly, forests are encroached upon to provide additional spaces for human settlement and farming. This predicament is further reinforced by anthropocentric destruction of the natural forests through uncontrolled lumbering, excessive consumption of wood fuel, and grazing animals in gazetted forests.[16] Such activities work in conjunction with other stressors and contribute immensely to the regressive growth pattern of forests across different regions in Uganda.

The aggressive and egotistical exploitation of the natural forests is an injustice to both the ecosystem and human beings. Obviously, such a statement is controversial as the latter are also the main perpetrators of forest destruction. The mutual relationship with nature in Uganda is breaking down. To many, the forest is life, and to destroy it means uprooting the very epicentre of their lives and livelihoods. It is therefore a threat to their own existence and continuity. In Uganda, the poor in communities around the forests often suffer lethal repercussions of its degradation[17] as they are reliant upon the forest to survive. Other very real impacts of forest degradation upon the poor include loss of specific vegetative habitats, increased temperatures, and drastic decline in rainfall; these, in turn, often lead to food insecurity, shortages of raw materials for their craft and industries, and extinction of traditional herbs used for medicinal purposes. This chapter does not discount the destruction of forests resulting from the wider dynamics of the Anthropocene age; rather, it boldly affirms that human beings everywhere in the world directly or indirectly endure the devastating impacts of forest degradation. In our view, such a statement is equally as development minded as it is theological. Therefore, the theological literature will now be explored.

African Theological Approaches

In search of a Pentecostal ecotheology to undergird sustainable development practice in Uganda relevant to forests, this chapter notes important contributions from African theological sources. African theology that includes the forest has a long history. Famously, in 1981, an illiterate Ghanaian midwife named Afua Kuma from the forest town of Obo-Kwahu released prayers and praises in a forty-six page volume entitled *Jesus of the Deep Forest*. In her psalm-like offering, the life of the people of God and the forest are clearly entwined.

---

16. Kayanja and Byarugaba, "Disappearing Forests of Uganda," 936.
17. Bamwesigye, "Willingness to Pay," 2.

In 2004, Ghanaian theologian Kwame Bediako encouraged Africans to engage with their own theologies (such as Kuma's) to further the missional conversation in the global South. He cites her text:

> As a dependable friend, Jesus ensures our wholesome growth.
> The Great Rock we hide behind:
> The great forest canopy that gives us cool shade.
> The Big Tree which lifts its vines to peep at the heavens,
> The magnificent Tree whose dripping leaves
> encourage the luxuriant growth below.[18]

Three themes from more recent African theological literature will be now explored as relevant to an ecotheology of the forest, with a synthesis proposed.

African theologians usually enter the debate about ecotheology via a constructive criticism of Western conceptions of the doctrine of *imago Dei*. According to them, the Western doctrine has fundamentally contributed to the anthropogenic environmental and ecological crisis facing the world today,[19] because it has imbued human beings with more power than other non-human creations. The result has not only jeopardized the flourishing of non-human actors, but also accelerated their extinction. It is important to note that human-centred egotistical detrimental acts are met with vehement resistance from non-human creations including the earth in the biblical passages.[20] There is need to deconstruct this old narrative and reconstruct a new one which prioritizes and establishes a strong symbiotic relationship between ecological and anthropocentric sustainability. In pursuit of this, African theologians propose the following (i) decolonizing the Western theological discourse on *imago Dei*, (ii) integrating the African concept of vital forces, and (iii) rediscovering the discourse of *missio Dei*.

Decolonizing the Western Theological Discourse of *Imago Dei*

Today, most environmentally-oriented African theologians constructively engage in serious conversation about decolonizing the theological discourse of the doctrine of creation inherent within the theological doctrine of *imago Dei* (Latin for "image of God"). They conclude that the prevalent discourse which

---

18. A. Kuma, *Jesus of the Deep Forest* (Accra: Asempa Publishers, 1981), 12.

19. T. C. Sakupapa, "Spirit and Ecology in the Context of African Theology: Christian Faith and the Earth," *Scriptura: Journal for Contextual Hermeneutics in Southern Africa* 111, no. 1 (2012): 422.

20. N. C. Habel, "Guiding Ecojustice Principles," *Spiritan Horizons* 11, no. 11 (2016): 106.

was deeply influenced by the West is anthropocentric in nature and therefore incongruent with African traditional reverence for non-human creations.[21] This position is in tandem with scholars who strongly assert that the Judeo-Christian construct of creation is profoundly responsible for the marginalization of nature.[22] In this telling, missionaries extensively propagated a domineering, dualistic, and anti-environmental worldview. This gradually and systematically resulted in the increased exploitation of non-human actors across the continent. The Christian faith moved extensively across the continent during colonization and wide-scale exploitation of Africa. Therefore, converts to the Christian faith often embarked on an exodus from their traditional practices of maintaining peaceful coexistence with the environment to adopt Western practices. Against this backdrop, African theologians anchor their revolutionary demand arguing to dethrone the alien and discriminatory Westernized interpretation of *imago Dei*. They seek to replace it with African theological ideology, which places both humans and nature on the same footing, giving both of them an equal worth, dignity, and preference.[23] Importantly, within this view, both are inseparable and mutually beneficial to each other.

Integrating the African Concept of Vital Force

The traditional African ontological paradigm recognizes a divine being or a vital force as the creator of everything. This is the equivalent of the biblical triune God. However, unlike the conception of the latter whose Spirit indwells only human creatures, the biblical God permeates and lives in all creation (Gen 2:7; Col 1:16–17; Acts 17:28) including, trees, rivers, forests, mountains, caves, and animals.[24] God provides all of creation with the necessary sustenance and resources for its flourishing. In this way, God's activity reaches to and is within the non-human as well as human. This view is antithetical to Western theological orientation, as elucidated previously, but it provides a fundamental grounding for the protection of the non-human. Because the thesis is, if God

---

21. C. J. Kaunda, "Towards an African Ecogender Theology: A Decolonial Theological Perspective," *Stellenbosch Theological Journal* 2, no. 1 (2016): 183.

22. P. Öhlmann, W. Gräb, and M.-L. Frost, *African Initiated Christianity and the Decolonisation of Development: Sustainable Development in Pentecostal and Independent Churches* (London: Routledge, 2020), 52.

23. A. C. Obiroa, and E. E. Emeka, "African Indigenous Knowledge System and Environmental Sustainability," *International Journal of Environmental Protection and Policy* 3, no. 4 (2015): 90.

24. Obiora and Emeka, "African Indigenous Knowledge System," 15.

cares about creation (here, the forests) to the extent of bestowing his Spirit upon them, it is imperative for humans to treat them with dignity and compassion. Through this theological revision, African scholars hypothesize, it may be possible to promote creation care practices that reverse the damage and the inaction of much of the church. Theologians seek to use this African hypothesis to motivate the reversal of widespread and unprecedented ecological damage, which are now "critical global moral and justice issues."[25] We believe it will do this, provided the proponents of ecotheology integrate this reformulation into their pursuit of an inclusive theology vested with the potential to liberate all creation from its groaning state.

Rediscovering the Discourse of Missio Dei

This in turn leads into a revision of the missional imperative in Africa. Beyond securing individual conversions only, a wider conception and expression of *shalom* is required. As explained earlier, with African theologians determining the Western-formulated concept of *missio Dei* is biased against non-human actors, then the question must also be asked as to how the non-anthropocene may fit into the missional task. A traditional domineering interpretation that focuses mainly on the redemption of human beings, ignoring the non-human, fundamentally undermines the normative view that God's mission is inclusive and seeks the restoration of all creation. Against this backdrop, African theologians passionately request that mission be rediscovered, reconstructed, and situated with its ecological context. In this suggested approach, substantial missiological and theological attention must be paid to the plight of nature. Such a missiology must provide the necessary biblical and theological grounding for practical initiatives aimed at redeeming, regenerating, reviving, restoring, and protecting the earth. We agree with this view because the present anthropogenic exploitation, overutilization, suppression, and oppression of the environment is entirely antithetical to God's unwavering love for all creation (see Ps 24:1–2; Gen 2:15). Thus, unless an anthropocentric Western doctrine of *missio Dei* is disrupted, many Christians are likely to remain either completely disengaged or passively involved in the narrative of creation and care for the earth.

---

25. K. J. Kaoma, "Towards an African Theological Ethic of Earth Care: Encountering the Tonga Lwiindi of Simaamba of Zambia in the Face of the Ecological Crisis," *HTS Teologiese Studies/Theological Studies* 73, no. 3 (2017): 1.

This section has outlined the African theological viewpoint as contextual to the proposed Pentecostal ecotheology. To identify an eco-missiology suitable for African practitioners in their non-Western cultural context, the authors started with a grounded approach and sought to centre the voices and practices of those in sub-Saharan Africa.

Methodology

As stated, this chapter was written in pursuit of a disruptive missionally-focused ecotheology suitable for Pentecostal practitioners in the African context. For this purpose, grounded theory was selected for our methodology: Glaser and Strauss famously introduced this method as a way of being more attentive to present realities. Although initially positivist (and therefore often anti-theist), now constructivist approaches are used in practical theology.[26] While a traditional grounded approach often discourages integration of the literature until after data collection, this study argues with Glaser, "all is data."[27]

The quest to identify a practical response to the climate crisis in East Africa was driven in part by our interdisciplinary location at the intersection of theology and development studies; both authors (one an Australian Pentecostal, the other a Northern Ugandan Anglican) are faculty members of the Masters of Transformational Development (MTD) at Eastern College, Australia. Although based in Melbourne, the MTD has a sub-Saharan African stream. In April 2023 both authors co-facilitated a Ugandan intensive "Climate Change, Justice and Sustainability."

The initial data for this study was drawn from our personal observations and conversations during this immersion trip in which students attended an Eastern Ugandan Pentecostal church at the invitation of facilitators Dr. Sara Kaweesa and Joy Chelangat, as outlined later. The authors sought to identify how representative this Pentecostal congregation's programme was of other regional approaches. We hoped to identify a range of responses from the sub-Saharan MTD students that we could present in the volume.

Our ethics approval was obtained 4 September 2023 via Christian Research Australia, approval number 147. Following, a group of ten consenting student practitioners who self-identified as Pentecostal and/or who worked in Pentecostal contexts engaged in a research-focused WhatsApp conversation.

---

26. B. A. Stevens, "Grounded Theology?: A Call for a Community of Practice," *Practical Theology* 10, no. 2 (2017): 127.

27. B. G. Glaser, "All is Data," *Grounded Theory Review* 6, no. 2 (2007): 1.

We invited them to identify Pentecostal approaches to environmental issues other than the one we had visited together. While there was initial interest, when it became clear we sought information from them on real world projects, most declined. In the end, two written responses were received, as outlined below (Participant 1 and 2). In order to gain more data, contemporaneous semi-structured interviews were undertaken via Zoom with Sara and Joy, our intensive presenters and key practitioners that we had visited (not included within the WhatsApp and thus not to be confused with the student practitioner group mentioned above nor the participants below) and who were working with a Pentecostal church in the Busia District of East Uganda. This allowed further discussion on the programme observed during the immersion trip of the intensive week. The findings from our participant data are outlined in the following section. This directed our search for relevant Pentecostal literature to explain the divergent practices observed, and which undergirds the authors' conclusions.

Findings
Student Practitioner Responses

The responses from our development practitioner participants identified no known Pentecostal environmental initiatives or programs in the region of sub-Saharan Africa. In fact, Participant 1 who was a Pentecostal pastor overseeing twenty-seven congregations in Zambia stated

> According to my experience working closely with the Pentecostal churches, they have less to do with ecological stewardship/conservation. This is evident in the way their programmes are structured – even in their Bible college, they put more emphasis on the work of the Holy Spirit. Only mainline churches are trying to educate people on the significance of conservation . . . My church and I have no engagement with any Pentecostals who are engaged in forest management, usually this is seen as a sector for the ungodly. We would prefer greeting ourselves in tongues whilst people are cutting our trees and exporting them abroad.

Participant 2 was heavily involved in conflict-reconciliation work amongst Pentecostals in Kenya. Despite an extensive network, she also knew of no Pentecostals engaged in forest management or any other conservation work.

> The issue [of forest management] does not feature a lot. Spiritual wellness is overly emphasized. People are getting ready for life in heaven thus little focus is placed on life here on earth.

However, both practitioners demonstrated awareness of the environmental challenges faced in Africa, citing various aspects of climate change including changes to rainfall patterns that affect the forest, high rates of deforestation (often due to poverty), and exploitation by "so-called investors." This knowledge had not translated into ecological projects. Practitioner 1 shared his ideas, including proposals for legal farming of the precious timber, mukula (a kind of Zambian rosewood).

Both participants supported the idea of Pentecostal churches actively undertaking sustainable development, explained as "development that takes care of the spiritual, physical, environmental, mental and psycho-social health of the target community"[28] and "managing natural resources . . . without depriving the future generation."[29] They considered a lack of ecotheology as the main barrier to this. These student practitioners advocated for an ecotheology rooted in the biblical text and motivating eco-praxis, but specifically action that "seeks to liberate nature from the abuse of humankind."[30] Similarly, both respondents supported the idea of churches partnering with NGOs. They hypothesized this would result in better environmental advocacy, with church reach and platform providing an asset to the NGOs[31] and NGOs reciprocating with knowledge and evidence-based assistance to churches on how best to stage and maintain environmental programs.[32] Still, both noted that such collaboration had not occurred to date in their regions. Participant 2 attributed this to NGO workers failing to identify well with the community ("workers live in urban areas and are basically tourists" while "pushing for their own projects"). Participant 1 noted that churches faced "lack of ownership amongst members" and setting aside finances was a challenge in under-resourced contexts. From this, it was clear that the Eastern Ugandan project offered a truly important case of a Pentecostal church engaged in forest management.

---

28. Participant 2.
29. Participant 1.
30. Participant 1.
31. Participant 2.
32. Participant 1.

Exploring the Eastern Ugandan Forest Management Program

At the heart of the Eastern Ugandan Pentecostal church's forest management project (and critical to its existence and success) are two Ugandan Christian development practitioners: Dr Sara Kaweesa (research scientist and team leader of her organisation, A Rocha Uganda) and Joy Chelangat (director of A Rocha's forest management programme). Our field trip to the Busia District first involved visiting a healthy forest with Dr Kaweesa who instructed us on the important measurements of its health, including soil and air quality, the intact canopy, and visible biodiversity of plants and insects (see image 1). Sara noted that A Rocha had sought the preservation of many kilometers of untouched East Ugandan forest; she demonstrated the forest's health by showing its butterflies, insects, and leaf litter. We then progressed to the church site where we met and shared reflections and lunch with the senior pastor and at least ten key members of the forest regeneration team. Finally, we walked with members of the committee past their village to view the forest regeneration program with Joy Chelangat (see image 2). The degradation of the forest in the areas adjacent to the church and village was obvious. In contrast to healthy forest areas, the replanted areas did not yet have canopy cover, and the soil and air quality were affected. However, we saw thousands of little newly planted trees with string attached and heard how the program volunteers were tracking the development of these native saplings. After observing these replanting efforts in the Busia District under Joy's direction and Sara's encouragement, we sought interviews with the two practitioners to understand their motivations and identify why the East Ugandan project had been so successful.

The motivations for Sara's and Joy's involvement in the project are pneumatological, that is, they emerge from a deep understanding of the Spirit animating creation. Sara stated that her desire to hold both her Christian faith and a passion for the non-human creation together had led her to supply practical and theological answers to the present ecological predicament. She explained how it led her to bring the international organization, A Rocha, to Uganda.[33] This organization originated in the early 1980s in Portugal. Its name "A Rocha" or "rock" represents Jesus Christ. The organization describes itself as "a global family of conservation organizations working together to live out God's calling to care for creation and equip others to do likewise." Representing

---

33. Sara stated, "I used to be an amateur ornithologist. I was counting marabou storks in Kampala, doing waterfall counts with my professor even before starting A Rocha. But then the calling to start A Rocha Uganda was just something that I felt, and I think it's a calling. So maybe that is the role of the Spirit."

various Christian traditions,[34] Sara noted that its ministry philosophy drew heavily upon Colossians 1. By 2025, the A Rocha Uganda program aims to replant twenty hectares (fifty acres) of East Uganda with 22,500 native trees.[35]

Sara described herself in varied terms including "charismatic," in contrast to Joy who declared she was "both Pentecostal and Spirit-filled . . . I believe in baptism by the Holy Spirit and His guidance." Joy articulated her motivation for environmental work as scriptural, but also originating from her childhood experiences:

> people within [my] community would go to the forest to cut trees for firewood, for timber, for poles, for construction. They would graze their animals. And over time this mountain forest became so degraded, and we started receiving long prolonged dry seasons compared to wet seasons. And at school I got to learn the effects of forest degradation and what I saw in my community is what I was told in class. So that really gave me a concern to protect the environment.

That both women had both pursued scientific training was important to Sara who emphasized, "I think we could say . . . it is the Spirit guiding me. But I am also qualified in these things because I am trained. I have years of experience, I have the paperwork, it's all there." She described this as "balance" between the scientific and spiritual aspects of their work.

During the interviews, it was clear the two practitioners had forged a deep friendship. Sara considered the success of the project as due to "mutual relationship to achieve a shared vision." When speaking about Joy, her affection was clear. She referred to her fondly as a "sister," "daughter," and a "dear friend" for whom she prays often. Similarly, Joy referred to Sara as "a mentor . . . [an] affectionate and concerned employer," and highlighted their shared passion for conserving the environment. During our field trip to the program, we observed them interacting on the field, their synergy in their teaching and activities, and their strong relationship with the church which now sustained the forest program.

---

34. Sara noted that evangelical, Pentecostal, Anglican and many other denominations were involved in the organisation.
35. See https://shop.arocha.org/product/trees-to-restore-west-bugwe-uganda/.

Image 1. Dr Sara Kaweesa Demonstrating the Health of the East Ugandan Forest

Image 2. Joy Chelangat at the Site of the Church's Forest Regeneration Programme

Photos Taken by Tanya Riches (used with permission)

The East Ugandan Pentecostal Church

Contact with the East Ugandan church was initiated by Sara, who described the greatest hurdle as general relationship building. Many actors (e.g. government departments, universities, the World Bank, and even the National Forestry Authority) had initiated projects in the area but these had not generated long term impact. Therefore, Joy noted that when they first explained their interest about the East Ugandan forest, these Pentecostals did not initially share their concerns, but did welcome them as fellow Christians. This ultimately led to the practitioners teaching biblical principles about creation care (e.g. Gen 2:15).

Both women maintained they had only given the village awareness ("sensitization") about their environment. But Joy described how things had changed.

> Up to now, they really support us so much in the project and in caring for God's creation because whenever we even organize meetings or trainings, it is this very church that supports us in coordinating and coordinating the community to participate.

Sara stated that she had always seen the church members as "co-workers" in the gospel. When asked to expand on how the work undertaken by the members of the church was related to the Spirit, Joy asserted

> The Holy Spirit teaches and reminds the church all things (John 14:26). God told man to protect nature (Gen 2:15) . . . take care of God's creation. Additionally, the Holy Spirit bears fruits in us (Gal 5:22) . . . the fruit of the Holy Spirit is love, joy, peace, long suffering, kindness, goodness, faithfulness, gentleness, and self-control . . . The church has self-control in the way she utilizes the forests and their resources, uses it in a way that its able to regenerate. For example, the church doesn't participate in deforesting the forest for charcoal production rather she is an advocate for its protection and sustainable use.

In this way, in East Uganda the fruits of the Spirit are evident in these Christians' lives and bear physical fruit for the community. Sara continued

> Pentecostals . . . they know that God speaks; even . . . walking down the forest and God speaks . . . They would not go and worship [the trees], but they know . . . all creatures are made by God. They are aware. But then I think maybe . . . how do they bring that home, how do they practice?

These practitioners described the project's work undertaken by the church as "forest liberation," which Joy explained as seeking out young saplings or trees and creating space for them by removing nearby invasive species (such as camara and pepper berry) and freeing them from climbers. Sara also explained it in more theological terms.

> We know that creation is eagerly waiting, longing to be liberated from the bonds of decay. So why is it Spirit-filled for me? It is very holy, it is supposed to be holy, it is supposed to be clean, beautiful, maintained. It's holy – doing its job praising God, pleasing to our eyes . . . but maybe when we cut [it], it is also lamenting.

Thus, the church's caretaking role was explained as ceasing some practices and also acting towards the forest's future benefit.

The forest regeneration programme has led to other livelihood projects in the community, such as beekeeping and agroforestry, when the church realized that poverty was the main reason for the degradation of the forest. In time, the community will receive income from these initiatives. Both development practitioners articulated a future goal of undertaking solar electricity initiatives in the area and forming university research partnerships that may measure and extend what had been accomplished at the site.

Sara described the relationship between forest and church now as "harmonious" and "mutually interdependent." Similarly, Joy emphasized an interdependent relationship between the environment, the church, and the village:

> Let me begin with the forest. The forest provides both the church and the village with the different products. For example, people in the village and the church go to the forest for products like firewood, herbal medicine, and wild foods. Then, the church is like a channel of communication where the village gathers and where information regarding the forest management is shared. Then, the village participates in the management of the forest through a program called collaborative forest management.

To tell the community's story this way, with the forest at its heart, does not mean that all forest-adjacent communities agree with or support this project. In fact, Sara mentioned Joy had at times suffered threats of violence. However, slowly, due to the size of this project, the church was having to reach out to adjacent communities and build a network of supporters to sustain the project's work. This relationality is resulting in a network of forest carers in the district.

Results/Discussion: In Pursuit of an African Pentecostal Ecotheology?

This section now turns back to the literature seeking to follow the recommendations from the practitioners regarding Pentecostalecotheology but also to better interpret the data uncovered on the ground. Three themes are discussed here. The first highlights the relational nature of a Pentecostal ecotheology and associated "green pneumatologies." The second expands this to note the distinctly African contribution of a "friendship" capable of embracing the non-human, including forests. Finally, we assess the contribution of this case to development practice in other faith-based (but particularly Pentecostal) contexts.

Even recently, global Pentecostal ecotheology was described as "relatively incipient."[36] Nevertheless, Davis asserts the "building blocks" do exist within the literature for a more comprehensive theological approach; she advocates engagement with the movement's "green pneumatologies." However, rather

---

36. A. Davis, "Pentecostal Approaches to Ecotheology: Reviewing the Literature," *Australasian Pentecostal Studies* 22, no. 1 (2021): 4–33, 4.

than entering the discussion via common Pentecostal practices, most authors – such as Davis – impose and critique Pentecostal theological doctrinal schema, for example, Jesus as saviour, healer, coming king, Spirit baptizer and sanctifier.[37] These can arguably reinforce the dichotomy between the material and spiritual (for example, where is Jesus as Creator?). Nevertheless, arguably, a nascent global Pentecostal ecotheology does exist. Notably, other thinkers like Aaron Swoboda call for "charismatic social justice," which arguably identifies Pentecostalism's contribution as its relational network.[38] For him, Pentecostal ecotheology often sounds as its glossolalia, "full of meaning, hard to distinguish, and in desperate need of a willing interpreter."[39] But rather than dismissing emphasis on the Spirit inbreaking into the material world, Swoboda concludes that the pneumatological imagination has potential to see the earth renewed. He notes "[Relationality is] the very strength of Pentecostal theology and practice . . . Ultimately that is the strength of the Spirit/creation theologies we have seen: renewed relationship."[40] The authors observed this relationality with an East African bent; how a deep connection between two development practitioners and the church (and by extension village or community) has resulted in the success of the forest regeneration program. While Swoboda's proposal is primarily a relationality between an individual and environment, the observed African Pentecostal relationality offers something more communal and far-reaching.

Pentecostal scholar Nimi Wariboko examines the embodied performative spirituality and communal relationality of sub-Saharan Pentecostals via the theme of "friendship" in his analysis of the "nature, dynamics, and logic" of Nigerian Pentecostalism.[41] He argues that, because invisible and material worlds constantly interact, the African Pentecostal must constantly discern between sources. He notes Pentecostals as "drawn to God by . . . desires" and "driven away by disgust," which in turn opens and closes relational possibilities.[42] Most significantly, Wariboko presents friendship here as a unique contribution: as the African Christian seeks fullness of life (echoing the vital

---

37. Davis, "Pentecostal Approaches to Ecotheology," 5.

38. A. J. Swoboda, *Tongues and Trees: Towards a Pentecostal Ecological Theology* (Blandford Forum: Deo, 2013).

39. Swoboda, *Tongues and Trees*, 14.

40. Swoboda, *Tongues and Trees*, 106.

41. N. Wariboko, *Nigerian Pentecostalism* (London: Boydell & Brewer, 2014), 208. His friendship is defined and described as "an activity of self-realisation, love and politics inspired by the value of spiritual practice that transcends . . . the Spirit-filled individual."

42. Wariboko, *Nigerian Pentecostalism*, 8.

life force in wider African cosmology and theology outlined earlier), he/she can move powerfully towards the love of neighbor. In other words, united by the Spirit, two people from differing locations can become oriented towards each other and also towards common goals. Therefore, he states

> tongues-speech is about openness and translation that bring[s] people together in mutuality. It is about constant interchange of talk and discourse among new friendships founded in the Spirit. It points to the activity of continued dialogue based on the gifts of the Spirit to unite citizens in the polis after Babel.[43]

In his view, such friendship "has an ontological and political status," providing a public politic based on mutual participation.[44]

It seems that the East Ugandan forest project offers exactly that – a new public politic based on an outward-focused and expanding relationality. We noted that it was the *friendship* between the two practitioners that had developed a wider circle encompassing the church, then village, and increasingly the region. This could be interpreted as an ever-expanding missional love that increases flourishing for both the human and the non-human in the relational network. Rather than incidental, this point is considered critical. Of course, such a proposal is complexified by the absence of value placed upon such relational and scientific work in some circles, with many Pentecostal pastors in Uganda noted as holding a distinctly "anti-intellectual" attitude[45] that emphasizes prosperity theologies to redress poverty.[46] Even as social engagement exists via extensive community programs in Uganda, much of the church is concerned with morality and its incorporation into national legislation. However, here Wariboko's volume provides explanation. There are overlaps between such initiatives if seen through the lens of relationality as the power to promote both inclusion and exclusion. These are two sides of the same power.

In light of the above, we assess whether the East African forest program can provide the basis for a uniquely Pentecostal approach to sustainable development. As stated, arguably, many Pentecostals have not yet engaged with ecological degradation. Additionally, in the non-Western context poverty and

---

43. Wariboko, *Nigerian Pentecostalism*, 206.

44. Wariboko, *Nigerian Pentecostalism*, 216, 167.

45. E. Kibirango, "An Exploration of Uganda's Pentecostal Pastors' Anti-Intellectual Attitude to Improve Desire for Additional Theological Education" (PhD diss., Lancaster Bible College, 2023), 126.

46. S. Bremner, "Transforming Futures? Being Pentecostal in Kampala, Uganda" (PhD diss., University of East Anglia, 2013), 126.

injustices become pressing concerns as part of everyday life. However, some Christian development practitioners see poverty and ecojustice as entwined: ecological issues that affect the forest are an issue of survival for the poor. Within Christian development studies, relationship has been highlighted as a key feature of better development practice. For example, Bryant Myers attributes his watershed book *Walking with the Poor* to two generative ideas from non-Western contexts – missiologist Paul Hiebert's critique of the Western "excluded middle" (resulting from the dichotomy between the spiritual and the natural in the Western worldview) and Jayakumar Christian's understanding of poverty as a relational breakdown.[47] Myers uses these ideas to interrogate the dichotomy of development practice that holds faith as its motivation for activity but operates largely as a secular practice. Notably, the East African case brings together the material and spiritual in a symbiotic way.

Filipino missiologist and development worker Al Tizon reinforces the idea that friendship changes the socioeconomic realities of the poor. He advocates the concept of solidarity, "at its best, solidarity paints a picture of true, mutually transforming partnership between the poor and the nonpoor, with the poor at the helm."[48] In his view, such a powerful transformation is Spirit-inspired.

> Christian solidarity means deep commitment, which can only come from genuine love of neighbor. It refers to nothing less than true friendship across conventional boundaries, a bond that sets the course for a hard, bumpy, sometimes bloody journey together toward justice. It means creating together a safe space, shared power, strategic linkages, and action toward social transformation.[49]

In the case of Eastern Uganda, the directionality of this relationality is reversed. In Joy's words, "Let me begin with the forest." A shared concern toward the liberation of the forest ignited a friendship capable of mobilizing a church, then a village, and now on to more villages. As the circle grows, both the material and spiritual realities of this friendship network are also deepened, widened, and opened to greater fullness of life. This provides a strong basis for a transformational and sustainable Pentecostal development approach.

---

47. B.Myers, *Walking with the Poor: Principles and Practices of Transformational Development* (Maryknoll: Orbis, 2011), 390.

48. A. Tizon, *Christ Among the Classes: The Rich, the Poor, and the Mission of the Church* (Maryknoll: Orbis, 2023), 132.

49. Tizon, *Christ Among the Classes*, 125.

Conclusions/ Recommendations

This chapter traces the possibilities for (East) African Pentecostals (and many others around the globe) to adopt an unconventional theological approach that values the life within the forest, seen here as a spirited "other" capable of a mutually life-giving friendship. This, of course, may bring up concerns of animism, particularly from those who may hold a theology in which the non-human is excluded. However, the practitioners could see and articulate clear differences. Rather than an object of worship, Joy's emphasis was upon the forest as a place in which Christians experience the Spirit of God. She noted that, in a traditional view, "forests grow by themselves and have no need for being tendered . . ." while [in contrast] "Christians consider forests as spiritual places where they can go worship God and also be refreshed." Crucially, "in a Christian view every creation on earth needs to be conserved and protected. [For the Christian], the Spirit of God plants and gives life to the forests including their ecosystems." In this way, the Christian partners with Jesus as Creator with benefit to the earth.

This study asked the question, "How are African Pentecostal churches and development workers engaging in environmental issues?" and "How does this interact with the forest?" The aim was to identify a Pentecostal missional ecotheology used by practitioners. To do so, we first attempted to grapple seriously with the context and contribution of African theologians, who seek to decolonize the idea of human dominance justified by the *imago Dei*, to recognize the vital life force within creation, and to reorient to the *missio Dei*. We sought practice-based approaches to the environmental crisis in the Pentecostal community.

On the field, we found Pentecostal communities were known to be largely inactive on environmental issues, but we also witnessed a church with (quite literally) dirt under its fingernails. These African Pentecostals engage ecojustice actively by unraveling tendrils from young saplings. In particular, one congregation in East Uganda was highlighted. It was set in context of the relationship with two development workers who are also firm friends. Notably, Sara (founder of A Rocha) did not elucidate aspects of the Colossians 1 text she cited as being the mission statement for her organization. However, the authors noted this chapter is directed by Paul to the faithful in Colossae. Its first section is written in gratitude due to the "love in the Spirit" between church members, which is Paul's continuing prayer for them. It goes on to identify Jesus as the first born of all creation, as well as Creator of all things "in heaven and on earth, visible and invisible." On this basis, it urges reconciliation for and between all, including creation. We believe this to be a clue. The shared passion for the non-human had sparked a Spirit-inspired friendship between two practitioners with the capacity to embrace and inspire a local East African Pentecostal church and its village, which has had great impact upon the forest. As the liberation of the forest continues, this program is slowly expanding to adjacent communities, lit by the same love.

The authors investigated whether this ecological relationship (proposed by Swoboda as the way of Pentecostal ecotheology) but more specifically a relationship of friendship (identified by Wariboko to be at work in African Pentecostalism) could undergird Pentecostal practices of ecojustice? Could friendship provide the basis for a mutual partnership that acts towards the common good by ameliorating poverty even as it restores the earth in the power of the Spirit? And to take this even further, if Pentecostals extend life force to the non-human and therefore view the forest *as friend*, can this have practical implications in reorienting both Christian discipleship and development work back into the environment/s that we live in? We believe so. However, this is posed as a question because it is still largely a potentiality. A Pentecostal imagination animated by the Spirit that includes forests, rivers, mountains, and oceans as friends indeed would have practical implications in reorienting Christian discipleship and development work within the very environments we live; however, the evidence of this love is yet to be fully seen or realized.

Bibliography

Bamwesigye, D. "Willingness to Pay for Alternative Energies in Uganda: Energy Needs and Policy Instruments towards Zero Deforestation 2030 and Climate Change." *Energies* 16, no. 2 (2023): 980.

Birungi, V., S. W. Dejene, M. S. Mbogga, and M. Dumas-Johansen. "Carbon Stock of Agoro Agu Central Forest Reserve, in Lamwo District, Northern Uganda." *Heliyon* 9, no. 3 (2023): 1–10.

Bremner, S. "Transforming Futures? Being Pentecostal in Kampala, Uganda." PhD diss, University of East Anglia, 2013.

Bush, G., Simon Nampindo, Caroline Aguti, and Andrew Plumptre. *The Value of Uganda's Forests: A Livelihoods and Ecosystems Approach*. Kampala: Wildlife Conservation Society, 2004.

Davis, A. "Pentecostal Approaches to Ecotheology: Reviewing the Literature." *Australasian Pentecostal Studies* 22, no. 1 (2021): 4–33.

Ghazoul, J., Z. Burivalova, J. Garcia-Ulloa, and L. A. King. "Conceptualizing Forest Degradation." *Trends in Ecology & Evolution* 30, no. 10 (2015): 622–32.

Glaser, B. G. "All is Data." *Grounded Theory Review* 6, no. 2 (2007): 1–22.

Habel, N. C. "Guiding Ecojustice Principles." *Spiritan Horizons* 11, no. 11 (2016): 92–109.

Kaoma, K. J. "Towards an African Theological Ethic of Earth Care: Encountering the Tonga Lwiindi of Simaamba of Zambia in the Face of the Ecological Crisis." *HTS Teologiese Studies/Theological Studies* 73, no. 3 (2017): 1–10.

Kaunda, C. J. "Towards an African Ecogender Theology: A Decolonial Theological Perspective." *Stellenbosch Theological Journal* 2, no. 1 (2016): 177–202.

Kayanja, F. I. B. and D. Byarugaba,. "Disappearing Forests of Uganda: The Way Forward." *Current Science* 81, no. 8 (2001): 936–47.

Kelly, P. K. "The Need for Ecojustice." *The Fletcher Forum of World Affairs* 14, no. 2 (1990): 327–31.

Kibirango, E. "An Exploration of Uganda's Pentecostal Pastors' Anti-Intellectual Attitude to Improve Desire for Additional Theological Education." PhD diss., Lancaster Bible College, 2023.

Kuma, A. *Jesus of the Deep Forest*. Accra: Asempa Publishers, 1981.

Lapola, D. M., P. Pinho, J. Barlow, et al. "The Drivers and Impacts of Amazon Forest Degradation." *Science* 379, no. 6630 (2023): 1–30.

Mawa, C., D. M. Tumuslime, and F. Babweteera. "Are Community Forests Delivering Livelihood Benefits? Insights from Uganda." *Forests, Trees and Livelihoods* 30, no. 2 (2021): 133–50.

Myers, B. *Walking with the Poor: Principles and Practices of Transformational Development*. Revised and Expanded ed.. Maryknoll: Orbis, 2011.

Nel, A., and D. Hill. "Constructing Walls of Carbon: The Complexities of Community, Carbon Sequestration and Protected Areas in Uganda." *Journal of Contemporary African Studies* 31, no. 3 (2013): 421–40.

Obiora, A. C., and E. E. Emeka. "African Indigenous Knowledge System and Environmental Sustainability." *International Journal of Environmental Protection and Policy* 3, no. 4 (2015): 88–96.

Obua, J., J. G. Agea, and J. J. Ogwal. "Status of Forests in Uganda." *African Journal of Ecology* 48, no. 4 (2010): 853–59.

Öhlmann, P., W. Gräb, and M.-L. Frost, eds. *African Initiated Christianity and the Decolonisation of Development: Sustainable Development in Pentecostal and Independent Churches*. London: Routledge, 2020.

Onen, O. W. "Poverty Eradication: Innovative Approach to Accelerate Poverty Alleviation in Uganda, Africa." In *SDGs in Africa and the Middle East Region*, edited by W. Leal Filho, Ismaila Rimi Abubakar, and Izael da Silva, 1–28. New York: Springer, 2023.

Sakupapa, T. C. "Spirit and Ecology in the Context of African Theology." *Scriptura* 111, no. 1 (2013): 1–12.

Smith, J. K. A. *Thinking in Tongues: Pentecostal Contributions to Christian Philosophy*. Grand Rapids: Eerdmans, 2010. Kindle Version.

Stevens, B. A. "Grounded Theology? A Call for a Community of Practice." *Practical Theology* 10, no. 2 (2017): 201–6.

Swoboda, A. J. *Tongues and Trees: Towards a Pentecostal Ecological Theology*. Leiden: Brill, 2019.
Tizon, A. *Christ Among the Classes: The Rich, the Poor, and the Mission of the Church*. Maryknoll: Orbis, 2023.
Wariboko, N. *Nigerian Pentecostalism*. London: Boydell & Brewer, 2014.

11

"Praying with Holy Ghost Fire in Ghana's Natural Environment"

A Potential African Pentecostal Contribution to Eco-Missiology

Kwame Oppong-Konadu & Sarah Korang Sansa

Pentecostalism is expanding rapidly, particularly in Africa, Latin America, and Asia.[1] Presently, in Ghana, a considerable number of the Christian population are Pentecostals.[2] An essential doctrinal trait in global Pentecostalism is Spirit baptism, often marked by praying in tongues, typically referred to as *glossolalia*.[3] Among some Ghanaian Pentecostals, glossolalia facilitates communication with God in the language of the Spirit via group or individual prayer sessions.[4] Aside from church auditoriums, we have observed that Pentecostal prayer services take place under trees, around open school fields or football pitches, and on prayer mountains quite distant from residential areas.

---

1. Steven J. Land, *Pentecostal Spirituality. A Passion for the Kingdom* (Cleveland: CPT, 2010), 10.

2. Ghana Statistical Service, "Ghana 2021 Population and Housing Census: General Report Volume 3C," 58–61.

3. Mark J. Cartledge, *Charismatic Glossolalia: An Empirical-Theological Study* (Aldershot: Ashgate, 2002), 187–205.

4. Kwame Oppong-Konadu, "Glossolalia: A Critical Reflection on the Gift of Speaking in Tongues in Ghanaian Pentecostalism" (Master's Thesis, Protestant Theological University, 2020), 40–56.

In these meetings within Ghana's natural environment, congregants usually stand throughout prayer sessions, praying together perceptibly in tongues with incredible vitality. A prevalent phrase during these prayer sessions, often considered spiritual warfare, is "Holy Ghost Fire."

Research on Pentecostals in Ghana has shown that there are pneumatological reasons behind prayer mountains, fields, and trees. The perception of God's presence around these quiet and serene spaces has been one of the main motivations for Pentecostal and charismatic prayer engagement in the natural environment.[5] This development looks like a positive paradigm for environmental protection in contemporary Ghana which is facing a massive and continuous degradation of forest resources.[6] Pneumatological prayer practices in the environment need critical examination due to their potential to help mitigate this challenge. Therefore, it is worthwhile to investigate such practices for new and unique insights that could enrich the conversation on creation care.

Theologians from the mainline Christian traditions (Roman Catholic, Orthodox, and Protestant) and even eco-feminists have contributed, and continue to contribute, to ecotheological discourses, however, these discourses have rarely considered the perspectives of Pentecostals and charismatics.[7] This chapter examines how Ghanaian Pentecostals might contribute to environmental sustainability in their lived theology. The main question the chapter seeks to answer is, "What role can the pneumatological practice of prayer in the environment among Ghanaian Pentecostals play in addressing environmental concerns in Ghana?"

Methodology

The chapter adopts an empirical-theological framework based on the philosophical and theological notion of dialectics to answer the above question. This approach is common among practical theologians as they prioritize experience and theological inquiry, frequently moving in a cyclical or spiral pattern. They begin with experience, investigate and reflect on it, offer a response, or des-

---

5. Michael Okyerefo, "I Experience Serenity and Convenience in the Forest: Achimota Forest Turned Sacred Space to Confront the Vicissitudes of Life," *Journal of the Sociology and Theory of Religion* 3 (2014): 3.

6. Patrick B. Cobbinah, Michael Poku-Boansi, and Charles Peprah, "Urban Environmental Problems in Ghana," *Environmental Development* 23 (2017): 33–46.

7. A. J. Swoboda, *Tongues and Trees: Towards a Pentecostal Ecological Theology* (Blandford Forum: Deo, 2013), 2–14.

ignate a praxis. This method connects with the Christian narrative, resulting in a dialectical interpretation and a call to fresh action. For Mark Cartledege, "The starting point for the process of practical theology as dialectics is the theologian(s) as they engage with the twin poles of the 'lifeworld,' the concrete reality, and the 'system,' or theological identity."[8]

The chapter appropriates the life history method to collect empirical data. It is "an internalized narrative integration of past, present and anticipated future which provides lives with a sense of unity and purpose."[9] The life history method offers valuable insights into individuals' experiences and perceptions, allowing actors to express themselves and their perspectives. The main weaknesses of this method include its individualistic nature and the fact that it looks problematic to view the individual as a source of objective "truth." Even so, it acknowledges that perspectives stem from a person's somewhat problematic experiences, focusing on the intersection of deterministic structures and individual agency, encompassing objective and subjective interpretations.[10] Building on this method, we present two distinct autobiographical narratives in our life histories about Ghanaian Pentecostal prayer engagements in the natural environment. We utilize the concept of "rescripting testimony" to analyze these narratives. This approach helps to ". . . move ordinary theology forward through a deeper analysis of its testimony mode and a broader dialogue with the Christian theological tradition, illuminated by the insights of the social sciences."[11]

The chapter has five sections. In laying the theoretical foundation for the empirical study, the first section describes the ecological crisis in Ghana and its impacts. The second section focuses on the African primal worldview and African Christian spirituality. The third section traces the emergence of the Pentecostal movement in sub-Saharan Africa, with a brief historical background of Ghanaian Pentecostals and their lived theology. The fourth section presents testimonies of the pneumatological practice of prayer in the environment among

---

8. Cartledge, *Practical Theology: Charismatic and Empirical Perspectives* (Eugene: Wipf & Stock, 2012), 27.

9. Dan P. McAdams, "The Development of Narrative Identity," in *Personality Psychology: Recent Trends and Emerging Directions*, eds. David M. Buss and Nancy Cantor (New York: Springer, 2012), 161.

10. Gill Musson, "Life Histories," in *Essential Guide to Qualitative Methods in Organizational Research*, eds. Catherine Cassell and Gillian Symon (London: Sage, 2004), 36.

11. Mark J. Cartledge, *Testimony in the Spirit: Rescripting Ordinary Pentecostal Theology* (Farnham: Routledge, 2010), 18.

Ghanaian Pentecostals. The fifth section, "Towards an Afro-Eco-Pentecostal Missiology," attempts to *rescript* these testimonies before concluding.

Overview of Ghana's Ecological Crisis and its Impacts

Ghana, for many years, has boasted a rich and diversified landscape. Covering a land area of 238,533 km², Ghana is well known for its several rivers, lagoons, lakes, and vegetation zones, which serve as habitats for various animal species and migratory birds.[12] The largest river in Ghana, River Volta, covers a length of 1600km and stretches across other rivers like the Pra, Tano, Offin, and Birim.[13] The country has sixteen homogenized protected areas managed by the Division of Wildlife, including: the Ankasa Forest Reserve; Bia, Kakum, and Mole National Parks; and the Gbele and Shai Hills Resource Reserves.[14] These protected areas frequently receive high numbers of tourists; good examples are Kakum National Park, well known for its distinctive canopy walkway in a semi-deciduous forest, and Mole National Park, serving as a habitat for diverse wildlife and indigenous tree species.[15]

For the past twenty years, the gradual destruction of the Ghanaian environment has become a national and local dilemma.[16] Constant exploitation of natural resources has resulted in increasing land degradation and intensified water and air pollution.[17] The nation's economic dependence on its natural resources has become a detriment to environmental sustainability: poor sanitation has developed into another significant environmental challenge that urban Ghana must cope with.[18] The majority of people living under poor conditions in rural and urban Ghanaian communities partake in unhygienic practices. One of these practices is open defecation, mostly along seashores, due to the lack of improved sanitation in various homes.[19] Improper waste disposal has become one of Ghana's greatest nightmares. Solid waste, including fecal waste

---

12. Edwin K. Eshun, "Religion and Nature in Akan Culture: A Case Study of Okyeman Environment Foundation" (Master's Thesis, Queen's University, 2011), 5–6.

13. Eshun, "Religion and Nature in Akan Culture," 6.

14. Philip Briggs, *Ghana: The Bradt Travel Guide* (Guildford: Globe Pequot, 2017), 36–37.

15. Briggs, *Ghana: The Bradt Travel Guide*, 36.

16. World Bank Group, *Ghana Country Environmental Analysis: Case Studies and Assessments* (Washington, DC: World Bank, 2020), xxii.

17. World Bank Group, *Ghana Country Environmental Analysis*, xix–xxii.

18. Cobbinah, Poku-Boansi, and Peprah, "Urban Environmental Problems in Ghana," 34.

19. Eugene Appiah-Effah, et al., "Ghana's Post-MDGs Sanitation Situation: An Overview," *Journal of Water, Sanitation and Hygiene for Development* 9, no. 3 (2019): 397–415.

and food scraps, is either dumped in open spaces or water bodies, or openly burned, often resulting in water pollution, destruction of aquatic habitat, flooding, and cholera outbreaks in some Ghanaian communities.[20] Quite recently, illegal small-scale gold mining has become another environment-damaging activity. This has raised tensions between the government of Ghana, the mining industry, and communities that are actively (whether directly or indirectly) involved in this act. Illegal mining has led to deforestation, biodiversity loss, accelerated soil erosion, sedimentation, and water pollution, continuously destroying Ghana's indigenous and prestigious forests while endangering the lives of animals in the ecosystem.[21]

The increasing rate of environmental degradation in Ghana has gradually and greatly affected Ghanaian society and economy. The major contributing factors to air and water pollution in Ghana are plastic waste fumes, solid waste disposal, the release of harmful chemicals, and the disposal of electronic waste, which has also resulted in (though not limited to) lost IQ points in children.[22] To address the ecological crisis in Ghana, an estimate of 4.2 percent of the Gross Domestic Product (GDP) is requisite for tackling air pollution, 3 percent GDP for tackling water pollution, and 1.2 percent GDP for gold mines, unmanaged solid waste, and other contaminated sites.[23] These estimations disclose that over 8 percent of government incomes received from Ghanaian taxpayers need to be allocated to help mitigate this ecological crisis. These monies could have been channelled to other sectors of the economy, like health, education, etc. to facilitate development.

There is a fear that, if not managed well, the continuing ecological destruction might lead to unexpected and unwanted health outcomes for Ghanaians. Meanwhile, the effects of climate change have been causing immense human suffering. The Ghana National Climate Change Adaptation Strategy indicates that Ghana has experienced a rise in temperature, a decreased amount of rainfall, a rise in sea level, and a high incidence of weather extremes due to climate change.[24] In Northern Ghana, droughts, excessive heat, and increasing

---

20. World Bank Group, *Ghana Country Environmental Analysis*, xxii.
21. World Bank Group, *Ghana Country Environmental Analysis*, xxv.
22. World Bank Group, *Ghana Country Environmental Analysis*, xix–xxii.
23. World Bank Group, *Ghana Country Environmental Analysis*, xix–xxii.
24. CC DARE, "Ghana National Climate Change Adaptation Strategy," United Nations Development Program, report, 9.

poverty have led to frequent rural–urban migration.²⁵ Women and children suffer greatly in rural Ghana due to excessive household labour and environmental health risks, causing respiratory problems among women.²⁶

Currently, there are ongoing governmental initiatives to respond to these environmental challenges. These include approaches ranging from "policy directions, conferences on climate change, and the formulation of various legal statutes."²⁷ An example is the legal Ghana National Environmental Action Plan, aimed at making Ghana's developmental strategy more environmentally sustainable.²⁸ Thus, despite the developmental projects that the nation seeks to achieve, the government has decided to ensure the continuity of its natural resources, which are prone to depletion if not closely monitored. The Ghana National Climate Change Policy, a climate change mitigation and adaptation action policy that seeks to provide strategic directions and coordinate climate change issues in Ghana, is one of the ways of balancing the country's quest for development with environmental consciousness.²⁹ On 1 March 2022, the Ministry of Lands, under the office and initiative of the president of Ghana, Nana Addo Dankwa Akufo-Addo, launched the 2022 "Green Ghana Day" initiative to plant over twenty million trees in Ghana; this initiative seeks to "create enhanced national awareness on the necessity for collective action towards the restoration of degraded landscape in the country."³⁰ However, despite these governmental interventions, mitigation efforts show that managing and addressing Ghana's ecological crisis has proven to be a complex endeavor. The reason is that governmental and non-governmental environmental protection agencies are facing complications in implementing laws at the grassroots. There have been political, national, and local tensions and barriers to advocating for

---

25. Mamudu A. Akudugu, Saa Dittoh, and Edward S. Mahama, "The Implications of Climate Change on Food Security and Rural Livelihoods," *Journal of Environment and Earth Science* 2, no. 3 (2012): 26.

26. Jacob Songsore, "Gender, Environment, and Human Security in the Greater Accra Metropolitan Area (GAMA), Ghana," in *Gendered Insecurities, Health, and Development in Africa*, eds. Howard Stein and Amal Hassan Fadlalla (London: Routledge, 2012), 147–48.

27. Eshun, "Religion and Nature in Akan Culture," 2.

28. Joseph R. A. Ayee, "The Formulation and Implementation of Environmental Policy in Ghana," *Journal of Africa Development/Afrique et Développement* 23, no. 2 (1998): 101.

29. Ministry of Environmental Science and Technology, *Ghana National Climate Change Policy* (Accra: Republic of Ghana, 2013), 1.

30. Ministry of Lands and Natural Resources, "Green Ghana Day 2022 Overview," *News Magazine*, news release, 2022, URL no longer available.

landscape restoration and community policy execution.[31] An example is the unemployment rate in Ghana, which has led many, including the young and old, into acts that destroy the environment, which sometimes lead to the loss of human lives.[32] This suggests that resolving Ghana's environmental crisis needs religious interventions, which include indigenous eco-religious practices and the Christian faith.[33]

African Primal Worldview and African Christian Spirituality

According to John V. Taylor, "primal" is a word that describes the common basal understanding of how the human being views God and the world.[34] This basic understanding reveals the spiritual makeup of an African. Hence, African primal spirituality denotes the spirituality of African people, communicating the underlying belief that "humanity is surrounded by a realm of spirits in which the Supreme God is thought to preside over a pantheon of sub-divinities and ancestral spirits."[35] In other words, African primal spirituality communicates a worldview of spirits (both bad and good). Sharing this notion, Kwame Bediako advanced Harold Turner's "six-feature analysis" of the primal worldview and argued that people live in the consciousness of both benevolent and malevolent spirits. By entering a union with the benevolent spirits, a person shares in its covering against evil mischiefs.[36] Putting it differently, people live with the understanding that there are good and evil spirits, and by establishing a relationship with the good spirits, one may find protection from the evil ones. John Mbiti attests to these religious beliefs by noting that "Africans are notoriously religious, with each people having their own religious system and a set of beliefs and practices."[37] For Harvey Cox, primal spirituality, including that of Africans, is usually expressed via "primal speech" (ecstatic utterances or *glossolalia*), "primal piety" (trances, visions, dreams, healing, etc.),

---

31. Gavin Hilson, "A Contextual Review of the Ghanaian Small-Scale Mining Industry," *Mining, Minerals and Sustainable Development* 76 (2001): 18–19.

32. Hilson, "A Contextual Review," 5.

33. Eshun, "Religion and Nature in Akan Culture," 2.

34. John V. Taylor, *The Primal Vision: Christian Presence Amid African Religion* (London: SCM, 1963), 18.

35. Peter J. Paris, "The Spirituality of African Peoples," *Journal of Black Theology in South Africa* 7, no. 2 (1993): 114.

36. Kwame Bediako, *Jesus in Africa: The Christian Gospel in Africa History and Experience* (Akropong-Akwapim: Regnum Africa, 2000), 87.

37. John S. Mbiti, *African Religions and Philosophy* (London: Biddles, 1989), 1.

and "primal hope" (unwavering optimism for a brighter future).[38] The African primal spirituality focuses on answering real African struggles (for example, fear of witchcraft, impotence, barrenness, etc.).

From an ecological perspective, Ebenezer Blasu defines primal spirituality as "a people's perception of and hence inner disposition about the reality of the 'geosphere' (the earth, its regions, and things in it in African thought), which informs their outer behaviour in their ecological communities (ecosystem)."[39] This definition implies that spirituality expresses the perception of the environment of a given society and how that informs their interactions with it. Hence, the belief in God as creator and the presence of his sub-divinities in creation is one of the main reasons for environmental care in African primal thought.[40] By implication, the African perception of the natural environment finds ground in their knowledge of God and his pantheon of spirits.

In the early eighteenth and nineteenth centuries, Africa received a seemingly new mode of worship called Christianity. It was a new religion that appeared on African soil with unfamiliarly dressed missionaries carrying a message and worldview distinct from that of Africans. For Mbiti, it was a time of massive "misinterpretation, misrepresentation and misunderstanding."[41] The African community did not fully understand the Christian message due to inadequate translation into African terms. The culture the missionaries met was alien and derogatory to them. Joshua Settles unveils this cultural struggle when he asserts that the African primal experience was ill-fitting for the Europeans.[42] Bediako clarifies this cultural mismatch by arguing that the African heritage was tagged as superstitious, ignorant, and savage, leading to a distorted transfusion of Christianity in the African culture.[43]

African Christian spirituality, thus, is a type of spirituality that emerged because of human connectedness to the African primal worldview. This type

---

38. Harvey G. Cox, *Fire from Heaven: The Rise of Pentecostal Spirituality and the Reshaping of Religion in the Twenty-First Century* (Reading: Addison-Wesley, 1995), 101–2.

39. Ebenezer Y. Blasu, *African Theocology: Studies in African Religious Creation Care* (Eugene: Wipf & Stock, 2020), 40.

40. Emmanuel Awudi, "Beyond Eco-Pneumatology: An Examination of Scripture with 'Green Eyes' and the Eco-Praxis of Some 'Indigenous African Churches' Towards the Development of an African Pentecostal Ecotheology" (PhD Diss., Akrofi-Christaller Institute, Akropong-Akuapem, 2023), 7.

41. Mbiti, *African Religions and Philosophy*, 10.

42. Joshua Settles, "Engaging Issues of Primal Spirituality and Identity: An Analysis of Short-Term Mission Training" (Master's Thesis, Akrofi-Christaller Institute of Theology, Mission and Culture, 2013), 14.

43. Bediako, *Christianity in Africa*, 6.

of spirituality developed as a response to missionary-influenced spirituality, as indicated above. For Toren and Tan, people ". . . will continue to believe many other elements of what made up their outlook of the world, but their overall worldview will receive a new flavor and structure because of the new constellation of . . . beliefs . . ."[44] Building on this argument, the primal past of a given people does not disappear after they have received a new religious experience. African spirituality is intrinsic and expressed in their recently developed religion. Yet, this new religion sieves the old practices to produce a finer and latest version that reveals the nature of the new religion. The old and the new practices are diverse, but some elements of the old produce a genuine religious outlook that is not abstract, but real and concrete. For instance, like the African primal spirituality, the African Christian spirituality also comes to give answers to real African existential issues like witchcraft, barrenness, sickness, and evil spirits, which Africans also fear in the primal worldview. It also promotes the freedom to express the African heritage in the service and worship of God. In African Christian Spirituality, "images of power appear prominent through singing or casting out of demons and often correspond with primal African needs for control and/or protection against ambiguous forces within an integrative cosmos."[45] This spirituality has traces within the Ghanaian Pentecostal movement.

The Origin and Lived Theology of the Pentecostal Movement in Sub-Saharan Africa, Ghana

Allan Anderson considers African Pentecostals as the "divergent African churches that emphasize the working of the Spirit in the Church, particularly with ecstatic phenomena like prophecy and speaking in tongues, healing, and exorcism."[46] Aside from the independent charismatic churches, Anderson's definition captures two other groups of Pentecostal churches that are relevant in this work: the AICs, often called "prophet-healing," "Spirit," or "Spiritual" churches, and the Western-originated classical Pentecostal churches. By featuring the AICs, African Pentecostalism details Africans' unique actions, efforts, and advancements to the expansion, relevance, and influence of Pentecostalism

---

44. Benno van den Toren and Kang-Sang Tan, *Humble Confidence: A New Model for Interfaith Apologetics* (Westmont: InterVarsity, 2022), 149.

45. Gregg A. Okesson, *Re-Imaging Modernity: A Contextualized Theological Study of Power and Humanity Within Akamba Christianity in Kenya* (Eugene: Pickwick, 2012), 21.

46. Allan H. Anderson, *An Introduction to Pentecostalism: Global Charismatic Christianity* (Cambridge: Cambridge University Press, 2004), 114.

as a worldwide movement. Native prophets, including William Wade Harris, promoted this version of Pentecostalism in Africa.[47] Ogbu Kalu corroborates this view, arguing that "Pentecostalism in Africa derived its colouring from the texture of the African soil and from the interior of its idiom, nurture, and growth; its fruits serve more adequately the challenges and problems of the African ecosystem than the earlier missionary fruits did."[48] Within Ghanaian Christianity, Kwabena Asamoah-Gyadu labels the AICs as "independent Indigenous Pentecostal churches." These Ghanaian-led churches actively embrace the Holy Spirit as an integral component of regular Christian engagement.[49] The efforts of African prophets who converted large numbers of people to Christianity marked the beginning of the Sunsum Sore (Spirit churches), the initial phase of Pentecostal Christianity in Ghana. The Twelve Apostles Church, Musama Disco Christo Church, and the Saviour Church are some of the most famous AICs in Ghana today. Ghanaian AICs reflect the beliefs of the global Pentecostal movement.[50]

The story of the emergence of Ghanaian Pentecostalism continues with Peter Newman Anim, a prominent local actor, who set the stage for the start of classical Pentecostalism in Ghana. Anim was a member of the Presbyterian Church, established earlier in Ghana, but left to form the Unity Prayer Group, uniting it with the Faith Tabernacle Church. However, after learning in 1928 of the Holy Spirit baptism through reading materials from the Apostolic Church, he broke away from the Faith Tabernacle Church because the Church was reluctant to countenance the doctrine of Spirit baptism in its operations. Anim later affiliated his group with the Apostolic Church, a product of the Welsh Revival in 1904 in the United Kingdom. The Apostolic Church sent Pastor James McKeown as a missionary to Ghana in 1937, the same year it started in the country. Yet, disagreements in doctrine caused a schism, resulting in the formation of the Christ Apostolic Church in 1939 by Anim. The McKeown-led Apostolic Church of Ghana subsequently seceded from the Apostolic Church in the UK and became known as the Church of Pentecost

---

47. Anderson, *Introduction to Pentecostalism* 127–28.

48. Ogbu Kalu, *African Pentecostalism: An Introduction* (Oxford: Oxford University Press, 2008), 178.

49. Johnson K. Asamoah-Gyadu, *African Charismatics: Current Developments within Independent Indigenous Pentecostalism in Ghana* (Leiden: Brill, 2005), 16.

50. Asamoah-Gyadu, *African Charismatics*, 19–21.

in 1962.⁵¹ The Apostolic Church was the first Western Pentecostal church to emerge in Ghana. However, Lloyd and Margaret Shirer, missionaries for the Assemblies of God, founded Pentecostal churches in Ghana in 1931 after arriving from Burkina Faso. It took them some time to become noticeable in the rest of Ghana, though, as their ministry concentrated on the less-developed northern region.⁵² In Ghana today, the Apostolic Church, Christ Apostolic Church International, the Assemblies of God, and the Church of Pentecost represent classical Pentecostalism.

The belief system of the worldwide Pentecostal movement, including the one in Ghana, highlights Holy Spirit baptism, a means by which people receive the Holy Spirit. For Frank Macchia, "Most Pentecostals view this as a revival or renewal experience in the Christian life and link it to involvement in the extraordinary gifts of the Spirit, especially speaking in tongues and divine healing."⁵³ Also, they consider Holy Spirit baptism as an eschatological sign, pointing to God's redemption before the *parousia*, or the second coming of Christ. Many Pentecostals see the Holy Spirit's presence in the cosmos as a sign of hope for the future, an ongoing process of creation, and a foretaste of the kingdom to come.⁵⁴ The inspiration behind their beliefs finds ground in the apostle Peter's Pentecost proclamation in which he reaffirmed Joel's prophecy (Acts 2:17). To continue the events of the book of Acts in the present day, Pentecostals strive to follow Acts' events, which linked early Jewish and Gentile encounters with the Spirit. As a first proof, speaking in tongues is the prime channel for advancing this course.⁵⁵ Pentecostals in Ghana demonstrate pneumatological prayer in the environment, including forests, under trees, on mountains, open fields, etc. by putting their belief in Spirit baptism and gifts of the Spirit into action. For example, it is typical to find Pentecostals praying

---

51. Opoku Onyinah, "Pentecostalism and the African Diaspora: An Examination of the Missions Activities of the Church of Pentecost," *Pneuma: The Journal of the Society for Pentecostal Studies* 26, no. 2 (2004): 225.

52. Alfred Koduah, "Classical Pentecostalism in Ghana," in *Christianity in Ghana: A Postcolonial History*, Vol. 1, ed. J. Kwabena Asamoah-Gyadu (Accra: Sub-Saharan Publishers, 2018), 139.

53. Frank D. Macchia, *Baptized in the Spirit: A Global Pentecostal Theology* (Grand Rapids: Zondervan, 2006), 27.

54. Althouse, *Spirit of the Last Days: Pentecostal Eschatology in Conversation with Jürgen Moltmann* (London: A&C Black, 2003), 162. Also see, Cartledge, *Testimony in the Spirit*, 172.

55. Macchia, *Baptized in the Spirit*, 64.

at Atwea Mountain in Ghana, although those from mainline traditions also pray there.[56]

For many Pentecostals, the presence of the Holy Spirit assures them that the God who hears their prayers and can meet their needs is with them. The psychology behind this confidence in the Holy Spirit is the fusion of the heart and mind during the act of prayer while anticipating answers.[57] This assertion implies that prayer is an engagement of all aspects of one's mind and heart, with the hope of visualizing results. The ontological dimension of heart-mind in prayer also constitutes worldviews (people's perceptions about the world passed on from generation to generation), the beliefs and expressions in their newly found faith, and their present conditions. These also include the belief in the sacrality of the natural environment, which has traces in the African primal worldview and has the tendency to give African Pentecostal Christians a plausible engagement with the Holy Spirit in their physical environment.[58] Biblical precedents, such as Moses's experience with the burning bush in Exodus 3:1–10, also help explain such sacred encounters in the environment. God manifested as a flame of fire, with Moses seeing a burning but not consumed bush. This miraculous sight drew Moses closer to the bush. Similarly, the miraculous signs of God's encounter in specific places in the environment prompt Ghanaian Pentecostal prayer engagements in these places. Again, considering Sallie McFague's metaphoric reference to the cosmos as "God's body," we can imagine that Ghanaian Pentecostals have the chance to view a portion of God's body, the cosmos, in these sacred spaces, just as Moses glimpsed God's back in Exodus 33:17–23.[59]

---

56. Cephas N. Omenyo, *Pentecost Outside Pentecostalism: A Study of the Development of Charismatic Renewal in the Mainline Churches in Ghana* (Zoetermeer: Uitgeverij Boekencentrum, 2002). See also Philip K. Okyere, "Pentecostalism, Pilgrimage to Prayer Mountains Pilgrims' Adherence to Holiness Ethics in Ghanaian Christianity," *Pentecostalism, Charismaticism and Neo-Prophetic Movements Journal (PECANEP)* 4, no. 2 (2023): 27–28.

57. Gerrit Immink, "Theological Analysis of Religious Practices," *International Journal of Practical Theology* 18, no. 1 (2014): 127–29.

58. Teddy Chalwe Sakupapa, "Spirit and Ecology in the Context of African Theology," *Scriptura* 111, no. 1 (2012): 423–28.

59. Sallie McFague, *The Body of God: An Ecological Theology* (Minneapolis: Fortress, 1993), 6.

Autobiographical Narratives on Ghanaian Pentecostal Prayer in Natural Environments
Autobiographical Testimony 1

I recall from my days in high school in the Bono region of Ghana a portion of land outside the school, with a big tree notably occupying some parts.[60] It was popularly called "Mango Down." Both male and female Christian students frequently trooped to this location to pray in the evenings. I observed the eagerness with which Ama, a close friend and roommate, went to Mango Down to pray in the evenings, usually joining a prayer group with other students. She mostly spent a long time praying with the group and would return to the dormitory late at night. I wondered about her excitement and drive for this Mango Down prayer gathering. She eventually invited me to this place after sharing her experiences with me. Such experiences included the perception that anytime she went there for group prayer she witnessed Spirit baptism and new Christian converts receiving the language of the Spirit. Deliverance sessions also took place there. I accepted her invitation and joined her in one of the prayer sessions.

At the prayer meeting, I observed that group members prayed in loud tones, and at some point, members began to speak in an unknown tongue as though they were under the Spirit's influence. There was also a noticeably prophetic exchange where some group members predicted unforeseen future events in the lives of other group members. These prophecies were bold, fierce, and uncontrollable utterances. I observed the gladness and joy with which the group leader followed proceedings in the prayer meeting. Later, he prayed for those prophesying and those receiving the prophecy. Toward the end of the meeting, the group leader called out individuals who had not yet received the gift of speaking in tongues to step forward for him to impart this spiritual gift to them. He also prayed for the sick and cast out demons from the lives of specific group members who, amid loud shouts, manifested what he called demonic possessions. This meeting did not surprise me because my Pentecostal background had exposed me to prayer groups of this nature. Yet, this particular prayer group fascinated me because of their unique style of worship under a mango tree.

---

60. The narrative in this section is the autobiographical testimony of the second author. She identifies as a Ghanaian Pentecostal and writes with an insider perspective. We use pseudonyms in our various narratives to conceal the identities of third parties since we do not have their permission to include them in this work.

Autobiographical Testimony 2

Powerhouse is a Pentecostal prayer group that Mr. Kofi Suro-Nipa pioneered in 2011. It is non-denominational and open to all and sundry. I joined this group at the invitation of a close relative and took part in prayer meetings for about four years, though not frequently.[61] This group convened every Monday and Thursday from 10 pm to 12 am for a unique prayer experience at a school field in the heart of a southern industrial city of Ghana. Lush vegetation glittering under the dark sky with beautiful stars surrounded this serene atmosphere. Congregants assembled in a circle, with artificial lights brightening the place. Upon arrival at the location, I would observe some congregants without footwear.

Although the prayer group did not have a formalized liturgy, I recall that the meeting usually started with an opening prayer by a volunteer congregant, after which a group of singers led a time of praise and adoration. It was a moment where an eruptive flow of spiritual energy aroused individuals, resulting in impulsive ruptures of adoration. Noticeably, some congregants bowed down while others lifted their hands in appreciation, with a distinct feeling of enthusiasm in the atmosphere. Then, the time came for testimonies, following the praise and adorations. The leader invited some congregants to recount their experiences of the miracles of God and responses to their prayers through health, marital, financial, and academic breakthroughs. It triggered a sense of wonder and thankfulness among congregants. The meeting later continued with the leader exhorting congregants with stories from the Bible, after which he ushered them into intense prayers. The prayers of congregants, spoken in diverse languages, rose in harmony. Individuals prayed for their needs, family, and friends and against spiritual forces hindering their progress, starting with the phrase (in the local dialect, Asante Twi language) "Awurade ee sɛ mebɔ men sam bɔ mpae a . . .," meaning "Oh God, if I clap my hands and pray . . ." This phrase took the congregants into another dimension of prayer. Aside from clapping hands, the leader sometimes asked congregants to move around or stamp their feet on the ground during prayer. At this point, the atmosphere became charged with loud prayers. The leader ended the warfare prayers, exclaiming loudly, "Holy Ghost," and the congregants responded, "Fire."

After vigorous prayers, the leader asked the congregants to be silent before God and stretch out their hands to receive an impartation, calling the Holy

---

61. The narrative in this section is the autobiographical testimony of the first author. He belongs to the Protestant (Methodist) tradition and identifies as a "friend" of Pentecostals, thus is an outsider.

Spirit to come upon them. During this encounter, some congregants fell under the unction of the power of the Spirit, bursting into loud cries and laughter, prophesying, and speaking in tongues. The leader expelled evil spirits lingering around some congregants, sometimes having a long confrontation with these spirits. He sometimes sprinkled anointing oil or water on these individuals while praying for them. He also prayed for healing for the sick, with some testifying to their instant healing. As a participant, I occasionally felt a sudden increase in atmospheric temperature, depicted through goosebumps. There was sometimes a scent of flowering plants delivered by soft winds, and I could smell it as the darkness grew. At some points, I used to imagine that perhaps the environment was demonstrating God's attendance at the meeting. The sound of leaves creaking seemed to reflect this belief. After the spiritual encounter, the leader closed the meeting with a word of prayer and gave the benediction. The congregants left the location for their homes with a revitalized feeling of commitment and fellowship. Previously an ordinary setting, the wide-open fields seem to have evolved into a hallowed area where congregants offered prayers, encountered God, and grew in faith.

Towards an Afro-Eco-Pentecostal Missiology

According to Ross Langmead, "Ecomissiology is an approach to mission which sees the mission of God in terms of reconciliation at all levels in a reality characterized by relationship and interdependence throughout."[62] Within the broader field of ecotheology, capturing eco-missiology, the *missio Dei* (God's mission) has a trinitarian interpretation.[63] Ecotheology stresses the involvement of God in creation, typically defined as "panentheism."[64] This perspective highlights the close relationship between the environment, humans, and God. However, as Jürgen Moltmann rightly argued, sin corrupts this God-human connection, affecting every aspect of the natural order and putting all creation in desperate need of God's reconciliation (Rom 8:19–22).[65] Even so, God initiates a reconciliation agenda for the entire cosmos through the person of

---

62. Ross Langmead, "Ecomissiology," *Missiology* 30 (2002): 505.
63. Langmead, "Ecomissiology," 506–8.
64. Jay McDaniel, *With Roots and Wings: Christianity in an Age of Ecology and Dialogue* (Maryknoll: Orbis, 1995), 97. Also see Langmead, "Ecomissiology," 506.
65. Jürgen Moltmann, *God in Creation: An Ecological Doctrine of Creation*, trans. Margaret Kohl (London: SCM, 1985), 233–34.

Christ (2 Cor 5:18–20). The Holy Spirit actively participates in the reconciliation agenda through the Spirit's association with creation and renewal.

Within the African Pentecostal mission, the Holy Spirit influences the praxis of spirituality through the Spirit's "transformative power," driving individual and corporate actions.[66] The Powerhouse prayer group corroborates this argument by appropriating the "Holy Ghost Fire" phrase. The descriptions of their prayer activities suggest that in Ghanaian Pentecostals' lived theology, the fire of the Holy Spirit has seemingly been perceived as a source of power to overcome evil forces that work against them. This observation affirms that worship engagements, enshrined in actions and statements, are how Africans interact with their spiritual world.[67] Also, religious practice in African (Ghanaian) Pentecostalism qualifies as establishing a connection to power sources and channels in the universe, just like in the primal worldview.[68]

Notably, the Powerhouse prayer group leader encourages congregants to end prayers with "Holy Ghost Fire" to move the "firepower" of God, empowering them to overcome evil forces. This scenario bears semblance to the Pentecostal experience of the early church portrayed in the book of Acts. With the early Christians, the Spirit empowered them for missions when they were hiding in fear. However, within the Powerhouse prayer group, the Spirit comes when people pray with great energy by clapping their hands, stamping their feet, and sometimes moving around, empowering them to battle evil forces. Also, while the early Christians had their first Pentecostal experience in the upper room, some Ghanaian Pentecostals first encountered the Spirit in the natural environment, similar to previous Pentecostal experiences elsewhere, such as the Azusa Street revival. This noticeable variation supports the assertion of Moltmann that "the experience of the Holy Spirit is as specific as the living beings who experience the Spirit and as varied as the living beings who experience the Spirit are varied."[69]

Furthermore, both narratives disclose the eagerness of members of these prayer groups to experience the divine in these sacred spaces. The ecstasy of falling into trances under the Spirit, the reception of the gifts of the Holy Spirit, such as speaking in tongues, the revelation of past and future events

---

66. Amos J. Markin, "Spirit and Mission: The Church of Pentecost as a Growing African Pentecostal Denomination" (PhD Diss., South African Theological Seminary, 2018), 294.

67. Mbiti, *African Religions and Philosophy*, 58.

68. Kwame Bediako, *Christianity in Africa. The Renewal of a Non-Western Religion* (Edinburgh: Edinburgh University Press, 1995), 106.

69. Jürgen Moltmann, *The Source of Life: The Holy Spirit and the Theology of Life*, trans. Margaret Kohl (Minneapolis: Fortress, 1997), 56.

(prophecy), healing, and deliverance in this sacred space motivate the prayer experience. At the Powerhouse specifically, marked by testimonies about God's divine provision, healing, academic and marital breakthroughs, freedom from demonic oppressions, etc., other members are encouraged and challenged to attend meetings regularly for results and testimonies. Also, many participate in these meetings because of the conviction that God is present in those sacred spaces, and their participation in those groups could solidify their bond with God through the Spirit. These two prayer groups reveal patterns of heart-mind engagement, which encompass their worldview (the way of seeing the world, including experiences and stories that have been told and passed on from generation to generation) and the outer disposition of their relationship with the divine and all life on earth.

Arguably, Ghanaian Pentecostal Christians who pray in the natural environment, with such pneumatological understanding, help enhance environmental respect in Ghana, an African country struggling with several forms of environmental degradation, as discussed previously. The preservation of natural resources in Ghana, including forest reserves like the Achimota forest, can be boosted if Ghana's Environmental Protection Agency (EPA) and other relevant agencies continually allocate spaces in the forest for prayer groups. The more prayer groups are encouraged to pray around vegetation zones, the more the EPA has leverage to achieve its environmental protection goal. Such an undertaking will help ensure the continuity of forest resources such as trees, streams, and wildlife species. Also, by transferring the perception of interacting with God in sacred spaces to their children through socialization, parents can contribute to conscientizing the younger generation to treat their environment, the body of God, with respect. It will help reduce individual activities that cause damage to the environment, including deforestation, *galamsey*[70] operations, water pollution, etc. Moreover, Ghanaian Pentecostal Christians, with a strong interest in prayer in the natural environment, could contribute to eco-missiology by consciously adopting these sacred spaces for their worship engagements and inviting others to join them in serving their triune God.

---

70. Galamsey refers to illegal small-scale gold mining. Historically, the term referred to traditional small-scale mining practices in which local communities searched for gold in rivers and streams however, over time, the term has taken on a broader meaning.

Conclusion

To answer the central question of this chapter, we argue that pneumatological prayer engagements in Ghana's natural environment could be a positive way of protecting environmental resources. Active prayer meetings in these sacred spaces can help reduce harmful practices like deforestation. Individuals who pray in parts of the environment seek to honour the God present with them in such spaces, who can reveal God's self through God's Spirit and come to their aid. Adding to eco-missiology discourses, we advocate an Afro-Eco-Pentecostal missiological approach in addressing environmental degradation in Ghana and sub-Saharan Africa. We argue that this approach seeks to contextualize eco-missiology within sub-Saharan Africa, recognizing the interplay between African indigenous worldview and Pentecostal spirituality in the interactions of Africans (Ghanaians) with a panentheistic God who often visits them through prayer engagements in sacred spaces and calls them to invite others to join them in worshipping their Lord. Yet, we acknowledge that the limited narratives in our life histories may not allow for generalizing the findings of this work to the Pentecostal community in Ghana or sub-Saharan Africa at large. Further research is necessary to provide a more profound analysis of the prospects of this Pentecostal prayer engagement, especially among the adherents.

Bibliography

Akudugu, Mamudu A., Saa Dittoh, and Edward S. Mahama. "The Implications of Climate Change on Food Security and Rural Livelihoods." *Journal of Environment and Earth Science* 2, no. 3 (2012): 21–29.

Althouse, Peter. *Spirit of the Last Days: Pentecostal Eschatology in Conversation with Jürgen Moltmann*. London: A&C Black, 2003.

Anderson, Allan H. *An Introduction to Pentecostalism: Global Charismatic Christianity*. New York: Cambridge University Press, 2014.

Appiah-Effah, Eugene, et al. "Ghana's Post-MDGs Sanitation Situation: An Overview." *Journal of Water, Sanitation and Hygiene for Development* 9, no. 3 (2019): 397–415.

Asamoah-Gyadu, Johnson K. *African Charismatics: Current Developments within Independent Indigenous Pentecostalism in Ghana*. Leiden: Brill, 2005.

Ayee, Joseph R. A. "The Formulation and Implementation of Environmental Policy in Ghana." *Journal of Africa Development/Afrique et Développement* 23, no. 2 (1998): 99–119.

Bediako, Kwame. *Christianity in Africa. The Renewal of a Non-Western Religion*. Edinburgh: Edinburgh University Press, 1995.

———. *Jesus in Africa: The Christian Gospel in African History and Experience*. Akropong-Akuapem: Regnum Africa, 2013.

Blasu, Ebenezer Y. *African Theocology: Studies in African Religious Creation Care.* Eugene: Wipf & Stock, 2020.

Briggs, Philip. *Ghana: The Bradt Travel Guide.* Guildford: Globe Pequot, 2017.

Cartledge, Mark J. *Charismatic Glossolalia: An Empirical–Theological Study.* Aldershot: Ashgate, 2002.

———. *Testimony in the Spirit: Rescripting Ordinary Pentecostal Theology.* Farnham: Routledge, 2010.

———. *Practical Theology: Charismatic and Empirical Perspectives.* Eugene: Wipf & Stock, 2012.

CC DARE. "Ghana National Climate Change Adaptation Strategy." United Nations Development Program, 2012. https://www.adaptation-undp.org/resources/ghanas-national-climate-change-adaptation-strategy-november-2012.

Cobbinah, Patrick B., Michael Poku-Boansi, and Charles Peprah. "Urban Environmental Problems in Ghana." *Environmental Development* 23 (2017): 33–46.

Cox, Harvey G. *Fire from Heaven: The Rise of Spirituality and the Reshaping of Religion in the Twenty-First Century.* Reading: Addison-Wesley, 1995.

Eshun, Edwin K. "Religion and Nature in Akan Culture: A Case Study of Okyeman Environment Foundation." Master's Thesis, Queen's University, 2011.

Ghana Statistical Service. "Ghana 2021 Population and Housing Census: General Report Volume 3C." https://census2021.statsghana.gov.gh/gssmain/fileUpload/reportthemelist/2021%20PHC%20General%20Report%20Vol%203C_Background%20Characteristics_181121.pdf.

Hilson, Gavin. "A Contextual Review of the Ghanaian Small-Scale Mining Industry." *Mining, Minerals and Sustainable Development* 76 (2001): 1–29.

Immink, Gerrit. "Theological Analysis of Religious Practices." *International Journal of Practical Theology* 18, no. 1 (2014): 127–38. https://doi.org/10.1515/ijpt-2014-0010.

Kalu, Ogbu. *African Pentecostalism: An Introduction.* Oxford: Oxford University Press, 2008.

Koduah, Alfred. "Classical Pentecostalism in Ghana." In *Christianity in Ghana: A Postcolonial History*, Vol. 1, edited by J. Kwabena Asamoah-Gyadu, 136–67. Accra: Sub-Saharan Publishers, 2018.

Land, Steven J. *Pentecostal Spirituality. A Passion for the Kingdom.* Cleveland: CPT, 2010.

Langmead, Ross. "Ecomissiology." *Missiology* 30 (2002): 505–18.

Macchia, Frank D. *Baptized in the Spirit: A Global Pentecostal Theology.* Grand Rapids: Zondervan, 2006.

Markin, Amos J. "Spirit and Mission: The Church of Pentecost as a Growing African Pentecostal Denomination." PhD Thesis, South African Theological Seminary, 2018.

Mbiti, John S. *African Religions and Philosophy.* London: Biddles, 1989.

McAdams, Dan P. "The Development of Narrative Identity." In *Personality Psychology: Recent Trends and Emerging Directions*, edited by David M. Buss and Nancy Cantor, 160–74. New York: Springer, 2012.

McDaniel, Jay. *With Roots and Wings: Christianity in an Age of Ecology and Dialogue*. Maryknoll: Orbis, 1995.

McFague, Sallie. *The Body of God: An Ecological Theology*. Minneapolis: Fortress, 1993.

Ministry of Environmental Science and Technology. *Ghana National Climate Change Policy*. Accra: Republic of Ghana, 2013. https://www.clientearth.org/media/p13faarf/national-climate-change-policy-ext-en.pdf.

Moltmann, Jürgen. *God in Creation: An Ecological Doctrine of Creation*, translated by Margaret Kohl. London: SCM, 1985.

———. *The Source of Life: The Holy Spirit and the Theology of Life*, translated by Margaret Kohl. Minneapolis: Fortress, 1997.

Musson, Gill. "Life Histories." In *Essential Guide to Qualitative Methods in Organizational Research*, edited by Catherine Cassell and Gillian Symon, 34–44. London: Sage, 2004.

Okesson, Gregg A. *Re-Imaging Modernity: A Contextualized Theological Study of Power and Humanity Within Akamba Christianity in Kenya*. Eugene: Pickwick, 2012.

Okyere, Philip K. "Pentecostalism, Pilgrimage to Prayer Mountains Pilgrims' Adherence to Holiness Ethics in Ghanaian Christianity." *Pentecostalism, Charismaticism and Neo-Prophetic Movements Journal (PECANEP)* 4, no. 2 (2023): 25–42.

Okyerefo, Michael. "'I Experience Serenity and Convenience in the Forest': Achimota Forest Turned Sacred Space to Confront the Vicissitudes of Life." *Journal of the Sociology and Theory of Religion* 3 (2014). https://uvadoc.uva.es/handle/10324/19757.

Omenyo, Cephas N. *Pentecost Outside Pentecostalism: A Study of the Development of Charismatic Renewal in the Mainline Churches in Ghana*. Zoetermeer: Uitgeverij Boekencentrum, 2002.

Onyinah, Opoku. "Pentecostalism and the African Diaspora: An Examination of the Missions Activities of The Church of Pentecost." *Pneuma: The Journal of the Society for Pentecostal Studies* 26, no. 2 (2004): 216–41.

Oppong-Konadu, Kwame. "Glossolalia: A Critical Reflection on the Gift of Speaking in Tongues in Ghanaian Pentecostalism." Master's Thesis, Protestant Theological University, 2020.

Paris, Peter J. "The Spirituality of African Peoples." *Journal of Black Theology in South Africa* 7, no. 2 (1993): 114–24.

Sakupapa, Teddy Chalwe. "Spirit and Ecology in the Context of African Theology: Christian Faith and the Earth." *Scriptura: Journal for Contextual Hermeneutics in Southern Africa* 111, no. 1 (2012): 422–30.

Settles, Joshua. "Engaging Issues of Primal Spirituality and Identity: An Analysis of Short-Term Mission Training." Master's Thesis, Akrofi-Christaller Institute of Theology, Mission and Culture, 2013.

Songsore, Jacob. "Gender, Environment, and Human Security in the Greater Accra Metropolitan Area (GAMA), Ghana." In *Gendered Insecurities, Health, and Development in Africa*, edited by Howard Stein and Amal Hassan Fadlalla, 131–53. London: Routledge, 2012.

Swoboda, A. J. *Tongues and Trees: Towards A Pentecostal Ecological Theology*. Leiden: Brill, 2019.

Taylor, John V. *The Primal Vision: Christian Presence Amid African Religion*. London: SCM, 1963.

Twum, Nana Sifa. "Green Ghana Project: Planting 20 million tree seedlings for generations." *GBC Ghana Online,* June 13, 2022. https://www.gbcghanaonline.com/commentary/green-ghana-project/2022/.

Van den Toren, Benno, and Kang-Sang Tan. *Humble Confidence: A New Model for Interfaith Apologetics*. Westmont: InterVarsity, 2022.

World Bank Group. *Ghana Country Environmental Analysis: Case Studies and Assessments*. Washington, DC: World Bank, 2020. https://www.ccacoalition.org/en/resources/ghana-country-environmental-analysis.

12

Eco-Ecclesiology

Repositioning Classical Ghanaian Pentecostal Ecclesiology toward Creation Care

Emmanuel Awudi

The work of Lynn White Jr. which placed the blame of ecological crises at the doorsteps of the Christian faith caused Christian scholars to re-examine ecclesiology and eco-care.[1] White contends that the Judeo-Christian faith which gives dominion over other creation to humanity led to the exploitation of the earth and its resources.[2] For him, the Judeo-Christian thinking of a transcendent God removed the idea of God from nature and allowed for its exploitation.

Though White's criticism of the faith led to a shift in theology and practice among many evangelical denominations,[3] Pentecostals were slow to this move until recently. One major reason for their late appearance on the ecological dialogue table is the priority they place on the winning of souls and prepar-

---

1. See Francis A. Schaeffer, *Pollution and the Death of Man: The Christian View of Ecology* (Wheaton: Tyndale, 1970); Richard L. Means, "Why Worry About Nature?," *Saturday Review*, essay, 2 December 1967.

2. Lynn White Jr., "The Historical Roots of our Ecologic Crisis," *Science* 155 (1967): 1203–7.

3. According to Amy Ross, ecotheology has become more prominent in evangelical missions, and they appear to have done better in this area than Pentecostals. Writing in 2012, she contends that the belief that creation care should play a role in the mission of God's people has well been established in the literature of evangelical theologians over the last twenty years. Amy Ross, "Integrating Ecological Mission into Mainstream Mission," *Australian Journal of Mission Studies* 6, no. 2 (2012): 48.

ing them for the return of Christ over efforts to heal the ailing earth.[4] Shane Clifton, made a similar assertion after reviewing about 108 monthly magazines published by the *Australian Evangel* magazine. He observed that none of the monthly issues published by the magazine out of this huge number touched on issues related to the environment except one which made reference to environmental degradation as a fulfilment of end-time prophecy.[5] This is because the majority of Pentecostals and charismatics see efforts to save the ailing earth as secondary to strategies that lead to the winning of souls. For many Pentecostals, ecological crises are signs of the second coming of Christ of which nothing can be done to mitigate its impact. Again, Pentecostals used to view with suspicion those who engage in activities other than soul winning as carnally minded believers.[6] Studebaker cites a personal example

> My sister and I were in college and graduated from school at roughly the same time. She earned degrees in environmental science and management and I in ministry and theology. Her work concentrated on tending the earth and mine on the church and "souls." I thought I had pursued a higher calling than hers and frankly thought her somewhat crazy for trying to "save" the spotted owls and old-growth forests. However, now I believe she was hearing the groans of the Spirit within Creation and "keep[ing] in step with the Spirit" (Gal 5:25, NIV).[7]

Yet in recent times, there is a growing realization within the tradition that such matters are very important and should no longer be swept under the carpet. Some denominations within the tradition are beginning to appreciate that the great commission works in tandem with the first commission to humanity; to keep and guard the earth and its inhabitants. For instance, the Vision 2023 of the Church of Pentecost (CoP), lists sanitation as one of the

---

4. Ben-Willie Kwaku Golo, "The Groaning Earth and the Greening of Neo-Pentecostalism in the 21st Century Ghana," *PentecoStudies* 13, no. 2 (2014): 202.

5. Shane Clifton, "Preaching the 'Full Gospel' in the Context of the Global Environmental Crises," in *The Spirit Renews the Face of the Ground: Pentecostal Forays in Science and Theology of Creation*, ed. Amos Yong (Eugene: Pickwick, 2009), 117.

6. Emmanuel Awudi, "Beyond Eco-Pneumatology: An Examination of Scripture with 'Green Eyes' and the Eco-Praxis of Some 'Indigenous African Churches' Towards the Development of an African Pentecostal Ecotheology" (PhD Diss., Akrofi-Christaller Institute, 2023), 88.

7. Steven M. Studebaker, "The Spirit in Creation: A Unified Theology of Grace and Creation Care," *Zygon: Journal of Religion and Science* 43, no. 4 (2008): 953.

strategies to community transformation.[8] The succeeding sections discuss the success and possibly the weaknesses of the CoP's annual creation care campaign and how to maximize the benefits.

The Creation Care Campaign of the CoP

In 2018, the leadership of the CoP launched the Vision 2023, "Possessing the Nations," with the focus of transforming every sphere of life with the values and principles of the kingdom of God. Creation care became one of the thematic areas of the vision.[9] The environmental campaign was launched on 22 November 2018 followed by a clean-up exercise on 8 December 2018 at Kasoa, a suburb of Ghana's Capital City, Accra. Other branches of the church organized the clean-up exercise in March 2019. Since then, the campaign has become an annual event, featuring prominently on the church's annual calendar of activities.

Aside from the clean-up exercises, in 2021, the church supported the Ghanaian government's "Green Ghana" project by planting 658,000 seedlings (out of a target of one million trees) across the country with about 81 percent survival rate. In 2022, the church planted 1,000,000 trees across the country. In 2023 and 2024, the focus of the campaign was on plastic waste management dubbed, "Buy Back." The church mobilized aggregators who helped in gathering plastics and sold them to waste management companies in the country for recycling.

In all, there was some level of education where both pastors and the laity were taken through some form of training and they in turn trained members of the church.

> Thus, topics on creation care were introduced in the training manuals for lay leaders . . . The manual for leaders in Advanced Level 3, which was prepared in May 2018 for the training of church leaders August 2018, included topics on creation care such as, "Taking Care of Our Father's Property," "Environmental Pollution

---

8. The Church of Pentecost, *Vision 2023: Five-Year Vision Document for the Church of Pentecost Covering the Period 2018–2023* (Accra: Pentecost Press, 2018), 62–63.

9. The Church of Pentecost, *Vision 2023*, 62–63.

and its Effects," "Assembly Bye Laws, Regulations, Principles and Personal Responsibility," and "Sanitation & Pollution."[10]

The Youth Ministry of the church also introduced topics on creation care into their annual devotional guides to help in educating the youth of the church on the biblical foundation for creation care.[11] These topics were also included in the annual Bible study outlines of the church to be studied in all local churches.

Though there has been some level of success with the CoP's environmental campaign, there are still areas that are yet to be addressed. The then General Secretary of the church, A. N. Y. Kumi-Larbi, argues that the environmental campaign of the church can only be sustained with attitudinal change. He made this remark three days after the first clean-up exercise in Kasoa (at a meeting of CoP pastors and officers in Kasoa Area at Mount Olives Assembly on 11 December 2018, which I attended), as he observed the filth remaining even at places that were cleaned.

Until 2018, nothing related to creation care featured in the previous visions of the church, except for a sermon note on stewardship in 2015 which admonished believers to be good stewards of God's creation.[12] The explanation of all the eleven tenets of the church are human-centred.[13] I argued in my thesis that the doctrines of Pentecostals in general do not motivate them to care for the other-than-human creation due to the anthropocentric hermeneutical principles embedded in them.[14] Emmanuel Anim attributes this to the prosperity gospel of the West. He writes,

> My thesis is that many African Pentecostal and Charismatic Christians have bought into the dominion theology or the prosperity gospel, which presents the most anthropocentric approach to reli-

---

10. Emmanuel Anim and Emmanuel Awudi, "Foundations and Practical Implications of the Ecological Work of the Church of Pentecost in Ghana," in *International Handbook on Creation Care and Eco-Diakonia: Concepts and Theological Perspectives of Churches from the Global South*, eds. Daniel Beros, et al. (Oxford: Regnum, 2022), 542.

11. Anim and Awudi, "Foundations and Practical Implications," 543. See also The Church of Pentecost, *Youth Ministry, Streams of Living Water 2021: A Daily Devotional Guide* (Accra: Pentecost Press, 2021), 336–45.

12. See Opuku Onyinah, *Christian Stewardship* (Accra: Pentecost Press, 2015), 104–11.

13. See Opuku Onyinah, Michael Ntumy, Alfred Koduah, Emmanuel Anim, eds., *Tenets of the Church of Pentecost* (Accra: The Church of Pentecost, 2019).

14. Awudi, "Beyond Eco-Pneumatology," 96.

gion and faith and thereby changed their attitudes to what was considered "sacred."[15]

This observation is common in all strands of Pentecostalism in Africa – whether classical Pentecostalism or charismatic. Thus, until Pentecostal-charismatic ecclesiology fully embraces ecotheology, there would be inadequate motivation in the tradition to care for creation.

Pentecostal-Charismatic Ecclesiology

Pentecostalism is one unique church tradition in the Christian faith today. Currently, it is the largest and the fastest growing church tradition in the world. As of mid-2023, it was estimated that 679,085,000 Christians in the world belonged to the Pentecostal/charismatic tradition, more than a quarter of the world's 2,604,381,000 Christian population.[16] Despite these large numbers, their influence in biodiversity conservation is minimal compared to some other church traditions.

Pentecostal-charismatic ecclesiology is defined and shaped by their Christology which they term as the "full gospel," anchored on five pillars – salvation, healing, sanctification, Spirit-empowerment, and the *parousia*. To be precise, the "full gospel," according to Jack Land, "consists of five elements – salvation, sanctification, healing, Holy Spirit baptism, and eschatology."[17] These elements of the "full gospel" have been the defining characteristics of Pentecostal-charismatic ecclesiology and missiology. It has informed their way of worship, how they pray, and the songs they sing.

However, I have argued that limiting the gospel of Christ to these five elements of Christology, short-changes Scripture.[18] Similarly, Kwame Bediako is of the view that any attempt to limit the explanation of the gospel to the New Tes-

---

15. Emmanuel Anim, "Environmental Sustainability and Eco-Justice: Reflections from an African Pentecostal," in *Kairos for Creation: Confessing Hope for the Earth*, eds. Louk Andrioanos, Thomas Sander, Juliane Stork, and Dietrich Werner (Wuppertal: United Evangelical Mission, 2019), 108.

16. Todd M. Johnson, Gina A. Zurlo, and Peter F. Crossing, "World Christianity 2023: A Gendered Approach," *International Bulletin of Mission Research* 47, no. 1 (2023): 71–80.

17. Steven J. Land, *Pentecostal Spirituality. A Passion for the Kingdom* (Cleveland: CPT, 2010), 7. However, the tradition often merges the sanctification element with the baptism of the Holy Spirit making the "full gospel" Jesus the Saviour, Jesus the Healer, Jesus the Baptizer of the Holy Spirit, and Jesus the Soon-Coming King – sometimes referred to as the "Four-Square Gospel."

18. Awudi, "Beyond Eco-Pneumatology," 7.

tament or the incarnation of Christ, runs the risk of over-simplification.[19] This has impacted also the way they treat the other-than-human species because doctrines believed and practiced determine how a person relates to others including the earth and its inhabitants. After analysing their oral and written theologies (songs, and tenets), I discovered anthropocentric tendencies in the explanations of their major doctrines, especially, the components of the "Full Gospel" as discussed in the next section of this chapter.

Impact of Pentecostal-Charismatic Ecclesiology on Creation Care

Even though, some African Pentecostal churches are involved in creation care campaigns, as seen in the previous sections, because they see these annual events as secondary to evangelistic activities, they are unable to yield the desired impact. Two major reasons for this inadequacy in African Pentecostal ecclesiology are a demarcation between what is sacred and secular, and the anthropocentric tendencies in their major doctrines. An analysis of the content of their "Full Gospel" shows a lack of ecological ethos in its explanation. Shane Clifton made a similar observation with Pentecostals in general as he avers that

> Traditionally, Pentecostals have proclaimed what is variously labelled the "fourfold" or "Full Gospel" which announced Jesus as Saviour, healer, baptizer in the Holy Spirit and a soon coming King. What is readily apparent is the way in which the various elements of the Pentecostal proclamation have been framed in a manner that excludes an ecological focus.[20]

He argues that the "full gospel" carries salvation in Christ as relating to only the human soul. For that matter, Pentecostals and neo-Pentecostals regard any other activity, including social actions directed at saving the earth as pre-evangelistic, rather than something which is connected with the gospel.

In most literature related to soteriology, Pentecostal-charismatic theologians and preachers have focused their attention on the reconciliation of humans to God. This is largely because of anthropocentric interpretations of the doctrine of sin. Charles Birch observed in 1990 that "Christians see themselves as having an obligation to work for the liberation of the oppressed. Yet there is one group that has caused little concern among Christians, who seem

---

19. Kwame Bediako, "What is the Gospel?," *Transformation* 14, no. 1 (1997): 4.

20. Shane Clifton, "Preaching the 'Full Gospel,' in the Context of the Global Environmental Crises," in *The Spirit Renews the Face of the Ground: Pentecostal Forays in Science and Theology of Creation*, ed. Amos Yong (Eugene: Pickwick, 2009), 118.

to have left the task of this particular liberation to secular movements."[21] What Birch implies is that mission to the marginalized needs to include the other-than-human community. In other words, the marginalized includes flora and fauna who have been groaning since the fall of Adam.

Even though, Scripture is explicit on the impact of Adam's sin on six relationships in the ecosystem,[22] the explanation of soteriology in the doctrinal statements of Pentecostal-charismatic churches is only concerned about the restoration of the relationship between the Creator and the human species. For instance, the doctrine of salvation is captured in the constitution of the Assemblies of God as "The Salvation of Man" and it states, "Man's only hope of redemption is through the shed blood of Jesus Christ the Son of God."[23] Both the title and the explanation of this doctrinal statement suggest that the focus is on the redemption of only humanity. Similarly, Ben-Willie Kwaku Golo argues that "The definition that neo-Pentecostals have of their existence is defined in terms of the spiritual salvation of man and preparing 'saved souls' for the *parousia*."[24] This makes the concern for winning souls and preparing them for heaven override efforts to save the groaning earth. Thus, Pentecostals carefully select and participate in activities that would either lead to the winning of souls or inure to their own benefits.

As seen with the doctrine of salvation, the doctrine of divine healing is not only anthropocentric but excludes the application of any other means except prayer. The position of the CoP on healing is explained as, "The healing of sicknesses and diseases is provided for God's people in the atoning death of Christ. The church is, however, not opposed to soliciting the help of qualified

---

21. Charles Birch, "Christian Obligation for the Liberation of Nature," in *Liberating Life: Contemporary Approaches to Ecological Theology*, eds. Charles Birch, William Eakin, and Jay B. McDaniel (Eugene: Wipf & Stock, 1990), 57.

22. The sin of Adam affected these relationships as discussed in the earlier paragraphs. These relationships include the relationship between God and humanity (Gen 3:8), human and his/her inner self (Gen 3:9–10), between human and human (Gen 3:12), God and other-than-human creation (Gen 3:14–15), human and other-than-human creation (Gen 3:17–19), and between other-than-human species within the ecosystem. See Emmanuel Awudi, "Building Creation Care Culture in the African Church: The Role of the Pulpit," *Journal of African Christian Thoughts* 26, no. 2 (2023): 23–25; Allison Howell, "The Bible and Care Creation," in *Bible in Mission*, eds. Pauline Hoggarth, Fergus Macdonald, Bill Mitchell and Knud Jørgensen (Oxford: Regnum, 2013), 176.

23. Assemblies of God, Ghana, *Constitution and Bye-Laws* (Accra: The Assemblies of God Literature Centre, 2013), 12–13.

24. Ben-Willie Kwaku Golo, "The Groaning Earth and the Greening of Neo-Pentecostalism in the 21st Century Ghana," *PentecoStudies* 13, no. 2 (2014): 202.

medical practitioners (2 Ki 20:7; Mk 9:12; Lk 10:34; Col 4:14)."[25] This explanation excludes the healing of the other-than-human species. Opoku Onyinah in expounding the doctrine of divine healing explains it as ". . . the healing of a physical or psychosomatic disease or condition through prayer."[26] Onyinah's definition is the prevailing understanding of healing among Classical Ghanaian Pentecostals and charismatics. "I grew up in a classical Pentecostal church where testimonies of healing implied that the use of medications indicated a lack of faith. Some individuals testified that they threw away their medications or refused caesarean operations during childbirth to show they had faith."[27] Their understanding was that healing that involved any procedure apart from prayer does not fall under divine healing. Thus, aside from the exclusion of medical procedures in divine healing, it is defined in anthropocentric terms. In other words, the healing of the other-than-human creation is excluded in the definition of divine healing among classical Pentecostals.

Pneumatology is one of the major points of divergence between Pentecostals and other denominations. It also remains arguably the most researched area among Pentecostals as far as the search for a Pentecostal Ecotheology is concerned. The constitution of the CoP states that "We believe in the Baptism of the Holy Spirit for all believers with the initial evidence of speaking in tongues (Joel 2:28, 29; Ac 2:3, 4, 38, 39; 10:44–46; 19:16), and in the operation of the gifts and the fruit of the Holy Spirit (Mk 16:17; Ac 2:4; 1 Co 12:8–11; Ga 5:22, 23)."[28] This largely reflects the view of the Pentecostal and charismatic churches.

My position is that even though the baptism of the Holy Spirit is a promise to only believers, the empowering work goes beyond the human community. However, this view is largely missing in Pentecostals' explanation of pneumatology. One thing that accounts for the missing ecological ethos in Pentecostal-charismatic pneumatology is that their interpretation of pneumatology usually begins from the New Testament; from the Lukan Scriptures.[29] Thus, they see the baptism of the Holy Spirit as power to proclaim the gospel and win souls. Though the sanctification role of the Spirit baptism is sometimes mentioned,

---

25. The Church of Pentecost, *The Constitution of the Church of Pentecost* (Accra: Pentecost Press, 2016), 9.

26. Opoku Onyinah, "Faith, Healing and Mission: Perspectives from the Bible," in *Christian Missions Ecumenism in Ghana: Essays in Honor of Robert K. Aboagye-Mensah*, ed. J. Kwabena Asamoah-Gyadu (Accra: Asempa, 2009), 213.

27. Awudi, "Beyond Eco-Pneumatology," 152.

28. The Church of Pentecost, *The Constitution of the Church of Pentecost*, 9.

29. Julie C. Ma and Wonsuk Ma, *Mission in the Spirit: Towards a Pentecostal/Charismatic Missiology* (Eugene: Wipf & Stock, 2010), 18–28.

what is mostly emphasized is power to cast out demons, heal the sick, and perform signs and wonders.[30] Thus, Pentecostals' conception of the Spirit baptism is that Jesus gives the believer power to evangelize and to cast out demons.

Owing to this understanding, early African Pentecostals deemed traditions, rules, rituals, and regulations that were used to conserve sacred forests and water bodies, as demonic, fit to be exorcized. Instead of converting these traceable primal environmental praxes, they condemned them without providing alternatives. This is evident in both their written and oral theologies as seen in the Ghanaian Pentecostal song below.

Nea Owui wɔ Kalvary sunsum no	The Spirit of the one who died at Calvary
Reyɛ anwanwa dwuma (2x)	Is performing wonders (2x)
Retu mmonsam, resa nyarewa	Casting out demons, healing the sick
Siw gyata ano, redum 'gya tum'	Shuts the mouths of lions, quenching raging fire
Reka ananafo mpasua nyinaa gu	Putting foreign armies to flight
Nea Owui wɔ Kalvary sunsum no	The Spirit of the one who died at Calvary
Reyɛ anwanwa dwuma[31]	Is performing wonders

Thus, African Pentecostals' understanding of the empowering role of the Holy Spirit is to enable them to heal the sick and cast out demons. This led to the exploitation and destruction of creation. My argument, however, is that the Spirit that creates, gives life, and empowers believers for service to all creation, is the same Spirit that groans with creation and intercedes on their behalf.

The last component of the "Full Gospel," which is the second coming of Christ, is least concerned about ecology. Similarly, Clifton argues that the worst aspect of the expatiation of the "Full Gospel" is eschatology, which Pentecostals understand as the rapture of the saints, followed by a total extermination of the earth and its inhabitants.[32] Though it is one of the major motivations for the evangelistic activities within the Pentecostals tradition, it affects their zeal towards creation care. Within the Pentecostal-charismatic circles, the dominant understanding of eschatology is the "salvation of the souls of the righteous from

---

30. Awudi, "Beyond Eco-Pneumatology," 86.

31. The Church of Pentecost Headquarters, *Pentecost Song Book* (Accra: Pentecost Press, 2016), 303.

32. Clifton, "Preaching the 'Full Gospel'," 120.

the torment of hell, followed by a total destruction of the present heaven and earth."[33] However, "An understanding of salvation as a flight from the earth and its inhabitants potentially leads to the exploitation of creation or less interest in what happens to them."[34] One aspect of eschatology which affects Pentecostals' zeal in eco-care is where humanity will spend eternity. The prevailing view among Pentecostals and charismatics is that believers will spend eternity in heaven. This is evident in many of their songs as seen below.

> I am traveling to heaven
> Heaven is my home
> There are storms on the way
> But with Jesus in my heart
> I have my salvation
> I am working my way through
> I shall be in heaven
> Heaven is my home[35]

As observed in the introduction, this worldview about eschatology has also created several blind spots in Pentecostal-charismatic ecclesiology and has affected how they relate to things here on earth.

Repositioning Pentecostal Ecclesiology Towards Creation Care

I concluded in my doctoral thesis that "Until creation care becomes a lifestyle, environmental campaigns and clean-up exercises alone cannot save the ailing earth. One sure way to making creation care a lifestyle is for ecotheology to be fully embraced by the tenets and major doctrines of all church traditions."[36] In the succeeding paragraphs, I shall propose strategies towards maximizing the impact of Pentecostal ecclesiology on creation care.

The first step to achieving this is to eliminate all anthropocentric tendencies in the doctrines of classical Pentecostals. As I pointed out earlier, the exclusion of the ecological framework in the "full gospel" renders it a "half-gospel."[37] To make the "full gospel" ecological, first, my doctoral study introduces a sixth component, Christ the Creator. Thus, instead of the "Full

---

33. Awudi, "Beyond Eco-Pneumatology," 189.
34. Awudi, "Beyond Eco-Pneumatology," 177.
35. The Church of Pentecost General Headquarters, *Pentecost Song Book*, 53.
36. Awudi, "Beyond Eco-Pneumatology," 195.
37. Awudi, "Beyond Eco-Pneumatology," 97.

Gospel" being pentagonal or foursquare, I propose a "hexagonal gospel" as the new paradigm for the "full gospel" – Jesus the Creator, Saviour, Healer, Baptizer of the Holy Spirit, the Sanctifier, and the soon coming King.[38] Christ the Creator has several biblical backings (Prov 8:22–31; John 1:1–3; 1 Cor 8:6; Col 1:15–16; Eph 1:10; Heb 1:2) and cannot be ignored as a component of the "full gospel." The plurality of the Godhead as represented by the Hebrew word, *Elohim* in Genesis 1:1 also confirms that Christ was with the Father right from the foundations of the universe.

Apart from the additional component of the "full gospel," there is also the need to reframe the other components to fully embrace ecotheology. First, the doctrine of salvation, which is the second component of the "full gospel," needs to be eco-friendly, roping all creation into the redemptive work of Christ. The understanding that sin affected all creation is important for the understanding of the purpose of the coming Messiah. This chapter posits that the rupture of relationships led to the expectation for a Messiah to mend all the affected relationships. The emphasis of salvation among classical Pentecostals has always been that Christ came to save sinners and not Christ came to save the world. "In other words, the church has always presented Christ as the Saviour of the fallen human community and not the fallen cosmos."[39] My proposed Eco-Soteriology is concerned about how the redemption of the human race is interwoven with and inextricably linked to the redemption of the groaning creation. The salvation of humans has never been divorced from that of the other-than-human community; they are inseparably knitted together. The Hebrew word, *yeshû'āh* meaning deliverance or rescue, refers to salvation that is all-creation inclusive.[40] The two major events which serve as the typology to salvation in Christ are the deluge in Genesis 7:1–5 and the deliverance of Israel from Egypt (Exod 12:38). In both instances, human beings were saved with other living organisms. The apostle Paul uses the Greek word, *apolutrōsis* in Romans 8:33 in reference to the rescuing of the whole universe from bondage. Paul understands redemption in Christ as encompassing all of God's creation. Thus, the destinies of humans and the other-than-human species are tied together. My argument, therefore, is that salvation is not deliverance from but with the cosmos. Holistic salvation encompasses reconciliation of the whole cosmos to God, the restoration of broken relationships, and the healing of the sick creation. Salvation in Christ

---

38. Awudi, "Beyond Eco-Pneumatology," 184.

39. Awudi, "Beyond Eco-Pneumatology," 183.

40. Stephen Renn, ed., *Expository Dictionary of Bible Words* (Peabody: Hendrickson, 2005), 849.

Jesus means rescuing of all creation including those on the periphery – both the marginalized in the human society and the current marginalized – the land, water bodies, flora and fauna.

The doctrine of healing among classical Pentecostals also need a reinterpretation in the light of ecology. As mentioned in the previous section, classical Pentecostals understanding of divine healing not only exclude the other-than-human species but also the use of medications and therapies. However, the Greek adjective, *theïkós*, which means "divine" when used to qualify anything, implies God has a hand in it.[41] My proposed Eco-Therapeuology proposes that healing, whether it is through prayers, or any other spiritual means or by therapy, diet or medical procedures, may be considered divine because God plays a role in the process. In my thesis, I argued that classical African Pentecostalism, rooted in continuity with the primal worldview, perceives healing as both cultural and multidimensional.[42] From this perspective, healing encompasses every available means to restore harmony and unity between God, the cosmos, creation, and humanity, ultimately recreating a just relationship.

There are biblical examples of how healing was extended to the other-than-human community. First, at Mara when the people of Israel could not drink water from the only available stream due to its bitter taste, God through Moses ministered healing to the water, changed the taste and made it drinkable (Exod 15:22–26). The second instance is when the prophet Elisha responded to the request of a group of prophets to heal their water and land (2 Kgs 2:19–21). Elisha requested salt and poured it into the river, which led to its healing. In these two instances, the healing of the other-than-human aspect of creation, led to the healing of the human species. These examples from the Old Testament come to support the understanding that healing, whether with herbs, drugs, or any other means is divine. It also shows that just as the ill health of creation affects the health of humanity, their healing also has significant effect on the human community.

Lastly, Pentecostal pneumatology also needs to include the other-than-human community in the empowering role of the Spirit. I posited in my doctoral studies that the empowering role of the Spirit is not just for church and piety or the ability to heal, see visions, cast out demons, or prophesy.[43] Pentecostals believe that one role that the Spirit plays is empowering believ-

---

41. Awudi, "Beyond Eco-Pneumatology," 152.
42. Awudi, "Beyond Eco-Pneumatology."
43. Awudi, "Beyond Eco-Pneumatology," 188.

ers for service.⁴⁴ They expect the Spirit to energize them to evangelize, win souls, baptize, and heal the sick. However, my proposed Eco-Pneumatology suggests that the Spirit empowers believers to render service to all creation. Thus, service to all creation is service to God. The Spirit enables believers to avoid behaviours that contribute to ecocides which can be embedded in the explanation of the sanctification role of the Spirit. The Spirit takes away enmity within the ecosystem and fosters a cordial relationship between humanity and the other-than-human species. The Spirit that dealt with the desolation, vacuity, and total darkness in the creation narrative is the same Spirit at work, reconciling both the human and non-human community to God.

This chapter draws attention to how the current understanding of eschatology among Pentecostals and charismatics affects their zeal in creation care. The understanding of eschatology as the rapture of saints to spend eternity in heaven, followed by a total annihilation of the earth are the major aspects of eschatology that need reinterpretation. In recent times, some Pentecostal scholars have also drawn attention to the fact that the burning of the earth is metaphoric; it relates to the annihilation of sin and the former things. For Brunner, Butler and Swoboda, eschatology is not a future destructive judgement but a future creating judgement.⁴⁵ Andrew Ray Williams also draws on Revelation 21:1 and 21:4 and concludes that the cosmos itself will not "pass away" but the "passing away of the former things" which includes sin, death, sorrow, sickness.⁴⁶

The creation story and the prototypes of eschatology in the Old Testament, Scripture does not envisage a world where human beings will exist without the non-human species. I also argued in my doctoral thesis that the disappearing of the sea is metaphoric, referring to the disappearing of things that create divisions among people.⁴⁷ It also refers to the destruction of the contributors to chaos and divisions among humanity. My position is that "Eschaton is not a flight from the earth and its inhabitants followed by their destruction. It is for the liberation, healing, and the restoration of creation that has been diseased

---

44. Allan H. Anderson, *An Introduction to Pentecostalism: Global Charismatic Christianity* (Cambridge: Cambridge University Press, 2004), 187. See also Assemblies of God, *Constitution and Bye-Laws*, 6.

45. Daniel L. Brunner, Jennifer L. Butler, and A. J. Swoboda, *Introducing Evangelical Ecotheology: Foundations in Scripture, Theology, History, and Praxis* (Grand Rapids: Baker Academic, 2014), 140.

46. Andrew Ray Williams, "Greening the Apocalypse: A Pentecostal Eco-Eschatological Exploration," *PentecoStudies* 17, no. 2 (2018): 216.

47. Awudi, "Beyond Eco-Pneumatology," 189.

from the fall of humanity till date."[48] The second coming therefore is not about pronouncing a destructive judgement on earth but a creative judgement that would purge the world of evil for righteousness to reign in the universe.

One other difficulty in Pentecostal eschatology is what John meant in Revelation 22:12. The Greek word *tachu* which is translated soon, quickly, swiftly, impromptu, or suddenly has always been interpreted as soon. This has created some urgency for the proclamation of the gospel since the emergence of Pentecostalism among Africans. However, it has led to the neglect of their responsibilities towards the universe. It appears the persecution of the church at the time might have caused the first century church to interpret the Greek word *tachu* as soon. However, relating this to Jesus's parables – the ten virgins (Matt 25:1–13) and the talents (Matt 25:14–30), shows that the return of Christ is impromptu rather than soon. My position, however, is that though Christian scholars may differ in their views on eschatology, such views must not negate Christians' responsibilities towards the earth.

Conclusion

Though Pentecostal-charismatic ecclesiology has not had the desired impact on creation care, there is still much opportunity to right the wrongs. It begins with the elimination of human-centred tendencies in their doctrines. It also has to do with the inclusion of ecological ethos in their ecclesiology to embrace both human and non-human species. The tenets of all church traditions need to fully embrace creation care as a way of influencing the worldviews of believers towards creation care.

Bibliography

Anderson, Allan. *An Introduction to Pentecostalism*. New York: Cambridge University Press, 2004.

Anim, Emmanuel. "Environmental Sustainability and EcoJustice: Reflections from an African Pentecostal." In *Kairos for Creation: Confessing Hope for the Earth*, edited by Louk Andrioanos, Thomas Sander, Juliane Stork, and Dietrich Werner, 107–19. Wuppertal: United Evangelical Mission, 2019.

Anim, Emmanuel, and Emmanuel Awudi. "The Foundations and Practical Implications of the Ecological Work of the Church of Pentecost in Ghana." In *International Handbook on Creation Care and Eco-Diakonia: Concepts and Theological Perspec-*

---

48. Awudi, "Beyond Eco-Pneumatology," 190.

tives of Churches from the Global South, edited by Daniel Beros, et al., 539–45. Oxford: Regnum, 2022.

Assemblies of God, Ghana. *Constitution and Byelaws*. Accra: The Assemblies of God Literature Centre, 2013.

Awudi, Emmanuel. "Beyond Eco-Pneumatology: An Examination of Scripture with 'Green Eyes' and the Eco-Praxis of Some 'Indigenous African Churches' Towards the Development of an African Pentecostal Ecotheology." PhD Thesis, Akrofi-Christaller Institute, Akropong-Akuapem, 2023.

———. "Building Creation Care Culture in the African Church: The Role of the Pulpit." *Journal of African Christian Thoughts* 26, no. 2 (2023): 23–29.

Bediako, Kwame. "What is the Gospel?" *Transformation* 14, no. 1 (1997): 1–4.

Birch, Charles. "Christian Obligation for the Liberation of Nature." In *Liberating Life: Contemporary Approaches to Ecological Theology*, edited by Charles Birch, William Eakin and Jay B. McDaniel, 57–72. Eugene: Wipf & Stock, 1990.

Brunner, Daniel L., Jennifer L. Butler, and A. J. Swoboda. *Introducing Evangelical Ecotheology: Foundations in Scripture, Theology, History, and Praxis*. Grand Rapids: Baker Academic, 2014.

Clifton, Shane. "Preaching the 'Full Gospel' in the Context of the Global Environmental Crises." In *The Spirit Renews the Face of the Ground: Pentecostal Forays in Science and Theology of Creation*, edited by Amos Yong, 117–34. Eugene: Pickwick, 2009.

Golo, Ben-Willie Kwaku. "The Groaning Earth and the Greening of Neo-Pentecostalism in the 21st Century Ghana." *PentecoStudies* 13, no. 2 (2014): 1–23.

Howell, Allison. "The Bible and Care Creation." In *Bible in Mission*, edited by Pauline Hoggarth, Fergus Macdonald, Bill Mitchell, and Knud Jørgensen, 168–77. Oxford: Regnum, 2013.

Johnson, Todd M., Gina A. Zurlo, and Peter F. Crossing. "World Christianity 2023: A Gendered Approach." *International Bulletin of Mission Research* 47, no. 1 (2023): 71–80.

Land, Steven Jack. *Pentecostal Spirituality: A Passion for the Kingdom*. Cleveland: CPT, 2010.

Lucas, Ernest. "The New Testament Teaching on the Environment." *Transformation* 16, no. 3 (1999): 93–99.

Ma, Julie C., and Wonsuk Ma. *Mission in the Spirit: Towards a Pentecostal/Charismatic Missiology*. Oxford: Regnum, 2010.

Means, Richard L. "Why Worry About Nature?" *Saturday Review*. 2 December 1967.

Onyinah, Opoku. "Faith, Healing and Mission: Perspectives from the Bible." In *Christian Missions Ecumenism in Ghana: Essays in Honor of Robert K. Aboagye-Mensah*, edited by J. Kwabena Asamoah-Gyadu, 213–23. Accra: Asempa, 2009.

Onyinah, Opoku, Michael Ntumy, Alfred Koduah, Emmanuel Anim, eds. *Tenets of the Church of Pentecost*. Accra: The Church of Pentecost, 2019.

———. *Christian Stewardship*. Accra: Pentecost Press, 2015.

Renn, Stephen, ed. *Expository Dictionary of Bible Words*. Peabody: Hendrickson, 2005.

Ross, Amy. "Integrating Ecological Mission into Mainstream Mission." *Australian Journal of Mission Studies* 6, no. 2 (2012): 48–55.

Schaeffer, Francis A. *Pollution and the Death of Man: The Christian View of Ecology*. Wheaton: Tyndale, 1970.

Studebaker, Steven M. "The Spirit in Creation: A Unified Theology of Grace and Creation Care." *Zygon: Journal of Religion and Science* 43, no. 4 (2008): 943–59.

The Church of Pentecost General Headquarters. *Pentecost Song Book*. Accra: Pentecost Press, 2016.

———. *The Constitution of the Church of Pentecost*. Accra: Pentecost Press, 2016.

———. *Vision 2023: Five-Year Vision Document for the Church of Pentecost Covering the Period 2018–2023*. Accra: Pentecost Press, 2018.

———. *Youth Ministry, Streams of Living Water 2021: A Daily Devotional Guide*. Accra: Pentecost Press, 2021.

Togarasei, Lovemore. "Paul and the Environment: An Investigation of his Christology and Eschatology." *Ghana Bulletin of Theology* 3 (2008): 143–55.

White, Lynn, Jr. "The Historical Roots of our Ecologic Crisis." *Science*, New Series 155, no. 3767 (1967): 1203–7.

Williams, Andrew Ray. "Greening the Apocalypse: A Pentecostal Eco-Eschatological Exploration." *PentecoStudies* 17, no. 2 (2018): 205–25.

13

Not of This World?

(Neo)Pentecostal Responses to Climate Change and Ecological Crises

Stian Sørlie Eriksen

In the broader strokes of Western Pentecostalism, environmental concerns often do not get centre-stage attention whenever Pentecostals meet or when commented upon from the outside. To some, environmental engagement and Pentecostalism sound like an oxymoron, like water and oil, or worlds apart. At best, Pentecostals have been perceived to take a back seat in current ecotheological and climate action-oriented discourses. In comparison, the broader ecumenical landscapes have called for awareness and action.[1] Pope Francis's *Laudato Si'*[2] and WCC's recent document "The Living Planet"[3] illustrate a wide consensus of urgency. Lutheran bishops in Norway have taken strong positions

---

1. Abbreviations used in this article include WCC (World Council of Churches), UN (United Nations), RCCG (Redeemed Christian Church of God), CoP (Church of Pentecost), PFN (Pentecostal Fellowship of Nigeria), BIU (Benson Idahosa University), CU (Covenant University), GEAPP (Global Energy Alliance for People and Planet), FHFL (Family Homes Funds Limited), ATR (African Traditional Religion), and SoMe (social media). For online sources, abbreviated forms are used even if they originally have longer titles.

2. Francis (pope), *Encyclical Letter Laudato Si' of the Holy Father Francis on Care for Our Common Home* (n.d.), https://www.vatican.va/content/francesco/en/encyclicals/documents/papa-francesco_20150524_enciclica-laudato-si.html.

3. World Council of Churches, "The Living Planet: Seeking a Just and Sustainable Global Community," 11th Assembly, Document No. PIC 01.2, rev., 31 August–8 September 2022.

against continued oil drilling.[4] Similarly, Catholic bishops in Ghana[5] and the Philippines[6] have voiced concerns on environmental and social issues. In recent years, ecotheology has emerged as a number one theological inquiry in the main streams of Christianity and other religious movements.[7] The bodies of research on ecotheology are becoming rather vast, including African contexts.[8]

Though an overstatement, historically, (classical) Pentecostals (and many evangelicals) have often been thought to emphasize the otherworldly, focusing on eternal salvation and Christ's imminent return, but neglecting caring for creation.[9] However, there seems to be growing awareness among Pentecostals of various kinds about the importance of attending to climate change and environmental issues, including Pentecostal scholarship.[10] Norwegian Pentecostal scholar Karl Inge Tangen highlights Pentecostal spirituality as a resource for ecotheology, and points out the Pentecostal origin of "Earth Day."[11] Exemplifying from the African context, Loreen Maseno and King'asia Mamati address

---

4. Peder Anker, "The Call for a New Ecotheology in Norway," *Journal for the Study of Nature and Religion* 7, no. 2 (2013): 187–207; Kjetil Fretheim, "Oil Dependence and Climate Change: Public Theology in Norway," *International Journal of Public Theology* 10, no. 2 (2016): 193–210.

5. "Ghana Catholic Bishops' Conference Launches Goal 6 of 'Laudato Si'," *NewsWatch GH*, 20 March 2023.

6. Brian Roewe, "Philippine Bishops Urge Church Finances to Disconnect from Fossil Fuels," *National Catholic Reporter*, 3 February 2022.

7. Tom Sverre Tomren, "From Environmental Activism to Environmental Education: A Historical Overview, Evaluations and a Suggestion for a Path Forward for the Religious Institutions as Partners for a Global Green Shift," *Consensus* 41, no. 1 (2020).

8. See Joshua Robert Barron and Akua Bi, "African Christian Creation Care: Ecotheology and Environmental Stewardship, A Bibliography" (Self-Published 2023; revised 13 November 2024).

9. For evangelicals, see John Copeland Nagle, "The Evangelical Debate over Climate Change," *University of St. Thomas Law Journal* 5, no. 1 (2008): 53–86; Michael Roberts, "Evangelicals and Climate Change," in *Religion in Environmental and Climate Change: Suffering, Values, Lifestyles*, eds. Gerten Dieter and Sigurd Bergman (New York: Bloomsbury Academic, 2012), 107–31.

10. See John D. Griffith, "All the Earth, Let Us Sing: Searching for a Latent Pentecostal Ecology in Australian Pentecostal Worship," in *Climate Crisis and Sustainable Creaturely Care: Integrated Theology, Governance and Justice*, ed. Christina Nellist (Cambridge: Cambridge Scholars, 2021), 81–102, and Anita Davis, "Pentecostal Approaches to Ecotheology: Reviewing the Literature," *Australasian Pentecostal Studies* 22, no. 1 (2021): 4–33.

11. Karl Inge Tangen, "Pentekostal Spiritualitet, Økoteologi og Miljøengasjement: Et Bidrag til Utvikling av en Pentekostal og Karismatisk Spiritualitet som kan Integrere Elementer av Økoteologi og Miljøetikk," *Scandinavian Journal for Leadership and Theology* 7 (2020); Jeffrey S. Lamp, "Ecotheology," in *The Routledge Handbook of Pentecostal Theology*, ed. Wolfgang Vondey (London: Routledge, 2020), 357–66; Loreen Maseno, "Prayer for Rain: A Pentecostal Perspective from Kenya," *The Ecumenical Review* 69, no. 1 (2017): 338.

an emerging ecotheological awareness among Pentecostal youth in Kenya.[12] In his enticingly entitled article "The Groaning Earth and the Greening of Neo-Pentecostalism," Ben-Willie Kwaku Golo addresses changing attitudes to environmental challenges in Ghana and how environmental action should be part of the churches' mission.[13]

Considering the global and diverse nature of Pentecostalism (or "Pentecostalisms"[14]), in many places where Pentecostalism grows, environmental degradation and effects of climate change represent issues more immensely felt than in the everyday affairs of suburban Western contexts. For delimiting purposes, I focus mainly on the African context, though the discussion concerns us more globally.[15] However, traveling to places like Madagascar, Malawi, or Nigeria, deforestation, water shortage, and waste management are daily real-life obstacles, often amplifying infrastructural and societal challenges. From the Nigerian context, Oyero et al. note that climate change "is perhaps the most serious environmental threat to the fight against hunger, malnutrition, disease and poverty in Africa."[16] This serves as a reminder that theology is always shaped by her lived contexts.[17]

---

12. Loreen Maseno and King'asia Mamati, "An Appraisal of the Pentecostal Ecotheology and Environmental Consciousness among Youths in Parklands Baptist Church, Kenya," *HTS Teologiese Studies/Theological Studies* 77, no. 2 (2021): a6840. See Kiambi James Thambura Atheru, Paul Maku Gichohi, and John Ngige, "Neo-Pentecostals' Religious Practices and Alleviation of Domestic Water Scarcity in Tigania West Constituency, Meru County, Kenya," *International Journal of Professional Practice (IJPP)* 9, no. 3 (2021): 87–99.

13. Ben-Willie Kwaku Golo, "The Groaning Earth and the Greening of Neo-Pentecostalism in the 21st Century Ghana," *PentecoStudies* 13, no. 2 (2014): 1–23. See also Dietrich Werner, "The Challenge of Environment and Climate Justice: Imperatives of an Eco-Theological Reformation of Christianity in African Contexts," in *African Initiated Christianity and the Decolonisation of Development: Sustainable Development in Pentecostal and Independent Churches*, eds. Philipp Öhlmann, Wilhelm Gräb, and Marie-Luise Frost, 51–72 (London: Routledge, 2020).

14. Allan Anderson, *An Introduction to Pentecostalism* (Cambridge: Cambridge University Press, 2004), 9–15.

15. See Harold D. Hunter, "Pentecostal Ecotheology from the margins," in *Contemporary Ecotheology, Climate Justice, and Environmental Stewardship in World Religions*, eds. Lucas A. Andrianos and Tom Svere Tomren et al.,Ecothee Volume 6th-Orthodox Academy of Crete Publications (Steinkjær: Embla Akademisk, 2021), 93–105.

16. Olusola Oyero, et al., "Behavioral Practices and Climate Change Awareness in Ado Odo/Ota, Ogun State, Nigeria: Implications for Communication and Development Agenda," presented to the International Conference on African Development Issues (CU-ICADI): Social and Economic Models for Development Track, 11–13 May 2015, 360.

17. See Michael Wilkinson and Peter Althouse, "Editorial: Pentecostalism as Lived Religion," *Canadian Journal of Pentecostal-Charismatic Christianity* 3 (2012): i–ii.

In recent decades, we have seen an exponential growth of contemporary forms of Pentecostalism, most known as neo-Pentecostalism.[18] Neo-Pentecostalism is both easy and difficult to define.[19] In the simple and traditional sense, neo-Pentecostalism denotes newer and independent Pentecostal-charismatic movements without formal ties to classical Pentecostal denominations. Socio-culturally, neo-Pentecostal churches represent modern, charismatic, often hierarchically, leader-driven, and media-savvy church networks that not only focus on church ministry but seek influence in various spheres of society.[20] While it is outside our scope to detail neo-Pentecostal theologies, key theological emphases often involve a more "realized" eschatology, expecting "God in the now" (though not denying the *parousia*). Emphasizing the here and now, neo-Pentecostals highlight human agency and dominion in the spiritual realm over sin, the demonic, life challenges (which may have spiritual causes), or political spheres of influence.[21] From this mindset, various shades of prosperity-oriented theologies emphasize this-worldly promises for life improvement, healing, and wealth (not necessarily in the extreme senses).[22] Visiting RCCG's Holy Congress at Redemption Camp in 2017, the overall theme was "On the Winning Side," proclaiming that submission to Christ should make believers and the church "win" in all areas of life.

Though contested (since Pentecostals themselves are scrutinized for their practices and lifestyles), Pentecostal churches often seek to be spiritual, ethical, and prophetic institutions holding back against secularization, spiritual and

---

18. See Michael J. McClymond, "Charismatic Renewal and Neo-Pentecostalism: From North American Origins to Global Permutations," in *The Cambridge Companion to Pentecostalism*, eds. Cecil M. Robeck Jr. and Amos Yong (Cambridge: Cambridge University Press, 2014), 31–51; J. Kwabena Asamoah-Gyadu, *Contemporary Pentecostal Christianity: Interpretations from an African Context* (Oxford: Regnum, 2013); André Droogers, "Essentialist and Normative Approaches," in *Studying Global Pentecostalism: Theories and Methods*, eds. Allan Anderson, Michael Bergunder, André Droogers, and Cornelis van der Laan (Berkeley: University of California Press, 2010), 42.

19. Benno van den Toren, "African Neo-Pentecostalism in the Face of Secularization: Problems and Possibilities," *Cairo Journal of Theology* 2 (2015): 111.

20. Cf. Rosalind I. J. Hackett, "Charismatic/Pentecostal Appropriation of Media Technologies in Nigeria and Ghana," *Journal of Religion in Africa* 28, no. 3 (1998): 258–77.

21. See Thomas D. Ice, "What is Dominion Theology?," *Article Archives* 74 (2009) and Andreas Heuser, "Outlines of a Pentecostal Dominion Theology," in *Political Pentecostalism: Four Synoptic Surveys from Africa, Asia, and Latin-America*, eds. Leandro L. B. Fontana and Markus Luber, Weltkirche und Mission 17 (Regensburg: Verlag Friedrich Pustet, 2021), 187–246.

22. Recent neo-prophetic movements may represent more extreme prosperity teachings compared with "mainstream" classical or even neo-Pentecostal churches. See Mookogo S. Kgatle and Allan H. Anderson, eds., *The Use and Abuse of the Spirit in Pentecostalism: A South African Perspective*, Routledge New Critical Thinking in Religion, Theology and Biblical Studies (London: Routledge, 2021).

structural evil, and moral decay in their societies. Reflecting the most expansive face of Pentecostalism makes neo-Pentecostalism a fascinating case for studying responses to climate change and environmental challenges, asking how "triumphalist" theologies may impact these churches' environmental engagement. Though generalizing, Golo, however, asserts that "the majority of neo-Pentecostals are preoccupied with concerns about economic liberation, material prosperity, and opulence as a benefit of spiritual faithfulness" and not the environment.[23]

My own interest in these issues springs from my (Western) Pentecostal background and my general interest in global Pentecostalism, mainly linked to these churches' presence in Western diasporas.[24] While being an outsider to African Christianity, I have worked closely with the Pentecostal migrant context for over two decades. Thus, studying the transnational contexts of these churches may provide insight concerning how churches from the global South impact Christianities in the North and what churches in the North can learn from churches in the South. Focusing on a few selected cases of transnational African neo-Pentecostal churches, the main thrust of this article asks what roles neo-Pentecostal churches can play concerning climate change and environmental challenges. Subsidiarily, I ask how we can understand neo-Pentecostal churches as actors concerning these issues and how neo-Pentecostal theology sheds light on these churches' engagement.[25]

Climate Change and Creation Care: A Question of Ethics

Research on neo-Pentecostal responses to climate change and environmental issues has generally been rather pessimistic, pointing to materialistic foci, prosperity-oriented Gospels, and a lack of action.[26] Comparing Catholics,

---

23. Golo, "Groaning Earth," 202; Hackett, "Charismatic/Pentecostal Appropriation," 259–60.

24. Cf. Frieder Ludwig and J. Kwabena Asamoah-Gyadu, eds. *The African Christian Presence in the West: New Immigrant Congregations and Transnational Networks in North America and Europe* (Trenton: African World, 2011); Frieder Ludwig and Stian Sørlie Eriksen, "Forschungszugänge zu Afrikanischen Transnationalen Gemeinden und Kirchen: Inbesondere in Grossbritannien, Deutschland und Norwegen," in *Migrationskirchen: Internationaliserierung und Pluralisererung de Christentums vor Ort*, eds. Gregor Etzelmüller and Claudia Remmelt (Leipzig: Evangelische Verlagsanstalt – Wissenschaft, 2022), 375–404.

25. I use "(neo-)Pentecostal" somewhat ambiguously, acknowledging that classification boundaries are blurry. I also use it theologically, extending its meaning to hint at "newness" as a framework for transformation.

26. For example, Ben-Willie Kwaku Golo, "Africa's Poverty and Its Neo-Pentecostal 'Liberators': An Ecotheological Assessment of Africa's Prosperity Gospellers," *Pneuma: The Journal of the Society for Pentecostal Studies* 35, no. 3 (2013): 366–84.

Anglicans, and Pentecostals' responses to climate change, George N. Nche noted that "Pentecostals seem not to have recognized climate change as an important issue, perhaps because there is yet to be a definite positive statement on climate change from their known and respected leaders."[27] Nche also points out the importance of how "theology affects perceptions" especially "in places where the impacts of climate change are directly visible."[28]

Creation care is fundamentally an ethical question – deeming and doing what is right facing current environmental dilemmas and crises. For Pentecostals (and believers in general), ethics are essentially spiritual and theological concerns. Referring to leading contemporary Pentecostal ethicist Nimi Wariboko, Christopher A. Stephenson summarizes that "ethical methodology is at its best [. . .] when it assumes the task of cultural criticism. To do so, ethics must leave aside the temptation only to understand the world without trying to change it."[29] Contrasting mere ethical theorization, this is "a contextual and comparative approach" seeking to solve "social problems through the best available theological, philosophical and social scientific insights."[30] One dimension of Wariboko's "Pentecostal principle" takes "pneumatology [as] the point of departure for the theological task," broadening the horizons for change, encompassing "a penchant for newness – the capacity to begin again."[31] Wariboko builds on Paul Tillich to hold that "all finite systems are necessarily open to transformation, "and ethical analyses should translate into new policies and actions to "overcome resistance to the common good."[32] Stephenson, however, adds Wariboko's observation that "current instantiations of Pentecostalism itself are not necessarily the most faithful representatives of the Pentecostal principle."[33]

In terms of epistemology, Wariboko speaks of a spirit-oriented rationality ("it-makes-spirit"), which is "that wisdom or horizon of knowability" that is found in God when relating to God as Spirit, complementing human

---

27. George C. Nche, "Beyond Spiritual Focus: Climate Change Awareness, Role Perception, and Action among Church Leaders in Nigeria," *Weather, Climate, and Society* 12, no. 1 (2020): 157.

28. Nche, "Beyond Spiritual Focus," 157.

29. Christopher A. Stephenson, *Profiles of Pentecostal Theology*, Brill Research Perspectives (Leiden: Brill, 2022), 37, referring to Nimi Wariboko, *The Pentecostal Principle: Ethical Methodology in New Spirit* (Grand Rapids: Eerdmans Publishing, 2012), 156–57.

30. Stephenson, *Profiles*, 37.

31. Stephenson, *Profiles*, 37.

32. Stephenson, *Profiles*, 36.

33. Stephenson, *Profiles*, 37.

sense-making ("it-makes-sense") limited by finitude.[34] A Spirit-infused ethical framework provides spiritual, theological, imaginative, and rational resources for spiritual and societal transformation. Catholic scholar of Pentecostalism Dimitry Sala notes that "the essence of Pentecostalism is God moving 'outside the box,' and us yielding to the wind of the Spirit (John 3:8)."[35] In this light, Sala argues that "anything Pentecostal – like all of Christianity has the specific assignment of transforming society and the world around."[36] Praying "Thy kingdom come, Thy will be done on earth . . . means here and not, not only 'in the sky, by and by,'" calling for "kingdom transformation" with "as much heaven to earth as possible."[37] Sala continues to note that believers are to be "the salt of the earth and the light of the world" (Matt 5:13, 14) where "the purpose and nature of salt is to change anything with which it comes in contact," thus speaking of the potential for transformational societal engagement by the (neo) Pentecostal movement.[38]

Neo-Pentecostals and African Worldviews

Considering contextual neo-Pentecostal approaches to environmental concerns, it is essential to note the close affinity of worldviews – a shared "spiritual ecology" – between (African) culture and religion and (African) neo-Pentecostals.[39] Van den Toren describes how "in traditional Africa, all areas of life were integrated and intertwined."[40] Similarly to neo-Pentecostal inclinations, African approaches to life tend to be "anthropocentric in the sense that religious practices are focused on the flourishing of the human being" and "pragmatic in the sense that religious practices are used in view of what they are intended to achieve: protection, healing, or blessing."[41] Similarly, for neo-Pentecostals,

---

34. Stephenson, *Profiles*, 128–29.
35. Dimitry Sala, "Pentecostal Culture, or Pentecost of Culture? Transformation, Paradigms, Power, Unity," *Spiritus* 6, no. 1 (2021): 114.
36. Sala, "Pentecostal Culture," 114.
37. Sala, "Pentecostal Culture," 114.
38. Sala, "Pentecostal Culture," 109.
39. Olufunke Adeboye, "'A Starving Man Cannot Shout Hallelujah': African Pentecostal Churches and the Challenge of Promoting Sustainable Development," in *African Initiated Christianity and the Decolonisation of Development: Sustainable Development in Pentecostal and Independent Churches*, eds. Philipp Öhlmann, Wilhelm Gräb, and Marie-Luise Frost (London: Routledge, 2020), 119.
40. van den Toren, "African Neo-Pentecostalism," 107–8.
41. van den Toren, "African Neo-Pentecostalism," 107–8.

religion is inseparable from and relevant to all spheres of life and society.[42] He further notes, however, that "religious practices often retain a strong sense of the supernatural" but can be "secularized" if used for secular goals, noting, for instance, how politicians may seek traditional ritualists to gain power and success.[43] For neo-Pentecostals with dualistic worldviews, such supernatural powers (e.g. present in sacred forests) may belong to God or the demonic realm but Spirit-filled believers have spiritual victory and dominion over hostile spiritual forces.[44] In a recent symposium on creation care I participated in, discussions problematized how this can result in complicated relationships with nature if neo-Pentecostals embrace a desacralizing (imperial/Western missionary), demonized (Pentecostal-charismatic), or materialistic (modern) view of nature, leading to lack of action, deforestation or other negative climate consequences. In the symposium, Golo and other presenters called for a reappreciation of indigenous knowledge to reclaim the "sacredness" (in the environmental sense) of nature, arguing for holistic theologies of the earth that could embrace nature preservation while remaining harmonious with Christian convictions and African worldviews.[45]

Selected Cases

Seeking to understand the role of neo-Pentecostal churches concerning climate change and environmental issues, I conducted an interdisciplinary media-oriented study, analyzing media posts, discourses, and publicly available materials from websites, SoMe (Facebook, Twitter/X, and Instagram), sermons (Facebook, YouTube), blogs, and news posts. In my search, I looked for materials that, in some ways, reflected neo-Pentecostal churches' engagement with environmental challenges. While searching broadly, I focused mainly on two strategically selected case churches, RCCG in Nigeria and CoP in Ghana. These were selected for their societal prominence, theological profiles, and transnational outlook and were churches I had previously interacted with in

---

42. van den Toren, "African Neo-Pentecostalism," 111–13, 115.

43. van den Toren, "African Neo-Pentecostalism," 107. Some discourses recount countless claims of Pentecostal pastors doing the same in secret.

44. Ben-Willie Kwaku Golo, "Taking Africa out of the African: Eco-Community, the Christian Heritage of Empire, and Neo-Pentecostalism in Africa," in *Wealth, Health, and Hope in African Christian Religion: The Search for Abundant Life*, ed. Stan Chu (Lanham: Lexington, 2017), 131–53.

45. Creation Care Symposium, "Religious Ecologies and Modernity: The Relevance of Religious Responses to Global Ecocrisis and Climate Change Today," Akfofi-Christaller Institute of Theology, Mission and Culture with A Rocha Ghana, Google Meet, 27 October 2023.

the diaspora. I also looked briefly at neo-Pentecostal higher education institutions. I focused on these churches and institutions' own materials, but outsiders' views were included. I also interacted with current research in the field and built on previous knowledge from relevant migration contexts, including previous visits to Nigeria, Malawi, and Madagascar.[46]

Studying these churches through media, there were limitations for me as an outsider and because I did not physically observe what took place on the ground. However, considering neo-Pentecostal churches' massive media presence, viewing these churches in their digital domains still made sense, even if representing a more two-dimensional approach. Doing digital research gave a bird's eye access to events that had already occurred across a chosen timespan and transcended geographical and cultural borders.[47] Since digital media represented extensions of these churches' presence, identities, and missions, this provided insight into how neo-Pentecostal ministries engage in society through media and how they were perceived.[48] Analyzing the material, I combined a theologically-oriented discursive and thematic approach.

Case 1: The Redeemed Christian Church of God (RCCG)

RCCG is one of today's most influential and fastest growing Pentecostal churches and among the most studied Pentecostal churches in Africa and the diaspora. Some argue that RCCG "straddles both the Classical and the Neo-Pentecostal divide," with some parishes remaining traditional while generally embracing more of a modern and "urbane outlook."[49] According to its website, RCCG has thousands of parishes in Nigeria, many places in Africa, and more than 190 nations, still aiming to expand.[50] The growth and success have been credited to the leadership of "Daddy GO," Enoch Adejara Adeboye, the international overseer who in 1981 took over an initially smaller church after

---

46. I also had informal conversations with leaders in respective churches.

47. Robert Kozinets, *Netnography: Doing Ethnographic Research Online* (London: Sage, 2009).

48. Stian Sørlie Eriksen, Tomas Sundnes Drønen and Ingrid Løland, "African Migrant Christianities: Delocalization or Relocalization of Identities?," in *Faith in African Lived Christianity Bridging Anthropological and Theological Perspectives*, eds. Karen Lauterbach and Mika Vähäkangas, Global Pentecostal and Charismatic Studies Series 35 (Leiden: Brill, 2019), 227–48.

49. Adeboye, "A Starving Man," 119.

50. The Redeemed Christian Church of God (RCCG), "The Redeemed Christian Church of God," website, https://www.rccg.org/.

the founder, Josiah Akindayomi.[51] RCCG holds a prominent role in Nigerian Pentecostalism, Adeboye being the spiritual "father" of several prominent Nigerian Pentecostal leaders. RCCG's attractiveness is linked both to the careful structure and organization of RCCG as well as to Adeboye's charismatic ministry. His *Open Heavens* devotional is cherished and often carried alongside the Bible. Monthly Holy Ghost Services are streamed worldwide. The transnational and digitized nature of RCCG is evident by being present on most SoMe platforms.

While RCCG undoubtedly is most known for her spiritual emphasis, scholars have noticed not only the growth and spiritual impact but also pointed out the increasing role RCCG has taken in society and on the national scene.[52] Mobolaji Oyebisi Ajibade comments more generally that "within the modern Nigerian Pentecostal movement, there is an ongoing broadening of emphasis – from just saving souls to saving the society; from signs and wonders in the church to service and influence in the society."[53] This "repositioning" may not only reflect a tactical and modernizing change, appealing to upward mobile Nigerians and the diaspora, but represent a transition of "religious creativity" shifting focus from "world-rejecting notions to world-accommodating ones."[54] In Ajibade's terms, churches like RCCG "have embraced secular values although they express them in religious language. They have succeeded in incorporating essentially secular elements, giving them a religious garb."[55] Thus, RCCG has become an important societal "agent of social transformation" not only for evangelization and discipleship but by contributing positively to local communities of RCCG parishes.[56] Seeking to be the salt and light of its community, merging the spiritual and the moral, RCCG has engaged in a variety

---

51. RCCG, "Our History," website, https://www.rccg.org/; Afe Adogame, "The Redeemed Christian Church of God: African Pentecostalism," in *Global Religious Movements Across Borders: Sacred Service*, eds. Stephen M. Cherry and Helen Rose Ebaugh (London: Routledge, 2014), 35–60.

52. Adeboye, "A Starving Man," 119; Babatunde A. Adedibu, "Approaches to Transformation and Development: The Case of the Redeemed Christian Church of God, Nigeria," in *African Initiated Christianity and the Decolonisation of Development: Sustainable Development in Pentecostal and Independent Churches*, eds. Philipp Öhlmann, Wilhelm Gräb, and Marie-Luise Frost (London: Routledge, 2020), 166–82.

53. Mobolaji Oyebisi Ajibade, "The Role of Pentecostalism in Sustainable Development in Nigeria," in *African Initiated Christianity and the Decolonisation of Development: Sustainable Development in Pentecostal and Independent Churches*, eds. Philipp Öhlmann, Wilhelm Gräb, and Marie-Luise Frost (London: Routledge, 2020), 153.

54. Adedibu, "Approaches," 141.

55. Ajibade, "The Role of Pentecostalism," 153.

56. Adedibu, "Approaches," 141.

of social development programs from microfinancing to healthcare, education, and various forms of empowerment.[57] This even includes filling gaps the government has been unable to fill, contributing to mending infrastructural shortcomings.[58] However, in contrast to mainline churches, churches like RCCG has often been less vocal in criticizing the government.[59]

One of the most noticed feats of RCCG's ever-expanding vision has been the construction of Redemption City (formerly Redemption Camp), a model city along the Lagos-Ibadan Expressway.[60] Visiting the camp in 2017, I witnessed a lively construction site for the vast "new auditorium" (the Arena), and expansive real estate development for residential and pilgrimage purposes. As an outsider, it was fascinating to observe construction trucks with RCCG logos and street names with biblical or spiritual references. Physically, spiritually, and symbolically, the camp illustrated "possessing the land," making it a place for Christian values and spiritual renewal. In sermons, I have heard Adeboye recount his extensive hours of prayers on the grounds, making it what it has become, spiritually (in terms of spiritual warfare, blessings, and miracles) and physically (in terms of expansion, peace, and prosperity).[61] According to Adeboye, the camp's origins were a "piece of land in a dense forest of snakes and other dangerous animals, which served as a den for robbers."[62] However,

---

57. Adedibu, "Approaches," 141–42, 144.

58. Adeboye, "A Starving Man," 125–26, 130. See also Ajibade, "The Role of Pentecostalism," 153; Cwesi Ofori, "Way to Go! RCCG Repairs Lagos-Ibadan Expressway," *Gospel GH*, 5 November 2015, https://gospelgh.com/way-to-go-rccg-repairs-lagos-ibadan-expressway/ (unfortunately, no longer accessible at the time of writing); and Perry Martins, "RCCG Repairs Lagos – Ibadan Express Way," *Gospel Buzz*, 6 November 2015, https://gospelbuzz.com/rccg-repairs-lagos-ibadan-express-way/.

59. Adeboye, "A Starving Man," 154. Notably, the former vice-president of Nigeria, Yemi Osinbajo, is ordained as an RCCG pastor and consulted Adeboye on political and spiritual matters, showing a close-knit relationship between religion and politics. As vice-president, he advocated for transition to cleaner energy sources (see X tweet @profosinbajo, 7 December 2021).

60. See Adedamola Osinulu, "The Road to Redemption: Performing Pentecostal Citizenship in Lagos," in *The Arts of Citizenship in African Cities: Infrastructures and Spaces of Belonging*, eds. Mamadou Diouf and Rosalind Fredericks (New York: Palgrave Macmillan, 2014), 115–35; Asonzeh Ukah, "Building God's City: The Political Economy of Prayer Camps in Nigeria," *International Journal of Urban and Regional Research* 40, no. 3 (2016): 524–40.

61. Cf. Asonzeh Ukah, "Redeeming Urban Spaces: The Ambivalence of Building a Pentecostal City in Lagos, Nigeria," in *Global Prayers: Contemporary Manifestations of the Religious in the City*, eds. Jochen Becker and Katrin Klingan (Zürich: Lars Müller Publishers, 2014), 178–97; Ukah, "Building God's City."

62. Bisi Daniels, "Adeboye at 81: The Building of Redemption City," *The Cable*, 14 March 2023.

expanding to build a city raises environmental questions.[63] Critical concerns about traffic jams and pollution have surfaced in conjunction with major events at the camp.[64] Though not unique to RCCG, it shows that churches must interact with governmental and other actors and deal with environmental concerns to expand their visions.[65]

Another example is taken from the educational series "Healthy Living" on RCCG's Dove television, illustrating how RCCG uses media to create climate awareness beyond the church walls.[66] In one session, the main guest was Simidu Stephen, a pastor and the head of RCCG's Environmental Health Section, even wearing a government-like uniform. The episode aimed at bringing awareness about UN World Environment Day (June 5) and how to "Save the Earth." Displaying a series of hashtags on the screen (#healthyliving, #savetheearth, and #educative), people were encouraged to interact by SMS or phone. Framed in prayer and pastoral concern, the host asked, "Why do we need to save the earth? We are already saved?"[67]

The conversation referenced Bible passages from Genesis about creation and science-proven facts on pollution, arguing that environmental care contributes to living healthy lives: "This is our earth. It is our home. It is our job to keep our Earth clean . . . before we move on to eternity . . . we don't have any other life to live."[68] More generally, they emphasized local tree planting to combat deforestation, training environmental officers to support the government, model waste management, conducting awareness events in parishes,

---

63. See Family Homes Funds Limited (FHFL) and Redeemed Christian Church of God (RCCG), "Environmental and Social Impact Assessment (ESIA) for the Green Pastures Housing Estate Development within The Redeemed Christian Church of God (RCCG), Redeemed Camp, Ogun State, Nigeria by Family Homes Funds Limited (FHFL) and Redeemed Christian Church of God (RCCG)," Ecosphere Consulting Ltd.report, December 2020.

64. Cf. Ibiyinka Olusola Adesanya, "Environmental Effects of Church Proliferation: The Redeemed Christian Church of God as a Case Study," *International Journal of Humanities and Social Science* 1, no. 15 (2011): 177–82; Osamolu Titilayo Fehintolu and Atuluku John, "An Appraisal of the Role of the Church in National Development: A Case of The Redeemed Christian Church of God in Nigeria," *Multidisciplinary Journal of Research Development* 25, no. 1 (2016): 75–85.

65. See Chinedum Uwaegbulam and Jesutomi Akomolafe, "RCCG Unveils 14-floor Trinity Towers, to Donate N2b Rental Income to Charity," *The Guardian*, 11 June 2022.

66. Dove Television, "Healthy Living: Save the Earth," Facebook, 5 May 2022. See also Kayode Oyero, "Nigerian Politicians Patronise Spiritual Leaders, Can't Ban Doomsday New Year Prophecies like Ghana – SANs," *Punch*, 31 December 2021, 360.

67. Dove Television, "Healthy Living."

68. Dove Television, "Healthy Living."

and facilitating educational programs in public and private schools.[69] Environmental stewardship was preached in churches, proclaiming, "The earth is the LORD's" (Ps 24:1–2).[70] In other words, being in a "place of dominion" did not give a license to exploit the environment, but rather the contrary.

Beyond Christian stewardship and practical action, perhaps the "most Pentecostal" responses to climate change were reflected in Enoch Adeboye's New Year's prophecies and RCCG's annual prayer and fasting periods. Going through the last decade's annual prophecies, natural catastrophes and extreme weather types were repeatedly mentioned for which the church should pray. During RCCG's 2023 50 days fasting prayer campaign, the prayer guide for 30 January (Day 20) focused on "Global climate change," asking,

> Why do we need to pray for climate change? Rising global temperatures, caused by climate change, is bringing major changes across the world. Changes to weather patterns disrupt harvests and put seasons out of balance. It makes weather unpredictable, which includes more frequent and heavy rain, intense heat of the sun, more floods, and more drought. These can cause shortage of food and eventually result in famine.[71]

The prayer points not only declared God's sovereignty over the weather, praying for a "favourable climate in Jesus's name" (cf. Matt 8:26) but admonished praying for forgiveness for sins that may have caused "unfavourable climate and weather conditions."[72] Encouraging prayer for the renewal of a damaged world, one should pray for a generation of competent, wise, and God-fearing leaders "that will cooperate with [Y]ou to correct all the errors of climate change."[73] The church should also pray for scientists and engineers to find "new discoveries that will result [in] a healthier climate on the Earth" and that those affected by severe climate change may be helped.[74] The prayer points

---

69. Rotary Club of Garden City (Georgetown) Guyana, "RCGCG Launches Children Environmental Handbook," 30 July 2022.

70. RCCG Sunday Service, "The Earth Is the Lord's," Sunday Service, Brandon MB, Facebook, video, 1 hour, 51 minutes, 8 seconds, 2 October 2022.

71. E. A. Adeboye, "RCCG Open Heavens Devotional Daily Open Heaven: Prayer Points and Declaration - RCCG 50 Days Prayers and Fasting Guide," *Open Heavens for Today*, 30 January 2023. See Flatimes, "RCCG Fasting Prayer Points for 9 February 2019 – DAY 30: Prayer for Climate Change," 9 February 2019, and RCCG_PR, "Day 22: Tuesday 24th November 2020," Instagram, 24 November 2020, for similar prayer points in 2019 and 2020.

72. Adeboye, "RCCG Open Heavens Devotional Daily."

73. Adeboye, "RCCG Open Heavens Devotional Daily."

74. Adeboye, "RCCG Open Heavens Devotional Daily."

also invoked spiritual warfare, "bind[ing] every demon assigned to scatter the works of creation on climate and weather with the blood of Jesus," terminating the works of "every spirit of fear of climate change, shifting our focus from your kingdom," and praying for the powers of nature to cooperate.[75] Following the church on Facebook, one could interactively participate in these prayers.[76]

Though one could criticize RCCG for lack of action and spiritualizing the climate crisis, one could argue that these prayers represented contextually relevant ways to raise awareness in the church in a (spiritual) language that made sense. The prayer guide revealed the complexities of neo-Pentecostal theology, pointing to natural, divine, or demonic causes and divine and human solutions. This must be understood at the juncture of the pneumatologically-oriented (Pentecostal) ethics and African worldviews noted previously, believing it is possible to change things by being in tune with the spirit realm. In other words, there is no distinction between praying for God's intervention and the human response of repenting, praying for leaders, doing spiritual warfare, or engaging in scientific breakthroughs.

Case 2: The Church of Pentecost (CoP)

The CoP in Ghana is another church that, like RCCG, has earned a transnational footprint, spreading worldwide, including Norway.[77] CoP statistics recount a steady growth with more than four million members in 151 countries.[78] Historically and theologically, CoP may most correctly classify as a classical Pentecostal church, but, like RCCG, has undergone modernizing transformations in recent decades. In media strategies and social engagement, CoP may better fit the neo-Pentecostal category.[79] CoP is also a notable actor in Ghana, ecclesiologically and elsewhere in society.

CoP recently renewed their current vision, "Possessing the nations," for a second period, advocating spiritual and societal transformation in the church

---

75. Adeboye, "RCCG Open Heavens Devotional Daily."
76. Redemption Television Ministry, "RCCG Fasting & Prayers. Day 20: Global Climate Change. With Pastor Awosusi Paul," Facebook, 30 January 2023, video, 15 minutes.
77. Stian Sørlie Eriksen, "The Church of Pentecost International: Fortellingen om en Migrantmenighet i Oslo," in *Kristne Migranter i Norden*, eds. Anders Aschim, Olav Hovdelien, and Helje Kringleboth Sødal (Kristiansand: Portal, 2016), 190–207.
78. Church of Pentecost (CoP), "Statistics," webpage, https://thecophq.org/statistics/.
79. Cf. Johnson K Asamoah-Gyadu, *African Charismatics: Current Developments within Independent Indigenous Pentecostalism in Ghana* (Leiden: Brill, 2005), 4.

and every sphere of society.[80] "Possessing the nations" is used literally for worldwide mission and figuratively for engaging various areas of society ("nations"). As captured by chairman Apostle Eric Nyameke, "In the coming years, [CoP] will strive to become a Church whose members go to possess or take their nations by influencing every worldview, thought and behaviour with kingdom principles, values and lifestyles, thereby, turning many people to Christ." CoP aims at combatting social ills by "deploying members as agents of transformation" through Christ-like living, moral integrity, community development, and cooperation with the government. Notably, this includes "a transformed society that is very concerned about the environment, keeping it clean and prompting others [...] to do same."[81] The vision is not limited to Ghana but concerns the church globally.

CoP's environmental focus has lasted for several years. Harold D. Hunter notes that CoP's former chairman, Apostle Opoku Onyinah, in 2017 "publicly opposed illegal mining and 'other practices,'"[82] contrasting previous lack of attention.[83] During the first phase of "Possessing the Nations," in 2018 CoP launched an "Environmental Care Campaign" involving the church's top leadership, calling for broad participation and cooperation between church, state actors, and NGOs addressing concerns such as sanitation, water, pollution, and waste management. Public representatives commended the church for highlighting environmental care and how Christian and traditional values aided its implementation.[84] As an outsider, I reminded myself of the markedly religious nature of Ghanaian society compared with most Western societies. I also noticed how faith was a critical (re)source for awareness and action.[85] Following CoP on SoMe platforms revealed admonishing hashtags, such as

---

80. Church of Pentecost General Headquarters, "The Church of Pentecost," webpage, https://thecophq.org/.

81. Church of Pentecost, *Vision 2023: Five-Year Vision Document for the Church of Pentecost Covering the Period 2018–2023* (Accra: Pentecost Press, 2018).

82. Harold D. Hunter, "Pentecostal Ecotheology from the Margins," in *Contemporary Ecotheology, Climate Justice, and Environmental Stewardship in World Religions*, eds. Lucas A. Andrianos and Tom Svere Tomren et al. Ecothee Volume 6th-Orthodox Academy of Crete Publications (Steinkjær: Embla Akademisk, 2021), 100–101.

83. Moses Kumi Asamoah, "Religious Environmentalism: The Church's Environmental Sustainability Paradigm (The Case of the Church of Pentecost in Ghana)," *European Journal of Business and Social Sciences* 2, no. 8 (2013): 59–76.

84. Church of Pentecost, "Environmental Care Campaign Launched," Facebook, 23 November 2018. See also 3News, "Church of Pentecost Launches Nationwide Environmental Care Campaign," 22 November 2018.

85. Church of Pentecost, "National Launch of Environmental Care Campaign," Facebook, 22 November 2018.

#MyEnvironmentMyResponsibility and #PlantATreeWhereYouLive, and provided examples of local implementations in various parts of Ghana.[86] I also witnessed CoP's focus on environmental stewardship on CoP's Norwegian youth website.

To further illustrate, from a "National Creation Care Conference" in Accra May 2023, CoP's websites and SoMe accounts referenced concerns about "the destruction of Ghana's natural resources, including illegal mining, deforestation, and pollution," seeking to "mobilize the Christian community, representing a significant portion of the country's population to . . . become a positive force in addressing environmental challenges."[87] Highlighting stewardship, the conference provided a know-how platform, connecting the church with outside agents, hoping to inspire "collective action to protect Ghana's environment for future generations."[88] CoP focused particularly on youth, education, and practical action.[89]

For CoP, there was no spiritual-secular divide between prayer, mission, and addressing environmental concerns, holistically approaching healing for all areas of life. Peter White notes CoP's strong missional emphasis by demonstrating Christian faith serving "in every geo-political and socioeconomic context," seeking the dominance of God's values in individuals, communities, and society.[90] Thus, CoP exhibited a theology of transformation as a resource for addressing environmental issues, while not exempting human responsibility, emphasizing holiness and repentance for restoration and healing. Taking centre stage in assuming responsibility, this included cooperation with "secular" partners.

---

86. Church of Pentecost – Goaso Manhyia, "On the Environmental Care Campaign," Facebook, 31 May 2019; CoP, "PIWC Tarkwa Climax of Environmental Care Day," Facebook, 15 May 2022; Timothy Ngnenbe, "Church of Pentecost Launches National Sanitation Campaign," *Graphic News*, 2 March 2020; Citi Newsroom, "UPPR Partners Church of Pentecost for Plastic Waste Collection," *CNR* 26 November 2022; "Pentecost Men's Ministry Embarks on Tree Planting Exercise," *NewsWatch GH*, 5 June 2021.

87. Church of Pentecost Twitter (X), social media post, 5 June 2023.

88. Church of Pentecost General Headquarters, "National Creation Care Conference Tackles Ghana's Environmental Crisis," *Church News*, 22 May 2023.

89. Church of Pentecost General Headquarters, "Odorkor Area Launches 2023 Environmental Care Campaign," *Church News*, 13 March 2023.

90. Peter White, "Missional Branding: A Case Study of the Church of Pentecost," *HTS Teologiese Studies/Theological Studies* 75, no. 4 (2019): 1–7.

Case 3: Neo-Pentecostal Universities

Several neo-Pentecostal institutions of higher learning have been established in recent decades. Ajibade comments that "the majority of Pentecostal Churches in Nigeria today are investing in education," adding that "education is one of the pillars and thrusts of sustainable development in any nation," and commending Pentecostal churches that do this.[91] Often, these universities are closely linked to their mother churches, and both RCCG and CoP have established universities, Redeemer University and Pentecost University. Pentecost University, for instance, is considered important for fulfilling CoP's "Possessing the nations" vision.[92]

While the academization of neo-Pentecostalism and the emergence of neo-Pentecostal universities need more comprehensive treatment, it is interesting to comment on the role that these have as societal actors and what roles these may have in dealing with issues of climate change and the environment. These institutions may serve as correctives to dated perceptions of anti-educational and anti-intellectual sentiments of Pentecostalism. They can also help us view neo-Pentecostal churches in their broader contexts so that we not only judge these churches' societal engagement based on the content of their sermons but also in light of their institutions. It is interesting to note that many high-profile neo-Pentecostal leaders (e.g. Enoch Adeboye), hold advanced academic degrees within the sciences or theology. Several institutions have, however, received criticism for charging high tuition fees in contexts of poverty.[93]

One of the first Nigerian neo-Pentecostal universities was Benson Idahosa University (BIU), established in 2002 in Benin City, and a direct heritage of Nigeria's Pentecostal "father" Benson Idahosa, and his Church of God Mission International, offering study programs within agriculture, education, leadership, engineering, law, and medicine.[94] Without further detailing BIU's history, it is interesting to note that BIU was part of an "Academia for Green Africa" (AFGA) initiative, resulting in the publication of *The African Environment Perspective* in 2011 which included "a compilation of environmental-inclined speeches and presentations" from the previously held AFGA conference at BIU

---

91. Ajibade, "Role of Pentecostalism," 154.
92. Church of Pentecost General Headquarters, "Possessing the Nations' Agenda Is the Heartbeat of Christ – Prof. Agyapong-Kodua," 13 July 2022.
93. Babatunde Aderemi Adedibu, "Nigerian Pentecostal Megachurches and Development: A Diaconal Analysis of the Redeemed Christian Church of God," *Religions* 14, no. 1 (2023): 70.
94. Benson Idahosa University (BIU), "Benson Idahosa University."

in 2010.[95] This initiative sought to identify "the role of academic institutions in Africa toward meeting and addressing the current global challenges of climate change and the environment" and was followed up later by a climate change summit in Copenhagen.[96] The research at BIU also reflects numerous scholarly contributions on climate change and environmental issues, particularly concerning law-related fields.[97] Overall, many BIU programs focus on "making a difference" in life and society. Similarly, David Oyedepo's Winners Chapel currently operates two universities in Nigeria, Covenant University (CU) and Landmark University, focusing on technical/engineering and agricultural studies. Highlighted on their website, CU displayed, for instance, the "Climate Champion" award given to CU as part of their participation in a significant climate change project in a UN youth program in Glasgow, Scotland in 2021. The project addressed climate change and food insecurity, calling for policy changes, cooperation, and concrete action.[98] Climate change also features in CU's research aims that seek to "offer solutions to society's big problems and be a leading, global educational institution" for solving "global food security problems, climate change, waste management, electronic governance, business, and poverty eradication. Although these are the 'big picture' challenges, there is a local aspect to each issue, which provides relevance and impetus."[99] These universities should, of course, be studied in their own right, but, concurrently, they should be viewed in light of their spiritual, ecclesial, and societal contexts. Listening to David Oyedepo and other neo-Pentecostal university founders, it became clear that these institutions are extensions of their wider ministries, which have distinct missional and spiritual goals. Consequentially,

---

95. Akanimo Odon and Sam Guodadia, *African Environmental Perspectives* (Self Published: AuthorHouse, 2011).

96. Odon and Guodadia, *African Environmental Perspectives*.

97. See Stella O. Idehen, "Determination of the Legal Implication of Sustainable Development as a Necessary Corollary to Human Development," *KB Law Scholars Journal* 1, no. 3 (2024), https://doi.org/10.60787/kblsj.v1i3.29; G. E. Okwezuzu, "Human Rights Perspective to Environmental Challenges: Emerging Trends," *East African Journal of Peace and Human Rights* 17, no. 2 (2011): 515–31; Adekunbi Imosemi, Nzeribe Abangwu, and Theo Nwanu, "Climate Change Mitigation: An Assessment of Global Legal Responses: So Far So Good?," *Journal of Research and Development* 1, no. 3 (2013): 79–96.

98. Covenant University, "Covenant University Emerges Climate Champion at COY 16," *Covenant News*, 6 May 2022.

99. Covenant University, "A Citadel of Spirituality, Knowledge, Leadership and Mental Productivity," Centre for Research, Innovation and Discovery, Website, 2023. Searching CU's research repository, we find numerous research contributions on environmental issues in the fields of engineering (e.g. Oyer et al., "Behavioral Practices"; Oloyede and CU, *Climate Change*; Ojo, "Impact of Climate Change"). In 2021, CU hosted an international conference on energy and sustainable environment, focusing on inclusive and innovative solutions.

these institutions can play vital roles, not only contributing to research and education but equally function as important bridges between the secular and the spiritual spheres and between the church and society. Raising awareness and facilitating action in matters of combatting environmental degradation, these institutions can mirror neo-Pentecostal theologies of "taking dominion" in various spheres of life, operationalizing theologies of human responsibility and energizing students and faculty to pursue these tasks within frameworks of spiritual empowerment and intellectual rigor.

Discussion

(Neo-)Pentecostal churches such as RCCG and CoP are undoubtedly important religious actors in their contexts. However, what can our brief study tell us about their roles concerning climate change and environmental challenges? Moreover, how can their theologies shed light on their engagement? Sociologically, there is no doubt that these churches hold positions of societal prominence. Considering their membership base and influence, they may initiate, mobilize, and sustain grassroots involvement in environmental care.[100] Potentially they may speak to governments and be prophetic voices in their time. If working together with other Pentecostals in their contexts,[101] they may even reverse Nche's poor statistics on Pentecostal engagement.[102] Nche's model for awareness, perception, and action (Figure 1) may here prove helpful for monitoring such efforts, as asked for by the CU students previously mentioned.

---

100. See Naomi Richman, "Nigerian Pentecostalism," *The Database of Religious History* (Vancouver: The University of British Colombia, 2020).

101. The Pentecostal Fellowship of Nigeria (PFN) serves an important function to be "the national body which binds all Christian churches, organizations and believers." See PFN, "About Pentecostal Fellowship of Nigeria," online article, 2022.

102. Nche, "Beyond Spiritual Focus," 150.

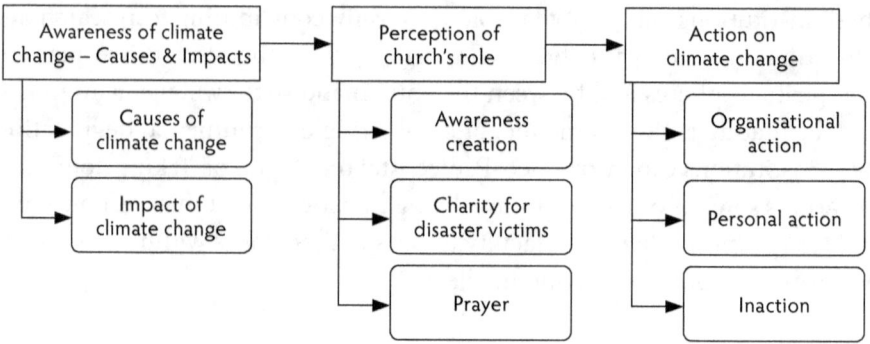

Figure 1. Church Involvement in Climate Change Issues[103]

Since Pentecostals represent a significant force on the national religious scenes, their actions bear more weight than in my own country, where Pentecostals represent a smaller minority to the majority Lutheran Church of Norway. The well-organized structures and prominence of leaders such as E.A. Adeboye, David Oyedepo, or Apostle Opoku Onyinah are tangible. Being vision-bearers, their ministries extend far beyond their local and national contexts, the diaspora, and even to the ears of foreign governments.[104] When Enoch Adeboye speaks, it is noticed; when he enters the stage, people come.[105] Recently (presumingly accidentally), Adeboye came "under fire" after a video went viral of him sharing a story of how God temporarily had suspended the winter when Adeboye had traveled to Colorado, USA because Adeboye did not like the cold.[106] Every year, national newspapers publicize (and keep count of) prominent pastors' New Year's prophecies, including Adeboye.[107] Thus, these leaders may attain leading roles not only spiritually but also in matters of climate change if speaking up to join forces with broader ecumenical initiatives. Our examples show a shift in neo-Pentecostal churches' engagement

---

103. Figure from George C. Nche, "Beyond Spiritual Focus: Climate Change Awareness, Role Perception, and Action among Church Leaders in Nigeria," *Weather, Climate, and Society* 12:1 (2020), 154. © American Meteorological Society. Used with permission.

104. In 2015, former UK PM David Cameroon visited RCCG's Festival of Life in London; Richard Burgess, *Nigerian Pentecostalism and Development: Spirit, Power, and Transformation* (London: Routledge, 2020).

105. I remember Adeobye visiting Oslo in 2010, packing a large national auditorium without much apparent advertisement.

106. Matthew Impelli, "Pastor Claims God Suddenly Stopped Winter for Him Because He Hates the Cold," *Newsweek*, 16 November 2023.

107. Interestingly, the practice of New Year's prophecies has been banned in Ghana; Oyero, "Nigerian Politicians."

with environmental affairs but may still reflect Wariboko's previously noted untapped potential for Pentecostals implementing Pentecostal ethics.[108] Within this theological-ethical framework, given the media analyses above, I will further discuss selected theological notions characterizing neo-Pentecostalism today. I admit I may be slightly bent on majoring on perceived potentials rather than engaging the conversation deeply and critically enough. I, however, do this in light of my material, which primarily represents the churches' propensities, plus, in my discussion, I seek to complement the larger research discourse in the existing literature on which I rely for more elaborate critical considerations.

The Earth is the Lord's

In my material, I found no disdain for nature, but sermons and awareness programs emphasized recognizing that "The Earth is the LORD's" (Ps 24:1–2), reminding followers about the sacredness of nature, calling for a greater appreciation for creation and Christian stewardship. This is not uniquely neo-Pentecostal but reflects a common Christian view of nature and a holistic worldview with interconnectedness between s/Spirit and earth. I agree with Golo and others who call for a revitalization of indigenous knowledge as correctives to Western materialistic mindsets.[109] Thus, neo-Pentecostal churches may adjust perspectives and practices when expanding their territories, considering not only government regulations but also acting theologically on the intrinsic value of God's creation. In the RCCG TV show I referenced, the rationale for creation care reflected not only nature's sake but also that proper environmental caretaking contributed to human flourishing realizing our dependence on a healthy environment for survival. This may reflect an "anthropo-theo-centric" view, in contrast to anthropocentric views with humans in focus, or ecocentric views with very high views of nature.[110] By caring for the environment, one honors God as Creator and God's mandate (stewardship) while recognizing this is for our own good.

---

108. Stephenson, *Profiles*, 37.

109. Creation Care Symposium, "Religious Ecologies and Modernity."

110. Andrew J. Hoffman and Lloyd E. Sandelands, "Getting Right with Nature: Anthropocentrism, Ecocentrism, and Theocentrism," *Organization & Environment* 18, no. 2 (2005): 141–62.

Thy Kingdom Come

Doctrinally, RCCG and CoP most correctly reflect classical Pentecostal eschatology, but awaiting the *parousia* does not suspend social action. Neo-Pentecostal focus on salvation and societal transformation reflects a (partially) realized eschatology, expecting God's kingdom to manifest in the now. Apart from extreme variants of prosperity preaching, most mainstream neo-Pentecostals value hard work and high work ethics as prerequisites for God's blessings; hence, the emphasis on education, entrepreneurship, and excellence. (These may also be culturally anchored expectations.) Ajibade notes that for Pentecostals, "prosperity comprises spiritual, mental and physical areas of life," believing that "God will reward faithful Christians with good health, financial success and material wealth 'according to his glorious riches in Christ Jesus' (Phil 4:19)."[111] Believing in progress (and not fate) provides incentives for innovation, upward mobility, and improvement for self and society. I find Golo and Novieto's discussion on neo-Pentecostal financial, cultural, and human capital very helpful. Without glossing over challenges accompanying neo-Pentecostal structures and theologies, these movements represent vast potentials for creating awareness for climate change in their contexts through entrepreneurialism and spiritual and community development.[112]

Why Do We Need to Pray for Climate Change?

In my material, I observed prayers for healing of and for the environment. The message of Pentecostalism and neo-Pentecostalism is undoubtedly one of healing and restoration, going back to faith healers such as T. L. Osborn, Oral Roberts, or Kenneth Hagin, but equally reflecting holistic African worldviews.[113] Praying, however, did not dissect trusting in God from human action but proposed a symbiotic relationship between faith and human solutions. Praying for environmental healing did not negate repentance, exemplary leadership, or new scientific discoveries, but brought awareness of societal ills (like climate change) and helped those praying to tap into spiritual and other resources for action. Illustratively, these churches responded to COVID-19 by praying for miracles while wearing face masks, just as participating in God's

---

111. Ajibade, "Role of Pentecostalism," 153.

112. Golo and Novieto, "Religion and Sustainable Development."

113. See Jacob Oladipupo, "Power in Neo-Pentecostalism and African Traditional Religion: A Nigerian Case Study," *International Journal of Science and Research (IJSR)* 7, no. 7 (2016): 431–41.

mission may include cooperating with "secular" governments. This reflects Wariboko's "contextual and comparative approach" to social problem-solving and a "pneumatological realism" making use of the best resources available, whether theological, spiritual or "secular" propounding "deeper cooperation across secular and sacred divides."[114] This may also reflect Wariboko's notion of "newness" with a potential for innovative solutions for environmental healing (and my play on "neo").[115] Hunter notes,

> How does the movement now respond to caring for God's creation when the sickness of creation damages our health and wellbeing? When pollution in various places caused me to be ill, my church would readily lay hands on me to recover. I welcomed this intervention, but I said that we must cure the curse because this same pollution is having a devastating effecting on those directly exposed to these monsters. Stated in a theological way, we acknowledge that God created humankind in the divine image. When we get sick, we are invited to pray for healing. God created this planet and said it was good. We were given water to drink and land on which to live. But we have brought many diseases into creation. Now we must seek the salvation of all creation.[116]

Possessing the Nations

A main theme throughout my material was an emphasis on transformation. The most vivid example was CoP's vision of "Possessing the Nations," seeking the transformation of all spheres of society. In the theological tradition of neo-Pentecostals, the dominion theologies of CoP and RCCG invited both prayer and societal action. To further illustrate, in an RCCG (adult) Sunday school lesson on "political dominion," Christians learned that occupying political positions for redemptive societal influence could be as important as preaching in the pulpit.[117] By this logic, being spiritually (and humanly) empowered to change failing policies or engage in societal transformation would make shar-

---

114. Adeboye, "A Starving Man," 132–33; Stephenson, *Profiles*, 37, 39; cf. Stephen M. Studebaker, *A Pentecostal Political Theology for American Renewal: Spirit of the Kingdoms, Citizen of the Cities* (New York: Palgrave, 2016).
115. Stephenson, *Profiles*, 37.
116. Hunter, "Pentecostal Ecotheology," 99–100.
117. RCCG Open Heavens Luton, "Political Dominion."

ing the gospel (mission) more effective and trustworthy.[118] However, from postcolonial perspectives, we may ask to what extent such "triumphalist" theologies represent new forms of spiritual "imperialism" or "colonialism," continuing missionary paradigms of conquest, though acted out from within.[119] In the material, these points were, however, not addressed as such.

Concluding Remarks: With God, All Things are Possible?

As mentioned, both Pentecostals and neo-Pentecostals are known for believing in the impossible and that "with God, all things are possible" (Matt 19:26 NIV). If daring to engage the epistemology and faith of the neo-Pentecostals we have interacted with, we could ask, what is possible with God in terms of climate change? I do not seek to speculate theologically but curiously ask how the neo-Pentecostal imagination may approach the question. Could "listening to the Spirit" stimulate the pursuit of new scientific discoveries, persuade someone to transform existing policies, or inspire renewed mobilizations for climate change action?

Regardless of the answers, studying Pentecostalism and climate change will remain important, not the least for Africa's young population and for future generations in the West. Not only is it necessary to follow Pentecostal churches and their involvement with climate change issues, both in the South and in the North, but it is essential to address these questions further and in more depth, theologically and sociologically.[120] For instance, what will the next generations of Pentecostals think of these issues, and what theologies will emerge from various contexts where Pentecostalism thrives? There is also great transnational potential for impact from cooperating with other Christians/Pentecostals globally and with the diasporas. As a Norwegian scholar and as a Pentecostal, I have not only gleaned insights from African neo-Pentecostals, but I was inspired to reflect further and learn from their theologies and involvement with propensities for change to create better worlds. Broadly envisioned, concerning these issues, we are all "insiders" living in the same world, hopefully joining hands across geographical, cultural, and theological divides to work for more research, education, prayer, and other sustainable forms of action.

---

118. In his current position, former Vice President Osinbajo serves as an advisor on clean energy questions, illustrating the (in)direct influence churches like RCCG can have through their members. See GEAPPP, "Former Vice President."

119. I am indebted to Karl Inge Tangen and Roald Kristiansen for engaging these points.

120. See Anderson, "Social, Political, and Economic Development."

Bibliography

3News. "Church of Pentecost Launches Nationwide Environmental Care Campaign." 22 November 2018. https://3news.com/church-of-Pentecost-launches-nationwide-environmental-care-campaign/#google_vignette.

Adeboye, E. A. "RCCG Open Heavens Devotional Daily Open Heaven: Prayer Points and Declaration - RCCG 50 Days Prayers and Fasting Guide." *Open Heavens for Today*. 30 January 2023.

Adeboye, Olufunke. "'A Starving Man Cannot Shout Hallelujah': African Pentecostal Churches and the Challenge of Promoting Sustainable Development." In *African Initiated Christianity and the Decolonisation of Development: Sustainable Development in Pentecostal and Independent Churches*, edited By Philipp Öhlmann, Wilhelm Gräb, and Marie-Luise Frost, 115–35. London: Routledge, 2020. DOI: 10.4324/9780367823825-9.

Adedibu, Babatunde A. "Approaches to Transformation and Development: The Case of the Redeemed Christian Church of God, Nigeria." In *African Initiated Christianity and the Decolonisation of Development: Sustainable Development in Pentecostal and Independent Churches*, edited By Philipp Öhlmann, Wilhelm Gräb, and Marie-Luise Frost, 136–50. London: Routledge, 2020. DOI: 10.4324/9780367823825-10.

———. "Nigerian Pentecostal Megachurches and Development: A Diaconal Analysis of the Redeemed Christian Church of God." *Religions* 14, no. 1 (2023). https://doi.org/10.3390/rel14010070.

Adesanya, Ibiyinka Olusola. "Environmental Effects of Church Proliferation: The Redeemed Christian Church of God as a Case Study." *International Journal of Humanities and Social Science* 1, no. 15 (2011): 177–82.

Adogame, Afe. "The Redeemed Christian Church of God: African Pentecostalism." In *Global Religious Movements Across Borders: Sacred Service*, edited by Stephen M. Cherry and Helen Rose Ebaugh, 35–60. London: Routledge, 2014.

Ajibade, Mobolaji Oyebisi. "The Role of Pentecostalism in Sustainable Development in Nigeria." In *African Initiated Christianity and the Decolonisation of Development: Sustainable Development in Pentecostal and Independent Churches*, edited by Philipp Öhlmann, Wilhelm Gräb, and Marie-Luise Frost, 151–63. London: Routledge, 2020. DOI: 10.4324/9780367823825-11.

Anderson, Allan. *An Introduction to Pentecostalism*. Cambridge: Cambridge University Press, 2004.

———. "Pentecostalism and Social, Political, and Economic Development." *Spiritus: ORU Journal of Theology* 5, no. 1 (2020): 121–36. DOI: https://doi.org/10.31380/2573-6345.1138.

Andrianos, Lucas A., and Tom Svere Tomren, et al. eds. *Contemporary Ecotheology, Climate Justice, and Environmental Stewardship in World Religions*. Ecothee Volume 6th-Orthodox Academy of Crete Publications. Steinkjær: Embla Akademisk, 2021.

Anker, Peder. "The Call for a New Ecotheology in Norway." *Journal for the Study of Nature and Religion* 7, no. 2 (2013): 187–207. DOI:10.1558/jsrnc.v7i2.187.

Asamoah-Gyadu, Kwabena J. *African Charismatics: Current Developments within Independent Indigenous Pentecostalism in Ghana*. Leiden: Brill, 2005.

———. *Contemporary Pentecostal Christianity: Interpretation from an African Context*. Regnum Series in Global Christianity. Oxford: Regnum, 2013.

Asamoah, Moses Kumi. "Religious Environmentalism: The Church's Environmental Sustainability Paradigm (The Case of the Church of Pentecost in Ghana)." *European Journal of Business and Social Sciences* 2:8 (2013): 59–76.

Atheru, Kiambi James Thambura, Paul Maku Gichohi, and John Ngige. "Neo-Pentecostals' Religious Practices and Alleviation of Domestic Water Scarcity in Tigania West Constituency, Meru County, Kenya." *International Journal of Professional Practice (IJPP)* 9, no. 3 (2021): 87–99.

Barron, Joshua Robert, and Akua Bi. "African Christian Creation Care: Ecotheology and Environmental Stewardship. A Bibliography Compiled by Joshua Robert Barron and Akua Bi." 2023. Revised 13 November 2024. https://www.academia.edu/54768825/African_Christian_Creation_Care_Ecotheology_and_Environmental_Stewardship?email_work_card=title.

Benson Idahosa University (BIU). "Benson Idahosa University." 2023. https://www.biu.edu.ng/.

Burgess, Richard. *Nigerian Pentecostalism and Development: Spirit, Power, and Transformation*. London: Routledge, 2020. DOI: https://doi.org/10.4324/9781315167299.

Church of Pentecost General Headquarters. "The Church of Pentecost Celebrates World Environment Day." 6 June 2023. https://thecophq.org/the-church-of-Pentecost-celebrates-world-environment-day/.

———. "The Church of Pentecost, IGP Plant Trees at National Police Training School." *Pentecost News*. 11 June 2021. https://thecophq.org/the-church-of-pentecost-igp-plant-trees-at-national-police-training-school/.

———. "National Creation Care Conference Tackles Ghana's Environmental Crisis." *Church News*. 22 May 2023. https://thecophq.org/national-creation-care-conference-tackles-ghanas-environmental-crisis/.

———. "Odorkor Area Launches 2023 Environmental Care Campaign." *Church News*. 13 March 2023. https://thecophq.org/odorkor-area-launches-2023-environmental-care-campaign/.

———. "'Possessing the Nations' Agenda Is the Heartbeat of Christ – Prof. Agyapong-Kodua." 13 July 2022. https://thecophq.org/possessing-the-nations-agenda-is-the-heartbeat-of-christ-prof-agyapong-kodua%EF%BF%BC/.

———. "Statistics." Webpage. https://thecophq.org/statistics/.

———. Untitled. X (formerly Twitter), Social Media Post, 5 June 2023. https://twitter.com/thecophq/status/1665657806857424896.

———. *Vision 2023: Five-Year Vision Document for the Church of Pentecost Covering the Period 2018–2023*. Accra: Pentecost Press, 2018. https://thecophq.org/vision-2023/.

Church of Pentecost. "'Environmental Care Campaign' Launched." Facebook, 23 November 2018. https://www.facebook.com/story.php/?id=100064559534854&story_fbid=2215797048438571&paipv=0&eav=AfYCkqz4NSGZEMTye0bODO3xiIeqETcaY6l8PFztGYn9o7PXwhkjA4IDOzAOUibQx_0&_rdr.

———. "National Launch of Environmental Care Campaign." Facebook. 22 November 2018. https://www.facebook.com/watch/live/?ref=watch_permalink&v=381222415951627.

———. "PIWC Tarkwa: Climax of Environmental Care Day." Facebook, 15 May 2022. https://www.facebook.com/piwctarkwa/videos/298353295827042.

Church of Pentecost – Goaso Manhyia. "On the Environmental Care Campaign." Facebook, 31 May 2019. https://www.facebook.com/100064402554101/videos/2386486951373698.

Citi Newsroom. "UPPR Partners Church of Pentecost for Plastic Waste Collection." *CNR*. 26 November 2022. https://citinewsroom.com/2022/11/uppr-partners-church-of-Pentecost-for-plastic-waste-collection/.

Conradie, Ernst M. *Christianity and Ecological Theology: Resources for Further Research*. Study Guides in Religion and Theology 11. Cape Town: Sun Press, 2006.

Covenant University. "A Citadel of Spirituality, Knowledge, Leadership and Mental Productivity." Centre for Research, Innovation and Discovery. 2023. https://www.covenantuniversity.edu.ng/about-us/operations/centre-for-research-innovation-and-discoveries.

———. "Covenant University Emerges Climate Champion at COY 16." *Covenant News*. 6 May 2022. https://covenantuniversity.edu.ng/information/more/covenant-news/439-covenant-university-emerges-climate-champion-at-coy-16.

Creation Care Symposium. "Religious Ecologies and Modernity: The Relevance of Religious Responses to Global Ecocrisis and Climate Change Today." Akrofi-Christaller Institute of Theology, Mission and Culture and A Rocha Ghana. Google Meet, 27 October 2023.

Daniels, Bisi. "Adeboye at 81: The Building of Redemption City." *The Cable*. 14 March 2023. https://www.thecable.ng/adeboye-at-81-the-building-of-redemption-city.

Davis, Anita. "Pentecostal Approaches to Ecotheology: Reviewing the Literature." *Australasian Pentecostal Studies* 22, no. 1 (2021): 4–33. https://apsjournal.com/index.php/APS/article/view/9572.

Dove Television. "Healthy Living: Save the Earth." Facebook, 5 May 2022. https://www.facebook.com/dovetv/videos/723036348827223.

Drooger, André. "Essentialist and Normative Approaches." In *Studying Global Pentecostalism: Theories and Methods*, edited by Allan Anderson, Michael Bergunder, André Drooger, and Cornelis van der Laan, 30–50. Berkeley: University of California Press, 2010.

Enate, Anselm A., and Taofeeq A. Amusa. "Challenges of Agricultural Adaptation to Climate Change in Nigeria: A Synthesis from the Literature." *The Journal of Field Actions: Field Actions Science Reports* 4 (2010). URL: http://journals.openedition.org/factsreports/678.

Eriksen, Stian Sørlie. "The Church of Pentecost International: Fortellingen om en Migrantmenighet i Oslo." In *Kristne Migranter i Norden*, edited by Anders Aschim, Olav Hovdelien, and Helje Kringleboth Sødal, 190–207. Kristiansand: Portal, 2016.

Family Homes Funds Limited (FHFL) and Redeemed Christian Church of God (RCCG). "Environmental and Social Impact Assessment (ESIA) for the Green Pastures Housing Estate Development within The Redeemed Christian Church of God (RCCG), Redeemed Camp, Ogun State, Nigeria by Family Homes Funds Limited (FHFL) and Redeemed Christian Church of God (RCCG)." Ecosphere Consulting Ltd. Report. December 2020. https://www.afdb.org/sites/default/files/documents/environmental-and-social-assessments/esia_summary_fhfl_rccg.pdf.

Fehintolu, Osamolu Titilayo, and Atuluku John. "An Appraisal of the Role of the Church in National Development: A Case of The Redeemed Christian Church of God in Nigeria." *Multidisciplinary Journal of Research Development* 25, no. 1 (2016): 75–85. https://www.globalacademicgroup.com/node/612.

Flatimes. "RCCG Fasting Prayer Points for 9 February 2019 – DAY 30: Prayer for Climate Change." 9 February 2019. https://flatimes.com/climate-change-rccg-fasting-prayer-points-9-february-2019/.

Francis (pope). *Encyclical Letter Laudato Si' of the Holy Father Francis on Care for Our Common Home*. N.D. https://www.vatican.va/content/francesco/en/encyclicals/documents/papa-francesco_20150524_enciclica-laudato-si.html.

Fretheim, Kjetil. "Oil Dependence and Climate Change: Public Theology in Norway." *International Journal of Public Theology* 10, no. 2 (2016): 193–210. https://doi.org/10.1163/15697320-12341442.

Ghana Catholic Bishops' Conference Launches Goal 6 of 'Laudato Si'." *NewsWatch GH*. 20 March 2023. https://newswatchgh.com/ ghana-catholic-bishops-conference-launches-goal-6-of-laudato-si/.

Global Energy Alliance for People and Planet (GEAPPP). "Former Vice President of Nigeria, H. E. Professor Yemi Osinbajo SAN, joins GEAPP as Global Advisor." Press release. 11 July 2023. https://energyalliance.org/professor-yemi-osinbajo-joins-geapp-as-global-advisor/.

Golo, Ben-Willie Kwaku. "Africa's Poverty and Its Neo-Pentecostal 'Liberators': An Ecotheological Assessment of Africa's Prosperity Gospellers." *Pneuma: The Journal of the Society for Pentecostal Studies* 35, no. 3 (2013): 366–84.

———. "The Groaning Earth and the Greening of Neo-Pentecostalism in the 21st Century Ghana." *PentecoStudies* 13, no. 2 (2014): 197–216. DOI:10.1558/ptcs.v13i2.197.

———. "Taking Africa out of the African: Eco-Community, the Christian Heritage of Empire, and Neo-Pentecostalism in Africa." In *Wealth, Health, and Hope in*

African Christian Religion: The Search for Abundant Life, edited by Stan Chu, 131–53. Lanham: Lexington, 2017.

Golo, Ben-Willie Kwaku, and Ernestina Novieto. "Religion and Sustainable Development in Africa: Neo-Pentecostal Economies in Perspective." *Religion and Development* 1, no. 1 (2022): 73–95. DOI: https://doi.org/10.30965/27507955-20220005.

Griffith, John D. "All the Earth, Let Us Sing: Searching for a Latent Pentecostal Ecology in Australian Pentecostal Worship." In *Climate Crisis and Sustainable Creaturely Care: Integrated Theology, Governance and Justice*, edited by Christina Nellist, 81–102. Cambridge: Cambridge Scholars, 2021.

Hackett, Rosalind I. J. "Charismatic/Pentecostal Appropriation of Media Technologies in Nigeria and Ghana." *Journal of Religion in Africa* 28, no. 3 (1998): 258–77. https://doi.org/10.2307/1581571.

Heuser, Andreas. "Outlines of a Pentecostal Dominion Theology." In *Political Pentecostalism: Four Synoptic Surveys from Africa, Asia, and Latin-America*, edited by Leandro L. B. Fontana and Markus Luber, 187–246. Weltkirche und Mission 17. Regensburg: Verlag Friedrich Pustet, 2021.

Hoffman, Andrew. J., and Lloyd E. Sandelands. "Getting Right with Nature: Anthropocentrism, Ecocentrism, and Theocentrism." *Organization & Environment* 18, no. 2 (2005): 141–62. https://doi.org/10.1177/1086026605276197.

Hunter, Harold D. "Pentecostal Ecotheology from the Margins." In *Contemporary Ecotheology, Climate Justice, and Environmental Stewardship in World Religions*, edited by Lucas A. Andrianos and Tom Svere Tomren, et al., 93–105. Ecothee Volume 6th-Orthodox Academy of Crete Publications. Steinkjær: Embla Akademisk, 2021.

Ice, Thomas D. "What is Dominion Theology?" *Article Archives* 74 (2009). https://digitalcommons.liberty.edu/pretrib_arch/74.

Idehen, O. Stella. "Determination of the Legal Implication of Sustainable Development as a Necessary Corollary to Human Development." *KB Law Scholars Journal* 1, no. 3 (2024). https://kblsp.org.ng/index.php/kblsp/article/view/29.

Imosemi, Adekunbi, Nzeribe Abangwu, and Theo Nwanu. "Climate Change Mitigation: An Assessment of Global Legal Responses: So Far So Good?" *Journal of Research and Development* 1, no. 3 (2013): 79–96. https://www.arabianjbmr.com/pdfs/RD_VOL_1_3/7.pdf.

Impelli, Matthew. "Pastor Claims God Suddenly Stopped Winter for Him Because He Hates the Cold." *Newsweek*. 16 November 2023. https://www.newsweek.com/nigerian-pastor-claims-god-changed-weather-him-hates-cold-1844386.

Kgatle, Mookogo S., and Allan H. Anderson, eds. *The Use and Abuse of the Spirit in Pentecostalism: A South African Perspective*. Routledge New Critical Thinking in Religion, Theology and Biblical Studies. London: Routledge, 2021.

Kozinets, Robert. *Netnography: Doing Ethnographic Research Online*. London: Sage, 2009.

Lamp, Jeffrey S. "Ecotheology." In *The Routledge Handbook of Pentecostal Theology*, edited by Wolfgang Vondey, 357–66. London: Routledge, 2020.

Ludwig, Frieder, and J. Kwabena Asamoah-Gyadu, eds. *African Christian Presence in the West: New Immigrant Congregations and Transnational Networks in North America and Europe*. Trenton: African World, 2011.

Ludwig, Frieder, and Stian Sørlie Eriksen. "Forschungszugänge zu Afrikanischen Transnationalen Gemeinden und Kirchen: Inbesondere in Grossbritannien, Deutschland und Norwegen." In *Migrationskirchen: Internationaliserierung und Pluraliserung de Christentums vor Ort*, edited by Gregor Etzelmüller and Claudia Remmelt, 375–404. Leipzig: Evangelische Verlagsanstalt – Wissenschaft, 2022.

Martins, Perry. "RCCG Repairs Lagos – Ibadan Express Way." *Gospel Buzz*. 6 November 2015. https://gospelbuzz.com/rccg-repairs-lagos-ibadan-express-way/.

Maseno, Loreen. "Prayer for Rain: A Pentecostal Perspective from Kenya." *The Ecumenical Review* 69, no. 1 (2017): 336–47. DOI: 10.1111/erev.12297.

Maseno, Loreen, and King'asia Mamat. "An Appraisal of the Pentecostal Eco-Theology and Environmental Consciousness among Youths in Parklands Baptist Church, Kenya." *HTS Teologiese Studies/Theological Studies* 77, no. 2 (2021): a6840. https://doi.org/ 10.4102/hts.v77i2.6840.

McClymond, Michael J. "Charismatic Renewal and Neo-Pentecostalism: From North American Origins to Global Permutations." In *The Cambridge Companion to Pentecostalism*, edited by Cecil M. Robeck, Jr. and Amos Yong, 31–51. Cambridge: Cambridge University Press, 2014. doi:10.1017/CCO9780511910111.005.

Nagle, John Copeland. "The Evangelical Debate over Climate Change." *University of St. Thomas Law Journal* 5, no. 1 (2008): 53–86.

Nche, George C. "Beyond Spiritual Focus: Climate Change Awareness, Role Perception, and Action among Church Leaders in Nigeria." *Weather, Climate, and Society* 12, no. 1 (2020): 149–69. https://doi.org/10.1175/WCAS-D-19-0001.1.

Ngnenbe, Timothy. "Church of Pentecost Launches National Sanitation Campaign." *Graphic News*. 2 March 2020. https://www.graphic.com.gh/news/general-news/church-of-Pentecost-launches-national-sanitation-campaign.html.

Odon, Akanimo, and Sam Guodadia. *African Environmental Perspectives*. AuthorHouse, 2011.

Ofori, Cwesi. "Way To Go! RCCG Repairs Lagos-Ibadan Expressway." *Gospel GH*. 5 November 2015. https://gospelgh.com/way-to-go-rccg-repairs-lagos-ibadan-expressway/.

Ojo, Aderemi Samuel. "Impact of Climate Change on Land-Use and Land-Cover of Yewa South Local Government Area, Nigeria." PhD Thesis, Covenant University, 2021.

Okwezuzu, G. E. "Human Rights Perspective to Environmental Challenges: Emerging Trends." *East African Journal of Peace and Human Rights* 17, no. 2 (2011): 515–31.

Oladipupo, Jacob. "Power in Neo-Pentecostalism and African Traditional Religion: A Nigerian Case Study." *International Journal of Science and Research (IJSR)* 7, no. 7 (2016): 431–41. https://www.ijsr.net/archive/v7i7/ART20183886.pdf.

Oloyede, Mary. "Climate Change and Tropical Coastal Vulnerability in the Gulf of Guinea, Nigeria." PhD Thesis, Covenant University, 2021.

Osinulu, Adedamola. "The Road to Redemption: Performing Pentecostal Citizenship in Lagos." In *The Arts of Citizenship in African Cities: Infrastructures and Spaces of Belonging*, edited by Mamadou Diouf and Rosalind Fredericks, 115–35. New York: Palgrave Macmillan, 2014.

Oyero, Kayode. "Nigerian Politicians Patronise Spiritual Leaders, Can't Ban Doomsday New Year Prophecies like Ghana – SANs." *Punch*. 31 December 2021. https://punchng.com/nigerian-politicians-patronise-spiritual-leaders-cant-ban-doomsday-new-year-prophecies-like-ghana-sans/.

Oyero, Olusola, Kehinde Oyesomi, Taiwo Abioye, et al. "Behavioral Practices and Climate Change Awareness in Ado Odo/Ota, Ogun State, Nigeria: Implications for Communication and Development Agenda." Presented to the International Conference on African Development Issues (CU-ICADI): Social and Economic Models for Development Track, 2015. https://eprints.covenantuniversity.edu.ng/6617/1/Prof%20Abioye%20T.%201.pdf.

Pentecostal Fellowship of Nigeria (PFN). "About Pentecostal Fellowship of Nigeria." Online Article. 2022. https://pfnlagosstate.org/about.

Pentecost Men's Ministry Embarks on Tree Planting Exercise." *NewsWatch GH*. 5 June 2021. https://newswatchgh.com/Pentecost-mens-ministry-embarks-on-tree-planting-exercise/.

Redeemed Christian Church of God (RCCG). "Global World Environment." RCCG House of Favour Headquarters, Facebook. Video, 55 minutes, 40 seconds. 31 May 2022. https://www.facebook.com/watch/live/?ref=watch_permalink&v=4519917754777550.

———. "Our History." https://www.rccg.org/our-history/.

RCCG Openheavens Luton. "RCCG Sunday School Lesson 19: Political Dominion." Teaching Material. 19 February 2023. https://openheavensluton.org/rccg-sunday-school-lesson-19-political-dominion/.

RCCG_PR. "Day 22. Tuesday 24th November 2020." Instagram. 24 November 2020.

RCCG Sunday Service. "The Earth Is the Lord's." Sunday Service, Brandon MB. Facebook. Video, 1 hour, 51 minutes, 8 seconds. 2 October 2022. https://www.facebook.com/watch/live/?ref=watch_permalink&v=1264989544253912.

The Redeemed Christian Church of God (RCCG). "The Redeemed Christian Church of God." https://www.rccg.org/.

Redemption Television Ministry. "RCCG Fasting & Prayers. Day 20: Global Climate Change. With Pastor Awosusi Paul." Facebook, 30 January 2023. Video, 15 minutes. https://www.facebook.com/watch/?v=1532655463879329.

Richman, Naomi. "Nigerian Pentecostalism." *The Database of Religious History*. The University of British Columbia, 2020. https://religiondatabase.org/browse/935.

Roberts, Michael. "Evangelicals and Climate Change." In *Religion in Environmental and Climate Change: Suffering, Values, Lifestyles*, edited by Gerten Dieter and Sigurd Bergmann, 107–31. New York: Bloomsbury Academic, 2012.

Roewe, Brian. "Philippine Bishops Urge Church Finances to Disconnect from Fossil Fuels." *National Catholic Reporter*. 3 February 2022. https://www.ncronline.org/news/earthbeat/philippine-bishops-urge-church-finances-disconnect-fossil-fuels.

Rotary Club of Garden City (Georgetown) Guyana. "RCGCG Launches Children Environmental Handbook." News Item. 30 July 2022. https://rotaryclubgardencitygy.org/stories/rcgcg-launches-children-environmental-handbook.

Sala, Dimitry. "Pentecostal Culture, or Pentecost of Culture? Transformation, Paradigms, Power, Unity." *Spiritus* 6, no. 1 (2021): 103–22. https://digitalshowcase.oru.edu/spiritus/.

Sheppard, Kylie. "Pentecostalism and Sustainability: Conflict or Convergence." PhD Thesis, Murdoch University, 2006.

Stephenson, Christopher A. *Profiles of Pentecostal Theology*. Brill Research Perspectives. Leiden: Brill, 2022.

Studebaker, Stephen M. *A Pentecostal Political Theology for American Renewal: Spirit of the Kingdoms, Citizen of the Cities*. New York: Palgrave, 2016.

Tangen, Karl Inge. "Pentekostal Spiritualitet, Økoteologi og Miljøengasjement: Et Bidrag til Utvikling av en Pentekostal og Karismatisk Spiritualitet som kan Integrere Elementer av Økoteologi og Miljøetikk." *Scandinavian Journal for Leadership and Theology* 7 (2020). https://sjlt-journal.com/index.php/sjlt/article/view/43.

Tomren, Tom Sverre. "From Environmental Activism to Environmental Education: A Historical Overview, Evaluations and a Suggestion for a Path Forward for the Religious Institutions as Partners for a Global Green Shift." *Consensus* 41, no. 1 (2020). DOI: 10.51644/QLZE3737.

Ukah, Asonzeh. "Building God's City: The Political Economy of Prayer Camps in Nigeria." *International Journal of Urban and Regional Research* 40, no. 3 (2016): 524–40. https://doi.org/10.1111/1468-2427.12363.

———. "Redeeming Urban Spaces: The Ambivalence of Building a Pentecostal City in Lagos, Nigeria." In *Global Prayers: Contemporary Manifestations of the Religious in the City*, edited by Jochen Becker and Katrin Klingan, 178–97. Zurich: Lars Műller, 2014.

Uwaegbulam, Chinedum, and Jesutomi Akomolafe. "RCCG Unveils 14-floor Trinity Towers, to Donate N2b Rental Income to Charity." *The Guardian*. 11 June 2022. https://guardian.ng/property/rccg-unveils-14-floor-trinity-towers-to-donate-n2b-rental-income-to-charity/.

van den Toren, Benno. "African Neo-Pentecostalism in the Face of Secularization: Problems and Possibilities." *Cairo Journal of Theology* 2 (2015): 103–20. http://journal.etsc.org.

Wariboko, Nimi. *The Pentecostal Principle: Ethical Methodology in New Spirit*. Grand Rapids: Eerdmans, 2012.

Werner, Dietrich. "The Challenge of Environment and Climate Justice: Imperatives of an Eco-theological Reformation of Christianity in African Contexts." In *African Initiated Christianity and the Decolonisation of Development: Sustainable Devel-*

opment in Pentecostal and Independent Churches, edited By Philipp Öhlmann, Wilhelm Gräb, and Marie-Luise Frost, 51–72. London: Routledge, 2020.

White, Peter. "Missional Branding: A Case Study of the Church of Pentecost." *HTS Teologiese Studies/Theological Studies* 75, no. 4 (2019): 1–7. https://dx.doi.org/10.4102/hts.v75i4.5278.

Wilkinson, Michael, and Peter Althouse. "Editorial: Pentecostalism as Lived Religion." *Canadian Journal of Pentecostal–Charismatic Christianity* 3 (2012): i–ix.

World Council of Churches. "The Living Planet: Seeking a Just and Sustainable Global Community." 11th Assembly, Document No. PIC 01.2 rev. 31 August–8 September 2022. https://www.oikoumene.org/sites/default/files/2022-10/ADOPTED-PIC01.2rev-The-Living-Planet-Seeking-a-Just-and-Sustainable-Global-Community.pdf.

Part IV

Ecumenical Perspectives

14

Pentecostal Climate Justice

Ecological Activism Meets Restitution

Harold D. Hunter

My youth in a small, radical Wesleyan-Pentecostal church was dominated by an official list of "29 [Bible] teachings made prominent."[1] The seventeenth such teaching, based on Scripture but often conveniently overlooked, was "restitution where possible." Although restitution was a hallmark of many early Pentecostal revivals in the USA including William J. Seymour's Apostolic Faith Mission, it has had a short shelf life for at least many white Pentecostals. The Pentecostal commitment to neighbors and communal wellbeing cannot be surrendered. It is to Jesus that we turn to lay on the altar our sins and seek forgiveness. Reform and restitution to those wronged by us or our ancestors must follow our repentance.[2]

The above is first and foremost the meaning of this teaching as it was originally understood. However, when looking at the biblical passages, it seems apparent that the theological intent can be extended to how we rob the earth. For example, how was such a concept applied by the Apostolic Faith Mission in South Africa when confronting apartheid? What about indigenous peoples

---

1. Compiled by the White Wing Publishing House and Press, *These Necessary Things: The Doctrine and Practices of the Church of God of Prophecy as set forth by the General Assembly*, 8th ed. (Cleveland: White Wing Publishing House, 1980), 12–13.

2. Restitution was in the original list of teachings published on 15 August 1910 in the Church of God Evangel and the 1911 Church of God General Assembly minutes, but not in 1909 court documents. See James M. Beaty, "Church Teachings and the Declaration of Faith: A History," Pentecostal Theological Seminary, lecture notes, 4, 8, 18 September 2010.

and the "boarding schools" on Turtle Island run by and including Pentecostals? How did the Church of God in Christ respond to the loss of their church in the 1922 Tulsa Massacre?

Those who think otherwise must ask indigenous peoples on their soil in the global South much as you would ask why African American Pentecostals are literal and not simply metaphorical about "freeing the captives." Notice that Luke 19:8 is where we have Zacchaeus saying he will give half of his possessions to the poor and "if I have defrauded anyone of anything, I will pay back four times as much" (NRSV). Various Reformed scholars speak of a Zacchaeus ecology sort of giving. The 11th World Council of Churches (WCC) Assembly in Karlsruhe, Germany, passed a reference to the "Zacchaeus tax" in one of their drafts for the new Commission on Climate Justice and Environmental Sustainability.[3]

Restitution must become an axiom of the Pentecostal mission to rescue climate justice refugees. Pentecostals must advance beyond simply confessing that global North Pentecostals sin against God's creation in the global North thereby creating climate justice refugees in the global South. The marginalized who are colonized by various economic realities and are victimized by the richest countries in the world cry out for justice.

During the 20 May 2022 WCC online seminar about climate justice and finances, James Bhagwan, General Secretary of the Pacific Conference of Churches, reflected that, in the Pacific region, people's spirit and faith are connected to the land and the ocean. "We cannot be forced to put at risk our children's future because of the desire for profit in the present," he said. "We ask you on behalf of our children in the Pacific: what kind of ancestors will you be?"[4] Representing the Pentecostal World Fellowship (PWF) at this discussion, I underscored how influential churches can be, adding with reference to the Zacchaeus tax idea: "The hour has come to repent and reform in order to restore all of God's creation."[5]

Many of us signed a United Nations Environment Programme (UNEP) statement in 2022 that began

---

3. See World Council of Churches, "ZacTax Toolkit," eBook (2021), https://www.oikoumene.org/resources/publications/zactax-toolkit; Harold D. Hunter, "Pentecostals at the WCC 11th Assembly in Karlsruhe, Germany 2022," WCC blog, 14 September 2022, https://www.oikoumene.org/blog/pentecostals-at-the-wcc-11th-assembly-in-karlsruhe-germany-2022.

4. Bhagwan's comments are part of WCC News, "Committing to Climate-Responsible Finance Sends 'Strong Signal of Hope to All,'" 23 May 2022, https://www.oikoumene.org/news/committing-to-climate-responsible-finance-sends-strong-signal-of-hope-to-all.

5. WCC News, "Committing to Climate-Responsible Finance."

The world is facing a triple "pandemic" of climate change, biodiversity loss and pollution. Those hardest hit are those who have caused the least damage. We have less than three years for our carbon emissions to start dropping from the peak, and yet emissions continue to rise. We have already exceeded several thresholds critical to a stable and functioning planetary system, and we are currently on a pathway to overshooting dangerous tipping points, with irreversible consequences for all life.[6]

A Pentecostal Pilgrimage

My first full-time seminary faculty appointment was at the Church of God School of Theology in Cleveland, Tennessee, now known as the Pentecostal Theological Seminary. I started teaching various theology courses in the fall of 1981. In the spring of 1982, I taught a course called Contemporary Theology. An original syllabus has survived, and it shows that I echoed the European colonial emphasis of my PhD studies at Fuller Theological Seminary School of Theology.

The next time I taught Contemporary Theology was in the summer of 1983. An original syllabus shows a complete redesign of the course that deconstructs colonial theologies dominating seminaries in the West at that time. This was facilitated by having created a ground-breaking course for the summer of 1982 titled "Theology of the Holy Spirit." The new Contemporary Theology syllabus began with influential theologians, then quickly moved on to issues important to Pentecostals, especially those in the pastorate, and sought to engage important developments around the world. I did not shy away from issues current at the American Academy of Religion/Society of Biblical Literature such as feminism, apartheid, sexuality, Palestine, conciliar ecumenism like the WCC, immigration, etc.

At the top of this new section was a lecture on "Environmental Issues," meaning ecology. I still have original lecture notes as I continued to expand this lecture when teaching this course at Oral Roberts University in 1986. While working as a Pentecostal church executive with extensive international travel, I put together a network of Pentecostal scholars on five continents. I flew to Geneva, Switzerland, in 1989 asking WCC General Secretary Emilio

---

6. From the UNEP-organized Stockholm+50 Interfaith meeting and its resulting statement. World Council of Churches, "Stockholm+50 Interfaith Statement:. 'Faith Values and Reach: Contribution to Environmental Policy,'" online document, June 2022.

Castro if I could run a conference adjacent to Canberra '91 that would bring together 100 Pentecostal scholars. That story is told elsewhere[7] but the result was the first global conference for Pentecostal scholars known as Brighton '91.

According to University of South Africa (UNISA) Professor M. L. Daneel's presentation at the Theological Stream of Brighton '91,[8] when it comes time for water baptism, one group of African Indigenous/Independent Church candidates in Zimbabwe confess not only personal sins, but things like "I chopped down 30 trees, but did not plant any"; "I ruined the topsoil." Then there is the Lord's Supper. A monstrous fire is built and 1,000s go running around this huge fire yelling out their sins. Along with familiar confessions to adultery, jealousy, and stealing, are wailings over ecological wizardry. Before taking the elements of communion, they must pass through a series of symbolic gates of heaven. Each gate has prophets who discern hidden sins not confessed when running around the bonfire. Those hidden sins include ecological sins!

Soon thereafter I taught at a series of Pentecostal schools in Central America, Ecuador, Puerto Rico, the Philippines, Romania, Singapore, South Korea, and elsewhere. Seeing in person the lives of climate change refugees had a dramatic impact on me, particularly what I witnessed firsthand in Nicaragua. These are simply early case studies of what I observed on my way to visiting 90 countries and I had long been aware of environmental racism.

My "Pentecostal Healing for God's Sick Creation?" published in a South Korean-based journal was the first academic, theological article by a PWF-type Pentecostal.[9] This was preceded by the First World Assemblies of God

---

7. Harold D. Hunter, "Foreword to the 2019 Reprint Edition," in *All Together in One Place: Theological Papers from the Brighton Conference on World Evangelization*, eds. Harold D. Hunter and Peter D. Hocken(Eugene: Wipf & Stock, 2019), 3.

8. M. L. Daneel, "African Independent Church Pneumatology and the Salvation of All Creation," in *All Together in One Place: Theological Papers from the Brighton Conference*, eds. Harold D. Hunter and Peter D. Hocken (Eugene: Wipf & Stock, 2019), 98–128. All Daneel quotes in this paragraph are from this source.

9. Harold D. Hunter, "Pentecostal Healing for God's Sick Creation?," *The Spirit and the Church* 2, no. 2 (2000): 145–67. My paper was based on that read at the 1998 Pentecostal World Conference in Korea. The useful study by Rice, "Ecology and the Future of Pentecostalism," unfortunately, gets the chronology wrong by pointing first to Amos Yong in 2005; it never mentioned my article. (See Jonathon Rice, "Ecology and the Future of Pentecostalism: Problems, Possibilities, and Proposals," in *Pentecostal Mission and Global Christianity*, eds. Wonsuk Ma, Veli-Matti Kärkkäinen, and Asamoah Gyadu [(London: Regnum, 2012], 360–79.) It did not help subsequent contributions that the journal that published my article was in Korea and stopped publication after a few years when the sponsoring Foursquare seminary closed unexpectedly. Anyway, Rice starts with Amos Yong, *The Spirit Poured Out on All Flesh: Pentecostalism and the Possibility of a Global Theology* (Grand Rapids: Baker Academic, 2005), 300. He then goes on to Wonsuk Ma, "The Spirit of God in Creation: Lessons for Christian Mission," *Transformation* 24, nos. 3/4 (2007): 227, and Steven M. Studebaker, "The Spirit in Creation: A Unified Theology

Prayer Rally held in 1994 in Seoul that witnessed to the importance of prayer for God's creation. Within two years, David Yonggi Cho, with some influence by Professor Jürgen Moltmann upon what was known as the "world's largest church," established a ministry team at Yoido Full Gospel to address environmental concerns. When enumerating six priorities of ministry at the 1999 Full Gospel Inchon church, its pastor, Song Kyu Choi, listed creation as number five.

There has long been a need to move toward organizing a global ecology group not unlike the PWF World Missions Commission Task Force on Development and Relief. One finds such with the World Evangelical Alliance (WEA), Lutheran World Federation (LWF), World Communion of Reformed Churches (WCRC), and the WCC. With the approval of the PWF executive committee and advisory board, a PWF Creation Care Task Force was created during the 26th Pentecostal World Conference (2022) hosted by the Yoido Full Gospel Church in Seoul, South Korea. All the global Christian groups engaged with the PWF have been notified about this launch.

Through the PWF Christian Unity Commission, I organized an ecology workshop at the October 2022 Pentecostal World Conference hosted by Yoido. Right before that, I organized a Brunnen workshop at the September 2022 WCC General Assembly in Germany. Initially, there were signs of making inroads into the WCC Commission on Climate Justice and Sustainable Development. However, despite a PWF nomination, there is no Pentecostal member of this commission.

The PWF Creation Care Task Force (PWF CCTF)[10] is being strangled by the fact that the PWF is not accredited by the UN. The same is true for the PWF WM Relief and Development group. The PWF CCTF could not send

---

of Grace and Creation Care," *Zygon: Journal of Religion and Science* 43, no. 4 (2008): 943–60, and so on. However, the correct sequence had already been published by A. J. Swoboda in his early work as he confirmed when I first met him at the Society for Pentecostal Studies. (See A. J. Swoboda, *Tongues and Trees: Towards a Pentecostal Ecological Theology* [Blandford Forum: Deo, 2013], 98; compare all of this with Anita Davis, "Pentecostal Approaches to Ecotheology: Reviewing the Literature," *Australasian Pentecostal Studies* 22, no. 1 [2021]: 4–33). Swoboda labels my work "exploratory," but I remain convinced that healing is a motif that resonates with our community. I also took note that the language was used with the unique group of global faith leaders of all religions organized in 2021 by the Vatican and referenced in this article. Prior to my article was Jean-Jacques Suurmond, "Christ King: A Charismatic Appeal for an Ecological Lifestyle," *Pneuma: Journal for the Society for Pentecostal Studies* 10, no. 1 (1998): 26–35. Suurmond told me he does not identify as a Pentecostal.

10. Once the PWF CCTF was approved by the PWF, individual members were nominated by the PWF Christian Unity Commission. The members in alphabetical order are Emmanuel Awudi (Ghana), Anita Davis (Australia), Benjamin Jacuk (Alaska Dena'ina traditional lands), Angela Maringoli (Brazil), Karen Reed (Canada), Elizabeth Salazar Sanzana (Chile), Joel Tejedo (Philippines), Sanna Urvas (Finland), Johannes Widlund (Sweden), Harold D. Hunter, chair.

someone to COP 29 – the November 2024 United Nations Climate Change Conference – nor even the sixth session of the United Nations Environment Assembly held in February 2024 in Kenya. How is it possible that the Church of God in Christ showed up at the 1945 launch of the UN and the WEA is fully accredited with the UN but not the PWF? In view of the lack of supporting Pentecostal institutions, this also impacts our ability to get major grants from the likes of the Lilly Endowment or Templeton Foundation.

"Faith and Science" Series

The series of Zoom sessions in 2021 titled "Faith and Science: Toward COP26" organized by the Vatican, UNEP, the Italian Embassy to the Holy See, and the British Embassy to the Holy See became an incredible encounter for all involved. A select group of no more than 50 global faith leaders from all religions seated around the globe along with eminent scientists met each month by Zoom with translation of various languages.

David Wells and Harold D. Hunter represented the PWF. Hunter did the primary presentation for the PWF about our engagement around the world and Wells reported on the Pentecostal Assemblies of Canada (PAOC). When addressing the Faith and Science group on behalf of the PWF, Hunter said we are not scientists, but speaking theologically, our faith tradition is drawn to language from Ecumenical Patriarch Bartholomew about sin against God's creation (more on Patriarch Bartholomew later). The spiritual discipline of fasting contributes to the healing of all of creation through the lens of those who seek the flourishing of all life.[11]

During the Zoom sessions with global faith leaders organized by the Vatican working toward COP26, prominent scientists focused on the food humans eat, the clothes humans wear, supporting biodiversity, transportation, seeking to be carbon neutral, and divesting from fossil fuels while moving toward investments in green energy. Oxford University economist Kate Raworth gave a ground-breaking presentation on an economy of life emphasizing thriving

---

11. Oral Roberts University's Professor of Religion Jeffrey Lamp has published more than most on the environment while assisting ORU students in such publications. See, for example, Jeffrey Lamp, Kathryn Moder, Megan Munhofen, Cade Rich, and Nathan Von Atzigen, "Creation Care as Caring for Human Beings: An Environmental Justice Case Study," *Spiritus: ORU Journal of Theology* 5, no. 1 (2020): 137–50 which adopts a "pro-life" narrative to chase Oklahoma politicians involved in determining the amount of mercury that is legally allowed. ORU's College of Science and Engineering offers a degree in Global Environmental Sustainability, and its president, William "Billy" M. Wilson, is also Chair of the PWF.

over growing which was warmly received by the faith leaders who were willing to challenge the axioms of capitalism.[12]

The scientist who created the most remarkable slides was Professor Riccardo Valentini. He shocked some of us when he said almost as many people die each year from obesity (29,000,000) as malnutrition (36,000,000). Valentini also mentioned that many modern city dwellers have little understanding regarding where food comes from. He argued, in light of the ecological impact of meat, that we need to get our food from trees and change our diet.

This series of meetings culminated in a meeting on 4 October 2021 at the Vatican with Pope Francis. Pope Francis delivered our "Joint Appeal" of the global faith leaders to His Eminence Alok Sharma, President of COP26. A Pentecostal bishop from Brazil signed the "Joint Appeal." The PWF did not sign this document, but Wells and Hunter were on the front row during the formal signing at the Vatican where otherwise the PWF seats would have been, very close to Pope Francis.

The United Nations Climate Change Conference held in Glasgow, Scotland, 1–12 November 2021, attracted many of the world's top political leaders among the 100+ countries that participated. The only two Pentecostals to travel to Glasgow for this event were Johannes Widlund and Mikael Jägerskog. They continue to advance a global network of Pentecostal ecology activists. Widlund is the environmental advisor for the Pingstmissionens Utvecklingssamarbete (PMU) – also known as the Swedish Pentecostal International Relief and Development Agency – and a member of the PWF Creation Care Task Force. Jägerskog is Head of Policy, Advocacy, and Learning, PMU, and an active member of the PWF World Missions Commission. Pointing to those in Sweden who celebrate Greta Thunberg, Ulrik Josefsson mentions one of the more outspoken Pentecostal influencers in this area is Micael Grenholm, an editor for an international network for peace and justice.

During the 2020 organizational phase, a "COP26 Faith Event – Final Non-Paper"[13] was circulated to those invited to the select group. A product of the "Faith and Science: Toward COP26" Zoom sessions with the global leaders,

---

12. Kate Raworth, "A Healthy Economy Should Be Designed to Thrive, Not Grow," TED-Talk, April 2018, https://www.ted.com/talks/kate_raworth_a_healthy_economy_should_be_designed_to_thrive_not_grow?language=en. See also Ciara Nugent, "Amsterdam Is Embracing a Radical New Economic Theory to Help Save the Environment. Could It Also Replace Capitalism?," *Time*, 22 January 2021, https://time.com/5930093/amsterdam-doughnut-economics/.

13. "COP26 Faith Event – Final Non-Paper," circulated 2020 by the Vatican's Secretaries of Relations with States, UNEP, the Italian Embassy to the Holy See, and the British Embassy to the Holy See.

the thesis of the "Final Non-Paper" stood tall on the following assertion that would be the cornerstone to the later "Joint Appeal" to all faith traditions and governments to protect the poor and marginalized

> The global temperature has already increased by one degree Celsius above the twentieth century average. With present National Determined Contributions (NDCs), the temperature will rise by 3 degrees, which will be catastrophic for the entire planet – humans, animals, and plants – especially the marginalized and poorest communities. COP26 aims to galvanize action to limit the rise to well below 2 degrees Celsius, and preferably 1.5 degrees Celsius.

The "Joint Appeal" presented to His Eminence Alok Sharma, President of COP26, included language drawn from a healing motif that is found in many like documents,

> We are caretakers of the natural environment with the vocation to care for it for future generations and the moral obligation to cooperate in the healing of the planet.
> We plead with the international community, gathered at COP26, to take speedy, responsible and shared action to safeguard, restore and heal our wounded humanity and the home entrusted to our stewardship.[14]

This healing theme should find resonance with Pentecostal churches and communities given the centrality of healing to Pentecostal spirituality.[15]

This statement by these global faith actors must consider the imposing holdings of faith communities while also engaging respective governments. The Roman Catholic Church has the largest holdings of any religious group on the planet. Speaking from the COP28 Faith Pavilion, Iyad Abumoghli, Founder and Director of the Faith for Earth Coalition of UNEP, offered these details:

- Six billion people (84 percent of the world's population) have a faith, religion, or values system.

---

14. Holy See Press Office, "Meeting on 'Faith and Science: Towards COP26', promoted by the Embassies of Great Britain and Italy to the Holy See, together with the Holy See 04.10.2021," summary of bulletin, press release, 4 October 2021, https://press.vatican.va/content/salastampa/en/bollettino/pubblico/2021/10/04/211004a.html.

15. For more Pentecostal perspective on the healing motif, see also Gani Wiyono, "Healing God's Creation: A Contribution of Pentecostal Understanding of Divine Healing to Ecotheology," in *Voices Loud and Clear: Papers from the Global Pentecostal Summit*, eds. Douglas Petersen and Byron D. Klaus, Regnum Studies in Mission (London: Regnum, 2024), 165–80.

- More than one-and-a-half million projects globally addressing climate change are run by faith groups.
- Faith groups own and are responsible for more than eight percent of Earth's habitable land.
- Faith groups own and are responsible for more than five percent of all commercial forests on the planet.
- More than four in ten health services (forty percent) in some countries are operated by faith groups.
- Half of schools worldwide (fifty percent) are owned or operated by faith groups – rising to sixty-four percent of schools in sub-Saharan Africa.
- Ten percent of the world's financial institutions are faith-related, making faith institutions the world's third largest investor; research shows that "faith-aligned" impact investment capital is valued at five trillion dollars worldwide.[16]

What the chief executive of Faith Invest, Martin Palmer, says more generally about the world's religious traditions is also important in this regard: "Faiths are key stakeholders in the planet. Globally, faiths run two-thirds of schools, provide significant health services – the Catholic Church alone runs a quarter of the world's health care – and manage eight per cent of the habitable land surface of the planet, including five per cent of commercial forests."[17] Some of what we have seen in this more recent "Faith and Science" initiative has been anticipated in part by various Pentecostal bodies in their growing interface with ecological and environmental issues; to some of these we now turn.

Official Ecology Statements from Select Pentecostal Churches and Organizations Around the World

Bishop George D. McKinney sponsored the 2013 Church of God in Christ General Assembly Resolution #042013–7 dedicated to the church's responsibility for climate change. "Be it resolved," it was agreed

> that the Church Of God In Christ, Inc. will engage in measurable stewardship actions that will reduce energy consumption, use sustainable practices in our houses, buildings and houses of

---

16. The preceding bulleted list is quoted directly from Iyad Abumoghli, "Call to Action/Sign-up!," 12 December 2023, email.

17. Joe Ware, "World Faith Leaders Point at Richer Countries to Solve the Climate Crisis," *Church Times*, 4 October 2021.

worship, and seek good council in peer-reviewed climate scientists that will increase our knowledge and actions to confront climate change (Proverbs 12:15; 15:22). In addition, the Church Of God In Christ, Inc. pledges to find ways to reduce the impact and risk of climate change through promoting good stewardship habits and increase awareness in our houses, businesses, relationships, and congregations.[18]

This is an official policy adopted by the Church of God in Christ General Assembly. It was not created in a vacuum as Bishop McKinney was a climate justice activist who took his case to the White House.

During the Pentecostal–Charismatic Churches of North America (PCCNA) conference, 2 October 1997, in Washington, DC, Bishop McKinney (d. 2021), then pastor of St. Stephen's Church of God in Christ in San Diego, California, gave an example of ecological injustice that he engaged that was subsequently published in the 1998 PCCNA magazine *Reconciliation*,

We have referred the issue of environmental justice, the pollution of our air, the water and the stockpiling of toxic waste materials to insensitive government agencies . . .

Public policies that allow low-income housing to be built and maintained on known toxic waste sites must be dismantled. About a year ago, a group of us traveled to Washington DC, and met with Vice President Al Gore regarding this injustice. We had with us a black pastor from Dallas who testified that he, his wife and their seven children did not know that the low-income housing in which they lived was built over a toxic waste site.

Now it's too late. All of the children in this family are affected with cancer or some other debilitating disease or deformity. The husband and wife, only in their late fifties, are dying from cancer. In their community, the cancer rate is twenty or thirty times higher than in the rest of the city. The tragedy of the situation was that the city of Dallas was aware that the location was a toxic dump, but no appropriate action was taken. The church, when it is aware of these circumstances, must bring pressure to bear upon

---

18. One Church of God in Christ document is identified as "Resolution Committee: General Assembly: Call Meeting 2013, Resolution #042013-7: Climate Change," a copy of which is in my possession (presumably, this will also be available in the COGIC official minutes from their archives).

those in power, demanding that justice be served to those who are defenceless.[19]

McKinney expressed these sentiments before the turn of the present millennium. Since then, a few Pentecostal churches and organizations around the world have addressed this matter. We will briefly summarize some of the developments.[20]

Oscar Corvalan confirmed that the Pentecostal Church of Chile has been involved with ecology for many decades.[21] The Pentecostal Church of Chile has been a member of the WCC since 1961 and is connected to the United Church of Christ in the USA. Things might have been quite different for this church had the International Pentecostal Holiness Church with headquarters in the USA kept its affiliation with the Pentecostal Church of Chile (signed in 1966 along with the Methodist Pentecostal Church) rather than terminating this agreement in 1968. Juan Sepulveda, an autochthonous Pentecostal from Chile who gave a Brighton '91 presentation on liberation theology, delivered a paper entitled "Romans 8:18–23, La Liberacion de la Creacion" at the Encuentro Pentecostal Latinoamerica in Brazil, 23–28 November 1992, perhaps one of the first theological papers on this topic by a Pentecostal scholar in Latin America.[22]

The official statement of the Pentecostal Movement in Norway may be found in a passage on creation care in the church's "Trosgrunnlag" (Statement of Faith). The relevant affirmation reads:

> We believe that God created heaven and earth, visible and invisible. Everything in the creation is intended to be good and beautiful. Humans are created in God's image and have an inherent worth from conception to natural death. We believe that God established the union between man and woman as the natural framework for life together. Humans are given the responsibility

---

19. George D. McKinney, "A God of Justice," *Reconciliation* 1 (1998): 5.

20. The Church of Pentecost in Ghana has been a leader in various respects, but I forego comment as there are chapters in this volume that elaborate in depth on what has happened there.

21. Conversation with Oscar Corvalan, Vitoria, Brazil, 26 October 2018, during RELEP Conference (Rede Latino-americana de Estudos Pentecostais) where I gave the keynote address on Pentecostal ecology.

22. Juan Sepulveda, "Romans 8:18–23, La Liberacion de la Creacion," Encuentro Pentecostal Latinoamerica (EPLA), conference presentation, Brazil, 23–28 November 1992. I have kept an original of this paper in my files; it was later published in *Evangelio y Sociedad* 16 (1993): 24–28.

of protecting and preserving God's creation. God continues to renew His creation, and one day He will recreate the whole world.[23]

While it is wonderful to know of and have the translation of this Norwegian commitment, any full account of the Pentecostal story is told in many languages, and this invites our attentiveness to developments around the world in languages other than English.

Stockholm+50[24] ran in the first week of June 2022. Swedish Pentecostal, Johannes Widlund, who presented a paper at the 2022 Pentecostal World Conference (PWC) hosted by Yoido Full Gospel Church,[25] was quite busy those days due to his Swedish Pentecostal Mission Development's (PMU) organizational involvement in this important celebration of the first UN event on climate change a half a century earlier in Stockholm. Those present in person and online witnessed a session moderated by another Pentecostal from Sweden, Esther Florres Sedman, that included a presentation by Festus Mukoya from the Free Pentecostal Fellowship in Kenya (both representing PMU). PMU itself has embraced what it calls the biblical vision of shalom that invites a holistic missional approach that embraces care for the Earth. This commitment is laid out in the PMU position paper in this way:

> Material and physical restoration: ensuring that all have the opportunity to participate in the stewardship of creation and to be sustained by it. This requires addressing systemic obstacles that limit people's ability to engage in stewardship and promoting the sustainable stewardship of resources.[26]

---

23. Pentecostal Church in Norway, *Visjon og Ordninger: Grunnlagsdokument for Pinsebevegelsen I Norge* [Vision and Arrangements: Constitutional Documents of the Pentecostal Church in Norway], 5, trans. Karl Inge Tangen.

24. The United Nations General Assembly convened this international meeting to commemorate the fiftieth anniversary of the 1972 United Nations Conference on the Human Environment (which made the environment a pressing global issue for the first time) and to discuss planetary ills affecting current and future prosperity and wellbeing.

25. Johannes Widlund's paper at the PWF Christian Unity Commission workshop was titled "Holistic Discipleship in the Environmental Crisis." Another presented in this workshop was by Finland's Sanna Urvas, titled "Our Concern for Creation: A Pentecostal Mariological Approach" (a revised version appears in this volume and will also be included in her monograph on Mariology). She also anchored a workshop for the PWF CCTF during the 2024 PWC held in Helsinki.

26. The PMU position paper, "Theological Basis for Understanding Human Poverty and Holistic Mission," was published by Niclas Lindgren. See Niclas Lindgren, "Theological Basis for Understanding Human Poverty and Holistic Mission: The Pentecostal Relief and Development Partners," *The Pentecostal Educator* 7, no. 2 (2022): 292.

The PAOC Statement of Essential Truths singles out creation care. The following was approved as Resolution #10 by the 2024 PAOC General Conference reflecting years of ecological activism: "CREATION – God created and sustains the heavens and the earth (15) which displays God's glory. Formed in the image of God, both male and female, humankind is entrusted with the care of God's creation as faithful stewards. As a result of human rebellion, sin and death entered the world, distorting the image of God and all of God's good creation."[27]

A. J. Swoboda, in his many publications, advances a distinctive Pentecostal pneumatology of the Spirit-baptized creation, the charismatic creational community, the holistic ecological Spirit, and the eschatological Spirit of ecological mission.[28] Swoboda is the founder and director of Blessed Earth Northwest, a centre that helps Christians think creatively and strategically about creation care issues in the Pacific Northwest. Alongside this work, he also served as the national director of the Seminary Stewardship Alliance, a consortium of Christian higher-ed schools that was devoted for a time to thinking strategically about Christian training in creation care. Swoboda's work has doubtless contributed to the coming "white paper" on ecology that others within his International Church of the Foursquare Gospel have informed me is being worked on. These kinds of organizational efforts, along with the ecclesial commitments noted above, invite us to return to the issue of climate justice with which this paper began.

Climate Justice for the Margins

The disproportionate impact of climate change on the poor and marginalized accounting for climate refugees is emphasized in the papal encyclical *Laudato Si'*,[29] and in a wide range of actions taken by the Green Patriarch, Ecumenical Patriarch Bartholomew. Maria Sereti gave a paper to the WCC Ecological Theology and Environmental Ethics (ECOTHEE) 2017 conference meeting

---

27. The resolution comes from David Wells's email to me and Karen Reed (29 February 2024); see also Pentecostal Assemblies of Canada, *Essential Truths: The PAOC Statement of Essential Truths* (Mississauga: Pentecostal Assemblies of Canada International Offices, 2023), 29.

28. A sign of the changing landscape for Pentecostal ecotheology by global North scholars writing in English are the forward steps taken by A. J. Swoboda, ed., *Blood Cries Out: Pentecostals, Ecology and the Groans of Creation* (Eugene: Wipf & Stock, 2014) which includes a chapter on Pentecostal ecological work in Africa (yet this is primarily the same AIC group noted by Daneel in his Brighton '91 paper).

29. After dominating the conversation for eight years, Pope Francis issued *Laudate Deum* on October 4, 2023. This is a remarkable encyclical that must be read by all persons of faith.

at the Orthodox Academy of Crete entitled "The Contribution of Ecumenical Patriarch Bartholomew I to the Configuration of an Ecumenical 'Integral Ecology.'"[30] "Integral ecology" was understood to speak of economic justice and, according to Sereti, was subsequently lauded by Pope Francis in his encyclical *Laudato Si'*, which was quoted during ECOTHEE '19. The clarion call for this basic concept has loudly come for many years from the WCC and others in the broader ecumenical movement. Sereti went on to link integral ecology to the eucharist which will not be discussed here even though it is echoed in the 1982 WCC Faith and Order "Lima Document."

The following are snapshots of Pentecostal ecotheology from around the world that also illustrate the Pentecostal mission to address climate refugees and environmental racism.[31]

Asia Pacific Theological Seminary professor in Baguio, Philippines, Joel Tejedo faithfully leaves the seminary behind and returns to his province, doing what he calls eco-farming or agro-ecology at his farm (e.g., planting rice, coconut, and other fruit-bearing trees, tilapia farming, etc.). His team is currently developing a living model that will integrate all forms of livelihood and livestock within their farm which will help local communities survive the global effect of the pandemic. Once they complete qualitative research by interviewing some practitioners then, perhaps, they can acquire some contextual theologies and practices of a robust Pentecostal ecotheology in the Philippines.[32]

I was present at a 2019 ecology conference sponsored by PRIDEMI (Programa Intensivo de Desarrollo Ministerial, or Intensive Ministerial Development Program) and hosted by the Pentecostal seminary SEMISUD outside Quito, Ecuador, which was focused on indigenous voices, and deserves more extended comment in any discussion of climate justice. The first speaker, Jonathan Suarez, a professor from Ecuador, offered a detailed deconstruction of (Ecuadorian) colonial history crushing indigenous peoples. He pointed to

---

30. See Maria Sereti, "The Contribution of Ecumenical Patriarch Bartholomew to the Configuration of an Ecumenical 'Integral Ecology,'" *The Ecumenical Review* 70, no. 4 (2018): 621–23.

31. Although Pentecostal activists and scholars are to be found all around the world, many are not included in this study due to the limited scope. A few more are named in my paper read to ECOTHEE-19, Orthodox Academy of Crete, 23–26 September 2019, and published as Harold D. Hunter, "Pentecostal Ecotheology from the Margins," *Cyberjournal for Pentecostal Charismatic Research* 27 (2020), reprinted in Lucas A. Andrianos and Tom Svere Tomren et al., eds., *Contemporary Ecotheology, Climate Justice, and Environmental Stewardship in World Religions*, Ecothee volume 6th-Orthodox Academy of Crete Publications (Steinkjær: Embla Akademisk, 2021), 93–105.

32. For a preliminary account, see Joel Tejedo, "Pentecostals, Civic Education, and Eco-Farming: The Case of Four Eco-Farming Institutions in Northern Luzon, Philippines," *Humanitas* 8, no. 2 (2022): 101–24.

Genesis 1:26 which was used to justify domination of creation and treating indigenous peoples as inferior. Suarez returned to parts of Genesis to advocate egalitarianism for all peoples and creation thus denying the sixteenth-century European interpretation of the early chapters of Genesis. He landed on Genesis 2:4–20 to link humans to all creation.

A Roman Catholic nun wearing a habit in the audience interjected that there are three indigenous peoples in Ecuador, and she said these indigenous peoples have no power and are even shunned by the government. One of the many videos stressed how indigenous communities respect creation. When they cut down a tree, this will be followed by a ceremony of apology acknowledging that global warming is a threat to humans. Anthropologist Michael Uzendoski looked at indigenous peoples around the world and pointed to the Quechua who say that plants have "souls" or are alive. The conference included a YouTube video that used animation to tell an indigenous story about Pachamama who gives rain, etc., and the essentials of life that is being destroyed by cities and suburbs.

The highlight was the panel of three Pentecostal indigenous leaders in Ecuador. The top leader, Byron Calo, said that for the Quechua, we are the land, not just part of the land. He said that their government allows white men to move Quechua out of their land, taking them far from the city and near the threatening volcano. He told of missionaries who said that to wear black as the Quechua do is bad so they must wear white. The Quechua say black is the colour of the land where we live, and they find it strange to say the colour white dominates heaven. Quechua think the colour of earth/soil (like brown or black) makes more sense for heaven. Luz Tipan (then a Pentecostal student from the Church of God) affirmed that Pachamama gives them life, food, etc. With their family and community, they ask for permission and say they are sorry for what they take so if they take potatoes then they must plant more. "We must return life to the earth that we take," my notes record Jose Chisaguano (another Church of God student then) telling of all the indigenous churches getting together for a celebration of Pachamama, noting their music comes from nature.[33]

Keynote speaker, the legendary Professor Boff, expounded on various global principles of twenty-first century life that could be better informed by

---

33. While some might feel a tension with regard to the Pentecostal practices described in this indigenous context, they seem less palpable for Pentecostal leaders from these communities in global conversations. For instance, more recently, I was in Assisi for a global ecumenical conference on Creation Day, where participant scholars and church leaders saw no tension in referring to Creation Day while affirming historic Christian doctrines like the Trinity.

indigenous peoples.[34] Social and ecological injustice are the perils of consumerism that threaten the very air that all inhabitants breathe as the heat of the planet increases.[35]

In my conversations with Māori (indigenous people of Aotearoa–New Zealand) theologians, Anglicans like Tamsyn Kereopa have told me: "the earth, the land and the entire creation is difficult to extract from ourselves which is one of the issues. There has been work done in Māori Christology recently which might be helpful, it looks at the land as ancestor. The sacredness of creation is central to any indigenous eco-theology as you know."[36] This is consistent with what Australian Pentecostal theologian Michael Frost reports from his research with Māori Pentecostals, for example the Māori proverb among the people of Te Ati Haunui-a-Pāpārangi "which expresses a deep and abiding connection to creation in stating, 'Ko au te awa, Ko te awa ko au' (I am the river, and the river is me)"; Frost also mentions that Māori theologian Henare Tate's argument that "there is no such entity as an isolated individual" as human identity "is only understood through relationship to Atua (God) and to *whenua* (land)."[37]

Echoes of Bishop McKinney are heard in Brazilian Professor Ângela Maringoli' s *Amazônia: Entre a crise e a teologia*, which she translates as *Amazonia on Fire!*[38] These, together with the cries of Pentecostal pastors in Nicaragua who are economic victims of climate change, constitute integral ecology, and link us to the economic justice lauded by Pope Francis in his encyclical, *Laudato Si'*, and endorsed by the "Green Patriarch" Bartholomew, and various WCC conciliar documents. From Brazil's Evangelical Pentecostal Manain Church, Maringoli's slightly earlier *Teoambientologia: Um Desafio para a Educação Teológica* (*Ecotheology: A Challenge for Theological Education*) addresses the urgent need to create spaces of theological education in Brazil for environmental responsibility, through a perspective of the transforming mission, presenting

---

34. See, for instance, Leonardo Boff's *Cry of the Earth, Cry of the Poor* (Maryknoll: Orbis, 2002) and Leonardo Boff and Mark Hathaway, *The Tao of Liberation: Exploring the Ecology of Transformation* (Maryknoll: Orbis, 2009).

35. The primary founder of SEMISUD in Ecuador, the regular PRIDEMI conference host, is David Ramirez, a top executive in Church of God (Cleveland, Tennessee). Ramirez retweeted a 2021 United Nations report that looked at increased temperature and the impact on severe storms concluding the "planet has only until 2030 to stem catastrophic climate change," and urging Pentecostal young people to respond accordingly.

36. Email from Tamsyn Kereopoa, 9 April 2021.

37. Frost, "Materiality or Materialism: Revising Pentecostal Eschatology, Renewing the Earth, and Saving the Planet from the Prosperity Gospel," *Australasian Pentecostal Studies* 22, no. 1 (2021): 112.

38. Ângela Maringoli, *Amazônia: Entre a Crise e a Teologia* (São Paulo: Recriar, 2020).

a holistic view of the knowledge contained in environmental education for the training of missionaries and seminarians in solving problems in the communities of the mission field.[39] With the help of this precious tool and informed by articles from the journalistic media, Maringoli unveiled actions against the magnificent Amazonian landscape, a natural heritage of humanity, home to a stupendous biodiversity, and reason for admiration and affection around the world. The destructive impetus that violates the precepts presented in Genesis and the suicidal attempt to replace the creation of God with the creation of humans show the poor knowledge about the role that the Most High has assigned to us, as well as the gap in the religious teachings received by many of us, and this prompts us to explore this issue from the theological point of view.

Final Reflection

Early in the twentieth century, white Keswickian and Wesleyan Pentecostals in North America were captivated by vigorous debates regarding "sanctification." Should one want to measure the status of upwardly mobile Pentecostals now in North America, it is illuminating to examine their views on restitution and redistribution. The faith tradition claiming to be the second largest Christian family in the world must "wash the saints' feet" when they are climate refugees or objects of environmental racism, rather than, like Pontius Pilate, "wash their hands" of their responsibility. How can a Pentecostal missional community fail to support the "Zacchaeus tax," especially in light of what has now been recounted in this essay (and also in this book)?

After initial attempts to organize the PWF were delayed by two world wars, the PWF beginnings became linked to relief work for those suffering from the devastation of war. An authentic Pentecostal mission cries out for a climate justice table that welcomes everyone. It is right to remember the ongoing plight of the marginalized who are ravaged by climate change. We should thereby

---

39. Ângela Maringoli, *Teoambientologia: Um Desafio para a Educação Teológica*, 2nd ed. (São Paulo: Recriar, 2019). Also see Ângela Maringoli, "The Feminine Evangelical Pentecostal Identity in the Preservation of the Environment in Latin America and Brazil and Its Empowerment," presentation at the Society for Pentecostal Studies annual meeting, 18–20 March 2021, Dallas, Texas, which includes a summary of the work of Marina Silva, a well-known Brazilian Assembly of God political and climate activist who was raised a Pentecostal. Cf. Ziporah Hildebrant, *Marina Silva: Defending Rainforest Communities in Brazil* (Albany: The Feminist Press at City University of New York, 2001).

affirm the theme of the 1991 WCC General Assembly influenced by Pentecostals in Latin America: "Come Holy Spirit, Renew Thy Whole Creation!"[40]

Bibliography

Beaty, James M. "Church Teachings and the Declaration of Faith: A History." Lecture, Pentecostal Theological Seminary, Cleveland, Tennessee. 18 September 2010.

Boff, Leonardo. *Cry of the Earth, Cry of the Poor*. Maryknoll: Orbis, 2002.

Boff, Leonardo, and Mark Hathaway. *The Tao of Liberation: Exploring the Ecology of Transformation*. Maryknoll: Orbis, 2009.

Daneel, M. L. "African Independent Church Pneumatology and the Salvation of All Creation." In *All Together in One Place: Theological Papers from the Brighton Conference on World Evangelization*, eds. Harold D. Hunter and Peter D. Hocken, 98–128. 1993. Reprint, Eugene: Wipf & Stock, 2019.

Davis, Anita. "Pentecostal Approaches to Ecotheology: Reviewing the Literature." *Australasian Pentecostal Studies* 22, no. 1 (2021): 4–33.

Frost, Michael J. "Materiality or Materialism?: Revising Pentecostal Eschatology, Renewing the Earth, and Saving the Planet from the Prosperity Gospel." *Australasian Pentecostal Studies* 22, no. 1 (2021): 104–21.

Hildebrant, Ziporah. *Marina Silva: Defending Rainforest Communities in Brazil*. Albany: The Feminist Press at City University of New York, 2001.

Hunter, Harold D. "Foreword to the 2019 Reprint Edition." In *All Together in One Place: Theological Papers from the Brighton Conference on World Evangelization*, edited by Harold D. Hunter and Peter D. Hocken, 1–9. 1993. Reprint, Eugene: Wipf & Stock, 2019.

———. "Pentecostal Ecotheology from the Margins." *Cyberjournal for Pentecostal Charismatic Research* 27 (2020). http://www.pctii.org/cyberj/cyberj27/hunter.html.

———. "Pentecostal Healing for God's Sick Creation?" *The Spirit and the Church* 2, no. 2 (2000): 145–67.

———. "Pentecostals at the 11th WCC Assembly in Karlsruhe, Germany 2022." WCC Blog. 14 September 2022. https://www.oikoumene.org/blog/Pentecostals-at-the-wcc-11th-assembly-in-karlsruhe-germany-2022.

---

40. This paper was initially presented to the Pentecostal World Fellowship (PWF) when as a participant in the 2021 "Global Faith Leaders of all Religions and Scientists" online event organized by the Vatican, I was invited to represent the Pentecostal World Fellowship at this event, among other organizations working towards COP26; our work, that culminated at Glasgow, 1–12 November 2021. Another version was presented at the annual meeting of the Society for Pentecostal Studies, Candler School of Theology at Emory University, 14–16 March 2024.

Lamp, Jeffrey S., Kathryn J. Moder, Megan R. Munhoffen, Cade A. Rich, and Nathan B. Von Atzigen. "Creation Care as Caring for Human Beings." *Spiritus* 5, no. 1 (2020): 137–50.

Lindgren, Niclas. "Theological Basis for Understanding Human Poverty and Holistic Mission: The Pentecostal Relief and Development Partners." *Pentecostal Education* 7, no. 2 (2022): 285–302.

Ma, Wonsuk. "The Spirit of God in Creation: Lessons for Christian Mission." *Transformation* 24, nos. 3/4 (2007): 223–30.

Maringoli, Ângela. *Amazônia: Entre a Crise e a Teologia*. São Paulo: Recriar, 2020.

———. *Teoambientologia: Um Desafio para a Educação Teológica*. 2nd ed. São Paulo: Editora Recriar, 2019.

———. "The Feminine Evangelical Pentecostal Identity in the Preservation of the Environment in Latin America and Brazil and Its Empowerment." Paper presented at the Society for Pentecostal Studies Annual Meeting, Dallas, Texas. 18–20 March 2021.

McKinney, George D. "A God of Justice." *Reconciliation* 1 (1998), 4–6. https://iphc.org/gso/wp-content/uploads/sites/5/2014/10/Reconciliation-Vol1-1998.pdf.

Pentecostal Assemblies of Canada. *Essential Truths: The PAOC Statement of Essential Truths*. Mississauga: Pentecostal Assemblies of Canada International Offices, 2023.

Pentecostal Church in Norway. *Visjon og Ordninger: Grunnlagsdokument for Pinsebevegelsen I Norge* [Vision and Arrangements: Constitutional Documents of the Pentecostal Church in Norway], translated by Karl Inge Tangen. Pentecostal Church in Norway n.d. https://pinsebevegelsen.no/_service/400418/download/id/485514/name/Grunnlagsdokument+2020_v01.pdf.

Rice, Jonathan W. "Ecology and the Future of Pentecostalism: Problems, Possibilities, and Proposals." In *Pentecostal Mission and Global Christianity*, edited by Wonsuk Ma, Veli-Matti Kärkkäinen, and Asamoah Gyadu, 360–79. London: Regnum, 2012.

Sepulveda, Juan. "La Liberación de la Creación: Estudio de Romanos 8:18–23." *Evangelio y Sociedad* 16 (1993): 24–28. http://www.sendas.cl/wp-content/uploads/2014/07/Revista_evangelio_y_-sociedad_numero16.pdf.

Sereti, Maria. "The Contribution of Ecumenical Patriarch Bartholomew to the Configuration of an Ecumenical 'Integral Ecology.'" *The Ecumenical Review* 70, no. 4 (2018): 621–23.

Studebaker, Steven M. "The Spirit in Creation: A Unified Theology of Grace and Creation Care." *Zygon: Journal of Religion and Science* 43, no. 4 (2008): 943–60.

Suurmond, Jean-Jacques. "Christ King: A Charismatic Appeal for an Ecological Lifestyle." *Pneuma: Journal for the Society for Pentecostal Studies* 10, no. 1 (1998): 26–35.

Swoboda, A. J. *Tongues and Trees: Toward a Pentecostal Ecological Theology*. Blandford Forum: Deo, 2013.

Swoboda, A. J., ed. *Blood Cries Out: Pentecostals, Ecology, and the Groans of Creation*. Eugene: Pickwick, 2014.

Tejedo, Joel A. "Pentecostals, Civic Education, and Eco-Farming: The Case of Four Eco-Farming Institutions in Northern Luzon, Philippines." *Humanitas* 8, no. 2 (2022): 101–24.

Ware, Joe. "World Faith Leaders Point at Richer Countries to Solve the Climate Crisis." *Church Times*. October 2021. https://www.churchtimes.co.uk/articles/2021/8-october/news/uk/world-faith-leaders-point-at-richer-nations-to-solve-the-climate-crisis.

White Wing Publishing House and Press, compiler. *These Necessary Things: The Doctrine and Practices of the Church of God of Prophecy as set forth by the General Assembly*. 8th ed. Cleveland: White Wing Publishing House, 1980.

Wiyono, Gani. "Healing God's Creation: A Contribution of Pentecostal Understanding of Divine Healing to Ecotheology." In *Voices Loud and Clear: Papers from the Global Pentecostal Summit*, edited by Douglas Petersen and Byron D. Klaus, 165–80. Regnum Studies in Mission. London: Regnum, 2024.

World Council of Churches. "ZacTax Toolkit." eBook. 2021. https://www.oikoumene.org/resources/publications/zactax-toolkit.

World Council of Churches News. "Committing to Climate-Responsible Finance Sends 'Strong Signal of Hope to All.'" 23 May 2022. https://www.oikoumene.org/news/committing-to-climate-responsible-finance-sends-strong-signal-of-hope-to-all.

World Council of Churches. "Stockholm+50 Interfaith Statement. 'Faith Values and Reach: Contribution to Environmental Policy.'" Online document. June 2022. https://www.oikoumene.org/resources/documents/stockholm50-interfaith-statement-faith-values-and-reach-contribution-to-environmental-policy.

Yong, Amos. *The Spirit Poured Out on All Flesh: Pentecostalism and the Possibility of a Global Theology*. Grand Rapids: Baker Academic, 2005.

15

Incarnation as a Metaphysical Key for Missional Pentecostal Ecotheology

A Marian Pentecostal Observation

Sanna Urvas

This chapter is a journey and a dialogue with three voices. It aims to vision a fresh way to tell the story of the love of God towards all people and creation. These voices are Pentecostal writers of eco-theology, missiologist Gregg Okesson and, most importantly, Ephrem the Syrian from the patristic era. In other words, this is a Pentecostal ecotheology engaging with Eastern Orthodoxy for the purpose of *missio Dei*.

Engaging in Conversation with Pentecostal Ecotheology Discourse

Pentecostal ecotheology is forming its voice and engaging with other Christian traditions to raise awareness of the crisis of our planet. Aaron J. Swoboda acknowledges in his doctoral thesis a need to develop a voice for Pentecostals to participate in this discourse. One recognizable paradigm is to draw from the sources of Pentecostal tradition and to "be centered on its own set of governing questions,"[1] per Swoboda. Swoboda acknowledges the newness of this theologi-

---

1. A. J. Swoboda, *Tongues and Trees: Towards a Pentecostal Ecological Theology* (Blandford Forum: Deo, 2013), 63.

cal field for Pentecostals and, likewise, the ability to engage new conversations with various avenues within cultures. Swoboda calls for Pentecostals to utilize their "unique perspective on the Holy Spirit and its role in the Christian story along with the particular view of experience within the Christian experience."[2] The aspect of Christian experience is utilized as a perspective in this paper.

Swoboda utilizes Amos Yong's hermeneutical method, namely pneumatological imagination, for his writing project. Yong forms his theological enterprise with the spiral movement which engages with Spirit, word and community.[3] The word "community" is understood widely including the theological voices from the past and invites Eastern Orthodox authors to the conversation table.[4] Swoboda notes in his thesis how both Walter Hollenweger and Edward Rybarczyk encourage Pentecostals to dialogue with Eastern voices.[5] Hollenweger argues that Eastern theological paradigm is constructed with "a more dignified, mystical, and respectful view of nature."[6] Rybarczyk, in turn, notes the sense of mystery being present in both traditions, Pentecostal and Eastern Orthodox, but that being situated differently. Eastern traditions envision the mystical Spirit holistically and in close reference to nature and creation while Pentecostal and charismatic spirituality emphasizes individual mystical experiences.[7] This paper attempts to join these two together by connecting the importance of a believer's mystical experience to understand the holistic nature of our cosmos veiled in mystery.

Another approach to ecotheology can be found from the proposal of Tony Richie who utilizes the Wesleyan-Pentecostal heritage and its Christ-centeredness. Richie's thesis employs "redemptive reality in Christ – that is, salvation, healing, sanctification/holiness, renewal, and restoration."[8] Christology is commonly the centre of Pentecostal worship and spirituality even if, theologically, the Spirit is more "up front." Martina Björkander demonstrates in her research of Pentecostal worship how *participatio Christi* and the *unio mystica* with divine

---

2. Swoboda, *Tongues and Trees*, 64. Swoboda is referring to Amos Yong, *The Spirit Poured out on All Flesh: Pentecostalism and the Possibility of a Global Theology* (Grand Rapids: Baker Academic, 2005) and Mark Cartledge, *Encountering the Spirit: The Charismatic Tradition* (London: Darton Longman & Todd, 2006).

3. Amos Yong, *Spirit–Word–Community: Theological Hermeneutics in Trinitarian Perspective* (Eugene: Wipf & Stock, 2002).

4. Yong, *Spirit–Word–Community*.

5. Swoboda, *Tongues and Trees*, 83, 89.

6. Swoboda, *Tongues and Trees*, 83–84.

7. Swoboda, *Tongues and Trees*, 89.

8. Tony Richie, "Radical and Responsible. A Wesleyan-Pentecostal Ecotheology," *Journal of Pentecostal Theology* 23 (2014): 234.

are central in Pentecostal experience, and that both are transformational in nature.[9] In this paper, Christ-centeredness is a key to join this holistic cosmology and individualistic experience. The metaphysical aspect of Christology found in the mystery of incarnation together with the experience of divinity functions as the crux. The engagement with an individualistic experience is located in the biblical example of Mary, *theotokos*, the mother of God.

Missiological Approach to Ecotheology, the Second Dialogue Partner

Pentecostalism is missional in its nature. Therefore, Pentecostal ecotheology needs to find its roots in the mission given to the church. This mission is not ontologically or cognitively separate from the nature of the Pentecostal message which is carried in the heart and heritage of the Pentecostal movement – a call to be filled with the Spirit. Therefore, the core is the experience of the divinity and the sense of transformation as noted by Björkander. The dialogue partner is missiologist Gregg Okesson who has elaborated the idea of public missiology.[10]

Okesson's main claim is that the Christian community needs to participate in the public life in its thickness and to become one with the suffering world.[11] "Thickness" means the complexity of public life; any thinly layered message of salvation which does not have the contact of point of reality is not sufficient to communicate the will of God accurately or the essence of God's kingdom. The thickness or, indeed, thinness, can be observed in the identity as well as in our message, holistic or not. The thickness of the identity for a community is a result of a knowledge and awareness of the complexity of the group. This emerges both from the layers of realities but also by the movement of these layers affecting the experiences of people. Okesson parallels this with the thickness of the public realm which "arises from the multiplicity of overlapping and interpenetrating publics."[12] There are no simple societies which could possess only one layer or one kind of reality which can be easily perceived and explained. Therefore, there is not one simple way to perceive, encounter, or address this complexity, and thick reality. The public space is present to all and everyone because "society" is the realm of togetherness that no-one can

---

9. Martina Björkander, *Worship, Ritual and Pentecostal Spirituality-as-Theology: A Rhythm that Connects Our Hearts with God* (Leiden: Brill, 2024). This case study project was in African context.

10. Gregg Okesson, *A Public Missiology. How Local Churches Witness to a Complex World* (Grand Rapids: Baker Academic, 2020).

11. Okesson, *A Public Missiology*, 23.

12. Okesson, *A Public Missiology*, 7.

avoid. Further, because of globalization one cannot escape the reality of this notion of sharing the same fate.[13] The estimates for the future of our planet are not promising whether one reads the data on climate change or on the decline of biodiversity or both together.[14] No-one has the privilege to be an outsider of this tragedy, but there is a message of salvation which informs and encourages each person to look after and care for the creation better. This would be a key to thicken a message in the public realm if a church, as the body of Christ, was found to be truly participating in Christ via an individual and corporate spiritual experience of divinity. This could be a path to grow in understanding of a shared connectedness in creation which would inform a concern of the welfare of all peoples and the environment. Experience is the key for a holistic and convincing message.

Okesson writes about the challenge of mixing religion into the public space and its discourses. The danger lies in the potential sacralization of harmful or oppressive politics. He points to the "psycho-social-spiritual forces" which exist under and within the global societies. Following the analogies of Walter Wink and Max Stackhouse, Okesson explains the potential demonic nature of these forces when/if they are destroying the order of God given to this world.[15] Therefore, answers for these problems need to be linked with an observation of the dynamics of the spiritual realm and not only practical efforts. The global church is part of the problem and it should be part of a solution as well.[16] The good news is that church communities can play their part in God's work of redemption if they understand their identity correctly, and their understanding and practice of life are orderly aligned with the will and vision of God.[17]

Amos Yong calls for trinitarian and pneumatological theologies to inform our theological reflections, including metaphysics. He insists that the validity of the Spirit's mission is equally important alongside the Son's and makes reference to Irenaeus's idea of two hands of the Father.[18] This can be seen as well in his concept *mission spiritus*, which lays attention to the acts of the Spirit

---

13. Okesson, *A Public Missiology*, 18, 23, 47.

14. For example, S. Habibullah, B. H. Din, S. H. Tan, "Impact of Climate Change on Biodiversity Loss: Global Evidence," *Environmental Science and Pollution Research* 29 (2022): 1073–86.

15. Okesson, *A Public Missiology*, 51–52.

16. For more about acknowledging the sinful nature of communities and single people and their relation to the demonic reality, see Urvas, "Theology of Sin and Evil in Classical Pentecostalism: Two Case Studies" (PhD Diss., University of Helsinki, 2020).

17. Okesson, *A Public Missiology*, 24.

18. Yong, *Spirit–Word–Community*, 73.

in mission.[19] Therefore, the Spirit is the key to understanding the role of the church and its empowerment in mission but, according to Okesson, the message needs to be holistic in order to be heard in the public space. Thus, it is a necessity that Christians embrace God's love for his creation also bodily, and not only intellectually, to truly understand the threat and sorrow of losing the richness of the created environment. Next, then, I turn to a bodily experience of Christological metaphysics, *theotokos*, which was made possible through the Holy Spirit.

Mary in the Light of the Writings of Ephrem the Syrian

The third dialogue partner is a voice from the past, Ephrem the Syrian. By this choice, I wish to bring alive the rich Christian theological heritage because Pentecostals are part of that tradition of Christianity which loves Christ and believes in both the sovereign God and the power of the Holy Spirit. There are also shared trends between theological hermeneutics and the general ethos. These are an appreciation of affective spirituality, a faithful understanding of the authority of Bible,[20] and a charismatic Christian faith. It is vital to remember that an appreciative attitude towards nature of the environment is not a modern phenomenon and, as such, alien to the Christian tradition. The early generations which fought against heretical gnostic voices valued the creation as a sign of the benevolence of God towards the created order. The opposite party regarded matter as evil and without any value or worth.[21]

Another perspective to the similarities between Ephrem's and Pentecostals' ethea is Ephrem's use of an affective style of writing which invites his reader to experience the mysteries of Christ and incarnation in a near-bodily manner. This reveals the beauty of Ephrem's literature as well as the similarity between

---

19. Amos Yong, *Mission after Pentecost. The Witness of the Spirit from Genesis to Revelation* (Grand Rapids: Baker Academic, 2019), 13–14.

20. Jeffrey Wickes writes how Ephrem's presentations to defend the divinity of Christ are constructed with dramatic New Testament narratives instead of abstract metaphysical and philosophical arguments. Jeffrey Wickes, *Bible and Poetry in Late Antique Mesopotamia: Ephrem's Hymns on Faith* (Oakland: University of California Press, 2019), 104–5.

21. David Litwa has studied the early Christian ideas of creator within minority interpretations of Bible. See David Litwa, *The Evil Creator Origin of an Early Christian Idea* (Oxford: Oxford University Press, 2021). See also Paul M. Blowers, "Doctrine of Creation," in *The Oxford Handbook of Early Christian Studies*, eds. Susan Ashbrook Harvey and David G. Hunter (Oxford: Oxford University Press, 2008), 906–31.

Pentecostal hermeneutics and narrative reading style.[22] Ephrem insisted on the importance of faith in the understanding of divine secrets. Yet another shared aspect is the holistic nature of doing theology. One does not only think with intellect but desires to feel the theology with the Holy Spirit in a holistic manner, with one's mind, spirit, and body. Pentecostal experience is often linked to the experience of the Spirit, but I challenge our theology to expand towards the Trinity and include the Christ as the key hypostatic dimension of the trinitarian mystery to Pentecostal affective theological hermeneutics. That is the reason I have chosen to listen to this one key writer from early Christianity, who embraced the experience of Christ and the mystery of the incarnation, through the experience of Christ's mother, Mary.

Ephrem of Syrian was born and lived during the turbulent times during the fourth century AD when the status of Christianity as a religion of Rome was being established. The church faced pressure from the Persian rulers but was relatively free from waves of persecutions. It was an era of heretical controversies within the church, and Ephrem is known to promote the orthodox doctrine of Christ and incarnation.[23] Unlike his contemporary philosophical writers, Ephrem's presentations to defend the divinity of Christ were constructed with dramatic New Testament narratives instead of abstract metaphysical and philosophical arguments.[24] His presentations demonstrate his roots, which were imbedded in the East and in Judaic biblical tradition rather than Greek philosophy.

Ephrem used poetry and prose as literary styles to write his theology in which a rich use of symbolism can be found.[25] He wrote only in Aramaic and he is an example of a Semitic form of Christianity, which according to Elena Narinskaya, developed free from Byzantine and Latin influence.[26] Ephrem's vision of incarnation was meant to communicate the orthodox understanding of two-nature Christology, but he included in his poetry aspects that expand his theology beyond these dogmatic debates of his time.

Incarnation encased a central argument during the patristic era to defend Christian orthodoxy against gnostic heretics. Another key doctrine was two-

---

22. Read more in Kenneth J. Archer, "Pentecostal Hermeneutics: Retrospect and Prospects," *Pentecostal Hermeneutics: A Reader*, ed. Lee Roy Martin (Leiden: Brill, 2013), 131–48.

23. Serafim Seppälä, *Elämän äiti – Neitsyt Maria Varhaiskristillisessä Teologiassa*, trans. S. Urvas (Helsinki: Maahenki Oy, 2010), 92.

24. Wickes, *Bible and Poetry*, 104–5.

25. Ephrem wrote also Bible commentaries, especially from the Old Testament and Torah.

26. Elena Narinskaya, *The Poetic Hymns of Saint Ephrem the Syrian: A Study in the Religious Use of Poetry in Fourth-Century Christianity* (New York: Edwin Mellen, 2013), 1.

nature Christology. Ephrem defended, utilized, and elaborated these two doctrines and formulated his theology with apophatic undertones which leave a space for the Holy Spirit to breath. He clearly announced God's favour towards the existence of the created matter. It is vital to remember that the growth of Mariology and the reason why Mary was used in early Christian theology are closely tied in defence of two-nature Christology.[27]

Therefore, Ephrem utilized Mary to connect these two natures and, likewise, two cosmological spheres – heaven and earth. Ephrem placed the connection in Mary's womb.

> If someone searches your hidden nature,
> behold, it is in heaven,
> in within the womb of divinity
> If someone searches your revealed body
> behold, it rests and appears from the tiny womb of Mary.[28]

Ephrem visioned Christ in the heavenly divine womb. It is the same Christ which rests in the womb of Mary as was before the incarnation and even before time. There are two doctrines combined together here: the eternal generation of the son which is a conciliar creedal formulation from the council of Nicaea (AD 325) and the incarnation, both expressed in two-nature Christology. The importance in this vision of a womb is the simultaneous distinction of situatedness and the spiritual dimension of divinity. This mystery is only possible to grasp through faith, but also through bodily experience if one identifies herself or himself with Mary. Ephrem wrote these secrets into the understanding of Christology and placed the words in the mouth of Mary.

> When I see your image, the created one,
> which is before my eyes,
> your invisible one is depicted in my mind.
> In your visible image I see Adam;
> in the invisible one I see your Father
> who is kneaded into you.[29]

---

27. Jaroslav Pelikan, *The Christian Tradition: A History of the Development of Doctrine*, vol. 1: *The Emergence of the Catholic Tradition (100–600)* (Chicago: The University of Chicago Press, 1971), 256–66.

28. Ephrem the Syrian, *Hymnen de Nativitate* 13:7, quoted in Seppälä, *Elämän*, 93; translation from the original language to Finnish is by Serafim Seppälä, to English S. Urvas.

29. Ephrem the Syrian, *Hymn of Nativity*, 16.3 in Narinskaya, *The Poetic Hymns of Saint Ephrem the Syrian*, 98; See also S. H. Griffith, "Spirit in the Bread, Fire in the Wine," *Modern Theology* 15, no. 2 (1999): 234.

Narinskaya notices how Ephrem refers to the human mind as having a capacity to see an invisible image of God. It is not a capacity of intellect but rather an ability of mind which is enlightened by faith.[30] This prophetic capacity enriched by faith is essential for understanding characteristics of Mary as a person through whose experience one can understand the nature of the incarnation as God's proclamation of his favour for the world. It is not only the fate of humanity through restoration, recapitulation, and resurrection, but also humanity in union and harmony with creation.

The Son is and was the base of creation of everything, along with the Spirit. Ephrem was an early writer, but he had a clear understanding of the full divinity and character of the Holy Spirit as a creative Spirit and a partaker in the creative action, as one *hypostasis* of Trinity. This question was another important debate of his time.[31] It is imperative to bring the method of creation to the contemporary conversation. Pentecostal orientation to ecotheology needs to be constructed with strong pneumatological orientation. Creation was and is a work of the Trinity; redemption and the eschatological future are as well. The Spirit has a role in all. Therefore, to talk about creation simultaneously incorporates talk about redemption and the eschatological future, and that is the path towards the cosmological dimension at the base of ecotheology.

To understand this, a metaphysical vision is needed to embrace the cosmological view which has both overlapping and linear continuity of redemptive actions of God. This is the cosmological base for my argument. The first level is the Christ. This level is both in the dimension of *logos* but also in the deeper sense of the divine mystery hidden in *ousia*. There is the wisdom of God, which we could call *Sophia*, as the third *hypostasis*, the Spirit. The divine plan of the universe, both in its material and nonmaterial spheres, is hidden in the trinitarian mystery. Christ before the time event of incarnation, was and is the base of all the matter, all that exists, and everything is held together because of him, according to Paul's letter to Colossians (Col 1:14–17). This is the reason why both Son and Spirit are necessarily present in creation, and why God is so keen to care and look after his created world. "The whole idea of everything" as a kind of intelligible entity rested within him, the Son, inside the deep mystery of the triune God. However, created matter is not divine, even if Son and Spirit were involved in the creative action. Ephrem wrote:

---

30. Narinskaya, *The Poetic Hymns of Saint Ephrem the Syrian*, 99, n. 143.
31. Pelikan, *The Christian Tradition*, 212–19.

> He was entirely in the deep
> and entirely in the high.
> He was entirely in everything and wholly in everybody.[32]

Sebastian Brock explains how Ephrem's poetry was profoundly theological and that he was highly aware of the sacramental character of the created order. It meant that everything in the created world has a capacity and potential to act as a witness and a pointer towards the Creator.[33] According to David Kiger, for Ephrem the natural world proclaimed the mystery of the incarnation. Ephrem used the reproduction system of worms as a metaphor for a nonsexual generation of baby Jesus. He meant to explain how the imagery of the Son is imprinted in creation and was fashioned by the Holy Spirit.[34]

> The Spirit spoke a parable in the worm, for it reproduces without sexual union; the type the Holy Spirit fashioned receives its meaning today.[35]

This is one important dimension and wisdom of these early church fathers' understanding of the importance of the creation. It does not make nature sacred in the sense that it would require devotion or worship. As Brock explains, Ephrem insisted that the core being of God stands outside creation and "thus lies beyond the ability of the created intellect to comprehend – and any claim to be able to do so is blasphemous."[36] This is the feature which connects Ephrem with the apophatic Greek tradition. God himself can only bridge the ontological gap through his initiative. Brock continues that this self-revelation is three-fold by means of types and symbols which operate in both the created order and the Scriptures, and also, finally, in the incarnation.[37] Yet again, without all three together, this self-revelation will be lacking. Therefore, this is a necessary reminder: if creation is distorted and neglected, it cannot bear this witness and revelation anymore, or not as clearly as it can if it is preserved and looked after.

Ephrem's Christological vision of creation is manifold. For him, Christ functions as a mediator, a voice, and a divine hand in creation of the world,

---

32. Ephrem the Syrian, *Hymnen de Nativitate*, 4:159.
33. Sebastian Brock, *Hymns on Paradise by St. Ephrem the Syrian* (New York: St. Vladimir's Seminary Press, 1990), 39.
34. David W. Kiger, "Fire in the Bread, Life in the Body. The Pneumatology of Ephrem the Syrian" (PhD Diss., Marquette University, 2020), 203.
35. Ephrem, *On Nativity*, 1.10, in Ephrem the Syrian, *Hymns*, 64.
36. Brock, *Hymns on Paradise*, 40–41.
37. Brock, *Hymns on Paradise*, 41.

living creatures and humanity. Ephrem saw Christ as a hand of the Triune Creator in forming the cosmos and, likewise, Adam or man, from the earth. This is the activity of the first-born Son of the Father. Ephrem employed the same words and phrases in the same manner when he described the Son forming in the womb of Mary and the forming of a new creation in a believer. The formation of a believer is an artistic act for Ephrem. He visioned man as a microcosmos of all created order and thus a representative of all creation. Therefore, the earth is seen as a mother who "bore" Adam, having thus a genetic relation between man and earth.[38] This brings forth a strong relational connecting point with humanity and the rest of creation.

There is yet one observation that needs to be made from Ephrem's theology of creation. Adam/the man is visioned to be a magnificent king in paradise. The concept of paradise is important to understand according to Ephrem's apophatic and spiritually orientated reading of Torah. Tryggve Kronholm explains.

> The Paradisiacal world is to him neither earthly/corporeally material, not spiritually immaterial, but of a particular spiritual substance, perceivable, palatable and enjoyable to endowed with a corresponding nature . . . Being connected with the terrestrial world the air of Paradise, indeed a "font of pleasures" is not only a source of life and fragrance in the Garden of Paradise, but reaches even down into the earthly sphere with Paradisiacal blessings, purifying and healing.[39]

Paradise was one biblical theme utilized by several patristic authors; it often referred to the spiritual nature of the church or initiation to the Christian faith.[40] This resonates beautifully with the Pentecostal holistic and supernatural worldview.[41]

Ephrem wrote that Adam was made the king of paradise because he had the ability of speech, which separated him from the beasts. But the role was not one of exploitation but rather to be servant in a priestly and pastoral manner. Adam's name-giving ability is closely connected to the living Word and *logos*

---

38. Tryggve Kronholm, *Motifs from Genesis 1–11 in the Genuine Hymns of Ephrem the Syrian*, Coniectanea Biblica Old Testament Series (Lund: CWK Gleerup, 1978), 51–55.

39. Kronholm, *Motifs from Genesis 1–11*, 69.

40. H. S. Benjamins, "Paradisiacal Life: The Story of Paradise in the Early Church," in *Paradise Interpreted: Representations of Biblical Paradise in Judaism and Christianity*, eds Gerard P. Luttikhuizen, Themes in Biblical Narrative (Leiden: Brill, 1999), 153–67.

41. Wolfgang Vondey, *Pentecostalism: A Guide for the Perplexed* (London: T&T Clark, 2012), 30–32.

given to him, not to be a ruler and abuser and owner of other creatures.[42] The importance of this vision of paradise is to understand the corporeal nature of human flourishing on one hand and, on the other hand, the fluid nature of the theology of time in which the eschatological future and the present time are overlapping through the existence of the kingdom of God.[43] Therefore, in order to be connected to this flow of purifying and healing Paradisiacal blessings, one needs to be connected and filled with the Spirit. But to be connected to this vision, creation is required to be in harmony with humanity. This is the message of Ephrem regarding the createdness of Adam as a microcosmos of all creation. God gave this task for humanity, but it is only possible through the redemption and reconciliation in Christ.

There is yet another aspect which needs attention before we can turn to the experience of Mary. Ephrem wrote about Adam as clothed in glory in creation. This did not make humanity divine even though God gave him this glory robe. But, due to the fall, this robe was taken away. Paradise – primordial, eschatological and everything in-between (as described earlier) – can be entered only by being clothed with the robe of glory. Yet, in turn, Jesus Christ was clothed with the flesh of Mary in incarnation, and through redemption and resurrection this flesh was reformed and now the entire humanity is invited to participate in this resurrected new reality which can become a robe of glory.[44]

The redemption provided by Christ is needed not only because of the fall of humanity but also because of the curse that was laid upon the earth due to Adam's and Eve's transgression. Ephrem wrote how earth was entirely innocent but became a victim of humanity's sinfulness, and now humanity suffers because of it. He wrote, "The earth, our mother, God disfigured together with us, the one that he cursed with the sinner he will bless through those who are righteous."[45] This has become a reality of humans when communities suffer from the illbeing of creation.

There is one interesting feature in Ephrem's vision of the paradise. It comes close to C. S. Lewis's Narnia world.[46] Ephrem wrote hymns about the fall, its consequences, and the loss of the glorious clothes given to Adam and Eve

---

42. Kronholm, *Motifs from Genesis 1–11*, 78–79.

43. Vondey writes about this Pentecostal understanding of natural and supernatural realities overlapping in time and existing reality and describes it as part of Pentecostal spirituality. There is the same undertone in Ephrem's theology which invites a reader to envision a world beyond our intelligible ability (*Pentecostalism*, 32).

44. Brock, *Hymns on Paradise*, 66–70.

45. Kronholm, *Motifs from Genesis 1–11*, 121.

46. C. S. Lewis, *The Chronicles of Narnia* (New York: HarperCollins, 1950–1957).

originally, who were offered substitutional garments by the fig trees (Gen 3:7). These trees appear almost as personal and intellectual qualities, because Adam is described as running to hide between trees. Ephrem visioned Paradise as a "bridal chamber of chastity" and "the fig tree took pity and gave them leaves" to cover their nakedness.[47] These trees are spiritual as is everything else in the garden and they serve as covering and protectors of Adam in his moment of humility and disgrace. Ephrem created a multitude of typological elements to express the spiritual connectedness of the message of salvation and the bond between humanity and creation, the trees and nature.[48] The reminder for humans is that the redemption of humankind is not alienated from the salvation story of the whole cosmos. Whether one imagines trees talking and acting on behalf of us or not, humanity shares the same destiny, in good and in bad.

It is utterly important to grasp the profound change that happened in incarnation. God created the world and had his breath and hidden presence in it, but he himself, as revealed truth, was not materially tied into creation. Everything changed in the incarnation. The whole order of the cosmos was realigned because now the second hypostasis of the triune ousia came to participate in the created order clothed in flesh. Something that was originally a source of everything became to exist in particularity. In other words, incarnation brings this everything within the existing matter. In other words, and now from a Marian perspective, Christ, as a logos, and metaphysically as a hypostasis of the hidden and concealed trinitarian ousia, is the dimension of all created beings. This was hidden in the womb of a woman, who went through a normal pregnancy in a biological sense, but not so normal as a spiritual experience.

As was mentioned above, the Pentecostal orientation to Marian observation needs necessarily to be both biblical and experiential in nature. Pentecostal Christology is strongly orthodox in its adherence to Mary's virgin birth and two-nature Christology. This experiential aspect is the feature to be underlined. Ephrem escorted his reader towards understanding Mary's thoughts and feelings when she carried the Christ under her heart and inside her womb. This creates a window to understand the unique and special relationship she had with Christ when she willingly offered her own flesh to clothe the divine Son when he was formed into humanity. The realization of this bridge between the primordial creation and the forming of the Son within Mary with the dust that originally belonged to Adam is the vision that inspired Ephrem to

---

47. Kronholm, *Motifs from Genesis 1–11*, 110–11.
48. Kronholm, *Motifs from Genesis 1–11*, 110–12.

write his cosmologically rich poems. But it can likewise inform and enrich the understanding of humanity's relationship to the created order.

Mary learned to love her son as all mothers do. She was in a unique place to realize the human connectedness with the creative act happening within her and being connected to the Creator forming within her as well. Therefore, there is nothing closer to the historical moment of connection between divinity and humanity and between the creator of the universe being formed within one created person than those nine months when Mary carried her first son. That can never be repeated, but the mystery that was revealed during the Christmas night can be revisited. By carrying Christ in one's heart, as Mary was carrying her child under hers, it is possible to create a deeper understanding of our relationship to the created order and to start to value that relationship, not only in one's mind but with actions as well. Mary was not forced to that role but she chose that role by accepting the offer and announcement of the angel (Luke 1:38).[49] This opportunity is offered to everyone, be it acceptance to participate in the redemptive mystery but equally by following the call to grow in harmony with the creation, and taking action to look after it until the whole universe is transformed and unified with Christ in eternity.

> From the Father learn the Son. For if the begetter is akin to creatures, it is found that also his Son is a companion to creatures. But if the Father is a stranger [to them], is his fruit akin [to them]? Were he far from him he would say, "He is not my Son" But when he calls out, He is [my] Son he has silenced the controversy.[50]

The connection of creation and humanity created in this experience of Mary can be observed through metaphysical theories presented by Amos Yong. Yong writes his vision of pneumatological semiotics by reading creatively Charles Sander Peirce's semiotics and Donald Gelpi's metaphysics of experience.[51] The importance for this study is the sense and structure of relationality, which is expressed with Peirce's "firstness" as possibility, "secondness" as actuality, and "thirdness" as reality. These can be utilized as signs and their relations to interpreters; but also as laws of existence and the potential

---

49. See more about Mary's role in redemption in E. L. Mascall, "*Theotokos*: The Place of Mary in the Work of Salvation," in *The Blessed Virgin Mary: Essays by Anglican Writers*, eds. E. L. Mascall and H. S. Box (London: Darton, Longman & Todd, 1963), 12–26.

50. Ephrem the Syrian, *Madrashe on Faith*, 61:5, in Wickes, *Bible and Poetry*, 110.

51. Yong has originally presented this in his *Spirit-Word-Community*, and further explained in many other published texts, e.g., Amos Yong, *The Spirit Poured Out on All Flesh: Pentecostalism and the Possibility of a Global Theology* (Grand Rapids: Baker Academic, 2005), 281–92.

dynamics between categories of perceived and experienced realities.[52] Mary's experience of her Son growing in her womb was a sign and a symbol of a created reality but it was also a sign of the benevolence of the creator and the blueprint of everything. Naturally, it wasn't the universe as a material entity but the mystical wholeness with the dynamics of this entirety was present within her, materialized in time. Incarnational reality in her was an unprecedented togetherness of the universal and the concrete. This is now present to us with eschatological dynamics.

Through the triad of Yong's system in which "Thirdness means that reality is dynamic, always becoming something else, as its laws and habits mediate the transformation of the present into the future,"[53] the connection between the community which is interpreting the reality and translating it into their communal life and praxis becomes the key for change. A community which is connected to paradise has access to a never-ending flow of goodness. Community members can become a source of this dynamic flow for the larger community within which they are living. This dynamic is a presence which communicates the salvific love of God. Okesson reminds his reader of the complicated goodness, which he sees in the local congregation.[54] This can and should be a counterforce for the complicated wickedness mentioned above. God's love residing in this manner in Christ-loving community is the strongest weapon needed for the spiritual warfare that God has ever provided for his people.

Concluding Thoughts

The Pentecostal global community now has tasks ahead. We need to embrace this Marian experience of carrying Christ under our hearts but enlarge its meaning as carrying the suffering of the world as well. We ought to love and care for the world, both humanity and the rest of the cosmos, and bring it to Christ for salvation and redemption. The Spirit enables us to embrace the healing powers of paradise but also encourages us to reach out to the created surroundings which suffer because of the sins of humanity. To be connected to the created order, one needs to be connected to the creator which is hidden in unseen reality but visible in creation for human eyes to perceive it. Christian communities need an honest and transparent acknowledgement of a failure

---

52. This interconnectedness of reality in Yong's theology is further explained in Urvas, "Theology of Sin and Evil," 101–7.
53. Yong, *The Spirit Poured Out on All Flesh*, 291.
54. Okesson, *Public Missiology*, 8.

to fulfil the commandment to look after their environment. All the layers of knowledge – wisdom provided by God, knowledge of the redemption, the humble realizations of sinful actions and neglect, together with the empowerment and wisdom from heaven – create the thickness that is needed to enter into the public realm. This is the message that can first transform a Christian community to make a difference in this world. Maybe then the world will believe that we truly know the creator of this world who wants to save us all.

Bibliography

Archer, Kenneth J. "Pentecostal Hermeneutics: Retrospect and Prospects." In *Pentecostal Hermeneutics: A Reader*, edited by Lee Roy Martin, 131–48. Leiden: Brill, 2013.

Benjamins, H. S. "Paradisiacal Life: The Story of Paradise in the Early Church." In *Paradise Interpreted: Representations of Biblical Paradise in Judaism and Christianity*, edited by Gerard P. Luttikhuizen, 153–67. Themes in Biblical Narrative. Leiden: Brill, 1999.

Björkander, Martina. *Worship, Ritual and Pentecostal Spirituality-as-Theology. A Rhythm That Connects Our Hearts with God*. Global Pentecostal and Charismatic Studies 48. Leiden: Brill, 2024.

Blowers, Paul M. "Doctrine of Creation." In *The Oxford Handbook of Early Christian Studies*, edited by Susan Ashbrook Harvey and David G. Hunter, 906–31. Oxford: Oxford University Press, 2008.

Brock, Sebastian. *Hymns on Paradise by St. Ephrem the Syrian*. New York: St. Vladimir's Seminary Press, 1990.

Cartledge, Mark. *Encountering the Spirit: The Charismatic Tradition*. London: Darton Longman & Todd, 2006.

Ephrem the Syrian. *Hymns*. Translated by Kathleen E. McVey. New York: Paulist, 1989.

Griffith, S. H. "Spirit in the Bread, Fire in the Wine." *Modern Theology* 15, no. 2 (1999): 225–46.

Habibullah, S., B. H. Din, and S. H. Tan. "Impact of Climate Change on Biodiversity Loss: Global Evidence." *Environmental Science and Pollution Research* 29 (2022): 1073–86. https://doi.org/10.1007/s11356-021-15702-8.

Kiger, David W. "Fire in the Bread, Life in the Body. The Pneumatology of Ephrem the Syrian." PhD Thesis, Marquette University, 2020.

Kronholm, Tryggve. *Motifs from Genesis 1–11 in the Genuine Hymns of Ephrem the Syrian*. Coniectanea Biblica Old Testament Series. Lund: CWK Gleerup, 1978.

Lewis, C. S. *The Chronicles of Narnia*. New York: HarperCollins, 1950–1957.

Litwa, David. *The Evil Creator. Origin of an Early Christian Idea*. Oxford: Oxford University Press, 2021.

Mascall, E. L. "Theotokos: The Place of Mary in the Work of Salvation." In *The Blessed Virgin Mary: Essays by Anglican Writers*, edited by E. L. Mascall and H. S. Box, 12–26. London: Darton, Longman & Todd, 1963.

Narinskaya, Elena. *The Poetic Hymns of Saint Ephrem the Syrian. A Study in the Religious Use of Poetry in Fourth-Century Christianity*. New York: Edwin Mellen, 2013.

Okesson, Gregg. *A Public Missiology. How Local Churches Witness to a Complex World*. Grand Rapids: Baker Academic, 2020.

Pelikan, Jaroslav. *The Christian Tradition: A History of the Development of Doctrine*, Vol. 1: *The Emergence of the Catholic Tradition (100–600)*. Chicago: The University of Chicago Press, 1971.

Richie, Tony. "Radical and Responsible. A Wesleyan-Pentecostal Ecotheology." *Journal of Pentecostal Theology* 23 (2014): 216–35.

Seppälä, Serafim. *Elämän äiti – Neitsyt Maria Varhaiskristillisessä Teologiassa*. Helsinki: Maahenki Oy, 2010.

Swoboda, A. J. *Tongues and Trees. Towards a Pentecostal Ecological Theology*. Journal of Pentecostal Theology Supplement Series 40. Blandford Forum: Deo, 2013.

Urvas, Sanna. "Theology of Sin and Evil in Classical Pentecostalism: Two Case Studies." PhD Thesis, University of Helsinki, 2020. http://urn.fi/URN:ISBN:978-951-51-6555-8.

Vondey, Wolfgang. *Pentecostalism: A Guide for the Perplexed*. London: T&T Clark, 2012.

Wickes, Jeffrey. *Bible and Poetry in Late Antique Mesopotamia: Ephrem's Hymns on Faith*. Oakland: University of California Press, 2019.

Yong, Amos. *Mission After Pentecost. The Witness of the Spirit from Genesis to Revelation*. Grand Rapids: Baker Academic, 2019.

———. *The Spirit Poured Out on All Flesh. Pentecostalism and the Possibility of Global Theology*. Grand Rapids: Baker Academics, 2005.

———. *Spirit–Word–Community. Theological Hermeneutics in Trinitarian Perspective*. Eugene: Wipf & Stock, 2002.

16

Cosmotheandric Eucharist, Contemplacostal Spirituality and the Call to Relational Solidarity

Aizaiah G. Yong

According to the Poor People's Campaign, we are living in an era of mass climate degradation wherein one-third of all those living the United States are in danger of being unable to afford running water and in which the ecological situation most impacts the poor.[1] One does not have to look far to notice rising sea levels, the dissolution of ice caps, drastic changes in temperature, and a seemingly continuous array of natural disasters ranging from hurricanes, earthquakes, and tornados. The Institute for Economics and Peace have predicted the likelihood of over one billion people becoming "climate refugees" over the next decades,[2] creating perhaps the most significant migration of people the world has ever seen, not by choice but due to unlivable environments in the places they used to call home. While these disturbing realities still often go unrecognized by many in modern life, indigenous communities and peoples have been raising the alarm for many years and they must be

---

1. Shailly Barnes and Saurav Sarkar, *The Souls of Poor Folk: Auditing America 50 Years After the Poor People's Campaign* (Washington, DC: Institute for Policy Studies, 2013).

2. See The Institute for Economics and Peace report, "Over One Billion People at Threat of Being Displaced by 2050 due to Environmental Change, Conflict, and Civil Unrest," news release, 9 September 2020.

engaged respectfully and collaboratively.³ The vulnerabilities threatening our environment, and us with it, will be with us for long into the future, even if we make every effort to adjust our ways of life now to ameliorate the ecological impacts of our activities. As these circumstances create mass trauma and despair for many as they are displaced and made vulnerable, I ask myself as a practical theologian and Pentecostal minister working especially (even if not only) across the spectrum of progressive evangelicals/Catholics to the so-called spiritual-but-not-religious of our time: What spiritual teachings can provide consolation and sustenance? What practices and spiritual visions[4] can ground us and offer us hope and empowerment? And further, what implications does all of this have on our understanding of missiology and the calling of the church to be a body which "constantly works . . . to affirm and safeguard life"?[5]

Panikkar's Cosmotheandic Eucharist

First, I turn to the world-renowned theologian, philosopher, Catholic priest, and interreligious spiritual giant of the twentieth century, Raimon Panikkar, as I believe he offers us powerful guidance in our present ecological situation. While he is famously known for his cosmotheandric vision (about which I have also written),[6] which contends that all of reality is three-dimensional comprised of the divine, the human, and the cosmos, which contends that all of reality is three-dimensional comprised of the divine, the human, and the cosmos, he sought to bear witness to the presence of Christ in unfamiliar ways and in cultural and religious traditions such as Hinduism.[7] Panikkar taught (and embodied) to those around him the presence of cosmic confidence, which he

---

3. See Cate Macinnis-Ng, Dan C. H. Hikuroa, and Tara McAllister, "Indigenous Knowledge Offers Solutions, but Its Use Must Be Based on Meaningful Collaboration with Indigenous Communities," *The Conversation*, Environment + Energy, research summary, 30 March 2023.

4. See my "Collective Despair and a Time for Emergence: Proposing a Contemplacostal Spirituality," *Religions* 15, no. 3 (2024): 349.

5. World Council of Churches, "Together Towards Life: Mission and Evangelism in Changing Landscapes," WCC Affirmation on Mission and Evangelism, 2012.

6. See Aizaiah G. Yong, *Multiracial Cosmotheandrism: A Practical Theology of Multiracial Experiences* (Maryknoll: Orbis, 2023), ch 2.

7. See Raimon Panikkar, *The Unknown Christ of Hinduism: Towards an Ecumenical Christophany* (Maryknoll: Orbis, 1981), which while controversial in its original (pre-Vatican II) context, anticipates much of the spirituality of the present era, as the rest of this chapter hopefully demonstrates.

believed was salvific because of the ways it enables living in full sacred communion with rather than being alienated from life.[8]

To expound, Panikkar taught that cosmic confidence was a way of knowing and presencing hope through connection to reality itself leading one to "realize our life has a meaning . . . even if we have been invited to the Banquet of Life just for a few moments."[9] According to Panikkar, the possibilities for attaining an experience of fullness in this life would be best accomplished through participation in an inclusive "banquet" open to all. Panikkar borrows the notion of a banquet or feast from the Christian tradition as Jesus often referred to a banquet motif throughout the Gospels (see John 2:1–2, Matt 22:1–14, and Luke 14:15–24). Panikkar was especially partial to this motif and would return to the vision of a banquet when communicating his sense that life is a rhythm of plenitude to receive and give ourselves unto. And, as a Catholic priest, Panikkar identified with the call to prepare oneself as a bride in preparation to be consummated with Christ at the wedding banquet (Rev 19:9). In other writings, Panikkar explained how it is the mother of Jesus, Mary, who teaches us best how to attend the banquet of life with an "unreserved, yes" – and how, if we follow her example in our own life, we can begin to experience the presence and union with Christ unexpectedly and often throughout our days and lives.[10] For Panikkar, a reference to the banquet did not mean that life contains unlimited resources for our consumption or is always festive and happy but rather that there is a generosity at the core of all things which results in making us humble, grateful, and loving in response.

Interestingly, Panikkar did not believe the invitation to the banquet of life was only reserved for human life. One of the primary reasons for this is that he did not believe reality itself centered around human beings, as he understood the human (conscious) dimension as inherent to all other beings as well. In fact, one of his most important neologisms was that of "ecosophy,"[11] or the wisdom of the earth. Panikkar differentiated ecosophy from ecology because he wanted to stress the importance of moving away from active speech and observa-

---

8. See Anthony Raj, "Cosmic Confidence in Interreligious Spirituality," The Role of Spirituality in Promoting Reconciliation Conference, conference presentation, Constanta, Romania, August 2015.

9. Raimon Panikkar, "A Self-Critical Dialogue," in *The Intercultural Challenge of Raimon Panikkar*, ed. Joseph Prabhu (Maryknoll: Orbis, 1996), 283–84.

10. Raimon Panikkar, *Mysticism and Spirituality*, Part Two, *Spirituality: The Way of Life*, Opera Omnia (Maryknoll: Orbis, 2014), 97–114.

11. See Raimon Panikkar, "Ecosophy," Raimon Pannikar Official Site, webpage, https://www.raimon-panikkar.org/english/gloss-ecosofi.html.

tion based in the rationalistic scientific method that he learned in the course of his PhD in chemistry in 1958. (This was the second of his three research doctorates which was sandwiched between an earlier doctorate in philosophy and a later one in theology.) He went to great lengths to advocate that human beings ought to become better listeners to nature (amid which humans live) and find harmony with all others who we share this earth. Panikkar intuited that many indigenous peoples were far more advanced ecosophically[12] and he encouraged all those who were caught up in the "technocratic acceleration" of modernity to spend much more time cultivating receptivity and the "yin" or "feminine dimension" enabling us to listen and heed the communication of more than human life.[13]

Additionally, in his theological anthropology, he elucidated how the whole human experience consists of a fourfold template of body, mind, the social, and the cosmic (the *Quaternitas perfecta*) recognized in many cultural traditions.[14] While much of modern civilization focuses on developing the first two, Panikkar encouraged the recovery of the latter in order to achieve fullness. Therefore, the banquet of life was something that was to be experienced in relation to all beings within life, because all are examples of the Christic principle – none excluded (even while Panikkar acknowledges it is up to each being to realize and achieve this in relationship with the divine).[15] Panikkar describes the Christic principle as a universal imprint which brings together heaven and earth within the innermost and acts in harmony with the outer world. For him, the Christ mystery is manifest in the historical Jesus of Nazareth but the Christ symbol permeates all of Reality and therefore other traditions bear witness to this in a way that contemporary Christians may not find familiar.

And it was in this awareness that Panikkar developed his own version of the ancient Christian spiritual practice known as the Eucharist. He would frequently invite his students, colleagues, and friends to join him in his own rendition of the banquet of life, incorporating many cosmic elements and interreligious insights to the process seeking to bear witness to the Christ mystery anew. Panikkar would lead these trinitarian and cosmotheandric liturgies

---

12. See Gerard Hall, Joan Hendriks, and Raimon Panikkar, *Dreaming a New Earth: Raimon Panikkar and Indigenous Spiritualities* (Preston: Mosaic, 2013).

13. Panikkar, *Mysticism and Spirituality*, 29.

14. Panikkar also recognized there were other homeomorphic equivalents to the human person outside of Greek philosophy and shares numerous examples such as jiva, altam, atman, and brahman or earth, water, fire, air (Panikkar, *Mysticism and Spirituality*, 302).

15. In his *The Unknown Christ of Hinduism*, Panikkar articulates more of his position that Christ is present far beyond Christianity or any one culture.

outside of any religious building or institution and with an open invitation for all who were interested to come together in a beautiful setting within nature (often on a hill or mountain overlooking the ocean) to deepen awareness of the gift of life and Christ's death and resurrection life at work in Reality (even though others may not describe it in this precise way nor was Panikkar looking for all to describe in the same ways as he understood God as beyond any final articulations in an apophatic sense). For Panikkar, this practice was ultimately kenotic and invited those to receive and pour out unto the world as a vessel of love continuing the sacrifice Jesus modeled. Panikkar was practicing a twentieth century version of *anamnesis*, or recalling the presence of the sacred within us, around us, and beyond each person (including but transcending the historical Jesus of Nazareth). Joseph Prabhu, a Hindu theologian and scholar, who was one of Panikkar's students, wrote in detail about his own experience at one of these gatherings reflecting, "it was a profound celebration with the human, cosmic, and divine dimensions of life being affirmed, reverenced, and brought into deep harmony."[16] In this testimony, it can be observed that Prabhu was a beneficiary of Panikkar's cosmotheandric eucharist and it was an occasion for Prabhu as a Hindu to discover his own sense of "cosmic confidence" and "ecosophy," tasting deep communion within himself, others, the sacred, and the whole of life. In other words, Panikkar's practice was not only meant to heighten consciousness of each Christic experience, but also to bring attention to the earth as our home, granting us sustenance through our interdependence.

While some Christians may be uncomfortable with the idea that non-Christians can adequately share in the Eucharist,[17] Panikkar's example is strangely resonant with some strands of Protestant Christian traditions which emphasize an "open table" such as the Christian Church (Disciples of Christ) movement of which I am an ordained minister, and there continues to be pentecostal leaders scattered among the movement primarily in communities of colour (especially in Puerto Rican and African-American congregations). For the Disciples, who were part of the twentieth century Protestant restorationist movement and emphasized unity within the church as of utmost importance, the ritual of communion was not intended to be exclusionary but inclusive. Disciples believe instead in the Lord's Supper as a concrete practice which strengthens recipients as "agents of transformation and renewal in relationships

---

16. Joseph Prabhu, "Raimon Panikkar, 'Apostle of Inter-Faith Dialogue,' Dies," *National Catholic Reporter*, 31 August 2010.

17. See Kenneth Kramer, "Of Lasting Value: Raimon Panikkar, Bruno Barnhart, and Donald Nicholl in Conversation about Eucharist," *Journal of Ecumenical Studies* 51, no. 1 (2016): 128–35.

through an encounter with the crucified and risen Jesus Christ."[18] Hence the practice of an open table carries a recognition of at least three truths:

1. The mystery of Christ is available to all freely and no one human being (or ecclesial body) is justified to sit in the place of judging who is in and who is out.[19]

2. The awareness that if we are truly in Christ then we are interrelated to all others in life and therefore to exclude any persons from participation is to exclude ourselves from participating in the Christ mystery.

3. The commitment and call to relational transformation at every level. It is important to note the connections between Panikkarian eucharist with the Disciples tradition as they both stress the more than human dimensions present within the practice of eucharist and also call each person toward social justice.

In the next section, I will draw from my own contemplacostal spirituality which draws upon the two strands identified here and adds another dimension (that of Pentecostal spirituality) which emphasizes relationality, creativity, and the empowerment of the Holy Spirit or *Paraclete*.

Contemplacostal Spirituality

In my own journey and growth as a Pentecostal minister, which has traversed many diverse Christian traditions, I have found many gifts through studying both the Christian contemplative tradition à la Panikkar and his emphasis on direct experience with the whole of life and the mainline Protestant Disciples tradition with their insistence on relationality, justice, and inclusion. Yet it appears one of the major gifts which Pentecostal-charismatic spiritualities can bring to strengthen both of these strands is the emphasis on the person of the Holy Spirit, the counsellor, advocate, comforter, and helper being the one who ultimately enables and leads any person to grow, heal, and transform. While it is evident that Pentecostal traditions affirm both the centrality of the personal and experiential nature of one's spirituality (along with the contemplative tradi-

---

18. D. Newell. Williams, "A Disciples of Christ View of Communion and Justice," *Teleios* 2, no. 1 (2022): 21–32.

19. The non-hierarchical, mutuality-based, and congregationalist polity of the Disciples tradition invites laity to administer the elements rather than depending on the clergy to do so. See also "Convenient Conversations for Disciples" held on the Christian Church (Disciples of Christ) website.

tion) as well as a radically open and democratic sensibility which honors the capacity of each person to minister through the anointing of the Spirit (akin to the Disciples tradition), what the Pentecostal-charismatics offer uniquely to both is a clearer articulation of the *how*. For Pentecostal-charismatics, the only way to experience Christ and to welcome others is through the Spirit's empowerment. And it is the emphasis upon the Spirit which enabled the early forms of Pentecostal Christianity to be more inclusive than the dominant culture of society was at that time (whether due to class, race, gender, or other categories). Keri Day's recent and groundbreaking study has noted that the early Pentecostal movement was characterized by racial diversity in a time of racial segregation, and others have shown how women were given prominent roles as founders and leaders of various strands in a time of deep patriarchy and exclusion of women.[20] Hence the widely diverse Pentecostal tradition was in its inception a movement for everyday people across many different walks of life to find empowerment in their own struggles and lives.[21]

In addition, the role of the Spirit is much more relatable across diverse religious and cultural (especially in Indigenous or non-theistic) traditions than God as Father or Christ as Son, thus opening new possibilities for intercultural learning.[22] Of course, one may ask the critical question of which spirit are those who do not identify as Christian calling out to, and while this is an important query in terms of embracing the diversity of ideological and religio-cultural traditions, for my purposes, I aim to build bridges with diverse others via discernment of the "fruit of the Spirit just as joy, peace, patience, kindness, long-suffering" and the opening to loving more of life toward mutual transformation.[23] As I look more fully at the example found in Christ and present at the day of Pentecost where many tongues were perceived and cherished, I see a life in full communion with the whole radiating with joy, hope, and a sense

---

20. See Keri Day, *Azusa Reimagined: A Radical Vision of Religious and Democratic Belonging* (Stanford: Stanford University Press, 2022), and Estrelda Alexander, *The Women of Azusa Street* (Cleveland: Pilgrim, 2005).

21. Documented in Grant Wacker, *Early Pentecostals and American Culture* (Cambridge: Harvard University Press, 2002), and Gastón Espinosa, *William J. Seymour and the Origins of Global Pentecostalism: A Biography and Documentary* (Durham: Duke University Press, 2014).

22. See Amos Yong, *Discerning the Spirit(s): A Pentecostal-Charismatic Approach to Christian Theology of Religions* (Eugene: Wipf & Stock, 2019).

23. The inter-spirituality movement is a modern example of this which espouses its practice as a form of new monasticism that embraces experiential, relational, and intercultural community building as essential for authentic twenty-first century spiritual communities. See Rory McEntee and Adam Bucko, *The New Monasticism. An Interspiritual Manifesto for Contemplative Living* (Maryknoll: Orbis, 2015).

of mutual enrichment where each person could hear the glory of God in their own languages. In my view, not only is a contemplacostal spirituality more inclusive, but it encourages those who may not consider themselves religious to reconsider the divine dimension of their experience. For example, we may think of those who were raised in Christianity but now identify with other cultural or religious traditions, therefore an emphasis on the Spirit (which is beyond any one religious group or culture) is something much more readily accessible than expecting others to adopt a particular confessional stance but rather to cultivate the outcomes of Spirit-empowerment and furthermore this even suggests that traditions with which we are not familiar have something to teach us about who the Spirit is and the creativity by which the Spirit moves (John 3:8). And as we have already witnessed through Panikkar, it is possible to reimagine the practice of the Eucharist while still maintaining the centrality of the Christ mystery so that it embraces the earthly and cosmic dimensions opening up participation with others in the world who do not subscribe to the Christian religious tradition which also provides important opportunities to learn from the cosmic indigenous wisdoms which have long been nourished by non-European traditions.

It is also my sense that an open contemplacostal practice of the Eucharist is also deeply aligned with what was actually at the heart of what Jesus was trying to do during the last supper. While he was inviting those with him to recall their love and solidarity with his life, death, and resurrection, Jesus began with gratitude for the bread and wine which was an emphasis on cultivating a participatory awareness of how life itself was a gift which can only be received through sacrifice, loss, and death, always promising seeds of new life. Jesus did not intend for this act to be a closed one as he instructed the disciples to go to the highways and byways inviting all to the banquet, to taste and celebrate for themselves (whatever their background was) this mystery. Finally, it was clear that Jesus had a very open posture to all he did: the last supper itself was shared fully with those who would later fall asleep on him leaving him in isolation, struggle with doubts about who he was, betray their trust in him, were morally questionable, and were ready to save their own lives and deny him. Therefore, the importance of communion is not on the qualifications which people bring to the table but was an invitation for each person to be met in the depths of being and as a path breaking down walls of separation within ourselves and in all our relations through the giving and receiving of Christ's love – transforming our waywardness connected to self-righteousness, fear, pride, or fragmentation. Interestingly, the Eucharist has a way of making space to engage these dynamics without getting mired in them, concluding with the expectation that through receiving the elements (the broken body and shed blood) we are granted an experience of connection, communion, and confidence (perhaps even cosmic) to participate in the renewal of all things.

Ecological Justice

Now why is all of this discussion important in the backdrop of ecological crisis and for a twenty-first-century missiology? We return to the theme of a banquet which was introduced to us first through Jesus and then brought back to remembrance through the work of Panikkar and the Disciples tradition. What would it look like to participate in plenitude during a time of scarcity and limitations of resources? Perhaps we need to return to oxymoric[24] thought, as Panikkar put it, which calls us to become open to the truth of abundance even amidst severe limitations; an embodied, rhythmic, and relational spiritual mood calling us to engage our own lived experiences (and those of all others) with a sense of reverence, connection, and mutuality. And it is in this backdrop, which I would like to promote at least four pragmatic needs that a new contemplacostal eucharistic practice can address:

1. It is of utmost importance that we recover practices which empower us to confront tragedy and suffering and are willing to go through the transformation which may accompany it.

2. The time is now to re-create practices that strengthen our awareness of our interdependence with (and affirmation of) life as a whole with no exceptions, overcoming tribalism and spiritual superiority complexes of any kind.

3. We cannot continue to live mind-dominant lives which know no limits and sever us from the embodied wisdom contained beyond our thinking self, beckoning us toward courageous transformation.

4. We are called to identify new ways of rediscovering the divine dimensions of life that are compatible and interested in the rich diversity in the world.

I will now spend time with each.

---

24. Another neologism of Panikkar which avoids anti-intellectualism and demonstrates the reality that rationalism is not king to reality. See Panikkar, "Oxymoric," Raimon Pannikar Official Site, webpage, https://www.raimon-panikkar.org/english/gloss-oxymoric.html.

Our current environmental situation continues to worsen and intensify and therefore radically inclusive missiology is an imperative. Although efforts should be made in every way possible to change our behaviours, rates of consumption, and the enormous commodification of matter, the scale on which we must change cautions us to consider that, unfortunately, we may not heed the ecosophy being offered until it is too late. If this is true, we must be prepared now with embodied rituals that metabolize the inevitable suffering we will continue to experience due to ecological degradation, re-weave us to celebration, and centre us in the dynamism of life (and its interrelationality with death) itself as trustworthy, returning us to the fullness of ourselves. A contemplacostal eucharist practice invites all those who will partake to be present with the moment as it is (including all of its loss, grief, and uncertainty) while also contemplating the creative force underlying and permeating life in all of its diverse forms. Whereas modernist responses to our environmental urgencies continue to attempt to master our problems, our own proposal presumes not only that things may get worse, but even if some kind of equilibrium is possible in the future, we will continue to absorb, and in that sense suffer from, the negative impacts of ecological upheaval. It will only be in the power of life itself (which is the mystery Jesus's life, death, and resurrection reveals as a symbol for all reality) that we will regain our strength to face the seemingly impossible and otherwise unthinkable.

Not only do we need rituals of relational empowerment, but we need to re-create rituals of communal[25] connection that assist us in remembering Christ anew. We cannot afford to be exclusionary, individualistic, or rationalistic only but are called to be flexible, culturally sensitive, and available to significant transformation in relationship with one another, trusting the power of the resurrection meets us where and when we least expect it and may even misrecognize it like the disciples who did not identify Jesus easily after he rose. We are invited to re-create rituals that in turn transform us, rituals that offer us a sense of belonging, are invigorating, and compel us to persevere towards justice and healing in a spirit of togetherness.[26] So much of our contemporary

---

25. Kramer, "Of Lasting Value," features three Christians discussing how communion can be a bridge toward other religious traditions as well as a way of rooting the human experience in community together.

26. Elsewhere I have co-written about the importance of convivencia with my colleague, Yohana Junker, and how we need to foster spaces of relationality in higher education and beyond as the key to deep transformation; see our chapter, Aizaiah G. Yong and Yohana Agra Junker, "Deepening Belonging: A Contemplative Practice of Relational Flourishing" in *Contemplative Practices and Acts of Resistance in Higher Education*, eds. Michelle G. Chatman, LeeRay Costa, and David W. Robertson-Morris (New York: Routledge, 2024), 63–71.

suffering comes from the felt sense of losing connection, of separateness, of isolation, and much of this arises from the dominant mentality that supposes humanity is above or superior to more than human life. We need rituals that remind us of our deep interdependence with each other and especially more than human life. We need practices that move us beyond finding solutions to uncertainties and usher us into shared vulnerability, mutuality, and communion. We have reviewed one such example that can remind and reveal to us the folly of our independent mind. We learn that our interdependence is not a curse, but a gift to honour and esteem. For it is through our deep interconnections where we find the most expansive joy and meaning.

In a time of despair and violence, the antidote is hope. This hope is grounded in what Panikkar calls cosmic confidence, which is not confidence in the cosmos, but the confidence of the cosmos itself as undergirding our own beings. Cosmic confidence is experiential and is the living power which resides in and through all of us calling forth renewal. When we live with cosmic confidence we feel our very lives as held and woven together with all others, including the divine, human, and cosmic dimensions. As Panikkar says, not "hope of the future but of the invisible dimension of reality itself."[27] Such is a hope that we can taste, touch, see, feel, and know personally. The embodied hope is what then generates within us the vision, creativity, boldness, and expansiveness to move beyond old models of competition and tribalism and into new expressions of life that have yet to be embodied.

Of course, in a time of ecological degradation, we are in deep need of creative responses rather than continuing down the same old destructive path, but this cannot even begin to be possible without practices that grant us hope. A contemplacostal eucharist practice can return us to experiences of relational nourishment beckoning us toward courageous transformation. Hope thus emerges from out of our contemplative experience of the fullness of life available to us wherever and with whomever we may find ourselves.

Finally, and perhaps most importantly it is imperative that we become re-enchanted with the divine dimension of life.[28] We must learn to listen again to the tales and wisdoms which come from beyond only the human. Within Christianity explicitly, there is a serious problem with our own hubris and

---

27. Raimon Panikkar, "Cultural Disarmament," Raimon Pannikar Official Site, https://www.raimon-panikkar.org/english/XXXV-2-Cultural-Disarmament.html. I discuss further Panikkar's cultural disarmament in *Multiracial Cosmotheandrism*, 22.

28. I appreciate Consiglio's *Rediscovering the Divine: New Ways to Understand, Experience, and Express God* (Maryknoll: Orbis, 2023), which encourages Christians to embrace embodiment and incarnation in fresh ways.

self-survival strategies which have moved us to the false position of domination over more than human life rather than a position of humility and service. It would do us well to follow Jesus's lead and consider the lilies and the birds who do not strive yet boast the glory of the divine (Matt 6:28–33). Further, to be sure, I am calling for the reintroduction of the religious dimension within life. This does not primarily mean we need to convert or proselytize so that others join institutional religion or that we should only teach explicitly religious materials such as the mystics hailing from various traditions (while it remains true that both can be helpful and warranted in many cases) but rather to tease out the spiritual core present in life itself (where it can often be found at work among the artists, prophets, the caregivers, and the storytellers) so that we can live in closer connection with the primordial creative (love) force at the depth dimension of all things. If we are to create new religious institutions, they should be ones which prioritize the experiences of the most vulnerable (including the more than human life!) and the seeming insignificant (in the eyes of the world) lest we believe that the divine is only reserved for an afterlife and not available fully in the here and now. The future of spiritual traditions should also be firmly committed to an ethic of nonviolence[29] where consent, agency, and mutuality is what enables relationships to grow and encourages a unique exploration of each person's encounter with the sacred. A remembrance of the divine also helps us in the overly reductionist era we find ourselves where scientism and technocracy dominate, and people have stopped looking to the religious dimensions of life believing that it cannot teach anything "new." In a real sense that is true, there is nothing "new" to be taught but there is a "new" experience to be lived and celebrated which can only happen through the uniqueness of each life. If we can create rituals that support people to lean into this, we may find promise and expectation of renewal regardless of what circumstances we may feel stuck in, and we can share in a satisfaction that is not materially quantifiable but salvific and total in its scope.

    I would like to take all four of these elements to now propose what I would term as relational solidarity. It is not a solidarity with only human life but a solidarity with the whole, including the divine. Solidarity is a sharing in the creational condition, not in order to triumph over or master but to persevere through the challenges and the pain, and to enjoy the mundane. And it is through sharing where we find communion and the greatest sense of belonging. My call is a movement away from individualist, monocultural, supremacist,

---

29. I agree with Howard Thurman, *Jesus and the Disinherited* (Boston: Beacon Press, 1996), who roots the religion of Jesus as one that is inherently nonviolent.

exclusive, or hierarchical ways of navigating our ecological moment and instead turn to the best of our spiritual traditions which guide us toward mutuality, vulnerability, creativity, and confidence.

Conclusion

Our world is both wonderful and finite but at the core of our ecological challenge is the awareness that our world is not an unlimited resource where we can simply extract and consume with no limits. Therefore, I end with an invitation to a cosmotheandric eucharist practice that involves sincerity, boundary crossing, and which leads us into depths of connection where joy, suffering, connection, hope, and justice making are sensed and deepened. Further, my invitation is that this practice would be supported by a contemplacostal spiritual vision that calls for a recovery of the divine and en-spirited dimension which many feel cut off from or distanced to because of imperial forms of religion but promises a power of new life if we are open. Not only does a contemplacostal spirituality invite intercultural and interreligious communities to practice mutuality together, but it also inspires empowerment through an acceptance of our vulnerability (that of human and more than human life) where we find all beings as inherently beloved. In conclusion, my proposal is simply one invitation toward practicing hope in an era of increasing despair and severe environmental degradation, but many others will be required. No one paradigm is sufficient. Let us together imagine practices that honour and embrace finitude as a sacred quality and lead us to treasure and celebrate the gift of life we have been offered through gratitude and ongoing cosmic renewal. While this posture will not promise an avoidance of difficulties, it does promise previously unimagined responses to the extended and persisting urgencies of our situation albeit now awakened to the promise of new life. And so it is.

Bibliography

Alexander, Estrelda. *The Women of Azusa Street*. Cleveland: Pilgrim, 2005.
Bon Air Christian Church. "Imagine God's Limitless Love. A Covenant Conversation for Disciples." Group Devotional Guide. 2021. https://cdn.disciples.org/wp-content/uploads/2021/05/10134223/A-Covenant-Conversation-for-Disciples.pdf.
Consiglio, Cyprian. *Rediscovering the Divine: New Ways to Understand, Experience, and Express God*. Maryknoll: Orbis, 2023.
Day, Keri. *Azusa Reimagined: A Radical Vision of Religious and Democratic Belonging*. Encountering Traditions. Stanford: Stanford University Press, 2022

Espinosa, Gastón. *William J. Seymour and the Origins of Global Pentecostalism: A Biography and Documentary*. Durham: Duke University Press, 2014.

Gupta Barnes, Shailly, and Saurav Sarkar. *The Souls of Poor Folk: Auditing America 50 Years After the Poor People's Campaign*. Washington, DC: Institute for Policy Studies, 2013.

Hall, Gerard, Joan Hendriks, and Raimon Panikkar. *Dreaming a New Earth: Raimon Panikkar and Indigenous Spiritualities*. Preston: Mosaic, 2013.

Institute for Economics and Peace, The. "Over One Billion People at Threat of Being Displaced by 2050 due to Environmental Change, Conflict, and Civil Unrest." News Release. 9 September 2020. https://www.prnewswire.com/news-releases/iep-over-one-billion-people-at-threat-of-being-displaced-by-2050-due-to-environmental-change-conflict-and-civil-unrest-301125350.html.

Kramer, Kenneth. "Of Lasting Value: Raimon Panikkar, Bruno Barnhart, and Donald Nicholl in Conversation about Eucharist." *Journal of Ecumenical Studies* 51, no. 1 (2016): 128–35.

Macinnis-Ng, Cate, Dan C. H. Hikuroa, and Tara McAllister. "Indigenous Knowledge Offers Solutions, but Its Use Must Be Based on Meaningful Collaboration with Indigenous Communities." *The Conversation*. Environment + Energy. Research Summary. 30 March 2023. http://theconversation.com/indigenous-knowledge-offers-solutions-but-its-use-must-be-based-on-meaningful-collaboration-with-indigenous-communities-201670.

McEntee, Rory, and Adam Bucko. *The New Monasticism: An Interspiritual Manifesto for Contemplative Living*. Maryknoll: Orbis, 2015.

Panikkar, Raimon. "Glossary." Vivarium Foundation. Online Resource. Accessed March 14, 2024. https://www.raimon-panikkar.org/english/glossary.html.

———. *Mysticism and Spirituality. Part Two Spirituality: The Way of Life*. Opera Omnia. Maryknoll: Orbis, 2014.

———. "A Self-Critical Dialogue." In *The Intercultural Challenge of Raimon Panikkar*, edited by Joseph Prabhu, 227–91. Maryknoll: Orbis, 1996.

———. *The Unknown Christ of Hinduism: Towards an Ecumenical Christophany*. Maryknoll: Orbis, 1981.

Prabhu, Joseph. "Raimon Panikkar, 'Apostle of Inter-Faith Dialogue,' Dies." *National Catholic Reporter*. 31 August 2010. https://www.ncronline.org/news/spirituality/raimon-panikkar-apostle-inter-faith-dialogue-dies.

Raj, Anthony. "Cosmic Confidence in Interreligious Spirituality." The Role of Spirituality in Promoting Reconciliation Conference. Conference Presentation. Constanta, Romania. August 2015. https://www.raimon-panikkar.it/news/cosmic-confidence-in-interreligious-spirituality/.

Thurman, Howard. *Jesus and the Disinherited*. Boston: Beacon Press, 1996.

Wacker, Grant. *Early Pentecostals and American Culture*. Cambridge: Harvard University Press, 2002.

Williams, D. Newell. "A Disciples of Christ View of Communion and Justice." *Teleios* 2 no. 1 (2022): 21–32.

World Council of Churches. "Together Towards Life: Mission and Evangelism in Changing Landscapes." WCC Affirmation on Mission and Evangelism. 2012. https://www.oikoumene.org/resources/documents/together-towards-life-mission-and-evangelism-in-changing-landscapes.

Yong, Aizaiah G. "Collective Despair and a Time for Emergence: Proposing a Contemplacostal Spirituality." *Religions* 15, no. 3 (2024): 349. https://doi.org/10.3390/rel15030349.

———. *Multiracial Cosmotheandrism: A Practical Theology of Multiracial Experiences*. Maryknoll: Orbis, 2023.

Yong, Aizaiah G., and Yohana Agra Junker. "Deepening Belonging: A Contemplative Practice of Relational Flourishing." *Contemplative Practices and Acts of Resistance in Higher Education*, eds. Michelle G. Chatman, LeeRay Costa, and David W. Robertson-Morris, 63–71. New York: Routledge, 2024.

Yong, Amos. *Discerning the Spirit(s): A Pentecostal–Charismatic Approach to Christian Theology of Religions*. Eugene: Wipf & Stock, 2019.

17

Ecological Imagination after Pentecost

Andy Lord

Pentecostals have been slow to engage with the development of theologies and missiologies that take seriously the current environmental crisis. Their emphasis upon the work of the Holy Spirit has been largely limited to the personal and communal domains without reference to the ecological issues that dominate our news. This has begun to change with Amos Yong notably pioneering theological approaches that take seriously the work of the Holy Spirit in all creation. These contribute to the wider discussions under the methodology of "after Pentecost" which develops his understanding of a "pneumatological imagination" rooted in the narratives of early Pentecostalism.[1] This is an approach also taken up by Wolfgang Vondey in his recent work that links narrative and the imagination, leading to creation as the starting point for a Pentecostal systematic theology. The narratives they work with tend to be those of early Pentecostalism rather than contemporary narratives so, when they turn to ecological issues, their theology remains rather abstract. The narratives of early Pentecostalism seem to have given way to more rigidly rational systematic approaches. Where have the narratives gone? They have largely gone outside the church. There are many who use creative forms of writing to motivate positive responses to the ecological crisis, perhaps engaging spiritual topics but often from beyond the usual Christian boundaries. This

---

1. Amos Yong, *Mission After Pentecost. The Witness of the Spirit from Genesis to Revelation* (Grand Rapids: Baker Academic, 2019).

chapter aims to ask how Pentecostals might constructively engage and learn from these in our systematic and ecological theology.

Central to this task is stretching our understanding of Pentecost and its imaginative resonances in contemporary writing and testimony. Many writers on the environment take what we might understand as an eschatological viewpoint – viewing the present from the perspective of a future in which the crisis has caused untold damage to our ecology. Ben Oki is one such writer and poet who sums up his powerful book on climate change through the refrain: "Can't you hear the future weeping? Our love must save the world."[2] He imagines a future life in which the earth is degraded and flooded and in which people live ordinary lives very different to ours. Pentecost perspectives would also want to highlight the work of the Holy Spirit, pouring out God's love in Christ today, the "last days" (Acts 2:17). The link between the present and the future and the need to observe, articulate, and imagine both today and possible futures with and without cooperation with the Spirit is vital to addressing the crisis. Here we focus on written reflective testimonies of those seeking to observe and articulate the present situation in order to stimulate positive action.

We start by outlining the systematic, missiological, and imaginative approaches of Yong and Vondey in the next section before turning to Robert Macfarlane, a leading contemporary nature writer. He is noted for his ability to observe, narrate, and engage in landscape with all its beauty, toughness, and crisis. The focus will be on passages resonant with Pentecost which illustrate what we might learn from such narratives. In order to further explore particularly Christian narratives in relation to nature we then turn to Thomas Merton, the twentieth century monk and writer, who engaged with the early environmentalist movement of the 1960s. This enables us to revisit our theological method to suggest how an ecological imagination might better enable future Pentecostal theology in ways that stimulate action in a time of environmental crisis.

---

2. Ben Okri, *Tiger Work* (London: Head of Zeus, 2023), 4, 37.

Pentecostal Theological Imagination

Ten years ago, Jonathan Rice argued that Pentecostalism was anti-ecological and this needed to change.[3] Some hold to an eschatology built on a dualism between spirit and matter that assumes that after the faithful have been raptured the earth will be annihilated.[4] Others distrust a social gospel in line with some North American cultural and political biases. There is a notable lack of ecological concern in Pentecostal missiology, reflecting the tendency to focus on narratives of personal conversion and communal transformation.[5] At the same time, Pentecostal involvement in the Lausanne movement has bridged the gap between evangelism and social issues with the theme of creation central to any holistic approach to mission.[6] A. J. Swoboda traces Pentecostal ecotheological engagements that have developed since the late 1970s out of the concern for social justice, particularly beyond the West.[7] The term "ecotheology" is often taken as covering contextual theologies that "take their bearings from cultural concerns about the environment and humanity's relationship with the natural world."[8] Here, we take an approach that appreciates the overlap between the ecological and the systematic, relating as they do the interconnected web of living organisms and the bringing together of different elements of Christian teaching. Rather than contextual theology, we are exploring here systematic theology and suggesting that it may be recast as ecological theology. Our interest here is in ecology and the imagination as theological method although one which is unavoidably joined to the ecological context through contemporary imaginative narratives.

---

3. Jonathan W. Rice, "Ecology and the Future of Pentecostalism: Problems, Possibilities, and Proposals," in *Pentecostal Mission and Global Christianity*, eds. Wonsuk Ma, Veli-Matti Kärkkäinen, and Asamoah Gyadu (London: Regnum, 2012), 360–79.

4. Jeffrey S. Lamp, "Ecotheology: A People of the Spirit for Earth," in *The Routledge Handbook of Pentecostal Theology*, ed. Wolfgang Vondey (London: Routledge, 2020), 357–61.

5. Although ecological concern is raised throughout *Pentecostal Mission and Global Christianity*, Rice's chapter stands out in its depth of treatment. In a similar way, Ma and Ma highlight the importance of creation to Pentecostal missiology but then proceed to focus on narratives that are personal and communal. Julie C. Ma and Wonsuk Ma, *Mission in the Spirit: Towards a Pentecostal/Charismatic Missiology* (Eugene: Wipf & Stock, 2010).

6. See here my summary of these developments and a proposed holistic charismatic missiology in Andy Lord, *Spirit-Shaped Mission: A Holistic Charismatic Missiology* (Carlisle: Paternoster, 2005).

7. A. J. Swoboda, *Tongues and Trees: Towards a Pentecostal Ecological Theology* (Blandford Forum: Deo, 2013), 95–96. See also Anita Davis, "Pentecostal Approaches to Ecotheology: Reviewing the Literature," *Australasian Pentecostal Studies* 22, no. 1 (2021): 4–33.

8. Celia Deane-Drummond, *Eco-Theology* (London: Darton, Longman & Todd, 2008), 10.

Yong has been a pioneering Pentecostal scholar for over twenty-five years and has been developing a "pneumatological imagination," a methodology for approaching a range of issues that surround the reality of God's interaction with the created world. This started with questions related to a theology of religions in which an imaginative approach "renders more plausible the idea of God as present and active in the world."[9] Yong has developed a complex methodological and metaphysical system resonant with the imaginative experience of early Pentecostals and charismatics. He has a particular interest in the overlap between science and Pentecostalism in relation to creation. In his earlier work, he applied the pneumatological imagination to "science in search of the Spirit," drawing on the Wesleyan tradition.[10] In later work, Yong developed an understanding of the spirit-filled cosmos through engagement with emergence theory. The creation narratives show God creating and working good by Spirit and Word with the spiritual dimensions of life being intensified with the appearance of humanity.[11] The biblical historical narratives make use of a variety of spirits, notably angelic spirits that minister God's salvific grace and demonic spirits that are divergent and oppose God's grace. Yong gives a key role to the church in God's work of redeeming the world, resisting the demonic, and delivering the oppressed. This is a glimpse of the "eschatological renewal of the whole creation" and is embodied in praxis on behalf of the environment, addressing ecological issues.[12] More recently, Yong's integrative approach has been developed through a deeper and more radical engagement with the Pentecost narrative.[13] What is significant for Yong here is the way in which the narrative brings God and the world together through a focus on the Holy Spirit. The Spirit is "environmentally situated" with the eschatological "last days" of Acts 2 pointing towards the "yearning for and reception of cosmic renewal by the divine breath."[14] Yong is moving to link imagination as method to praxis building on the early church narratives.

---

9. Amos Yong, *Discerning the Spirit(s): A Pentecostal–Charismatic Approach to Christian Theology of Religions* (Eugene: Wipf & Stock, 2019), 29.

10. Amos Yong, *The Spirit Poured Out on All Flesh: Pentecostalism and the Possibility of a Global Theology* (Grand Rapids: Baker Academic, 2005), 269–80.

11. Amos Yong, *The Spirit of Creation: Modern Science and Divine Action in the Pentecostal–Charismatic Imagination* (Grand Rapids: Eerdmans, 2011), 209–17.

12. Yong, *Spirit of Creation*, 228.

13. Amos Yong, "Pneumatological Imagination: The Logic of Pentecostal Theology," in *The Routledge Handbook of Pentecostal Theology*, ed. Wolfgang Vondey (London: Routledge, 2020), 152.

14. Yong, "Pneumatological Imagination," 159.

Vondey follows a similar Pentecostal approach to Yong, utilizing more fully the narratives of early Pentecostalism that have been summarized in terms of the full gospel, narratives that see Jesus as saviour, sanctifier, Spirit baptizer, healer, and coming king. Vondey notes a crisis of the imagination from antiquity to the modern age in which context Pentecostalism represents a revival of the imagination, particularly through its narratives seen as a story of the Holy Spirit.[15] He develops this through an exploration of the idea of play which enables a way of living motivated "by an unlimited imagination . . . oriented towards the fulfilment of God's own imagination."[16] Vondey notably starts his systematic approach with a consideration of creation, starting with a Pentecostal cosmology that addresses the lack of ecological consciousness in much previous Pentecostal theology. He draws on Pentecostal narratives to suggest that "creation can be seen as the economy of salvation, as it were, the cosmic altar of redemption, sanctification, empowerment, transformation, and eschatological mission."[17] Christians are empowered through Spirit baptism to engage with God's sanctifying work in creation – with holiness having a cosmological as well as anthropological value.[18] They will challenge evil through spiritual warfare and join in the divine healing of the cosmos. This is a holistic approach to healing that is a prophetic work in creation including "liberation from social, political, economic, and institutional injustice and the restoration of relationships among all of God's creatures into the eternal fellowship of the Spirit."[19]

Yong and Vondey place imagination central to their theological method, drawing on the biblical and early Pentecostal narratives. This is being stretched in the direction of ecological concern and praxis, connecting with the more popular understanding of imagination as that which brings together in the mind different ideas and feelings in ways that provoke creative work and action.[20] At the same time, it is notable how their theologies remain abstract

---

15. Wolfgang Vondey, *Beyond Pentecostalism: The Crisis of Global Christianity and the Renewal of the Theological Agenda*, Pentecostal Manifestos Series (Grand Rapids: Eerdmans, 2011), 17–34.

16. Wolfgang Vondey, *Pentecostal Theology: Living the Full Gospel* (New York: Bloomsbury, 2017), 13.

17. Vondey, *Pentecostal Theology*, 156.

18. Vondey, *Pentecostal Theology*, 161–66.

19. Vondey, *Pentecostal Theology*, 170–71.

20. A point picked up by Swoboda who notes that our "imaginative attitude has been what has shaped our attitude towards creation" in A. J. Swoboda, *Tongues and Trees Towards a Pentecostal Ecological Theology* (Blandford Forum: Deo, 2013), 212.

and distant from contemporary imaginative narrative and testimony. How are we to bridge the gap between past and contemporary narratives in theological method? Many approaches are possible but here our interest is in learning from the contemporary ecological narratives that remain absent from our theology from the perspective of "after Pentecost." In this regard, the approach of Ben Quash is helpful from his *Found Theology* that combines the imagination, the Spirit, and history.[21] He is seeking to connect the Spirit "found" in historical context with the "givens" of Christian Scripture and tradition, exploring art and poetry in different contexts. His concern, like ours, is to bridge the gap between the contemporary Spirit and that explored in systematic theology. Quash encourages us to seek the Spirit without measure (John 3:34) in the world and bring articulations of this into our theological conversation. To undertake theology is to seek the Spirit in Scripture, the past traditions, and the current realities. Given the lack of contemporary Pentecostal narratives, it is helpful to seek the Spirit in the narratives of contemporary "nature writers" who imaginatively bring together history, geography, geology, politics, and personal experience in narrative form.

This seeking of the Spirit on the edges beyond the church is in line with the narrative of Pentecost. Consider those on the edge of the crowd that first Pentecost who would have noticed people and aspects of creation being brought together in fresh ways – there were tongues of fire that anointed people and a wind that blew them out into the world. There would have been a sense of "something more" going on in the world than was obvious at first sight, a challenge to look deeper, that resulted in many coming to faith. Pentecostal theology needs an openness to finding the Spirit at work in narratives from the edge in ways that are then brought into conversation with the traditions that shape us.

Finding the Spirit on the Edge

We turn now to consider Macfarlane who has written a series of best-selling books relating the landscape and the soul which have won many international awards. He is a professor in Cambridge, UK, who engages with personal, historical, geographic, geological, political, and religious narratives to suggest how our interactions with the land around us shapes our thinking and living, leading to ethical actions that can transform the world at a time of environ-

---

21. Ben Quash, *Found Theology: History, Imagination and the Holy Spirit* (London: T&T Clark, 2013).

mental crisis. He is someone deeply aware of nature with a gift for articulating the connections between disciplines, histories, and peoples that come together in specific places.[22] In terms of methodology, he uses forms of journey narratives that give testimony to new ways of imagining and acting on behalf of the environment. These are rooted in particular landscapes but open us up to something more universal. The rootedness of Nan Shepherd in the Cairngorms that resulted in *The Living Mountain* inspires Macfarlane across many of his books.[23] He notes that "Shepherd was a localist of the best kind: she came to know her chosen place closely, but that closeness served to deepen rather than limit her vision."[24] She captured landscape as one interconnected entity through a very focused attention. Macfarlane draws this into narratives that play with forms to communicate a holistic and open vision that raises the challenge to respond. There are overlaps here with the Holy Spirit found in the particular, but with universal intent, at Pentecost.[25] Whilst Macfarlane is moving towards a more spiritual understanding, this is not within a Christian framework but through an interest in the new animist thinking which will be explored in his forthcoming book *Is a River Alive?*[26] Our focus here is on a few narratives that illustrate links with our after Pentecost perspective, pointing in the direction of further theological development.

One journey took place beneath the northeast coast of England and is narrated in *Underland*.

> Neil wanted to drive the Paris–Dakar Rally back in the day. Neil is steering a stripped-down doorless Ford Transit van in a subterranean desert maze more than 600 miles in extent, Neil is a matter of weeks from retirement . . . We take the ramps fast enough to lift up as we come over them. We leave the tunnels behind us clouded

---

22. The term "nature" is here being used when reference is made to those operating outside a Christian worldview whereas "creation" is more usual within the Christian tradition. For a detailed consideration of issues relating to this, see Veli-Matti Kärkkäinen, *A Constructive Christian Theology for the Pluralistic World*, vol. 3, *Creation and Humanity* (Grand Rapids: Eerdmans, 2015).

23. Nan Shepherd, *The Living Mountain: A Celebration of the Cairngorm Mountains of Scotland* (Edinburgh: Canongate, 2011).

24. Robert Macfarlane, *Landmarks* (London: Penguin, 2016), 56.

25. A theme I explored in Lord, *Spirit-Shaped Mission*.

26. Robert Macfarlane, *Is a River Alive?* (London: Penguin, Hamish Hamilton, 2025).

with dust. Instead of slowing down for the corners, Neil just leans on the horn. *Paaaaarp!*[27]

This is an exciting journey through halite geology towards the potash seams that are used in fertilizers and whose cutting machines are left to decay in the tunnels of mined out seams. Macfarlane ponders what future geologists will make of the old machines and collapsed tunnels millions of years into the future. In the present we create the "trace fossils" of the future that will speak the memories of our lives.[28] Humanity will leave its mark on the strata to come, full of plastic, smog, fertilizers, and radionuclides. In many ways the book is asking the questions: If we look at the present in the light of the future, what might we see? How might this change the way we live? It is a similar approach to Okri that we noted in the introduction, one that resonates with the Pentecost concern for the eschatological Spirit, the Spirit of the last days (Acts 2:17). The Spirit's sustaining of creation is witnessed to in the eschatological strata of rocks that record the mix of the creative Spirit and humanity's less creative actions.

At the same time and in the same maze of tunnels there is a searching back in time:

> More than half a mile under the earth, in a laboratory set into a band of translucent silver rock salt left behind by the evaporation of an epicontinental northern sea some 250 million years earlier, a young physicist is trying to look into a void. He sits watching a computer screen, close to a larger silver cube. The cube's name is DRIFT and it is a breath-catcher. The young physicist is trying to catch the faint breath of a particle wind sent blowing across space from a constellation called Cygnus, the Swan, many light years distant from Earth.[29]

This is a wonderfully evocative passage on how we might imagine the Spirit blowing through the universe over centuries from one star system to another. The scientific search for the origins and working of the universe can only be glimpsed through the almost mythic sense of hidden movements across time and space. Expansive connections link past, present, and future with some kind of faith being needed to know that which seems beyond knowing. For Macfarlane, these are linked to the breath of his sleeping young son when he

---

27. Robert Macfarlane, *Underland: A Deep Time Journey* (London: Penguin, Hamish Hamilton, 2019), 69–70.
28. Macfarlane, *Underland*, 78–79.
29. Macfarlane, *Underland*, 55.

returns home from the journey. At first, beside his bed, there seems to be no breath but then he feels it on his hands: "*Breathe. Breathe again.* My heart slowing back down. Starlight silvering the fine down on the edge of his skin. Everything causing a scintillation."[30] Surely this is a method of expressing the "wonders in the heavens above" in ways that connect to all people "on the earth below" (Acts 2:19) – the scintillating breath of the Spirit that connects all things in everlasting movement.

We can helpfully relate this breath of the Spirit to Macfarlane's journeys that sought out wild places. Initially, he had sought to experience the wild in the vast, remote, and isolated places in the British Isles.[31] These are places beyond our usual historied lives that connected with his desires to get away and discover hope in untouched places of the world. What Macfarlane needed to learn to see was the wild in life more generally, "the wildness of natural life, the sheer force of ongoing organic existence, vigorous and chaotic. This wildness was not about asperity, but about luxuriance, vitality, fun."[32] An example is a limestone gryke, a small vertical fissure less than half a meter in length.

> We lay belly-down on the limestone and peered over its edge. And found ourselves looking into a jungle. Tiny groves of ferns, mosses and flowers were there in the crevasse – hundreds of plants, just in the few yards we could see, thriving in the shelter of the gryke: cranesbills, plantains, avens, ferns, many more I could not identify, growing opportunistically on wind-blown soil. The plants thronged every available niche, embracing one another into indistinguishability. Even on this winter day, the sense of life was immense.[33]

There are resonances here with the wild Spirit who at Pentecost both shook the disciples' world and rooted them more deeply in the languages of those they are living alongside.[34] The Spirit moves us to discover the truth of the wildlife that is closer than we imagine.

Macfarlane was criticized by Kathleen Jamie who describes him in terms of a "lone enraptured male" who, she suggests, like Christian saints is seeking an individual spiritual experience without regard to community or social

---

30. Macfarlane, *Underland*, 83.
31. Robert Macfarlane, *The Wild Places* (London: Granta, 2017), 7.
32. Macfarlane, *The Wild Places*, 316.
33. Macfarlane, *The Wild Places*, 168.
34. A number of writers have explored the nature of the "wild Spirit" such as the charismatic Russ Parker, *The Wild Spirit* (London: Triangle, 1997).

realities.[35] This may have some force in relation to Christian testimonies that are purely personal without reference to the Pentecost drive to establish community and transforming the world. Whilst the critique does have merit in relation to Macfarlane's earlier writing, he increasingly sees himself as part of wider communities, learning from friends, and contributing to causes that address social ills. His narratives are carefully constructed and imaginative artworks that draw together many experiences and disciplines to motivate ethical action on behalf of all creation. The few examples given here are suggestive of how his work resonates with Pentecost and within which we might find the Spirit speaking to us, integrated with given theological themes such as eschatology, creation, Scripture, and community.

Spiritual Ecological Narratives

These excerpts from Macfarlane suggest fresh ways into theology rooted in contemporary narratives. However, we have been using the term "narrative" in a general way and it is worth reflecting further from a Christian perspective. Pentecostals are used to narrative testimonies, Spirit(ual) narratives, which often take the form of the story of life prior to meeting Christ and the transformative effect of this encounter on further life.[36] Such approaches are often traced back to Augustine's *Confessions* in bringing the self into the larger story of God's redeeming providence, perhaps (at times) more influenced by Romanticism with its focus on restoring the authentic self.[37] Recent thinking has asked questions about what such narratives omit, silence, rewrite, or marginalize. Such narratives can also present experiences as if they can be abstracted from their social contexts – the cultures, economics, classes, races, and genders – that shape the stories. We need a little more chaos and varied forms and structures in our narratives.[38] Macfarlane structures the chapters of each of his books differently, combining narrative extracts of his journeys with historical interludes, philosophical reflections and, more recently, myths

---

35. Kathleen Jamie, "A Lone Enraptured Male," *London Review of Books* 30, no. 5 (2008): 25–27.

36. Mark J. Cartledge, *Testimony in the Spirit: Rescripting Ordinary Pentecostal Theology* (Farnham: Routledge, 2010).

37. Heather Walton, *Not Eden: Spiritual Life Writing for This World* (London: SCM, 2015), 9–17.

38. Another way of phrasing this is we need narratives with a sense of mystery to be explored as argued by Douglas Christie, "Nature Writing and Nature Mysticism," in *Routledge Handbook of Religion and Ecology*, eds. Mary Evelyn Tucker, John Grim, and Willis Jenkins (London: Routledge, 2018), 227–34.

used to communicate challenging experiences. His writing bears similarities to the spiritual life writing that Heather Walton describes as that of "adaptive borrowers" who use a variety of sources brought together in ways that may be fragmented but "evocative, inspiring, and imaginative."[39] This often requires that fictional techniques may be needed to communicate the lived experience that is more complex, messy, and harder to translate into words than is often assumed. Pentecostals face a theological challenge to both engage with contemporary narratives in ways that take account of relevant critiques and draw their own narratives creatively into the theological process.

We might ask what form this will take given the Pentecostal rooting in the Christian tradition, unlike Macfarlane. There will no doubt be many, but it is worth considering the example of Thomas Merton, a well-known Catholic monk and writer from the last century. The son of two artists, Merton grew up in France, England and the USA. His worldly living did not make him the obvious convert to Christ, but he later gave testimony to the way God graciously led him to join the Trappist monastery in Kentucky. His best-selling early autobiography led to a life of writing that was gradually integrated with his monastic calling to silence and obscurity.[40] Influenced by the early Romantic poets, Merton developed a mystical approach to contemplation through which all is brought together in its particularity.[41] From the late 1950s onwards, he turned more to issues in the world, initially those of race and war. Through reading *Silent Spring* in 1962 and exchanging letters with Rachel Carson, he began to address environmental issues.

Here we look at some examples of his later writing in relation to engagement with the environment and the Spirit through narrative.[42] Given our concerns, a good place to start is with Merton's "Prayer on the Vigil of Pentecost":

> Today, Father, the blue sky lauds you. The delicate green and orange flowers of the tulip poplar tree praise you. The distant blue hills praise you, together with the sweet-smelling air that is full of brilliant light. The bickering flycatchers praise you with the lowing cattle and the quails that whistle over there. I too, Father,

---

39. Walton, *Not Eden*, 20.

40. Thomas Merton, *The Seven Storey Mountain* (New York: Harcourt, Brace and Company, 1948).

41. Ross Labrie, *Thomas Merton and the Inclusive Imagination* (Columbia: University of Missouri Press, 2001).

42. For a wider introduction to and engagement with his thought, see Andy Lord, *Transforming Renewal: Charismatic Renewal Meets Thomas Merton* (Eugene: Wipf & Stock, 2015).

> praise you, with all these my brothers, and they give voice to my own heart and to my own silence. We are all one silence, and a diversity of voices. You have made us together, you have made us one and many, you have placed me here in the midst as witness, as awareness, and as joy. Here I am. In me the world is present and you are present. I am a link in the chain of light and of presence.[43]

This praise testimony was written as he was living in a hermitage in the woods of the monastery he was rooted in for his monastic life. He would often sit outside and say some of the seven daily offices of prayers that are based on the Psalms. There would be space for silent contemplation of the familiar world around him and here we witness a combination of what we might call the inner, the outer, and the incarnational. The inward life of awareness and joy is linked to the outer description of creation and the incarnational presence of God in that place. It is this latter that takes us beyond Macfarlane whose eyes have not been deeply formed through the illumination and purification of the Christian traditions, rituals, and experience. The prayer connects with Merton's teaching on the mystical tradition, particularly the theme of *theoria physica* that explores the contemplation of God in nature.[44] It is a narrative prayer on the day of the Spirit that testifies to an ecological vision.

Merton's contemplative narratives are grounded in a lifetime of refined contemplative practice that faced the challenge of seeing rightly. To see clearly what is in front of him required the monastic disciplines that aim at "purity of heart."[45] Narration (and the environment crisis) demands a clarity of sight that sees creation in itself, not simply in its usefulness to humanity. We see this in the fragmented journal of Merton's travels from California to New Mexico just months before his death.

> It was a quiet flying to Eureka yesterday afternoon in a half empty plane . . . The redwood lands appear. Even from the air you can see that the trees are huge. And from the air too, you can see where the hillsides have been slashed into, ravaged, sacked, stripped, eroded with no hope of regrowth of these marvelous trees.[46]

---

43. Thomas Merton, *Conjectures of a Guilty Bystander* (London: Burns & Oates, 1968), 177.

44. Thomas Merton, *The Inner Experience: Notes on Contemplation*, ed. William H. Shannon (London: SPCK, 2003), 67–68; Thomas Merton, *Introduction to Christian Mysticism*, ed. Patrick F. O'Connell (Kalamazoo: Cistercian, 2008), 121–24.

45. It is here that Merton's study of Zen and its benefits for a Christian consciousness fit. See Thomas Merton, *Zen and the Birds of Appetite* (New York: New Directions, 1968).

46. Thomas Merton, *Woods, Shore, Desert* (Santa Fe: Museum of New Mexico, 1982), 11.

We see a dedication to godly observation where the Spirit can be found in all that is before Merton as he slowly moves on his journey without any seeming rush to conclude. Such observations are placed alongside suggestive connecting reflections and testimonies that can be seen through a communion that joins them together in the Spirit. There is perhaps a confidence that the communion the reader has with the same Spirit will enable them to enter into the narrative in transformational ways.

This sense of shared communion, a connectedness in the Spirit that communicates, is central to Merton's well-known 1958 "Epiphany in Louisville."

> In Louisville, at the corner of Fourth and Walnut, in the centre of the shopping district, I was suddenly overwhelmed with the realization that I loved all those people, that they were mine and I was theirs, that we could not be alien to one another even though we were total strangers. It was like waking from a dream of separateness, of spurious self-isolation in a special world, the world of renunciation and supposed holiness. The whole illusion of a separate holy existence is a dream.[47]

This is often presented as a testimony to a direct encounter with God that transformed Merton, marking his "turn to the world." As such, it is a significant narrative that contributes to how we might see a greater ecological consciousness amongst Christians. However, the narrative is more complex in its composition and resonances in ways that might nuance our ways forward. I have quoted from the published narrative that Merton edited from his original (at the time) more private journal.[48] The original gives more theological content in its links to incarnation and sophia (wisdom) as linked to greater appreciation of the feminine. The process of creating narrative from experience is complex for Merton, as for Macfarlane, and requires deep reflection, reworking, and a careful grasp of language and theology. This particular narrative has been refined to highlight the connections of love that unite all people and, indeed, all creation. The ordinary – a shopping street – remains itself whilst pointing people to other ordinaries, the people in other places, through transformational epiphanies in the Spirit.[49] There is much to learn from Merton even if

---

47. Merton, *Conjectures of a Guilty Bystander*, 156–57.

48. Thomas Merton, *A Search for Solitude: Pursuing the Monk's True Life*, ed. Lawrence S. Cunningham, The Journals of Thomas Merton 3 (San Francisco: Harper, 1996), 181–82.

49. These are the "epiphanies of connectedness" that are seen in this narrative and Merton's wider writing by Mary C. Grey, *Prophecy and Mysticism: The Heart of the Postmodern Church* (Edinburgh: T&T Clark, 1997).

his approach remains at a distance from ecological action and is at times overly positive. These were still early days in environmental consciousness; we need to turn to more recent writers to help us find ways forward.

Douglas Christie explores contemplative practices that might develop a contemplative ecology, an imagination in our terms, that might help us see the world more clearly and motivate action to protect the environment.[50] From a more Reformed perspective, Belden Lane emphasizes the role of the storyteller in developing a religious imagination that will connect people with the environment.[51] There is more work to be done but the aim has been to illustrate how nature writing generally and as developing with the Christian tradition might contribute towards a greater ecological imagination within Pentecostalism.

Reimagining Ecotheology After Pentecost

This chapter has identified a problem in Pentecostal theological method in regard to ecological issues, notably that, despite their inherent narrative basis, they lack contemporary narratives that feed imaginative action. We have suggested a way forward through finding the Spirit at work on the edge, with some examples from the writing of Macfarlane illustrating how narratives might help us reimagine Pentecost. This was developed further through the spiritual narratives of Merton whose faith-shaped narratives also have much to contribute. We have moved from method to its use although remain guilty, like Yong and Vondey, of abstaining from recommendations for action. The aim is to clear the way for better future action alongside those beyond the church, for which other examples are given in this book.

Reflecting further on methodology, there needs to be a move in Pentecostal systematic theology from grounding method in narrative (notably Pentecost and early Pentecostalism) towards including the ecological voices on the edge. These should form a vital part of the "many tongues" that together shape the pneumatological imagination and stimulate further theology and performative action.[52] If we are to take seriously Pentecost as "the core symbol of Pentecostalism" which needs to be taken "seriously for an articulation of Pentecostal theology," then we need to appreciate how this "given" interacts

---

50. Douglas E. Christie, *The Blue Sapphire of the Mind: Notes for a Contemplative Ecology* (New York: Oxford University Press, 2013).

51. Belden C. Lane, *Landscapes of the Sacred: Geography and Narrative in American Spirituality* (Baltimore: Johns Hopkins University Press, (1988) 2002).

52. To use the terminology of Yong, "pneumatological imagination."

with the "found."[53] At the heart of Pentecost the Holy Spirit is "found" and discerned within and beyond the followers of Jesus, but articulated in ways that bring (reflected on) experience into dialogue with the "givens" of Scripture and tradition.[54] This naturally overlaps with aspects of practical theology, although the concern here is to stretch systematic approaches.[55] In terms of ecological issues, it is vital that Pentecostal theology is brought into dialogue with the Spirit discerned in contemporary nature writing as well as Pentecostal testimony to environmental change. To develop an environmental theology without these would be to leave the imagination starved of life-giving insights, as has sadly often been the case.

I have suggested that this development might lead to an ecological theology, one approach within the wider ecotheological landscape where ecology is a concept rooted in connectedness before it is applied to either the environment or theology. This concept has a rich history rooted in the development of contemporary views of nature, including the Romantic movement that influenced Merton.[56] Theologically, we can see this concept beneath many approaches to the nature and work of the Holy Spirit, the "go-between God" who is always moving between Father and Son, between the triune God and all in the world, sustaining and enlivening.[57] There is room here to develop our understanding of the ecological Spirit as the "connector" in classical theology as well as in much contemporary theology of the Spirit's creative presence. All can be brought together in life through the moving breath/wind of the Spirit who anoints all flesh with flames of love and truth. Living as we do after Pentecost, it is incumbent on us to stretch our imaginations through fresh engagement with the Pentecost narrative, the narratives of early Pentecostalism, and the narratives of today.

---

53. To extend the approach of Vondey, *Pentecostal Theology*, 282.

54. Pointing here in the direction of an integration of Pentecostal theology and Quash's *Found Theology*.

55. For a movement in the opposite direction (from practical to deeper theological engagement) see Mark J. Cartledge, *Mediation of the Spirit: Interventions in Practical Theology*, Pentecostal Manifestos Series (Grand Rapids: Eerdmans, 2015).

56. Here the narrative historical work of Andrea Wulf is significant. See *The Invention of Nature: The Adventures of Alexander von Humboldt, the Lost Hero of Science* (London: John Murray, 2015) and *Magnificent Rebels: The First Romantics and the Invention of the Self* (London: John Murray, 2022). There are also recent relevant philosophical insights such as Timothy Morton, *Being Ecological* (London: Pelican, 2018). I am grateful to Dr Rich Genyer, a biological geographer, for this reference.

57. John V. Taylor, *The Go-Between God: The Holy Spirit and the Christian Mission* (London: SCM, 1972).

This resonates with the development of ecological missiology that expands its concern from personal conversion narratives, communal (church) transformation narratives, and even social action narratives towards creative ecological narratives. Mission has often been articulated through the narratives arising from the missionary movement and more recent missional and contextual church practice. For some, these have given rise to a shift from mission to world Christianity whilst often still neglecting narratives of ecological engagement.[58] There needs to be a further shift towards ecological mission that will engage more fully with the Spirit of creation who is testified to in narratives of action that are both local and global in nature. In this task, dialogue with the narratives of writers beyond the church who share ecological concerns offers the promise of imaginative approaches that bring the future and present together in creative action.

Conclusion

This chapter has explored a missing element in Pentecostal systematic theology, namely, engagement with contemporary narratives in relation to nature. Given the Pentecostal roots in narrative, we have suggested the need for testimonies at a time of environmental crisis to form an integral part of our theological and missiological method. How this might work has been explored in relation to one contemporary nature writer and one early Christian contributor to the environmental movement. This is a challenge to our methodology, challenging us to find the Spirit at work in a wider sphere than we often assume. It is a challenge to our imaginations which often lack connection with the land we live in and the changes that affect us all. Finally, it is a missional challenge to reimagine action from a position of seeing more clearly both the needs and our part in the crisis, as well as the beauty and connections that already exist and point to a better future. There is still much to be done but human creative imagination continues to flourish as does more engaged Pentecostal theology and mission practice. May the Spirit continue to breathe life into our minds, hearts, and hands as we face the future of the world together.

---

58. A good introduction to the shifts in mission thinking over recent decades can be found in Joel Cabrita, David Maxwell, and Emma Wild-Wood, *Relocating World Christianity: Interdisciplinary Studies in Universal and Local Expressions of the Christian Faith* (Leiden: Brill, 2017).

Bibliography

Cabrita, Joel, David Maxwell, and Emma Wild-Wood. *Relocating World Christianity: Interdisciplinary Studies in Universal and Local Expressions of the Christian Faith.* Leiden: Brill, 2017.

Cartledge, Mark J. *The Mediation of the Spirit: Interventions in Practical Theology.* Pentecostal Manifestos Series. Grand Rapids: Eerdmans, 2015.

———. *Testimony in the Spirit: Rescripting Ordinary Pentecostal Theology.* Farnham: Routledge, 2010.

———. *Testimony: Its Importance, Place and Potential.* Cambridge: Grove, 2002.

Christie, Douglas E. *The Blue Sapphire of the Mind: Notes for a Contemplative Ecology.* New York: Oxford University Press, 2013.

———. "Nature Writing and Nature Mysticism." In *Routledge Handbook of Religion and Ecology*, edited by Mary Evelyn Tucker, John Grim, and Willis Jenkins, 227–34. London: Routledge, 2018.

Davis, Anita. "Pentecostal Approaches to Ecotheology: Reviewing the Literature." *Australasian Pentecostal Studies* 2, no. 1 (2021): 4–33.

Deane-Drummond, Celia. *Eco-Theology.* London: Darton, Longman & Todd, 2008.

Grey, Mary C. *Prophecy and Mysticism: The Heart of the Postmodern Church.* Edinburgh: T&T Clark, 1997.

Jamie, Kathleen. "A Lone Enraptured Male." *London Review of Books* 30, no. 5 (2008): 25–27.

Kärkkäinen, Veli-Matti. *A Constructive Christian Theology for the Pluralistic World*, Vol. 3, *Creation and Humanity.* Grand Rapids: Eerdmans, 2015.

Labrie, Ross. *Thomas Merton and the Inclusive Imagination.* Columbia: University of Missouri Press, 2001.

Lamp, Jeffrey S. "Ecotheology: A People of the Spirit for Earth." In *The Routledge Handbook of Pentecostal Theology*, edited by Wolfgang Vondey, 357–66. London: Routledge, 2020.

Lane, Belden C. *Landscapes of the Sacred: Geography and Narrative in American Spirituality.* 1988. Reprint, Baltimore: Johns Hopkins University Press, 2002.

Lord, Andy. *Spirit-Shaped Mission: A Holistic Charismatic Missiology.* Carlisle: Paternoster, 2005.

———. *Transforming Renewal: Charismatic Renewal Meets Thomas Merton.* Eugene: Wipf & Stock, 2015.

Ma, Julie C., and Wonsuk Ma. *Mission in the Spirit: Towards a Pentecostal/Charismatic Missiology.* Eugene: Wipf & Stock, 2010.

Macfarlane, Robert. *Is a River Alive?* London: Penguin, Hamish Hamilton, 2025.

———. *Landmarks.* London: Penguin, 2016.

———. *Underland: A Deep Time Journey.* London: Penguin, Hamish Hamilton, 2019.

———. *The Wild Places.* London: Granta, 2017.

Merton, Thomas. *Conjectures of a Guilty Bystander.* London: Burns & Oates, 1968.

———. *The Inner Experience: Notes on Contemplation*, edited with notes by William H. Shannon. London: SPCK, 2003.

———. *A Search for Solitude: Pursuing the Monk's True Life*, edited by Lawrence S. Cunningham. The Journals of Thomas Merton 3. San Francisco: Harper, 1996.

———. *The Seven Storey Mountain*. New York: Harcourt, Brace and Company, 1948. London: Sheldon, 1975.

———. *Woods, Shore, Desert*. Santa Fe: Museum of New Mexico, 1982.

———. *Zen and the Birds of Appetite*. New York: New Directions, 1968.

———. *An Introduction to Christian Mysticism*, edited and introduced by Patrick F. O'Connell. Kalamazoo: Cistercian, 2008.

Morton, Timothy. *Being Ecological*. London: Pelican, 2018.

Okri, Ben. *Tiger Work*. London: Head of Zeus, 2023.

Parker, Russ. *The Wild Spirit*. London: Triangle, 1997.

Quash, Ben. *Found Theology: History, Imagination and the Holy Spirit*. London: T&T Clark, 2013.

Rice, Jonathan W. "Ecology and the Future of Pentecostalism: Problems, Possibilities and Proposals." In *Pentecostal Mission and Global Christianity*, edited by Wonsuk Ma, Veli-Matti Kärkkäinen, and J. Kwabena Asamoah-Gyadu, 360–79. Oxford: Regnum, 2014.

Shepherd, Nan. *The Living Mountain: A Celebration of the Cairngorm Mountains of Scotland*. Edinburgh: Canongate, 2011.

Swoboda, A. J. *Tongues and Trees: Toward a Pentecostal Ecological Theology*. Journal of Pentecostal Theology Supplement Series 40. Blandford Forum: Deo, 2014.

Taylor, John V. *The Go-Between God: The Holy Spirit and the Christian Mission*. London: SCM, 1972.

Vondey, Wolfgang. *Beyond Pentecostalism: The Crisis of Global Christianity and the Renewal of the Theological Agenda*. Pentecostal Manifestos. Grand Rapids: Eerdmans, 2011.

———. *Pentecostal Theology: Living the Full Gospel*. London: T&T Clark, 2017.

Walton, Heather. *Not Eden: Spiritual Life Writing for This World*. London: SCM, 2015.

Wulf, Andrea. *The Invention of Nature: The Adventures of Alexander von Humboldt, the Lost Hero of Science*. London: John Murray, 2015.

———. *Magnificent Rebels: The First Romantics and the Invention of the Self*. London: John Murray, 2022.

Yong, Amos. *Discerning the Spirit(s): A Pentecostal–Charismatic Contribution to Christian Theology of Religions*. Journal of Pentecostal Theology Supplement Series 20. Sheffield: Sheffield Academic Press, 2000.

———. *Mission After Pentecost: The Witness of the Spirit from Genesis to Revelation*. Mission in Global Community. Grand Rapids: Baker Academic, 2019.

———. "The Pneumatological Imagination: The Logic of Pentecostal Theology." In *The Routledge Handbook of Pentecostal Theology*, edited by Wolfgang Vondey, 152–62. London: Routledge, 2020.

———. *The Spirit of Creation: Modern Science and Divine Action in the Pentecostal–Charismatic Imagination*. Grand Rapids: Eerdmans, 2011.

———. *The Spirit Poured Out on All Flesh: Pentecostalism and the Possibility of Global Theology*. Grand Rapids: Baker Academic, 2005.

18

Knowing God's Mission as Creation Care

A Missional Pentecostal Ecclesiological Conversation

Eugene Baron

The relation between God's mission (*missio Dei*), and the positionality of the church, has taken shape through the discourses on mission theology and missional ecclesiology. One of the positions taken is that the church is an important agent in God's mission to the world, including the care for his creation. Nevertheless, the challenge that this chapter wrestles with is *how* the church allows congregants during worship services to become aware of such a reality and their responsibility in the *missio Dei* in terms of creation care. In pursuit of this objective, the chapter first discusses the role of the church as God's agent (missionary nature of the church) in caring for creation. The second section of the chapter discusses the worship service as a locus for missional consciousness. The third section discusses different epistemologies that could function in the worship service of churches as a space for preparing congregants for God's mission. Section four assesses the missional worship discourses of ecumenical scholars in terms of the epistemological dimensions and perspectives in relation to missional worship. The conclusive argument of the chapter is that multiple *episteme* should be explored to communicate and assist congregants to understand their mission as creation care during worship services, but that a Pentecostal perspective is still quite under-utilized and under-prioritized in discourses of missional worship. We take into account that missional worship is still a discourse dominated by ecumenical scholars.

The Church is God's Participant in the *Missio Dei*

The church has been argued by numerous scholars to be God's agent in the world.[1] This is not taken for granted as there are different perspectives on the positionality of the church in terms of the *missio Dei* discourse.[2] Some argue for the primacy of the church as part of the *missio Dei* in the world, but further argue that the church should be tilted towards the world (kingdom of God). However, other mission theologians radicalize the view of Hoekendijk[3] and argue that God is at work in the world, whether the church is part of the *missio Dei* or not. This discourse suggests that the church could be circumvented in God's mission in the world.[4] This has been labelled as a secular view and conceptualization of the *missio Dei*. George Vicedom, and more especially Karl Barth's work at the Brandenburg Conference in 1932, is credited for the former understanding of the *missio Dei*, in which the church is at the centre of God's mission in the world. The chapter is framed within such a missiological paradigm.

This discussion was taken further in the 1990s through the Gospel in Our Culture Network (GOCN) that took up this task after scholars such as

---

1. The most prominent scholar that defends this view is found in the work of Wilhelm Richebacher, "The Basis of Mission Theology or the Wrong Path," *International Review of Mission* 92, no. 367 (2009): 599–605. See also works such as Johannes J. Knoetze and Paul Verryn, "Migrants, Missio Dei and the Church in South Africa," in *The Human Dilemma of Displacement: Towards a Practical Theology and Ecclesiology of Home*, ed. Alfred R. Brunsdon (Durbanville: AOSIS, 2021), 171–87; Godfrey Harold, "An Evangelical Understanding of the Missio Dei as the Inclusion of Social Justice: A Critical Theological Reflection," *Pharos Journal of Theology* 100 (2019): 1–10; and C. J. P. Niemandt, "Ontluikende Kerke – 'n Nuwe Missionêre Beweging, Deel 1: Ontluikende Kerke as Prototipes van 'n Nuwe Missionêre Kerk," *Verbum et Ecclesia* 29, no. 1 (2008): 139–71.

2. See Richebacher, "The Basis of Mission Theology or the Wrong Path," in which he considers the main tensions on the role of the church in the *missio Dei* discussion.

3. See his work, J. C, Hoekendijk, *The Church Inside Out: Adventures in Faith* (London: SCM, 1976).

4. See these opposing views and perspectives in the work of Richebacher, "The Basis of Mission Theology or the Wrong Path." See also the discussion of Michael W. Stroope in *Transcending Mission: The Eclipse of a Modern Tradition* (Downers Grove: InterVarsity, 2017), 7, in which he writes "Describing mission as the action of God in world history or as Jubilee proclamation captures this wide and inclusive sense of the term. The focus is on God's liberating acts in world history through a myriad of forms and many agents. Such action may or may not include human participation and may even exclude the church."

Lesslie Newbigin became concerned about the re-evangelizing of the West. The GOCN and the Fresh Expressions of Church (FXoC) movement in the United Kingdom (UK) have reflected on the nature of the church in different contexts. This was not aimed merely at their own North American and UK (in terms of the FXoC) contexts, it also became a way in which scholars in the global South were encouraged to embrace such a particular (missional) discourse and praxis. In the terms of such a discourse, the nature of the church should shift radically – from church-centered to God-centred. The missionary nature of the church was interpreted to be a focus on the kingdom of God, not an ecclesiocentric vision. This idea of the missionary nature of the church was not merely adopted in its embryonic stages by Reformed (GOCN) and Anglican (especially FXoC) ecclesial traditions, but also by some Pentecostal churches. There are examples in the South African context where one of the mainline Pentecostal churches, the Apostolic Faith Mission, for instance, adopted such an agenda, cooperated, and created vision plans/statements for their denomination.[5] Nevertheless, this could not be said to be the same in all cases, especially the independent Pentecostal churches which do not always subject themselves to academic, theoretical discourses in the same way as Reformed churches. However, without drawing them into an existing ecclesiological paradigm, and perhaps even stifling their own agency in terms of contributing to the missional church paradigm, it might be useful to reflect on how they could contribute as an ecclesial tradition, and most particularly their epistemological contribution.

One of the arguments of missional church scholars is that the church is not an enclave,[6] but a dialectic community in the world.[7] This is congruent with Newbigin's description of the local church as a "hermeneutic of the gospel," one that is involved in the "concerns of the neighbourhood" and that exercises

---

5. The AFM-SA states on its website, "The AFM is a missional movement with a passion for soul winning. This missionality is the foundation and underlying motivation of everything we do as a church. The 'One AFM Game Plan' is the name we use for a communication process that aims to re-focus the church on all its leadership levels, with the original calling of the AFM. At the heart of its intent lies the Great Commission, a desire to see the AFM returning to its missional roots, where every AFM member is a powerful witness and soul-winner in their community and on the marketplace." See their webpage for this information: https://afm-ags.org/leading-the-afm/one-afm-game-plan/.

6. This has often been the critique that has been launched at the ecclesiological understanding of Stanley Hauerwas.

7. See, for instance, Tormod Engelsviken who supports this perspective in "Missio Dei: The Understanding and Misunderstanding of a Theological Concept in European Churches and Missiology," *International Review of Mission* 92, no. 367 (2003): 481–97. However, in my own view, his rhetoric rather suggests an ecclesiocentric view of mission.

"priesthood in the world."[8] Yong stretches the argument when he engages Newbigin's notion and argues that this hermeneutic of the gospel is made possible by the engineering of the Spirit of God and the Spirit's indwelling in the church (congregants).[9] He traces the pneumatological dimension in the trinitarian mission of Newbigin, which allows the epistemology of mission (as *missio Dei*) to find a home in a Pentecostal mission and ecclesiology. However, it is in this sense that Yong's proposal for a "pneumatological imagination" could assist the re-imagination and the possibility of such a dialogical relationship between the church and the world, not as mutually exclusive but through mutual interdependence. The church/world/science dialogical relationship is possible through the Pentecost event (Acts 2), where the Spirit made possible a hermeneutic for the plurality of the gospel during the embryonic stages of the church.

Furthermore, one of the progenitors of GOCN, Darrell Guder describes the church as incarnational.[10] In terms of his argument, the church is therefore simultaneously shaped by its social context as it also shapes its local context. The church that shares in the *missio Dei* should be in a dialogical relationship with the rest of the inhabited world in which God is actively participating. It is in this sense that the role of God's agents, including the church, is argued to play a role in God's creation as well. God's mission as creation care has been affirmed by Niemandt[11] with his reference to "deep incarnation" as a missional approach. It is to reimagine God as reaching into the depth of the cosmos through the incarnation of Jesus Christ and therefore Jesus's sensitivity towards all of creation. From a Catholic perspective, Schlesinger[12] engages Pope Francis's encyclical of *Evangelii Gaudium* to also discuss how ecological concerns have been articulated by the Pope (official Catholic position) as part of the *missio Dei*. In terms of the Pope, the *missio Dei* has to do with the "decentering of humans" as well as the salvation of humans (from their anthropocentric positioning) in an attempt to explore God's agenda for the

---

8. Lesslie Newbigin, *The Gospel in a Pluralist Society* (Grand Rapids: Eerdmans, 1989), 222–33.

9. Amos Yong, "Pluralism, Secularism, and Pentecost Newbigin-ings for Missio Trinitatis in a New Century," in *The Gospel and Pluralism Today: Reassessing Lesslie Newbigin for the 21st Century*, eds. Scott W. Sunquist and Amos Yong (Downers Grove: IVP Academic, 2015), 153.

10. Darrell L. Guder, *Missional Church: A Vision for the Sending of the Church in North America* (Grand Rapids: Eerdmans, 1998), 14.

11. Niemandt, "The Missio Dei as Flourishing Life," *Eccesial Futures* 1, no. 1 (2020): 11–30.

12. Eugene R. Schlesinger, "A Trinitarian Basis for a 'Theological Ecology' in Light of Laudato Si,'" *Theological Studies* 79, no. 2 (2018): 339–55.

flourishing of creation. This is quite an interesting perspective of a tradition that has been argued to place a high premium on the salvation of the church to firmly support the idea of a church in community with the rest of creation, society, and the world.

The Church's Worship Service and Liturgy as Locus of Missional Consciousness

In a *missio Dei* paradigm, mission and worship are not distinct activities, in fact, for Schattauer mission *is* worship.[13] The matter of church worship (through liturgy) in which members become conscious of their agency in the *missio Dei* has become also a crucial conversation in missional theology.[14] Meyers,[15] who also ground her work mainly on that of Schattauer,[16] argues that missional worship is not in essence about techniques, but about a different approach to liturgy; it is when the congregation during their worship "enact and signify the love of God for the world." This, she argues, comes close to the root meaning of the Latin word for "liturgy" to imply "public service," which supports the understanding of liturgy as the church's offering on behalf of the world.

Schattauer has made some significant contributions to the connection between mission theology and worship and argues that the worshipping assembly is the locus of the *missio Dei*.[17] It is the place where God, during the worship and fellowship of the local assembly, "manifests his reconciling love," and where the emphasis is not per se on the activity of the local assembly, but on "seeing God at work."[18] In his description, the experience(s) of God during worship from members of the congregation, is in fact how they experience God's mission (worship *is* mission). However, perhaps interestingly, he discusses other ways in which scholars have articulated the relationship between mission and worship where (1) the worship service prepares and nurtures congregants to go out and do mission or (2) where mission is brought into the worship ser-

---

13. Thomas Schattauer, ed., *Inside Out: Worship in An Age of Mission* (Minneapolis: Fortress, 1999), 3.

14. See other contributions of Eugene Baron on the notion of missional consciousness, for example, "The Call for African Missional Consciousness through Renewed Mission Praxis in URCSA," *Studia Historiae Ecclesiasticae* 45, no. 3 (2019): 1–19.

15. Ruth Meyers, *Missional Worship, Worshipful Mission: Gathering as God's People, Going Out in God's Name* (Grand Rapids: Eerdmans, 2014).

16. Schattauer, *Inside Out*.

17. Schattauer, *Inside Out*, 36.

18. Schattauer, *Inside Out*, 36.

vice, for example "seeker" services, or social justice activities in the church. His preference is for the experience of God during worship as an expression of the *missio Dei* (missional worship).

Schattauer's argument is that the church is assembled amidst the world and is God's visible locus of his work in the world. There is for Schattauer not an abyss between church, world, and mission, but these three are integrated during the worship service.[19] Often these three are argued to be mutually exclusive within many theological traditions but, within missional theology and particularly apparent in the work of Schattauer, these three find integration in a *missio Dei* paradigm and are *not* mutually exclusive.[20] It is in this regard that Pentecostal worship might be able to contribute more to this discussion – because of its integration of those three elements – at least its praxis.[21] Numerous missional church theologians argue that the dichotomy of the "world, church (worship), mission" should be deconstructed because through worship we engage the "real world" and simultaneously engage with God's world which is not a "pie-in-the-sky." Though this discussion becomes more and more relevant through the work of Protestant theologians, this has become a praxis within Pentecostal worship services because of its *experiential* epistemology, which many missional theologians from the Reformed Protestant tradition might be still struggling to deconstruct and to reimagine ecclesiology. In Pentecostal scholarship, this discussion has already received attention. For instance, the ethnographic work of Björkander on how praise and worship in Pentecostal worship contribute to theology, as much as other theological modes, such as academic teaching of theology.[22] Furthermore, Pentecostal scholarship has engaged the issue of mediated experience in terms of how the context influences the experience of God during worship.

---

19. Schattauer, *Inside Out*, 36.

20. See, for instance, van Engen on the visibility and invisibility of the church, as one that is beyond its institutionality, but one that is invisible as the salt and the light of the world. It is different from that which dialectic theologians, such as Barth, conceptualize between faith and religion, church and the secular (world). Charles van Engen, *Mission on the Way: Issues in Mission Theology* (Grand Rapids: Baker Academic, 1996), 223–24.

21. The latest substantive source on Pentecostal worship can be seen in the work of Martina Björkander, *Worship, Ritual, and Pentecostal Spirituality-as-Theology: A Rhythm that Connects Our Hearts with God* (Leiden: Brill, 2024).

22. Björkander, *Worship, Ritual*.

Epistemological Routes to *Missio Dei*: A Pentecostal Epistemological Contribution

This section focuses primarily on the work of James Smith, as well as Yong's engagement with the trinitarian missiology of Newbigin, to discuss the epistemological contribution of Pentecostalism. Smith contests the idea that rationality can only be articulated and framed in terms of intellectualism.[23] He laments the notion that *to know* is primarily acquired through propositions and the following of the strict principles of logical positivism (intellectualism). This is a fallacy that is proclaimed through the rhetoric of modernity. The epistemology of Western Christianity framed in the project of modernity (intellectualism) was aimed at countering superstition, myths, and faith systems – often expressed through religion. This epistemology of Western Christianity (intellectualism) would reject all *other* forms of knowing.

Newbigin argues that, as a result of claims of their irrelevance for the public sphere, faith traditions and religion were relegated to the private sphere since they were regarded as having no social value.[24] The epistemology that was embraced by Western Christianity reduced human beings to "thinking things." Other epistemologies have always been ridiculed; the Pentecostal tradition was since its inception rejected/ridiculed for making their truth claims on experiential knowledge. Nonetheless, the Pentecostal theologian Peter Neumann would refer to numerous ecumenical theologians to argue that the epistemology of experience is not novice since someone such as James Cone developed his contextual, black theology through his argument that the black, oppressed people are shaped by their black experience.[25] The notion of the cultural-linguistic approach by George Lindbeck (and subsequently numerous ecumenical theologians) serves as another fruitful theological discourse that paves the way for embracing an experiential epistemology. The notion implies that people relate to, construct, and give expression to their faith in terms of the culture and language they are situated in and interact with. Through various ecumenical theologians, such as Smith (himself a Reformed Christian philosopher), Neumann developed his argument on the legitimacy of experience as an epistemological category for Pentecostalism and, for that matter, Christian theology.

---

23. James K. A. Smith, *Thinking in Tongues: Pentecostal Contributions to Christian Philosophy* (Grand Rapids: Eerdmans, 2020).

24. See Lesslie Newbigin, *Foolishness to the Greeks: The Gospel and Western Culture* (Grand Rapids: Eerdmans, 1986).

25. Peter D. Neumann, *Pentecostal Experience: An Ecumenical Encounter* (Eugene: Wipf & Stock, 2012).

In his own postmodern approach, Smith provides room for discussion on other forms of episteme, beyond what modernism provided. He argues that the modernist epistemology has long been rejected by Pentecostalists because at the heart of their approach was a subjective, embodied, and emotive form of knowledge. This is observable in their worship services. Their worship services are mostly loosely structured and do not subscribe to rigid forms of worship.[26] My own experience as a regular attendee of such worship services was that congregants would often deliver their testimonies attesting to how God provided for their material needs through emotive, embodied storytelling; this could be as simple as the provision of "bread and sugar" at times when they did not know how they could put some food on the table. In their testimonies and their stories, the story of God (*missio Dei*) finds integration. Their bodies will tell the story of the goodness of the Lord – which some Reformed churches would regard as unfitting for a worship service and relegate it rather to some other "secular" mural activity and labelling it as "disorderly" and not proper theology.[27] However, the well-known Pentecostal scholar, Hollenweger, vehemently disagrees with the above, arguing that the opposite of a written form of liturgy is not chaos but part of oral theology.[28]

Although there are various cases of abuse of the mode of testimony in Pentecostal worship – for instance, self-glorification[29] and eccentric actions during worship services forming part of the sharing of testimonies and/or other parts of the liturgy of Pentecostal churches – there also might be various abuses in Reformed congregational worship. This forms some of the major critiques from some Reformed and ecumenical theologians and academics, labelling Pentecostalism as an irrational faith tradition, which Smith vehemently rejects as a distorted perception of what testimonies mean for the Pentecostal church. In terms of my own argument, it is not merely a matter of stories or experience per se but it is, in missiological terms, a storied missiology – a method of knowing God's action in the world.[30] It is this narrative approach (which might

---

26. This varies sociologically from Pentecostal-Charismatic churches that have been established by classical Pentecostal traditions, such as Assemblies of God and the Full Gospel Church. This can be seen in the description of the Pentecostal churches that Björkander researched in Kenya that had more structured liturgical services.

27. J. Kwabena Asamoah-Gyadu, *Contemporary Pentecostal Christianity: Interpretations from an African Context* (Oxford: Regnum, 2013).

28. Walter J. Hollenweger, *Pentecostalism: Origins and Developments Worldwide* (Peabody: Hendrickson, 1997), 271.

29. See Eugene Baron, *Becoming a Resilient Christian Community: A Narrative Approach* (Munster: LitVerlag, 2023), 21.

30. Eugene Baron, *Narrative Missiology* (Leiden: Brill, 2025).

constitute story *forms* or other forms like poetry, drama, etc.) that is conducive to unthink the Western forms of church and life, rejecting an epistemology that always reduces human beings to merely intellectual bodies that renders them irrelevant for their context. The missiological dimension in Smith's argument on stories is perhaps captured in his argument that the purpose or objectives of stories for Pentecostals is to make sense of God's involvement in the world. This can be traced back to how Peter (in Acts 2) went about explaining the disciples' experience to the audience that wanted to understand the happenings with them on Pentecost, weaving it into the "larger received narrative" (in history) to be able to say, "that is that."[31] Yong and other Pentecostal scholars use the same Pentecost event as a hermeneutic, a "pneumatological imagination" to understand the *missio Dei*.

Furthermore, the emphasis for Smith is on stories or testimonies as embodied by Pentecostals.[32] This form of knowledge should not be understood as merely another means to arrive at concepts and propositions, but functions as *legitimate knowledge* in itself, able to produce theology, that is, God-knowledge. Like Hollenweger, Smith situates Pentecostal theology within the confines of a "narrative theology" as opposed to discursive theology, that is, one not based on a system of thinking but theology through stories and songs.[33] This Pentecostal epistemology is affirming materiality and embodiment as a necessity to experience the Spirit's work and God's presence. For Pentecostalism, through one's bodily experience one comes to experience the truth of God. As Kwabena Asamoah-Gyadu argues, worship for Pentecostals is an authentic encounter with God.[34] Though Pentecostal adherents would be criticized for not spending too much time in intellectual or dogmatic forms of worship, they find their theology or mission of God in such embodied practices and liturgies. The ethnographic research of Prosén on Pentecostal worship as a mode of theology attests to the above argument.[35] Nevertheless, Crites's work on the *Narrative Quality of Experience* (1971) also shows the integration of reason and experience: the conflation of body and mind working in synchronization to construct

---

31. Smith, *Thinking in Tongues*, 52.
32. Smith, *Thinking in Tongues*, 52.
33. Hollenweger, *Pentecostalism*, 196.
34. J. Kwabena Asamoah-Gyadu, *African Charismatics: Current Developments within Independent Indigenous Pentecostalism in Ghana* (Leiden: Brill, 2005.)
35. Martina Prosén, "Pentecostal Praise and Worship as a Mode of Theology as a Mode of Theology," in *Faith in African Lived Christianity: Bridging Anthropological and Theological Perspectives*, eds. Karen Lauterbach and Mika Vähäkangas (Leiden: Brill, 2020), 167.

knowledge.[36] However, he argues that it is through one's bodily experience that one would first know and come to know reality and truth. In Pentecostalism, one's own bodily experiences connect you with the story of God.[37]

The rationality operative in a story or other aesthetics, which Smith[38] argues is present in Pentecostal epistemology, can be detected in two ways. He explains firstly that the exposure to certain emotions by congregants trains them how to act, behave, and function in certain circumstances and spaces in the future. Secondly, experience through storytelling is already a construal of the world and reflects the world as one knows it, but it also suggests how the world should be interpreted outside the worship service.

In various theological circles the idea and discussion around different forms of knowledge systems (Wittgenstein)[39] might be an issue to concede to, but the challenge of Smith's work is to see this being performed in worship services.[40] It is there where this embodied liturgy will be able to demonstrate God's mission in the world. Those who will wait for the delivery of the traditional sermon might feel awkward when at a Pentecostal worship service there might not be a sermon – because the knowledge has been performed, and in an intelligent way (rationality?): the story of God's redemption was constructed, or co-constructed, together by the Pentecostal worshiping community. The kind of bodily or embodied epistemology is already intelligent, as Smith would argue that the knowledge is already construed in the experience.

However, Smith goes further to suggest how Pentecostal spirituality through aesthetics and inclusive of drama, et cetera, can serve as an episteme within worship services. His argument that this form of epistemology can lead to re-imagination of the world and serve as epistemic grammar is quite interesting. According to Smith,[41] the re-imagination that Baron and Maponya[42] suggest is required for churches to become missional in nature could best happen through an experiential epistemology.

---

36. Stephen Crites, "The Narrative Quality of Experience," in *Why Narrative? Readings in Narrative Theology*, eds. Stanley Hauerwas and L. Gregory Jones (Grand Rapids: Eerdmans, 1989), 291.

37. See also Allan H. Anderson, *Introduction to Pentecostalism: Global Charismatic Christianity* (Cambridge: Cambridge University Press, 2004), 14.

38. Smith, *Thinking in Tongues*, 52.

39. See Ludwig Wittgenstein, *Philosophical Investigations* (Oxford: Basil Blackwell, 1958).

40. See Baron, *Becoming a Resilient Christian Community*.

41. Smith, *Thinking in Tongues*, 80–85.

42. Eugene Baron and Moses S. Maponya, "The Recovery of the Prophetic Voice of the Church: The Adoption of a 'Missional Church' Imagination," *Verbum et Ecclesia* 41, no. 1 (2020): 8.

Pentecostalism is already a "showing" and "displaying" and manifesting religion.[43] It is a religion that wants to feel, touch, see, et cetera. Therefore, it is confirmed implicitly by Pentecostals that "we are embodied, imaginative, affective, and narrative animals."[44] Thus, we can be drawn by narratives and dramas that get hold of our attention through our emotions and desires into a new world, and we can make assumptions about our world, the future world, and our actions. Through this, Pentecostals can be instrumental in re-narration and counter-narrations to competing stories. It would not be pointless to produce some good arguments, but in most cases, it would be more effective to have themed services and demonstrate the effects of ecological degradation on the environment within the church worship service. It would be further prudent to connect within the liturgy, sermons, and worship songs in creative ways to the creation narrative in Scripture, for example, with regard to the current water crises in the world. Smith therefore argues that a Pentecostal aesthetic also has a futuristic element attached to it as do cinematic movies, using metaphor to create hope in a world to come. Smith argues that the eschatological orientation of Pentecostalism and its worldview creates a hopeful positionality.[45] It positions its adherents towards an openness to possibilities, what Hermans would describe as a positionality of contingency.[46] In exercising a Pentecostal epistemology here, as well, or in support thereof, it might be more appropriate to conduct an action research project in which exposure is given to environmental crises and the ways in which they affect and move (or not) Pentecostal adherents to confront society with such challenges.

Yong's engagement on Pentecostal epistemology deserves some attention.[47] Yong's contribution to the epistemological dimension of Pentecostalism is done in conversation with Newbigin's discussion on a different "plausible structure"[48] in a pluralist society than that which the project of modernity provided. The idea of Newbigin that the gospel should be told and engage the larger narrative, including science, seems to be the motivation behind Yong's proposal that the Pentecostal event, the gift of languages, which presumes cultural and

---

43. Smith, *Thinking in Tongues*, 81.

44. Smith, *Thinking in Tongues*, 83.

45. Smith, *Thinking in Tongues*, 82.

46. Chris A. M. Hermans and Kobus Schoeman, eds., *Theology in an Age of Contingency*, International Practical Theology 21 (Zürich: LIT Verlag, 2019), 15.

47. Amos Yong, "Pluralism, Secularism, and Pentecost."

48. See Newbigin's discussion in his book *Foolishness to the Greeks* on the fact that to believe, or commit yourself to a particular knowledge system, whether it is facts or faith, is a plausible structure that needs its believers to legitimize it.

religious pluralism, serves as proof for Newbigin's argument that stories of the sciences and engagement with various sciences should be embraced by the church (which is the hermeneutic of the gospel). According to Yong, it is in this sense that these two (religion and science/creation) seem to impose an intersubjective social reality. Furthermore, it is through the Spirit that such knowledge of science is facilitated. It is the Spirit that mediates knowledge, the truth, through materiality, historicity, and the sociality of human integratedness. It is the Spirit who indwells Christians and guides us towards a plurality (in science and faith knowledges) of reason, experience, Scripture, and tradition. The notion and perspective of pneumatological imagination address the issue that experience is mediated through our traditions and subcultures, a concern for Neumann if we only suggest an experiential epistemology without including Yong's view.[49] The challenge of mediated experience has been also resolved by the Swedish Pentecostal, Martina Prosén.

Prosén would bring into her discussion the element of Pentecostal worship that is, in essence, serving as an epistemological resource to *know* God.[50] In her work, she emphasizes the ongoing process between text and context when it comes to constructing theology. These processes, she argues, take place where theology is lived, expressed, and reflected upon. This is therefore not merely in creeds, critical reflection upon Scriptures, or in confessions, but also in their expression through praise and worship, songs,[51] and testimonies. Yong argues in quite similar vein that the doctrines and theology of Pentecostal churches are present in their singing, worship, and personal lives and the gap between liturgy and theology could be much more narrow than might be assumed.[52] However, what Prosén's thesis shows is that theology emerges from the communal-spiritual experiences of believers.[53] Kwabena Asamoah-Gyadu describes worship in his chapter "Signs of the Spirit: Worship as Experience" as

---

49. See Peter D. Neumann's discussion on the mediation of experience through our own cultural-linguistic situatedness in his book, *Pentecostal Experience*, ch. 1.

50. See her book, resulting from her doctoral thesis, Björkander, *Worship, Ritual, and Pentecostal Spirituality-as-Theology*. See also Prosén's chapter, "Pentecostal Praise and Worship as a Mode of Theology."

51. For other work from Pentecostal scholars on the role of Pentecostals and music, see Monique Ingalls and Amos Yong, eds., *The Spirit of Praise: Music and Worship in Global Pentecostal-Charismatic Christianity* (University Park: The Pennsylvania State University Press, 2015).

52. Amos Yong, "Improvisation, Indigenization, and Inspiration: Theological Reflections on the Sound and Spirit of Global Renewal," in *The Spirit of Praise: Music and Worship in Global Pentecostal-Charismatic Christianity*, eds. Monique Ingalls and Amos Yong (University Park: The Pennsylvania State University Press, 2015), 281.

53. Björkander, *Worship, Ritual, and Pentecostal Spirituality-as-Theology*, 57.

an encounter and experience with the Spirit.⁵⁴ He also describes experience as a Spirit-infused encounter, which is inspiring and transformative in the life of the congregants.⁵⁵ All these conversations of Pentecostals show that experience is indeed mediated by the Spirit of God in relation to context and Scripture.

Ecumenical Contributions to Episteme and Missional Worship

The worship service is a moment where clergy and laity meet in a sacred space to be open to reimagining their participation in God's mission.⁵⁶ This has largely been a space for using one's intellectual and cognitive abilities to grasp their roles as members of the church. Shenk argues that modern mission practitioners and missiologists find themselves in the environment of the Enlightenment, following the same "spirit" of advancing the idea of reason against faith.⁵⁷ They were/are carriers of the rationalistic view of life. However, Langmead deems this approach (propositionally) as inadequate and suggests the use of imagination, and especially poetry, as essential episteme to make people aware of God's mission in the whole of creation.⁵⁸ It is important to keep these two paradigms (reason and experience) together, either striking a balance that keeps them in creative tension or equally accepting both modes as legitimate epistemological pathways to understanding God's mission. The Western approach, especially one that could be found in the missional church discourses, does make room for imagination, but it seems to be always an outcome of a propositional modernistic knowledge framework and process. It is not in a narrative form or an embodied form of knowledge expressed and articulated as a form of epistemology in the discourse on missional ecclesiology.

The following authors, mostly ecumenical, have written about missional worship, discussing how they have been able to integrate (or not) an experiential epistemology. In the missional church discourse, discussion on missional hermeneutics is crucial to understanding how people come to understand the purpose of God in the world. In the work of scholars such as Michael Goheen,

---

54. Asamoah-Gyadu, *Contemporary Pentecostal Christianity*, 18.

55. Asamoah-Gyadu, *Contemporary Pentecostal Christianity*, 19.

56. The most recent Pentecostal theology of worship that also addresses some of the missional dimensions of worship is that of Steven Felix-Jager, *Renewal Worship: A Theology of Pentecostal Doxology*, Dynamics of Christian Worship (Downers Grove: IVP Academic, 2022).

57. Wilbert R. Shenk, "The Relevance of a Messianic Missiology for Mission Today," in *The Transfiguration of Mission: Biblical, Theological, and Historical Foundations*, ed. Wilbert R. Shenk (Scottdale: Herald, 1993), 19.

58. Ross Langmead, "Ecomissiology," *Missiology* 30 (2002): 505–18.

the focus is on a particular hermeneutical reading of the Bible to understand God's purpose in Scripture, especially in understanding our (readers in front of the text's) role in God's mission on earth. In such cases, someone like N. T. Wright will refer to the meta-story of God's redemptive history to understand the biblical account of the *missio Dei*.[59] Nevertheless, the authors on missional hermeneutics do not necessarily discuss the dimension of experiential epistemology within the ecclesial and worship context. Although in the work of Yong as a Pentecostal theologian, Scripture and the epistemological category of experience find integration in his notion of pneumatological imagination, it is still questionable how ecumenical theologians have used this as another epistemological category when discoursing on missional worship.[60] Let me now discuss some contributions on missional ecclesiology and worship, and how some ecumenical theologians discuss epistemological dimensions in missional worship discourse. The following is drawn from a literature review on missional worship with the goal of understanding whether experiential epistemology has been integrated into such discourses.

Schattauer, as a Lutheran missional theologian, has embarked on understanding how missional worship can engage culture or contemporary life.[61] He commenced by discussing how the assembly is the locus of the *missio Dei*, focusing on the eucharistic prayer in which the assembly proclaims and remembers the liberating mission of God. The "assembling" of the congregation itself is God's work (*missio Dei*) as well as the eschatological element of the eucharist in which the assembly focuses, not merely on the past but on the present and the future as well. The symbolic aspects of the liturgy remind the assembly of a different reality, an eschatological one. Schattauer argues that what is still missing is how the manifestation of God is integrated with his world and contemporary life and how that happens.

Wepener, a Reformed theologian in South Africa, draws his research data from missional church discussions in South Africa, arguing that missional liturgy is primarily God directed and focused upon discernment regarding calling and mission and exactly who God is. Then he cautions that one should

---

59. See the following authors who focus on the missional reading of the Bible: Christopher J. H. Wright, *The Mission of God: Unlocking the Bible's Grand Narrative* (Downer Grove: IVP Academic, 2018); Michael W. Goheen, *A Light to the Nations: The Missional Church and the Biblical Story* (Grand Rapids: Baker Academic, 2011); Dean Flemming, *Why Mission?* (Nashville: Abingdon, 2015); and Michael J. Gorman, *Becoming the Gospel: Paul, Participation, and Mission* (Grand Rapids: Eerdmans, 2015).

60. See discussion in Yong, "Pluralism, Secularism, and Pentecost."

61. Schattauer, *Inside Out*, 37.

be conscious of all the kinds of distraction within the liturgy, also because of the possibility that one of these distracting poles is sometimes dished up to congregations and worship leaders as being "missional."[62] It is not quite clear what he means by distracting poles; however, from commentaries on worship from Reformed theologians, it might be the focus on more bodily expressions. Nevertheless, his Reformed roots are apparent in the way he discusses how congregants come to a missional consciousness during worship. He argues that the liturgy should allow the Word [Scripture] to assist the congregation in understanding what is expected of them and let the epistemological or hermeneutical process incarnate into the worship act and into worshippers' lives. He further suggests that *to know* God's mission happens through a pneumatological interaction between worshippers and the Scripture. I quote, "preaching should take the world of secularised people into account and invite them to become part of God's kingdom in the world."[63] Interestingly so, the *how* is not explicitly articulated at all. A noteworthy challenge in his discussion on missional epistemology is the dichotomizing of the theological and the anthropological dimensions in the liturgy, especially such an understanding and the physical movement in Pentecostal worship. Nevertheless, one is left to believe that Wepener's appropriation of missional worship is that God's voice can also be discerned in "culture and creation" and not, as expected from a Reformed theologian, in a narrow articulation of the notion of *sola scriptura*.[64]

Closer to an experience epistemology in the discourse of missional ecclesiology is Lisel Joubert's attempt as a Reformed theologian to look at ways in which spirituality operated in the early church.[65] One of her discoveries is how early Christians reflected on God through metaphorical language about God, converting it to metaphors, rhyme, and art. Through this, she argues, God became proclaimed beyond mere words and conceptualizations via aesthetics. Joubert acknowledges that the idea of God as beauty does not sit well with Protestant theologians, because God (in terms of their epistemology) can only be accessed through a rational (intellectual) process, which makes any other epistemological means elusive.[66] As a rhetorical device in her work, she

---

62. Cas Wepener, "Towards a Missional Liturgy," *NGTT: Dutch Reformed Theological Journal* 49, no. 1/2 (2008): 213–17.

63. Wepener, "Towards a Missional Liturgy," 214.

64. Wepener, "Towards a Missional Liturgy," 216.

65. Lisel Joubert, "Ecclesiology, Spirituality, and the Early Church," in *Missional Ecclesiology: Participation in the Mission of the Triune God*, extended version, eds. Coenie Burger, Frederick Marais, and Pieter van der Walt (Wellington: Bible Media, 2021), 68.

66. Joubert, "Ecclesiology, Spirituality, and the Early Church," 69.

conducts a historical review of the performance of the worship of the early church through the means of aesthetics to convince her Reformed readers interested in missional ecclesiology. As an insider of the Reformed school of thought, Joubert courageously pushes for an understanding of worship as a witness (mission). If this is done, it would be possible to even employ aesthetics to reimagine a new vision of God in the world.

Another contribution from a Reformed scholar on missional worship is Muller's discussion on the contribution of the African Independent Churches (AIC).[67] His work is interesting because, as a Reformed scholar, he endorses a different epistemology within the missional ecclesiological discourse, mainly for a Reformed audience. His discussion equalizes Reformed missional worship with that of Pentecostal expressions found in the worship services of the AIC. In terms of his argument, it is evident that their embodied worship practices and their experiences of God through activities of the Spirit are not merely means to an end (a Sola Scriptura approach), but ends in themselves.[68]

Brown, who is a Presbyterian, discusses how people in a worship service can be concientized and prepared to understand God's presence outside of church walls.[69] Her discussion is relevant to missional worship since it addresses the way in which the worship service could make congregants aware of God's mission in the world. Though she mentions numerous conditions, let us for the relevance of this chapter, focus on two. She first argues that the rhetoric of worship services should not emphasize what *we* must do, but what God has *already* done, *is* doing, and *will* do to make future things new. The epistemological dimension is introduced when she suggests the inclusion of the arts of poetry, song, images, and dance as ways in which worship leaders/ liturgists could make congregants aware of the promises of the triune God. The missional dimension of such worship finds expression in the awareness of congregations that God who gives life to the dead not only sends us, but

---

67. Harvey G. Cox, *Fire from Heaven: The Rise of Spirituality and the Reshaping of Religion in the Twenty-First Century* (Reading: Addison-Wesley, 1995) described the AICs as an African expression of the global Pentecostal movement.

68. Reteif Muller's "African Initiated Churches in South Africa: Giving Expression to an Embodied Gospel," in *Missional Ecclesiology: Participation in the Mission of the Triune God*, eds. Coenie Burger, Frederick Marais, and Pieter van der Walt (Wellington: Bible Media, 2021), 168–83, is argued by Smith to be the contribution of Pentecostal epistemology in which stories are not part of scaffolding towards the truth, but the truth is in that kind of epistemology (i.e. narratives). He argues that it is often the narrative forms which are most often embedded in metaphor – poetry, music, and theatre – that allow us to re-imagine.

69. Sally A. Brown, "Discerning the Public Presence of God," *Theology Today* 70, no. 1 (2013): 35.

precedes us, into our urban streets, suburban playgrounds, and coastal flood plains. With eyes wide open to God's presence and promise, we can move into such spaces filled not with apprehension but with courage and creativity, ready to act as agents of redemptive hope.[70]

Bradley, a Baptist scholar, also provides some interesting perspectives on the missional qualities of music, something in which Pentecostals were a forerunner, in terms of the contextualization that music provides and the embodiment of doctrines and beliefs, that is, performing the gospel.[71] This is perhaps something that we do not see within Reformed churches that propose missional worship. He argues that music has a way to draw those even outside of the boundaries of the church. But how do songs assist us in knowing God's mission? Bradley argues that music by itself is a missional agent in shaping theological views and helping our missional positionality, and therefore songs should be written that will shape such behaviours and attitudes.

Nevertheless, the most influential and important work documented by the missional church theologians is in the book *Missional Church: A Vision for the Sending of the Church in North America* (1998), which is the product of the research group GOCN, particularly in one of its contributions focusing on how missional communities are cultivated. One of the arguments is made of the experiential nature of practices that cultivate and engender missional communities.[72] In GOCN's view, the focus should be on the physical and emotional presence of members in the church services as participating in communal practices is needed to develop missional communities – communities that will be directed towards the world and God's concerns. Since this book is a "primer" contribution to the field of missional ecclesiology, one expected a more robust inclusion of an experiential epistemological discussion within it.

Conclusion: Missional Worship, Epistemology and Creation Care

Though Marumo and van der Merwe would not employ the concept of missional church, linking the church's role to that of the concept *missio Dei* suffices to illustrate how they would argue for missional worship to serve as space for

---

70. Brown, "Discerning the Public Presence of God," 37.

71. C. Randall Bradley, *From Memory to Imagination:. Reforming the Church's Music* (Grand Rapids: Eerdmans, 2012), 142.

72. Guder, *Missional Church*, 156.

addressing ecological degradation.[73] Written from a Reformed perspective with one of these authors being a Reformed minister, their approach is interesting in the way that they argue for ritual/liturgy to be instrumental in awareness of ecological degradation and one's contribution to God's mission. Though this is laudable, they have not written much on how they perceive and prioritize such forms of knowledge through song and rituals/liturgy. They do mention hymns and biblical passages that speak to the issues of the environment.

What Smith does not do is establish the link between epistemology and the sciences/creation within a Pentecostal paradigm.[74] However, this conversation is eloquently articulated in the work of Yong[75] when he discusses a dialogical model between a pneumatological imagination and the sciences/creation debate.[76] He provides first a biblical basis for the Spirit as part of creation (in the Genesis narrative), which encourages an appreciative approach by human beings towards creation. However, he goes further in discussing how a pneumatological imagination suggests a metaphysics of experience in contrast to a modernist epistemological framework which does not make room for such an imagination as he proposes.[77] In this way, he brings at least the discussion on experiential epistemology into dialogue with the science/creation discussion within a pneumatological/Pentecostal framework.

The Lutherans Rhoads and Rossing have been able to make the link between worship and creation care.[78] They argue that among transforming acts of preaching, teaching, witnessing, and advocacy worship should also be transformative if the church worldwide wants to address the ecological

---

73. Phemelo Olifile Marumo and Sarel Van der Merwe, "True Disciples, Nature, and Leiturgia: Preservation of the Earth," *Missionalia* 45, no. 2 (2017): 154–67.

74. Smith, *Thinking in Tongues*, 81.

75. Yong, *The Spirit Poured Out on All Flesh*, 270.

76. Through the work of Peirce, he argues that a pneumatological imagination can be empirically confirmed. Though Peirce has listed four methods of settling doubt (tenacity, authority, a priori, scientific), he argues that there are external objects/truths and, if we have sufficient experience and reason about it, we would be able to come to a full conclusion. In this way, we sway between realism and idealism. This might more be inclined towards Hiebert's missiological epistemology of critical realism. In fact, the epistemological process of re-imagining by many missional theologians is not discussed at length: one is left with the assumption that the process happens through some form of rational intellectual appropriation. See Yong, *The Spirit Poured Out on All Flesh*, 270.

77. Yong, *The Spirit Poured Out on All Flesh*, 277.

78. David M. Rhoads and Barbara R. Rossing, "A Beloved Earth Community: Christian Mission in an Ecological Age," in *Mission After Christendom: Emergent Themes in Contemporary Mission*, eds. Ogbu U. Kalu, Peter Vethanayagamony, and Edmund Kee-Fook Chia (Louisville: Westminster John Knox, 2010), 130.

crises. They resolve that the church should 1) be conversant with the scientific perspectives of the natural world; 2) use the same logic of social justice for a human being for the rest of the created world; 3) adhere to the biblical mandate to a soteriology of all of creation (not merely humans) to build relationships with nature (through spiritual disciplines); 4) re-address the theology of creation. Significantly, they argue for the role that indigenous knowledge systems can and should employ in informing our theology of creation. It is in this instance that the work of Prosén is relevant, especially her argument that context – which includes testimony, praises, and worship – informs Pentecostal theology.[79] The question is "How can the personal/communal stories on environmental degradation find integration within Pentecostal testimonies, praise, and worship?" This is not merely a philosophical question; it has been tested and employed by Björkander using ethnographic research methods. Bjorkander states these testimonies, praise, and worship have been argued by Kwabena Asamoah-Gyadu as being informed in Africa by primal imagination.[80] Björkander therefore argues that the context that he is referring to is made up of African traditional religion and culture, especially for the Pentecostal churches in Africa.[81] This allows Pentecostal adherents to integrate their primal worldview in relation to creation care within their worship (through testimony, praise, and worship, etc).

While a lot has been said, it is evident through a literature review on missional worship, epistemology, and creation care that there remains still a considerable amount of research to be done to include an experiential epistemology to address ecological degradation.[82] This might be supplemented by including more Pentecostal voices and contributions to enhance the discussion on missional worship and creation care. It was the purpose of the chapter to demonstrate that through an experiential epistemology in a worship service the church can allow for its members during worship to reimagine themselves

---

79. Prosén, "Pentecostal Praise and Worship as a Mode of Theology," 167.

80. Asamoah-Gyadu, *Contemporary Pentecostal Christianity*, 25. He also takes from the argument of Bediako's chapter, "The Primal Imagination and the Opportunity for a New Theological Idiom," in Kwame Bediako, *Jesus in Africa: The Christian Gospel in African History and Experience*, Regnum Studies in Mission (Minneapolis: Augsburg Fortress, 2013), 85–96.

81. She did her research in Kenya, Africa.

82. See Yong's question: "If music and worship are as central to human activity and meaning making as this volume suggests (and as many of us as readers can attest), then why has not more consideration been given among renewal theologians to the resonances between musical and worship styles and theological methodologies?" Yong, "Improvisation, Indigenization, and Inspiration," 282.

as God's agents caring for creation.[83] The Pentecostal church's worship services are prime examples of this and should be embraced by other liturgical forms in addressing ecological degradation. We need to realize that without this we will not reach Christians theologically regarding care for creation, especially those who are intellectually impaired, disabled, illiterate or mostly non-reading, not inclined to intellectualism, who are not lovers of reading, or who are too old to read but could still use other senses.

Bibliography

Anderson, Allan H. *An Introduction to Pentecostalism: Global Charismatic Christianity*. Cambridge: Cambridge University Press, 2004.

Asamoah-Gyadu, J. Kwabena. *African Charismatics: Current Developments within Independent Indigenous Pentecostalism in Ghana*. Leiden: Brill, 2005.

———. *Contemporary Pentecostal Christianity: Interpretations from an African Context*. Oxford: Regnum, 2013.

Baron, Eugene. *Becoming a Resilient Christian Community: A Narrative Approach*. Munster: LitVerlag, 2023.

———. "The Call for African Missional Consciousness through Renewed Mission Praxis in URCSA." *Studia Historiae Ecclesiasticae* 45, no. 3 (2019): 1–19.

———. *Narrative Missiology*. Leiden: Brill, 2025.

Baron, Eugene, and Moses M. Maponya. "The Recovery of the Prophetic Voice of the Church: The Adoption of a 'Missional Church' Imagination." *Verbum et Ecclesia* 41, no. 1 (2020): 1–11.

Bediako, Kwame. *Jesus in Africa: The Christian Gospel in African History and Experience*. Akropong-Akwapim: Regnum Africa, 2000.

Björkander, Martina. *Worship, Ritual, and Pentecostal Spirituality-as-Theology: A Rhythm that Connects Our Hearts with God*. Leiden: Brill, 2024.

Bradley, C Randall. *From Memory to Imagination. Reforming the Church's Music*. Grand Rapids: Eerdmans, 2012.

Brown, Sally A. "Discerning the Public Presence of God." *Theology Today* 70, no. 1 (2013): 30–37.

Cox, Harvey G. *Fire from Heaven: The Rise of Pentecostal Spirituality and the Reshaping of Religion in the Twenty-First Century*. Reading: Addison-Wesley, 1995.

Crites, Stephen. "The Narrative Quality of Experience." In *Why Narrative? Readings in Narrative Theology*, edited by Stanley Hauerwas and L. Gregory Jones, 65–88. Grand Rapids: Eerdmans, 1989.

---

83. See for instance Neumann's argument that Pentecostals allow both Scripture and experiences of the Spirit to inform their actions and life.

Engelsviken, Tormod. "*Missio Dei*: The Understanding and Misunderstanding of a Theological Concept in European Churches and Missiology." *International Review of Mission* 92, no. 367 (2003): 481–97.

Felix-Jager, Steven. *Renewal Worship. A Theology of Pentecostal Doxology: Dynamics of Christian Worship*. Downers Grove: IVP Academic, 2022.

Flemming, Dean. *Why Mission?* Nashville: Abingdon, 2015.

Goheen, Michael W. *A Light to the Nations: The Missional Church and the Biblical Story*. Grand Rapids: Baker Academic, 2011.

Gorman, Michael J. *Becoming the Gospel: Paul, Participation, and Mission*. Grand Rapids: Eerdmans, 2015.

Guder, Darrell L. *Missional Church. A Vision for the Sending of the Church in North America*. Grand Rapids: Eerdmans, 1998.

Harold, Godfrey. "An Evangelical Understanding of the *Missio Dei* as the Inclusion of Social Justice: A Critical Theological Reflection." *Pharos Journal of Theology* 100 (2019): 1–10.

Hermans, Chris A. M., and Kobus Schoeman, eds. *Theology in An Age of Contingency*. International Practical Theology 21. Zürich: LIT Verlag, 2019.

Hoekendijk, J. C. *The Church Inside Out. Adventures in Faith*. London: SCM, 1976.

Hollenweger, Walter J. *Pentecostalism: Origins and Developments Worldwide*. Peabody: Hendrickson, 1997.

Ingalls, Monique, and Amos Yong, eds. *The Spirit of Praise: Music and Worship in Global Pentecostal-Charismatic Christianity*. University Park: The Pennsylvania State University Press, 2015.

Joubert, Lisel. "Ecclesiology, Spirituality, and the Early Church." In *Missional Ecclesiology: Participation in the Mission of the Triune God*, extended version, edited by Coenie Burger, Frederick Marais, and Pieter van der Walt, 63–74. Wellington: Bible Media, 2021.

Keum, Jooseop, ed. *Together Towards Life: Mission and Evangelism in Changing Landscapes. With a Practical Guide*. Geneva: World Council of Churches, 2013.

Knoetze, Johannes J., and Paul Verryn. "Migrants, *Missio Dei* and the Church in South Africa." In *The Human Dilemma of Displacement: Towards a Practical Theology and Ecclesiology of Home*, edited by Alfred R. Brunsdon, 171–87. Durbanville: AOSIS, 2021.

Langmead, Ross. "Ecomissiology." *Missiology* 30 (2002): 505–18.

Marumo, Phemelo Olifile, and Sarel Van der Merwe. "True Disciples, Nature, and *Leiturgia*: Preservation of the Earth." *Missionalia* 45, no. 2 (2017): 154–67.

Meyers, Ruth A. *Missional Worship, Worshipful Mission: Gathering as God's People, Going Out in God's Name*. Grand Rapids: Eerdmans, 2014.

Muller, Retief. "African Initiated Churches in South Africa: Giving Expression to an Embodied Gospel." In *Missional Ecclesiology: Participation in the Mission of the Triune God*, extended version, edited by Coenie Burger, Frederick Marais, and Pieter van der Walt, 168–83. Wellington: Bible Media, 2021.

Neumann, Peter D. *Pentecostal Experience: An Ecumenical Encounter.* Eugene: Wipf & Stock, 2012.

Newbigin, Lesslie. *Foolishness to the Greeks. The Gospel and Western Culture.* Grand Rapids: Eerdmans, 1986.

———. *The Gospel in a Pluralist Society.* Grand Rapids: Eerdmans, 1989.

Niemandt, Cornelius Johannes Petrus. "The *Missio Dei* as Flourishing Life." *Ecclesial Futures* 1, no. 1 (2020): 11–30.

———. "Ontluikende Kerke – 'n Nuwe Missionêre Beweging, Deel 1: Ontluikende Kerke as Prototipes van 'n Nuwe Missionêre Kerk." *Verbum et Ecclesia* 29, no. 1 (2008): 139–71.

Prosén, Martina. "Pentecostal Praise and Worship as a Mode of Theology." In *Faith in African Lived Christianity: Bridging Anthropological and Theological Perspectives*, edited by Karen Lauterbach and Mika Vähäkangas, 156–79. Leiden: Brill, 2020.

Rhoads, David M., and Barbara R. Rossing. "A Beloved Earth Community: Christian Mission in an Ecological Age." In *Mission After Christendom: Emergent Themes in Contemporary Mission*, edited by Ogbu U. Kalu, Peter Vethanayagamony, and Edmund Kee-Fook Chia, 128–43. Louisville: Westminster John Knox, 2010.

Richebacher, Wilhelm. "The Basis of Mission Theology or the Wrong Path." *International Review of Mission* 92, no. 367 (2009): 588–605.

Schattauer, Thomas, ed. *Inside Out: Worship in An Age of Mission.* Minneapolis: Fortress, 1999.

Schlesinger, Eugene R. "A Trinitarian Basis for a 'Theological Ecology' in Light of Laudato Si.'" *Theological Studies* 79, no. 2 (2018): 339–55.

Shenk, Wilbert R. "The Relevance of a Messianic Missiology for Mission Today." In *The Transfiguration of Mission: Biblical, Theological, and Historical Foundations*, edited by Wilbert R. Shenk, 17–36. Scottdale: Herald, 1993.

Smith, James K. A. *Thinking in Tongues: Pentecostal Contributions to Christian Philosophy.* Grand Rapids: Eerdmans, 2020.

Stroope, Michael W. *Transcending Mission: The Eclipse of a Modern Tradition.* Downers Grove: InterVarsity, 2017.

Van Engen, Charles. *Mission on the Way: Issues in Mission Theology.* Grand Rapids: Baker Academic, 1996.

Wepener, Cas. "Towards a Missional Liturgy." *NGTT: Dutch Reformed Theological Journal* 49, no. 1/2 (2008): 206–19.

Wittgenstein, Ludwig. *Philosophical Investigations.* Oxford: Basil Blackwell, 1958.

Wright, Christopher J. H. *The Mission of God: Unlocking the Bible's Grand Narrative.* Downers Grove: InterVarsity, 2006.

Yong, Amos. "Improvisation, Indigenization, and Inspiration: Theological Reflections on the Sound and Spirit of Global Renewal." In *The Spirit of Praise: Music and Worship in Global Pentecostal-Charismatic Christianity*, edited by Monique M. Ingalls and Amos Yong, 278–88. University Park: The Pennsylvania State University Press, 2015.

———. "Pluralism, Secularism, and Pentecost: Newbigin-ings for Missio Trinitatis in a New Century." In *The Gospel and Pluralism Today: Reassessing Lesslie Newbigin for the 21st Century*, edited by Scott W. Sunquist and Amos Yong, 147–70. Downers Grove: IVP Academic, 2015.

———. *The Spirit Poured Out on All Flesh: Pentecostalism and the Possibility of Global Theology*. Grand Rapids: Baker Academic, 2005.

Appendix

Possible Next Steps for Spirit-Filled Witness vis-a-vis the Environment

Readers of this book might wonder, what else might they be able to do to respond to the invitation to participate in the mission of God to save the world in ways that faithfully anticipates also the coming new heavens and new earth? The contributors to this book provide the following suggestions:

As individuals, we might consider, if we have not already, the following:

1. Do we recycle, and if yes, how can we do even better?
2. How might we generally reduce our consumption habits and, more specifically, redirect them away from fossil fuels toward renewable energy resources, both for smaller purchases and larger investments (e.g., what kind of apartment or house we live in)?
3. Are there ways we can incorporate vegetarian meal days into our meal plans, or perhaps consider adopting a vegetarian lifestyle?
4. How can we be more deliberate in sourcing our food by choosing fresh, seasonal produce from local growers, integrating organic pantry staples where possible, and prioritizing local and/or organic suppliers that support both sustainable farming practices and the ethical treatment of animals?
5. What about having more native-to-our-region plants in our gardens that will support butterflies, bees, etc., crucial to the pollination process that benefits us and other organisms in our environment?
6. Can we shift to public transit or toward electric vehicles?
7. Can we minimize our air travel and thereby do our part in reducing the planet's carbon footprint?

8. What else can I do to raise awareness about environmental degradation among family, friends, and other conversations I am a part of?
9. Is it possible for me as an individual, or for my family collectively, to take active steps to be in solidarity with or advocate on behalf of Indigenous communities or groups working on environmental justice in our region?

As church members or leaders, we might consider, if we have not already, the following:

1. How might we encourage more teaching/preaching on this topic in our churches?
2. Can we prompt or extend conversations about what it means for our church to be "green" committed?
3. What about organizing retreats that encourage participants to connect with God through nature, and that provide opportunities for reflection, prayer, and education about the importance of creation care?
4. Might we open discussion about making plant-based food the default for church events, and giving people the choice to opt in for meals with animal products, instead of having to opt out of them? Can we source our food by choosing fresh, seasonal produce from local growers, integrate organic pantry staples where possible, and prioritize local and/or organic suppliers that support both sustainable farming practices and the ethical treatment of animals?
5. If your church or organization has yard space, should we develop a garden plan that includes native-to-our-region plants and trees that will both support butterflies, bees, etc., crucial to the pollination process for us and other organisms in our environment, and also provide food and shelter for native birds and other wildlife?
6. How can we encourage the younger generation to consider the sciences and technology for their future careers, with the focus on understanding our planet better (e.g., climate, ocean, and mountain research) and developing new techniques and innovations to reduce the consumption of our planet's nonrenewable resources?
7. Do we have or can we join conversations with local churches or others in the community about ways to support city or local environmental efforts, from animal rescue, rehabilitation, and therapy

Possible Next Steps for Spirit-Filled Witness vis-a-vis the Environment

initiatives, to clean-up drives, tree planting events, and wildlife corridor creation, and beyond? Is it possible for us as a church to take active steps to be in solidarity with or advocate on behalf of Indigenous communities or groups working on environmental and species conservation, restoration, and protection in our local region?

8. What about opening up or extending discussions with our sister denominational or network churches about how our participation in the mission of God to save the world includes, rather than excludes, the environment?

As those formally engaged in mission endeavors, working in mission/development organizations, or leading mission initiatives, whether ecclesial, parachurch, in NGOs, or other venues, we might consider, if we have not already, the following:

1. How do we have or extend conversations about if and how ours is a "green" organization?

2. Should we revisit our organizational mission to explore if and how the environment might be added or could be further engaged?

3. Which projects or organizations – locally, nationally, and globally – that we are already committed to and partnering with are also working in this direction and how can we strengthen our collaboration, learn from them, and extend our efforts?

4. Is it possible to take active steps to be in solidarity with, or advocate on behalf of, Indigenous communities or groups working on environmental justice, particularly those from more socioeconomically marginalized communities struggling to meet basic needs and access resources which production is being reduced overall due to over-consumption by other communities?

Langham Literature and its imprints are a ministry of Langham Partnership.

Langham Partnership is a global fellowship working in pursuit of the vision God entrusted to its founder John Stott –

> *to facilitate the growth of the church in maturity and Christ-likeness through raising the standards of biblical preaching and teaching.*

Our vision is to see churches in the Majority World equipped for mission and growing to maturity in Christ through the ministry of pastors and leaders who believe, teach and live by the word of God.

Our mission is to strengthen the ministry of the word of God through:
- nurturing national movements for biblical preaching
- fostering the creation and distribution of evangelical literature
- enhancing evangelical theological education

especially in countries where churches are under-resourced.

Our ministry

Langham Preaching partners with national leaders to nurture indigenous biblical preaching movements for pastors and lay preachers all around the world. With the support of a team of trainers from many countries, a multi-level programme of seminars provides practical training, and is followed by a programme for training local facilitators. Local preachers' groups and national and regional networks ensure continuity and ongoing development, seeking to build vigorous movements committed to Bible exposition.

Langham Literature provides Majority World preachers, scholars and seminary libraries with evangelical books and electronic resources through publishing and distribution, grants and discounts. The programme also fosters the creation of indigenous evangelical books in many languages, through writer's grants, strengthening local evangelical publishing houses, and investment in major regional literature projects, such as one volume Bible commentaries like *The Africa Bible Commentary* and *The South Asia Bible Commentary*.

Langham Scholars provides financial support for evangelical doctoral students from the Majority World so that, when they return home, they may train pastors and other Christian leaders with sound, biblical and theological teaching. This programme equips those who equip others. Langham Scholars also works in partnership with Majority World seminaries in strengthening evangelical theological education. A growing number of Langham Scholars study in high quality doctoral programmes in the Majority World itself. As well as teaching the next generation of pastors, graduated Langham Scholars exercise significant influence through their writing and leadership.

To learn more about Langham Partnership and the work we do visit **langham.org**

www.ingramcontent.com/pod-product-compliance
Lightning Source LLC
Chambersburg PA
CBHW050134240426
43673CB00043B/1658